Slavic Cultures
in the Middle Ages

California Slavic Studies
Editorial Board

Henrik Birnbaum
Robert O. Crummey
Hugh McLean
Nicholas V. Riasanovsky
Ronald Vroon

Christianity and the Eastern Slavs
in three volumes

Editorial Board

Boris Gasparov
Robert P. Hughes
Irina Paperno
Olga Raevsky-Hughes
Nicholas Riasanovsky
Theodore Taranovsky
Donald W. Treadgold

Contents of the Volumes

Volume I
Slavic Cultures in the Middle Ages
Edited by Boris Gasparov and Olga Raevsky-Hughes

Volume II
Russian Culture in Modern Times
Edited by Robert P. Hughes and Irina Paperno

Volume III
Russian Literature in Modern Times
Edited by Boris Gasparov, Robert P. Hughes,
Irina Paperno, and Olga Raevsky-Hughes

CALIFORNIA SLAVIC STUDIES XVI

Christianity and the Eastern Slavs

VOLUME I

Slavic Cultures in the Middle Ages

Edited by

Boris Gasparov and Olga Raevsky-Hughes

UNIVERSITY OF CALIFORNIA PRESS

Berkeley   Los Angeles   Oxford

University of California Press
Berkeley and Los Angeles, California

University of California Press, Ltd.
Oxford, England

© 1993 by
The Regents of the University of California

Library of Congress Cataloging-in-Publication Data

Christianity and the Eastern Slavs.

    p. cm. — (California Slavic studies; 16–)

    Based on papers delivered at two international conferences held in May 1988 at the University of California—Berkeley and the Kennan Institute for Advanced Russian Studies to commemorate the millennium of the Christianization of Kievan Rus'.

    Includes bibliographical references and index.

    Contents: v. 1. Slavic cultures in the Middle Ages / edited by Boris Gasparov and Olga Raevsky-Hughes.

    ISBN: 978-0-520-30247-1 (pbk. : alk. paper)

    1. Slavs, Eastern—Civilization—Congresses. 2. Christianity and culture—Congresses. 3. Orthodox Eastern Church—Slavic countries—Congresses. 4. Russian literature—History and Criticism—Congresses. 5. Russia (Federation)—Civilization—Congresses. 6. Millennium of Christianity in Kievan Rus', 988–1988—Congresses. I. Gasparov, B. II. Raevskaia-Kh'iuz, O. (Ol'ga) III. Series.

DK4.C33 vol. 16, etc.

947 s—dc20
[947]
                                                                            92–20504
                                                                               CIP

CONTENTS

Acknowledgments — ix

Abbreviations — xi

Introduction
  Boris Gasparov — 1

I. History of Christianity

Universal Witness and Local Identity in Russian Orthodoxy (988–1988)
  †John Meyendorff — 11

Крещение Руси: мировоззренческие и эстетические аспекты
  Aleksandr Panchenko — 30
  Summary — 41

Christianity before Christianization: Christians and Christian Activity in Pre-988 Rus'
  Henrik Birnbaum — 42

The Spirituality of the Early Kievan Caves Monastery
  Fairy von Lilienfeld — 63

When Was Olga Canonized?
  †John Fennell — 77

Why Did the Metropolitan Move from Kiev to Vladimir in the Thirteenth Century?
  Donald Ostrowski — 83

The Origins of the Muscovite Ecclesiastical Claims to the Kievan Inheritance (Early Fourteenth Century to 1458/1461)
  Jaroslaw Pelenski — 102

Religion and Identity in the Carpathians: East Christians in Poland and Czechoslovakia
  Paul Robert Magosci — 116

II. Church Slavic and the Medieval Literary Tradition

([Church] Slavonic) Writing in Kievan Rus'
  Dean S. Worth 141

On the Place of the Cyrillo-Methodian Tradition in Epiphanius's *Life of Saint Stephen of Perm*
  Harvey Goldblatt 154

The Corpus of Slavonic Translations Available in Muscovy: The Cause of Old Russia's Intellectual Silence and a Contributory Factor to Muscovite Cultural Autarky
  Francis J. Thomson 179

Церковнославянизмы в украинском языке
  Pavel Sigalov 215
  Summary 238

III. Christianity and Medieval Cultural Paradigms

Солярно-лунарная символика в облике русского храма
  Boris Uspenskii 241
  Summary 251

The Notion of "Uncorrupted Relics" in Early Russian Culture
  Gail Lenhoff 252

Justice in Avvakum's Fifth Petition to Tsar Aleksei Mikhailovich
  Priscilla Hunt 276

Традиционность и уникальность сочинений протопопа Аввакума в свете традиции Третьего Рима
  Maria Pliukhanova 297
  Summary 327

The Evolution of Church Music in Belorussia
  Guy Picarda 328

Notes on the Contributors 357

Index 361

ACKNOWLEDGMENTS

A debt of gratitude is owed the following funding organizations: the National Endowment for the Humanities; the Kennan Institute for Advanced Russian Studies; the I. V. Koulaieff Educational Foundation (San Francisco); the Center for Slavic and East European Studies (University of California, Berkeley).

We gratefully acknowledge the assistance of Keith Goeringer, Catherine Gordis, David Mayberry, William Nickell, Anthony Vanchu, Glen and Irina Worthey, and G. Patton Wright. Vail Palomino was the coordinator of our efforts, and we wish to express our thanks to her.

We are especially grateful to Hugh McLean, Nicholas Riasanovsky, Theodore Taranovsky and Donald W. Treadgold for reading the manuscripts and for their numerous editorial suggestions.

B.G.
R.P.H.
I.P.
O.R.-H.

ABBREVIATIONS

AB	*Analecta Bollandiana*
BAN	Biblioteka Akademii nauk
ByzSl	*Byzantinoslavica*
ChOIDR	*Chteniia Moskovskogo obshchestva istorii i drevnosti rossiiskikh* (Moscow)
CSHB	*Corpus Scriptorum Historiae Byzantinae*
DOP	*Dumbarton Oaks Papers*
ELMB	*Entsyklapediia literatury i mastatstvy Belarusi* (Minsk, 1984–)
GBL	Gosudarstvennaia biblioteka imeni V. I. Lenina, Moscow
GIM	Gosudarstvennyi istoricheskii muzei, Moscow
GPB	Gosudarstvennaia publichnaia biblioteka imeni N. E. Saltykova-Shchedrina, Leningrad
HUS	*Harvard Ukrainian Studies*
IORIaS	*Izvestiia Otdeleniia russkogo iazyka i slovesnosti* (St. Petersburg, 1896–Leningrad, 1927)
LVR	*Letopisets' velikii rus'skii*
NPL	*Novgorodskaia pervaia letopis' starshego i mladshego izvodov*, ed. M. N. Tikhomirov (Moscow and Leningrad, 1950)
PG	*Patrologia Graeca*
PL	*Patrologia Latina*
PLDR	*Pamiatniki literatury Drevnei Rusi* (Moscow, 1978–)
PSRL	*Polnoe sobranie russkikh letopisei*
RIB	*Russkaia istoricheskaia biblioteka*
RO MGAMID	Rukopisnyi otdel, Moskovskii glavnyi arkhiv Ministerstva inostrannykh del
SG	*Slavica Gandensia*
SR	*Slavic Review*
TL	*Troitskaia letopis'. Rekonstruktsiia teksta*, ed. M. D. Priselkov (Moscow and Leningrad, 1950)
TODRL	*Trudy Otdela drevnerusskoi literatury*
TsGADA	Tsentral'nyi Gosudarstvennyi Arkhiv Drevnikh Aktov
ZhPA	*Zhitie protopopa Avvakuma im samim napisannoe i drugie ego sochineniia*, ed. N. K. Gudzii (Moscow, 1960)

INTRODUCTION

BORIS GASPAROV

This publication in three volumes originated in papers delivered at two international conferences held in May 1988, at the University of California, Berkeley, and the Kennan Institute for Advanced Russian Studies (Washington, D.C.). Like many other conferences organized that year in the United States, Europe, and the Soviet Union, they were convened to commemorate the millennium of the acceptance of Christianity in Rus' (the event occurred in 988 or 989, depending on differing chronological calculations). We believe that this collection of essays will throw light on the enormous, truly unique role which the Christian tradition has played throughout the centuries in shaping the nations which spring from Kievan Rus'—the Russians, Ukrainians, and Belorussians. Although these volumes devote greater attention to Russian culture, the investigation of the issues in the history of Christianity in Ukrainian and Belorussian cultures occupies an important and integral part of the project.

* * *

For a thousand years Christianity has played a central role in the cultural consciousness of the Eastern Slavs. Its impact can be seen in the structures of their social life and institutions, in their cultural and literary traditions, and in the formation and development of their languages. After the adoption of Christianity by Rus', throughout seven centuries of Kievan Rus' and Muscovy, the region's allegiance to Orthodoxy remained a crucial component of its political and cultural development. Eventually, political life and social institutions were secularized; this process took place over the course of the seventeenth century and was completed by Peter the Great. Yet the Eastern Orthodox tradition remained an all-encompassing spiritual environment to which virtually every political, social, or cultural phenomenon related in one way or another. Even in times of vehement denial of this heritage (such as the populist era of the third quarter of the nineteenth century or the Soviet period), the Christian underpinnings remained crucial.

A vast reservoir of concepts, images, and expressions derived from the

Christian tradition; and ecclesiastical literature has remained a common stock in the nations' memories, shaping their languages, the symbolism of their literatures and art, and their world outlook. The variegated and often semiconscious usage of this stock both ensured continuity of the cultural tradition and helped to shape newly emerging ideas and institutions. Even the reception of those political, literary, and social ideas that came from the West bore the imprint of the Eastern Orthodox environment into which they were brought on Slavic soil.

Thus, many (if not all) of the major achievements of Russian culture of the nineteenth and early twentieth centuries were the result of such transplantations of Western concepts into a cultural context shaped by the Orthodox Christian tradition. This trend became especially clear and productive at the turn of the twentieth century, when a resurgence of interest in Christianity among the Russian intellectual and artistic elite merged with neo-Kantian trends in philosophy, utopian social ideas, and the advent of Modernism in literature and art, and produced a cultural movement, unique in its intensity and originality, now widely known as the Russian "Silver Age."

No less important was the role played by the Church and the Christian tradition of the other East Slavic nations. Eastern Orthodox Christianity played a vital role in shaping the national self-consciousness of Ukrainians and Belorussians as distinct nations, influenced the path of their development, and left a powerful imprint on their cultural memory.

The history of Rus' and of the East Slavic nations that developed in its territories has, of course, many features in common with the histories of other Christian peoples. However, the distinctive features of this branch of universal Christianity can be discerned in the ways in which the Christian tradition functioned in society and manifested its influence on various aspects of national culture, ideology, and civic life.

It may be that the most characteristic feature of the Christian tradition among the Eastern Slavs, apparent from its very origin and evident in the whole span of its thousand-year history, is its "implicitness": the absence or insufficient development of the codifying mechanisms that would define the functioning of the Church and its place in the life of society. In East Slavic Christianity there was no clear-cut boundary between the ecclesiastical and secular spheres; the rights and responsibilities of the Church in its relations to secular powers and civil life were equally vague. The ecclesiastical sphere itself—questions of dogma, liturgy, the dissemination and editing of the sacred books, and the manner and content of religious education—lacked strictly defined regulatory mechanisms, clearly formulated principles, and legitimate institutional structures. In all of these domains, both the Church itself and the religious sphere of social life generally relied more on the continuity of tradition and the collective mind of its members than on objectified and abstracted regulations and institutions. The absorption of tradition, its direct assimilation through existing texts, was more highly valued than the ability explicitly to formulate rational principles and subsequently to adhere to these principles.

This special—implicit and amalgamative—character of the Christian tradition is revealed in the properties of the sacral language of Slavonic religious books, Church Slavonic. The translation of holy books into Church Slavonic was accomplished in the South and West Slavic territories one hundred years before the acceptance of Christianity in Rus'. It was an act neither of creating Christian texts in a language that already had a literary tradition and was codified in that tradition, such as Greek or Latin, nor of translation into any sort of "living" contemporary language, as in the cases of the Armenian translation of the Gospels in the fourth century, the Gothic Bible of the fifth century, or the translations of the Latin Bible into living languages during the Reformation. It was an artificial language created for the purpose and accordingly distinguished by uncertainty and plasticity in its structure and contents. It was a language comprehensible to all Slavs, but at the same time unlike any one living ideolect; it was a language meant specifically for written use, and existed exclusively in the sphere of sacred books; yet it was not governed by the norms that usually comprise an integral part of a written tradition.

On Russian territory, Church Slavonic remained in this condition for eight hundred years. In the Ukraine and Belorussia, under the influence of Roman Catholic culture and the Reformation and Counter Reformation, the raising of philological and theological problems, the compilation of dictionaries and grammars, the organization of regular instruction in Church Slavonic began earlier, at the end of the fifteenth century. These processes reached Muscovy only in the second half of the seventeenth century, as a result of the spreading influence of centers of education and scholarship which had been established in the western and southwestern borderlands of the East Slavic region. Until then such aspects of Church Slavic culture as the dissemination in manuscript of the sacred and religious-didactic texts, the performance of the liturgy, the instruction, the oratory tradition, and the tradition of religious and didactic literature were maintained and developed predominantly on the basis of texts at hand.

The members of this culture were not men of learning and professional competence in the strict sense of these terms, but rather "initiates" in the tradition. The religious and professional baggage of one thus initiated consisted of an indefinitely large number of texts and traditional skills handed down through practice and learned with various degrees of accuracy (or inaccuracy). Training in literacy took place in the course of memorizing and copying of texts, a process that also involved an introduction to the ideological, dogmatic, and philosophical problems of Christianity. The norms that guided the scribes of the sacred books did not exist in the form of an abstract codex; they were drawn directly from the texts and comprised a certain level (never clearly defined) of what might be called "mnemonic competence." Any linguistic, textological, dogmatic, or procedural problem connected with the maintaining of church culture and rites was decided by appealing to this rich but vague store of experience, which was accepted as the common property of the community of the initiated—those invested if not with clear-cut powers, then at least with due authority.

The absence of normative mechanisms, which could have defined and set limits to the various spheres of religious activity, has imbued the Orthodox Christian self-consciousness with a synthesizing character, one disposed to holistic generalizations and linkages. A religious cognition of the world comes about not as the result of gradual and purposeful efforts, but as an instantaneous and total "transfiguration." Thinking seeks to encompass all aspects of existence, to leave nothing out, so as at once to discover a universal and radical solution.

This aspect of the East Slavic cultural consciousness, intimately linked with the Christian tradition, is manifest throughout the whole span of Russian history. The ethics of Tolstoy or the cosmic utopia of Nikolai Fedorov are examples in modern culture. This same feature may be seen in the pervasive interpretation, expressed in the religious literature of ancient Rus', of the acceptance of Christianity as a renovation of the entire world. This maximalist holism of thought is evident in the extraordinary energy of the long-lived Russian apocalyptic and eschatological tradition and in the religious and social movements connected with it.

The weak points of the religious tradition described here are obvious. They have been manifested many times, particularly in periods of crisis in the history of Russian and East Slavic Christianity. An outsider viewing the centuries-long history of Kievan and Muscovite Rus' is struck by the scarcity of mechanisms traditionally associated with learning: the lack of interest in abstract philosophical, theological, and philological problems, the dearth and low quality of translations from foreign languages, even the suspicious and hostile attitude toward "floridity" and "philosophizing" as attributes of an alien and hostile world (the West). At first glance it seems inexplicable that out of this apparently barren soil could arise the philosophical and ethical problematics of modern Russian literature, the religious philosophy of the beginning of the twentieth century, and, finally, Russian philological scholarship.

However, this unformed character of the intellectual and normative instruments of the Christian tradition that developed in the territory of Rus' ensures the total, if only implicit, presence of this tradition in the life of society. Thus, on one hand, Church Slavonic, with its purely mnemonic norms, could not preserve its integrity and was poorly protected from contamination by the vernacular; an erosion of the sacral language, its "corruption" occurred. On the other hand, in the course of this very process the words, idioms, rhetorical locutions of Church Slavic penetrated all spheres of everyday speech and brought with them those religious values that for centuries had been passed on through the tradition of memorizing and reproducing the sacred texts. In sum, anyone speaking and writing one of the East Slavic languages may himself not realize to what degree his consciousness is permeated by turns of thought that have been assimilated thanks to the presence of the Church Slavic substratum in his speech.

The Christian worldview, manifested less in precisely formulated categories and norms than in the collective memory of texts, permeates the whole of public and private life. Even a direct denial of the Church rests on moral categories, rhetorical turns of thought, and language in which the memory of the Christian tradition is present. It is a well-known fact that many of the Russian revolutionaries emerged from the clergy and relied on rhetoric borrowed from ecclesiastical texts. One may also recall the extraordinary activization of a Church Slavic linguistic layer in the Bolshevik Revolution's oratorical style and in the ideological language of the Soviet period. But most striking are the messianic aspirations of the Russian revolutionary movement and Soviet ideology. Social reconstruction is understood as a total transfiguration that creates the new man and a new earth. The radical transformation of the spiritual and physical nature of man (up to achieving physical immortality) and an equally radical transformation of the face of the earth and the entire cosmos are expected as the necessary result of revolutionary renovation.

It is no exaggeration to say that Christianity forms the foundation of what is called "Russian culture," the aggregate of concepts, ideas, and spiritual values associated with such names as Dostoevsky and Tolstoy, Vladimir

Soloviev and Nikolai Fedorov, Boris Pasternak and Mikhail Bakhtin. Thus, we might say that Christianity underlies the specific "voice" of Russian and East Slavic cultures in dialogue with the various West European cultural traditions. The essence of this voice lies in the effort to avoid an excessively rigid rationalism that would strictly distinguish between "rule" and "usage," the general and the individual, subject and object. Russian thought attempts to find solutions at the intersection between the individual and the collective, between knowledge and action. Individual efforts dissolve in the tradition, and they follow this tradition not according to any clearly established program. Any act of cognition draws upon what is a common reservoir of collective memory. Such concepts as *sobornost'* ("conciliarity," originally advanced by the Slavophiles) and Bakhtinian "dialogism," both of which are widely used in the discussions of the distinguishing qualities of Russian culture, may serve as approximate designations for this difficult-to-define phenomenon; its vague and amorphous character is an attribute as intrinsic to it as its exceptional plasticity and aptitude for integration and synthesis.

The editors of the present publication believe that the contents of the three volumes offered here mirror this character of the East Slavic Christian tradition. The publication is structured as a dialogue of scholars from several disciplines—historians, linguists, and specialists in various areas and periods of Russian and other East Slavic literatures and cultures. Our goal has been to integrate several fields of knowledge that ordinarily exist separately, to integrate not by means of holistic generalizations, but rather by juxtaposing and interlacing various themes, objects, and spheres of study usually compartmentalized in different disciplines and studies of various historical epochs. Our hope is that this "polyphonic" composition of the volumes may allow the reader to see interconnections and echoes between different dimensions of the national histories and cultures informed by Orthodox Christianity. It is an attempt to explore the multistructured and multivalent linguistic, symbolic, and ideological infrastructure which comprises the Christian tradition of the Eastern Slavs.

* * *

Volume I is devoted to the period from Kievan Rus' to the seventeenth century in the history of the Eastern Slavs. The papers that comprise the three sections of the volume deal with issues in the history of Christianization, the linguistic problems associated with the adoption of Christianity in the medieval period and at later stages, and the influence of the Christian tradition on cultural paradigms established in the period following Christianization. Volumes II and III deal with modern times and include investigations in Russian culture. The papers gathered in Volume II concern various issues in the history of culture from the eighteenth to the twentieth century: cultural institutions and cultural life (section one) and ideological paradigms and cultural mythology (section two). Volume III contains papers that focus on literary texts and literary movements; the three sections are devoted to the nineteenth century, the age of Modernism (ca. 1890–1920), and the period from 1920 to 1960.

* * *

The editors of this volume have had to deal with a difficult problem for which there is perhaps no simple and universal solution: the problem of how to render personal and geographical names whose original form is in the Cyrillic alphabet. Various articles in the volume use Church Slavic (of different epochs and national traditions), Old Russian (medieval East Slavic), Ukrainian, Ruthenian, Belorussian, Bulgarian textual, cultural and bibliographic materials. Often there co-exist several conflicting traditions of rendering proper names from these languages into the Latin alphabet—traditions reflecting the complicated political and cultural history of the respective areas and peoples. The plurality of names for Lvov (the form adopted from Russian and conventionally used in English), L'vov (Russian name in transliteration), L'viv (Ukrainian name in transliteration), Lwów (Polish), Lemberg (German)—each name reflecting a certain historical perspective, is perhaps the best-known case among innumerable examples of such controversies. To ignore this plurality, to impose on the volume as a whole, for the sake of "consistency," a uniform set of rules for rendering proper names, would result, in our opinion, in losing important historical and cultural overtones which sometimes are related to the very core of an article's argument.

Another dilemma is whether to render personal names as they were adopted in English or in transliteration according to their original form: should it be Epiphanius the Most Wise, or Epifanii the Most Wise, or Epifanii Premudryi; Metropolitan Jonas or Iona; Prince Alexander Nevsky, Aleksandr Nevsky, or Aleksandr Nevskii? Again, the editors felt that the answer depends on the character of the article—whether it is dedicated to problems of history and ideology not closely connected with language, or deals with close philological analysis.

There is, however, one area in which uniformity is necessary—bibliographical references; to make references in many languages available for the readers, they must be presented precisely in the way they appear in library catalogues.

As a consequence, we have adopted different strategies for rendering proper names in the main text (including expository text in notes), on the one hand, and in bibliographical references, on the other. The main text of each article retains the orthography of proper names chosen by the author and reflecting his/her treatment of the subject. At the same time, for all bibliographical data in languages with the Cyrillic alphabet the uniform rules of transliteration adopted by the Library of Congress were used throughout the whole volume. Finally, references to works in languages with the Latin alphabet preserve the orthography of proper names employed in the titles of those works.

This means that the same personal or geographic name may appear in several different forms within one article: one form in the main text; others in transliterations from the Russian, Bulgarian, Ukrainian, etc. sources referred to; still others in the titles of works in English, French, German, Polish, Czech, etc., for instance: the monk Hrabr (conventional English orthography), Khrabr (in Russian titles), Khrabăr (in Bulgarian titles), Xrabr, Chrabr (in German, French, etc.).

We believe that in spite of the apparent "inconsistency," this strategy allows a reasonable compromise between retaining various stylistic and semantic overtones, expressed through different orthographic modes, and maintaining a uniform and precise scholarly apparatus. Such a compromise in itself reflects the complexity of problems and the plurality of approaches dealt with in this volume.

PART I
History of Christianity

Universal Witness and Local Identity in Russian Orthodoxy (988-1988)

†JOHN MEYENDORFF

On the day of Pentecost the one Gospel preached by the disciples of Jesus was heard and understood by those gathered in a variety of tongues. Indeed, the apostolic preaching had to reach the "ends of the world." Since that time —inasmuch as universality necessarily implied cultural and linguistic pluralism—the issue of the legitimate human *diversity* vis-à-vis God-established *unity* remained crucial for defining *what* the Christian Church is and how its mission is to be performed on a universal scale.

The early Christian community confessed and practiced what we call today *eucharistic ecclesiology*. In each place, the disciples gathered together to hear the Word and partake of the Eucharist of the Mystery of Christ's Risen Body. Indeed, he had promised them that "where two or three are gathered together in my name, there am I in the midst of them" (Matt. 18:20). This experience of Christ's presence in the midst of the local community gave rise to the original use of the term "catholic" applied to the Church. Writing around the year 100 A.D., Saint Ignatius of Antioch said: "Where Christ is, there is the catholic church" (Epistle to the Smyrnaeans 8:2). Coming from the adverbial Greek form καθόλου, the adjective "catholic" referred to "fullness" and "completeness" as the result of Christ's personal presence. In the local eucharistic assembly, the *whole* Body of Christ was made manifest, not a part or a segment. It is this notion of local catholicity distinct from an interpretation of catholicity in the sense of geographic universality which explains the general and unopposed acceptance throughout the Christian world in the second century of a uniform pattern of ecclesial structure: the local Eucharist was to be presided over by a single person called "bishop" (ἐπίσκοπος, "overseer") occupying the seat of Jesus himself and reflecting his position in the midst of his disciples at the last supper. And since, in the Greco-Roman world, the *city* was conceived as the primary social unit, eventually everywhere there would be one bishop in each city.[1] Then the original eucharistic assembly, which was unique, would split into several "parishes."

Realized in each community, this local fullness implied and required unity of faith and action between the communities on a universal scale. The apostle Paul's concern with one original Judaeo-Christian community of Jerusalem contained an important expression of this sense of universal unity. As the Jerusalem center disappeared, an unchallenged consensus was reached which recognized that an alternate point of universal reference existed in the "very ancient" church of Rome, located in the imperial capital—the international center par excellence—where the principal apostles Peter and Paul had died as martyrs.

In the pre-Constantine Church, however, neither Jerusalem nor, even less, Rome would exercise any form of disciplinary or administrative power. Their prestige was moral and was mentioned only occasionally in the available sources. But the young Christian Church, in spite of many internal controversies and external troubles, was highly concerned with its universal unity, which manifested itself in councils and other forms of frequent direct contacts between the local churches.

With the establishment of Christianity under Constantine and with the transfer of the imperial capital from ancient Rome to Constantinople, the new Rome, the empire began to take an active and forceful role securing Christian unity. Roman imperial universalism and the Christian demand for an apostolic and missionary expansion of the faith to the ends of the world were merged. The emperor began to call together ecumenical councils. Local churches began to organize themselves within the provinces, the dioceses, and the prefectures, matching the administrative division of imperial territories. The bishops of major cities—Alexandria, Rome, Antioch, and, later, Constantinople—became archbishops or patriarchs.

It is against this background that the East and the West began to be drawn apart. Rome ceased to be the imperial capital, as barbarian invasions swept the West. The bishops of Rome assumed a new role, as the principal custodians of both Christianity and Roman universality in that new "barbarian" environment. More and more explicitly, they would invoke the prestige of their church as the place where Peter and Paul were martyred. Eventually, in eleventh century, it was assumed in the West that the Roman Pope possessed not only moral prestige, but actually direct administrative power over all the local churches and that this power was of divine origin and that it could express itself even in political or military terms. The East, meanwhile, maintained the principle of equality of all bishops, recognizing, however, that coordination between them was to be assured through a patriarchal pluralism, defined by and responsible to church councils. In practice, also, the empire was understood to be a principal agent of Christian unity and Christian missionary expansion.

In Kievan Rus', Christianity became formally the state religion precisely when this bifurcation between East and West was gradually taking permanent form. The famous account, in many ways legendary, found in the *Primary Chronicle* does reflect two major and undoubtedly historical aspects of the event: 1) Prince Vladimir and his government were searching for the *universal* religious form that would allow the Kievan State to become part of world civilization; 2) in their search they faced alternatives—Islam, Judaism, and the two branches of Christianity—which involved four different forms of universalism. According to the author of the *Chronicle,* a not unbiased observer but a committed Orthodox monk of the late eleventh century, the choice was made in favor of Byzantine Christianity because a Greek scholar sent to preach Christianity to Vladimir had succeeded in showing the intellectual and cultural superiority of his church and because the same cultural and aesthetic power had been witnessed in St. Sophia of Constantinople by Vladimir's own envoys: "We knew not whether we were in heaven, or on earth," they reported to the Kievan prince.[2]

Of course, other factors of a geo-political, personal, and economic nature also contributed to what we call today the "baptism of Rus'." It is useful to remember that the historical event did not occur in a vacuum. Similar conversions of princes, followed by their nations, occurred in northern and eastern Europe throughout the ninth and tenth centuries. All of them renounced their local tribal religions in favor of a universal religious and cultural family. The Moravians and the Bulgarians, like the Russians, chose the Byzantine affiliation, whereas the Scandinavians, Poles, and Hungarians turned to the Latin (in fact, Germanic) West. Others, like Volga-Bulgars, became Muslims, and the Khazars chose Judaism.

This short paper is not intended as a discussion of the historical significance of the "baptism of Rus'," even less as a history of Russian or Ukrainian Christianity. My only purpose is to present some observations concerning an issue of central importance in the history of Christianity as a whole: How does the universal nature of the Gospel relate to the concrete realities of political history and civilization? How did Christian Russians understand the tension, manifested in the miracle of Pentecost, between the legitimate cultural identity of their nation and the universal unity of the Church?

No one would deny that this issue is of crucial importance, particularly for Russia. The original close connection with the Byzantine empire after the baptism of Saint Vladimir, the conquest by the Mongols, the subsequent rise of the Muscovite empire, the stormy and self-conscious relations with western Europe throughout the modern period, and, finally, the status of superpower, achieved in the twentieth century, all involve the problem of national self-consciousness. Furthermore, if one looks at the problem from the point of view of Christian ecclesiology, as is proper as we mark the millennium of Russian Christianity, one is bound to raise questions concerning not only the place of national churches within the one universal Church, but also the issue of primacies, legitimate or illegitimate, of the old Rome, the new Rome, Constantinople, the *de facto* influence of the Russian Church within Eastern Orthodoxy, which expressed itself sometimes in the theory of a "third" Rome, and finally, of the witness of Russian Christianity in the modern world.

The most logical way to comment upon these aspects of the Russian historical odyssey is to follow a chronological order, starting with the events of 988 and the Russian connection with Byzantium.

988-1448: The Cyrillo-Methodian Legacy and the "Byzantine Commonwealth"

The Christianization of the various "barbarian" nations that occupied the territory of Europe from the fourth to the tenth century was partly a spontaneous and partly an organized process. The conversion of the Goths to Arianism, for example, was connected with the accidental fact that the Roman empire, centered in Constantinople, had itself embraced Arianism by the year 360 A.D. But catholic or orthodox Christianity had also made inroads, without direct imperial sponsorship, in remote places of the British Isles and Gaul (as well as in faraway countries of the East: Armenia, Georgia, Ethiopia, India). Irish monks undertook, on their own initiative, the conversion of many nations of northern and central Europe. Only later, in the seventh and eighth centuries, with the mission of Saint Augustine of Canterbury to England and Saint Boniface to Germany, did missionary expansion in western Europe acquire a firm connection with and dependence upon the See of Rome. Competition between Arian and orthodox Christianity ended with the defeat of Arianism. In connection with that defeat the Latin language also triumphed as the only language of the Catholic Western Church, distinct from the "Gothic" Arian Church, which used the Gothic Bible of Ulfilas (Wulfila) and a liturgy in Gothic (perhaps because it was already following the Eastern practice accepted in Constantinople of translating the liturgy into the vernacular).

Christian expansion in the East followed a slightly different pattern because of the role played by the still powerful empire of Constantinople. There were spontaneous missionary forays beyond the imperial borders, and the imperial government was always ready to give them support, which involved some control and some centralization. The emperors understood their role in terms of preserving a Christian—and a "Roman"— unity. In the missionary field they even disregarded the tragic schism between Chalcedonians and Monophysites. Actively concerned with healing the schism, the emperors, particularly Justinian (527–560), nevertheless supported Monophysite missions in Nubia, Persia, and the Arabian peninsula. The Islamic invasion ended Christian missionary expansion in the Middle East, but in the ninth and tenth centuries Byzantine Christianity spread to the North. This spectacular expansion witnessed to the continuous universal and missionary consciousness of the Byzantine Orthodox Church, a consciousness that other Eastern Christian groups, reduced to the ghetto-like survival within Islamic society, were not able to preserve.

Thus, for a long time Eastern Christianity was more centralized around Constantinople than was Western Christendom around Rome. This was still the case in the ninth and tenth centuries when the mission to the Slavs occurred so successfully. But administrative and cultural centralization did not lead to linguistic uniformity. The well-known mission of Saints Cyril and Methodius (863), although it could not develop in German-dominated Moravia, gave rise to a spectacular development of Slavic Christian civilization in Bulgaria. As witnessed by the *Primary Chronicle*, the Cyrillo-Methodian mission was viewed, by the Russians as well, as the starting point of Christianity in all Slavic lands.[3]

For the principality of Kiev and its dependencies, particularly Novgorod, the baptism of Saint Vladimir implied both a permanent entry into a world community of Christian nations and the beginning of literacy and literature. The event of 988 was, of course, preceded by several preliminary steps, including particularly the baptism of Princess Olga (957), which involved contacts between East and West. However, the marriage of Vladimir and the sister of Emperor Basil II, the establishment in Kiev of a Greek ecclesiastical hierarchy, the building under Vladimir's son, Iaroslav, of the Cathedral of Saint Sophia, the founding of the Monastery of the Caves, and many other contemporary decisive steps made the Kievan state into a permanent member of what Obolensky called the "Byzantine Commonwealth."

Indeed, the "Commonwealth," always centered in Constantinople, implied a sharing of cultural values and priorities inherited from but also replacing the old Roman *imperium*. During almost the same period, the West was gradually developing its own formula, which also replaced the imperial system that the Carolingians and the Ottonians attempted to restore for a while: a system of *papal* monarchy, both religious and political, which resulted from the "Gregorian reformation" of the eleventh century.

The "Commonwealth" had a recognizable and unquestionable center in Constantinople. This implied strict adherence to the orthodox faith, reflecting in this regard the tradition of early Christianity, in which unity of faith was the basic link between local churches conditioning all canonical or administrative structures. The unity of faith was expressed in liturgical uniformity and also in the acceptance of Byzantine art, music, and translated literature as prevailing cultural patterns. However, as mentioned earlier, there was no linguistic uniformity, and the Cyrillo-Methodian tradition of translations was generally maintained. Politically, there were several solutions for defining relations between the Constantinopolitan imperial center and the member states: from direct military conquest and annexation (whenever that was possible) to the establishment of competing Slavic centers such as Preslav, Ohrid, Trnovo, and Skoplje, or Greek centers like Thessalonika or Trebizond, or the distant Georgian center of Mtskheta. The existence of the Commonwealth did not prevent tensions and conflicts, but the principle of a single Christian empire was not challenged. From the ecclesiastical point of view, centralization under the "ecumenical" patriarch of Constantinople was always the solution preferred by the Byzantines. However, the emergence of independent patriarchates could not be prevented beyond the borders of the empire: in Georgia (fifth century), Preslav and Ohrid (tenth century), Trnovo (thirteenth century) and Serbia (fourteenth century). These national centers were reluctantly recognized, but eventually suppressed (except for the distant Georgian patriarchate) whenever circumstances allowed.

Compared with the southern Slavs, both the Kievan and the Muscovite Russians remained more consistently loyal to Constantinople. Never politically controlled by the empire, they recognized the emperor as the God-established symbolic head of the Christian universe. His name was mentioned in churches, and his involvements in ecclesiastical affairs, including the affairs of the Church in Russia, were not challenged. Indeed, the patriarchate of Constantinople was the main channel of administrative and cultural ties with Byzantium: the head of the Church in Russia during the entire period was the "metropolitan of Kiev and all Rus'," a prelate appointed from Constantinople and generally a Greek. The role of the emperor, and not only of the patriarch, in the appointment of metropolitan and the definition of the extent of his jurisdiction was well documented in the sources, especially for the late medieval period.[4] Except for a brief military confrontation under Iaroslav in 1051, there were no direct political conflicts between Byzantium and Kiev comparable to the numerous wars fought by the Greeks, the Bulgarians, and the Serbs. The Russians made no serious attempts at establishing ecclesiastical independence before 1448. This tradition of ecclesiastical loyalty was broken only briefly, in the cases of (perhaps) Metropolitan Hilarion (1051) and (certainly) Metropolitan Clement Smoliatich (1147–1155), and within the borders of Lithuania, in the case of Gregory Tsamblak (1415-1419). Caused by local and episodical conflicts, these incidents were not real challenges to the system under which the metropolitanate of Kiev was conceived as a province of the patriarchate of Constantinople.

During the entire period, although it was administered mostly by Greeks, the Russians never felt the Church as a "foreign" body. Quite the opposite, it represented the only administrative structure that held together the politically divided "land of Rus'." Extending from the Carpathian Mountains to the Volga and from the Baltic to the southern steppes, controlled by Cumans and Patzinks, the Kievan realm, following the death of Iaroslav (1054), became divided into numerous "appanages." Unity was preserved for a time, under a single Grand Prince of Kiev, head of the princely family. However, the sack of Kiev in 1169 by Prince Andrei Bogoliubsky of Suzdal led to the establishment of two regional centers of Rus': the northeastern Suzdalian grand-principality, where Andrei built a new capital Vladimir-on-the-Kliazma; and the southwestern principality of Galicia-Volhynia, united by Prince Roman in 1199. Soon the divided country was to face the Mongol conquest (1237–1240). The northeast became solidly a part of the Mongol empire, whereas Galicia-Volhynia, as well as Novgorod, succeeded in preserving some degree of autonomy. In the fourteenth century the Lithuanian pagan dynasty of Gedyminovichi succeeded in gathering a vast part of Rus', including Kiev itself, under its control, while Poland eventually annexed Galicia. Understandably, none of the states actually ruling the former territory of Kievan Rus' could claim to represent fully the Kievan legacy and legitimacy. The Church alone could make the claim. Its unity was, for understandable reasons, challenged by the various pretenders to political leadership, but its head, the metropolitan, appointed from Byzantium, was generally able to remain above the competitions of local powers. He also profited from the religiously tolerant respect of the Mongol Khans who maintained commercial and political ties with Constantinople and for whom the metropolitan was a respectable intermediary in foreign diplomatic contacts. The Byzantine authorities dealt very skillfully with the situation in

Russia, appointing alternatively Russian and Greek metropolitans, and, after some hesitation, endorsing Moscow as the most reliable and secure residence for the head of the Church.[5] Whether the Byzantines realized it or not at the time, their choice would contribute greatly to the rise of the Muscovite empire.

During the period of the Mongol rule, the Church could exercise its unifying role precisely because it was attached to a legitimate center of Christian universality and because it was a province of the Byzantine patriarchate. It incarnated values that were higher than those of petty local political interests and power struggles. The "catholic" values of Orthodoxy manifested themselves particularly in the spiritual figure of Saint Sergius of Radonezh (ca. 1314–1392), in the missionary labors among the Finnic tribes of Zyrians by Saint Stephen of Perm' (1340–1396), in the monastic revival inspired by the "hesychasm" of Mt. Athos, in the opportunities given to a great painter, Theophanes the Greek, to develop his talent and to spur the achievements of Andrei Rublev and the Rublev school.

But it was certainly the "system," the ecclesiastical structure itself, that made possible the extraordinary role of the Church. Some metropolitans of the period stand out personally as real makers of history. Metropolitan Cyril (1242–1281), although a nominee of southern Prince Daniel of Galicia, spent most of his tenure in the north, established ties between the families of Daniel and of Alexander Nevsky, Grand Prince of Vladimir, and secured unity and survival under the Mongol rule. Among his successors, the metropolitans of Kiev, now residing permanently in Moscow, the names of Peter (1308–1325) and Alexis (1354–1378) stand out prominently in Muscovite hagiography, which is colored by a somewhat narrower concept of "nationhood" accepted since the sixteenth century. Both rendered great services to the rise of Moscow.

Perhaps even more outstanding is the personality of Metropolitan Cyprian (1375–1406). A Bulgarian by birth, Cyprian was known not only as a "friend of the Byzantine Empire" (φιλορώμαιος ἄνθρωπος),[6] but also as the author of a "Praise" (Ἐγκώμιον) in honor of the predecessor, Saint Peter, architect of Moscow's supremacy in Russian ecclesiastical affairs.[7] But Cyprian also succeeded in remaining a "friend" of Polish King Jagiello, in spite of the latter's conversion to Roman Catholicism.[8] Cyprian secured the ecclesiastical unity of all Russian dioceses, including even Galicia, which was under Polish rule. Together with Saint Sergius, he led the principality of Moscow away from its dependence upon the Mongols; and in his scholarly achievements, as writer and translator, he is unparalleled among Russian bishops of the period. It is noteworthy from the ideological point of view that the sponsorship of Metropolitan Cyprian allowed the compilation (*svod*) in 1408 of the various regional chronicles into a single chronicle (the so-called *Troitskaia Letopis'*), as the history of a single nation. Indeed, Cyprian was a "catholic metropolitan of Russia,"[9] a guardian of unity in the name of the Church, and an upholder of Orthodox Christian universality at its best, in the Cyrillo-Methodian tradition.

The achievements of Cyprian were maintained by his successor, the Greek Photius (1408–1431), but they did not survive the tenure of Isidore (1436–1441), as world events of the first magnitude were changing the fate of Russian Christianity for centuries to come. A participant in the Council of Florence (1438–1439) and an architect of the Union concluded there, Isidore would be rejected upon his return to Moscow (1441).

1448-1721: Instability and Transition

In the eyes of the Russians, the capitulation of the highest civil and ecclesiastical authorities of Constantinople before the papacy in Florence (1438–1439) and the fall of Byzantium (1453) were connected events with mystical significance. The vision of an Orthodox world of which Russia was only a part lost its concreteness. To preserve Orthodoxy, Moscow was now on its own. Initially, it could claim to represent in its entirety a "Russia" that included both Kiev and Moscow and had maintained its ecclesiastical unity, against many odds, under Metropolitan Cyprian. Indeed, in 1448, Jonas was elected "metropolitan of Kiev and all Russia" in Moscow, independently from Constantinople, after the rejection of the Uniate Isidore, and was recognized for a time by all the dioceses controlled by Poland. But a competing "metropolitan of Kiev and all Russia," Gregory Bolgarin, was soon consecrated in Rome (1458) by the exiled "uniate" patriarch of Constantinople, and he assumed power over what would later become the Ukraine and Belorussia. Eventually, Gregory switched allegiance from Rome to the Orthodox ecumenical patriarchate, now prisoner of the Turks (1470), not to Moscow. Henceforth, there would be two "Russian" churches, not one, as before.

What is remarkable is that Moscow assumed its lonely role of the last rampart of Orthodoxy with reluctance and little self-assurance. Following the rejection of Isidore in 1441, the Muscovites waited seven years before proceeding with the independent election of Jonas. Before taking the step, the Grand Prince wrote several deferential and apologetic letters to Constantinople about the matter. Following the fall of Byzantium the idea of

Muscovite ecclesiastical independence gained strength and *de facto* legitimacy; however, only at the end of the fifteenth century did ideas about a *translatio imperii* to Moscow begin to emerge. This theme appears in the so-called *Legend of the White Cowl*, circulated within the Latin-oriented court of the archbishop of Novgorod, Gennadius (1484-1504). Its intention, however, was not to exalt Moscow but to affirm the supremacy of the episcopate over the princely power.[10] Referring more explicitly to the power of the Muscovite Grand Prince, the famous letters of the monk Philotheus of Pskov, written to Basil III in the first years of the sixteenth century, are more apocalyptic than political in tone and in context: Moscow is not only the "third" Rome, but also the *last*, and for a very short time, because the end is near. The letters of Philotheus are anything but a political program; rather they provide a warning or even a threat; the Grand Prince is called to spiritual vigilance because there will be no recourse following a new betrayal similar to that of the first two Romes, but only judgment.[11] If anyone expressed the notion of a *translatio imperii* to Moscow as a clear-cut political theory, it is the ecumenical patriarch of Constantinople, Joasaph, but only in 1561, by affirming the legitimacy of the imperial title of Ivan IV, on the basis of his descent from Anna, the wife of Saint Vladimir and sister of Emperor Basil II.[12]

In Russia itself the idea of the third Rome seems to have expressed a sort of nostalgic and, at the same time, apocalyptic dream, as if the traditional Byzantine universalist scheme could be maintained in spite of all the historic catastrophes and the obviously new cultural and political realities of the sixteenth and the seventeenth centuries.

These realities were dominated by the rapid and deliberate transformation of Muscovy into a nation-state. This transformation and its implicit secular development and growth stood as the main concern of the founders of Moscow's greatness: Ivan III, Basil III, and Ivan IV. All three were convinced "Westernizers" in terms of establishing political and commercial ties with western European states. Ivan III's marriage with Zoe-Sophia Palaeologine, the niece of the last Byzantine emperor (1478), was not used very explicitly to enhance a continuity between Byzantium and Moscow. It rather served to enhance cultural Italian influence in Moscow since Zoe had been educated in Italy. Ivan's and Zoe's son Basil sponsored the development of a "German" free settlement in the suburbs of Moscow, through which Western ideas and technology gained access to Muscovite society. The awesome personality of Ivan IV, the "Terrible" (1533–1584), dominated the sixteenth century. He was the first Muscovite Grand Prince to be formally crowned "tsar," or emperor, according to a modified Byzantine ceremonial (16 January 1547), but very characteristically he took the title of "tsar of all Russia," not that of "Roman Emperor," as the theory of a third Rome would require, and his general policies were inspired more by Machiavelli—whom he personally appreciated—than by any Byzantine legacy.

In fact, throughout the sixteenth century, the visionaries who either lived the spiritual reality of Orthodox universality (like Saint Nil Sorsky and the trans-Volgan elders, or the great Maximus the Greek), or dreamed the myth of a continued Byzantine imperial legacy (the few churchmen who developed the idea of a third Rome) were all marginalized in Muscovite society. This is best illustrated by the circumstances of the establishment of the Moscow Patriarchate in 1589. The theory of the third Rome would imply the transfer of the ecumenical patriarchate from Turkish-held Constantinople to Russia. Patriarch Jeremiah II Tranos, who was visiting Moscow in that year, was offered the opportunity to make that move himself. As he refused, the Russians rather easily settled for a national patriarchate, the "patriarchate of Moscow and all Russia," formally established not by the tsar, but by the Greek patriarch, and occupying the *fifth*, not the first, place among the Orthodox patriarchs. National self-affirmation, not Byzantine universality, was the foremost concern of Boris Godunov, the powerful minister of Tsar Theodore, who engineered the proceedings of 1589.

Such national self-affirmation was in full conformity with the contemporary history of Europe. It could also find some legitimacy in the Cyrillo-Methodian tradition, which, by admitting the multiplicity of liturgical languages, endorsed the principle of national churches as well. But at the time of Cyril and Methodius, Christian universality was also finding its incarnation in the patristic and medieval sense of what the Christian faith implied. In post-Renaissance Europe, the state and the nation became ends in themselves, and the Church of Russia, isolated and defensive, from the middle of the fifteenth century gradually fell deeper under the state's domination.

The utter confusion of the "Time of Troubles," which included dynastic instability, Polish and Swedish invasions, the establishment of the Polish-dominated power of the False Dimitri in Moscow, led to compensatory resurgence of the Church's power, as the last resort of the nation's dignity and survival. But it was a fiercely defensive and insecure Church, lacking theological leadership, unconsciously receptive to Western ideas while externally anathematizing the Latins as heretics. All this inner weakness manifested itself in the tragic conflict between Patriarch Nikon and the "Old Believers."

The mystical and apocalyptic vision of Russia as the guardian of Orthodoxy in the few remaining years before the Last Judgment, as held by a few churchmen, stood as a clear inner contrast with the very practical and ambitious national growth of the Muscovite tsardom. In the seventeenth century Tsar Alexis Romanov (1645–1676) and Patriarch Nikon (1652–1658) made a last attempt at overcoming the contrast by giving concrete reality to Moscow's claim to be really the third Rome.

The deep crisis within both church and society created by this attempt showed clearly that the issue went much beyond the minor liturgical reform engineered initially by Nikon and pursued with quite unnecessary fierceness by the tsar after Nikon's deposition. The problem was of a spiritual nature and concerned the very nature of "Orthodox Russia" vis-à-vis Christian universality.

Increased contacts with both the Orthodox patriarchates of the Middle East and the Westernized Ukrainian clergy (eastern Ukraine was incorporated in 1654) raised the problem of liturgical uniformity between the local Orthodox churches. Actually Muscovite Russians were preoccupied with the state of their liturgical books since the sixteenth century. Lacking any competence or sound advice in the matter, Nikon decided, with the tsar's support, to achieve unification by simply adjusting all Russian texts and practices to those accepted at the time by the Eastern patriarchates. He pretended to "return to ancient Greek laws," whereas, in fact, he had no knowledge of or access to the true traditions of Orthodox Byzantium. Greek liturgical practices and the Greek books published in Venice incorporated some Latin texts and usages. His goal, like the tsar's, was to restore Russian prestige in Orthodox Christendom, but millions defending the existing Russian practices (which were often closer to the "ancient" ones than the neo-Greek habits) asked several questions: If, in order to be Orthodox, one has to follow those same Greeks who betrayed the Church at Florence and were punished by the Turkish conquest, what really happens to the theory of the third Rome? Were the Russians not Orthodox before Nikon's reforms? Or rather, was not the patriarch a heretic, and the tsar the Antichrist, whose coming had been forecast so often in Russian apocalyptic literature, including particularly the letters of the monk Philotheus about Moscow, the third Rome?

These questions were answered in the affirmative by the "Old Believers." Patriarch Nikon was soon disillusioned with the reforms. His dream of building up a strong church able to control the activities of the state became unacceptable to the tsar who had him defrocked. Russian Christianity was deeply wounded not only in its institutions but in its very soul. The reforms had been ridiculously minor: the sign of the cross with three fingers instead of two, *Alleluia* said thrice and not twice. They could not be compared with the substantial changes that historically had often taken place in the liturgy, such as the introduction in the fourteenth century by Patriarch Philotheos and Metropolitan Cyprian of the Palestinian rule, replacing the old practices of Constantinople. No one protested them at the time because the "catholic" sense of the universal church was not questioned. But in the seventeenth century there was no longer any spiritual assurance, no longer confidence in the ecclesiastical leadership, but an unhealthy defensiveness which suppressed, on both sides, the most elementary sense of history and tradition.

The Great Council of 1666–1667, presided over by Patriarchs Paisios of Alexandria and Macarios of Antioch, confirmed the reforms and assured formal universal Orthodox unity, but at the price of anathematizing millions of Russian "Old Believers." Facing merciless persecutions, splitting into a multitude of mutually exclusive sects, the schismatics found refuge in an apocalyptic withdrawal from history. As Florovsky rightly remarks, the Schism was not a survival of ancient Russia, but a dream and an escape from reality. The "Old Believers" lived in what they thought was the past or else in the apocalyptic future, but they rejected the present. They represented a *new* divisive phenomenon that had little to do with Holy Tradition.[13]

But the Orthodox Church itself, which had lost many of its members and was intellectually leaderless, was hardly prepared to face the coming radical challenge of Westernization. The idea of transient "Romes" proved to be an anachronistic myth; the Russians themselves did not know how to apply it to reality. The attempt was inconsistent from the start and ended in spiritual tragedy.

1721–1988: The Challenge of the West

Most historians describe the ecclesiastical reforms of Peter the Great as the ultimate humiliation of the Russian Church. Indeed, the suppression of the patriarchate and the establishment of a regime similar in every way to that of Protestant northern Europe were truly revolutionary. More dangerous than the administrative reforms themselves was a pervasive spirit of deliberate secularization imposed by the state, with police methods used extensively to fight "superstition," to limit the growth of monasticism, to impress—by force and great contempt for the past—a mentality coming from the Enlightenment. The intent was to promote a true Reformation. The so-called "Spiritual Regulation" (*Dukhovnyi Reglament*), a set of detailed by-laws for the Church composed by a Protestant-minded friend of Peter, Feofan Prokopovich, is a real manifesto of this new spirit.[14] Paradoxically, however, the network of theological schools established by Peter would teach primarily a Latin theology, with Latin as the language of instruction. This school methodology, manned almost exclusively by Ukrainian graduates of the Kievan Academy, would in fact perpetuate a spirit of the "Counter Reformation."

The whole reform amounted to a massive inoculation of Western culture and Western problematics. Actually, the process had begun much earlier and had provoked purely defensive, anti-Western reactions. The Russians attempted to freeze history in the "Council of the Hundred Chapters" (*Stoglav*), to solve all ethical problems in the *Domostroi*, to reassert the "third Rome" theory by imitating the Greeks (Nikon), or to withdraw from history altogether (the Old Believers). The challenge brought about by Peter required a more serious response, the emergence of a truly "catholic" and creative manifestation of the tradition of the Church, i.e., the ability to live Orthodox Christianity in a meaningful way within the new irreversible fact that Russia had entered modernity. This response could not be achieved overnight, but required the gradual uncovering of the authentic potentials of Russian Christianity, an ability to use Western problematics critically, to witness within the concrete realities of history, and to criticize the Russian past.

It is impossible to summarize the results fully, but I would affirm my strong conviction that during the post-Petrine time, Russian Orthodoxy won more authentic spiritual victories in terms of Christian witness to its people and to the world than in the preceding two centuries of its existence. Here are a few of the most obvious examples particularly relevant to the topic of this paper: the "catholicity" of the Christian tradition in Russia.

(1) As the Middle East and the Balkans fell under Islam, the Russian Church remained alone among the Orthodox churches able to pursue missionary expansion. It never stopped this mission. Continuing the work of great missionaries of the earlier period, like Saint Stephen of Perm and Saint Trypho of Pechenga, and following the Cyrillo-Methodian model of translating Scripture and Liturgy into vernacular languages, Orthodox missionaries evangelized the peoples of northeastern European Russia and Siberia. Of course, these missions were not always successful, and Russian missionaries, like the European missionaries in Asia and Africa, have been accused of actually pursuing colonial policies of Russification. Recent and more objective studies, however, have recognized their large measure of success.[15] Furthermore, the work accomplished by the two greatest missionaries of the

nineteenth century, Innocent Veniaminov and Nicholas Kasatkin, can still be seen today beyond the borders of Russia in Alaska and Japan and was quite independent of political considerations.

(2) The period following the Petrine reforms can rightly be described by the expression "Western captivity of Orthodox theology" used by Florovsky. The Protestant mentality permeating the reforms themselves and the Latin methodology adopted by the schools, while contradicting each other, had a common Western background. The fact remains, however, that once the Western thinking and methodology had been "digested," Russian theological schools produced by the end of the nineteenth century innumerable historical and patristic studies of the highest caliber. Their biblical translators had published a Russian Bible. The Russian clergy, although socially marginalized by the system, received an excellent theological education. Furthermore, Russian theologians were fully cognizant of contemporary Western theology, whereas very few Roman Catholic or Protestant scholars thought that anything useful could be read in the Russian language (Adolf Harnack is an exception; he studied Russian specifically to be able to read Glubokovsky's dissertation on Theodoret of Cyrrhus). The emergence, after the middle of the nineteenth century, of a "lay" theology—with people like Alexis Khomiakov and, later, the school of Vladimir Soloviev—also contributed to making Russian theology, in spite of its wandering away from the Byzantine patristic tradition (as mercilessly described by Florovsky in his *Ways of Russian Theology*), a diversified, but meaningful and hopeful witness to Orthodoxy, not only within Russia but also on a global scale.

(3) Peter the Great and his eighteenth-century successors attempted by administrative means to curb Russian monasticism as the main promoter of "superstition." The number of communities was reduced; their recruitment was strictly limited by the state, and their land holding secularized. Such measures became a factor provoking the emigration to Moldavia of the great Paisii Velichkovskii, translator of the Greek *Philokalia* into Slavonic.[16] When drastic limitations were imposed upon monastic institutions, the "hesychastic" contemplative trend, inspired by Mt. Athos and the Russian tradition of "Non-Possessors," developed anew, not only through the translations of Paisii, but also in the case of such remarkable personalities as Saint Tikhon of Zadonsk who knew how to combine his strong and conscious affinity with contemporary Western spirituality (particularly Johann Arndt and German pietism) with Orthodox monastic tradition.[17] In the nineteenth century Saint Seraphim of Sarov and the "elders" of Optino would represent the most

authentic link of Orthodox spirituality in Russia with the early Christian and Byzantine tradition. The strength and influence of that tradition in Russian society is another victory over the constraining "system" instituted by Peter.

(4) In spite of the excruciating crisis of the seventeenth century and the aggressive secularization imposed in the eighteenth, Russia produced a modern literature, which in its quasi entirety and in the persons of its most prominent representatives is a Christian literature, not because it treats exclusively religious subjects, but because it shows awareness of the transcendent nature of human destiny and because it expresses adequately and pertinently what is authentic in religion itself. In spite of some nasty aberrations of the young Pushkin or the delusions of the old Tolstoy, the overall message of Russian literature as a whole, a message not only to Russia, but indeed to the world, is that man lives not by bread alone and that the solution to the human tragedy is to be found in Christ's cross and resurrection. Remarkably the Russian classics have remained so for the Russians of today, and most of what is truly valuable in contemporary Russian literature continues that great tradition. Such signals coming from a country where materialism is state dogma reveal that a thousand years of Christianity in Russia were a millennium of inner, spiritual struggle—certainly not a triumph only. But cannot the same be said of the *two* thousand years of historical Christianity seen as a whole?

(5) The ultimate trial of Russian Christianity, however, came during the last seventy years. Did it pass the test, not only in terms of a survival of the Church as an important element of the Russian national tradition, but as a "catholic" witness to the power of faith? I think it can be said that it did. Not only Marxist theoreticians, but also many Western historians have said (and sometimes continue to say) that the Orthodox Church of Russia was so tightly identified with the old tsarist regime that it was actually doomed as soon as the revolution triumphed. This view overlooks the fact that the Church was in many ways marginalized and brutalized by that old regime and that its clergy were not an "ally of the exploiting classes" at all, but a social group spiritually close to the mass of the people. The revolutionary and post-revolutionary fears made millions of political victims, but also thousands upon thousands of authentic martyrs, who will certainly be one day publicly recognized as the seed of Orthodoxy's perseverance and revival. Their witness is important not only for the future of Christianity in Russia, but also for a triumphant faith in the midst of a century where secularism seems to have the upper hand in post-Christian Western society.

Conclusion

A century passed after the Petrine reforms before the Russian intellectual elite undertook, at the beginning of the last century, a formal debate about the place of Russia in world history. In his *History of the State of Russia* (1816–1829), N. M. Karamzin brilliantly showed that Russia had indeed a pre-Petrine past. Although erudite medieval historians began to study ancient chronicles, some doubted the cultural value of that past altogether. For Chaadaev, Russia "does not belong to any of the big families of humanity," since (before Peter the Great) "nothing happening in Europe ever reached" it. Its centuries-old isolation might still give Russia the advantages of youth and freshness, but for Chaadaev its future lay in Europe and with Europe. This view of the so-called Westerners was from the 1840s fiercely attacked by Slavophiles, whose reaction significantly was not only to defend the Russian past, but also to restore a holistic sense of the Church, in which they saw not only a product of history but a divine-human reality. Orthodoxy, therefore, according to the Slavophiles, is that which gives Russian history a meaning—precisely that which Peter's reforms attempted to suppress.

As one looks now at this famous debate between the Westerners and the Slavophiles, one discovers, of course, that the two groups were not so far from each other as it appeared at the time. As Florovsky notes, "from ancient times, the Russian soul lives and dwells in many centuries and many ages simultaneously."[18] In the nineteenth century particularly, practically every member of the Russian elite, including those who embraced the Slavophile ideology, spoke English, wrote in French, and thought in German. In his poem "Scythians," Blok said: "We understand all things—the sharp Gallic mind, and the nebulous German genius . . . ." These words were said not without "messianic" arrogance, but they also reflected what Florovsky calls the "nomadic habits" of the Russian intelligentsia, the tendency to change their dwellings often, and their faddism.

Protection against the danger of nomadism could be found only in the wholesome vision of the Church, which the older Slavophiles defended and which they themselves acquired both by reading the Fathers and by becoming intimately familiar with the problematics and tragedies of Western Christendom. Better than others, they understood that *independence* from Western intellectual captivity did not imply *estrangement* from the problems of Christendom as a whole. The witness to Christian truth reacquires a witness of Catholic Orthodoxy, which is able to save the world, and not only Russia.

Of course, the nationalistic and messianic temptation became quite strong in the later politicized Slavophilism of the 1860s and the 1880s, when it began to be accepted as a political ideology by the state. Nothing was more foreign to its original roots, which could be characterized as ahistorical and Romantic, but not nationalistic. Simplification and reduction of the mystery of the Church to political, social, and earthly realities are most incompatible with "catholicity." Such temptations are sometimes present in Russian Orthodoxy today. More than ever, the straight line must be discovered in the integrity and wholesomeness of the ecclesial tradition itself and in that capacity for self-criticism and self-purification that characterized mature Russian religious thought in the past and that, more than ever, is needed for its future.

Notes

1. I have discussed this basic principle of orthodox ecclesiology in *Catholicity and the Church* (Crestwood, N.Y., 1983), pp. 111–120.

2. *Povest' vremennykh let*, ed. D. S. Likhachev and B. A. Romanov (Moscow and Leningrad, 1950), vol. 1, p. 75; S. H. Cross and O. P. Sherbowitz-Wetzor, trans., *The Russian Primary Chronicle* (Cambridge, Mass., 1953), p. 111.

3. The *Russian Primary Chronicle* includes a detailed account of the Cyrillo-Methodian mission to Moravia, although the latter was not directly concerned with Russia (except for a controversial mention of "Russian letters" brought by the brothers from an earlier mission to the Crimea).

4. For instance, in 1347 Emperor John Cantacuzenos issued a "chrystobull" defining the borders of the Russian dioceses and their relationship with the metropolitan of Kiev residing in Moscow. The Russian grand prince is addressed as "the very beloved nephew of Our Majesty." (Text in K. E. Zachariae von Lingenthal, *Jus graeco-romanum,* vol. 3 [Leipzig, 1860], 700–703; English translation in J. Meyendorff, *Byzantium and the Rise of Russia. A Study of Byzantino-Russian Relations in the Fourteenth Century* [Cambridge, 1981], 280–282).

5. For a detailed discussion of the history of the Russian metropolitanate in the fourteenth century, see Meyendorff, *Byzantium and the Rise of Russia,* 73ff.

6. See D. Obolensky, "A *Philorhomaios anthropos:* Metropolitan Cyprian of Kiev and all Russia," *DOP* 32 (1979):79–98. The expression appears in the draft of a letter by Patriarch Matthew to Cyprian written in 1400 (Miklosich-Müller, *Acta Patriarchatus Constantinopolitani* (Vienna, 1862), vol. 2, p. 369.

7. Text in *Velikie Minei Chet'i* (Moscow, 1868), 21 December, cols. 1942–1946; earlier shorter version in G. Prokhorov, *Povest' o Mitiae* (Leningrad, 1978), pp. 214–215; partial English translation in Meyendorff, *Byzantium and the Rise of Russia,* pp. 300–302.

8. See a letter of Patriarch Anthony to Jagiello, dated 1397, in Miklosich-Müller, vol. 2, p. 283.

9. Μητροπολίτης Ῥωσίας καθολικός, ibid., pp. 192–194.

10. See an accessible English translation in S. Zenkovsky, *Medieval Russia's Epics, Chronicles, and Tales* (New York, 1974), pp. 323–332.

11. For pertinent remarks on the letters, see G. Florovsky, *Puti russkogo bogosloviia* (Paris, 1937; rpt. 1981), pp. 10–11.

12. Most recent edition of the patriarchal letter in A. A. Takhiaos, Πηγὲς ἐκκλησιαστικῆς ἱστορίας τῶν ὀρθοδόξων Σλάβων (Thessaloniki, 1984), vol. 1, pp. 161–162.

13. Florovsky, pp. 67–69.

14. See the English translation of the *Reglament* in: James Cracraft, ed., *The God and Peter the Great. The Works of Thomas Consett, 1723–1729* (New York, 1982), pp. 1–203.

15. See for instance O. Kobtzeff, "Ruling Siberia: The Imperial Power, the Orthodox Church and the Native People," *St. Vladimir's Theological Quarterly* 30, no. 3 (1986):269–280.

16. See S. Chetverikov, *Moldavskii starets Paisii Velichkovskii, ego zhizn', uchenie i vliianie na pravoslavnoe monashestvo* (Paris, 1976) (*Starets Paisii Velichkovskii: His Life, Teachings, and Influence on Orthodox Monasticism.* Translated by V. Lickwar and A. Lisenko [Belmont, Mass., 1980]). For a complete and highly informative compendium of materials on Paisii, including his unpublished autobiography, see A. Tachiaos, *The Revival of Byzantine Monasticism among Slavs and Romanians in the XVIIIth Century* (Thessaloniki, 1986).

17. On Tikhon, see particularly N. Gorodetsky, *The Humiliated Christ in Modern Russian Thought* (London, 1938).

18. Florovsky, p. 500.

Крещение Руси: мировоззренческие и эстетические аспекты

ALEKSANDR PANCHENKO

Относительно ментальности древнерусского общества в период крещения существуют прямо противоположные мнения. Одно гиперскептическое, настаивающее на том, что решение Владимира повергло большинство населения в пессимизм. В доказательство приводят тот фрагмент «Повести временных лет», согласно которому новую веру вводили принудительно, и Владимир, побуждая киевлян креститься, прибег к угрозе: не явившиеся на реку объявлялись врагами князя. Когда же понадобились отроки «на ученье книжное», своего рода бурсаки, Владимир употребил силу. Он набирал будущих причетников из семей «нарочитой чади», социальной элиты. «Матере же чад сих плакаху по них, еще бо не бяху ся утвердили верою, но акы по мертвеци плакахуся».[1] Комментируя этот фрагмент, Б. А. Успенский сопоставил деяния Владимира с деяниями Петра: «Здесь возникает разительная аналогия с процессом европеизации при Петре I, одним из моментов которого также было насильственное обучение».[2]

В качестве доказательства привлекается и археологический материал, будто бы подтверждающий позднее, считавшееся баснословным известие Иоакимовской летописи о вооруженном сопротивлении крещению (Путяте и Добрыне) жителей Софийской стороны Новгорода: они расправились с прихожанами Спасского храма, который до 988-989 гг. мирно уживался с языческим большинством. В. Л. Янин пишет: «Археологические раскопки выявили ряд существенных реалий, соответствующих этому рассказу. Церковь Спаса может быть локализована только на Разваже улице, где в дальнейшем существовал храм с тем же названием. В этом районе были произведены раскопки широкой площадью и ... обнаружены следы пожара 989 г., уничтожившего здесь всю застройку. Важнейшей следует признать находку в слоях, предшествующих пожару 989 г., христианского креста-тельника, свидетельствующего о наличии здесь христиан до официального акта крещения».[3]

Гиперскептики полагают, что Русь пережила крещение как драму и даже трагедию. Это весьма сомнительно. Матери всегда оплакивают разлуку с детьми. Тогда, при Владимире, слезы могли быть особенно горьки и обильны, потому что детям предстояло новое поприще, которого страшились как раз из-за его новизны. Петр тоже посылал «в новизну», и наблюдение Б. А. Успенского резонно. Однако мы знаем, что никаких общественных потрясений отправка дворянских недорослей в Европу не вызвала. Продолжая аналогию, можно допустить, что в исходе X в. все обошлось более или менее спокойно. Конечно, есть соблазн истолковать слова «акы по мертвеци» семиотически (переход из одного мира в другой). Но по меньшей мере равноправно и другое толкование, житейское: матери не просто плакали, они голосили, как голосят по покойнику (или начиная с Петра по забритому в рекруты).

Что до «увязки» позднелетописного баснословия и новгородского пожарища, сделанной В. Л. Яниным, — ее надлежит счесть излишне смелой. Археологическая датировка с точностью до года в данной ситуации невероятна. Невероятно, между прочим, и крещение новгородцев «мечом и огнем». Ни у Добрыни, ни у его державного племянника-князя для этого не было никаких возможностей. Ошибочно видеть в киевском князе самодержца вроде Петра. Князь очень зависел от веча, народ был вооружен, и ополчение по силе превосходило дружину.[4]

Не будем рассматривать (по причине явной недостоверности) «миссионерскую» точку зрения, согласно которой крещение вызвало всеобщий энтузиазм (как на полотне В. М. Васнецова). Гораздо вернее полагать, что Русь отнеслась к акту Владимира с большим спокойствием, частью с любопытством, частью равнодушно, поскольку этот акт не затронул большинства. Вся сумма исторических свидетельств — а эта сумма велика — подтверждает, что именно так и было на самом деле.

Есть три вехи на пути человека — рождение, брак, смерть. Их обрядовое обрамление необходимо и достаточно для оценки религиозной ориентации общества. Из правил митрополита Иоанна II известно, что в поколениях внуков и правнуков Владимира венчание в храме оставалось прерогативой социальной элиты. Простой же народ продолжал «играть» свадьбы без попа, притом, как показывают новейшие исследования, обязательно со скоморохом (впрочем, датировка этого обыкновения не ясна). Любопытно, что этот глагол употреблялся только с существительным «свадьба» и не применялся ни к какому другому празднику. Языческий ореол глагола очевиден из Даниила Заточника, который «уравнивал как запретные 'богу лгати' и 'вышним играти'».[5]

Масса сельских жителей и покойников своих хоронила по-язычески. Крестики в домонгольских погребениях в общем редки (хотя от столетия к столетию их становится больше). К тому же они как бы уравнены в правах с амулетами, например с медвежьими клыками. Это делается чисто по-русски, «на всякий случай», по принципу «на том свете разберут». Даже когда дело касается погребений заведомо крещеных людей, например, новгородских посадников, строгости в обряде не наблюдается: погребают с оружием, не опасаясь обвинений в неправославии.

Что до рождений, у нас нет материала, дабы судить о том, сколько из них сопровождалось крещением младенцев, а сколько нет. Однако в нашем распоряжении всегда остается именослов, источник беспристрастный и красноречивый, и мы еще обратимся к соотношению мирских и крестных имен в княжеском роду.

У новообращенных народов можно считать почти правилом появление «Юлиана Отступника», когда государь, наследующий первому христианину из правящей фамилии, пытается реабилитировать и восстановить язычество. Так, например, было в Болгарии, в Польше, в Чехии, так было и в Швеции XI века после падения династии Инглингов. Но Русь являет собою исключение из этого правила; она не последовала примеру соседей и родственников (имею в виду династические и этнические узы). Казалось бы, нет ничего естественнее, чем обвинение в неоязычестве Святополка Окаянного, убийцы первых киевских святых Бориса и Глеба. Однако в борисоглебских памятниках, единодушно и резко враждебных убийце, такого обвинения не находим — потому, несомненно, что для него не было ни малейших оснований и что оно никому не пришло в голову. Значит, религиозная ситуация не осознавалась как ситуация проблемная. Если общество ею не очень интересовалось и не использовало ее для хулы либо хвалы — ведь и Бориса с Глебом не пытались изобразить замученными за Христа, — то общество ею было довольно.

Важно также, что Русь, ставши ордынской провинцией, не знала характерного для славянского Юга «потурченства», хотя при хане Узбеке и его преемниках переход в ислам мог быть для иных весьма выгодным. Но все или почти все остались верны православию, опять-таки потому, что оно им было по душе.

О причинах «пониженной драматичности», характерной для крещеной Руси, надлежит задуматься. Бесспорно, что христианство распространилось в Киеве задолго до Владимира «как вера частная, о бок и рядом с господствующим язычеством».[6] Бесспорно, что отношение к христианству киевской знати, князя и дружины, менялось. Из договоров с греками видно, что при Игоре оно было сочувственным, часть его дружинников клялась Перуном, часть же церковью Илии, а при Святославе равнодушным, но всегда терпимым. «Живяше же Ольга с сыном своим Святославом, и учаше и мати креститися, и не брежаше того ни во уши приимати; но аще кто хотяше креститися, не браняху, но ругахуся тому ... Якоже бо Ольга часто глаголашеть: 'Аз, сыну мои, Бога познах и радуюся; аще ты познаеши, и радоватися почнешь'. Он же не внимаше того, глаголя: 'Како аз хочю ин закон прияти един? А дружина моа сему смеятися начнуть'».[7] Христианство, с точки зрения Святослава, смешная вера («ругахуся» тоже говорит не о брани, но насмешке). Святослава можно понять, если сопоставить походную и кровавую жизнь этого сурового и жестокого воина с десятисловием и тем более Нагорной проповедью. Но важен эмоциональный и эстетический подтекст ответа князя: христианство не страшно, оно смешно, а со смешным не борются, его терпят.

Положение резко изменилось при Владимире. Именно он, будущий креститель Руси, обагрил руки кровью христиан. На протяжении одного десятилетия он провел две конфессиональные реформы — сначала языческую, в 988 г. христианскую. Побуждения, надо полагать, оба раза были схожими: Владимир считал, что единению Руси может и должна соответствовать и способствовать единообразная культура, в тогдашних условиях — единая вера. Монокультура всегда навязывается сверху и обычно сопровождается насилием. Крайнее его проявление — убийство киевских первомучеников, двух варягов-христиан — сына, которого собирались принести в жертву кумирам, и отца, который защищал своего отпрыска. «И осквернися кровию земля Руська», — гласит летопись.

Почему Владимир так скоро отрекся от своего днепровского «Олимпа»? Во-первых, монокультура, как показывает исторический опыт, вообще недостижима, тем более на языческой основе. Если даже для маленькой античной Греции была характерна гетерогенность культов, что же тогда говорить о бескрайней Русской равнине? Во-вторых, языческая реформа не могла не встретить отпора: не зря же о кровавых жертвоприношениях не забывали и в летописные времена. К тому же Владимир был крайне непопулярен. Об этом говорят описания его смерти и похорон, сетования «Повести временных лет» на киевлян, которые его «не прославили». Об этом говорит и борисоглебская трагедия: если Владимирова дружина, узнав о смерти князя, бросила его любимого сына на произвол судьбы, значит, она ждала этой смерти и радовалась ей.

С отпором и с неприязнью Владимиру приходилось считаться. Это одна из причин осторожности и колебаний перед второй реформой, того, что принято называть «выбором вер». Презумпция, конечно, была монотеистической, но ситуация состязания между иудаизмом, исламом, латинством и греческим обрядом соответствует реальному положению Руси. Пусть недостоверны миссионерские речи, избрание «мужей добрых и смысленых, числом 10», пусть вымышлены и посольства (хотя полагают, что посольства в Булгар и Хорезм имели место), — все же контакты с четырьмя монотеистическими вероисповеданиями — не выдумка. Когда киевского князя именуют «каганом», то подразумевается, что Киевская держава выступает в роли государственной правопреемницы Хазарии, данниками которой еще сравнительно недавно были днепровские поляне. Государственный континуитет может предполагать и континуитет конфессиональный — по крайней мере, в качестве проблемы. Мусульманский мир был знаком Руси не хуже, хотя бы потому, что она граничила с Волжской Булгарией. Нет сомнений и относительно культурного обмена с Германией, т.е. с латинством: это и посольство княгини Ольги к Оттону I в 959 г., и какие-то германские планы убитого Владимиром Ярополка, быть может, одновременно брачные и конфессиональные.[8]

Владимир был очень осторожен; во второй раз ошибиться опасно. Он боялся обмануться, тем более что внутри и мусульманства, и христианства были действительно «опасные» ответвления — исмаилизм, манихейство, богомильство, альбигойство. Предпочтение Византии вовсе не было неизбежностью. На Руси это понимали, как явствует из текста митрополита Илариона: тот, не сомневаясь в Божественном Промысле, рассматривал религиозные реформы и как цивилизационные вехи. Они совершаются «во времена своа»,[9] т.е. на определенном этапе исторического пути народов и стран. Насколько сильна была эта цивилизационная точка зрения, видно из фрагмента о «гибели» иудаизма. Причина ее не только в том, что непризнанный Христос был распят иудеями, но и в превратностях их земной судьбы, государственной и этнической, в пленении и в разрушении римлянами Иерусалима: «Иудейство оттоле погыбе, и закон по семь ... погасе, и расеяни быша иудеи по странам».[10] По Илариону, на смену дряхлеющим народам приходят народы юные, у которых все в настоящем и все впереди. Такова Русь. Это, в сущности, современная концепция о возрастах этноса.[11]

Владимир решился тогда, когда ему представилась возможность сделать суверенный выбор. Византия не навязывала Руси свою веру, да и не в силах была ее навязать. После разысканий А. В. Поппэ дело представляется следующим образом.[12] В 987 г. Василий II был императором без империи. Узурпатор Варда Фока занял всю Малую Азию. Корсунь (Херсонес Таврический) держала сторону претендента. Последней надеждой императора был киевский князь. Один отряд Владимир отправил на Босфор, а сам во главе другого покарал корсунских мятежников летом или весной 989 г. Платой за помощь была рука порфирогенетки Анны, которая, видимо, прибыла в Киев летом предыдущего года. До этого Владимир крестился и стал Василием (возможно, в день Богоявления 6 января 988 г.). Что до крещения киевских жителей, то из предлагаемых А. В. Поппэ дат самой приемлемой кажется мне 27 мая 988 г., день Пятидесятницы. Во-первых, в конце мая в Днепре вода уже теплая — надо же было посчитаться с чувствами и здоровьем земляков! Во-вторых, Пятидесятница, когда Святой Дух снизошел на апостолов и они вдруг заговорили на разных наречиях, это реабилитация (по сравнению с Вавилонским столпотворением) наций и национальных языков. Крестится «язык нов», притом и хвалить Бога он будет не по-гречески, не по-латыни, а на своем или почти своем языке. Выбор дня Пятидесятницы — еще одна благодатная для Руси отметина.

Владимир не добивался Анны, император сам ее навязал своему спасителю, хотя византийская матримониальная доктрина строго запрещала выдавать порфирородных девиц за варваров. Коль скоро Византия зависела от Владимира, то он волен был проводить реформу по собственному разумению. Какие религиозные и культурные идеи ее оплодотворяли и сопровождали, можно судить по летописной «Речи философа». Сознавая, что это краткое, облегченное, считающееся с уровнем неофитов изложение, мы все же не должны забывать о чрезвычайной важности этой «Речи». Ее надлежит расценивать как «русский вариант православия» (дело не в догматике, а в культуре).

Начнем с негативных моментов, т.е. с вероучительных купюр. Чего нет в «Речи философа»? В ней нет буквально ни слова о нравственности, ни слова о десяти заповедях и Нагорной проповеди. Следовательно, Владимир не воспринимал крещение в качестве этического обновления и этического обязательства. В сфере этики неофиты были свободны и могли следовать обычаю, преданию, т.е. национальной традиции. В этой связи примечательно, что многие десятилетия спустя летописец-христианин (притом монах) не настаивает на связи нравственности с конфессией. Со ссылкой на Георгия Амартола он пишет о том, что одни народы руководствуются письменным законом, другие

— устным обычаем, и не эти «руководства» определяют черты их нравственных физиономий. Хороши поляне: «Своих отець обычай имуть кроток и тих». Легко возразить, что это самовосхваление (полянам — хвала, соседям древлянам — хула). Но апологию сирийцев никакими человеческими слабостями не объяснить (сирийцы «закон имуть — отець своих обычай: не любодеяти и прелюбодеяти, ни красти, ни оклеветати, ни убити, ни зло деяти весьма»). Значит, это историософская концепция.

Это показатель того, что христианизация не осознавалась как перерыв традиции. Хотя первые русские писатели охотно пользовались расхожими этикетными оппозициями «тьма — свет», «мрак — заря», но состояние язычества в их представлении не было состоянием варварства. Именно поэтому у Илариона в культурной памяти нации равноправны и «просветитель» Руси Владимир, и его предки-язычники «старый Игорь» и «славный Святослав». Если «худость» внеположна язычеству, она внеположна и его устной культуре. Это убеждение отобразилось, в частности, в скудости или лаконизме летописных сведений о славянской письменности. Летописцы, скорее всего, не видели в ней чего-то экстраординарного (в ценностном аспекте). Они не без оснований полагали, что упорядоченная жизнь в сфере устной культуры не только возможна, она имеет даже некоторые преимущества: тренирует память, создает привычку к афористической речи; княжеские речи перед битвой, «дипломатические ноты» того же Святослава отмечены словесным изяществом. Не случайно человечество чтит людей, не оставивших ни строчки — Сократа или Христа.

Что до позитивного момента «Речи философа», он очевиден: это историзм. Начав с дней творения, Философ заканчивает проповедью апостолов. Это сухой и невыразительный перечень, включающий рассказ о грехопадении, о Каине и Авеле, потопе, Вавилонской башне, праотцах и египетском пленении, Моисее, Иисусе Навине, о Давиде и Соломоне, о пророках, предсказавших воплощение Иисуса Христа, о его земном служении и страстях, воскресении и вознесении. Это эмоционально нейтральная, даже олимпийски бесстрастная речь, но она заключает в себе множество цивилизационных идей. Среди них первенствует идея, согласно которой мир познаваем, и человеку ведомы его начала и концы. Значит, религиозная реформа — не просто приращение знания, но принципиальная переоценка человека. Раньше он был игрушкой судьбы, каких-то неведомых сил, «страшилищ», говоря по-старинному, — теперь он овладел историей.

Иной позитивный момент «Речи философа» касается бессмертия души. Завершается «Речь» рассказом о судном дне, после которого праведники обретут «царство небесное, и красоту неизреченьну, веселье бес конца, и не умирати в веки». Грешникам уготована мука вечная, но кто — грешник? Тот, кто не верует в Христа и отказывается от крещения. Как видим, для вечного блаженства достаточно веры, о «добрых делах», о нравственных заслугах опять-таки речи нет.

Можно, конечно, считать, что это уловка и приманка для неофитов. Но плодотворнее стать на точку зрения этих неофитов и попытаться сделать выводы, которые делали они. Крещение есть спасение — вот главный вывод, о чем некогда писали Н. К. Никольский и М. Д. Приселков.[13] Это, конечно, вольномыслие, потому что крещение есть лишь одно из условий спасения. Однако это вольномыслие имело немаловажные эстетические и культурные последствия.

Основываясь на постулате «крещение есть спасение», современники и потомки Владимира избавлялись от страха перед смертью и загробным существованием; «историзм» избавлял их от страха перед существованием земным. Перед русским человеком представал мир, лишенный противоречий и оппозиций; точнее говоря, существовала оппозиция христианин — язычник, крещеный — некрещеный, но не было оппозиции хороший христианин — плохой христианин. Соответственно появлялась возможность создавать искусство, в основу которого не был положен контраст, то искусство, которое в Древней Руси именовалось «умиленным». Такая возможность была реализована по крайней мере в пении, в церковной монодии: контраст и драматизм намечен в ней слабо. Только патриарх Никон завел на Руси музыку с контрастом мажорных и минорных ладов. Хотя «черно-белый» принцип использовался в литературе, в иконописи, все же этот ранний этико-эстетический импульс безусловно сказался в радостном и светлом восточнославянском искусстве домонгольской поры. Митрополит Иларион назвал своих пребывавших в язычестве земляков «безнадежниками». Христианство принесло с собою «надежду», «упование», т.е. культурный оптимизм, который стал мощным цивилизационным импульсом.

Сделанные мной выводы — обычная ученая спекуляция. Она может быть верной, может быть и неверной. Но «Повесть временных лет» позволяет нам услышать «глас народа», и этот глас возвещает о том, что Русь приняла христианство за красоту: «И придохом же в Греки, и ведоша ны, идеже служать Богу своему, и не свемы, на небе ли есмы были, ли на земли: несть бо на земли такаго вида ли красоты такоя, и недоумеем бо сказати ... Мы убо не можем забыти красоты тоя, всяк бо человек, аще вкусить сладка, последи горести не приимаеть...».

У русского человека появилась возможность пребывать в состоянии красоты — в храме, где услаждаются слух, зрение, обоняние — и где воспаряет душа. Но неверно было бы заключить, что храм и храмовое поведение резко противопоставляются миру и мирскому поведению. В русском варианте православной культуры этого не произошло. Для доказательства самое время вернуться к именослову.

Для летописца Владимир и после крещения остался Владимиром, хотя его надлежало именовать Василием. История помнит не Георгия, а Ярослава Мудрого, не Романа и Давида, а Бориса и Глеба (их канонизация под именами мирскими, а не крестными, как и почитание св. Ольги, а не св. Елены — красноречивое свидетельство о русской свободе в церковных и духовных делах). Эта двоименность, сохранившаяся у рязанских князей вплоть до XV в., а у дворян и крестьян почти до Смуты, осознавалась, бесспорно, как культурное сосуществование «обычая» и «закона».

«Аз худый дедом своим Ярославом, благословленым, славным, нареченый в крещении Василий, русьскым именемь Володимир...» — так начал свое «Поучение» Мономах.[14] Соответственно двоименности автора оно разделено на две не похожих одна на другую части. Про первую можно сказать, что она написана Василием: это в основном коллаж из цитат, прежде всего из Псалтири. Впрочем, даже здесь нет аскезы. По Мономаху, для спасения души достаточно трех добрых дел — покаяния, слез и милостыни. Они «не бо суть тяжка; ни одиночство, ни чернечьство, ни голод, яко инии добрии терпять, но малым делом улучити милость Божию». Мономах отделяет себя от монашествующих лиц. Их правила — не для него. Но заметим, что пост он простодушно называет «голодом»! Вторая часть написана князем Владимиром, воином и охотником. Достаточно прочесть ее, чтобы увидеть: на этот текст десятисловие и Нагорная проповедь не распространяются. Но это — не двойничество. Это — «двоеверие».

Напомню, что автор термина «двоеверие» — Феодосий Печерский. Когда князь Изяслав Ярославич обратился к нему с вопросом о «вере варяжской, какова есть», игумен бранил варяжскую (она же латинская) веру и заключил так: «Аще ли кто хвалить их веру, таковый обретаеться свою хуля; или начнеть хвалити непрестанно чюжаа веры, отреченныа православнаго христианьства, таковый обретаеться двоиверець и близь ереси есть ... И аще ти речеть кто: 'Сию веру и ону Бог дал', ты же рьци ему: 'Ты кто еси, кривоверне? Мниши Бога двоеверна?'».[15]

Изяслав (кстати, любимец Феодосия) занял киевский стол в 1054 г., когда схизма расколола христианскую Европу. Вопрошание было, так сказать, ко времени, к тому же Изяслав был западником и по родственным связям, и по культурным симпатиям. Но запрет печерского игумена никак не повлиял на него, как не сказался этот запрет на матримониальной и культурной практике этого и ближайших поколений русских князей. Они оставались «двоеверны», т.е. терпимы к чужим конфессиям. Тем более терпимы были они к своей традиции, о чем красноречиво свидетельствуют сочинения Василия-Владимира Мономаха.

Крещение не было отречением. Русь создала свой вариант православия, терпимый и открытый, создала «равновесную» культуру, одушевленную оптимизмом.

Примечания

1. *ПЛДР*, т. 1. *XI-начало XII века* (М., 1978), стр. 132. Далее цитаты из «Повести временных лет» (в упрощенной транскрипции — это распространяется и на другие памятники) даются по этому изданию без ссылок.

2. Б. А. Успенский, *Языковая ситуация Киевской Руси и ее значение для истории русского литературного языка* (М., 1983), стр. 13, прим. 1.

3. В. Л. Янин, «Крещение Новгорода и христианизация его населения». В кн.: *Введение христианства у народов Центральной и Восточной Европы: Крещение Руси. (Сборник тезисов)* (М., 1987), стр. 62.

4. См.: И. Я. Фроянов, *Киевская Русь. Очерки социально-политической истории* (Л., 1980).

5. Ю. М. Лотман, Б. А. Успенский, «Новые аспекты изучения культуры Древней Руси», *Вопросы литературы*, 1977, No. 3, стр. 161.

6. Е. Голубинский, *История русской церкви* (М., 1880), т. 1, ч. 1, стр. 55.

7. См.: А. Н. Новосельцев, «Взаимоотношения Древней Руси со странами Востока и принятие Русью христианства». В кн.: *Введение христианства у народов Центральной и Восточной Европы*, стр. 30–31.

8. А. В. Назаренко, «Проблема христианизации Руси и русско-германские отношения второй половины X в.», *Введение христианства...*, стр. 24–26.

9. Цит. по: А. М. Молдован, *«Слово о Законе и Благодати» Илариона* (Киев, 1984), стр. 86.

10. Ibid., стр. 86–87.

11. См.: Л. Н. Гумилев, *Этногенез и биосфера Земли*, изд. 2-е, исправ. и доп. (Л., 1989).

12. А. В. Поппэ опубликовал несколько работ на эту тему (и на разных языках). Главная из них: Andrzej Poppe, *The Rise of Christian Russia* (London, 1982).
13. См., например: *Россия и Запад*, т. 1 (Пгр., 1923), стр. 36–56.
14. *ПЛДР*, т. 1, стр. 392.
15. *ПЛДР*, т. 2, *XII век* (М., 1980), стр. 614–618.

Aleksandr Panchenko/Summary: The Baptism of Rus': Ideological and Aesthetic Aspects

The native population's reaction to the baptism of Rus' was undramatic. Conversion to Christianity was soon perceived not only as preordained by Divine Providence, but also as providing a civilizing impetus and cultural direction (Metropolitan Hilarion). The "Rech' filosofa" of the Chronicle account does not speak of moral issues. In the sphere of ethics the neophytes were free to follow indigenous traditions. Religious reform brought a profound re-evaluation of human destiny. Earlier, man was a plaything of fate; now he becomes a part of history. Baptism was equated with salvation, and from this stemmed a basic characteristic of Old Russian art that can be described as *umilenie*. This is the source of the radiant and joyful character of the East Slavic art of the pre-Mongol period. Old Russian Orthodoxy is characterized by tolerance for tradition, openness, and optimism.

Christianity before Christianization

Christians and Christian Activity in Pre-988 Rus'

HENRIK BIRNBAUM

That there were Christians and some Christian activity in Rus' prior to the conversion of 988 has long been established. What remains controversial is the nature, point of entry, ethnic base, extent, and significance of the Christian presence in East Slavic territory and of events associated with Christianity or Christian personages in the period preceding the momentous achievement of the Kievan ruler Vladimir (Volodimier). As is well known, that achievement earned him the epithet "the Saint" in Russian and Ukrainian history and brought about his being venerated, though not by the act of formal canonization.[1] However, his cult probably did not begin as early as the eleventh, but in all likelihood only by the late thirteenth century.[2] It is some of the much debated issues just indicated that the following remarks will address.

The earliest traces of a Christian presence in Rus', and notably in Kiev, are associated with the names of the semi-legendary rulers Askold and Dir (in the second half of the ninth century, chronological details remaining controversial) and, later, with those of Prince Igor (912–945) and, particularly, his widow, Princess Olga (acting as regent for her minor son, Sviatoslav, from 945 to 962). Olga herself converted to Christianity, though the precise date and place of her baptism have been a matter of continued controversy,[3] as are her request to King Otto I for a Christian bishop and its immediate consequences. After Sviatoslav's death in 972, his oldest son, Iaropolk, seems to have been well disposed toward Christianity, being himself married to a Christian Greek. It has even been suggested that he may have been baptized and that evidence to that effect could subsequently have been suppressed after his assassination in 980 at the behest of Vladimir. The martyrdom of

---

This essay also appears in the author's *Aspects of the Slavic Middle Ages and Slavic Renaissance Culture* forthcoming from Peter Lang Publishing, Inc. and reprinted by permission of the publisher.

two Christian Varangians, father and son, recorded in the Primary Chronicle (PVL) under the year 983, is additional proof of the existence of a Christian community in Kiev at that time; it can be viewed in the context of Vladimir's early, markedly anti-Christian attitude.

There is, of course, nothing unusual in the fact that in medieval times Christian missionaries dispatched to heathen lands would preach the gospel, make some converts, and possibly even found small Christian congregations, but nonetheless fail (or not even attempt) to convert the country as a whole to the new faith. Sweden, linked to early Rus' by dynastic and other ties, can serve as a telling example. Its "apostle," Ansgar, paid a first visit to Birka in 829–831, but the country as a whole did not effectively embrace Christianity until sometime toward the end of the eleventh century.[4] Similarly, it should come as no surprise that some early traces of a Christian presence can be found in Rus' prior to the official introduction of Christianity in 988. It is to the credit of N. K. Nikolsky to have first drawn attention to the distinction between, on the one hand, the formal conversion of Rus' to Christianity, its official "baptism" (*kreshchenie*), which undoubtedly was brought about by Byzantium and led to the establishment of the Kievan metropolitan eparchy subordinate to the patriarchate of Constantinople, and, on the other, the considerably earlier entry and spread of Christian beliefs and practices, the first "enlightenment" (*prosveshchenie*) with which we are concerned here. Nikolsky made this distinction in his important yet controversial study on the PVL as a source for the early history of Russian writing and culture.[5] In it he considered the account referred to as *Skazanie o prelozhenii knig na slavianskii iazyk*—entered in the chronicle text under the year 898 and held by A. A. Shakhmatov to be a later interpolation attributable to the Vydubichi abbot Silvestr—an isolated remnant of an earlier, suppressed historiographic tradition, Slavophile in outlook (to use a modern concept) and contrasting with a Grecophile and, by the same token, pro-Varangian tendency prevailing at the Caves and Vydubichi Monasteries. Contrary to that latter tendency, it stressed Slavic unity and the close ties of Rus' to other Slavic peoples, notably Christian Moravia (as well as Pannonia, the two regions mistakenly conceived as part of the Roman province of Illyricum) and Bulgaria. While Nikolsky's emphasis on the early Western connection of Christianity in Rus' was challenged by some scholars,[6] others were, explicitly or implicitly, inclined to accept the main thrust of his argument, albeit in part with significant qualifications.[7] Of the various views expressed about the origin of the *Skazanie*, the opinion voiced by B. N. Floria appears to be the most compelling. According to him, the

Skazanie was originally written at the Sázava Monastery in Bohemia long after the events of 988.[8] In this particular respect Floria is thus in disagreement with Nikolsky's chronological notions, as he also does not concur with O. Králík about the controversial Legend of Saints Václav and Ludmila by Christian, extant in a Latin version, as being one of the sources of the *Skazanie*. Though chronologically irrelevant, therefore, to pre-988 phenomena and developments in Rus', its subsequently inserted 898 entry notwithstanding, the significance of the *Skazanie* as an isolated testimony in the PVL to early links with the Christian tradition among the Western (and Southern) Slavs was correctly recognized by Nikolsky. Equally, if not even more important is his notion of the transforming impact that Christian culture had on society in Old Rus' even before 988.

The attempt made by K. Ericsson to construe "the earliest conversion of the Rus' to Christianity" as having taken place in connection with, or rather as a consequence of, a claimed unsuccessful attack on Constantinople in 834, during the reign of the last iconoclast Byzantine emperor, Theophilus, launched by Kyi, the legendary indigenous ruler of the Poliane, is highly speculative and generally unconvincing.[9] Ericsson invokes, among other things: (1) a problematic equation of the names Theophilus and Bogoliub, the latter said to be echoed in the byname of Prince Andrei Bogoliubskii—conceived as another Kyi—and also in the name of his village, Bogoliubovo; (2) the plausible assumption that the Rus' (*Rhōs*) envoys who accompanied a Byzantine embassy and were recommended to Emperor Louis the Pious by Emperor Theophilus upon their arrival at the Frankish court in Ingelheim in May of 839, as mentioned in the *Annales Bertiniani,* must have been Christians; (3) a questionable identification of the two hundred or so people baptized by Constantine-Cyril in 861 at the Khazar court in Derbent with remnants of a Christian community of Poliane, also assuming that the much debated gospel and psalter texts shown to the Byzantine emissary at Cherson could in fact have been written in an early form of East Slavic (and not in Syriac or Gothic);[10] (4) Methodius's allusion to another, earlier prince who was forcibly baptized as a captive on foreign soil—thus allegedly referring to Kyi's supposed christening in Constantinople—when warning the pagan ruler of the Vistulans; (5) certain chronological considerations based on the unreliable dates of the PVL (and discrepancies with the Novgorodian chronicle tradition that in part draws on more ancient sources;[11] (6) some additional factors thought to be suggestive of this hypothesis.

The reference to Kyi's alleged military exploits, including his journey—at first warlike—to Constantinople, is found only in the late (sixteenth century), comprehensive Nikonian Chronicle, which also indicates that the legendary ruler of the Poliane received great honors from the emperor.[12] However, the chronicle does not reveal the nature of these honors, and it is only Ericsson who—on flimsy grounds—surmises that Kyi's great honors implied baptism.[13] In this context it should also be recalled that it is far from certain that the legendary Kyi of the chronicle text, whether styled a regional ruler or just a simple ferryman, was indeed an historical figure and not merely a construct invented by one of the chroniclers to account for the origin of the name of the city on the Dnieper.[14]

We are on firmer, yet still controversial, ground when it comes to the acceptance of Christianity by some of the Rus' (*Rhōs*) people—apparently Norsemen for the most part—following the failed attack, in 860, on Constantinople headed by the Kievan rulers Askold and Dir, or perhaps by just one of the two.[15] Here, we have the testimony of Patriarch Photius, who not only in two homilies, "On the attack of the *Rhōs*"[16] described the Varangian assault and siege of Constantinople, but also in an encyclical letter of 867 directed to the three Oriental patriarchs advised them of the conversion and baptism of the *Rhōs*.[17] As Obolensky points out:

> The pattern which we have seen operating so often in the conversion of barbarian peoples to Byzantine Christianity was thus repeated in the case of the Russians: In Photius' eyes their acceptance of the Christian religion and of a bishop from Constantinople made them, however independent their rulers may have been in practice, citizens of the Byzantine Commonwealth and thus subjects to the emperor. These religious and political links were further strengthened about 874, when the Russians concluded a formal treaty with Byzantium and accepted an archbishop, sent to their country by the patriarch Ignatius.—The status and prerogatives of this prelate are unknown, but it may be assumed that they were comparable to those enjoyed by the archbishop whom the same Ignatius some four years earlier had dispatched to head the Bulgarian Church. It is natural to assume that he resided in Kiev, where, if the Russian chronicle can be trusted, Askold and Dir ruled jointly at that time. Whether one or both of these princes formally accepted Christianity is also unknown. Nor can we follow, in the absence of reliable evidence, the fate of this first Byzantine ecclesiastical organisation on Russian soil; most probably it was submerged, later in the century, by a wave of paganism which swept away the pro-Christian rulers of Kiev and replaced them with a rival group of Scandinavians from North Russia, headed by Oleg. Yet . . . this bridgehead which Byzantine Christianity had secured on the middle Dnieper was probably never wholly destroyed, for a Christian community survived and even increased, at least in Kiev, during the fifty years before Russia's final conversion in the late tenth century.[18]

By and large, this analysis appears well-founded and to the point. However, rather than speaking of "the Russians" it would be more appropriate to refer here to the Rus' (or *Rhōs*), who at that time were still predominantly made up of Varangians, with at most a smattering of an East Slavic (but not yet specifically Russian) admixture. Thus, still a half-century later, all the fifteen Rus' names appearing as signatories to Prince Oleg's treaty of 911 with the Byzantine Emperors Leo and Alexander are purely Scandinavian in origin.[19] Likewise, it would be more proper in this context to speak of East Slavic than of "Russian" soil. Also, the rulers on the Dnieper did not consider themselves formal subjects, or vassals, of the Byzantine emperor; at most, they were spiritually under his authority and that of the patriarch, presuming that they had converted to Christianity.[20] Whether the archbishop who, according to Constantine Porphyrogenitus's not always reliable information (found in his *Life of Emperor Basil*), was dispatched to Rus' by Patriarch Ignatius did in fact head a short-lived eparchy, subordinate directly to the patriarch of Constantinople (which if so came to an end with the overthrow of Askold and Dir by Oleg, presumably in 882), is not quite clear, even though some scholars, for example, L. Müller, are inclined to believe so.[21]

How far apart the pertinent views still are can best be illustrated by the different assessments of Askold and Dir. In part at least, this discrepancy of opinion reflects the age-old Normanist controversy. Thus, O. Pritsak not only assumes that they were Varangians whose Old Norse name forms were Hǫskuldr and Dýr, but also identifies them with two historical figures, placing them in a Scandinavian context into which Oleg and Riurik fit as well. Thus, in Pritsak's imaginative conception Askold was the Viking Hasting who later returned to England and ultimately wound up in France where he was known by the pagan title Guthrum (Guthurm or Gormr) and subsequently by the Christian name of Athelstan. Dir is said to have been identical with the Viking king Bjǫrn, known as Berno Nortmannus from the Frankish annals, the older of the two, son of the famed Ragnarr Loðbrók. Hasting-Askold, coming from Denmark, and Bjǫrn-Dir, from Aldeigja (Old Ladoga), supposedly met at Polotsk before jointly launching their attack on Constantinople. After the unsuccessful raid on the Imperial City, Bjǫrn-Dir is said to have returned to Ladoga and to have died in Rus' (not in Frisia, as erroneously claimed in the Norman tradition) while, as indicated, Hasting-Askold went west.[22]

Contrasting with this extreme Normanist view is the opinion recently expressed by P. P. Tolochko (1987: 21–24) who, making reference to A. A. Shakhmatov, B. A. Rybakov, and M. N. Tikhomirov, claims that Askold and Dir were native, i.e. East Slavic, rulers of Kiev.[23] Allegedly, this opinion is corroborated by a statement found in the Polish fifteenth-century historiographer Jan Długosz's *Annales,* where we read that after the death of Kyi and his brothers their direct descendants ruled in Kiev until the power shifted to two brothers, Oszkald (= Askold) and Dir.[24] However, this passage can be interpreted differently, namely that after three generations of indigenous rulers the reign was taken over by two newcomers to the area.[25]

In my opinion, Askold and Dir were indeed Varangians, though obviously they did not belong to the clan of Riurik. Their identification with historical Scandinavian (Viking) figures, as suggested by Pritsak, appears much less convincing, however. Possibly they did not even rule simultaneously in Kiev but succeeded each other, so that even the date of 882 when, according to the PVL, Oleg disposed of them is not necessarily accurate.[26] It seems likely, though, that they, or at any rate Askold, were/was killed when Oleg assumed power in Kiev. And even if Askold's and Dir's reign was shared and thus simultaneous, they must have arrived in Kiev considerably earlier than the attack on Constantinople of 860, probably in or about 850.[27] Apparently they were not of princely descent, according to Varangian notions, as is also suggested by Oleg's telling them: "You are not princes nor even of princely stock, but I am of princely birth."[28] Considering Kiev part of the princely family patrimony of Riurik and Igor, Oleg may have suspected that Byzantium was attempting to usurp his right of inheritance, or rather that of Igor, by designating Askold and Dir as princes, since the Byzantine emperor had the prerogative of creating new princes. Oleg could thus have surmised that Askold and Dir, if Askold or both brothers had converted to Christianity, had submitted themselves to Byzantine suzerainty, and had in reward been given princely titles. Yet there is no indication in Photius's encyclical letter that any such titular distinctions had been conferred upon the Kievan rulers.[29] Echoing a view earlier expressed by the eighteenth-century historian V. N. Tatishchev, Tolochko suggests that Oleg's successful coup was not so much due to some uneven power constellation—the northern detachment cannot, after all, have been particularly numerous (some reinforcements from the tribe of the Krivichi and the exaggerated description in the PVL notwithstanding) and Kiev was certainly easily defended and probably had a well-manned garrison—as it was to Askold's (and Dir's?) own Kievan boyars from the ranks of the East Slavic tribe of the Poliane, who were not prepared to accept Christianity. Tolochko takes it for granted, therefore, that the leadership of Rus' in

Kiev—the Varangians, but not the majority of the local Slavic nobles—had embraced Christianity.[30]

From another document, the Charter of Vladimir, preserved in copies from the twelfth to the fourteenth centuries and later,[31] we know that the first bishop sent by Patriarch Photius to Kiev was probably Michael, as corroborated by some other documents, or possibly Leo (or Leontius), even though in the charter he is wrongly thought to have been sent only to the court of Vladimir more than a century later.[32] Much more information about Askold and Dir than in the PVL is found in the considerably later Nikonian Chronicle, which may have drawn on some additional sources from the south of Rus' not available to the compilers of the PVL.[33] Thus, in the entry for 876, we find the tale about how a miracle performed by the Byzantine bishop sent to the Rus' eventually swayed them to accept Christianity. The original version of this tale is to be found in Constantine VII Porphyrogenitus's biography of his grandfather, Emperor Basil I. Also, in the entry for 881, the story of Oleg's deceptively overcoming Askold and Dir is told at greater length than in the PVL.[34] It seems indeed likely that Askold, and perhaps also Dir, as well as the rest of the Varangian leadership in Kiev, had accepted Christianity; so this may actually be considered the first conversion of Rus', as long as Rus' is understood here to refer either exclusively or at any rate primarily to the Varangian element in the mid-Dnieper region and not, or at most only secondarily, also to the East Slavic Poliane.[35] It is possible that any record of this early conversion might have been suppressed in or expunged from the text of the pro-Byzantine and pro-Varangian PVL and later Russian chronicle texts echoing it in order not to detract from Vladimir's 988 achievement.[36]

Clearly, the reigns of Oleg and Igor (together thought to extend over a period from 882 to 945) implied a major setback for the cause of Christianity in Rus'. Yet there is evidence that a Christian community continued to exist in Kiev also during that time. That many of the Varangian Rus' retained their Christian faith is suggested and in part unequivocally borne out by some of the statements made in the PVL in connection with the conclusion of Oleg's treaty (of 911, entered under the year 912) with Byzantium and, in particular, Igor's subsequent agreement of 944 (entered under the year 945). Thus we read after the insertion of the treaty text in the entry for 912:

> The Emperor Leo honored the Russian envoys with gifts . . . and placed his vassals at their disposal to show them the beauties of the churches, the golden palace, and the riches contained therein. They thus showed the Russes much gold and many palls and jewels, together with the relics of

our Lord's Passion: the crown, the nails, and the purple robe, as well as the bones of the Saints. They also instructed the Russes in their faith, and expounded to them the true belief.[37]

To be sure, this passage may be interpreted as displaying the Byzantines' proselytizing zeal vis-à-vis as yet pagan foreigners, especially as no reference is made to any form of Christianity among the Rus'. Note also that in the entry for 904–907, in the preliminary peace agreement (concluded in 907), it is stated that "According to the religion of the Russes, the latter swore by their weapons and by their god Perun, as well as by Volos, the god of cattle, and thus confirmed the treaty."[38] Yet, it is also conceivable that among the envoys from Rus' there were some who had embraced, or were familiar with, the Christian faith and for whom, therefore, the showing of Christian churches and relics as well as instruction in things Christian would have been genuinely meaningful. However, D. S. Likhachev in his commentary to the PVL surmises that the compiler of the PVL (as opposed to the author of the earlier version known as *Nachal'nyi svod*, where the treaty text is missing) simply added these concrete details patterned on the account of Vladimir's mission to Constantinople in 988.[39] More recently, A. N. Sakharov even doubts that a special Rus' mission was dispatched to Constantinople in connection with the treaty of 911.[40] Quite unreliable, in this context, is an Arabic source, the geographer Marwazī, according to whom the Rus' had embraced Christianity in 912/913, i.e. shortly after the conclusion of the 911 treaty.[41]

Matters are less equivocal when it comes to the treaty of 944 concluded between Prince Igor and Byzantium. Thus, immediately following the treaty text we read:

> Those of us who are baptized have sworn in the Cathedral, by the church of St. Elias, upon the Holy Cross set before us, and upon this parchment, to abide by all that is written herein, and not to violate any of its stipulations. May whosoever of our compatriots, Prince or common, baptized or unbaptized, who does so violate them, have no succor from God, but may he be slave in this life and in the life to come, and may he perish by his own arms.—The unbaptized Russes shall lay down their shields. ... If any of the princes or any Russian subject, whether Christian or non-Christian, violates the terms of this instrument, he shall merit death by his own weapons, and be accursed of God and of Perun because he violated his oath ... The Russes laid down their weapons ... and Igor and his people took oath (at least, such as were pagans), while the Christian Russes took oath in the church of St. Elias, which is above the creek, in the vicinity of the Pasyncha square and the quarter of the Khazars. This was, in fact, a parish church, since many of the Varangians were Christians.

The preamble of this treaty states explicitly: "If any inhabitant of the land of Rus' thinks to violate this amity, may such of these transgressors as have adopted the Christian faith incur condign punishment from Almighty God in the shape of damnation and destruction forevermore."[42]

Regarding the English rendition of the Old Russian text it should be remarked that the phrase "... in the Cathedral, by the church of St. Elias ..." (*tserkov'iu sviatago Il'ie v sborniei tserkvi*) is misleading, since the chronicler did not refer here to any cathedral but merely to one and the same parish church (*sbornaia tserky*), as also follows from the continuation of the text. Further, "and the quarter of the Khazars" is probably indeed the correct translation of *i kozare,* appearing in the Laurentian Copy superscribed after the words *konets' pasyn"che besiedy,* though in some editions, in accordance with other manuscripts of the PVL, the reference to the Khazars is added after the mention of the Christian Varangians.[43] Obviously, therefore, of the fifty-one, mostly Scandinavian-named members of the Rus' appearing as signatories to this treaty, headed by Ivor (ON Ivarr), the personal representative of Igor, many were Christian. Regarding these Christians, Cross and Sherbowitz-Wetzor note that "Christians among the Russes are mentioned in this treaty for the first time; no such reference to them was made in the instrument of 911. Cosmas of Prague attests to their presence in Kiev (*MGH,* NS., II, xxii, 44). These Varangian Christians belonged more likely to the Latin rite than to the Byzantine ... The location of the church of Saint Elias (which was probably a wooden structure) can be only approximately defined ..."[44] It seems, though, that Saint Elijah's Church was located in the lower town, the Podol district of Old Kiev, that is, the city's commercial sector on the Pochaina Creek, a tributary of the Dnieper.[45] The question of whether the Christian Varangians of Rus', including Olga soon thereafter, were adherents of the Roman (Latin) or the Greek (Byzantine) rite is not easy to settle and perhaps also not particularly relevant.[46] For they could very well have been influenced both by their—sporadically Christianized—Scandinavian contacts and by their experience from visits to, wars with, and service in Byzantium. Very possibly the question did not really arise yet in the tenth century as Christianity was essentially still considered but one religion. Therefore, the story of the conversion of Vladimir in the PVL, where Catholic Christianity (represented by Germans, not Western Slavs!) and Byzantine Christianity (advocated by Greeks) are presented as different religions, like Judaism and Islam, bears the unmistakable mark of a post-1054 anachronism. Yet there can be little doubt that as regards the liturgical form, the Varangians and their East Slavic followers must have been deeply impressed by what they had seen and heard in Byzantium. Finally, the presence of some Christian scribes, presumably Bulgarian monks, in Kievan Rus' is rendered likely by the fact that the treaties of 911, 944, and 971 were presumably drafted in two versions, one Greek and the other one in Old Bulgarian, perhaps with an admixture of a few East Slavic vernacular elements.[47]

With Princess Olga's regency (945–962) we encounter the first Christian ruler of a unified Rus'. Many details of her own baptism and subsequent request for a Christian bishop from Germany have remained controversial until now, however. What can be said with some assurance, though, is that the date of 955 found in most chronicles of Old Rus' (from the PVL onward) is incorrect at least as regards Olga's first visit to Constantinople. As far as the place of Olga's baptism is concerned—Kiev or Constantinople—scholars still differ in their opinion. The incorrect date goes back to a miscalculation—or merely rough, approximate count—by James the Monk (Iakov Mnikh), the author of a memorial eulogy of Prince Vladimir, *Pamiat' i pokhvala kniaziu rus'komu Volodimieru* (in its extant form probably compiled only in the thirteenth century). He indicated that Olga had lived her last fifteen years as a Christian, the princess having died, as James himself correctly established, on 11 July 969. Recently, however, it has been suggested on paleographic grounds that even the figure fifteen may be due to a misreading (or incorrect copying) and that James himself had indicated nine years as the time that had elapsed between Olga's baptism and her death, thus dating the former to the year 960, a date now favored by D. Obolensky on other grounds as well.[48] Of all annalistic writings in Rus' only a few are known to have an indirect reference to what is possibly the correct date of Olga's baptism. One is the late (seventeenth century) so-called Hustyn Chronicle (*Gustinskaia letopis'*), which notes: "i kresti iu sam patriarkh Polievkt". The same Patriarch Polyeuctus (consecrated on 3 April 956) is also mentioned in connection with Olga's baptism in two other late (seventeenth century) chronicle compilations, the Kievan Synopsis and the *Mazurinskii letopisets*. These may echo earlier sources not reflected in the PVL. Since the reliable, precise dates for Olga's visits to the Byzantine emperor mentioned in the most detailed description of the two events, the second Book of Ceremonies (*De caerimoniis aulae Byzantinae*, chapter 15), authored—or at any rate edited—by Emperor Constantine VII Porphyrogenitus (944–959), are Wednesday, 9 September, and Sunday, 18 October, but with no year indicated, scholars have speculated whether to date these visits to 946 or 957, the only potential years when these dates fell on

Wednesday and Sunday, respectively. Surprisingly and perhaps significantly, however, there is no mention in the emperor's account of the Rus' princess' baptism during her stay in Constantinople. Some researchers have suggested that Olga visited Constantinople in 957, but was subsequently baptized only in 959 in Kiev.[49] Or they have left the question of the place of her baptism open.[50] Another scholar, while at first also not taking a stand concerning the place and time of her conversion, preferred to date Olga's two audiences with the Byzantine emperor to 946, but subsequently opted for Olga's baptism in Constantinople in 954/955.[51] O. Pritsak argues that Olga in fact visited Constantinople twice: in 946, when she was received by the emperor on Wednesday, 9 September, but was still a pagan, and in 957, when she saw the emperor on Sunday, 18 October, by now a newly converted Christian. The baptismal act itself would have been administered by Patriarch Polyeuctus just a day or so before. According to Pritsak, the first trip to Byzantium was apparently prompted mostly by the need to reconfirm the stipulations of the 944 agreement concluded in behalf of Prince Igor, her husband, slain the following year (945). Her second visit, during which she, in a private ceremony, would have become a Christian (and in that capacity, herself of Varangian stock, joined that portion of the Varangian-Rus' community in Kiev which already was converted), is not to be seen, so Pritsak reasons, as in any way inconsistent with her soon-to-follow embassy to the German king, Otto I. Olga is said to have returned to Kiev from Constantinople toward the end of 957.[52]

In early 958, she most probably discussed with her close advisers the possibility of introducing Christendom on a large scale in Rus'. She then could have dispatched her envoys to Frankfurt-am-Main in the late fall of that same year as they arrived at Otto's court by the early summer of 959. At that time, the Byzantine ruler, Emperor Constantine VII, maintained friendly relations with Otto I, whom he greatly admired. And after the official peace of the Church had been proclaimed in 920, the schism between an Eastern and a Western Church, clearly felt to have existed in Photius's days—in the second half of the ninth century—had for the time being been averted. According to Pritsak, "Olga was baptized in October 957 in Constantinople by Patriarch Polyeuctus. This was a personal, private conversion. When Olga later wanted to baptize her entire realm, she turned to the professional missionaries of Otto I, following the advice of the Byzantine emperor Constantine VII."[53] The eventual failure of this attempt, despite Otto's great interest in eastern missionary activities, may well have led to, or sped up, Olga's dismissal from power by her son Sviatoslav, who resisted her urgings to turn Christian.[54]

Concerning Olga's mission to King (and since 962, Emperor) Otto I, we read in the so-called Lothringian Chronicle, compiled by the anonymous continuator of Abbot Regino of Prüm, usually identified with Adalbert of Trier, who subsequently became the first archbishop of Magdeburg: "Legati Helenae reginae Rugorum [Russorum, H.B.], quae sub Romano imperatore Constantinopolitano baptizata est, ficte, ut post claruit, ad regem venientes episcopum et presbiteros eidem genti ordinari petebant."[55] Helena was the name Olga had assumed in baptism, presumably in honor of the mother of Emperor Constantine I the Great, Saint Helena, and/or as a gesture of courtesy toward the ruling emperor, Constantine VII (Porphyrogenitus), whose spouse's name was also Helena. The mention of Romanus II rather than of his father, Constantine VII, is remarkable insofar as Romanus died in March of 963, whereas the annalistic entries in Regino's continuator, Adalbert, run through 967. Still, this apparent inaccuracy may perhaps be explained by the fact that Romanus II (b. 939) was accorded the title of co-emperor, *basileus,* as early as 945, i.e., prior to the death of Constantine in 959. However, this problem is resolved if we accept Obolensky's new date for Olga's baptism, the year 960, when Romanus II was sole emperor.[56] As is known, Otto I responded to Olga's request favorably by having the monk Libutius consecrated missionary bishop to Rus'. Yet, for some reason he was first detained and then suddenly died in early 961. As his replacement the aforementioned Adalbert of Trier was selected to take on the task of going to Kiev. He did leave for Rus' but returned the following year, 962, his mission having failed. As Pritsak indicates, Adalbert's entry for 959 was probably written between late 962 (when he returned from Rus')—hence his aside *ficte, ut post claruit*—and mid-March of 963, when Emperor Romanus II, identified as the current ruler of Byzantium, died.[57] Olga is further said to have founded the Church of the Holy Trinity in her native town of Pskov and to have had a chapel built at Askold's gravesite in Kiev. Tradition, moreover, has it that a church already existed in Novgorod in Olga's time.[58]

The reasons for the failure of Adalbert's mission are not entirely clear.[59] Nor do we know whether Olga's being removed from power by her pagan son Sviatoslav was a direct consequence of her failure, as well as the German bishop's, to convert Rus', or whether that failure itself was prompted by the political takeover in Kiev. Be this as it may, Sviatoslav's ten-year rule (962–972) marked a setback for Christianity and yet another reversion to paganism, even if we can assume that a Christian, still predominantly Varangian, community continued to exist in Kiev, though now under less favorable conditions.[60] Yet it may have been reinforced by some of Sviatoslav's returning warriors, who during his Balkan campaigns had come across many Christians. For, as I have suggested elsewhere, "it should be noted . . . that during the five years (966-971) spent among Christians in Bulgaria, some of Sviatoslav's warriors were surely exposed to Christian influences, and upon their return to Rus' may have maintained an interest in, or even involvement with, that religion."[61] J. Fine also points out that "connections between Bulgarians and Russians, resulting from Sviatoslav's activities in Bulgaria, must be considered as an important part of the background to the official conversion of the Russians."[62]

This, then, brings us to the relatively brief rule (972-980) of Iaropolk, Sviatoslav's oldest son. He was initially assigned to Kiev and the surrounding land of the Poliane as his patrimonial inheritance. There is some hint in the chronicle text that Iaropolk himself may have embraced the Christian faith or that he at least had Christian sympathies. Thus, Iaropolk's feud with his brother Oleg is said to have had a natural explanation: Oleg had for no good reason killed the son of Sveinald, Sviatoslav's field commander. Therefore, Sveinald, who had joined Iaropolk after Sviatoslav's death, egged him on to attack his brother and to take possession of his inherited property. Yet when Oleg was inadvertently killed in a struggle with Iaropolk, the latter, upon learning of his brother's death, "wept over him" and reproached Sveinald for having his, not Iaropolk's, wish fulfilled. Also, we are told that Iaropolk had a Greek wife, a former nun, whom Sviatoslav had brought back from one of his Balkan campaigns because of her beauty.[63] Subsequently, Iaropolk, though forewarned, went to submit to his brother Vladimir and, when entering, was slain by two Varangian assassins.[64] Iaropolk's action, as described in the chronicle, doubtless brings to mind the irrational—but godly—behavior of the first native martyred princes, Boris and Gleb. That his possible Christian affiliation would subsequently have been suppressed by the compiler of the PVL, extolling his murderer, the "baptizer" of Rus', would only be natural.

However, there is one puzzling event reported in the PVL under the year 1044, which seems to contradict the assumption that Iaropolk possibly could have been converted to Christianity: "The bodies of the two princes Yaropolk and Oleg, sons of Svyatoslav, after their remains were baptized, were laid in the Church of the Holy Virgin."[65] Why would Iaroslav have the remains of his two uncles exhumed? To be sure, Oleg had been killed unintentionally, but Iaropolk was, at least legally, albeit posthumously, the father of Iaroslav's archenemy, Sviatopolk, whom Iaroslav had defeated and who was responsible for the death of Boris and Gleb. In actual fact, though, it was Vladimir, who, according to the chronicler's account, had begotten Sviatopolk, having had intercourse with Iaropolk's widow.[66] In his attempt to view the legendary Kyi as a convert to Christianity, Ericsson suggests that "both Kyi and Volodimer, the murderer, as a Christian, could inherit the heavenly kingdom, but not his victims, the two brothers who had died as pagans."[67] Perhaps we do not have to resort to that explanation, however. For even if Iaropolk had in fact—perhaps secretly—turned Christian (which Iaroslav may or may not have been aware of) it was a charitable deed by the Christian Iaroslav to have the bones of his uncles exhumed, baptized, and reinterred at a consecrated place, the Church of the Holy Virgin (or the Tithe), even if one of them happened to have been the legal (but, as Iaroslav perhaps knew, not the natural) father of his erstwhile enemy, and a man whom Iaroslav's father, while still a pagan, had callously and cunningly murdered. In other words, the postmortem baptism, or rebaptism, of Iaropolk is not necessarily definite proof that he had not in his lifetime converted. There is also no real positive evidence—at most a few vague hints—that he had in fact turned Christian. Still, most scholars, while acknowledging Iaropolk's friendly attitude toward Christianity or even assuming his intent of becoming a Christian, think that he was not actually baptized.[68]

Finally, we have the case of the two Christian Varangians martyred just five years before the conversion of Rus'. As it happened, celebrating the victory over the Baltic tribe of the Jatvingians, Vladimir and his people were busy sacrificing to the pagan idols, and a handsome Varangian youth was chosen by lot to be sacrificed to the gods. When his father resisted and gave an impassioned speech for Christianity (which he had embraced in Byzantium) and against pagan idolatry, the enraged mob moved on them and killed both father and son.[69] Whether this account was originally part of the chronicle narrative or, as Shakhmatov believed, was inserted there secondarily (since it is also known, adding the two Varangians' names, from a Prolog text for 12 July[70]) there is no reason to doubt its authenticity—and thus the existence of a Christian, still primarily Varangian, community in Kiev also in the rabidly pagan days of Vladimir's early rule, only three years after he had strengthened the worship of pagan deities in Kiev, Novgorod, and elsewhere.[71]

We can conclude that Christianity began to penetrate into Rus' long before its official introduction in 988. The earliest recorded mention of the

Rus' (*Rhōs*), i.e., Varangian Northmen residing in East Slavic territory and, to judge by Emperor Theophilus's concern, themselves Christians, dates to the year 839, when members of that ethnic group accompanied a Byzantine embassy to Emperor Louis the Pious at Ingelheim.[72] It is therefore possible that Christian influences from Byzantium had begun to be felt in the mid-Dnieper region some years earlier, though any assumption of a full-fledged conversion of Rus', or even its top echelon, in the time of the dubious ruler Kyi, about 834, belongs at best to the realm of legend. Christian impulses possibly reached East Slavic territory also from the Slavic West, echoed in the *Skazanie o prelozhenii knig na slavianskii iazyk,* which, however, probably was inserted into the Old Russian chronicle text only in the eleventh century, originating in the Sázava Monastery. There is hardly any reason to assume that Christianity in its Czech version, directly continuing the Cyrillo-Methodian tradition, would have reached Novgorod earlier than it spread to Kiev, more ample traces of Glagolitic writing in the Volkhov city notwithstanding. There are good grounds to assume the establishment of a permanent Christian, predominantly Varangian, community in Kiev no later than in the days of Askold and Dir (ca. 850–882), presumably in connection with the Rus' attack on Constantinople in 860. At that time the Rus' leadership may have converted *en bloc.* This Christian congregation appears to have weathered the shifting anti- and pro-Christian moods and attitudes of various rulers (Oleg, Igor, Olga, Sviatoslav, Iaropolk, Vladimir), as testified to, in particular, by the explicit and detailed reference to the numerous Christian Rus' and to the Church of Saint Elijah in the wording of Prince Igor's 944 treaty with Byzantium. In this connection it is also worth noting that in Prince Sviatoslav's much briefer treaty with Emperor John I Tzimisces of 971, there is no mention of any Christian Rus'. On the contrary, the only deities invoked there are "the god in whom we believe, namely . . . Perun and Volos, the god of flocks."[73] The reference to the two Christian Varangians, martyred in Vladimir's early, pagan reign, is nonetheless further evidence of the fact that Christian Norsemen (and by that time presumably also some local native Slavs) continued to reside in Kiev when there was a renewed upsurge of—now reformed—paganism. After the conversion in 988, paganism, in the form of adherence to heathen beliefs and practice of pagan rites and customs, remained strong throughout Rus', giving rise to the century-long coexistence of the two religions, official Christendom and henceforth largely subdued heathendom, this contrast and blend being known in the history of Russian religion as *dvoeverie.*[74]

The decisive step was taken on 6 January 988, the Day of Epiphany, by

Prince Vladimir who, after some three months of catechetical preparation in late 987, had himself (and presumably some of his high-ranking nobles) baptized in Kiev, not, as has also been suggested, in Cherson, which at that time was still held by the Byzantine usurper Bardas Phocas. Vladimir thus fulfilled the basic precondition for his marriage to the purple-born Princess Anne, the sister of Emperor Basil II. The mass baptism of the Kievans in the waters of the Dnieper followed possibly on Easter Sunday, 8 April, but more likely —given the water temperature of the river—on Whitsunday, 27 May 988.[75]

Notes

1. V. Vodoff, "Pourquoi le prince Volodimer Svjatoslavič n'a-t-il pas été canonisé?" *Proceedings of the International Congress Commemorating the Millennium of Christianity in Rus'-Ukraine*, ed. O. Pritsak and I. Ševčenko, *HUS* 12/13 (1988/1989): 446–466. Only after the present essay was completed did I have an opportunity to acquaint myself with the important monograph by V. Vodoff, *Naissance de la Chrétienté russe* (Paris, 1988). In particular, its first chapter, "Les Débuts du christianisme russe" (pp. 29–61), bears on the topic of the present study.

2. L. Müller, *Zum Problem des hierarchischen Status und der jurisdiktionellen Abhängigkeit der russischen Kirche vor 1039* (Cologne and Braunsfeld, 1959), pp. 48–52 [= Osteuropa und der deutsche Osten, 3:6]; idem, *Die Taufe Rußlands. Die Frühgeschichte des russischen Christentums bis zum Jahre 988* (Munich, 1987), p. 104; A. S. Khoroshev, *Politicheskaia istoriia russkoi kanonizatsii (XI–XVI vv.)* (Moscow, 1984), pp. 48, 55; J. Fennell, article in this volume.

3. Müller, *Die Taufe Rußlands*, pp. 72–82; O. Pritsak, "When and Where Was Ol'ga Baptized?" *HUS* 9 (1987): 5–24; D. Obolensky, "Olga's Conversion: The Evidence Reconsidered," *HUS* 12/13 (1988/1989): 145–158.

4. B. Sawyer et al., eds., *The Christianization of Scandinavia* (Alingsås, 1987); B. Sawyer, "Scandinavian Conversion Histories," *HUS* 12/13 (1988/1989): 46–60; P. Sawyer, "The Organization of the Church in Scandinavia after the Missionary Phase," ibid., pp. 480–487.

5. N. K. Nikol'skii, *Povest' vremennykh let, kak istochnik dlia istorii nachal'nogo perioda russkoi pis'mennosti i kul'tury. K voprosu o drevneishem russkom letopisanii*, 1, (Leningrad, 1930) [= *Sbornik po russkomu iazyku i slovesnosti*, vol. 2, no. 1], sec. 1–9.

6. See, for example, G. Il'inskii, Review of Nikol'skii, *Povest' vremennykh let*, in *ByzSl* 2 (1930): 432–436; V. M. Istrin, "Moravskaia istoriia slavian i istoriia Poliano-Rusi, kak predpolagaemye istochniki nachal'noi russkoi letopisi," *ByzSl* 3 (1931): 308–332; D. S. Likhachev, *Vozniknovenie russkoi literatury* (Moscow and Leningrad, 1952), pp. 168–169; N. K. Gudzii, "Literatura Kievskoi Rusi i drevneishie inoslavianskie literatury," in *Issledovaniia po slavianskomu literaturovedeniiu i fol'kloristike* (Moscow, 1960), pp. 8–14.

7. See, for example, R. Jakobson, "Minor Native Sources for the Early History of the Slavic Church," *Harvard Slavic Studies* 2 (1954): 39–73, rpt. in *Selected*

Writings (Berlin, New York, and Amsterdam, 1954–1985), vol. 6, pt. 1, pp. 159–189; O. Králík, "Privilegium Moraviensis ecclecis," *ByzSl* 21 (1960): 219–237; idem, "Povest' vremennykh let i legenda Kristiana o sviatykh Viacheslave i Liudmile," in *Russkaia literatura XI–XVII vekov sredi slavianskikh literatur* (Moscow and Leningrad, 1963) [= *TODRL* 19]: 177–207; A. S. L'vov, "Cheshsko-moravskaia leksika v pamiatnikakh drevnerusskoi pis'mennosti," in *Slavianskoe iazykoznanie. VI Mezhdunarodnyi s"ezd slavistov (Praga, avgust 1968 g.). Doklady sovetskoi delegatsii* (Moscow, 1968), pp. 316–338; B. A. Larin, *Lektsii po istorii russkogo literaturnogo iazyka (X–seredina XVIII v.)* (Moscow, 1975), pp. 10–12; A. V. Isachenko [Issatschenko], "Esli by v kontse XV veka Novgorod oderzhal pobedu nad Moskvoi (Ob odnom nesostoiavshemsia variante istorii russkogo iazyka)," *Wiener Slavistisches Jahrbuch* 18 (1973): 51, n. 3; idem, *Geschichte der russischen Sprache,* vol. 1, *Von der Anfängen bis zum Ende des 17. Jahrhunderts* (Heidelberg, 1980), pp. 35–36; B. N. Floria, "Skazanie o prelozhenii knig na slavianskii iazyk. Istochniki, vremia i mesto napisaniia," *ByzSl* 46 (1985): 121–130; B. A. Uspenskii, *Istoriia russkogo literaturnogo iazyka (XI–XVII vv.)* (Munich, 1987), p. 44 [= *Sagners Slavistische Sammlung,* vol. 12].

8. The role of the Sázava Monastery as a disseminator of Church Slavonic writing in Rus' was the subject of the paper by V. Vavrínek, "The Monastery of Sázava as Transmitter of Slavonic Culture to Kievan Rus'," delivered at the Ravenna Congress.

9. K. Ericsson, "The Earliest Conversion of the Rus' to Christianity," *The Slavonic and East European Review* 44 (1966): 98–121.

10. Cf. H. Goldblatt, "On 'rus'skymi pismeny' in the *Vita Constantini* and Rus'ian Religious Patriotism," in *Studia Slavica Mediaevalia et Humanistica Riccardo Picchio Dicata,* ed. M. Colucci et al. (Rome, 1986 [1987]), pp. 311–328. Goldblatt suggests that the phrase *rus'skymi pismeny* of the *Vita Constantini* (ch. 8) indeed refers to Early East Slavic, but that this passage, or the entire *Vita,* in the version attested by the majority of extant manuscripts, represents a Russocentric ideological tradition of a later period.

11. Cf. S. V. Bakhrushin, *Trudy po istochnikovedeniiu, istoriografii i istorii Rossii epokhi feodalizma (Nauchnoe nasledie),* ed. B. V. Levshin (Moscow, 1987), pp. 15–35, 203–206.

12. S. A. Zenkovsky, *The Nikonian Chronicle: From the Beginning to the Year 1132,* vol. 1, ed. S. A. Zenkovsky, trans. S. A. and B. J. Zenkovsky (Princeton, 1984), pp. 6–7.

13. Ericsson, p. 104.

14. Note also his folklorically colored first mention, like that of Riurik, as one of three brothers. For a compelling argument against the existence of Kyi, see H. Trunte, "Kyj—ein altrussischer Städtegründer? Zur Entmythologisierung der slavischen Frühgeschichte," *Die Welt der Slaven* 33 (1988): 1–25.

15. A. A. Vasiliev, *The Russian Attack on Constantinople in 860* (Cambridge, 1946) [= Mediaeval Academy of America, *Publications,* vol. 46].

16. S. Aristarches, ed. Τοῦ ἐν ἁγίοις πατρὸς ἡμῶν Φωτίου πατριάρχου Κονσταντίνου πόλεως λόγοι καὶ ὁμιλίαι ὀγδοήκοντα τρεῖς, vol. 2 (Constantinople, 1900), no. 51, pp. 5–27; no. 52, pp. 30–57; C. Mango, ed. and trans., Homilies 3 and 4 in *The Homilies of Photius, Patriarch of Constantinople* (Cambridge, 1958), pp. 82–110, esp. pp. 74–82.

17. *PG*, vol. 102, cols. 736D–737A; B. Laourdas and L. G. Westrink, eds., *Photii patriarchae Constantinopolitani epistulae et amphilochia*, vol. 1, *Epictualrum pars prima* (Leipzig, 1983), p. 50; Zenkovsky, p. lviii. See also D. Obolensky, *The Byzantine Commonwealth: Eastern Europe, 500–1453* (New York, 1971), pp. 182–184; H. Rüss, "Das Reich von Kiev" in *Handbuch der Geschichte Rußlands*, ed. M. Hellmann et al. (Stuttgart, 1979–1980), 1:180, 283–286.

18. Obolensky, *The Byzantine Commonwealth*, p. 184.

19. S. H. Cross and O. P. Sherbowitz-Wetzor, eds. and trans., *The Russian Primary Chronicle: Laurentian Text* (Cambridge, 1973), pp. 65–66, 236, n. 38; Isachenko, *Geschichte der russischen Sprache*, 1:30; A. N. Sakharov, *Diplomatiia drevnei Rusi, IX–pervaia polovina X v.* (Moscow, 1980), pp. 147–180.

20. A. A. Vasiliev, "Was Old Russia a Vassal State of Byzantium?" *Speculum* 7 (1932): 350–360; W. K. Hanak, "Some Conflicting Aspects of Byzantine and Varangian Political and Religious Thought in Early Kievan Rus," *ByzSl* 37 (1976): 48–49.

21. Müller, *Zum Problem des hierarchischen Status*, pp. 21–22; idem, *Die Taufe Rußlands*, pp. 57–66; see also Rüss, p. 285.

22. O. Pritsak, *The Origin of Rus'*, vol. 1: *Old Scandinavian Sources Other than Sagas* (Cambridge, 1981), pp. 175–182. For a different, more realistic view of whence the Rus' attacked Constantinople in 860, see Vasiliev, *The Russian Attack on Constantinople*, pp. 169–175.

23. P. P. Tolochko, *Drevniaia Rus'. Ocherki sotsial'no-politicheskoi istorii* (Kiev, 1987), pp. 21–24.

24. J. Długosz, *Roczniki czyli Kroniki sławnego Królewstwa polskiego* (Warsaw, 1961), p. 184; idem, *Annales seu Cronicae incliti regni Poloniae* (Warsaw, 1964), p. 121.

25. For discussion of the history and recent state of the unabating Normanist controversy, see H. Lowmianski [Kh. Lovmianskii], *Zagadnienie roli Normanów w genezie panstwo slowianskich* (Warsaw, 1957), pp. 35–186; idem, *Rus' i normanny*, ed. V. T. Pashuto et al. (Moscow, 1985), pp. 5–22, 57–247, 252–290; *Varangian Problems. Scando-Slavica*, suppl. 1: Report of the First International Symposium, "The Eastern Connections of the Nordic Peoples in the Viking Period and Early Middle Ages" (Copenhagen, 1970); H. R. E. Davidson, *The Viking Road to Byzantium* (London, 1976), pp. 11–173; Rüss, pp. 267–282.

26. Rüss, p. 284; Tolochko, *Drevniaia Rus'*, p. 22; A. P. Vlasto, *The Entry of the Slavs into Christendom: An Introduction to the Medieval History of the Slavs* (Cambridge, 1970), p. 245.

27. Ericsson, p. 113.

28. Cross and Sherbowitz-Wetzor, p. 61.

29. Hanak, pp. 49–50.

30. Tolochko, *Drevniaia Rus'*, pp. 22–24; cf. Rüss, pp. 284–286.

31. Ia. N. Shchapov, *Kniazheskie ustavy i tserkov' v drevnei Rusi, XI–XIV vv.* (Moscow, 1972), pp. 12–135, esp. pp. 115–116.

32. Zenkovsky, pp. lvii–lviii.

33. Cf. ibid., p. xxxvi, with references to work by B. A. Rybakov and B. N. Kloss.

34. Ibid., pp. lvii–lx, 12–13, 17–18, 25–26 and n. 78, 29–30.

35. Müller, *Die Taufe Rußlands*, pp. 57–66.

36. On Askold and Dir, see Vasiliev, *The Russian Attack on Constantinople,* pp. 177–182.
37. Cross and Sherbowitz-Wetzor, pp. 68–69.
38. Ibid., p. 65; see also Müller, *Die Taufe Rußlands,* pp. 67–68.
39. Likhachev, *Povest' vremennykh let,* pt. 2: *Prilozheniia. Stat'i i kommentarii* (Moscow and Leningrad, 1950), p. 280.
40. Sakharov, pp. 179–180.
41. A. A. Vasiliev, *The Second Russian Attack on Constantinople* (Cambridge, 1951), p. 175 [= *DOP,* vol. 6]; Vlasto, *The Entry of the Slavs into Christendom,* p. 395, n. 81; A. Ducellier, "Byzance face au monde musulman à l'époque des conversions slaves: L'example du Khalifat Fatimide," *HUS* 12/13 (1988/1989): 373–386.
42. Cross and Sherbowitz-Wetzor, pp. 74, 77.
43. Likhachev, *Povest' vremennykh let,* p. 187, n. 22a.
44. *The Russian Primary Chronicle: Laurentian Text,* p. 238, n. 53.
45. P. P. Tolochko, *Drevnii Kiev* (Kiev, 1976), pp. 46–47; A. V. Kudryts'kyi, ed., *Kyiv. Istorychnyi ohliad* (Kiev, 1982), p. 18 and map of eighteenth-century Kiev. See also Müller, *Die Taufe Rußlands,* pp. 70–72.
46. Cross and Sherbowitz-Wetzor, p. 240, n. 64.
47. A. P. Vlasto, *A Linguistic History of Russia to the End of the Eighteenth Century* (Oxford, 1986), pp. 24, 348; B. A. Uspenskii, *Istoriia russkogo literaturnogo iazyka (XI–XVII vv.)* (Munich, 1987), pp. 24–25.
48. D. Obolensky, "Olga's Conversion."
49. J.-P. Arrignon, "Les relations internationales de la Russie Kiévienne au milieu du Xe siècle et le baptême de la princesse Olga," in *Occident et Orient au Xe siècle. Actes du IXe Congrès de la Société des historiens médiévistes de l'enseignement supérieur public, Dijon, 2–4 juin 1978* (Paris, 1979–1980); idem, "Les relations diplomatiques entre Byzance et la Russie de 860 à 1043," *Revue des études slaves* 55 (1983): 129–137.
50. D. Obolensky, "Russia and Byzantium in the Mid-Tenth Century: The Problem of the Baptism of Princess Olga," *Greek Orthodox Theological Review* 28 (1983): 157–171; idem, "The Baptism of Princess Olga of Kiev: The Problem of the Sources," in *Philadelphie et autres études,* ed. H. Ahrweiler (Paris, 1984), pp. 159–176 [= *Byzantina Sorbonensia,* vol. 4].
51. G. G. Litavrin, "Puteshestvie russkoi kniagini Ol'gi v Konstantinopol'. Problema istochnikov," *Vizantiiskii vremennik* 42 (1981): 46–48; idem, "O datirovke posol'stva kniagini Ol'gi v Konstantinopol'," *Istoriia SSSR* 5 (1981): 179–183; idem, "Russko-vizantiiskie sviazi v seredine X veka," *Voprosy istorii* 6 (1986): 41–52.
52. O. Pritsak, "When and Where Was Ol'ga Baptized?" See also F. Tinnefeld, "Die russische Fürstin Olga bei Konstantin VII. und das Problem der 'purpurgeborenen Kinder,'" *Russia Mediaevalis* 6 (1987): 1, 30–37.
53. O. Pritsak, "When and Where Was Ol'ga Baptized?" p. 21. Pritsak's notion that Byzantium would in fact not have minded if Olga turned to the Holy Roman Empire (and thus to the pope), rather than to Constantinople (and to the patriarch), for the official conversion to Christianity of her country, does not seem overly persuasive, however. For a similar view, see G. v. Rauch, "Frühe christliche Spuren

in Rußland," *Saeculum* 7 (1956): 65–66. A somewhat different view is expressed by Rüss, "Das Reich von Kiev," pp. 292–293.

54. For a discussion of Olga's diplomatic activities, including the reasons for her conversion, see Sakharov, pp. 259–298, 349–353. Here it should be noted that L. Müller continues to maintain that Olga was baptized shortly after her husband's death, i.e., probably still in 945 and in Kiev, and that she visited Constantinople in 946 already a Christian. See Müller, *Die Taufe Rußlands*, pp. 72–86, esp. pp. 80, 83.

55. *Quellen zur Geschichte der sächsischen Kaiserzeit*, ed. A. Bauer and R. Rau (Darmstadt, 1971), p. 214 [= *Ausgewählte Quellen zur deutschen Geschichte des Mittelalters. Freiherr vom Stein-Gedächtnisausgabe*, vol. 8].

56. See note 50, above.

57. O. Pritsak, " When and Where Was Ol'ga Baptized?" p. 8. See also R. Holtzmann, *Geschichte der sächsischen Kaiserzeit (900–1024)* (Munich, 1941), pp. 187–188. On this passage, and in particular the phrase *ficte, ut post claruit*, see M. Picchio Simonelli, "Gli Slavi in alcune fonti occidentali del X secolo," in *Studia Slavica Mediævalia et Humanistica Riccardo Picchio Dicata*, ed. M. Colucci et al. (Rome, 1986 [1987]), pp. 579–580.

58. Cf. v. Rauch, p. 66.

59. For a partial, cogently argued explanation, see Müller, *Die Taufe Rußlands*, pp. 85–86.

60. Ibid., pp. 87–88.

61. H. Birnbaum, "When and How Was Novgorod Converted to Christianity?" *HUS* 12/13 (1988/1989): 505–530.

62. J. V. A. Fine, Jr., *The Early Medieval Balkans: A Critical Survey from the Sixth to the Late Twelfth Century* (Ann Arbor, 1983), p. 187. Here, "Rus' " instead of "Russians" would be more accurate.

63. Cross and Sherbowitz-Wetzor, pp. 90–91.

64. Ibid., p. 93.

65. Ibid., p. 139.

66. Ibid., p. 93.

67. "The Earliest Conversion of the Rus' to Christianity," p. 104.

68. Cf. Müller, *Die Taufe Rußlands*, pp. 88–91.

69. Cross and Sherbowitz-Wetzor, pp. 95–96.

70. Ibid., p. 244, n. 87.

71. Ibid. (*sub anno* 980), pp. 93–94. See also B. A. Rybakov, "Iazycheskaia reforma Vladimira," in *Iazychestvo drevnei Rusi* (Moscow, 1987), pp. 412–454; Müller, *Die Taufe Rußlands*, pp. 92–94. On the martyred Varangians in particular, see V. Putsko, "Les Martyrs varègues de Kiev (983)," *AB* 101 (1983): 363–385.

72. See Müller, *Die Taufe Rußlands*, pp. 19–24. A. V. Riasanovsky's argument that the testimony of the *Annales Bertiniani* does not necessarily bear out that the Rus' at Ingelheim were Varangians is not persuasive. See "The Embassy of 838 Revisited: Some Comments in Connection with a 'Normanist' Source of Early Russian History," *Jahrbücher für Geschichte Osteuropas* 10 (1962): 1–12. For a more realistic view of the earliest penetration of Finnic, East Slavic, and Turkic settled territories in eastern Europe by Norsemen, see T. S. Noonan, "Why the Vikings First Came to Russia," *Jahrbücher für Geschichte Osteuropas*, n.s. 34 (1986): 321–348. On Byzantine

countermeasures, see D. W. Treadgold, "Three Byzantine Provinces and the First Byzantine Contacts with the Rus'," *HUS* 12/13 (1988/1989): 132–144.

73. Cross and Sherbowitz-Wetzor, p. 90. Cf. the similar formula in the preamble to the agreement of 907, cited above.

74. D. Obolensky, "Popular Religion in Medieval Russia," in *The Religious World of Russian Culture,* vol. 2: *Russia and Orthodoxy* (Festschrift G. Florovsky), ed. A. Blane (The Hague and Paris, 1975), pp. 51–52; Rybakov, pp. 455–782. On the shift from the pre-Christian to the Christian era in Rus', the clear break as well as the lingering echoes of the earlier epoch in the later one as reflected in literature, see Putsko, pp. 363–385.

75. Cf. Müller, *Die Taufe Rußlands,* pp. 111–116, esp. p. 112. For a compelling chronological reconstruction, see A. Poppe, "The Political Background to the Baptism of Rus': Byzantine-Russian Relations between 986 and 989," *DOP* 30 (1976): 195–244, rpt. as Chapter 2 in *The Rise of Christian Russia* (London, 1982).

The Spirituality of the Early Kievan Caves Monastery

FAIRY VON LILIENFELD

For the modern Ukrainian, Russian, or Belorussian reader, the spirituality of the Kievan Caves Monastery (KCM) is to be found in the Kievan Caves Patericon (KCP).[1] As is generally known and as I underlined at the Symposium on the Millennium of the Baptism of Rus' in Rome,[2] this patericon in its present manuscript form dates only from the fifteenth century, as does its name.

Strangely enough, the pieces included in this *paterik* not earlier than the end of the fourteenth or the beginning of the fifteenth century are those representing the oldest layer of witness to the earliest spirituality of the KCM.[3]

The literary nucleus of what is called a *paterik*[4] of the KCM by fifteenth- and sixteenth-century copyists is the *poslanie* of Bishop Simon of Suzdal to Monk Polikarp of the KCM, with stories of monks of the KCM integrated into it, and the "continuing" collection of stories which Polikarp himself wrote down as a sort of answer to Simon, but addressed to Akindin, the abbot, with an introductory *poslanie*. None of these stories by Simon and Polikarp were recorded until about 1225, though some of them surely go back to an older oral tradition. The keynote of spirituality of the work of Old Rus' literature, which I will call the "Poslaniia of Simon and Polikarp" (PSP), had already changed: it is the worship of the holy place of the KCM, the holy fathers who lived there and whose relics rest there, admiration for the miraculous foundation and building of the *katholikon* of the monastery, which was erected above the original caves and crypts. A heavy emphasis is put here upon the close connection of the monastery with Constantinople.

The criteria for identifying the oldest stories of the PSP are to be found precisely in those narratives that in the later redactions of the KCP are connected with the name of Nestor the Chronicler, but must belong to an even older layer of the *Povest' vremennykh let* than its redaction by Saint Nestor.[5] They are:

1. the tale recounting why the monastery was called Caves Monastery,[6]
2. the tale of the death of Saint Feodosii,[7] combined with
3. the tale about life in the KCM and some of the outstanding monks in it.[8]

Nearly as old as this collection of tales is another source about life in the KCM from the eleventh century: the *Life of Feodosii Pecherskii*, written by Nestor at the end of the eleventh century.[9]

The distinctive characteristics of the KCM in comparison with other monasteries founded at that time in Kievan Rus' are clearly expressed in the first tale of the *Povest' vremennykh let* under the year 6559 (1051). After telling us about the digging of the first crypt by the later Metropolitan Ilarion, the Chronicle continues:

> Not many days afterwards, there was a certain man, a layman of Liubech, in whose heart God had inspired the desire to go on a pilgrimage. He made his way to Mount Athos, beheld the monasteries there, and upon examining them and being charmed by the monastic life, he entered one of the local monasteries and begged the prior to confer upon him the monastic habit. The latter complied with his request and made him a monk, calling him Antonii, and after he had admonished him and instructed him in his monastic obligations, he bade him return to Rus' accompanied by the blessing of the Holy Mount, that many other monks might spring from this example. The prior blessed him and dismissed him, saying: "Go in peace."
>
> Antonii returned to Kiev and reflected where he should live. He went about the monasteries and liked none of them, since God did not so will, and subsequently wandered about the hills and valleys, seeking the place which God should show him. He finally came to the hill where Ilarion had dug the crypt, and liked this site, and rejoiced in it. He then lifted up his voice in prayer to God, saying amid his tears: "Oh Lord, strengthen me in this place, and may there rest upon it the blessing of the Holy Mount and of the prior who tonsured me."
>
> Thus he took up his abode there, praying to God, eating dry bread every other day, drinking water moderately and digging the crypt. He gave himself rest neither day or night but endured in his labor, in vigil, and in prayer . . .[10]

The Chronicler then tells of the growth of the monastery. Of Antonii personally he says:

> Thus he acquired distinction as the Great Antonii and those who drew near him besought his blessing . . . Brothers joined him, and he welcomed and tonsured them. Brethren thus gathered about him to the number of twelve. They dug a great crypt and [built] a church, and cells, which exist to this day in the crypt under the old monastery.

When the brethren had thus assembled, Antonii said to them: "God has gathered you together, my brethren, and you are under the blessing of the Holy Mount, through which the prior at the Holy Mount tonsured me and I have tonsured you also. May there be upon you first the blessing of God and second that of the Holy Mount."

And he added this injunction: "Live apart by yourselves, and I shall appoint you a prior, for I prefer to go alone to yonder hill, as I formerly was wont when I dwelt in solitude." So he appointed Varlaam as their prior, and he betook himself to the hill, where he dug a grotto, which is under the new monastery, and in which he ended his life, enduring in virtue, and for the space of forty years never issuing forth from the crypt in which his bones lie to the present day.[11]

What we have here before us is the typical account of the life of a hermit and the founding of a monastery "of the desert." It is true that this monastery was not so far from town as the monasteries of the deserts of Egypt, Sinai, Palestine, and Syria were from their respective provincial capital towns, or Mount Athos from Constantinople. But the desert (*eremos*) is represented in the case of the KCM by the crypts, catacombs and grottoes, that Antonii and his disciples built.

As in the period of the early Church, so in Byzantine medieval times, monks chose life in the "desert" as an alternative to life in a large town or village amid agricultural land—all that was the *kosmos,* where one could not live a life of repentance, permanent prayer, and asceticism. Only in the desert, which was uninhabitable land for the inhabitants of the *kosmos,* could one try to lead a totally new life, following strictly the teaching of Jesus Christ and his way of life and preparing for the New World of God ("the desert—the City of God"[12]) living as "Angels on Earth"[13] in an eschatological anticipation of life in Heaven. Such a life could be realized only in the distance that the "desert" gave one from the life of the *kosmos,* the large towns and the agricultural land. Only in the desert could one lead a life of deep and permanent repentance (*metanoia*) "in perpetual remembrance of death" and of the Last Judgment, a life according to the commandments of Christ (*entolai tou Kyriou*), in order to realize the true Christian "way of life" (*politeia*).[14]

To understand fully our text from the *Povest' vremennykh let*, we must remember that there were in Byzantium of the tenth and eleventh century—that is, in the time of the Baptism of Rus'—mainly three types of monastic life:

1. There were large monasteries in or near towns of the Empire, especially the capital, Constantinople. They were usually orga-

nized as *coenobia* in a more or less strict sense. They had a function in the life of the town, providing hospitality for travelers, hospital treatment for the sick, and a home for the aged, especially for the founders of the monastery. These monasteries also played an active role in the commercial life of their towns, as they manufactured earthenware vessels, cordage, and other articles of everyday use, as well as objects of pilgrims' art. These monasteries were also centers of worship and pilgrimage of the people, of confession and pastoral care of all men and women. Thus, while being monasteries, they were functionally linked to the "world" to procure salvation and welfare (*Heil und Wohl*) for its inhabitants.

2. Apart from these town monasteries, there were the "hermits" or "solitaries" who went far away from their native towns to the "desert" to live a life of prayer and asceticism. These hermits, however, did not stay alone all the time. As our text describes Antonii and the "beginning" of the KCM, so it was in all times of desert monasticism: the saintly living monk became famous. As it is said here: "Good men noticed his conduct," "he was remarked and revered . . . ," "celebrated" throughout Rus', and so he got disciples, "brothers joined him," and Antonii, like all famous hermits before him, could not turn them away, for Christ's sake he could not.

3. And there was a third type of monastic life, the life of "the elder" (*gerōn, dikaîos; starets*) and his disciples in a small community in the same desert. This small monastery in the desert cannot be called really "coenobitic" because not all the criteria of coenobitism are applicable to this "colony of hermits."

The latter two types of monastic life were very similar and closely related to each other. We find them in Byzantium of that time in opposition to that of the large, highly developed monasteries of the town. Compared to the monks of these monasteries, the hermits and elders led a primitive, archaic life in which personal poverty and the poverty of the community were combined.

It is typical for this tale of the beginning of the KCM that Antonii in the end left the brethren he had gathered. Hermits like him are always in the end disturbed by the clamors (*thoryboi*) inside even a small desert convent. All sorts of things happen with the younger, inexperienced monks. The elder whom they choose as their teacher and who has no spiritual right to reject disciples feels distracted from his purpose in life: prayer, tears of repentance, contemplation of the *magnalia Dei,* his personal asceticism. When he thinks he has already stabilized the ascetic life of his disciples, and if he finds a person among them who is already advanced in his own spiritual life (*prokopsas*) and whom he trusts entirely, he installs him as new prior and leaves to go "deeper into the desert," as was said in the lives of the old Monks of the Desert.

Our narrative about Antonii of the KCM and the first years of the KCM is a witness to the fact that Antonii was a typical hermit and that he acted just as they had acted in former centuries. We find in it also a clear awareness of the distinction between town monasteries and desert monastic bodies. A little later we are told in the same passage of the *Povest' vremmenykh let*:

> Now when the monastery [the KCM] was completed during the priorate of Varlaam [the successor whom Antonii had chosen] [Prince] Iziaslav founded the monastery of Saint Demetrios and appointed Varlaam prior therein, since he intended, by virtue of his material wealth, to make it superior to the ancient monastery. *Many monasteries have indeed been founded by emperors and nobles and magnates, but they are not such as those founded by tears, fasting, prayer and vigil* [italics added]: Antonii had neither silver nor gold, but accomplished his purpose through tears and fasting, as I have recounted.

The italicized portion renders the deciding sentence in Russian Church Slavonic:

> мнози бо манастыри от цесарь и от бояръ и от богатьства поставлени, но не суть таци, каци суть поставлени слезами, пощеньемь, молитвою, бдѣньемь.[15]

That means that the KCM realized the original sense of monastic life, saving one's soul for life eternal: "tears, fasting, prayer, vigil." We should hear it in the original voice of the old Greek sources of early monasticism: *dakyra, enkrateia, proseuchē, kai nēpsis.*

In this type of monasticism the "rule" it follows, its *politeia*, its *zhitie*, is to be found in the behavior and habits of its elder, the teacher and spiritual leader of his disciples in a small desert monastery, a shining example for them and for the later inhabitants of this hermit's society. Therefore the Chronicler tells us about Antonii:

> He took his abode there, praying to God, eating dry bread every other day, drinking water moderately and digging the crypt. He gave himself rest

neither day [n]or night, but endured in his labors, in vigil and prayer. . . . [Antonii was] enduring in virtue, and for the space of forty years never issuing forth from the crypt.[16]

Because of just such behavior Saint Feodosii was chosen the third abbot of the KCM. He is the next outstanding figure among the holy fathers of the KCM:

> When Varlaam had departed to Saint Demetrios', the brethren held a council, and then once more visited the ancient Antonii with the request that he should designate them a new prior. He inquired whom they desired. They replied that they desired only the one designated by God and by his own selection. Then he inquired of them: *"Who among you is more obedient, more modest, and more mild than Feodosii? Let him be your prior"* [italics added]. ["кто болии въ васъ, акъ же Феодосии, послушливыи, кроткыи, смѣреныи, да сь будеть вамъ игуменъ."][17]

We find this ideal and example of monastic behavior again when the Chronicler tells us about the death of Feodosii (under the year 6582 [1074]) and about his placing the monastery in the hands of Stephen, the leader of the monastery choir. He then continues his story:

> While Stephen governed the monastery and the pious flock that Feodosii had gathered, these monks shone out like bright stars throughout the lands of Rus'. Some of them were constant in fasting every other day or every third day, others living on bread and water only, still others in subsisting solely on boiled vegetables, and others only on raw food. They dwelt in love, while the young brethren obeyed the elder, not venturing to speak in their presence, but always comporting themselves obediently and with great consideration. Likewise the elder also gave proof of their love for their younger associates, admonished them, and consoled them like beloved sons. If any brother fell into some sinful way, they consoled him, and three or four of them shared the penance of one brother out of great affection to him. Such was the brotherly love and such the continence in this monastery. If any brother quit the monastery, all the rest were deeply afflicted on his account, sent in search of him, and recalled him to the monastery. All the brethren then appeared before the prior, and kneeling at his feet, they besought him in their brother's behalf, and received him in the community with joy. Such was their charity, their continence, and their austerity.[18]

Later we shall return to this text, but let us for the moment pay attention to some of the other monks' way of living, as the Chronicler describes it in the text that follows the description quoted above: "I shall mention a few eminent figures from their number . . . [Priest Damian] was so austere and temperate that he lived only on bread and water till his death . . ."[19]

The same sort of remark about the personal asceticism of a monk is to be found in certain similar stories about monks in the PSP. There we read, for instance, about Saint Afanasii the Recluse, who was seemingly dead for two days and then came to life again, that apparently after having lived through something similar to anticipating the Last Judgment, he "went to the crypt and blocked the door after himself and stayed in the crypt without talking at any moment to anybody, and so for twelve years . . ."[20] Thus he found his personal *askesis*, or training. To his brethren, however, he gave another rule of life, when after finding him alive, they asked him what he had seen while he seemed to be dead. He said to them quite in the tone and style of the *pneumatophoroi*, of the old Fathers of the Desert:

> "Strive for salvation!" [спаситеся!] The brethren implored him to tell them what had happened, and said that this would serve their spiritual advancement. And he said to them: "You will not believe me, if I tell you." The brethren swore to him: "We will preserve all you will tell us." He answered them: "Be obedient in all things to the prior, live in repentence all the time and pray to the Lord Jesus Christ and to His most pure Mother and to Saint Antonii and Saint Feodosii, that you may end your life here and may be held worthy to be buried in the Crypt with the holy fathers."[21]

So all we hear about the idea of true *askesis* in the first generations of the KCM is typical for the life of the Monks of the Desert, for the Desert monasteries and hermit colonies, and for the solitary hermits. It is what is called in the *paterika* of the old church *idiorhythmia*, the "idiorhythmic" way of monastic life; that is, each monk eventually finds his personal way of *enkrateia*, of *въздержание*. His way of life is a model of monastic rule to those who follow his example. Reading and hearing stories of the "old famous fathers" gives a young beginning monk or an advancing monk seeking deeper experience a choice of possibilities, how he can progress in the ascetic way of life.

The several ways of fasting in the KCM, of which we were told by the *Povest' vremennykh let* in the text quoted above, represent in fact such a list of possible choices: "Some of them were constant in fasting, some in vigil, some in genuflexion, some in fasting every other day or every third day, others living on bread and water only, still others in subsisting solely on boiled vegetables, and others on raw food . . ."[22] This is said by the Chronicler *after* he has told us about Feodosii's procuring the typikon of the Studios Monastery in Constantinople for the KCM. There has been much misunderstanding in scholarly literature about this introduction of the Studios typikon and about the changing of the life of the monastery to coenobitism.[23] These texts quoted from the *Povest' vremennykh let* indicate that the monastery remained, in any case at this early time of its existence, an "idiorhythmic" one.

It is true that under the priorship of Saint Feodosii, the great disciple of Saint Antonii, the monastery was structured anew. Saint Feodosii gave to it the functions of a charitable institution—or perhaps more accurately he admitted that it had become an institution of charity for the poor. He made the monastery take care of prisoners of the princely court of justice, and he did not allow the monks to have personal riches, especially when such riches had been obtained in a non-righteous way; nevertheless they continued to have such possessions, as the tales from PSP inform us. Saint Feodosii also did not shun relations with princes, especially the grand princes of Kiev, but he exhorted them as rulers to be guided by Christian social ethics and to be righteous in their personal lives.

The *Life of Saint Feodosii*, written by Saint Nestor the Chronicler in the 1080s (also a very ancient source for the early spirituality of the KCM, though it was included in the KCP relatively late)[24] tells us a great deal about the relations of Saint Feodosii to Prince Iziaslav. Feodosii makes Iziaslav pay attention to the monastery's schedule. When the monks have their rest after the services and labor of the morning, even Iziaslav is not to disturb it and is made to wait outside the walls until vespers begin. Then he has to hear the office, and only then may he talk to Saint Feodosii.[25] Feodosii also gives orders that the prince and his escort are to be given special attention and even served special dishes, though the prince may also have shared the frugal meal of the brethren.

Feodosii was an eager advocate of the right of the eldest brother to inherit the throne of Kiev and an adversary of the Varangian-Rus' custom that permitted the most powerful and victorious prince to aspire to this throne, usurping it from its legal holder. When Sviatoslav, Iziaslav's brother, drove Iziaslav from Kiev, forcing him to seek asylum at the court of the Polish king, Feodosii did not commemorate the new Grand Prince of Kiev in the liturgy. His brethren subsequently strove to convince him that he should acknowledge that the new ruler was well established and indeed exercised power in Kiev and, consequently, over the KCM. Feodosii's only concession to their pleas, however, was that he would commemorate Sviatoslav too, but only *after* naming his elder brother, the legal ruler in his eyes.[26]

Very often in the *Life of Saint Feodosii* (LF), we find Iziaslav at the feet of Feodosii listening to his teaching, eager to learn the Gospel of Christ and to hear the exhortations to a worthy Christian way of life.

From the oldest tales of the *Povest' vremennykh let* and the LF, it is quite clear that the first generation of monks in the KCM felt themselves absolutely free from princely influence and overlordship. For them the monastery simply belonged to another world. We recall the Chronicler's statement cited above: "Many monasteries have indeed been founded by emperors and nobles and magnates, but they are not such as those founded by tears, fasting, prayer and vigil. Antonii had neither silver nor gold, but accomplished his purpose through tears and fasting, as I have recounted."

But the monastery did need the prince when it became crowded and had to establish buildings outside the Crypt, on the hill above it. Antonii had to send to Iziaslav to beg him to give "the hill," that is, the surface of the hill inside of which the first crypts were situated, to the monastery as its property.[27] The prince and the boyars made rich donations to the monastery and, of course, they gained influence. But in this early time the sources always show us a clear limitation of this influence; the monastery and its priors remain sure that they belong to a totally different sphere of life and espouse totally different values.

To return to our original themes of coenobitism and idiorhythmia in the KCM in the eleventh century, we must recall the fact that in Eastern monasticism there had taken place a "reconciliation" between the two old conceptions of monasticism, coenobitism and solitary desert life. It had taken place not later than in the sixth or seventh century. From that time on, monastic life occurred in the following stages: A young monk entered a *coenobion*, then his prior allowed him to lead a more idiorhythmic life under the direction of an elder in a hermits' colony, and if very advanced and experienced in spiritual life, he was even allowed to live in absolute solitude.[28] In the case of the KCM this usually meant that he could go away from the monastery to live in some other lonely place. This Antonii himself did, for example, at least twice in his monastic life, and he ended as a recluse in the hill not too far from the site of the first crypt. Eunuch Efrem and the "Great Nikon" went quite far away from the KCM to an "isle near Constantinople" and to the "isle of Tmutorakan'." The LF shows us also—as I noted already concerning the tales of the *Povest' vremennykh let* and PSP—that life in the KCM under Feodosii was not that of a strict *coenobion* in the sense of Saint Pachomios or Saint Benedict, not even in the sense of Saint Basileios the Great, to cite only the most classical proponents of coenobitism.

Let us remember that coenobitism is characterized by the following: common property, a common roof (under which all monks sleep), common worship, common manual work (also in agriculture), and common practice of ascetic *enkrateia* under the direct command of the abbot.[29] In the KCM there is much individual working, reading, and praying, according to these sources; there are those who lead the extreme life of a fool in Christ or a life of exceptional poverty. Though the ideal of absolute obedience to the abbot remains, there are also examples of personal guidance of a young monk by an elder or instances of personal friendship between two monks which bring spiritual progress for one or both of them.

The severity of Saint Feodosii is not the severity of a monastery aware of its social obligations and needing provisions and money to fall back upon in times of deprivation or catastrophe. Feodosii's monastery observes the strictness of the "desert": not only each monk, but also the whole monastery must be poor; it must live by the grace of God from day to day, from donation to donation; it must give away to the needy whatever it has. Feodosii does not allow any hoarding of supplies "for a black day," as the Russians say. LF is full of examples of this radical, "non-possessive" behavior of the monastery as a whole; it is full of stories about living in absolute poverty from one day to the next.

The *Povest' vremennykh let* harps upon the fact that the KCM had been founded by the "blessing of the Holy Mount Athos," which Antonii had brought from the prior who had tonsured him. We should note that on Mount Athos at this time the same forms of monastic communal living prevailed as we find in the KCM.[30] Sometimes the ideal of solitary life and the actual practice of living in hermits' groups clashed with the ideal of coenobitism, but advocates of both ideals sometimes agreed on a common program, with stages of increasing rigor leading toward individual perfection.

An important aspect of the life of the old monks of the desert (fourth to sixth centuries) is to be found also in the oldest nucleus of narratives about monks of the KCM: it is the presence of several charismatic gifts granted by the Holy Spirit. Damian the Presbyter, for instance, had the gift of healing "sick and suffering children" by his prayers; Brother Eremiia, "who remembered the conversion of Rus' "[31] had the gift of prophecy and insight into the hearts of his fellow brothers. Brother Matfei also had the gift of insight into the spiritual background of events, especially into the machinations of the devil and his demons.

Special gifts were granted to the former Prince of Chernigov, Sviatosha (named Nikolai as a monk). He was the first Russian monk we hear of who constantly repeated the Jesus Prayer, "O Jesus Christ, Son of God, have mercy upon me!" He does not use it in the way we know from roughly contemporary Byzantine sources, where this prayer was said by illiterate or temporary Byzantine sources, where this prayer was said by illiterate or nearly illiterate monks as a substitute for reading the offices or the cell "pravilo," because Simon tells us that Sviatosha "had many books in his cell"[32] and quite obviously read them also. Sviatosha also had the gift of seeing into the hearts and hidden thoughts of men, especially his fellow monks, when looking at them or talking to them.

The PSP notes that the monk Kuksha possessed a special charismatic gift for conducting missionary work among the heathen. The introductory part of PSP, the *poslanie* of Bishop Simon itself, tells us of the martyr's death of Bishop Leontii of Rostov, one of numerous bishops who came from the KCM. Many other stories of the PSP are full of accounts of the monks' giving witness to the Christian faith before non-believers of all nationalities who came in contact with them and of the conversion of many heathen.

In this context we should stress that the KCM itself admitted not only monks from Kiev and other towns of Rus', but also men of other nationalities—Polovtsy, Torks, Volga-Bolgars, Hungarians, Scandinavians (*Variazi*), Armenians, Syrians, and Jews (or Khazars!).[33]

As in the early Church, monasticism in the KCM was not national but multinational. Peoples of all tongues were called by the monks of the KCM, as true disciples of Christ, to believe in the Lord and be saved. To stress this fact is especially important, because in the thirteenth century, there arose in eastern Europe a new exclusiveness, a consciousness of "Rus'" nationality—whatever this means in the thirteenth century!—and of Orthodoxy. Nothing of the sort is to be found in the KCM in the eleventh and twelfth centuries, according to the oldest sources, and not even in the PSP (thirteenth century) or in the KCP (fifteenth century).

So the monks of the KCM and their priors truly maintained the spirituality of the early Church, which continues the Pentecost experience. All nations hear, can hear, and have the right to hear the Good News of salvation in Christ. Likewise in early desert times monks of all nationalities lived together in good neighborliness with cell colonies and in common worship in Sunday and festal services. The same sense of multinational belonging as Christians is found in the KCM from the very beginning of its existence. The evidence of literary sources is confirmed by that of archeology, which continues to bear witness to this multinational tradition, continuing in times when PSP and KCP had already taken definite form.

One should note another feature of early monasticism that the PSP has in common with the missionary traditions of eastern Christianity and with Syriac monastic spirituality and its followers in Armenia and Georgia: the repeated heavy stress on total sexual abstinence as a feature of the Christian life of a new convert. Just as in the apocryphal Acts of the Apostles, the passions of the Eastern Martyrs, and the lives of Eastern saints, we find in the stories of the PSP the idea that non-believing "people of this world" lead a disorderly sexual life without any restraint. They try to seduce the newly tonsured monk (or nun) by sexual enticements. We find two especially expressive stories on this topic in the LF and the PSP: (1) some details in the story of Varlaam, the boyar's son, whom his parents try to prevent from becoming a monk by bidding his wife to "seduce" him anew to married life.[34] (2) the story of Moisei the Hungarian, quite a novella with details borrowed from the Potiphar story of the Old Testament.[35]

The PSP is also full of stories about unworthy and bad monks, some from a rather early period of the monastery's life. These monks fall to two main temptations: (1) the accumulation of personal wealth and the estimation of wealthy people, especially wealthy monks, higher than poor people and poor monks; (2) the desire to leave the monastery and to go "back to the world." As the PSP tells us rather frequently, it is especially in this context that monks have to fight demons. It is a special sign of virtue and spiritual courage when a monk "remains in his place" despite the assaults of demons, when he resists their seduction without fleeing from it.

As already stated, the PSP has the literary form of exhortation illustrated by simple stories, and its central message is the promise of forgiveness of sins for the repenting monk—and the layman! Its stories about bad and blundering monks are full of this promise of forgiveness for the sinner. Both the PSP and the LF transmit faithfully the central message of Christ: "Repent your sins [*metanoeite*] and believe in the Kingdom of God!" Christ's love for sinners, witnessed in his bitter, sacrificial death for their salvation, is a major theme in these stories. Saints Antonii and Feodosii, as well as some other saintly monks, embody this "love of mankind" in their meeting and treating sinners.

It is interesting to note that stories of this kind contain more realistic details about Kievan and Russian life than any other kind of monastic story in the PSP and LF. The ideal saintly monks from other stories seem to be more "timeless"; they could have lived in any society and any century of the medieval church. But here, in the sinners' stories we sense the pulsating Kievan life of that time. In the whirl of its "worldly" events the grand priors, elders, and monks of the first generations of the KCM represented the "living icon," the convincing image of the humility and love of Jesus Christ.

Notes

English translations of the texts from the *Povest' vremennykh let* are taken from S. H. Cross, O. P. Sherbowitz-Wetzor, *The Russian Primary Chronicle, Laurentian Text* (Cambridge, Mass., 1953), 138–142, 159–164. The translations from the *Life of Feodosii* and the KCP are mine.

1. I quote its text from the currently most accessible edition: *PLDR* 2 (1980): 412–623. This is a reprint (without the textual apparatus of the original edition, which I always consulted) from the scholarly standard edition edited by D. I. Abramovich, 2d ed. (Kiev, 1931). D. I. Abramovich issued in 1911 an edition of the text, which was not so complete as the revised first edition of 1929.

2. F. von Lilienfeld, "The Spirituality of the Kievan Caves Patericon," a paper delivered in May 1988 at the Rome Symposium of the Italian Institute of Medieval Studies and the Polish Institute of the History of European Christianity in Rome.

3. See the introduction by D. I. Abramovich to his 1929 edition. Also: D. K. Prestel, "A Comparative Analysis of the 'Kievan Caves Patericon,'" Ph.D. diss., University of Michigan, 1983, especially pp. 32–72, and the literature cited on pp. 385–400.

4. The Old Russian *paterik* is derived from the Greek word *paterikon*, which means "Book of the Fathers." But I have shown in my paper for the Millennium Conference of the Institute of World Literature in Moscow, 1–3 June 1988, that the literary genre of the old Greek *paterika* was not understood in the original sense by the Russian redactors of the final corpus of the KCP. What had been in Greek and Oriental *paterika* a collection of apophthegmata, i.e. of short sayings of the "fathers" of the first monastic generations, the "Fathers of the Desert," or very short records of their behavior and their miracles, in Russia of the fifteenth and following centuries had become a collection of stories and other texts for the praise of one monastery as a sacred place where so many holy fathers had lived, whose imperishable relics rested there even in the redactor's time. The monastery's churches had been miraculously built; it was not only a stronghold of piety, but also of "the Constantinople connection," i.e., of the "Greek faith," opposed to the Latin one or to the Russian self-will. The redactor took no note of the literary genre of the various texts compiled in the KCP.

5. I do not go here into the intricacies of the different theories and hypotheses about the origin and further development of the several redactions of the *Povest' vremennykh let* presented by A. A. Shakhmatov, V. M. Istrin, M. D. Priselkov, D. S. Likhachev, and L. Müller, to name only the most outstanding scholars, who have coped with this theme. Here it is sufficient to acknowledge that there is every evidence in the text that the "Nestor Chronicle" is a compilation of various texts composed during the eleventh and the beginning of the twelfth century, and that we can easily discern some stages of its early formation in the 1030s–1040s, the 1070s–1080s, and at the end of the eleventh century, fixing Nestor's personal contribution to this late eleventh-century redaction in the first decades of the twelfth century (Shakhmatov proposes the date 1111; Likhachev, ca. 1113).

6. *PLDR* 1 (*Povest' vremennykh let*, Moscow, 1978): 168–174, under the year 6559 (=1051); *PLDR* 2 (KCP):432–440 (Slovo 7).

7. Ibid., 1:116–200 under the year 6582 (=1074). In KCP this tale is incorporated into Nestor's "Life of Saint Feodosii" (Slovo 8).

8. Ibid., 1:202–210 under the year 6582 (=1074); cf. ibid., 2: 468–472 (Slovo 12).

9. Ibid., 1 (*Zhitie Feodosiia Pecherskogo,* edited from the text of the famous twelfth-thirteenth century "Uspenskii sbornik," with corrections from the edition of the "Life" by D. I. Abramovich in his KCP [cf. note 1]): 304–390.

10. Ibid., 1:170.

11. Ibid., 1:170, 172.

12. See D. J. Chitty, *The Desert a City. An Introduction to the Study of Egyptian and Palestinian Monasticism under the Christian Empire* (Oxford, 1966).

13. See K. S. Frank, *Aggelikos bios. Begriffsanalytische und begriffsgeschichtliche Untersuchung zum "engelgleichen Leben" im frühen Mönchtum* (Münster, 1964).

14. See F. von Lilienfeld, *Zur Spiritualität des frühen Wüstenmönchtums,* Oikonomia 18 (Erlangen 1983).

15. *PLDR* 1:172.

16. Ibid., 1:170, 172.

17. Ibid., 1:172s.

18. Ibid., 1:200s.

19. Ibid., 1:202.

20. Ibid., 2:496 (Slovo 19).

21. Ibid., 2:496.

22. Ibid., 1:200.

23. On the strict idea of coenobitism, see pp. 71–72 with note 29 below.

24. See n. 9. I quote this source also below from *PDLR* 1:304–390.

25. Ibid., 1:338, 340.

26. Ibid., 1:376–382.

27. Ibid., 1:172.

28. Of course, one finds in Byzantine lives of saints and in Byzantine historiographical literature also other examples of monks who remained hermits from the beginning to the end of their monastic lives.

29. See P. de Meester, *De monachicu statu iuxta disciplinam byzantinam,* Sacra Congegatione per la Chiesa Orientale, Codificazione canonica orientale, Fonti. Ser. 2, fasc. 10 (Vatican City, 1942).

30. Cf. A. Kazhdan, "Hermitic, Cenobitic and Secular Ideals in Byzantine Hagiography of the Ninth through the Twelfth Century," *Greek Orthodox Theological Review* 30 (1985): 473–487, especially p. 476.

31. *PLDR* 1:202.

32. Ibid., 2:500.

33. It is to be remembered that the khans and notables of the Khazars had adopted Judaism; so that they could be meant by the KCP term of "Jews."

34. *PLDR* 1 (LF):322–328.

35. Ibid., 2:542–554.

When Was Olga Canonized?

†JOHN FENNELL

The date of Saint Olga's canonization, like that of Saint Vladimir's, has plagued serious scholars for over a hundred years—almost as much as has the vexed question of the date and place of her baptism. No one, from Golubinsky, Vasiliev, and Serebriansky[1] to the present-day investigators, has been able to do more than say that she was probably numbered among the saints some time after, or even before, the Mongol invasion—and this only on the strength of the fact that the date of the earliest copies of the short Prologue *zhitie* cannot be established earlier than the end of the thirteenth century.

The reasons for this vagueness are not hard to find. First, little or nothing is known by scholars about the very process of canonization in the Byzantine world—and this applies as well of course to the early Russian Church. We do not know what the requirements were, who could authorize canonization, whether local bishop, metropolitan, or patriarch—or what the conditions were. We can assume that in all probability miracles such as the healings performed at the grave, the incorruptibility of remains, and the odors of sanctity exhaled by the body, were a *sine qua non*, or that canonization was extremely difficult without them. We can also assume that in most cases local veneration—that is, in the diocese itself or even in the precincts of the church where the burial took place or of the church to which the relics may have been translated—preceded universal recognition of sanctity, i.e., pan-Orthodox canonization.

Second, we know even less about Olga's canonization than we do about her grandson Vladimir's. The sources give little or no information: such epithets as *blazhennaia, preslovushchaia v premudrosti,* which are sprinkled in chronicles from the eleventh to the sixteenth century, are uninformative and in all probability simply decorative icing on the cake applied by scribes from the fourteenth century onwards. Even in Metropolitan Ilarion's *Slovo*, written between 1046 and 1051 with the—unsuccessful—aim of creating a favorable atmosphere for Vladimir's canonization, the only tiny fleeting mention of Olga seems, *pace* Ludolf Müller, to have been a later interpolation;[2] and surely Vladimir's grandmother was worthy of at least a mention in a work which refers to Christian Iaroslav and his wife (who had no claims to sanctity whatsoever) as well as to pagan Igor and Sviatoslav, Olga's husband and son respectively? From the eleventh through the seventeenth century, no churches, no monasteries were dedicated to Saint Olga, unlike the Sofias, Marinas, Irinas, Anastasiias, Varvaras, Nadezhdas, Liubovs, and Kseniias, all of whom had churches or monasteries named after them. Even the name Olga seems to have been avoided: chronicles record only two Olgas in the twelfth century and two in the thirteenth. As for iconography, there are no known portrayals of either Vladimir or Olga before the fifteenth century, with one possible exception: on the wall of the northern nave of the twelfth-century Church of Saint Kirill near Kiev, there is a fresco of Saints Vladimir and Olga, both with haloes, painted in the 1880s over, it is believed, an original fresco of the twelfth century. Unfortunately none of the experts in the *Kirillovskaia tserkov'* (*filial* of the Sofiiskii Museum in Kiev) can give any guarantee of the correspondence between the nineteenth-century painting and what may be beneath it.

Now what sources are there which mention Olga after her death in 969? First, of course, there is the *Povest' vremennykh let* and later chronicles, which add little or nothing to the original version. The account of her death and burial is followed by a standard encomium, clearly written, as D. S. Likhachev has pointed out,[3] by whoever wrote the encomium to Vladimir, *sub anno* 1015. In it she is described as the forerunner of the Christian land, the morning star before the sun, dawn before light, a pearl in the dung (*biser v kale*). The only significant element is the hint of a miracle: "All men glorified her lying [incorrupted] in her body for many years."[4] This is repeated in the eulogy to Vladimir, written originally by the monk Iakov in the third quarter of the eleventh century (the earliest copy of which, alas, stems from the 1470s), with the additional information that believers visiting her grave in the *Desiatinnaia tserkov'*, whither Vladimir had translated her relics, can see her imperishable body through an aperture in the sarcophagus; for unbelievers, however, there is no opening, and they can see only the outside of the sarcophagus itself.[5] As for the earliest Prologue or Synaxarion brief *Life* of Olga, this exists only in a South Slavic version datable to the end of the thirteenth century or the beginning of the fourteenth, probably deriving from an earlier Kievan version.[6] Unfortunately this contains no new information and no indications as to when or why Olga was canonized: it consists merely of a brief version of her baptism in Constantinople, a comparison to Helen, the mother of Constantine the Great, and a few eulogistic phrases. Later north-Russian redactions (fourteenth–sixteenth centuries) of the Prologue *Life*, as well as the full *zhitie* composed in the sixteenth century, give no further information of any value.

What conclusions can be drawn from the above? First, in all the sources there exists a strong link between Olga and her grandson Vladimir. As mentioned above, the eulogy of Olga in the *Povest' vremennykh let* was almost undoubtedly written by whoever wrote Vladimir's encomium: both the contents and the phraseology are similar. The link is stronger still in Iakov's *pokhvala*. Here Vladimir is portrayed as being inspired to accept Christianity by Olga's trip to Constantinople and her baptism; the proximity between Olga and Helen is stressed, and Vladimir and Olga are portrayed as doing what Constantine and Helen did. Both were generous to the poor, the halt, the blind, widows and orphans. Moreover, of course, it is stressed that Olga's bones were eventually laid to rest by Vladimir in the Kiev Tithe Church founded by him.[7]

In both the chronicle and the *pokhvala* of Iakov, the only striking difference between the two future saints is the fact that the miraculous imperishability of Olga's remains is stressed, whereas the unwillingness of the Russians to render proper homage to Vladimir at his death is given as the reason why God declined to have Vladimir glorified with a miracle. In the eulogy to Vladimir following the description of his death in 1015, the chronicler remarks: "We, having become Christians, do not give homage to Vladimir worthy of his deed. Had we had zeal enough and prayed to God for him on the day of his death, then God would have seen our zeal towards him and would have glorified him"[8]—that is, with a miracle, the true sign of his sanctity. This is sure evidence that Vladimir's canonization was not even under consideration at the time that part of the *Povest' vremennykh let* was redacted.

So, in spite of the close links between Olga and Vladimir in the minds of those who wrote about them, there was only one great difference between them. Vladimir's death was clearly undistinguished by any sort of miracle, whereas Olga's seemingly contained the true marks of sanctity. Still, how can we tell what the prototypes of *any* of the sources in fact contained? How can we possibly know what was added by the pious hands of later scribes who after the eventual canonization attempted to add to their lustre in the earlier writings? We don't know. Maybe in the protograph of Iakov's *pokhvala* there was even no mention of any miracles at Olga's grave?

My conclusions, therefore, are that the two future saints, both later to be styled *ravnoapostol'nye* and who were linked together by the close relationship of grandmother/grandson and by similar exploits—baptism in a pagan milieu—were officially admitted to the company of the saints at the same time. But when?

Recently at a conference in Germany in anticipation of the millennium, I put forward the thesis that a date could be found for Vladimir's canonization. I will briefly repeat my findings.

There are two sources which give us *termini ad quem* and *a quo*. Under the year 1311, the earliest redaction of the Novgorod First Chronicle states that the archbishop of Novgorod built a stone church dedicated to Saint Vladimir.[9] This must mean that by 1311 Vladimir had been canonized. But what about the earliest date? In the version of Aleksandr Nevsky's *zhitie* found in the Laurentian Chronicle under the year 1263, the beginning of the campaign against the Swedes in 1240 is described as follows: "and he [Aleksandr] marched against them on Sunday, the day of the 630 holy fathers of the Council in Chalcedon and of the holy martyrs Kirikos and Iuletta and of the holy prince Vladimir [*sviatogo kniazia Vladimira*] who baptized the Russian land, having great faith in the martyrs Boris and Gleb."[10] As one can see, this just does not make sense: "having great faith in Boris and Gleb" is far from the subject it should qualify, Aleksandr Nevsky.

Now as Kirikos's and Iuletta's day is 15 July and as Vladimir died on 15 July, it has been thought by most scholars that the Novgorodians (or more likely Aleksandr himself) decided to institute the church celebration of Saint Vladimir shortly after the Neva battle; thus, 1240 is taken as the date of his canonization.

However, in *all* accounts of the battle on the Neva, Aleksandr's victory is ascribed to the spiritual assistance *not* of Vladimir, but exclusively of Boris and Gleb. More important still, the Laurentian Chronicle version, although the earliest of all chronicles to carry Aleksandr's *zhitie* (the chronicle was copied in 1377, undoubtedly straight from its final redaction of 1305), does not carry the earliest version of the *Life*. According to Begunov,[11] the version closest to the prototype of the *zhitie* is that contained in the Pskov Second Chronicle where we read: "And he marched against them on Sunday 15 July, having great faith in the martyrs Boris and Gleb."[12] This makes sense, omits *all* mention of Kirikos and Iulitta and the (wrongly dated) Chalcedon Council, and, above all, "Saint" Vladimir.

Now it has been established that the original *zhitie* of Aleksandr Nevsky was written in 1283. As the prototype contains *no* mention of Vladimir, it would appear that by 1283 Vladimir was not yet recognized in Novgorod— or anywhere else, for that matter—as a saint. It follows that the copyist of the final redaction of the Laurentian Chronicle (1305) added—probably from a Novgorodian source—Saint Vladimir's day to the dating of the Neva battle some time between 1283 and 1305. In other words Vladimir was recognized as a saint some time in the twenty-two years between these two dates.

When? In 1283, a Greek, Maxim, was appointed metropolitan of Kiev and all Rus'. In 1299, in the wake of a Tatar attack on Kiev, he transferred his see to northeast Russia where he died in 1305. In other words, the dates of his metropolitanate, 1283–1305, are the same as the dates between which Vladimir—and, I suggest, Olga too—were canonized.

Now we know that in 1284 Maxim summoned all the Russian bishops to a council in Kiev. Unfortunately, the only source to mention it (the Nikon Chronicle) is silent on the reason for the summoning,[13] but I would suggest that it was to decide on the admittance of Vladimir and Olga, and perhaps others too, to the company of saints.

The 1280s were a period of civil war and disintegration in northeast Russia: neither of the two sons of Aleksandr Nevsky who alternated as grand prince had the ability or strength to unite Suzdalia or to resist the ever-increasing advances of the Tatars. In spite of the splintering of the Kipchak Horde after Mangu Temir's death in 1280, the Russians began to lean ever more heavily on Tatar military support for their disastrous interprincely feuds and thus still more to weaken the state. At the same time the Church in Byzantium had recently disavowed the union with Rome and reaffirmed the orthodoxy of the patriarchate.[14] Might not then the decision at long last to canonize Vladimir be considered, so to speak, as a gift to depressed and flagging Russia from the buoyant Byzantine Church eager to reaffirm its orthodoxy? It was the only recorded council of Russian bishops chaired by the metropolitan which took place between 1283 and 1305—and such a council, with the blessing of the patriarch, was presumably a requirement for full canonization.

In the next year, 1285, Maxim is reported as visiting "all the Russian land (i.e., Suzdalia, northeast Russia), teaching, instructing and administering,"[15] and spreading the news of the canonization of Vladimir and Olga. Especially noted in the chronicles is his visit both to Novgorod where Vladimir's memory was already held in honor and where the first church dedicated to him was built in 1311, and to Pskov where Olga was born.

So I would suggest that Olga was formally canonized together with her grandson, both of them "equal to the apostles," in 1284 in Kiev, the city where both ruled.

Notes

1. E. Golubinskii, *Istoriia kanonizatsii sviatykh v Russkoi Tserkvi* (Moscow, 1903), pp. 56–57. V. Vasil'ev, *Istoriia kanonizatsii russkikh sviatykh,* in: *Chteniia v imperatorskom obshchestve istorii i drevnostei rossiiskikh* (1893), bk. 3, pp. 73–75. N. Serebrianskii, *Drevne-russkiia kniazheskiia zhitiia* (Moscow, 1915), vol. 1, 22 ff.
2. *Des Metropoliten Ilarion Lobrede auf Vladimir den Heiligen und Glaubenskenntnis,* ed. Ludolf Müller (Wiesbaden, 1962), pp. 23, 118–19.
3. *Povest' vremennykh let,* ed. V. P. Adrianova-Peretts (Moscow and Leningrad, 1950), 2:316.
4. *PSRL,* 1: cols. 68–69.
5. A. A. Zimin, "Pamiat' i pokhvala Iakova mnikha i zhitie kniazia Vladimira po drevneishemu spisku," *Kratkie soobshcheniia Instituta Slavianovedeniia,* 37 (1963): 69–70.
6. Serebrianskii, vol. 2 (*Teksty*), pp. 6–13.
7. Zimin, pp. 69–70.
8. *PSRL,* 1: col. 131.
9. *NPL,* 93.
10. *PSRL,* 1: col. 479.
11. Iu. K. Begunov, *Pamiatnik russkoi literatury XIII veka, "Slovo o pogibeli russkoi zemli"* (Moscow and Leningrad, 1965), 12 ff.
12. *Pskovskie letopisi,* vol. 2, ed. A. N. Nasonov (Moscow, 1955), p. 12.
13. *PSRL,* 11:162.
14. J. Meyendorff, *Byzantium and the Rise of Russia* (Cambridge, 1981), p. 43.
15. *PSRL,* 11:166; cf. 1: col. 526.

Why Did the Metropolitan Move from Kiev to Vladimir in the Thirteenth Century?

DONALD OSTROWSKI

The chronicles report that in 1299 the metropolitan of Kiev moved his residence from Kiev to Vladimir-on-the-Kliazma.[1] Subsequently, the metropolitan's taking up residence in Moscow had enormous consequences for the political and religious history of the Rus' land. Historians have expressed diverse opinions concerning the circumstances of the move of the metropolitanate from Kiev. Since no survey of those opinions has been made, and since historians have expressed their views, for the most part, in isolation without reference to previous accounts of this issue, it is worthwhile to consider that historiography briefly.

* * *

N. M. Karamzin, in his *History of the Russian State*, follows the chronicle account in writing that Metropolitan Maksim (1282–1305) went with his entourage (*kliros*) to Vladimir and that "the majority of Kiev's inhabitants fled to other towns."[2] Karamzin asserts that Maksim left Kiev so as not to be a martyr and victim of the intolerable Mongol tyranny. If that is the reason the metropolitan left Kiev, then it is not clear why he would wait until 1299, when Mongol control in the area was declining and the Lithuanians were moving into the area. S. M. Soloviev, in contrast, sees the move of 1299 being prepared already under Metropolitan Kirill (1242–1280): "when the significance of Kiev and Southern, Dnepr Rus' declined conclusively," Kirill "turned greater attention to Northern Rus'."[3] In support of this assertion, Soloviev cites chronicle references to Kirill's travels to Chernigov, Riazan', the Suzdal' land, and Great Novgorod, as well as references to Kirill's being in Vladimir in 1255 and at Nevsky's funeral in 1263, "after which he went to Kiev; the chronicler speaks about his return from there [to the Council of Vladimir] under 1274."[4] Soloviev also mentions Kirill's travel from Kiev to Pereiaslavl'-Zalesskii where he died, and that he "was buried in Kiev." Soloviev concludes, rather ambiguously:

> If on the basis of this information we do not have the right to say that Kirill transferred the [metropolitan's] residence from Kiev to Vladimir, then at least we see that he appears in the north several times and very probably that he lived here if not more, then as much as in the south.[5]

When Maksim became metropolitan, according to Soloviev, he "at first indicated that the capital of the Rus' metropolitanate should remain in Kiev."[6] Soloviev mentions that the chroniclers attribute the move to Vladimir to Maksim's wish to avoid violence from the Tatars in Kiev. But then Soloviev raises the question whether that violence was worse in 1299 than earlier. He concludes that "Maksim made a decisive, final step clearly testifying to the fact that the vital forces had completely poured out [*otlili*] from the south to the north."[7]

The idea that a large transfer of population occurred during this time shows up in the work of V. O. Kliuchevsky who writes that Kievan Rus' "was completely devastated as a result of the Mongol incursions." Kliuchevsky seems to consider these incursions as only the final blow to the emptying of Kievan Rus', which he sees as having been going on since the mid-twelfth century. This situation, he continues, led to the "flight of the Kievan population northwards," which carried the metropolitan with it.[8] As evidence to support his assertion, Kliuchevsky refers to the chronicles' description of the move of Metropolitan Maksim in 1299. He then quotes from the chronicle that "all the city of Kiev did flee also." Kliuchevsky does imply that some people either remained in Kiev or returned at a later time, because he writes that "the disturbed state of the times rendered care of the South Russian pastorate as necessary as ever . . . so that the metropolitan had to make frequent journeys to the south to visit his Kievan eparchies."[9]

One finds at least three problematic aspects of Kliuchevsky's depiction. He does not acknowledge Soloviev's description of earlier activities in the north of the metropolitanate under Kirill, Maksim's predecessor. Also, he seems so convinced that a mass movement of population from Kiev to the northeast occurred that he overlooks the fact that the chronicle entry relates only that "all Kiev fled" (*razbiezhesia*), but does not indicate a direction.[10] In fact, the only direct evidence we have of anyone's moving from Kiev to the northeast during the last half of the thirteenth century is the chronicle account of the move of the metropolitan and his entourage. Finally, Kliuchevsky makes no effort to account for the apparent time delay between the Mongol sack of Kiev in 1240 and the move of the metropolitan fifty-nine years later. If conditions in Kiev were so bad, one would think that the metropolitan would have moved sooner.

E. E. Golubinsky is in agreement with Soloviev's suggestion that Kirill resided as much in the north as in the south, but makes no reference to Soloviev's work. He asserts that Metropolitan Kirill left Kiev because it was "unsafe for habitation,"[11] and, at first, divided his time between the grand prince of Galicia, Danylo, and the grand prince of Rus', Aleksandr Nevsky. Furthermore, Golubinsky decides that Kirill lived more or less continuously in the north between 1250 and 1263. It was only after the death of Nevsky, according to Golubinsky, that Kirill returned to Kiev.[23] Golubinsky argues that the vacancy of the Vladimir eparchy until 1274 is evidence that Kirill was contemplating an official move of the metropolitan's residence there.[13] Then, in 1299, fleeing Tatar attacks, which dispersed the entire town of Kiev, Metropolitan Maksim sought refuge in Vladimir.[14] Thus, Golubinsky argues for three moves: from Kiev to Vladimir around 1250, from Vladimir to Kiev after 1263, then back to Vladimir in 1299. But Golubinsky provides no rationale for why Kirill, if he had established himself in Vladimir in the 1250s would want to move back to Kiev in the 1260s, especially if Kiev was so unsafe.

M. D. Priselkov, in contrast, suggests that Kirill resided in Vladimir from 1250 on, and made only infrequent trips south to Kiev.[15] D. S. Likhachev follows Priselkov on this point and offers a possible explanation for why the metropolitan would move north in the 1250s—the agreement between Danylo and the papacy according to which Danylo would receive the title of king. Likhachev argues that this agreement "was not able to meet and did not meet with sympathy among the Rus' clergy."[16] He concludes that Kirill moved to the north in opposition to the policies of union with Catholicism that Danylo seemed to be undertaking. George Vernadsky asserts that Kirill found "Kiev completely devastated and unsuitable for the establishment of the diocesan administration" and, therefore, "went to East Russia instead."[17] Vernadsky adds that Kirill's "disapproval of Daniel's negotiations with the pope was an additional motive for his decision." Steven Runciman places the initial leaving of the metropolitan in the twelfth century. He asserts that after Andrei Bogoliubsky's sack of Kiev in 1169, the metropolitan had "to reside in the capital of whatever Grand Prince was dominant at the moment." This "nomadic life" of the metropolitan, according to Runciman, "weakened the organization of the Church."[18] Iu. A. Limonov, in contrast, asserts that Kirill went to Vladimir in 1250 and "remained in the northeast for the entire period of the reign of Aleksandr Nevsky."[19] Limonov cites only two of Kirill's activities in the north (his coming with Nevsky to Novgorod in 1251 and his participation in the ceremony when Nevsky became prince of Vladimir in 1252) to support his assertion.[20] But Limonov does not explicitly say whether he believes that Kirill returned to Kiev after the death of Nevsky or remained in Vladimir. None of these historians attempts to explain the chronicle entry concerning the move of the metropolitan from Kiev in 1299.

Ivan Wlasowsky, in his history of the Ukrainian Orthodox Church, also asserts that Kirill "rarely visited Kiev, residing most of the time in Vladimir on the river Kliazma," but stops short of arguing that Kirill transferred the metropolitan's official residence there. Instead, Wlasowsky asserts that Kirill "prepared the groundwork for the formal transfer."[21] Wlasowsky's interpretation is a decidedly nationalistic one. He sees a similarity between Kirill's activities as metropolitan and subsequent "Ukrainian Church prelates who ... played a significant role in the political strengthening and cultural improvement of the Muscovites." He is referring to the period after 1649 when Ukrainian and Belorussian clerics went north to Muscovy.[22]

Wlasowsky refers to unnamed "Russian historians" who "explain ... [the move of the metropolitan] by the decline of Kiev, the constant disturbances of the Tatars in the south, and the need of the metropolitan's counsel and administration in the north where Church life was rising and spreading in the new state . . . ." He disputes the last point of the "Russian historians" by arguing that "there were also demands of Church life in the Galician-Volhynian state" where the Tatars were not so strong and where "pressure against Orthodoxy had begun to be exerted by the Latin Church."[23] He, thus, seems implicitly to accept the first two points, which concern the need for the metropolitan to move from Kiev, but he does not agree with the last point, the direction of the move.

Wlasowsky does not provide any other explanation but suggests that the metropolitan had betrayed Ukrainian state interests, which Wlasowsky associates with Galicia-Volhynia: "Because of its political position and also because of the greater distance from the Tatar Horde, Ukrainian culture was able to develop at this time only in the Galician-Volhynian state, which embraced exclusively Ukrainian territories with a Ukrainian population . . ."[24] Then he speculates that the princes of Galicia and Volhynia, Danylo and Vasyl'ko, nominated Kirill "for the good of their people and their state and not for the Suzdalian north." He concludes that Kirill, although "born a Ukrainian in Galicia and an able prelate, did not fulfill the hopes and expectations of the Galician-Volhynian princes."[25] Wlasowsky repeats this same argument in regard to the nomination of Peter as metropolitan in 1305 who "as a son of the Galician lands" it was expected would "care for the church-religious life of his own people." But their "expectations, as in the case of Kirill III, were not fulfilled" because Peter went north to help Ivan Kalita in "the realization of his political-state plans."[26] Given the betrayal of Ukrainian state interests by Kirill, Wlasowsky deems it appropriate that "Maksim followed in his footsteps, all the more so since he was a Greek who had been sent from Constantinople and thus felt no particular connection to Kiev or moral obligation to the Ukrainian people."[27] What Wlasowsky does not provide is a motivation for this "betrayal" on the part of the metropolitans, in particular Kirill and Peter, who for Wlasowsky are the apparent villains in the piece. It is doubtful, however, that anybody in the thirteenth century was thinking in terms of Ukrainian-versus-Russian state interests.

One of the few historians to deal directly with other historians' interpretations on this issue has been Joseph Fuhrmann. He challenged Priselkov and Likhachev's suggestion that Kirill resided more or less permanently in the north by pointing out that the Nikon Chronicle entry for 1280 states that Metropolitan Kirill "as was his custom, left from Kiev and travelled to all the towns of Rus'." Fuhrmann also states that the entry for 1274 indicates that Kirill left Kiev to hold a council in Vladimir.[28] Besides these two entries, he could also have pointed to the entry under 1274 where the Novgorod I Chronicle reports that "they [the Novgorodians] sent Kliment to Kiev for confirmation."[29] Under 1276, the chronicles state that Kirill consecrated Kliment in Kiev.[30] In addition, when Kirill died in Pereiaslavl'-Zalesskii in 1280, the chronicles report that "they bore him to Kiev."[31] If the metropolitan's residence had been in Vladimir, then there would have been no reason to transport his body to Kiev. The Nikon Chronicle treats Maksim, Kirill's successor, the same way: in 1284 "all the bishops of Rus' were summoned to Kiev to Maksim."[32] One notes that Maksim does not leave Vladimir to go to Kiev; the other bishops come to him in Kiev. Under 1285, some chronicles report that "Metropolitan Maksim came from Kiev to Novgorod."[33] Finally, the chronicle reports indicate that other bishops besides Kliment were consecrated in Kiev.[34] If the metropolitan had moved to Vladimir as early as 1250, then we would have to explain why the chronicles place the move in 1299, a full forty-nine years later and why they continue to treat Kiev as the *de facto* as well as *de jure* residence of the metropolitan.

John Meyendorff acknowledges that Kirill "had transferred the centre of . . . [his] activities as metropolitan to the north-east . . . and to Novgorod."[35] But Meyendorff asserts that the metropolitan had not resided there officially, nor resided in Kiev "since the Mongol conquest . . ."[36] Thus, if one understands Meyendorff correctly, the metropolitan had no official residence from 1240 to 1299. Instead, because Kirill's activities in the north are "mentioned so often in the chronicles," Meyendorff concludes "that he undoubtedly sojourned there for several consecutive years."[37] He points out that although Danylo appointed Kirill as metropolitan, Kirill "did not feel bound by the policies of his princely sponsor."[38] But the "decisive shift" that Kirill made to the northeast "could not possibly be a purely personal decision."[39] Meyendorff does not see it as a betrayal of Galicia, as Wlasowsky does, because Kirill "promoted the unity" of the Galician princes with those in the north through royal marriages. Nor does Meyendorff think the shift can be explained by any "anti-Western sympathies" on the part of Kirill. Instead, he proposes "wider and long-term considerations of *Realpolitik*,"[40] among which were that a "vast majority" of the metropolitan's flock was now under control of the Kipchak Khanate and that "tradition and canonical ties" of Rus' with Byzantium "could only be enhanced by a policy of loyalty to the Mongol empire."[41] Meyendorff cites the Laurentian Chronicle for the establishment by Maksim of "his permanent residence in Vladimir."[42] He recaps without editorial comment the reason given by the chronicler for the move, that is, "that Tatar devastations made his sojourn in Kiev impossible."[43] While Meyendorff is the first investigator to emphasize the importance of Byzantine-Mongol relations as a significant component of the decision to move the metropolitan's residence, he leaves several questions unasked. In particular, why could not the metropolitan have promoted unity from Galicia? Why was Vladimir the city of choice rather than, say, Novgorod or Tver'? And he does not consider why Maksim would establish the metropolitan's official residence in the northeast only in 1299 rather than earlier or later.

Thus, we see no real agreement in the historiography concerning the circumstances of the move. In particular, had Metropolitan Kirill previously moved to Vladimir? If so, then did he move back to Kiev? Why would the metropolitan move north to Vladimir instead of west to Galicia? And, finally, the question of "Tatar violence" (*nasilie*) has hardly been addressed at all. As Soloviev asked, what was worse about the Tatar violence of 1299 than previously that provoked the metropolitan to move?

* * *

Most likely, the idea behind the move of the seat of the metropolitanate to the north was to get the head of the Rus' Church, the metropolitan, and the nominal Christian ruler of Rus', the grand prince, to reside in the same place,⁴⁴ just as the Patriarch of Constantinople resided in the same city as the Byzantine Emperor. The idea, which was expressed in the chronicles, that the metropolitan moved because Kiev had been made unsafe by "Tatar violence,"⁴⁵ which Golubinsky and others understood to mean "plundering" (*razgrablenie*)⁴⁶ would seem to be belied by two considerations. First, the metropolitan, at least officially, resided some fifty-nine years in Kiev after the sack of 1240 and traveled extensively throughout Rus' lands in apparent safety. Metropolitan Kirill's extensive traveling as head of the Rus' Church led the Church historian Filaret to remark that he "scarcely spent a year in one place."⁴⁷ Second, the northeast suffered frequent Mongol intrusions during this period. From 1273 to 1298, we have accounts of at least sixteen punitive raids by the Mongols on towns in the northeast.⁴⁸ Vladimir, Moscow, and other towns in the northeast were sacked as late as 1293; Moscow was sacked again in 1298. If, as Vernadsky argues, Kiev was "completely devastated and unsuitable for the establishment of the diocesan administration," then Vladimir seems to have been no better off after its destruction in 1238.⁴⁹ The Mongols were no less violent in the north than they were in the south.

Much of the argument that Kiev was unsafe in the year 1299 is based on Carpini's description of Kiev in 1246: "Kiev . . . has been reduced almost to nothing, for there are at the present time scarce 200 houses there and the inhabitants are kept in complete servitude."⁵⁰ However, there is no other extant description of Kiev at this time, so there is no way to confirm Carpini's description or indeed that he was describing Kiev or some other town he was told was Kiev. It is possible that the Mongols were aware of the quasi-military reconnaissance purpose of Carpini's mission and may have tried to deceive him.⁵¹ There is no evidence in Carpini's account, such as a description of the Sophia Cathedral, that connects the town he saw with Kiev itself.⁵² Carpini, however, may have seen a Kiev that was relatively undevastated, but disappointing in appearance when compared with Western cities that were more densely populated.⁵³ William of Rubruck provides supporting evidence for the conjecture that western Europeans of the time were unimpressed with the size of non-Western European towns. In his *Journey*, Rubruck states that the capital of the Mongol Empire, Karakorum, "is not as large as the village of Saint Denis."⁵⁴ Besides, we do not find such a description of Kiev in the first redaction manuscript copies of Carpini's work.⁵⁵ In the following passage, the italicized part is an insertion of the second-redaction copies of his "History":

> Subduing this country, they attacked Rus', where they made great havoc, destroying cities and fortresses and slaughtering men; and they laid siege to Kiev, the capital of Rus'; after they had besieged the city for a long time, they took it and put the inhabitants to death. *When we were journeying through that land we came across countless skulls and bones of dead men lying about on the ground. Kiev had been a very large and thickly populated town, but now it has been reduced almost to nothing, for there are at the present time scarce two hundred houses there and the inhabitants are kept in complete servitude.* Going on from there, fighting as they went, the Tatars destroyed the whole of Rus'.

As one can see, without the italicized words, the text continues smoothly from "and put the inhabitants to death." to "Going on from there . . ." The passage that begins with "When we were journeying . . ." and ends with "in complete servitude" is a later insertion into Carpini's text and creates a break in the narrative. One also notes the contradiction between the first-redaction wording that the Mongols "put the inhabitants to death" and the second-redaction statement that "the inhabitants are kept in complete servitude." One would have to conjecture that only some or even most of the inhabitants were put to death, and the rest kept in complete servitude; however, that changes the implication of the first-redaction narrative that all the inhabitants were put to death.

Let us allow for the sake of further argument that Carpini wrote this passage and that he was accurately describing Kiev in 1246. If he did see a devastated Kiev, then that would create a situation where the Tatars were raiding a town "reduced almost to nothing." To be sure, this implied situation would reinforce the image the chroniclers tried to create of the Tatars being destructive and irrational. However, given the evidence we have about the Mongol Empire and its concern for international trade,[56] it would be a highly unlikely circumstance that they would continue to raid a town that had already been destroyed.

On the one hand, it might be possible to postulate an economically revived Kiev. That is, Kiev of the 1240s and 1250s may have been devastated, as reported in Carpini's text, and unfit for diocesan administration, as Vernadsky suggests. In this scenario, Metropolitan Kirill would have moved to Vladimir, remaining there until the 1260s or 1270s when he would have returned to a revived Kiev. Metropolitan Maksim then moved back to Vladimir because of renewed Tatar attacks on this revived Kiev. Such a hypothesis could be supported by the point that from 1238 to 1274, no new bishop of Vladimir was appointed. That the metropolitan acted as the bishop of Vladimir during that period is evident from the chronicle entry for

1299 where it states that Maksim took over the eparchy of Vladimir and sent Semen who was then bishop of Vladimir to become bishop of Rostov.[57] This hypothesis would also obviate Fuhrmann's objections against the argument that the metropolitan resided in the north, because the two chronicle entries he cites to show that the metropolitan traveled from Kiev are from the years 1274 and 1280, and the others I cited are from after 1274, that is, after this postulated return to Kiev.

On the other hand, it could be argued that the move from Kiev in 1299 may have resulted from a decline in the commercial power of Kiev. For, when the Mongols established their administration over Rus', they seem also to have re-established the dominance of the Volga trade route over that of the Dnepr.[58] Given the shift of trade to the Volga route, a revival of Kiev as a commercial center toward the end of the thirteenth century remains to be demonstrated. Again, if we accept second-redaction additions as the work of Carpini himself, then we have testimony that Kiev remained, at least until 1246, a stopping-off place for merchants who traveled to Rus':

> In addition, there are as witnesses the merchants from Vratislavia, who accompanied us as far as Kiev . . . and also many other merchants, both from Poland and from Austria, who arrived at Kiev after we had gone to the Tatars. Further witnesses are the merchants from Constantinople who came to Rus' via the Tatars and were in Kiev when we returned from the land of the Tatars. The names of these merchants are as follows: Michael the Genoese and Bartholomew, Manuel the Venetian, James Reverius of Acre, Nicolas Pisani, are the chief; the less important are: Mark, Henry, John, Vasius, another Henry Bonadies, Peter Paschami. There were many others . . .[59]

This passage would seem to indicate that Kiev must have retained some importance as a trading center and that it must not have been all that dangerous to live in immediately after the sack of 1240 if merchants from Constantinople, Genoa, Venice, Poland, and Austria were traveling there.[60] And it would seem to contradict the previously mentioned second-redaction addition that "Kiev . . . has been reduced almost to nothing." As a result of their dissonant nature in relation to the text of the first redaction, and as a result of my study of the other changes in the second redaction, I have come to the conclusion that neither passage is the work of Carpini, but of a subsequent editor who was trying to enhance Carpini's testimony.[61] In the first case, this editor probably wanted to emphasize the destructiveness of the Mongols; thus, he inserted descriptions of human bones by the roadside as well as the sorry plight of Kiev itself. In the second case, the editor tried to support the authenticity of the description by providing names of merchants who had seen Carpini in Kiev. Thus, we have no direct evidence that indicates how extensively Kiev was affected by the sack of 1240 or that it was unsuitable for habitation. Indeed, if we eliminate the second-redaction additions, Carpini nowhere states that he visited Kiev at all.[62]

The three-move hypothesis, which Soloviev and Golubinsky suggest, would seem to be a complicated one. In particular, if the metropolitan moved to Vladimir in the 1250s, there seems to be no clear motivation for him to move back to Kiev in the 1260s or 1270s. Besides, the metropolitans do not seem to have abandoned Kiev all that easily. If it was clear already by the 1250s that the grand prince, as the appointee of the Kipchak Khan, was residing in the north and that Kirill and Maksim spent a large amount of time there, then it is also clear that the metropolitans were maintaining Kiev as their official residence, that is, as the religious capital, perhaps in hope that the political capital could be returned to Kiev (tradition played an important role in Rus').

To be sure, the only evidence we have of the metropolitan's activities between 1250 and 1274 concerns his activities in the north. The chronicles report that Kirill was in Vladimir in 1250, 1252, 1255, and 1263, and in Novgorod in 1256, but they do not mention his being in Kiev at all. However, to conclude then that Kirill resided continuously in Vladimir and not in Kiev is a specious use of the argument from silence. There is very little mention of Kiev in the chronicles in the decades immediately following the sack of 1240.[63] Nor do we have chronicles of this time from Kiev, which could mean either that no chronicle writing was being done in Kiev— evidence of the bad situation there—or that whatever chronicles were written there did not survive. We really cannot say which is the case.

* * *

It seems to me that the metropolitans would not leave Kiev unless they had to. Whatever destruction Kiev underwent in 1240, it was not enough to chase the metropolitan, let alone the merchants or people of Kiev, away permanently. Given that the Mongol khans protected the Rus' Church,[64] it would take a breakdown in that protection to force the metropolitan to leave Kiev. This hypothesis is speculative to be sure, but there may be some evidence to support it.

We have the testimony of Nikephoros Gregoras to the effect that southern Rus' at the end of the thirteenth century was being devastated by the Mongols.[65] What might be meant here, as well as the testimony of the chronicles concerning Tatar "violence," may be the so-called second war waged in the steppe south of Kiev between Nogai and Tokhta from 1299 to 1300.[66] This war ended in a victory for Tokhta at Kukanlyk (Kaganlyk), which Vernadsky identifies as the Kagamlyk River, a tributary of the Dnepr, in Poltava Province.[67] Vernadsky's view about the location of the battle is not an uncontested one.[68] Yet, if Nogai's and Tokhta's armies were fighting each other in the area, then we would expect devastation and generally unsafe conditions to be the result. This conflict would seem a better interpretation of "Tatar violence" than punitive raids on Kiev or Mongol hostility to the Rus' Church, which it had been protecting for almost fifty years.[69] In a civil war, however, that protection could no longer be guaranteed. At least two other possibilities must be considered. First, Tokhta, the winner of the steppe war, may have wanted the head of the Rus' Church located in the area he more clearly controlled, that is, northeastern Rus', rather than an area, Kiev, associated with his recently defeated foe, Nogai. However, if Maksim moved at the behest of Tokhta, then that would leave the chronicler's explanation, that it was because of violence, unaccounted for. One might also consider the impact of Lithuanian advances in the Kievan area as a component of the metropolitan's decision. Kiev, during this period (at least until 1320), was in the "no man's land" between the Duchy of Lithuania and the Kipchak Khanate. Yet, such an explanation would not account for the apparent precipitousness of the move in 1299.

There seems to be evidence that the metropolitan's move was a precipitous and sudden one. In 1295, he appointed Semen as the new bishop of Vladimir.[70] If the metropolitan were planning a move to Vladimir, then it would not seem likely that he would appoint a new bishop there, only to oust him five years later and take over his diocese.[71] He could have more easily moved immediately to Vladimir in 1295 while the see was vacant. In addition, the chronicle entry provides at least two indications that the move was not well thought out in advance. First, the entry states that "the metropolitan went from Kiev to Briansk, and from Briansk he went to the Suzdalian land."[72] The mention of Briansk seems unnecessary unless the chronicler wanted to indicate that the metropolitan spent some time there, perhaps deciding where to go or whether to return to Kiev. The second indication of indecision is the statement in the entry for 1299. The people of Novgorod with their prince had nominated a new archbishop, Feoktist. They wanted the metropolitan's blessing, so "they petitioned him [Maksim] and seated him [Feoktist] at the bishop's court until they found out where Maksim, Metropolitan of Kiev and all Rus', was."[73] The residence of the metropolitan would not seem to have been a question if the metropolitan were at that time located in Vladimir and had been so since the 1250s. Nor would it seem to have been a problem if the metropolitan had been spending most of his time in the north in Vladimir.

The most likely explanation is that the metropolitan resided both officially and unofficially in Kiev until the year 1299. At that time, the metropolitan made a sudden decision to leave Kiev, apparently without a clear notion of his destination. He headed north because the main area of conflict of the steppe war between Nogai and Tokhta was in the south. He could have headed west to Galicia, but then the Lithuanians, who were still pagans, might not have allowed him and his entourage through. Besides, even if he had reached Galicia, he would have been cut off from the larger part of Rus' and its grand prince by the Lithuanians. It may be of some significance, however, that when it came time to make the decision to leave Kiev, the metropolitan, Maksim, was someone who did not owe his nomination to the Galician prince. Such a lack of connection with Galicia may have made his decision to move north easier and established a precedent for his successor, Peter, who although nominated by the Galician prince, continued the metropolitan's residence in the north.

Also, considerations of Byzantine Church policy may have entered into the metropolitan's decision. After the determination was made in Nicaea in the late 1240s to cooperate with the Kipchak Khanate, a policy that remained generally in effect throughout the late thirteenth and fourteenth centuries,[74] it was incumbent on the metropolitan to work with the khan's appointee as ruler in Rus' (the grand prince), and *not* to foment opposition from Galicia. The head of the Rus' Church was obliged to obey the policies of the Byzantine Church. The north, which was safe not so much from Mongol punitive expeditions, but from the devastations of all-out steppe warfare, whether between Mongol armies or between the Mongols and Lithuanians, was a logical choice for the metropolitan to choose.

Then the decision had to be made exactly where in the north to set up the new official residence of the metropolitan. As far as the Byzantine Church was concerned, it did not much matter in which town the metropolitan of Rus' resided;[75] his duties covered the entire Rus' land. If the political capital was no longer in Kiev, but in Vladimir, then the most likely place for the metropolitan would be where the political ruler resided, at least ostensibly.[76] The move also had a symbolic meaning. Although the metropolitan maintained the title "of Kiev and all Rus'" until the middle of the fifteenth century,[77] the move effectively meant the end of the hope, if any remained, that

Kiev would once again be both the political *and* the religious capital of Rus'. We continue to see the effects of that decision "to this day," as the chroniclers would have put it.

Notes

1. Most of the chronicles agree that the move occurred in 6807, that is, sometime between 1 March 1299 and 28 February 1300. The Laurentian and the Simeonov Chronicles, which place it under the year 6808, and the Kholmogory Chronicle, which has it under 6805, disagree. See *PSRL*, vol. 1 (2d ed.), col. 485, vol. 18, p. 84, and vol. 33, p. 77. But these differences can be attributed, in the case of 6808, to an ultra-March dating and, in the case of 6805, to scribal error. Through the fourteenth century, Rus' chroniclers used either the ultra-March or March year, with the latter predominating. See N. G. Berezhkov, *Khronologiia russkogo letopisaniia* (Moscow, 1963), pp. 122, 322–323, n. 168. In addition, two sixteenth-century chronicles, the Voskresensk and the Typography, mention 18 April as the date Maksim arrived in Vladimir. See *PSRL*, vol. 7, p. 182 and *PSRL*, vol. 24, p. 106. However, the absence of such a date in other and earlier chronicles makes that date suspect. The Mazurin Chronicle records the move under the year 6791 (1282/83) and changes Maksim's destination to Moscow (*PSRL*, vol. 31, p. 77). See also M. N. Tikhomirov, *Kratkie zametki o letopisnykh proizvedeniiakh v rukopisnykh sobraniiakh Moskvy* (Moscow, 1962), pp. 51–52. We can dismiss both the assertions of this chronicle as faulty interpolations.
2. N. M. Karamzin, *Istoriia gosudarstva rossiiskogo* (St. Petersburg, 1892), vol. 4, p. 106.
3. S. M. Solov'ev, *Istoriia Rossii s drevneishikh vremen* (Moscow, 1960), vol. 3, p. 562.
4. Ibid., p. 563.
5. Ibid.
6. Ibid.
7. Ibid., p. 564.
8. V. O. Kliuchevskii, *Sochineniia* (Moscow, 1956–1959), vol. 2: *Kurs russkoi istorii*, pt. 2, p. 23.
9. Ibid., p. 24.
10. *PSRL*, vol. 1 (2d ed.), col. 485; *PSRL*, vol. 7, p. 182; *PSRL*, vol. 18, p. 84; *PSRL*, vol. 24, p. 106. See also *PSRL*, vol. 10, p. 172 (where *razbiezhesia* has been changed to *razydesia*). Cf. *PSRL*, vol. 3, p. 130; *PSRL*, vol. 4, p. 46; and *PSRL*, vol. 5, p. 203. Kliuchevskii discusses what he believes is evidence for the migration earlier in this work (*Sochineniia*, vol. 1, pp. 282–291). The view that some kind of mass migration of people from Kiev fleeing to the northeast, where they became the basis of the Great Russian nationality, had been given fuller exposition in the works of Soloviev and M. P. Pogodin. See especially the latter's "Zapiska o drevnem iazyke russkom (pis'mo k I. I. Sreznevskomu)," *Izvestiia Akademii nauk po Otdeleniiu russkogo iazyka i slovesnosti*, vol. 5, pt. 2 (1856): 70–92. For a discussion of the development of this schema, see Natalia Polońska-Vasylenko, *Two Conceptions of the History of Ukraine and Russia* (London, 1968), pp. 30–37. Also see Mykhailo S.

Hrushevsky, "Zvychaina skhema 'russkoï istoriï' i sprava ratsional'noho ukladu istoriï Skhidn'oho Slovianstva," *Stat'i po slavianovedeniiu*, ed. V. I. Lamanskii, vol. 1 (St. Petersburg, 1904), pp. 298–304; reprinted as "The Traditional System of 'Russian' History and the Problem of a Rational Organization of the History of Eastern Slavs," in *Annals of the Ukrainian Academy of Arts and Sciences in the U.S.*, vol. 2 (1952), pp. 355–364. Besides the lack of direct evidence for such a large transfer of population, it would seem unlikely the people of Kiev, if they were fleeing the Mongols, would flee to an area the Mongols already controlled. Furthermore, as the archaeologist A. A. Spitsyn has argued: "the possibility of the migration of the population along the Dnepr to the far north is completely inadmissible" since it would involve their abandonment "of abundant black soil for clay and sand, the comfortable for the demanding, the steppe for the forest, the warm for the cold, bountiful harvests for sparse ones, the ox for the horse, the cottage for the hut, large villages for isolated settlements, easy work for hard labor" ("Istoriko-arkheologicheskie razyskaniia," *Zhurnal Ministerstva narodnogo prosveshcheniia* [1909], no. 1, p. 95).

11. E. E. Golubinskii, *Istoriia russkoi tserkvi* (Moscow, 1900–1911), vol. 2, pp. 55, 56.

12. Ibid., p. 57.

13. Ibid., pp. 57–58.

14. Ibid., p. 95.

15. M. D. Priselkov, *Istoriia russkogo letopisaniia XI–XV vv.* (Leningrad, 1940), pp. 104–105.

16. D. S. Likhachev, "Galitskaia literaturnaia traditsiia v zhitii Aleksandra Nevskogo," *TODRL* 5 (1947): 51. Fennell seems to be in agreement with Likhachev's interpretation. See John Fennell, *The Crisis of Medieval Russia 1200–1304* (London, 1983), pp. 103, 112.

17. George Vernadsky, *A History of Russia* (New Haven, 1943–1969), vol. 3, *The Mongols and Russia*, p. 147.

18. Steven Runciman, "Byzantium, Russia and Caesaropapism," *Canadian Slavonic Papers* 2 (1957): 6.

19. Iu. A. Limonov, *Letopisanie Vladimiro-Suzdal'skoi Rusi* (Leningrad, 1967), p. 169.

20. Ibid., p. 170.

21. Ivan Vlasovs'kyi [Wlasowsky], *Narys istoriï Ukraïns'koï pravoslavnoï tserkvy*, vol. 1 *(IX–XVII)* (New York, 1955), p. 102.

22. Ibid. For Ukrainian influence on Muscovy in the seventeenth century, see K. V. Kharlampovich, *Malorossiiskoe vliianie na velikorusskuiu tserkovnuiu zhizn'* (Kazan', 1914). See also Frank B. Kortschmaryk, *The Kievan Academy and Its Role in the Organization of Education in Russia at the Turn of the Seventeenth Century* (New York, 1976).

23. Vlasovs'kyi, *Narys istoriï*, p. 102.

24. Ibid., pp. 101–102.

25. Ibid., p. 102.

26. Ibid., p. 104.

27. Ibid., p. 102.

28. Joseph T. Fuhrmann, "Metropolitan Cyril II (1242–1281) and the Politics of Accommodation," *Jahrbücher für Geschichte Osteuropas* 24 (1976): 166–167, n. 29. More exactly, the chronicles do not mention Kirill's coming to Vladimir for the Council of 1274, although that is a likely reason. They mention only his coming with Serapion and appointing him bishop of Vladimir, Suzdal', and Nizhnii Novgorod. For the entry of 1280 cited by Fuhrmann, see *PSRL*, vol. 10, p. 157. But compare *PSRL*, vol. 7, p. 174; *PSRL*, vol. 18, p. 77; *PSRL*, vol. 20, p. 168; *PSRL*, vol. 24, p. 102; *PSRL*, vol. 25, p. 152; *PSRL*, vol. 30, p. 96, where the entry merely states: "Metropolitan Kirill came from Kiev to the Suzdal' land." For the entry of 1274, see *PSRL*, vol. 7, p. 172; *PSRL*, vol. 10, p. 152; *PSRL*, vol. 15 (2d ed.), pt. 2, col. 404; *PSRL*, vol. 18, p. 74; *PSRL*, vol. 20, p. 168; *PSRL*, vol. 23, p. 89; *PSRL*, vol. 25, p. 151; *PSRL*, vol. 28, pt. 1, p. 61; *PSRL*, vol. 28, pt. 2, p. 220; *PSRL*, vol. 30, p. 95; and *Troitskaia letopis'. Rekonstruktsiia teksta* (hereafter *TL*), ed. M. D. Priselkov (Moscow and Leningrad, 1950), p. 332. Fuhrmann, in what must be a typographical error, refers the reader to *PSRL*, vol. 2, col. 476; but there is no such information in that (the Hypatian) chronicle.

29. *NPL*, p. 323. Cf. *PSRL*, vol. 10, p. 152, which provides a more elaborate rendition.

30. *PSRL*, vol. 5, pt. 2, p. 199; *PSRL*, vol. 10, p. 153; *PSRL*, vol. 20, p. 168; *PSRL*, vol. 25, p. 151; *PSRL*, vol. 28, pt. 1, p. 61; *PSRL*, vol. 28, pt. 2, p. 220; and *NPL*, p. 323. No reason is provided why it would take two years from the time Kliment was sent to Kiev to the time when he was consecrated and returned to Novgorod.

31. *PSRL*, vol. 7, p. 175; *PSRL*, vol. 10, p. 157; *PSRL*, vol. 18, p. 77; *PSRL*, vol. 20, p. 169; *PSRL*, vol. 23, p. 91; *PSRL*, vol. 24, p. 102; *PSRL*, vol. 25, p. 153; *PSRL*, vol. 28, pt. 1, p. 61; *PSRL*, vol. 28, pt. 2, p. 221; *PSRL*, vol. 30, p. 96; and *TL*, p. 338.

32. *PSRL*, vol. 10, p. 162.

33. *PSRL*, vol. 23, p. 93; *PSRL*, vol. 28, pt. 1, p. 63; *PSRL*, vol. 28, pt. 2, p. 222. The Nikon Chronicle reports that in 1285 Maksim "according to his custom traveled throughout the Rus' land" (*PSRL*, vol. 10, p. 166). Other chronicles also report that Maksim came to Novgorod but do not say from whence he came. See *PSRL*, vol. 5, pt. 2, p. 201; *PSRL*, vol. 7, p. 178; *PSRL*, vol. 25, p. 156.

34. For the consecration of Iakov in Kiev in 1288, see *PSRL*, vol. 10, p. 167. For the consecration of Taras in Kiev in 1289, see *PSRL*, vol. 10, p. 167. For the consecration of Andrei in Kiev in 1289, see *PSRL*, vol. 7, p. 179; *PSRL*, vol. 10, p. 167; *PSRL*, vol. 18, p. 82; *PSRL*, vol. 20, p. 171; *PSRL*, vol. 24, p. 105; *PSRL*, vol. 25, p. 157; *PSRL*, vol. 30, p. 98; and *TL*, p. 344.

35. John Meyendorff, *Byzantium and the Rise of Russia: A Study of Byzantino-Russian Relations in the Fourteenth Century* (Cambridge, 1981), p. 43.

36. Ibid., pp. 78–79.

37. Ibid., p. 42. Meyendorff mentions some of these activities in the north: traveling to Vladimir in 1250; celebrating the marriage of the grand prince Andrew with Danylo's daughter in 1251; "close ties" with Aleksandr Nevsky; presiding over Nevsky's funeral in Vladimir in 1263; and dying in Pereiaslavl'-Zalesskii in 1281.

38. Ibid.

39. Ibid., p. 43.
40. Ibid., p. 44.
41. Ibid.
42. Ibid., p. 46.
43. Ibid., p. 46, n. 33.
44. From the Mongol invasion until 1326, the grand prince's ostensible residence was Vladimir. And the grand prince maintained "of Vladimir" as part of his title well into the fifteenth century.
45. *PSRL*, vol. 1 (2d ed.), col. 485. Compare *PSRL*, vol. 7, p. 182; *PSRL*, vol. 10, p. 172; *PSRL*, vol. 15 (2d ed.), pt. 1, col. 35; *PSRL*, vol. 15 (2d ed.), pt. 2, col. 407; *PSRL*, vol. 18, p. 84; *PSRL*, vol. 20, pt. 1, p. 172; *PSRL*, vol. 23, p. 95; *PSRL*, vol. 24, p. 106; *PSRL*, vol. 28, pp. 64, 223; *PSRL*, vol. 30, p. 99; *PSRL*, vol. 33, p. 77; *PSRL*, vol. 34, p. 104.
46. Golubinskii, *Istoriia russkoi tserkvi*, vol. 2, p. 95. The term *nasilie* can also mean oppression and coercion. See I. I. Sreznevskii, comp., *Materialy dlia slovaria drevne-russkogo iazyka po pis'mennym pamiatnikam* (St. Petersburg, 1893–1912), vol. 2, col. 230. Since the Church was neither oppressed nor coerced, it seems "violence" is the more likely meaning here. Such an understanding of *nasilie* in this context is supported by the evidence of a gloss on *nasilie tatarskoe* at this point in the text of the Mazurin Chronicle (see n. 1 above): *radi tatarskiia obidy i nepokoia* (because of Tatar enmities and disruptions).
47. Filaret [Dmitrii G. Gumilevskii], *Istoriia russkoi tserkvi*, 2d ed. (Moscow, 1849–1853), vol. 2, p. 126.
48. Lawrence N. Langer, "The Medieval Russian Town," in *The City in Russian History*, ed. Michael F. Hamm (Lexington, Ky., 1976), p. 15; V. V. Kargalov, *Vneshnepoliticheskie faktory razvitiia feodal'noi Rusi* (Moscow, 1967), p. 193.
49. See A. N. Nasonov, *Mongoly i Rus' (Istoriia tatarskoi politiki na Rusi)* (Moscow and Leningrad, 1940), p. 39.
50. Fr. Iohannes de Plano Carpini, "Ystoria Mongalorum," in *Sinica Franciscana*, vol. 1: *Itinera et relationes fratrum minorum saeculi XIII et XIV*, ed. P. Anastasius van den Wyngaert (Firenze, 1929), p. 72; and John of Plano Carpini, "History of the Mongols," in *The Mongol Mission: Narratives and Letters of the Franciscan Missionaries in Mongolia and China in the Thirteenth and Fourteenth Centuries*, ed. by Christopher Dawson (London, 1955), pp. 29–30. My translation of passages from Carpini's text follows but does not completely coincide with the translation found in *The Mongol Mission*. Cf. "Libellus historicus Joannis de Plano Carpini," in *The Principal Navigations Voyages Traffiques and Discoveries of the English Nation*, ed. Richard Hakluyt (Glasgow, 1903–1905), vol. 1, pp. 110–111, 152–153. On the basis of Carpini's description, Cahun proposes that the Venetians prevailed upon the Mongols to destroy Kiev in order to eliminate a rival for trade in the Crimea. Léon Cahun, *Introduction a l'histoire de l'Asie: Turcs et Mongols des Origines à 1405* (Paris, 1896), pp. 349–350. For a survey of the arguments and rather inconclusive archaeological evidence concerning the impact of the Mongol sack of Kiev in 1240, see M. K. Karger, "Kiev i mongol'skoe zavoevanie," *Sovetskaia arkheologiia* 11 (1949): 55–102.
51. On the gathering of military information by Carpini to help an anti-Mongol

alliance, see James J. Zlatko, "The Union of Suzdal, 1222–1252," *Journal of Ecclesiastical History* 8 (1957): 45–47.

52. Compare, e.g., Lassota's extensive description of Kiev, which he passed through in 1594. *Habsburgs and Zaporozhian Cossacks: The Diary of Erich Lassota von Steblau*, trans. Orest Subtelny, ed. Lubomyr R. Wynar (Littleton, Colo., 1975), pp. 74–78.

53. The conclusion that Kiev was less densely populated than western European towns and cities can be drawn from recent archaeological research. See P. P. Tolochko, *Kiev i kievskaia zemlia v epokhu feodal'noi razdroblennosti XII–XIII vekov* (Kiev, 1980), pp. 76–89. Tolochko, nonetheless, estimates Kiev's population at close to 50,000 by the year 1200.

54. "Itinerarium Willelmi de Rubruc," in *Sinica Franciscana*, vol. 1, p. 285; and "The Journey of William of Rubruck," in *The Mongol Mission*, p. 183.

55. "Ystoria Mongalorum," p. 72 (n. a). See also Denis Sinor, "John of Plano Carpin's Return from the Mongols: New Light from a Luxemburg Manuscript," *Journal of Royal Asiatic Society* (1957):199.

56. See, inter alia, Wilhelm Heyd, *Geschichte des Levantehandels im Mittelalter* (Stuttgart, 1879), vol. 2, pp. 77–78.

57. When the metropolitan began to reside in Moscow, he again appointed a bishop in the Vladimir eparchy. Pavel Stroev, *Spiski ierarkhov i nastoiatelei rossiiskie tserkvi* (St. Petersburg, 1877), col. 653. Later, in 1352, Metropolitan Feognost appointed Aleksei bishop in Vladimir as successor designate. Stroev, *Spiski ierarkhov*, cols. 653–654. See also *PSRL*, vol. 7, p. 217; *PSRL*, vol. 10, p. 225; *PSRL*, vol. 20, p. 187; *PSRL*, vol. 23, p. 111; *PSRL*, vol. 24, p. 121; *PSRL*, vol. 25, p. 179; *PSRL*, vol. 28, pp. 73, 234; *PSRL*, vol. 33, p. 78.

58. Thomas S. Noonan, "Russia's Eastern Trade, 1150–1350: The Archeological Evidence," *Archivum Eurasiae Medii Aevi* 3 (1983): 201–264; Janet Martin, "The Land of Darkness and the Golden Horde: The Fur Trade under the Mongols, XIII–XIV Centuries," *Cahiers du monde russe et soviétique* 19 (1978): 401–422.

59. Carpini, "History of the Mongols," p. 71; "Ystoria mongalorum," p. 129.

60. According to van den Wyngaert, Manuel the Venetian, James Reverius of Acre, and Nicolas Pisani were all from Venice. "Ystoria mongalorum," p. 129, n. 2.

61. For further discussion of this problem, see my "Second-Redaction Additions in Carpini's *Ystoria Mongalorum*," *HUS* 14 (1990): 522–550.

62. We would, however, be able to conclude that he did pass through Kiev from the testimony of Benedict the Pole. See *Sinica Franciscana*, vol. 1, p. 135; and *The Mongol Mission*, p. 79. But, then, a second-redaction editor would have been able to conclude likewise.

63. The Galician-Volhynian Chronicle makes only incidental mention of Kiev until 1259, then no mention at all through 1292. The Novgorod I Chronicle makes no mention of Kiev from 1246 through 1273. In the Laurentian Chronicle, there is only one incidental mention of Kiev from 1241 through 1298. The northeastern chronicles (Simeonov, Voskresensk, Vladimir, Moscow compilation of the end of the fifteenth century, Nikon, and so forth) make no mention of Kiev from 1250 through 1273.

64. On this protection, see the recent article by Sergei Hackal, "Under Pressure from the Pagans?—The Mongols and the Russian Church," in *The Legacy of St.*

Vladimir: Byzantium, Russia, America, ed. J. Breck, J. Meyendorff, and E. Silk (Crestwood, N.Y., 1990), pp. 47–56.

65. Nikephorŏs Gregoras, *Historiae Byzantinae,* 3 vols., ed. Ludwig Schopen and Immanuel Bekker (*CSHB,* vols. 6–7, 48) (Bonn, 1829–1855), vol. 3, pp. 513–516.

66. Rashid al-din reported that in 698 A.H. (1298–1299), Tokhta gathered "nearly 30 *tumĕns* [or 300,000 troops at full complement] on the [left] bank of the River Uzï" [Dnepr]. The following year, again according to Rashid al-din, Tokhta "crossed the Uzï with an army of 60 *tumĕns*" (or 600,000 troops at full complement). Rashid al-din, *The Successors of Genghis Khan,* trans. John Andrew Boyle (New York, 1971), pp. 127–128. For a discussion of this steppe war, see C. d'Ohsson, *Histoire des Mongols. Depuis Tchinguiz-Khan jusqu'à Timour bey ou Tamerlane,* 4 vols. (Amsterdam, 1834–1835), vol. 4, pp. 755–758; and N. I. Veselovskii, "Khan iz temnikov Zolotoi Ordy Nogai i ego vremia," *Zapiski Rossiiskoi Akademii nauk,* 8th ser., vol. 13 (1922) pp. 48–49. See also V. G. Tizengauzen [Tiesenhausen], *Sbornik materialov, otnosiashchikhsia k istorii Zolotoi Ordy,* vol. 1 (St. Petersburg, 1884), pp. 112–114, 122–123, 159. The date for the campaign of Tokhta supplied by Tiesenhausen, according to the Chronicle of Beybars by Rukn al-Din, is 699 A.H., that is, 28 September 1299 to 16 September 1300. On the conversion of Islamic years to Christian years, see E. I. Kamentseva, *Khronologiia* (Moscow, 1967), pp. 110–113 and table 2. On the one hand, this year for the final events of the war leads me further to discount 18 April as the date when the move of the metropolitan was completed, unless 18 April 1300 was meant (see above n. 1). On the other hand, the "second" steppe war may have been only a continuation of the "first" steppe war. That is, more or less continuous fighting may have been going on between Nogai and Tokhta from 1297 to 1300, where the reference to "699 A.H." may represent only the year in which the decisive battle took place. If the latter is the case, then the date the metropolitan left Kiev represents approximately the time when the venue of the war, which had begun on the Don River, reached the area south of Kiev.

67. Vernadsky, *The Mongols and Russia,* p. 188 and n. 197. On the location of the Kagamlyk River, see P. P. Semenov, *Geograficheskо-statisticheskii slovar' Rossiiskoi imperii* (St. Petersburg, 1863–1865), vol. 2, p. 409; and V. P. Semenov, *Rossiia. Polnoe geograficheskoe opisanie nashego otechestva* (St. Petersburg, 1899–1914), vol. 7, pp. 311, 415, and 416.

68. Bruun asserts that the battle was near where Odessa is located today. F. K. Brun [P. K. Bruun], "Chernomor'e. Sbornik issledovanii po istoricheskoi geografii Iuzhnoi Rossii," *Zapiski Imperatorskogo Novorossiiskogo universiteta* 30 (Odessa, 1880): 356. Spuler places the battle at the Terek River in the Caucasus. Bertold Spuler, *Die Goldene Horde. Die Mongolen in Rußland* (Leipzig, 1943), p. 76. Groussett, however, agrees with Vernadsky that the battle was near the Dnepr. René Grousset, *The Empire of the Steppes: A History of Central Asia,* trans. Naomi Walford (New Brunswick, 1970), p. 403.

69. For the Mongol promise of protection of the Church, see V. A. Kuchkin, "Skazanie o smerti mitropolita Petra," *TODRL* 18 (1962): 77. The *iarlyki* contained the stipulation to the metropolitans that the clergy should pray for the well-being of the khans and their families. In return, the khans extended their protection to the Rus' Church and exempted it from taxation. Cf. *PSRL,* vol. 1, cols. 474–475, 524.

On the *iarlyki*, see, for example, M. D. Priselkov, *Khanskie iarlyki russkim mitropolitam* (St. Petersburg, 1916), pp. 96–98 for the text of the *iarlyk* from Khan Mengu-Temir to Metropolitan Kirill, and more recently A. I. Pliguzov, "Kratkoe sobranie iarlykov ordynskikh khanov, dannykh russkim mitropolitam i dukhovenstvu," in *Russkii feodal'nyi arkhiv* (Moscow, 1986–1988), vol. 3, pp. 585–594, esp. pp. 588–589, concerning tax exemptions and other economic guarantees. See also Nasonov, *Mongoly i Rus'*, pp. 14–15; G. A. Fedorov-Davydov, *Obshchestvennyi stroi Zolotoi Ordy* (Moscow, 1973), pp. 34–35; and Meyendorff, *Byzantium and the Rise of Russia*, p. 45.

70. Stroev, *Spiski ierarkhov*, col. 653.

71. *PSRL*, vol. 1 (2d ed.), col. 485; *PSRL*, vol. 7, p. 182; *PSRL*, vol. 10, p. 171. Semen was made bishop of Rostov and Iaroslavl', which eparchy had been vacant since 1295. Stroev, *Spiski ierarkhov*, col. 326.

72. *PSRL*, vol. 1 (2d ed.), col. 485; *PSRL*, vol. 10, p. 172; *PSRL*, vol. 18, p. 84.

73. *NPL*, pp. 90, 330. See also *PSRL*, vol. 10, p. 172.

74. Two exceptions to the policy of friendly relations are the alliance of the Mongols and Bulgarians against Byzantium in 1264–1265 and the Venetian-Genoese War of 1348, in which Genoa allied with the Khanate against Byzantium and Venice. On the war of 1264–1265, see George Vernadsky, "Zolotaia orda, Egipet i Vizantiia v ikh vzaimootnosheniiakh v tsarstvovanie Mikhaila Paleologa," *Sbornik statei po arkheologii i vizantinovedeniiu, izdavaemyi Seminariem imeni N. P. Kondakova* (Prague, 1927), p. 79. On the Venetian-Genoese War, see Costas P. Kyrris, "John Cantacuzenus, the Genoese, the Venetians, and the Catalans (1348–1354)," *Byzantina* 4 (1972): 333–336. The shift in Byzantine policy seems to have resulted from the Genoese capture of Chios and several other locations nearby, which gave Genoa control of the Hellespont Straits, and thus of the western outlet of Black Sea trade. Byzantium was not in a position to expel the Genoese from these strongpoints, at least not without Venetian help.

75. One thinks in particular of the decision of the Church Council of 1380, which states that the metropolitan in Moscow must use the designation "of Kiev and Great Rus'." That decision seems to have had nothing to do with where the metropolitan actually resided, but rather with the hope that the two metropolitanates, that of Great Rus', on the one side, and that of Lithuania and Little Rus', on the other, would soon be reunited. See Meyendorff, *Byzantium and the Rise of Russia*, pp. 214–221. The decision of the council can be found in *Acta patriarchatus Constantinopolitani*, ed. Franz Miklosich and I. Müller (Vienna, 1862), vol. 2, pp. 12–18. See also *Russkaia istoricheskaia biblioteka*, vol. 6, supplement, cols. 165–183.

76. Although the Nikon Chronicle reports that Peter, when he was first chosen metropolitan, "resided" (*siade*) briefly in Kiev in 1308 (*PSRL*, vol. 10, p. 176), earlier chronicles report that he merely went there after being consecrated and before continuing on to Vladimir. See *PSRL*, vol. 7, p. 185; *PSRL*, vol. 20, p. 173; *PSRL*, vol. 23, p. 97; *PSRL*, vol. 25, p. 159; *PSRL*, vol. 28, p. 224; *PSRL*, vol. 30, p. 101.

77. Stroev, *Spiski ierarkhov*, col. 3. See also A. I. Pliguzov, "O titule 'Mitropolit Kievskii i vseia Rusi,'" *Russkii feodal'nyi arkhiv*, vol. 5 (forthcoming).

The Origins of the Muscovite Ecclesiastical Claims to the Kievan Inheritance

(Early Fourteenth Century to 1458/1461)

JAROSLAW PELENSKI

One of the principal concerns of Muscovite Russia's national and imperial ideology was her preoccupation with the Kievan heritage and the resulting formulation of official claims to Kievan Rus', at first ecclesiastical but later secular. This concern was subsequently transmitted to modern Russian national consciousness and historical thought. Although the ideological and historiographic controversies over the Kievan inheritance date back to the nineteenth century, concrete antiquarian and conceptual inquires into the origins of Muscovy's preoccupation with the Kievan inheritance did not begin until the post-World War II period. At that time D. S. Likhachev attempted to show that Muscovite chronicle-writing and culture were permeated by a new historicism that served as evidence for his hypothesis about the existence of the early Renaissance in Muscovite Russia in the late fourteenth and fifteenth centuries.[1] (As a matter of fact, Likhachev's hypothesis has been questioned in scholarship,[2] and the topic has been apparently abandoned by the author). Aside from the conceptual differences of opinion, the new literature on the origins of Muscovy's claims to the Kievan inheritance has tended to concentrate on the official secular claims to Kievan Rus'. Likhachev dates these claims to the late fourteenth or early fifteenth century,[3] whereas I suggest the second half of the fifteenth.[4] Still, for a better understanding of the problem, it is necessary to consider the official ecclesiastical claims as well. Therefore, in this article I shall discuss Muscovy's ecclesiastical claims to the Kievan inheritance, concentrating on four major areas in which they were manifested: 1. the transfer of the Metropolitanate of Kiev and all Rus' to Moscow, and the enhancement of the city of Moscow; 2. the contest for the heritage of the Metropolitanate of Kiev and all Rus'; 3. the canonization of three metropolitans; and 4. the Kiev–Suzdal'–Vladimir–Muscovy continuity theory in early Muscovite chronicle-writing.

The Transfer of the Metropolitanate of Kiev and All Rus'

This transfer from Kiev to Moscow was accomplished in two stages. First, a transition from Kiev to Vladimir took place following the establishment of the Mongol-Tatar supremacy over the states of Rus', an accommodation between the Golden Horde (or the Kipchak Horde), Byzantium, and the Grand Principality of Suzdal'-Vladimir in the realm of ecclesiastical policies, and the implementation of the Western-oriented policies of the Galician-Volhynian rulers like Danylo Romanovych (ruled 1238–1264) and Iurii I (1303–1308), both of whom assumed the title of king after the acceptance by Danylo of a royal crown from Pope Innocent IV (1253). Kirill was the first metropolitan of Kiev and all Rus' (1242–1281) to move from the coreland of Kievan Rus' to the northeastern Grand Principality of Vladimir where he performed his duties as the chief ecclesiastical official of Rus' during the greater part of his tenure and until his death in Pereiaslavl'-Zalesskii in 1281. In Vladimir, among other things, he presided over Grand Prince Aleksandr Nevsky's funeral (1263) and held in that city in 1274 an important council of Russian bishops.

The transfer of the Metropolitanate of Kiev to Vladimir was completed by Kirill's successor Metropolitan Maksim (1283–1305), who, according to the Vladimirian Chronicles (while keeping his title Metropolitan of Kiev and all Rus') left the Metropolitan see and escaped from Kiev in 1300, because "he could not endure the Tatar oppression."[5] This explanation of the metropolitan's move by the Vladimirian chroniclers is rather anachronistic and ideologically motivated since the Mongol-Tatars were not oppressing the Church and because Vladimir, to which Maksim moved, was located much more deeply in their sphere of influences than Kiev.

In the second stage of its transition, the Metropolitanate of Kiev and all Rus' was moved from Vladimir to Moscow. This transfer was undertaken under the auspices of Metropolitan Petr (1308–1326) who had opted for the Muscovite side in the struggle between Moscow and Tver' for the Grand Principality of Vladimir.[6]

This move had an extraordinary significance for Moscow's rise, growth, and victory in the struggle for supremacy in northeastern Russia, in particular, and for the lands of all Rus', in general. An institution like the metropolitanate would serve in the long run as an ideological, cultural, and, at times, administrative center of the Muscovite state. Among immediate consequences of this transition, the status of Moscow and the Muscovite Grand Principality was greatly enhanced. This is best attested by the selection of

Moscow by Metropolitan Petr in 1322 to be the permanent residence of the Metropolitanate of Kiev and all Rus', the attention paid by early Muscovite ideologies to Petr's special concern for the city of Moscow as a chosen city at the time when Moscow was still struggling for recognition as one of the principal centers of northeastern Rus', and, finally, by the cult of Petr as hierarch-saint of Moscow and the Suzdal' land.

Petr's role as a hierarch-saint is best attested in the "Praise for Petr," contained in the second recension of the so-called *Pouchenie Petra Mitropolita* (Admonition of Metropolitan Petr). Paraphrasing other admonitions and to some extent the famous "Praise of Volodimer I" by Metropolitan Ilarion, the Muscovite author, writing probably at the end of 1330s, exclaimed:

> O great miracle. Rome prides itself in having the Supreme Apostle Peter, Damascus proudly philosophizes about having the light of the entire universe—Apostle Paul. The city of Thessalonica rejoices in having the Christian martyr Demetrius, Kiev takes pride in having the new Christian martyrs Boris and Gleb, the Rus' Princes—the healers. Rejoice o city of Moscow in having the great hierarch—Petr.[7]

Metropolitan Petr's pivotal role in the enhancement of Moscow was magnified by Kiprian, another metropolitan of Kiev and all Rus', who wrote an expanded *Vita* of Metropolitan Petr in 1381. In it he inserted the famous prophecy about the future greatness of Moscow, allegedly made by Petr in an exchange with Ivan Danilovich Kalita, the ruler of Moscow:[8]

> And so, my son, take my advice, and build a church in your city of Moscow, and you shall be glorified above all other princes, and your sons and grandsons for generations to come. And this city will be glorified in all the cities of Rus', and hierarchs will reside in it, and their arms will be raised above the shoulders of their enemies, and God will be glorified in it, and, finally, my bones will laid to rest in it.[9]

The *Vita* of Metropolitan Petr by Kiprian became one of the most popular biographies in old Russian literature, as attested by its inclusion in both the *Great Menology* (*Velikie minei chetii*) and the *Book of Degrees* (*Kniga stepennaia*). Paradoxically, both Petr, the author of the ideological enhancement of Moscow, and Kiprian, the author of Petr's influential *Vita*, were not even Muscovites by origin. Metropolitan Petr was, in fact, a native of Volhynia or Galicia who originally had made his ecclesiastical career under the auspices of King Iurii of Galicia but subsequently abandoned the King for an even higher office, this time under the sponsorship of the Muscovite ruler. Kiprian, the Bulgarian—who by his own interpretation of Petr's life and deeds, among other things, contributed immensely to the enhancement of Moscow's position and the creation of the myth of Moscow—is perceived in scholarship as a relatively even-handed individual in the execution of his duties vis-à-vis the Orthodox of all Rus'. It deserves mention that the Muscovite tradition, including the writings of Metropolitan Kiprian, attempted to play down Metropolitan Petr's Galician connection by emphasizing his Volhynian origins and by stressing his sponsorship by a Volhynian prince. In reality, it was King Iurii of Galicia who championed Petr's promotion to the position of Metropolitan of Galicia.

The Contest for the Metropolitanate of Kiev and All Rus'

The origins of this contest coincided with the emergence of the Muscovite patrimonial state and the struggle on the part of the Muscovite dynasty for the Vladimir Grand Principality and supremacy over the various lands of Rus'. They also chronologically coincided with the political-ideological revival of the Galician-Volhynian Rus' under the auspices of King Iurii I and with the transformation of the Lithuanian polity into a dual Lithuanian-Ruthenian state. From 1322 to 1458, the Metropolitanate of Kiev and all Rus' was based (with some interruptions) in Moscow and contested by various contenders: Galicia-Volhynia, Poland, the Lithuanian-Ruthenian state, and the Polish-Lithuanian union state. In 1458/1461, the Metropolitanate was finally divided into Metropolitanate of Kiev and all Rus'—under the auspices of Lithuania and later the Polish-Lithuanian Commonwealth—and the Moscow-based Metropolitanate of Kiev and all Rus'. For almost 150 years, the Muscovite court in collaboration with the Metropolitanate of Kiev and all Rus' had conducted a protracted struggle for the Kievan ecclesiastical inheritance, as represented by the unity and indivisibility of that Metropolitanate. They had also made all possible efforts to prevent its division and the creation of other metropolitanates with a claim to the Kievan succession.[10]

One of them was the Metropolitanate of Halych, a separate ecclesiastical entity, independent of the Metropolitanate of Kiev and all Rus' and established in 1303 at the request of King Iurii I with the Byzantine Patriarch's approval. It was suppressed in 1347 by the Byzantine empire in a display of open power politics and revived in 1371 by the Byzantine patriarchate under political pressures of King Kazimierz of Poland. The Metropolitanate of Halych was not a lasting organizational success. Originally, it had been created to remove Galicia and Volhynia from the jurisdiction of the Metropolitanate of Kiev and all Rus', which was under Tatar and Muscovite control, and to provide the Orthodox faithful of Galicia with the necessary organizational framework, headed by an ecclesiastical leader, independent of any secular authority outside of the Galician-Volhynian state and later the Polish Kingdom. Unlike the Muscovite dynasty and the Moscow-based Metropolitanate, which were engaged in the contest for the heritage of the entire Metropolitanate of Kiev and all Rus', the Galician-Volhynian rulers and their Polish successors limited their contest to the land under their control (partial inheritance of Kiev and all Rus').

Another competitor in the contest for the heritage of the Metropolitanate of Kiev and all Rus' was the Grand Principality of Lithuania, eventually the Lithuanian-Ruthenian state. At first, the Lithuanian dynasty was involved, like Galicia-Volhynia, in the contest for a partial inheritance of the Kievan Metropolitanate which resulted in the establishment of the first Metropolitanate "of the Lithuanians" (1300, or rather 1315–1319). However, the continuous expansion of Lithuania into the lands of old Kievan Rus', particularly the attempts by Grand Prince Olgierd (1345–1377) to rule over *omnia Russia*, led to an extension of the Lithuanian aims. Olgierd and his successors, grand princes of Lithuania and joint rulers of the Polish-Lithuanian union state, endeavored and intermittently succeeded in establishing under their own auspices a Metropolitanate of "Kiev and all Rus'," "all Rus'," or "Rus'" (1352?; 1355–1362; 1376–1380s?; 1415–1421; 1432–1435). Their grand design ("Kiev and all Rus'") was in some respects similar to that of the Muscovite dynasty, as they continued to participate in the contest with Muscovy for the lands of Kievan Rus'.[11]

Muscovy's efforts in the contest for the preservation of a unitary status of the Metropolitanate of Kiev and all Rus' under the exclusive control of the Muscovite dynasty and government were greatly facilitated by the policies and ideological approach of the Byzantine Empire and Patriarchate in the framework of which the Metropolitanate of Kiev and all Rus' functioned. From the creation of the Metropolitanate of Kiev and all Rus' throughout the period of the contest for the Kievan ecclesiastical inheritance, both the Empire and the Patriarchate consistently adhered to the doctrine of a unitary status of the Metropolitanate of Kiev and all Rus' (so conveniently explicated by John Meyendorff[12]), which they defended against attempts to create competitive metropolitanates in the realm of old Rus', such as the one by Andrei Bogoliubsky.[13] Only in exceptional circumstances, as in the case of the titular metropolitanates in the eleventh century,[14] or in situations of strong political pressures, did they consent to the formation of competing and independent Ruthenian metropolitanates, not subject to political and ideological control of the Moscow-based Metropolitanate of Kiev and all Rus' and the Muscovite ruler.

Byzantium's insistence on the unitary nature of the Moscow-based Metropolitanate of Kiev and all Rus' reflected primarily her political and ideological interests and not the religious and organizational-ecclesiastical needs of the Orthodox Christians of the various Rus' polities, except for Muscovy proper. From the Byzantine perspective, Moscow potentially had a good chance to be victorious in the contest for the supremacy over the various Rus' polities, and Byzantine emperors and patriarchs acted accordingly. Such an approach seemed to be obvious. Another imperial power, the Golden Horde, had previously drawn exactly the same conclusions from the struggle for hegemony in the Russian realm and after some vacillations had decided to make the Grand Prince of Moscow the Khan's principal native executive vassal in the lands of Rus'.

The Canonization of Three Metropolitans

Muscovy's ecclesiastical claims to the Kievan inheritance were greatly facilitated not only by the institutional *translatio* of the Metropolitanate of Kiev and all Rus', but also by the politics of canonization of saints in the framework of that institution. Significantly, three metropolitans of Kiev and all Rus' of the Muscovite period were canonized as saints of the Russian Church, prior to the establishment of the Patriarchate of Moscow in 1589: Petr (in office, 1308–1326), Aleksei (1354–1378), and Iona (1448–1461).

Immediately following his death, Petr was canonized by the Council of Vladimir in 1327. That his canonization was confirmed in Constantinople already by 1339[15] attests to his exceptionally good reputation at the court of the Byzantine patriarch. His *Vita*, as already mentioned, was authored by Kiprian, another prominent metropolitan of Kiev and all Rus'.

Aleksei, who served in the capacity of Metropolitanate of Kiev and all Rus' for twenty-four years, who during the period when Grand Prince Dmitrii Ivanovich was a minor acted as a regent and *de facto* head of the Muscovite government, and who was one of the leading Muscovite statesmen, was canonized as a saint of the Russian Church by Iona, the last Moscow-based metropolitan of Kiev and all Rus'.[16] Iona arranged for Aleksei's canonization immediately following his own ascension to the Metropolitanate of Kiev and all Rus' in 1448. Like Metropolitan Petr, Aleksei came from the Ukrainian Rus'. He was an offspring of a Chernigovian boyar family that had voluntarily migrated to the north where his father, Fedor Biakont, entered the services of the Muscovite ruler. Metropolitan Aleksei's life and activities became the subject of a series of hagiographic and ideological works: a *Vita* by Pitirim, bishop of Perm, written most probably at the time of his canonization; another *Vita* by Pakhomii the Serbian (Logofet), written at the request of Metropolitan Iona in 1459; an expanded version of the latter, written at the request of Metropolitan Makarii and included in the *Book of Degrees,* the most extensive of all the *Vitae* of metropolitans in that work;[17] and another *Vita,* composed at the end of the seventeenth century by monk Evfimii, a disciple of Epifanii Slavinetsky.

Unlike Petr and Aleksei, Iona was from Riazan'. He was a Great Russian and the first metropolitan of Moscow not confirmed by the Byzantine patriarchate.[18] He was also a prominent Muscovite politician during the age of Vasilii II and a staunch supporter of that Muscovite ruler. During their tenures the division of the Metropolitanate of Kiev and all Rus' was finalized. Metropolitan Iona was canonized in two stages: the first stage took place in the period 1472–1479; the second coincided with the Church Council of 1547, conducted under the auspices of Metropolitan Makarii. Iona's life and accomplishments were also eulogized in various recensions of his *Zhitie.*[19]

These three metropolitans had distinguished themselves by a devotion to the Muscovite cause, service to the Muscovite ruler, and a deep involvement in the struggles for the supremacy of Moscow, in which they unhesitatingly and decisively used the weapon of excommunication against the enemies of the Muscovite rulers. As far as the problem of Kievan ecclesiastical inheritance was concerned, they fought with determination for the preservation of the unitary status of the Moscow-based Metropolitanate of Kiev and all Rus' under sponsorship of the Muscovite dynasty and against all efforts on the part of the Ruthenian, Lithuanian, and Polish rulers to create metropolitanates for Kiev and other Rus' lands, independent from the Muscovite state. In other words, they were the coarchitects of the all-Russian version of Muscovite ideology and politics. Their canonizations were based on their political and ideological achievements, rather than religious contributions. The similarity of their careers and contributions was clearly recognized by Iov, another Muscovite master politician, the first patriarch of Muscovite Russia (1589–1605), at whose request Prince Semen Ivanovich Shakhovskoi composed a joint *Vita* and *Praise* of the three metropolitans.[20] The integration of their *Vitae* into a single work attests to their being regarded as presenting a unity of purpose and achievement.

The Continuity Theory in Early Muscovite Chronicle-Writing

The fourth major factor in facilitating Muscovy's struggle for the Kievan inheritance in the ecclesiastical realm (as well as the secular) was the formulation under the sponsorship of the Metropolitanate of Kiev and all Rus' of the Kiev–Suzdal'–Vladimir–Moscow continuity theory. The theory was first construed in the codex known as the *Troitskaia letopis'* (*TL*), apparently compiled in the metropolitan's chancery mainly under the auspices of Metropolitan Kiprian[21] from the end of the fourteenth to the beginning of the fifteenth century, and concluded in 1406–1408.

The *TL* represented an official or semiofficial codex. Its only existing copy, used by the Russian historian N. M. Karamzin who quoted extensively from it in his *Istoriia gosudarstva rossiiskogo*, was destroyed in the Moscow fire of 1812. However, the discovery of the Simeonov Chronicle by A. A. Shakhmatov greatly facilitated the study of the *TL*, particularly his findings that for the years 1177–1393 the two chronicles were virtually identical. These findings, in turn, immensely helped M. D. Priselkov reconstruct the *TL* text on the basis of Karamzin's quotations, the Simeonov Chronicle, and other materials.[22] The *TL* included as its first component the *Povest' vremennykh let* (*PVL*) (the *Narration of the Bygone Years*), according to the *Lavrent'evskaia letopis'* (the Laurentian Chronicle), or a closely related text, covering the period to the year 1110. From about 1110 to about 1204, it incorporated Suzdalian and Vladimirian chronicle materials, also based on the Laurentian Chronicle or a closely related compilation, like the prototype of the Radziwiłł Chronicle. From 1203 to 1205, it followed the Suzdal'-Vladimir historical material, although in an edited version. From 1206 to 1263, it again very closely followed the Suzdal'-Vladimir chronicle-writing until the death of Aleksandr Nevsky in 1263. For the period 1263–1305, it used materials of the Laurentian Chronicle, as well as materials of other chronicles from northeastern Rus'. Its entries for the years 1305–1408 represent a valuable historical source material: until its destruction in 1812, the *TL* was the only surviving Muscovite chronicle covering that period. The *TL* included information pertaining to the history of Muscovy, the Rus' lands under the sovereignty of the Lithuanian Grand Principality and of other Russian states, like Tver', Riazan', and Novgorod.

What is significant about the *TL* is the approach taken by its authors and compilers, especially by Metropolitan Kiprian, to the post-1110 history of the Kievan Rus'. They, first of all, did not use the *Kievskaia letopis'* (the Kievan Chronicle) (1118–1198 [1200]), or a closely related text for inclusion into the *TL*. On the contrary, they adapted for their purposes the Suzdal'-Vladimirian Chronicle(s), constituting the second major component of the Laurentian Chronicle for the time period 1111–1203/1204 (or parts of the prototype of the Radziwiłł Chronicle), which treat Kiev, the Kievan land, and "Kievan Rus'" from an exclusively Suzdal'-Vladimirian point of view. For example, the *TL* contains accounts (*skazaniia*) of the sacks of Kiev of 1169 and 1203 to be found in the Suzdal'-Vladimirian Chronicle(s).[23] In other words, the *TL* not only verbally accepted the Suzdal'-Vladimirian interpretations of those events, but also treated the entire history of twelfth-century Kievan Rus' from the generally hostile and anti-Kievan point of view of the Suzdal'-Vladimirian Chronicles.[24] The *TL*'s treatment of the time period between 1206 and the mid-1260s, as well as some later periods, with regard to certain lands and polities of Rus', was even more biased. For example, the entire history of the Galician and Volhynian Rus' from 1205 to 1340 was virtually eliminated from the *TL*. Its accounts for the period 1206–1263 deal with the history of the northeastern Rus', viewed primarily from the Suzdal'-Vladimirian perspective and interpret it for the benefit of the Grand Principality of Vladimir. For the period from 1269 to the end of the thirteenth century, the *TL* concentrates on selected developments in northeastern Russia, with emphasis on the Vladimir Grand Principality, however without a particular preferential treatment of princely competitors for the Grand Principality of Vladimir. Scholars have argued that from 1305 to 1408 the *TL* reflected the all-Russian view, however not so much of the Muscovite, as of the Moscow-based Metropolitanate of Kiev and all Rus'. This opinion needs qualification. Whereas the compilers of the *TL* did indeed include in it materials pertaining to other Russian states, such as Tver' and Novgorod, as well as to the Lithuanian-Ruthenian state, the overall orientation of the *TL* was clearly pro-Muscovite.

As far as the interpretation of the ecclesiastical claims to the Metropolitanate of Kiev and all Rus' was concerned, the authors and editors of the *TL*'s component pertaining to the period 1300/1305–1408 emphasized that it had to be based first in Vladimir and then in Moscow, and that it must remain indivisible and by implication, under the auspices of the Muscovite ruler. However, they did not advance any secular dynastic claims for Moscow to the Kievan Rus'. They simply referred to Muscovite rulers as rulers of Moscow and stressed the Vladimirian connection of the Muscovite dynasty, particularly as reflected in the annalistic necrologs for the Muscovite rulers, for example.[25] The direct dynastic link to Kiev and claims concerning unification with Kiev were to be developed in Muscovite chronicle-writing much later,[26] specifically in connection with the takeover and annexation of Novgorod in 1470s.[27]

The principal contribution of the authors and editors of the *TL*, as well as its sponsor, Metropolitan Kiprian, is the advancement of the first known Kiev–Suzdal'–Vladimir–Muscovy continuity theory in Russian history. This can be established on the basis of the analysis of the entry under the year 1392 in the *TL* which includes a reference to a certain *Letopisets' velikii rus'skii* (*LVR*) stating that it covered historical events "from [the time of] Iaroslav the Great to this present prince [Muscovite Grand Prince Vasilii I Dmitrievich, who began to rule in 1389]."[28]

Traditionally, it has been assumed that the reference to "Iaroslav the Great" applied to Iaroslav I Volodimerovich, the Wise (1019–1054). Therefore, D. S. Likhachev has concluded that the lost *LVR* was the first historical work to provide a "full survey of all Russian history" from the Kievan to the Muscovite period.[29] On the basis of this lost work, the *TL* and some other inconclusive evidence have dated the origins of the official secular Muscovite claims to Kievan Rus' into the late fourteenth–early fifteenth century, namely the period of the hypothetical early Renaissance in Muscovite Russia.[30] If one were to accept the traditional interpretation of the reference to "Iaroslav the Great" in the *TL*, then the lost *LVR*, compiled probably in the 1380s, would be the first work to have advanced the Kiev–Suzdal'–Vladimir–Muscovy continuity theory.

However, an analysis of the relevant entry in the *TL* by G. M. Prokhorov, and in particular his identification of "Iaroslav the Great" as Iaroslav II Vsevolodovich of Vladimir (1190–1238/1246),[31] has established that the lost *LVR* had begun with the Vladimirian and not the Kievan period. In fact, the same applies to the annalistic necrologs for the Muscovite rulers, included in the *TL*.[32] Therefore, it can be concluded that the *TL* is the first known work to have advanced the Kiev–Suzdal'–Vladimir–Muscovy continuity theory in Russian history. To be sure, at that initial stage of its development this continuity theory was still rudimentary and unsophisticated. Only later, in the sixteenth century such Muscovite works as the *Voskresenskaia letopis'* (*Voskresensk Chronicle*), *Nikonovskaia letopis'* (the *Nikon Chronicle*), the *Book of Degrees,* and the *Great Menology* provided more accomplished interpretative versions of the continuity theory. Nonetheless, the first continuity theory devised at the end of the fourteenth and the beginning of the fifteenth century proved in the *TL*, regardless of its inconsistencies, crudity, and naive simplicity, was to make an extraordinary career not only in Russian historical and political thought, but also in Western historiography until the present time.

This analysis of the origins of Muscovy's claims to the Kievan inheritance has concentrated on the discussion of the ecclesiastical institution of the Metropolitanate of Kiev and all Rus' and on historical-ideological works composed within its framework and by its members. The development of the secular official claims to the Kievan inheritance, which I have discussed elsewhere, came much later.[33] Its first major phase falls into the period from the mid-fifteenth century to the beginnings of the sixteenth, which means that the beginnings of the formulation of the secular claims to Kiev and all Rus' coincided with the division of the Metropolitanate of Kiev and all Rus' in 1458/1461. Thus, the origins of Muscovy's ecclesiastical claims to the Kievan inheritance preceded the origins of her secular claims to Kievan Rus' by about a century and a half. This, indeed, reflects the status of Russian culture and the level of its development in that period.

Notes

1. D. S. Likhachev: *Natsional'noe samosoznanie drevnei Rusi: ocherki iz oblasti russkoi literatury XI–XVII vv.* (Moscow and Leningrad, 1945), pp. 68–81. *Kul'tura Rusi epokhi obrazovaniia russkogo natsional'nogo gosudarstva: Konets XIV–nachalo XVI v.* (Moscow and Leningrad, 1946), pp. 40–41, 57–97, 103–104; *Russkie letopisi i ikh kul'turno-istoricheskoe znachenie* (Moscow and Leningrad, 1947), pp. 293–305; *Kul'tura vremeni Andreia Rubleva i Epifaniia Premudrogo: Konets XIV–nachalo XV v.* (Moscow and Leningrad, 1945), pp. 4, 6, 11–12, 17, 19–20, 90–115, 142–146, 161–170; *Die Kultur Rußlands während der osteuropäischen Frührenaissance vom 14. bis zum Beginn des 15. Jahrhunderts* (Dresden, 1962), pp. 6, 8, 13–14, 18–19, 20–21, 90–117, 145–152, 167–175; "Predvozrozhdenie na Rusi v kontse XIV–pervoi polovine XV veka," in *Literatura epokhi vozrozhdeniia i problemy vsemirnoi literatury* (Moscow, 1967), pp. 136–182.

2. J. Pelenski, "The Origins of the Official Muscovite Claims to the 'Kievan Inheritance'," *HUS* 1, no. 1 (1977): 29–52; Ch. J. Halperin, "Kiev and Moscow: An Aspect of Early Muscovite Thought," *Russian History*, 7, no. 3 (1980): 312–321, especially p. 313, n. 8; J. Meyendorff, *Byzantium and the Rise of Moscow* (Cambridge, 1981), p. 128.

3. See note 1 above.

4. See J. Pelenski, "The Origins," pp. 29–52; idem, "The Emergence of the Muscovite Claims to the Byzantine-Kievan 'Imperial Inheritance'," *HUS* 7 (1983): 520–531; idem, "The Sack of Kiev of 1482 in Contemporary Muscovite Chronicle Writing," *HUS* 3–4 (1979–1980): 638–649.

5. *PSRL*, vol. 1, pt. 1 (1926/1962), col. 485. For a convenient discussion of the circumstances pertaining to the transfer of the metropolitan, see Meyendorff, *Byzantium and the Rise of Moscow*, pp. 29–72.

6. For Metropolitan Petr's life and career, as well as the literature on the subject, see "Petr," in N. Barsukov, *Istochniki russkoi agiografii* (St. Petersburg, 1882), cols. 431–453; E. Golubinskii, *Istoriia russkoi tserkvi,* vol. 2, pt. 1 (1900), pp. 98–144; V. A. Kuchkin, "Skazanie o smerti mitropolita Petra," *TODRL* 18 (1962): 59–79; Meyendorff, *Byzantium and the Rise of Moscow,* pp. 149–154; G. M. Prokhorov, "Petr," in D. S. Likhachev, ed., *Slovar' knizhnikov i knizhnosti drevnei Rusi,* no. 1 (XI–pervaia polovina XIV v.) (Leningrad, 1987), pp. 325–329.

7. Cited in V. A. Kuchkin, "Skazanie o smerti mitropolita Petra," *TODRL* 18 (1962): 64.

8. L. A. Dmitriev, "Rol' i znachenie mitropolita Kipriana v istorii drevnerusskoi literatury (K russko-bolgarskim literaturnym sviaziam XIV–XV vv.)," *TODRL* 19 (1963): 215–254, especially pp. 236–254. For a recent text edition of Kiprian's *Zhitie mitropolita Petra,* see G. M. Prokhorov, *Povest' o Mitiae* (Leningrad, 1978), pp. 204–215. See also G. M. Prokhorov, "Drevneishaia rukopis' s proizvedeniiami mitropolita Kipriana," in *Pamiatniki kul'tury. Novye otkrytiia. Ezhegodnik za 1978* (Leningrad, 1979), pp. 17–30. For the text in the *Kniga stepennaia,* see *PSRL,* vol. 21, pt. 1 (1908), pp. 321–332. Two recent works related to the themes of this article have erroneously characterized Metropolitan Kiprian's attitudes as unfriendly toward Moscow and have failed to appreciate the significance of the *Vita* in question, as well as the insertion of the prophecy about Moscow in it (N. S. Borisov, *Russkaia tserkov' v politicheskoi bor'be XIV–XV vekov* [Moscow, 1986], pp. 106–111, 113–118, 132–139; A. S. Khoroshev, *Politicheskaia istoriia russkoi kanonizatsii [XI–XVI vv.]* [Moscow, 1986], pp. 101–104).

9. G. M. Prokhorov, *Povest' o Mitiae,* pp. 211–212; *PSRL,* vol. 21, pt. 1 (1908), p. 328.

10. The titles "Metropolitan of all Rus'," or "Metropolitanate of all Rus'," or "Metropolitan of Kiev and all Rus'" were used interchangeably (J. Meyendorff, *Byzantium and the Rise of Moscow,* pp. 73–95). The concept "Metropolitan of Kiev and all Rus'" was applied more consistently since 1347, and especially since the early 1390s, when in the course of the contest for the Metropolitanate of Kiev and all Rus' the concepts "Metropolitan of all Rus'" and "Metropolitan of Kiev and all Rus'" acquired more specific meanings (for a discussion of the use of the titles in the sources, see A. Pliguzov, "O titule 'Mitropolit kievskii i vseia Rusi'" [unpublished paper].

11. For a discussion of the history of various contending metropolitanates and the relevant literature, see A. S. Pavlov, "O nachale Galitskoi i Litovskoi mitropolii i o pervykh tamoshnikh mitropolitakh po vizantiiskim dokumental'nym istochnikam XIV-go veka," *Russkoe Obozrenie* 3 (May 1894): 214–251; N. D. Tikhomirov, *Galitskaia Mitropoliia, Tserkovno-istoricheskoe issledovanie* (St. Petersburg, 1985); K. Chodynicki, *Kościół prawosławny a Rzeczpospolita Polska, 1370–1632* (Warsaw, 1934), p. 374; I. Nazarko, "Halychka Metropoliia," *Analecta Ordinis S. Basilii Magni,* ser. 2, sec. 11, vol. 3 (1–2), 145–225; M. Giedroyć, "The Arrival of Christianity in Lithuania: Between Rome and Byzantium (1281–1341)," *Oxford Slavonic Papers,* n.s., 20 (1987): 14–20, idem, "The Influence of Ruthenian-Lithuanian Metropolitanates on the Progress of Christianization (1300–1458)" (unpublished paper).

12. *Byzantium and the Rise of Moscow,* pp. 73–95. See also D. Obolensky, "Byzan-

tium, Kiev, and Moscow: A Study in Ecclesiastical Relations," *DOP* 11 (1957): 21–78.

13. For a discussion of Andrei Bogoliubsky's attempt to create a competitive metropolitanate, and the literature on the subject, see J. Pelenski, "The Contest for the 'Kievan Succession' (1155–1175): The Religious-Ecclesiastical Dimension," *Proceedings of the International Congress Commemorating the Millennium of Christianity in Rus'-Ukraine, HUS* 12–13 (1988–1989): 761–780.

14. A. Poppe, "Zur Geschichte der Kirche und des Staates der Rus' im 11. Jh.: Titularmetropolen," *Das heidnische und christliche Slaventum* (Wiesbaden, 1970), pp. 64–75.

15. V. A. Kuchkin, "Skazanie," pp. 71–75; G. M. Prokhorov, "Petr," p. 327. Contradictory assessments regarding the relationship of church and state and the interconnected problem of the canonization politics in Muscovite Russia have recently been offered in scholarship. Contrary to the preponderance of the available evidence, N. S. Borisov has questioned the established view about the close cooperation between church and state in Muscovite Russia, particularly in the fourteenth century, but also in the fifteenth. Borisov has advanced the hypothesis that the Orthodox Church's support for state policies was "rather modest" and that especially in the fourteenth century the prevailing attitude of the Metropolitans of Kiev and all Rus' toward Moscow was characterized by a "temporizing neutrality" (*Russkaia tserkov'*, p. 188 and "Moskovskie kniaz'ia i russkie mitropolity XIV veka," *Voprosy istorii*, no. 8 [1986]: 30–43, especially p. 43). A. S. Khoroshev, however, has maintained that the canonization of Russian saints was a "political institution," that the primary criterion for the canonization of Russian saints was political, and that there existed a most intimate relationship between church and state in Old Rus' (*Politicheskaia istoriia russkoi kanonizatsii*, pp. 189–190. See also idem, *Tserkov' v sotsial'no-politicheskoi sisteme Novgorodskoi feodal'noi respubliki* (Moscow, 1980).

16. For Metropolitan Aleksei's life and career, as well as the literature on the subject, see Barsukov, cols. 27–32; E. Golubinskii, *Istoriia russkoi tserkvi*, vol. 2, pt. 1 (1900), pp. 171–225; idem, *Istoriia kanonizatsii sviatykh v russkoi tserkvi* (Moscow, 1903), pp. 74–75; A. E. Presniakov, *Obrazovanie velikorusskogo gosudarstva* (Petrograd, 1918), pp. 290–317; G. M. Prokhorov, "Zhitie Alekseia mitropolita," in D. S. Likhachev (ed.), *Slovar' knizhnikov i knizhnosti drevnei Rusi*, no. 2 (*vtoraia polovina XIV–XVI vv.*), pt. 1 (A-K) (Leningrad, 1988), pp. 243–245. N. S. Borisov has treated the close cooperation of church and state and their symbiotic relationship during the tenure of Metropolitan Aleksei as an exception in the history of church-state relations of the Muscovite period (*Russkaia tserkov'*, pp. 79–99).

17. *PSRL*, vol. 21, pt. 2 (1913), pp. 346–386.

18. For Metropolitan Iona's life and career, as well as the literature on the subject, see N. Barsukov, *Istochniki russkoi agiografii*, cols. 266–272; E. Golubinskii, *Istoriia russkoi tserkvi*, vol. 2, pt. 1 (1900), pp. 469–515; Ia. S. Lur'e, "Iona," in *Slovar' knizhnikov i knizhnosti drevnei Rusi*, no. 2, pt. 1 (A-K) (1988), pp. 420–426; Ia. S. Lur'e, "Zhitie Iony," ibid., pp. 270–273. N. S. Borisov's and A. S. Khoroshev's treatments of the activities and the canonization of Metropolitan Iona are rather brief and offer no new insights.

19. N. Barsukov, *Istochniki russkoi agiografii*, cols. 266–272; E. Golubinskii, *Istoriia kanonizatsii sviatykh v Russkoi Tserkvi*, pp. 79–80.

20. N. Barsukov, *Istochniki russkoi agiografii,* cols. 31–32, 271, 449.

21. For Metropolitan Kiprian's life and career, and the literature on the subject, see E. Golubinskii, *Istoriia russkoi tserkvi,* vol. 2, pt. 1 (1900), pp. 297–356; L. A. Dmitriev, "Rol' i znachenie mitropolita Kipriana," *TODRL* 19 (1963): 215–254; D. Obolensky, "A *Philorhomaios anthropos:* Metropolitan Cyprian of Kiev and all Russia," *DOP* 32 (1979): 79–98. G. M. Prokhorov, *Povest' o Mitiae;* N. F. Droblenkova, "Bibliografiia," G. M. Prokhorov, "Kiprian," in "Letopistsy i istoriki XI–XVII vv.," *TODRL* 39 (1985): 53–71; also "Kiprian," in *Slovar' knizhnikov i knizhnosti drevnei Rusi,* no. 2, pt. 1 (A-K) (1988), pp. 464–475.

22. For the text of the reconstructed *Troitskaia letopis',* see M. D. Priselkov, *Troitskaia letopis': Rekonstruktsiia teksta* (Moscow and Leningrad, 1950). The most important scholarly contributions to the study of the *Troitskaia letopis'* are the following: M. D. Priselkov, "Letopisanie XIV veka," in *Sbornik statei po russkoi istorii posviashchennykh S. F. Platonovu* (1922), pp. 24–39: "O rekonstruktsii teksta Troitskoi letopisi 1408 g., sgorevshei v Moskve v 1812 g.," *Uchenye zapiski Gosudarstvennogo pedagogicheskogo instituta im. Gertsena* (1939): 542; M. D. Priselkov, *Istoriia russkogo letopisaniia XI–XV vv.* (Leningrad, 1940), pp. 113–142; Priselkov, *Troitskaia letopis',* Introduction, pp. 7–49; S. I. Kochetov, "Troitskii pergamennyi spisok letopisi 1408 g.," *Arkheograficheskii ezhegodnik za 1961 god* (1962), pp. 18–27; G. N. Moiseeva, "Otryvok Troitskoi pergamennoi letopisi perepisannyi G. F. Millerom," *TODRL* 26 (1971): 93–99; Ia. S. Lur'e, *Obshcherusskie letopisi XIV–XV vv.* (Leningrad, 1976), pp. 17–66; G. M. Prokhorov, "Letopisets Velikii Rus'skii: Analiz ego upominaniia v Troitskoi letopisi," in *Letopisi i khroniki* (Moscow, 1976), pp. 67–77; C. J. Halperin, "The Russian Land and the Russian Tsar: the Emergence of Muscovite Ideology, 1380–1408," *Forschungen zur osteuropäischen Geschichte* 23 (1976): 5–103, especially pp. 58–68; Ia. S. Lur'e, "Letopis' Troitskaia," in D. S. Likhachev (ed.), *Slovar' knizhnikov i knizhnosti drevnei Rusi,* no. 2 (*vtoraia polovina XIV–XVI v.*) (1989), pt. 2 (L-Ia) (Leningrad, 1989), pp. 64–67. Kiprian's role as a sponsor of the *TL* and the latter's significance in the history of Muscovite chronicle writing and ideology has been almost completely overlooked by N. S. Borisov (*Russkaia tserkov'*) and A. S. Khoroshev (*Politicheskaia istoriia*).

23. *PSRL,* vol. 1 (1926), cols. 354–355, 418–419; *TL,* pp. 244–245, 285–286.

24. For a discussion of these interpretations and views, see J. Pelenski, "The Sack of Kiev of 1169: Its Significance for the Succession to Kievan Rus'," *HUS* 9, no. 3–4 (December 1987): 303–316.

25. J. Pelenski, "The Origins," pp. 36–37, 41.

26. Ia. S. Lur'e, *Obshcherusskie letopisi XIV–XV vv.,* pp. 120–121.

27. J. Pelenski, "The Origins," pp. 46–48.

28. *TL,* p. 439.

29. Likhachev, *Russkie letopisi,* p. 295.

30. See note 1 above.

31. Prokhorov, "Letopisets Velikii Rus'skii," pp. 67–77, especially pp. 71–74.

32. See J. Pelenski, "The Origins," pp. 36–7, 41.

33. See J. Pelenski, "The Origins," pp. 29–52; idem, "The Emergence of the Muscovite Claims," pp. 520–531; idem, "The Sack of Kiev," pp. 638–649.

Religion and Identity in the Carpathians

East Christians in Poland and Czechoslovakia

PAUL ROBERT MAGOSCI

> The worst thing that has happened in the world during the past few years is the appointment of the Pole, Wojtyla, as Pope. His aggressive brand of Catholicism has had a particularly negative impact on our people.
> —Comments of an Orthodox priest in Czechoslovakia, 1986

This uncompromising statement by a popular young priest in a small mountain village in northeastern Czechoslovakia captures in essence the centuries-old religious animosities that persist in the Carpathian region. The message is undeniable and reflects a reality known to many—that the tension between the Orthodox and Catholic cultural and religious spheres remains great and that any successes garnered by one side are inevitably viewed by the other as a direct threat to the national as well as religious concerns of Eastern Orthodox Christians living in Poland and Czechoslovakia's Carpathian region.

The Carpathian region refers to the mountains and valleys of the north-central Carpathian ranges inhabited by East Slavs who historically have been known as Rusnaks or Rusyns and who in modern parlance are referred to as Ukrainians.[1] According to political boundaries established at the close of World War II, this East Slavic inhabited Carpathian region includes territories in far southeastern Poland, northeastern Czechoslovakia, and the far western Ukraine, in particular the Transcarpathian *oblast'*.

In language and culture, the inhabitants of this region belong to the sphere of the East Slavs. Some of their earliest ancestors (supplemented by later waves of migration from the east) have inhabited the Carpathians since the time of dispersal and resettlement of the Slavs during the sixth and seventh centuries. Then with the initial entry of the Slavs into the Christian world during the ninth and tenth centuries, the Carpathian region became firmly part of the sphere of Eastern Christianity.

This essay is a revised version of one originally published under the same title in *Cross Currents* 8 (1988). Reprinted by permission of the editor.

The strong sense of religious and ethnic conceptual bonding as expressed through the terms Rusnaks/Rusyns remained undisturbed until the last decades of the nineteenth and the outset of the twentieth centuries, when local leaders influenced by the idea of nationalism and by the statistical and other demands of modern state bureaucracies began to argue that the traditional religious mode of self-identity was too vague and that the populace must think instead in terms of ethnolinguistic or national categories.

Thus began attempts at terminological precision and the formulation of a national identity alongside a religious one. The practical result, however, has not been clarity, but profound confusion that to a large degree still exists. This confusion is reflected by the fact that the East Slavs in the Carpathians have been described by others and by themselves as either Rusyns, Rusnaks, Lemkos, Ruthenians, Russians, or Ukrainians, terms which are at certain times and for some member of the group mutually exclusive national identities and at other times complementary identities that form and reflect a kind of hierarchy of multiple loyalties. Looked at in another way, the terminological question can be seen as a struggle between the religious-based universalism of the faithful Eastern Christian masses as expressed in their association with concept of Rus', and the attempts of an often secular intelligentsia that prefers to emphasize the ethnonational particularities of the group. Nonetheless, the people themselves have seemed historically to prefer Christian universalism to ethnic particularism. Here we will use the historic terms Rus' or Carpatho-Rusyn to describe the population of the Carpathian region.

Today basically two Eastern Christian Churches, the Orthodox and Greek Catholic, serve the East Slavic Rusyns in the Carpathian region. Although both derive from the same theological base, they are divided along jurisdictional lines that bring to the fore the whole question of Western Catholic and Eastern Orthodox spheres of religious and cultural influence in Europe. Indeed, the presence of Christianity in the Carpathians, whether the result of the ninth-century mission of Cyril and Methodius and their disciples or that of the post-tenth century arrival of Christian migrants from Kievan Rus', predates the division between the Eastern Orthodox and Western Catholic worlds that began in 1054.[2] While the Carpathian region remained Eastern Christian, it was politically part of Roman Catholic Poland and Hungary, located in the Orthodox borderlands of those states in an area that witnessed periodic attempts at church union between the thirteenth and fifteenth centuries: Galicia in 1247; Constance, 1414–1417; and Florence, 1439.

Finally, a qualified success in these unionistic efforts took place in 1596, when at Brest in the Polish-Lithuanian Commonwealth, several Orthodox bishops agreed to enter into union with Rome. The resultant Uniate Church, as it was known, switched its jurisdictional allegiance from the Orthodox ecumenical patriarch in Constantinople to the Catholic pope in Rome, but it was allowed to retain its Eastern Christian practices, including the liturgy of Saint John Chrysostom (said in Church Slavonic, not in Latin), a married priesthood, and the Julian calendar. The 1596 Union of Brest that affected lands in the Polish-Lithuanian Commonwealth was followed half a century later by the Union of Užhorod in 1646, which affected the lands in the Hungarian Kingdom.[3]

It should be stressed that the introduction of the union between 1596 and 1646 took on from the outset the negative characteristics of an all-or-nothing situation. Backed by the Polish and later Hungarian Roman Catholic hierarchies and secular governments, the Uniates were initially recognized as the only legal form of Eastern Christianity in the region. For the most part, the adherents of the "old faith" (*stara vira*)—Orthodoxy—were forced either to accept the union or to emigrate eastward to Slavic lands under the control of Muscovy. In the Carpathian region, however, Orthodox adherents with their own hierarchs were able to survive until the late eighteenth century.[4] By then all Carpatho-Rusyn villages became Uniate or Greek Catholic, as the church came to be officially called in the Austrian Empire, which by 1722 had come to control the whole area.

It should also be remembered that from the very beginning, local Orthodox prelates considered the Union of Brest and Union of Užhorod to be uncanonical and therefore illegal. When there were no longer any local Orthodox hierarchs left in the region, the anathematic views toward the Uniates/Greek Catholics were maintained by the hierarchy of the Russian Orthodox Church in Muscovy and later the Russian Empire. It is not surprising, therefore, that after the partition of Poland (1772–1795), when the Russian Empire gained large territories inhabited by Greek Catholics, the tsarist government gradually banned their church. Before 1796, this was accomplished unilaterally through governmental decrees and later in the 1830s with the assistance of the Greek Catholic and Russian Orthodox hierarchies. The last Greek Catholic diocese on Russian territory (Chełm/Kholm) was abolished in 1875.[5]

Despite the persecution in the Russian Empire, the nineteenth century proved to be the best era in the history of Greek Catholicism. This was connected with the policy of the Austrian government, in particular the Josephine reforms and enlightened ideas that dominated state policy when in 1772 the Habsburgs acquired Galicia and the vast majority of Greek Catholics. Already one year before, the Habsburg rulers had raised Mukačevo to the status of an independent Greek Catholic diocese (previously it had been subordinated to the Roman Catholic archbishopric of Eger), while in Galicia, the Greek rite was made equal to the Roman rite, and by 1808, the metropolitan status of L'viv-Halych was restored in Galicia.[6]

Initially, however, such positive government intervention helped only to continue a trend that had existed in Greek Catholic circles since the Church had come into being in 1595; namely, the tendency for hierarchy and priesthood to assimilate culturally and linguistically to the dominant culture. In the case of Galicia, this meant Polish culture; south of the mountains in the Hungarian Kingdom it meant Hungarian culture. Part of the assimilation included changes in Eastern Christian liturgical practices, such as the adoption of the Western Gregorian calendar, replacement of Church Slavonic with Polish, Hungarian, or Slovak, and in the twentieth century the imposition of celibacy for the priesthood. These trends occurred with various speeds, and, in some cases, were reversed or never even implemented. For instance, the trend toward Polonization of the Greek Catholic hierarchy ended with the onset of Austrian rule in Galicia in 1772, then began again at the outset of the nineteenth century until it was definitively reversed after 1848, so that under the leadership of two metropolitans, Hryhorii Iakhymovych and Andrei Sheptyts'kyi, the Church became a catalyst of national consciousness and stood in the forefront of the Rus'-Ukrainian national movement in Galicia.[7] Thus, at least in Galicia, the Greek Catholic Church, which during the first half of the nineteenth century was an instrument of cultural assimilation, had by the outset of the twentieth century become the popular symbol of Ukrainian nationhood.

South of the mountains in Hungary, however, this same period saw the Greek Catholic Church become an instrument of national assimilation, while some of the hierarchs and many priests of the Diocese of Mukačevo became leading magyarones and helped promote state efforts to magyarize the local Rusyn population. Part of this trend witnessed the creation of a new Greek Catholic vicariate in 1873 and the diocese at Hajdúdorog in 1912. Hungarian gradually replaced Church Slavonic as the liturgical language, and the local Rusyn population became completely magyarized.[8]

The point is that in the eyes of many Rusyn patriots, whether among the intelligentsia or the masses, the Greek Catholic Church had become or was becoming the symbol of compromise and subservience to the Roman Catholic world of Poland and Hungary, and that changes in religious practices seemed sure to be followed by linguistic and national assimilation and the eventual disappearance of the Rusyns as an East Slavic people. It was attitudes such as these that led to a search for some kind of Eastern spiritual renewal, which in part took the form—depending on one's views—of a "descent into the *schisma* of Orthodoxy" or a "return to the Orthodox faith of our fathers."

Throughout all the Greek Catholic territories in the Austro-Hungarian Empire, it was precisely in the Carpathian region where the Orthodox revival had its greatest following. This was due to several factors: (1) the return of immigrants from America who had converted to Orthodoxy in the New World; (2) the interest of Pan-Slavic circles in the Russian Empire; and (3) the innate conservatism of the Carpathian mountain inhabitants who instinctively felt themselves different—and therefore suspicious of non-mountain dwellers, whether or not they happened to be of the same faith or nationality.[9] Moreover, from the very outset, the "return to Orthodoxy" was often a conscious religious and national act since Orthodoxy was depicted by the apologists and came to be viewed by its new adherents as the "true faith" of the East Slavic Rus' *qua* Russian people. Such views not only coincided with the late nineteenth-century brand of Russian Pan-Slavism and Neo-Slavism, but also responded to the Christian universalist preference of the Rusyn masses since the Russian Orthodox Church integrated within its fold many ethnic elements, the dominant Slavic component of which was considered part of a so-called common Russian people (*obshcherusskii narod*).[10]

Therefore, by the twentieth century the following symbolic dichotomies prevailed throughout Carpathian society. From the perspective of Greek Catholics, their church represented the perfect compromise for Eastern Christianity, because it allowed for the survival of the Eastern rite and of the East Slavs, whether as Rusyn or Ukrainians, in a Western Christian political and cultural environment. Based on such premises, Orthodoxy was considered not only the misguided faith of schismatics from the fold of "universal" Catholicism, but also a potential if not actual threat to Austria-Hungary because it preached the ethnonational unity of Rusyns and Russians and looked forward to the day when tsarist Russia would expand its despotic grasp to and beyond the Carpathians.

The Orthodox felt that their church represented a return to the "original" faith of Rusyns and all East Slavs so that its existence served as a guarantee against foreign or Western (that is, Polish or Hungarian) national assimilation. In that context, argued the Orthodox, the Greek Catholics not only were preparing the ground for assimilation to Polish or Hungarian culture (Ukrainian was, by the way, viewed as an artificial bastardized form of the Polish language and its acceptance as a sure step to eventual, complete Polonization), they also slowly but surely were dropping all the tenets and practices of Eastern Christianity until it would not be long before Greek Catholics would be no different from Roman Catholics.

As long as the Austro-Hungarian Empire existed, the Orthodox revival in the Carpathians was kept to a minimum, even if it required trials from time to time against its adherents whose religious conversion was equated with state treason.[11] However, with the collapse of Austro-Hungary in 1918 and the creation of relatively religiously tolerant new political authorities in the Carpathian region—Poland north of the mountains and Czechoslovakia to the south—the Greek Catholic-Orthodox rivalry took on a new dynamism. The Rusyn masses began to express their national as well as religious preferences by large-scale "conversions" to Orthodoxy. Thus, among Rusyns south of the mountains in Czechoslovakia, nearly one-quarter (112,000) of the 460,000 Greek Catholics became Orthodox during the 1920s, while during the same period north of the mountains in Poland, about the same percentage, one-quarter (30,000) of the Rusyns, known locally as Lemkos, did the same.[12]

Moreover, the religious change was often marked by violence, as parishioners locked Greek Catholic priests out of their churches, drove them from their parish houses, and installed Orthodox priests (*popy*), often newly-arrived refugees from lands farther east that had come under Soviet control.[13] South of the mountains in Czechoslovakia, the pro-Orthodox movement was in large part a reaction against the pro-Hungarian tendencies of the Greek Catholic hierarchy and village priesthood—a reaction, moreover, that for its own political reasons was welcomed and at times directly supported by the Czechoslovak authorities. North of the mountains in Poland, the pro-Orthodox movement was motivated by a reaction against the Westernizing liturgical orientation and Ukrainian national preferences of certain circles in the Greek Catholic Church, in particular within the Diocese of Przemyśl-Sambir-Sanok, which had jurisdiction over the Lemko Rusyns.[14] Because they considered Ukrainianism as a separatist and anti-Russian (therefore in peasant eyes anti-Rusyn as well) phenomenon, the local Lemko Rusyns saw in Orthodoxy their national as well as spiritual salvation.

Not surprisingly, the Vatican was alarmed by the seemingly wholesale flight to Orthodoxy. To stem that tide, in Czechoslovakia it replaced the former pro-Hungarian (magyarone) bishops of the two Greek Catholic dioceses (Mukačevo and Prešov) with nationally pro-Rusyn and politically pro-

Czechoslovak candidates.[15] In Poland, Rome felt obliged to take a more radical step by detaching the Lemko-inhabited Carpathian region from the jurisdiction of the Ukrainian-dominated Greek Catholic Diocese of Przemyśl. The result was the creation in 1934 of a Lemko Apostolic Administration, placed directly under the Vatican and headed by a pro-Lemko Rusyn (that is, not a sympathizer of the Ukrainian national orientation), whose presence was intended to suggest to the remaining Greek Catholics that their Church and their children would not be turned into instruments of Ukrainianization.[16]

Considering its own traditional anti-Ukrainian orientation, the Polish government welcomed the Lemko Apostolic Administration as a limited but positive step in controlling Ukrainian influence in the southeastern part of the country. Ukrainian spokespersons, however, branded the apostolic administration as a Polish-inspired Vatican plot to tribalize, divide, and eventually assimilate the Ukrainian nationality, of whom Lemko Rusyns were considered a part.[17] As for the Lemko Rusyn population, it generally welcomed the creation of what was now considered its "own" Greek Catholic Church.[18] This move by the Vatican, based on precedent among immigrants from the Carpathian region in the United States, did in fact contribute to stabilizing membership and in cutting further losses to Orthodoxy.[19]

Hence, by the 1930s, a tenuous balance was reached between the two variants of Eastern Christianity in the Carpathian region. Some villages became all Orthodox or all Greek Catholic; others were split between the two orientations, each of which had its own church. However, this balance and relative stability was brutally upset after World War II with the arrival of a new political force in the area—the Soviet Union.

By late 1944, all the Greek Catholic territory that formerly had been part of the Austro-Hungarian Empire came firmly under the control of the Red Army. Within one year, most of that territory was incorporated into the Ukrainian S.S.R., leaving at most about 300,000 Rusyns beyond direct Soviet control within the new boundaries of Poland (approximately 180,000 in the Lemko Region) and Czechoslovakia (120,000 in northeastern Slovakia).

Although the officially atheistic Soviet Union at best tolerated Russian Orthodoxy, especially after the *modus vivendi* reached between Stalin and the Church during World War II, it was certainly not going to allow on its territory what was now hailed as the historic instrument of Polish and Hungarian feudal domination over the Rus' people and at present the agent of Vatican and Western imperialism—namely, the Greek Catholic Church. Thus, the Soviet government followed the precedent of tsarist Russia and—

aided by the Russian Orthodox Church hierarchy, which never recognized the legality of the Union of Brest and Greek Catholicism—organized in 1946 a church *sobor* in L'viv, which abrogated the 1596 union.[20]

As a result of the 1946 L'viv *Sobor*, the Greek Catholic priests in former eastern Galicia (L'viv, Przemyśl, and Stanyslav dioceses) were given the choice to become Orthodox, and 1,111 (37.6 percent) of the 2,950 accepted the offer. As for the remainder who refused, a few hundred went underground; another 1,600 were imprisoned, where they lingered with few exceptions until their deaths in Soviet camps.[21] Three years later, in Soviet-controlled Transcarpathia (formerly Subcarpathian Rus' in Czechoslovakia), the Greek Catholic Diocese of Mukačevo was liquidated and the church and its faithful officially transformed into Orthodox. Unlike in Galicia, there was no *sobor* held in Transcarpathia as had been the case in L'viv. Instead, the "act of reunion" was simply declared to be in effect following the reading of a proclamation during a service on 28 August 1949 in the cathedral church in Užhorod.[22]

With Greek Catholicism officially eliminated in Soviet territory, it survived for the moment only in the Carpathian region of southeastern Poland and northeastern Czechoslovakia. However, since that time the situation in both these countries has been particularly complicated.

After the new Soviet-Polish and Soviet-Czechoslovak borders were formed in 1945, efforts were made on both sides to follow the trend at the time in international relations, which favored the transfer of populations in an effort to make political and ethnic boundaries coincide, that is, to eliminate the problem of national minorities that—so it was felt—had contributed to if not caused World War II. In this regard, Rusyns from the Carpathian region (in return for Poles and Czechs from Soviet territory) were given the option to emigrate eastward to the Soviet Ukraine. In Poland's Lemko region, about 120,000 opted or were administratively encouraged to go east; in northeastern Czechoslovakia, only 12,000 Rusyns accepted the invitation. This eastward trek to the Soviet Union from Poland took place in 1945–1946 and from Czechoslovakia in 1947. Nonetheless, about 40,000 Lemko Rusyns still remained in southeastern Poland and another 110,000 in northeastern Czechoslovakia.[23]

As for Poland, the new pro-Soviet government resolved the problem in a simple way. Claiming that the local Lemko Rusyns were aiding anti-Soviet Ukrainian partisans who were holed up in the Carpathian Mountains, during the spring and summer of 1947, the Lemkos were forcibly removed from their homes and resettled in the so-called "Recovered Lands" (*Ziemie Ody-*

skane), the formerly German territories of Silesia (especially near Wrocław) and along the Baltic Sea that had become part of Poland in 1945.[24] Therefore, with regard to the historic Eastern Christianity churches in Poland's Carpathian region, the problem was resolved. There ceased to be any problem because there were no more Eastern Christians.

In legal terms, Poland's Communist authorities accepted the Soviet view that after the L'viv *Sobor* of 1946 the Greek Catholic Church ceased to exist in historic Galicia, which included lands in post-1945 Poland that had been under the jurisdiction of the Diocese of Przemyśl and Lemko Apostolic Administration. Based on such a premise, Polish government decrees were issued in 1947 and 1949, which respectively nationalized Greek Catholic church property and then legalized the seizure on the grounds that it belonged to "juridical persons" whose "existence and activities lost their purposes as a result of resettlement of their members to the Soviet Union."[25] As a result of these decrees, the Greek Catholic Church in Poland was "delegalized," allowing for the official "non-recognition" of the Greek Catholic rite in Poland from that time until the present.

In practice, after 1947, the Lemko Greek Catholic Apostolic Administration (with its 1129 parishes and 127,580 faithful as of 1943) ceased to exist. Church property in the depopulated Lemko Rusyn villages was left to decay and eventually disappear. In those Lemko villages resettled by Poles, former Greek Catholic churches were often appropriated by the Roman Catholic Church, in a few instances given to the Orthodox Church, or in the case of wooden ones, left to decay or be torn down, using what remained of the structures for firewood.[26]

South of the border in Czechoslovakia, the vast majority of the population remained in place. There were two reasons for this. In contrast to the historic tradition of antagonism between Poles and East Slavic Rusyns and Ukrainians north of the Carpathians, on the southern slopes of the mountains the past was marked by friendly relations between Slovaks and Rusyns. Moreover, the isolated extremist views directed at Rusyns living on "Slovak land"[27] were neutralized in the new postwar political situation in Czechoslovakia in which the powerful Communist party had a relatively high number of functionaries of Rusyn background.[28] Therefore, aside from the truly voluntary nature of the eastward emigration of 12,000 Rusyns in 1947, there was to be no attempt at forced deportation to the Soviet Union or westward to other parts of the Czechoslovak republic.

However, after Czechoslovakia came to be ruled exclusively by a Communist regime in February 1948, the Soviet model in religious affairs was soon adapted. This sealed the fate of the Greek Catholic Church. In April 1950, Czechoslovakia's Communist officials invited eighty Greek Catholic priests to a "peace rally" in Prešov. By previous agreement with local Orthodox leaders, the "peace rally" was transformed into a church council (*sobor*) and, following the Soviet model, the union with Rome was abolished, making all former Greek Catholics become Orthodox. Like the rest of Orthodox Church in Czechoslovakia, the new Orthodox parishes initially became part of the Russian Orthodox Moscow Patriarchate.[29] Of the 301 Greek Catholic priests at the time, one-third became Orthodox. The remainder who refused to convert were arrested and, when finally released, forbidden to serve as priests. Bishop Pavel Gojdič and his suffragan, Vasyl Hopko, were also arrested, the former dying in prison in 1960.[30]

Thus, by 1950, it seemed that Greek Catholic problem had been resolved in east-central Europe. The homeland where the church had flourished was now firmly in Orthodox or, in part, Roman Catholic hands. Ironically, within the Soviet bloc, it was only in ostensibly anti-Slavic Hungary (where the Diocese of Hajdúdorog had long ago taken on a purely Hungarian character) and otherwise staunchly pro-Soviet Bulgaria (whose adherents in union with Rome numbered fewer than 5,000) that Greek Catholicism survived as a legal church.[31] However, despite their Communist governments and even strongly pro-Stalinist orientation, neither Poland nor Czechoslovakia was the Soviet Union. As a result, the relatively less rigid approach of Warsaw and Prague to religious matters allowed for new movement on the Eastern Christian front.

In Poland, following the political changes in October 1956, a church-state *modus vivendi* provided a "tolerated but not recognized" status to the Greek Catholic rite within the Roman Catholic Church. This meant that Lemko Rusyns and fellow Greek Catholic Ukrainians scattered throughout the western and northern parts of the country were permitted to have services conducted at some fifty "pastoral points" by the approximately fifty surviving Roman Catholic priests now designated bi-ritual assistants in Roman Catholic parishes. In practice, Greek Catholic services were held in Roman Catholic chapels, provided that the resident priest agreed.[32] In effect, the hierarchy of the Polish Roman Catholic Church was mildly tolerant of these activities, whereas the response among the lower echelons of the Polish priesthood ranged from Christian solidarity with to fierce opposition against their Greek Catholic brethren.

Also, beginning in 1956, some Lemkos were allowed to return to their ancestral village—provided they could arrange to convince Polish families to sell them back their confiscated homesteads. By the mid-1960s, about 3,000 had returned, a resettlement in the Carpathian homeland that has continued so that today there are about 10,000 Lemko Rusyns living once again on the northern slopes of the Carpathians.[33] This has meant that the Eastern Christian presence, which had been physically removed by 1947, has now returned in the form of both a semi-legal Greek Catholic and a fully legal Orthodox community.

The numbers are small, and the estimated 10,000 Lemko Rusyns living in the Carpathians are divided more or less evenly among Orthodox, Greek Catholics, and non-believers. In response to this mini-revival, the Polish Autocephalous Orthodox Church established (or reestablished) in 1983 a new Eparchy of Przemyśl and Nowy Sącz, specifically for the Lemko Carpathian region. It is based in Sanok, has thirty-three parishes served by fourteen priests, and is headed by a bishop of Lemko Rusyn background, Adam Dubec.[34] In 1985, a symbolically major event took place in the small Lemko Rusyn village of Zyndranowa where the first Orthodox church newly constructed in the region since before World War II was opened. Two other Orthodox churches are under construction in Krynica and Gorlice.

This activity among the Orthodox has caused concern within Polish Roman Catholic circles and has forced slight change in their traditionally intolerant attitude toward Greek Catholics. When the first Greek Catholics began returning to the Carpathian region, it was not uncommon to find Roman Catholic Polish priests—often under the influence of their own parishioners—refusing access to chapels in their churches for Greek Catholic services. With the recent increase in Orthodox activity, however, the Roman Catholics think that such "schismatic" activity needs to be stopped and that allowing Greek Catholics to function might be the best way to achieve that goal. Moreover, the favorable pronouncements of Pope John Paul II toward Ukrainian (Greek) Catholics in the West, as well as the four recent visitations by the secretary of the Vatican's Congregation for the Oriental Churches (Archbishop Myroslav Marusyn) to Poland's Greek Catholics, have raised the latter's status. These developments culminated in 1989 with the pope's appointment of Msgr. Ivan Martyniak as bishop to Poland's primate, Cardinal Glemp, with responsibility for Greek Catholics throughout the country.[35]

Despite such improvements in their status, the Greek Catholics in Poland remain under the jurisdiction of the Polish Roman Catholic Church. In the Carpathian region, there are today thirteen parishes served by three priests. Of those parishes, two (Komańcza and Krempna) managed somehow to survive throughout the postwar events; five (Kulaszne, Łosie, Nowica, Pętna, Uście Gorlickie) were established in the 1960s following the initial return of the Lemkos, and six (Gładyszów, Gorlice, Krynica, Olchowiec, Rozdziele, Rzepadź) have come into being since 1979.[36] All but one of the Greek Catholic parishes carry on their services in Roman Catholic churches, that is, at the discretion of the local Roman Catholic priest. It was therefore of great symbolic importance when a large new Greek Catholic church, the first of its kind to be constructed since World War II, was opened in 1989 in the village of Komańcza.

On the southern slopes of the Carpathian Mountains in Czechoslovakia, the fate of Eastern Christianity in the past four decades has been significantly different. The efforts at political liberalization in the 1960s that culminated in the Prague Spring of 1968 also prompted Czechoslovakia's former Greek Catholics to demand the restoration of their church. In June 1968, their efforts met with success when the Dubček government legalized the existence of the Greek Catholic Church.[37]

One immediate question that arose concerned church property. Who now had the legal right to it—the Orthodox who held it since 1950 or the Greek Catholics who wanted it back? This thorny issue was to be resolved by the mechanism of a plebiscite. Among the first symbolic steps of the plebiscite was the return of the Prešov diocesan cathedral church to the Greek Catholics in July 1968. In the next year, plebiscites were held in about 210 parishes, only five of which opted to remain Orthodox. In the end, the government recognized the existence of 205 Greek Catholic and eighty-seven Orthodox parishes.[38]

In many ways, the political and cultural turmoil that marked Czechoslovakia's Prague Spring played itself out in Rusyn villages through the mode of religion and a return to the Orthodox-Greek Catholic conflicts that had characterized the interwar years. Immediately after the legalization decree was issued, a delegation of one hundred Orthodox priests delivered a protest to the president of Czechoslovakia against the reestablishment of the Greek Catholic Church.[39]

At the village level, while there were peaceful transfers of property from the Orthodox to Greek Catholics, there were also several cases marked by assaults and the physical removal of Orthodox priests, breaking down of church doors, stoning of services, and in at least one instance the death of a Greek Catholic curate at the hands of an Orthodox priest. The situation was made even more ominous in that most of the plebiscites were carried out after 12 August, that is, in the presence of Soviet armed forces throughout the country. While it is known that some Orthodox priests garbed in sacred vestments greeted the Soviet troops as "liberators and defenders of Orthodoxy," vicious rumors soon began to circulate according to which the Orthodox supposedly had invited the Soviets and that it was they who were now identifying to the interventionist forces the Greek Catholics as "counterrevolutionaries."[40]

Nonetheless, despite the return beginning in early 1970 to a Soviet-style regime in Czechoslovakia and its repeal of many of the achievements of 1968, the restoration of the Greek Catholic Church has not been rescinded. It continues to function openly and with its own ecclesiastical structures, although like many Czech and Slovak Roman Catholic dioceses it did not have its own bishop until the revolutionary events of 1989. Moreover, the existence of a legal Greek Catholic Church in eastern Slovakia in the decades since 1968 proved to be a source of embarrassment to Soviet authorities in neighboring Transcarpathia where an underground Greek Catholic Church was, since the 1970s, increasing its activity. The movement in Soviet Transcarpathia was, in part, encouraged by the improved status of its co-religionists and co-nationals on the other side of the border in Czechoslovakia.[41]

But why did Czechoslovakia's Communist authorities—more precisely in the post-1968 federalist situation, the Slovak authorities—allow ties for the survival of the Greek Catholic Church in their country? The answer, in part, is to be found in the nationality problem, and this, in turn, leads to a further question: how has the restoration of Greek Catholicism and therefore the renewal of the Orthodox Greek Catholic dichotomy in the Eastern Christian world of the Carpathians affected the way in which the local population views itself and is viewed by others with regard to the question of national identity? Whereas there are some aspects of the conflict over national ideology evident in Poland's Lemko region, the number of Rusyns living there is too small to make any conclusive judgments.[42] South of the mountains in Czechoslovakia, however, the critical mass is large enough to see some trends.

First of all, it should be remembered that as part of the post-World War II Soviet influence in Poland and Czechoslovakia, the nationality question, like the religious question, was ostensibly resolved as a result of the so-called "iron laws" of Marxist historical evolution, albeit helped along by administrative decree and legal enforcement. This meant that the nearly century-old question of who the East Slavic Rus' population of the Carpathians was in national terms—Russian, Ukrainian, or a distinct Rusyn nationality—was decided. They were Ukrainian. But like the religious question, the nationality question turned out to be not so easily resolved.[43]

When in 1952 the Rusyn population of northeastern Czechoslovakia was administratively declared to be Ukrainian—a decision that meant among other things having Ukrainian instead of Russian taught in the nearly 322 elementary and secondary schools—large numbers of people reacted by voluntarily declaring themselves to be Slovak. They demanded and received Slovak schools in their villages. By 1966, there were only seventy-two elementary and secondary schools left in Rusyn communities that were not Slovak and provided instruction in Ukrainian. Then, with the heady days of the Prague Spring when demands of all kinds were being made to correct the injustices of the neo-Stalinist past, alongside the demand for a return of the Greek Catholic faith, there was a call for the return of Rusyn schools and for recognition of Rusyns as a distinct nationality. Indeed, planning was begun to restore instruction in the local Rusyn dialect in the schools, which would have meant a rejection of Ukrainian instruction and the return of Slovak schools. The Warsaw Pact intervention, however, put an end to those and all other "counterrevolutionary" ideas. As we have seen, Czechoslovakia's Rusyns did get back their Greek Catholic Church, but at what cost?

The price, in fact, has been to see that church become an instrument of Slovakization. Indeed, the general trend toward assimilation was already well underway. For instance, if in the 1930 census, 91,079 persons in northeastern Czechoslovakia claimed Rusyn as their nationality, in 1959–1960, when Ukrainian was the only possible choice, a mere 35,435 opted to do so.[44] It is uncertain whether the several proposals for changes away from the Ukrainian cultural and educational policy made in 1968–1969 would have made any difference in an individual's decision to emphasize a sense of Rusyn identity. The brutal destruction of the Czechoslovak experiment from the East only convinced many traditionally pro-Czechoslovak Rusyns that they had better throw their lot fully with their West Slavic brethren by identifying with them nationally as well as linguistically and politically.

In this context, the Greek Catholic Church has been an unwitting partner in the assimilation process. At the moment of its restoration in June 1968, the question of who was to serve as bishop in the restored diocese of Prešov became acute. The last bishop, Pavel Gojdič had died in prison in 1960, but his auxiliary and successor, Vasyl' Hopko, survived, released in 1964 from confinement in an old-age home, and finally in 1968 rehabilitated and allowed to return to Prešov to lead the restoration process of the Greek Catholic Church. However, from the very outset, pro-Slovak forces within the Church vowed that no Rusyn should ever again head the diocese.

To justify their views, the Slovak Greek Catholic faction pointed to official

Czechoslovak nationality statistics that allowed under Communist rule only for a Ukrainian identity, not a Rusyn one. Accordingly, in 1960 there were only 35,000 Ukrainians in northeastern Czechoslovakia, representing a mere eleven percent of the total Greek Catholic population estimated at 315,000.[45] Slovak Greek Catholic activists, who were generally suspicious of most data statements issued in the past by the Czechoslovak Communist authorities, accepted at face value the official statistics. As for the "Rusyn revival" of 1968, whose spokesmen challenged Slovak views on statistics and other matters, it was dismissed as the machinations of anti-Slovak extremists or perhaps even pro-Soviet agitators.

Such attitudes were not only held by Slovak Greek Catholics in eastern Slovakia, but were also promoted by powerful Slovak financial circles in the West, which put pressure on the Vatican to appoint a Slovak to head the restored Greek Catholic Diocese of Prešov.[46] In the end, the recently released and rehabilitated Bishop Hopko, who was allowed to return to Prešov in 1968 to lead the movement to restore the Greek Catholic Church and who was to be recognized as bishop by the Dubček government, was finally allowed to travel to Rome in December 1968 for an audience with the pope. However, when the bishop returned home a few weeks later, he discovered that (according to a letter of the Sacred Congregation for Oriental Churches, dated 22 December 1968) he was removed as head of the Prešov Diocese and made subordinate to a Slovak administrator, the Reverend Ján Hirka.[47] Thus, the chance to have the appointment of a Greek Catholic bishop to the Diocese of Prešov recognized by the Czechoslovak government was missed in 1968-1969 because of internal nationality controversies. Bishop Hopko was effectively removed from any real influence and died in 1976.

In the absence of a bishop, the diocesan authorities under administrator Hirka gradually engaged in the Slovakization of church practices throughout all parishes, including the estimated seventy-five in Rusyn villages. While the liturgy remained in Church Slavonic in both Rusyn and Slovak parishes, the homilies and other non-liturgical parts of the service became Slovak.[48] Church publications were also increasingly Slovakized, with the largest printings of the monthly journals (the Slovak edition *Slovo* and Ukrainian *Blahovistnyk*) and the annual almanacs being today in Slovak instead of in Ukrainian or in Rusyn dialect as had been the case in the early years of the Church's restoration after 1968.[49]

Finally, in the wake of Czechoslovakia's Velvet Revolution of November 1989 and the end of Communist rule, the Vatican was able to raise Hirka to the rank of bishop. Not surprisingly, at his massive and well-publicized installation in February 1990, the Slovak aspect of the Greek Catholic Diocese of Prešov was clearly emphasized. The newly won freedoms in Czechoslovak society have also encouraged some Greek Catholic priests and lay persons to prepare translations of Rusyn-language liturgical and prayer books and to demand their use in Rusyn parishes. Although Bishop Hirka has promised to respond to the needs of all his flock, including Rusyns, it is still too early to know whether the Greek Catholic officials who surround him are able or willing to reverse the pro-Slovak orientation within their church.[50]

In response, the Orthodox Church, with its approximately 20,000 faithful, its own cathedral churches in Prešov and Michalovce, and its seventy-four parishes spread throughout the countryside, prides itself once again as the defender of the East Slavic Rus' world in the face of Vatican and Slovak religious and national assimilationist encroachments as carried out through the medium of the Greek Catholic Church.[51] After all, for the Orthodox world, Greek Catholicism remains the bastard child of Roman Catholic Jesuit machinations in Eastern Europe, and for many Orthodox it seems particularly ironic that Greek Catholicism has been allowed to survive and do its "destructive work" among Eastern Slavs in Poland and Czechoslovakia right on the doorstep of the "Orthodox" Soviet Union. Furthermore, the traditional Rus'-Russian orientation of many Rusyns in Czechoslovakia makes such views quite palatable, and it seems no coincidence that those villages that were most reluctant to accept Slovak schools and a Slovak identity are precisely those that have remained Orthodox.

Thus, when all is said and done, the nationality question and problems of national identity that were ostensibly resolved in the Carpathian region just after World War II continue to be expressed consciously or unconsciously through the medium of religion. As in the past, so too in the present, Christianity and its temporal structures remain a shield for nationalist passions and, alas, national hatreds.

Notes

1. On the question of nomenclature, see Paul R. Magocsi, *The Shaping of a National Identity: Subcarpathian Rus', 1848-1948* (Cambridge, Mass., 1978), pp. 277-281.

2. The question of the beginnings of Christianity in the Carpathians is a controversial one. Local church historians have accepted as a given the introduction of Christianity by Cyril and Methodius or by their disciples in the late ninth century, with both the eparchies of Mukačevo south of the mountains and Przemyśl to the north supposedly having come into existence already in the ninth century. The earliest written records derive from a much later period—eleventh century for Przemyśl and later fourteenth century for Mukačevo. For the popular version of the Cyril and

Methodian mission, see the interwar history textbook by Ìryneĭ Kondratovych, *Istoriia Podkarpatskoĭ Rusy dlia naroda* (Užhorod, 1924), pp. 10–14. The most systematic scholarly critique of this popular view is found in Aleksei L. Petrov, *Drevneishiia gramoty po istorii karpato-russkoi tserkvi i ierarkhii, 1391–1498 g.* (Prague, 1930), esp. pp. 1–5. Most recently, a Greek Catholic historian in Czechoslovakia has argued not only that the Byzantine missionaries were in the Carpathian region, but that they went there *before* going to Moravia (863) and that it was *from* Carpathian Rus' that Kiev received Christianity one century later. See Stepan Pap, *Pochatky Khrystyianstva na Zakarpatti* (Philadelphia, 1983).

3. For details on these unions, see Halecki, *From Florence to Brest,* and Michael Lacko, *The Union of Užhorod* (Cleveland and Rome, 1968); and a discussion of the basic problems and literature in Paul Robert Magocsi, *Galicia: A Historical Survey and Bibliographic Guide* (Toronto, 1983), pp. 81–86.

4. An Orthodox eparchy with its own bishop survived in the eastern part of Subcarpathian Rus' (Transcarpathia) under the protection of Protestant Transylvania until 1711, while north of the mountains the Orthodox Eparchy of Przemyśl had throughout the seventeenth century an Orthodox as well as Greek Catholic bishop until 1691, when it became definitively Greek Catholic.

5. For details, see W. Lencyk, *The Eastern Catholic Church and Czar Nicholas I* (Rome and New York, 1966).

6. The metropolitanate of L'viv-Halych, established in 1303, had ceased to exist in 1404.

7. See John-Paul Himka, "The Greek Catholic Church and Nation-Building, 1772–1918," *HUS* 8, nos. 3–4 (1984): 426–452.

8. Magocsi, *Shaping of a National Identity,* pp. 55–58; Atanasii V. Pekar, *Narysy istoriĭ tserkvy Zakarpattia,* vol. 1 (Rome, 1967), pp. 95–112; Imre Timko, ed., *A Hajdúdorogi Bizánci Katholikus Egyházmegye jubileumi emlékkönyve 1912–1987* (Nyíregyháza, 1987), esp. pp. 17–29 and 159–181.

9. The impact of returning Carpatho-Rusyn immigrants on the Orthodox revival in the homeland deserves scholarly attention. The role of Orthodox sympathizers in the Russian Empire (in particular Count Vladimir Bobrinskoi) also should be analyzed. For some interesting insights, see the statement of a contemporary Russian Orthodox activist: Mikhail Sarych, *Bratskii priviet bratiam i sestram-karpatorussam, zhivushchim v predielakh karpatskikh gor i v Amerikie* (St. Petersburg, 1893); and the annual reports: *Otchet o dieiatel'nosti Galitsko-russkago Blagotvoritel'nago Obshchestva v S.-Peterburgie,* 2 vols.: *za 1912/1913–1914 god* (St. Petersburg, 1913–1914).

10. For the best explanation of the Orthodox East Slavic ideology as it pertains to the Carpathian region, see O. Monchalovskii, *Sviataia Rus'* (L'vov, 1903).

11. The first of these trials occurred in 1882 in L'viv (against Olga Grabar and others) followed by Marmaroš Sighet in 1913–1914 (against Archimandrite Aleksei Kabaliuk and others) and L'viv in 1914 (against Simeon Bendasiuk and others). Cf. Rene Martel, "La politique slave de la Russie d'avant-guerre: Le procès ukrainien de Marmaosz-Sziget," *Affaires étrangères,* 6, no. 10 (1936): 623–634 and 7, no. 1 (1937): 58–64; Bohdan Svitlynskii, "Avstro-Uhorshchyna i Talerhof" in *Voennye prestupleniia gabsburgskoi monarkhii, 1914–1917 gg.* (Trumbull, Conn., 1964), annex, pp. 1–40; Konstantin M. Beskid, *Marmarošsky proces* (Chust, 1926).

12. For the situation in the Carpathian region in Czechoslovakia, see Magocsi, *Shaping of a National Identity*, pp. 178–185; and Ivan Vanat, *Narysy novitn'oï ïstoriï ukraintsiv Skhidnoï Slovachchyny, 1918–1938*, vol. 1 (Bratislava and Prešov, 1979), pp. 175–189. For the situation in Poland, see Ivan Teodoric, "Lemkovskaia Rus'," *Nauchno-literaturnyi sbornik Galitsko-russkoi matitsy*, 8 [69] (1934): 16–23.

13. The center of the Orthodox movement south of the Carpathians was in the village of Ladomirova, just outside the Svidník in northeastern Czechoslovakia, where in the early 1920s Archimandrite Vitalii Maksimenko established the Holy Trinity Monastery and printshop to propagate the faith. See Paul R. Magocsi, *The Rusyn-Ukrainians of Czechoslovakia* (Vienna, 1983), pp. 40–41; and Vanat, *Narysy*, vol. 1, pp. 178–179.

14. The bishop of the Greek Catholic Diocese of Przemyśl-Sambir-Sanok was actually a Lemko, Josyfat Kotsylovs'kyi (1876–1947, consecrated 1917), who was one of leading "westernizers" in the Greek Catholic Metropolia of L'viv-Halych, favoring celibacy and other Latin-rite influences in opposition to the "easternizing" predilections of Metropolia Sheptyts'kyi. As for the diocesan priesthood, it was for the most part deeply embued with a Ukrainian national sentiment. Tadeusz Duda, "Stosunki wyznaniowe wśród Łemków greckokatolickich zamieszkałych na terenie obecnej diecezji tarnowskiej w XIX i XX wieku," *Tarnowskie Studia Teologiczne* 10, no. 1 (1986): 240–243.

15. The pro-Hungarian Greek Catholic bishops of Prešov, Istvan Novak (1879–1923, consecrated in 1913) and of Mukačevo, Antál Papp (1867–1945, consecrated in 1912), each of whom refused to swear an oath of allegiance to the new Czechoslovak state, were replaced eventually by Petro Gebei (1864–1931, consecrated in 1924) in Mukačevo and by Pavel Gojdič (1888–1960, consecrated in 1927) in Prešov.

16. The first apostolic administrator was the Lemko-born Reverend Vasylii Masciuk (1899–1936), who was followed in 1936 by another Lemko, the Reverend Iakiv Medvets'kyi (1880–1941). The new Greek Catholic administration included 111 parishes and 127,305 faithful. See the statistics and historical survey (stressing the distinctiveness of Lemkos and their Christian descent from the mission of Saints Cyril and Methodius) in *Shematyzm Greko-Katolytskoho dukhovenstva Apostol'skoï administratsiï Lemkovshchyny 1936* (L'viv, 1936).

17. For a summary of the Ukrainian position, see the introduction by Vasyl' Lenchyk to the reprinted edition of the 1916 *Shematyzm* (Stamford, Conn. 1970), and the earlier Mykola Andrusiak, "Der westukrainische Stamm der Lemken," *Südost-Forschungen* 6, 3-3 (1941): 536–575.

18. For the contemporary Lemko view strongly critical of "Ukrainian infiltration," see "Sto musyme o sobi znaty y pamiataty!," *Kalendar 'Lemka' na zvychainyi rok 1935* (Przemyśl, 1934), pp. 133–134; and the discussion by one of the clerical supporters of the Apostolic Administration, I. F. Lemkyn [Ioann Polians'kyi], *Istoryia Lemkovynŷ* (Yonkers, N.Y., 1960), pp. 168–170. For a non-partisan review of those events, see Duda, "Stosunki," pp. 243–246.

19. It was in part the realization that Rusyn Greek Catholic immigrants from south of the Carpathians who were living in the United States could not get along with their increasingly Ukrainian-oriented religious brethren from Galicia that prompted the Vatican to establish separate administrations (1916) and then dioceses

(1924) for immigrants from Austrian Galicia and the Hungarian Kingdom today, the Ukrainian Catholic Church and the Byzantine Ruthenian Catholic Church. Accepting pre-World War I political boundaries, Lemko immigrants were separated from their Rusyn brethren and placed within Galician Ukrainian dioceses.

20. The proceedings of L'viv Sobor were published first in *Diianyia Soboru hreko-katolyts'koï tserkvy u L'vovi, 8–10 bereznia 1946* (L'viv, 1946) and more recently in a revised version: *L'vivskyi tserkovnyi sobor: dokumenty i materialy, 1946–1981* (L'viv, 1984), with a slightly abridged English version: *The Lvov Church Council: Documents and Materials, 1946–1981* (Moscow, 1983).

21. *Martyrolohiia ukraïns'kykh tserkov*, vol. 2: *Ukraïns'ka katolyts'ka tserkva: dokumenty, materialy, khrystyians'kyi samvydav Ukraïny*, ed. Osyp Zinkevych and Taras R. Lonchyna (Toronto and Baltimore, 1985), p. 74. For greater details, see *First Victims of Communism: White Book on the Religious Persecution in Ukraine* (Rome, 1959).

22. For the Greek Catholic view of these events, see Pekar, *Narysy*, pp. 159–170; Vasyl' Markus, "Nyshchenn'ia hreko-katolyts'koï tserkvy v Mukachivs'kii Ieparkhiï v 1945–50 rr.," *Zapysky Naukovoho tovarystva im. Shevchenka* 169 (1962): 386–405; and Michael Lacko, "The Forced Liquidation of the Union of Užhorod," *Slovak Studies* vol. 1: *Historica*, No. 1 (Rome, 1961), pp. 145–157. For the Russian Orthodox view in praise of historically justified return to the true faith, see Bishop Savva (of Mukačevo and Užhorod), "30th Anniversary of the Reunion of the Zakarpatskaya Region Greek Catholics (Uniates) with Russian Orthodox Church," *Journal of the Moscow Patriarchate*, no. 1 (1980): 21–24.

23. For a discussion of the Lemko Rusyn eastward migration in the context of other European population movements at the time, see Joseph B. Schechtman, *Postwar Population Transfers in Europe, 1945–1955* (Philadelphia, 1962), pp. 151–179. On the lesser known emigration from northeastern Czechoslovakia, see Vanat, *Narysy*, vol. 2: *1938–1948* (1985), pp. 264–266.

24. Although it seems that plans for the deportation of Lemkos (and Ukrainians from neighboring lands in postwar southeast Poland) were already prepared, it was the death of General Karol Świerczewski in a battle with the Ukrainian Insurgent Army (the Banderite UPA) in March 1947 that provided the official justification for removal. The forced deportation was carried out between April and July 1947 (often with only a few hours' notice), despite the fact that the remaining Lemkos in Poland lived primarily in the western Lemko region (west of the Dukla Pass) where the UPA carried on only limited activity and where the local population was traditionally anti-Ukrainian. On the deportation and the new life of Lemkos in the "Recovered Lands" see Andrzej Kwilecki, "Fragmenty najnowszej historii Łemków," *Rocznik Sądecki* 8 (1967): 274–287; idem, *Łemkowie: zagadnienie migracji i asymilacji* (Warsaw, 1974); and Kazimierz Pudło, *Łemkowie: proces wrastania w środowisko Dolnego Śląska, 1947–1985* (Wrocław, 1987).

25. Cited with further details in Bohdan R. Bociurkiw, "The Suppression of the Greek Catholic Church in Post-war Soviet Union and Poland," in Dennis J. Dunn, ed., *Religion and Nationalism in Eastern Europe and the Soviet Union* (Boulder, Colo. and London, 1987), p. 106.

26. In the palatinate of Rzeszów, which included most of the Carpathian Lemko

region as well as former Ukrainian-inhabited villages beyond the San, the vast majority of the 220 churches that disappeared between 1939 and 1972 were not destroyed as a result of World War II, but because of neglect during the post-1947 decades of peace. Ryszard Brykowski, "Zabykowe cerkwie," *Architektura* 37, no. 5 (1983): 53–58. For a useful introduction to what occurred in Lemko villages after the deportations and resettlement by Poles, see C. M. Hann, *A Village without Solidarity* (New Haven, 1985), pp. 17–39.

27. Ostensibly, the leader of the Slovak nationalists during the interwar years, the Reverend Andrei Hlinka, had once quipped that it might be preferable to ship the Rusyns eastward. This attitude resurfaced at times of political instability as during the deportation of Lemkos and the Banderite problem in neighboring Poland (1943–1947) and the Prague Spring (1968–1969).

28. On Slovak attitudes and the high number of Rusyn Communist activists after World War II, see Pavel Macu, "National Assimilation: the Case of Rusyn-Ukrainians of Czechoslovakia," *East-Central Europe* 2, no. 2 (1975): 126–127.

29. The Orthodox jurisdictional question south of Carpathians was complicated. With the expansion of Orthodoxy during the interwar years in both eastern Slovakia and Subcarpathian Rus', the new church with its Eparchy of Mukačevo-Prešov was placed in 1931 under the Serbian patriarch in Belgrade. In 1945–1946, the Orthodox in Soviet Transcarpathia (Subcarpathian Rus') and in Eastern Slovakia were released from the jurisdiction of the Serbian Orthodox Church to become respectively the Eparchy of Mukačevo and the Czechoslovak Exarchate of the Russian Orthodox Moscow Patriarchate. Finally, in 1951, the Orthodox in Eastern Slovakia organized into the Eparchies of Prešov and of Michalovce, became part of a distinct Czechoslovak Autocephalous Orthodox Church, retaining since then close ties with the mother church in Moscow. See Pavel Aleš, "Cesty k autokefalite," in *Pravoslávny tsirkevný kalendár 1981* (Bratislava, 1980), pp. 79–86; and Andrew Sorokowski, "Ukrainian Catholics and Orthodox in Czechoslovakia," *Religion in Communist Lands* 15, no. 1 (1987): 59–60.

30. For the Greek Catholic view of these events, see Pekar, *Narysy,* pp. 170–176; Lacko, "The Forced Liquidation," pt. 2: "Liquidation of the Diocese of Prešov," pp. 158–185; and Julius Kubinyi, *The History of the Prjašiv Eparchy* (Rome, 1970), pp. 169–178. For the local Orthodox view, see Aleš, "Cesty," p. 84 and Iliya Kačur, *Stručný prehľad historie pravoslavnej cirkvi v byvalom Uhorsku a v Československu* (Prešov, n.d.), pp. 166–171. For the Czechoslovak Marxist view, see Ivan Bajcura, *Ukrajinská otázka v ČSSR* (Košice, 1967), pp. 128–132.

31. In neighboring Romania, the union was abolished and the Greek Catholic faithful absorbed into the Romanian Orthodox Church in October 1948, while in Yugoslavia, which had broken with the Soviet bloc in 1948, the Greek Catholic Diocese of Križevci (which included Rusyn communities originally from south of the Carpathians as well as local Croats and Ukrainian immigrants and their descendants from Galicia) continued to function.

32. By 1977, large concentrations of Greek Catholics were identified in the 156 Roman Catholic parishes, including sixteen located in the Tarnow and Przemyśl Roman Catholic dioceses, which cover the Lemko region. See Bociurkiw, "The Suppression," pp. 107 and 118, n. 57.

33. Kwilecki, "Fragment najnowszej historii," pp. 287–288; and idem, *Lemkowie*, pp. 198–200.

34. The Orthodox understanding is that the eparchy in 1983 is a restoration of what ceased to exist in 1691. Mykola Syvits'kyi "Vidrodzhennia peremys'koï ieparkhiï," *Tserkovnyi kalendar na 1985 rik* (Sanik, 1984), pp. 165–169.

35. Archbishop Marusyn's visitations took place in 1984, 1985, 1986, and 1987, and some included the Lemko region. An important indication of support for Poland's Greek Catholics occurred during the last visit of Pope John Paul II to Poland (June 1987), when he attended mass at the Basilian Greek Catholic Church in Warsaw.

36. See the statistics in the first Greek Catholic Church almanac published in Poland since before World War II, *Hreko-Katolyts'kyi tserkovnyi kalendar 1987* (Warsaw, 1987), pp. 74–78.

37. The texts of the resolution of Greek Catholic clergy requesting the legal reconstitution of their church, dated 10 April 1968, and of the Czechoslovak governmental decree, signed by then vice-prime minister (and later president) Gustav Husák, approving the restoration and dated 13 June 1968, appeared in *Kalendar Gréskokatolíkov 1969* (Trnava, 1968), pp. 46–50. An English translation of the governmental decree is found in Michael Lacko, "The Re-establishment of the Greek Catholic Church in Czechoslovakia," *Slovak Studies* 9; *Historica*, no. 8 (1971): 164–165.

38. Ibid., pp. 166–171.

39. For the Orthodox view of the Prague Spring, including opposition to restoration of the Greek Catholic Church, aided by the arrival in Czechoslovakia during early 1968 of "107 church figures—Vatican agents who were wolves in sheep's clothing," see the articles by the Orthodox Rusyn lay activist in Prague, Ivan S. Shlepets'kyi, sent by him in 1968 to the Prešov Ukrainian newspaper, *Nove zhyttia*, but published only in the West: "Komu potrebna unyia s Rymom na Priashevshchyni?" *Karpatorusskyi kalendar Lemko-Soiuza na hod 1970* (Yonkers, N.Y., 1970), pp. 77–80 and "V spravakh demokratyzatsyy Priashevshchyny," *Karpatorusskyi kalendar Lemko-Soiuza na hod 1969* (Yonkers, N.Y., 1970), pp. 35–59.

40. For details, see Lacko, "The Re-establishment," pp. 164–165; and Athanasius B. Pekar, "Restoration of the Greek Catholic Church in Czechoslovakia," *Ukrainian Quarterly* 29, no. 3 (1973): 284–288; and the rejection of the such accusations by the Orthodox in their official organ, *Zapovit sv. Kyryla i Mefodiia*, vol. 11, nos. 5, 6, 7 (Prešov, 1968).

41. By the second half of the 1970s, Greek Catholic laymen in the western regions of the Ukrainian S.S.R. led by Josyf Terelia of the Transcarpathian oblast were at great personal risk (often resulting in imprisonment and exile) openly sending official requests to the Soviet government, the United Nations, and the governments of Western countries, requesting the restitution of the Greek Catholic Church in the Soviet Union. Subsequently, in the era of Gorbachev's *glasnost'*, the underground Greek Catholic hierarchy has revealed itself publicly, holding an increasing number of liturgies and ordaining new priests, including even several from the Ukrainian emigration in the West. At present, discussions are underway between the Vatican, the Soviet authorities, and the Russian Orthodox Church about full legalization for

the Greek Catholic Church in the Soviet Union, although the precise jurisdictional format of a renewed church is still to be determined. See *Martyrolohiia,* pp. 531–589 and 651–665; and the monthly newsletter, *Church of the Catacombs/Ukrainian Press Service* (St. Catherine's, Ont., 1986–present).

42. In an atmosphere of political discussion that has prevailed since 1980 in Poland during and even after the rise and fall of the Solidarity movement, the question of the Lemkos has been revived once again. The issue concerns whether they should be considered Ukrainians (as they have been officially designated by the Polish government since 1945) or a distinct Lemko Rusyn nationality with the right to their own organizations. So far, it seems that this debate (carried on among Lemkos and among interested Poles and Ukrainians) has been the concern of the secular intelligentsia, without any particular role being played by either the Greek Catholic or the Orthodox Church. For details, see the series of articles in the *Carpatho-Rusyn American* 10, nos. 1, 2, 3, 4; and 11, no. 1 (1987–88).

43. The following discussion is based largely on Maču, "National Assimilation." See also Magocsi, *Rusyn-Ukrainians,* pp. 49–55; Bajcura, *Ukrajinská otázka,* pp. 132–134 and 149–160; and Pavel Uram, "K niektorým otázkam vývoja ukrajinského školstva v ČSR v rokoch 1945–1960," *Zbornik prac učitel'ov UML UPJS* 5 (1978): 243–252.

44. Maču, "National Assimilation," pp. 104, 129–130.

45. Based on the relatively reliable statistics of 1930, and taking into consideration natural increases and post-World War II emigration, there should have been approximately 130,000 Rusyns in Slovakia in 1968. See Magocsi, *Rusyn-Ukrainians,* p. 64, n. 91.

46. See the interview with the leading activists, the Canadian industrialist, Stephen B. Roman, and then auxiliary Greek Catholic Bishop of Toronto, Michael Rusnak, in Benedykt Heydenkorn, "Rozmowy z biskupem Rusnakiem i St. Romanem," *Kultura* 1/2 [256/257] (1969): 148–153.

47. For opposing interpretations of Hopko's fate in 1968–1969, see the Slovak view by Lacko, "The Re-establishment," p. 174; and the Rusyn/Ukrainian views by A. Pekar, *Bishop Basil Hopko, S.T.D., Confessor of the Faith* (Pittsburgh, Pa., 1979), pp. 15–30, idem, "Restoration," pp. 288–296; and anon., *Tragedy of the Greek Catholic Church in Czechoslovakia* (New York, 1971), pp. 25–66.

48. The figure for the number of Rusyn Greek Catholic parishes was provided to me during an interview in Prešov (June 1988) with administrator Hirka, who based his calculations on data from the *Schematizmus slovenskych katolíckych diecéz* (Trnava and Bratislava, 1978), pp. 417–456. According to the administrator, the reason for increasing Slovakization is that he is unable to find priests who are able or willing to speak in Rusyn.

49. In an interview with me (August 1989), the administrator Hirka blamed the decline in the printing of *Blahovistnyk* on its editor, the Reverend Stepan Pap, who dropped the sections written in Rusyn dialect and transformed the monthly into a Ukrainian publication which, according to Hirka, readers did not want. Also according to Hirka, Pap's Ukrainian-language *Bibliinyi katykhyzm dlia hrekokatolykiv* (Trnava and Bratislava, 1982) and *Taina pokaiannia: iak spovidatysia* (Trnava and Bratislava, 1984) simply sat in storage gathering dust because of a lack of reader

demand. The Reverend Pap (who has died since) told me in August 1989 that as former editor he was not allowed to publish in Rusyn because government-owned printing shops refused to print works in an "unofficial" language.

50. Bishop Hirka stated in 1988 that he had commissioned several Rusyn-language religious books (in the Latin alphabet) that were slated for publication in early 1989. They have still not appeared. The priests and laypersons who have prepared their own Rusyn texts (in the Cyrillic alphabet) say that the bishop refuses to grant them the required episcopal imprimatur in order that they be printed and used in services. See the discussion of these matters in "The Revolution of 1989," *Carpatho-Rusyn American* 12, no. 4 (1989): 7-8; "Revolution of 1989 Update," *Carpatho-Rusyn American* 13, no. 2 (1990) 4-7; and the interview with Bishop Hirka on the eve of his installation and entitled: "Ia liubliu rusyniv," *Nove zhyttia* (Prešov), 16 February 1990, p. 5.

51. The statistical data is drawn from the *Pravoslávny cirkevný kalendár 1981* (Bratislava, 1980), pp. 57-61. While it is true that most Orthodox parishes use only Church Slavonic in the liturgy and Rusyn dialect (often heavily mixed with Church Slavonicisms) for homilies, Orthodox publications (including the monthly *Zapovit Kyrila i Mefodiia,* annual almanacs, and its first catechism, *Cesta k Bohu* (Bratislava, 1984) are now primarily or exclusively in Slovak.

PART II
Church Slavic and the Medieval Literary Tradition

([Church] Slavonic) Writing in Kievan Rus'

DEAN S. WORTH

1. Introduction

The importance of the Christianization and Byzantinization of Kievan Rus', as the first great "macroevent" of East Slavic cultural history, is obvious.[1] Nevertheless, it is important not to take Christianization as the only decisive factor in the development of medieval Russian cultural life. Specifically, this is true of early language history and the developments that would lead to the creation of the so-called Russian literary language.[2]

Received opinion has it that literacy came to the Eastern Slavs with the introduction of Christianity and that for centuries thereafter the written culture of Rus' was recorded in Russian Church Slavonic, that is, in a language the primary function of which was ecclesiastic ("Church") and the form of which was a Russified variant of the South Slavic written language known as Old Church Slavonic ("Russian . . . Slavonic"). Scholars tend to operate with the conceptual and terminological equation "written" = "Slavonic" = "religious," as opposed to and hermetically sealed from its triadic opposite, the "spoken" = "East Slavic" = "secular" native East Slavic vernacular.[3] This, it seems to me, is an oversimplification and an exaggeration of the role of the Church, and of Church Slavonic, in the development of East Slavic verbal culture as we know it from the preserved texts.

In what follows I shall approach this topic from a somewhat different perspective. Without denying the obviously fundamental importance of Christianization for East Slavic cultural history in general, I shall argue that, in the specific area of verbal culture, Christianization was by no means the only, and perhaps not even the prime, motivating force. My argument, offered here in a preliminary version, has several components: (1) what was introduced into Kievan Rus' was not an ecclesiastic writing system that could, marginally, be used for other purposes as well, but primarily a writing system that served several purposes, only one of which was propagation of the faith—that is, "writing" cannot be equated with "Church"; (2) not all culturally significant writing, and not even all religious writing, was in Slavonic, but much was, instead, written either in the vernacular or, importantly, in a language unmarked by features that would qualify it as either Slavonic or vernacular—that is, "writing" cannot be equated with "Slavonic"; (3) Slavonic writing was not all religious, but was used for a variety of secular purposes, and in such "mixed genres" as the chronicles—that is, "Slavonic" cannot be equated with "Church"; (4) the very variety and complexity of the sociolinguistic situation in Kievan Rus' is what made further development possible. Had the opposition of "high" and "low" language variants been as absolute as asserted in the theory of diglossia,[4] it is hard to imagine how the attested interpenetration of Slavonic and vernacular elements could have occurred, for example in Russian legal texts,[5] and even more prominently in such linguistically heterogeneous works as the chronicles,[6] the *Molenie Daniila Zatochnika*,[7] and such later hybrid works as Kotoshikhin's *O Rossii* . . .[8] or ambassadorial reports from the sixteenth and seventeenth centuries.[9]

2. Written and Spoken Language in Rus'

Before examining the pseudo-equation "written" = "Slavonic" = "religious" more closely, it seems appropriate to dwell briefly on the opposition of written to spoken language.

The opposition of written to oral language is generally self-evident, provided one takes the two terms literally. "Written" refers to the surviving texts in the broad sense (including epigraphic material), regardless of content and style; this material is, by and large, rather well studied. "Oral" refers to the spoken language of various segments of the medieval Russian population; in the framework of our present topic, we know next to nothing about this material and can at best work only by inference. It is important not to assume that the "spoken" material in our written sources (for example, the princely speeches in the chronicles or the *Igor Tale*) is related in any statable fashion to the way people actually spoke in Kievan Rus', all the more so since the distinction between direct and indirect speech is often unclear in Old Russian.[10] Recent studies by Zemskaia and her colleagues provide striking evidence of the difference between official (e.g., literary) recordings of spoken Russian and the way highly educated Russian intellectuals actually talk.[11] There is no reason to assume the situation was any different nine hundred years ago.

It would be equally naïve to equate non-Slavonic secular texts with the spoken language of that period, as is often done in the case of the *Russkaia Pravda* and the Novgorod birchbark letters. The *Russkaia Pravda*—even aside from the fact that the oldest copy (in the 1282 Novgorod *Kormchaia*) is a quarter millennium younger than the presumed first written text of Iaroslav's time—was, even in the eleventh century, almost certainly an archaic and highly stylized language intended for easy memorization and oral transmission. Furthermore, typology tells us that legal language is usually both archaic and arcane, serving not only to codify and transmit the legal code, but also to ensure the livelihood of its interpreters. Why should the *Russkaia Pravda* have been an exception? (Indeed, this—and not merely our own ignorance of Russian—may explain the oft-noted difficulty of assigning unambiguous readings to some of the *Russkaia Pravda*'s syntax.)[12] The birchbark letters, as recent studies have shown,[13] are more coherently organized by epistolary conventions than was previously recognized, and even to the extent they are not so organized, there is no reason to assume that they are any more a direct reflection of the spoken language than are our own scribbled notes or telegrams.

None of the above is to deny the obvious fact that some varieties of text were closer and others more distant from spoken Russian, which itself, conversely, must have existed in more or less "literary," sc., "written" variants. What is claimed here is simply that the border between the categories written vs. spoken, as filtered through the preserved texts, is far too indistinct to serve as a classificatory principle and cannot reasonably be equated with the distinctions between religious and secular works and between Slavonic and East Slavic linguistic features.

3. Written Language and Religious Function

The oversimplified equation of written texts with religious function is probably due to the term *tserkovnoslavianskii iazyk* itself. This label first appeared in the work of Nadezhdin and Maksimovich in the 1830s.[14] It is no coincidence that the term appeared only after the Russian literary language had become firmly established and the meaning of "Slavonic" had been restricted to only those elements of Old Russian or Middle Russian Slavonic that had *not* been incorporated into the new standard language. In other words, the term "Church Slavonic" came into being at a time when it made sense, when Slavonic had become the language of the Church and only of the Church. This was not at all the situation in previous centuries.

The earliest writing among the Eastern Slavs was not even Slavonic, much less religious in purpose. Two uses are attested. First, Cyrillic letters are used to identify a tenth-century amphora from the Gnezdovo excavation site as a container for oil, for peas, or as belonging to a certain Gorun, depending on the interpretation one accepts.¹⁵ Second, the Novgorod excavations have uncovered wooden merchandise-sack seals inscribed with owners' or destinaries' names and records of the sacks' contents.¹⁶ There are also early inscribed coins, but these are of little value for a discussion of East Slavic literacy.¹⁷ Of greater cultural importance are the early treaties between Rus' and Byzantium (912, 945). These are written in a language which shows Church Slavonic (genetically, South Slavic) features alongside vernacular forms, e.g. полоняникъ обою страну держим есть . . . и возвратять искупное лице во свою сторону (911), да входять в городъ . . . входяще же Русь в градъ (945).¹⁸ These and similar passages, assuming the preserved copies are an accurate rendition of the original (from the 912 treaty to the 1377 Laurentian Ms. is, after all, 465 years!), show Slavonic and vernacular forms more or less in free alternation, and one can probably assume that the South or East Slavic orientation was irrelevant to the purpose at hand. In any case, the two treaties demonstrate, as did the epigraphic material adduced above, that early East Slavic writing was not necessarily connected with the propagation of Christianity or its rituals. One can only agree with B. A. Uspensky that the existence of pre-Christianization treaties with Byzantium and of *veritel'nye gramoty* from the mid-tenth century shows that "Church Slavonic [may] not yet [have been] connected exclusively with Christian culture [and] did not form part of the antithesis sacral/secular, as was to become the case later, but simply fulfilled the function of a written language, that is, of the language used in the written recording (*pis'mennaia fiksatsiia*) of a text." Uspensky, however, considers this written-record function to be only an occasional, pre-Christianization phenomenon, whereas in general "the tradition of writing arises in Rus' after the Christianization."¹⁹ The somewhat different point of view espoused here is that the language of written documentation (Slavonic and vernacular) arose in response to various economic and social situations, only one of which—albeit an important one—was the introduction of the Christian faith.

Writing in ancient Rus' was not in and of itself a religious activity, but was available for any purpose, secular or ecclesiastic. When Iaroslav decided to have the traditional oral legal code set down in writing in mid-eleventh century, there was a ready-made writing system in place, one that could codify on parchment the archaic formulae of the inherited oral law just as easily as it did the rhetorical devices of Hilarion's newly nationalist sermon. Similarly, when members and servants of the wealthier classes learned to read and write in Novgorod, they did not hesitate to use the same alphabet that they found in their Gospel lectionaries for recording who owed whom how many *kuny* or for asking their wives to send them a horse. In short, writing very soon entered the public domain, where it was available for profane as well as sacred purposes.

We have seen that writing was introduced in Kievan Rus' prior to, and developed independently of, Christianization. Further evidence of this independent development can be found in the organization of yearly entries in the *Primary Chronicle*. Although the annual dating of the older parts of the *Chronicle* is well known to be a secondary temporal grid imposed on preexistent written material, the extent to which written records were kept in the chanceries of the early princes is reflected in the presence or absence of regular annual entries in the *Chronicle,* as shown in Table 1. Entries for the first hundred and ten years are scattered haphazardly across the time axis, with small entry clusters following the 911 expedition and treaty and Igor's Byzantine campaign in 941. More or less systematic recording begins with Sviatoslav's adult reign in 964, but is not kept up by Iaropolk (972–979). Volodimir's chancery keeps yearly records approximately until—interestingly—the official Christianization, after which record-keeping again becomes spotty. Only with the advent of Iaroslav the Wise in 1016 does the princely chancery consistently keeps annual records. We can conclude that regular record-keeping began in the mid-tenth century, i.e., well before the official Christianization, and was regularized as a bureaucratic institution only in the early eleventh century, a generation thereafter. Christianization itself appears to have nothing to do with the regularization of this form of writing.

4. Non-Slavonic Writing in Rus'

It is clear from this evidence in §3 that several types of documentation in Kievan Rus' were written not in Slavonic but either in some form of stylized vernacular (*Russkaia Pravda,* birchbark letters, various epigraphic material) or in a mixed language with both Slavonic and vernacular features (the treaties with Byzantium). The inaccuracy of the equation "written" = "Slavonic" has been established and need not be re-argued here. Instead, I wish to examine more closely than is usual the actual linguistic facts that lie behind the distinction of "Slavonic" and "vernacular."

The distinction between "(Church) Slavonic" and vernacular writing is usually taken as a binary opposition between two identifiable kinds of text. This is, however, an oversimplification, apparently resulting from failure to examine the actual linguistic evidence for the distinction. This evidence is so obvious that one is surprised that it has not yet been exploited. There are,

Table 1. Annual Entries in the Primary Chronicle
("+" = entry exists for given year)

852+	891	930	968+	1005	1043+	1082+
853	892	931	969+	1006	1044+	1083+
854	893	932	970+	1007+	1045+	1084+
855	894	933	971+	1008	1046	1085+
856	895	934+	b——b	1009	1047+	1086+
857	896	935	972+	1010	1048	1087
858+	897	936	973+	1011+	1049	1088+
859+	898+	937	974	1012	1050+	1089+
860	899	938	975+	1013	1051+	1090
861	900	939	976	1014+	1052+	1091+
862+	901	940	977+	1015+	1053+	1092+
863	902+	941+	978	d——d	1054+	1093+
864	903+	942	979	1016+	1055	1094+
865	904	943+	c——c	1017+	1056	1095+
866+	905	944+	980+	1018+	1057+	1096+
867	906	945+	981+	1019+	1058+	1097+
868+	907+	946+	982+	1020+	1059+	1098+
869+	908	947	983+	1021+	1060+	1099+
870	909	948	984+	1022+	1061+	1100+
871	910	949	985+	1023+	1062	1101+
872	911+	950	986+	1024+	1063+	1102+
873	912+	951	987+	1025	1064+	1103+
874	913+	952	988+	1026+	1065+	1104+
875	914+	953	989+	1027+	1066+	1105+
876	915+	954	990	1028+	1067+	1106+
877	916	955+	991+	1029+	1068+	1107+
878	917	956	992+	1030+	1069+	1108+
879+	918	957	993	1031+	1070+	1109+
880	919	958	994	1032+	1071+	1110+
881	920+	959	995	1033+	1072+	1111+
882+	921	960	996+	1034	1073+	1112+
883+	922	961	997+	1035	1074+	1113+
884+	923	962	998	1036+	1075+	1114+
885+	924	963	999	1037+	1076+	1115+
886	925	a——a	1000	1038+	1077+	1116+
887+	926	964+	1001+	1039+	1078+	1117+
888	927	965+	1002	1040+	1079+	
889	928	966+	1003+	1041+	1080+	
890	929+	967+	1004	1042+	1081+	

a——a beginning of Sviatoslav's adult reign
b——b death of Sviatoslav
c——c beginning of Volodimir's reign
d——d beginning of Iaroslav's reign

in fact, not two but four kinds of relevant linguistic artifacts. A single word, or an entire text, must fall into one of not two, but four categories: (1) it contains one or more identifiable Slavonic features, and no identifiable vernacular features, e.g., градъ, освѣщение; (2) it contains one or more identifiable vernacular features and no identifiable Slavonic features, e.g., городъ, свѣча; (3) it contains no identifiable Slavonic or vernacular features, e.g., рука, богъ; (4) it contains both Slavonic and vernacular features, e.g., прѣдьрьжащии, ограженис.[20] In markedness, such words fall into one of the four categories shown in Table 2.

Table 2. Markedness of Slavonic and Vernacular Features

	Slavonic	Vernacular
рука, богъ	–	–
градъ, освѣщение	+	–
городъ, свѣча	–	+
прѣдьрьжащии, ограженис	+	+

Texts of varying lengths can (indeed, must) equally well be divided into these same four categories, although it is obvious that the longer the text, the more likely is it to contain both Slavonic and vernacular elements, if only in the form of scribal errors; some quantitative measure must be added to the feature distinctions.

The characterization of complete texts in terms of +/– Slavonic and +/– vernacular will obviously require much further refinement and will be the subject of a separate study. If the first scribe of the "Life of Feodosii" in the *Uspenskii Sbornik* not only uses the regular Russian Church Slavonic *ž* reflex of **dj* but also lets an occasional pleophonic form slip into his text (и бѣ самъ съ братиею дѣла|я и городя дворъ манасты|рьскыи и се же разграже|ну бывъшю манастырю [48b.18–21]), we would still want to characterize his text as Slavonic with occasional lapses. When the second scribe, however, consistently writes **tьrt* and **tьrt* groups with second pleophony (привезо|ша .г. возы пълъны | суще кърьчагъ съ винъмь, ихъ же посъла же|на нѣкая, иже бѣ прѣ|дьрьжаща вься въ дому [51v.10–14]), we would have to call this a predominantly Slavonic but nonetheless hybrid text. Such complexities go far beyond the framework of this paper, but we can attempt at least a preliminary taxonomy.

A text that contains only marked Slavonic, but no marked vernacular forms (i.e., a text containing only +S/–V and –S/–V forms) is to be considered "Slavonic" (for example, the Gospel texts). Conversely, texts containing only –S/+V and –S/–V forms are "vernacular" texts (for example, the *Russkaia Pravda*). In this sense, "Slavonic" texts are not only not vernacular but also "anti-vernacular" (all their forms are –V): vernacular texts are not only not Slavonic but also "anti-Slavonic" (all their forms being –S). Texts containing any combination of +S/–V, –S/+V and +S/+V, with or without –S/–V forms, are "mixed" texts, since they contain forms marked both as Slavonic and as vernacular (both the *Uspenskii Sbornik* and the *Primary Chronicle* illustrate this category, the vital difference between them being due to the different frequency and distribution of the various formal classes). If they exist (and they would have to be brief), texts containing only –S/–V forms could be termed "neutral" texts. Mixed and neutral texts are neither Slavonic nor vernacular; they are "non-Slavonic" without being "anti-Slavonic" and "non-vernacular" without being "anti-vernacular." As time passes, an increasing proportion of Old and Middle Russian texts fall into the mixed category.

5. Non-Religious Slavonic Writing

The third of the pseudo-equations with which we began is that of "Slavonic" and "Church," the term "Church Slavonic" itself implying that identifiably Slavonic texts are compatible only (or primarily) with religious functions. The equation of "Slavonic" with "religious" inheres in the terminology itself (*tserkovno*slavianskii, slavon *d'église, Kirchen*slavisch, *Church* Slavonic), but confuses form with function. On the one hand, "Slavonic" is a formal linguistic term referring to (1) a well-known set of phonological and morphological features distinguishing South from East Slavic (SSl *grad*, **tj* → *št* : ESl *gorod*, **tj* → *č*, etc.) and (2) a set of syntactic and lexical features derived from Greek and distinguishing Slavonic from any vernacular (of the Saloniki suburbs in 860 or the Kiev court in 988). "Church," on the other hand, is a sociolinguistic term that defines the social function of some given text in terms of the speech situation or some system of genres.

Overall, it seems clear that even if we define "Slavonic" narrowly, as in §4 above (that is, containing only markedly Slavonic +S/–V and neutral –S/–V forms), the functional range of such written texts extends far beyond the religious sphere. Here, for example, is a brief passage from Flavius Josephus's "Jewish War" in Old Russian translation:

Римляне же[,] мятежником бѣжавшим къ граду и цьркъви горящи и всѣм окрьстным мѣстомъ, и вознесше истуканная своя и поставиша во цьркъви противу въсточным вратом, и пожроша имъ ту. И Тита прославиша великыми похвалами, и нарекоша и самодержца. И воини же вси исполнишася богатства плѣнением и въсхыщением, яко въ Асуриистѣи земли плѣняшеся злато[21]

Here, a passage from the *Izbornik* of 1076 (Xenofont speaking):

Не прѣзьрѣхъ ништиих, ни оставихъ страньна, и печальна не прѣзьрѣхъ никъгда же, и иже въ тьмьницахъ заклжчении, потрѣбьная имъ даяхъ.[22]

Here, a few lines from the *Aleksandriia*:

ставшема ся ѡбѣма странама на браннѣмь състоупѣ, не вдас[т] Александръ ни единому плъкоу пристоупити к нимъ ... и быс[т] брань велика междоу ими, и бьющеса гонаху, ѡво на сю страну, ѡвѡ же на ѡноу, ѡбои же оубо побѣждающеса расхождаахоу[.][23]

Here, a seduction scene from the *Kiev Caves Paterikon*:

Яко се власть пріимши на немь, и повелѣваеть ему причтатися себе, и раздрѣшивши же его от узъ и въ многоцѣнныя ризы его облъкъши и сладкыми брашны того кормяще, и нужденіем любовным того уобьемлющи, на свою похоть нудящи.[24]

One could continue in this vein almost indefinitely, but the point is already clear: Slavonic was not only the language of the Church, but the language of writing things down in general. In a word, Slavonic from the very beginning was, *pace* Issatschenko, *polyfunctional*.[25]

In the diglossic framework, one would expect the *iazykovoi kollektiv* to accept Slavonic and Russian as varieties of a single language, whereas the twentieth-century linguist would recognize them as two separate, albeit genetically related languages. The problem with this distinction is that one twentieth-century linguist (e.g., Uspensky), may hold this view, whereas another, (e.g., Lunt), may not.

A concomitant of Slavonic polyfunctionalism was that Slavonic itself could easily become internally differentiated. To an extent, this had been true from the very beginning of Slavic writing: the simple narrative texts of the New Testament Gospels were broadly and easily accessible to the masses they were intended to help convert, whereas the theological treatises of the Church fathers were available only to those who had studied such matters, and probably only to those with an active command of Greek.[26]

Slavonic polyfunctionalism, combined with the fact that one and the same writing system was used for more and less prestigious secular, as well as for religious works, facilitated the intermingling of genetically South Slavic and genetically East Slavic forms in a variety of genres. In more traditional terms, this is the interpenetration of Church Slavonic and vernacular elements that—regardless of which of the two is taken as primary and which secondary, i.e., regardless of whether one adopts the Shakhmatov or the Obnorsky view—eventually resulted in the amalgam called standard literary Russian. Had Slavonic been not polyfunctional, but restricted to more narrowly religious texts, the authority of the Church, seeing the written word as the divine message, could not easily have tolerated the mutual accommodation of what would have had to be viewed as mutually incompatible linguistic elements.

6. Conclusion

We have argued against the widespread assumption that Christianization was the major motivating force in the development of verbal culture in Kievan Rus'. Instead, we have proposed that it was the introduction of a writing system itself, used for a variety of secular as well as religious purposes, that brought this culture into being. *Writing itself was polyfunctional* and was not necessarily either sacral in purpose or Slavonic in form. Furthermore, Slavonic itself was not restricted to a religious function, that is, *Slavonic was itself polyfunctional,* albeit across a narrower range of functions than writing in general. To assert this is not to deny the importance of sacral writing in the prehistory of the Russian literary language, but merely to restrict such writing to its proper place as one of several factors in the creation and evolution of Russian verbal culture.

Notes

1. D. S. Worth, "Towards a Social History of Russian," in Henrik Birnbaum and Michael S. Flier, eds., *Medieval Russian Culture,* California Slavic Studies, vol. 12 (Berkeley, Los Angeles, London, 1984), pp. 227–246, esp. 238 ff. In this view, subsequent macroevents were secularization and Europeanization in the seventeenth–eighteenth centuries and technicalization and internationalization in our own time.

2. "So-called," because no one has yet defined this term such that it would be equally applicable to the medieval and modern periods. The only specific definition known to me is that of A. V. Isachenko, "Kakova spetsifika literaturnogo dvuiazychiia v istorii slavianskikh iazykov?" *Voprosy iazykoznaniia,* 1958, no. 3:42: a literary language must be (1) normalized, (2) stylistically differentiated, (3) polyvalent (i.e., applicable to various sociolinguistic functions), and (4) obligatory for all members of the given *socium.* Symptomatic of the near-universal inattention to this fundamen-

tal definitional necessity is the first chapter (pp. 3-25) of the late F. P. Filin's last book, *Istoki i sud'by russkogo literaturnogo iazyka* (Moscow, 1981), where the term "russkii literaturnyi iazyk" is used over sixty times without once being defined.

3. On the problems of such dichotomic oppositions, see Worth, "Towards a Social History," 231 ff.

4. Most thoroughly and convincingly expounded by B. A. Uspenskii, *Iazykovaia situatsiia Kievskoi Rusi i ee znachenie dlia istorii russkogo literaturnogo iazyka* (Moscow, 1983), and *Istoriia russkogo literaturnogo iazyka (XI–XVII vv.)* [= *Sagners slavistische Sammlung*, vol. 12] (Munich, 1987). See also Gerta Hüttl-Folter, "Diglossiia v drevnei Rusi," *Wiener slavistisches Jahrbuch* 24 (1978): 108–123; K.-D. Seeman, "Diglossie und gemischtsprachige Texte im Kiever Rußland," *Festschrift für Herbert Bräuer zum 65 Geburtstag am 14. April 1986*, ed. R. Olesch and H. Rothe (Cologne and Vienna, 1986), 515–526; A. A. Gippius, A. B. Strakhov, O. B. Strakhova, "Teoriia tserkovnoslaviansko-russkoi diglossii i ee kritiki," *Vestnik moskovskogo universiteta, Filologiia*, 1988, no. 5: 34–49. Reservations have been expressed by D. S. Worth, "On 'diglossia' in Medieval Russia," *Die Welt der Slaven*, 23 (1978): 371–393, Horace G. Lunt, "The Language of Rus' in the Eleventh Century: Some Observations about Facts and Theories," to appear in the proceedings of the Ravenna Conference, and A. A. Alekseev, "Pochemu v Drevnei Rusi ne bylo diglossii," *Problemy istoricheskogo iazykoznaniia*, no. 3, *Literaturnyi iazyk Drevnei Rusi* (Leningrad, 1986), pp. 3–11. Other anti-diglossia articles in this same collection, by Klimenko, Kolesov, and Rusinova, are concerned more with political patriotism than with scholarship and can be ignored here.

5. D. S. Vort [Worth], "O iazyke russkogo prava," *Voprosy iazykoznaniia*, 1975, no. 2: 68–75.

6. Gerta Hüttl-Folter, *Die trat/torot Lexeme in den altrussischen Chroniken* (Vienna, 1983).

7. K. F. Taranovskii, "Formy obshcheslavianskogo i tserkovnoslavianskogo stikha v drevnerusskoi literature XI–XIII vv.," *American Contributions to the Sixth International Congress of Slavists, Prague, 7–13 August 1968*, vol. 1: Linguistic Contributions, ed. H. Kuchera (The Hague, 1968), pp. 377–394.

8. A. E. Pennington, *Grigorii Kotoshikhin, O Rossii v tsarstvovanie Alekseia Mikhailovicha. Text and commentary* (Oxford, 1980).

9. D. S. Worth, "Slavonisms in Russian Diplomatic Reports, 1567–1667," *Slavica Hierosolymitana* 2 (1978): 3–12.

10. D. S. Worth "Vernacular and Slavonic in Kievan Rus'," *The Formation of the Slavonic Literary Languages: Proceedings of a Conference in Memory of Robert Auty and Anne Pennington at Oxford, 6–11 July 1981*, UCLA Slavic Studies, vol. 11 (Columbus, 1985), pp. 233–241.

11. E. A. Zemskaia et al., *Russkaia razgovornaia rech'. Obshchie voprosy. Slovoobrazovanie. Sintaksis* (Moscow, 1981); idem, *Russkaia razgovornaia rech'. Teksty* (Moscow, 1978).

12. A. V. Issatschenko, *Geschichte der russischen Sprache. 1 Band. Von den Anfängen bis zum Ende des 17. Jahrhunderts* (Heidelberg, 1980), pp. 112–115.

13. A. A. Zalizniak, "Novgorodskie berestianye gramoty s lingvisticheskoi tochki zreniia," in V. L. Ianin, and A. A. Zalizniak, *Novgorodskie gramoty na bereste (iz raskopok 1977–1983 gg.)* (Moscow, 1986), pp. 89–219; idem, "O iazykovoi situatsii v drevnem Novgorode," *Russian Linguistics* 11 (1987): 115–132; D. S. Worth, "Incipits in the Novgorod Birchbark Letters," *Semiosis: Semiotics and the History of Culture: In Honorem Georgii Lotman* (Ann Arbor, 1983), pp. 320–332; idem, "Mirror Reversals in Novgorod Paleography," *Language and Literary Theory. In Honor of Ladislav Matejka*, [= *University of Michigan Papers in Slavic Philology*, no. 5] (Ann Arbor, 1985): 215–22-2.

14. A.I. Gorshkov, "Otechestvennye filologi o staroslavianskom i drevnerusskom literaturnom iazyke," in L. P. Zhukovskaia, ed., *Drevnerusskii literaturnyi iazyk v ego otnoshenii k staroslavianskomu* (Moscow, 1987), p. 8.

15. Various interpretations of this inscription are neatly summarized by Horace G. Lunt, "The language of Rus' in the Eleventh Century . . ."; see also B. A. Uspenskii, *Istoriia russkogo literaturnogo iazyka*, p. 24.

16. A. A. Medyntseva, "Novgorodskie nakhodki i dokhristianskaia pis'mennost' na Rusi," *Sovetskaia arkheologiia*, 1983, no. 4: 49–61; V. L. Ianin, "Nadpisi na dereviannykh 'schetnykh' birkakh," in V. L. Ianin, and A. A. Zalizniak, pp. 81–86.

17. Lunt, *op. cit.*

18. V. P. Adrianova–Peretts, ed., *Povest' vremennykh let* (Moscow and Leningrad, 1950), 1:28, 36.

19. B. A. Uspenskii, *Istoriia russkogo literaturnogo iazyka*, p. 25.

20. What is characterized as Slavonic and what as vernacular will obviously depend on the time period and manuscript type one deals with. An East Slavic feature like the third person ending *-tь* is characteristic of Russian Church Slavonic manuscripts from the very beginning, whereas the **dj* reflex *žd* is diagnostically Slavonic, i.e., opposed to *ž*, only from the fifteenth century.

21. N. A. Meshcherskii, ed., *Istoriia iudeiskoi voiny Iosifa Flaviia v drevnerusskom perevode* (Moscow and Leningrad, 1958), p. 422 (folio 699v). In this text, **tьrt* and **tьrt* groups are not diagnostic for the Slavonic : vernacular opposition but are an accepted feature of Russian Slavonic.

22. *Izbornik 1076 goda*, ed. V. S. Golyshenko et al. (Moscow, 1963), p. 476 (folio 109v).

23. Cited from S. P. Obnorskii, S. G. Barkhudarov, *Khrestomatiia po istorii russkogo iazyka*, vol. 1 (Moscow, 1952), p. 176.

24. *Das Paterikon des Kiever Höhlenklosters*, nach der Ausgabe von D. Abramovič neu herausgegeben von Dmitrij Tschiževskij (Munich, 1964), p. 143.

25. "Im Gegensatz zur 'Polyvalenz' des Kirchenslavischen bei den Südslaven, die zur Bildung einer wirklichen Schriftsprache bei Bulgaren und Serben im Mittelalter geführt hat, blieb das Kirchenslavische bei den Ostslaven im wesentlichen

auf den sakralen Bereich beschränkt." (A. V. Issatschenko, *Geschichte der russischen Sprache* . . . , 1:73). Note that this view of Slavonic as polyfunctional does not necessarily imply the view that Slavonic and Russian were either two separate languages (Shakhmatov, Obnorsky, Unbegaun, Uspensky, Shevelov) or a single one (Vinogradov, Lunt, most Soviet scholars). The solution to this argument hinges on the psycholinguistic perceptions of those who used these languages—or this language—many centuries ago and is therefore not susceptible to scientific investigation in our day. There seems to be no evidence that Slavonic and the vernacular were considered two separate entities prior to the late sixteenth and seventeenth centuries; Maksim Grek's associate Sylvan said he had translated John Chrysostom "на рускои языкъ" and praised Maksim for his expertise not only in Greek and Latin, but also "в сладчаишем мне руском" (A. V. Issatschenko, *Geschichte der russischen Sprache* . . . , 1:77).

26. On the internal differentiation of Slavonic in the seventeenth century, see D. S. Worth, "Stylistic Variants within Russian Church Slavonic (On the Language of the *Solovetskii Paterik*)," *Wiener slawistischer Almanach* 12 (1984): 323–331.

On the Place of the Cyrillo-Methodian Tradition in Epiphanius's *Life of Saint Stephen of Perm*

HARVEY GOLDBLATT

I

An oft-repeated interpretative tradition informs us that, paradoxically, the Cyrillo-Methodian patrimony and ideology survived most securely among the East Slavs, a part of the Slavic world where the mission was never active.[1] In particular, scholars frequently have emphasized that the image and deeds of Constantine-Cyril the Philosopher, the "first pastor and teacher of the Slavic people"[2] and "inventor of Slavic letters,"[3] were best preserved in the "Russian Lands."[4] They also have pointed out that the preservation of this cultural heritage was linked with a "revival" or "reawakening" of literary activity in the Russian lands in the late fourteenth and the fifteenth century —commonly subsumed under the historiographic formulae "Second South Slavic Influence,"[5] "East European Pre-Renaissance,"[6] or "Orthodox Slavic Revival"[7]—which stood in sharp contrast to the cultural stagnation characteristic of the preceding period of feudal fragmentation and Tatar domination.

Indeed, the evidence from this period of literary revival reveals not only renewed interest in Saint Cyril's apostolic and teaching achievements but also attempts to emphasize the philosopher's prominent role in affirming a "Russian" culture. One should bear in mind that many documents of the fifteenth century aim to link Constantine the Philosopher's activity directly with Rus'.[8] It is important to recall, in this regard, Chapter 8 of *Vita Constantini*, where in all extant textual witnesses of the work it is stated that, during his stay in Cherson (Chersonesus), a Byzantine possession in the Crimea, Saint Cyril "found a Gospel and Psalter written in Russian letters."[9] Nor should one forget that in two fifteenth-century chronicles the "philosopher," who in the East Slavic Primary Chronicle (*sub anno* 6494 [988 A.D.]) aims to persuade Vladimir to accept Byzantine Christianity, is given the name "Cyril."[10] Likewise, in some apocryphal versions of the story of "Solomon's Chalice"—that is, the story that figures so prominently in Chapter 13 of *Vita Constantini*—in which Constantine succeeds in interpreting three enigmatic verses engraved on a mysterious chalice, the "philosopher" called "Cyril" who finally deciphers the inscription is said to have visited Rus' and instructed Vladimir.[11] Finally, in certain texts Saint Cyril appears as the creator of "Russian letters" and as the translator from Greek into the "Russian language."[12]

It should also be noted, however, that in some of the documents from this period of literary revival in the Russian lands—a period when the spiritual leadership of the Orthodox Slavic community gradually was being transferred from the Balkan Slavic lands to the East Slavic area—references to Constantine-Cyril's activity are not used merely as part of a "nationalistic desire of the Russians to claim some of his accomplishments."[13] Indeed, a number of texts, whether explicitly or implicitly, aim not to celebrate Constantine's contributions to the "Russian" people but rather to minimize his achievements, often comparing them unfavorably to those of Grand Prince Vladimir or even transferring them to the "apostle of the Russian people." In other words, an equally forceful and important thesis that appears to have developed in the fifteenth century is that Rus' had had no need of a "foreign" apostle, such as Saint Cyril, for the true faith had been revealed to the lands of Rus' by none but God the Almighty through the inspired actions of Saint Vladimir.

This is the principal idea expressed in the *Tale on Russian Writing*, a document preserved in at least six codices, all of East Slavic origin, dating from no earlier than the middle of the fifteenth century.[14] In this work Constantine is seen not as an active participant in the creation of a tradition—that is, the inventor of the Slavic alphabet and the translator of Greek books into Slavic —but as a passive carrier of "Russian writing" to the Western Slavs whose mark on the affairs of the "Moravians, Liakhs, and Czechs" quickly was effaced by the actions of the "Latin bishop Voitiekh."[15] The depreciation of Constantine's accomplishments in relation to the inspired actions of Prince Vladimir is perhaps most clearly evidenced by the differences between this work and the description of the philosopher's activity found in Chapter 8 of *Vita Constantini*.[16] At the same time, by suggesting that Constantine had learned "Russian writing" (*gramota rouskaia*) from a "Russian" (*rousin*) in Cherson, the *Tale on Russian Writing* provides the correct ideological context in which one must understand Constantine's discovery of a "Gospel and Psalter written in Russian letters."[17] The notion that Constantine the Philosopher had found "Russian letters" in Cherson, or that he had studied with a man to whom God had revealed "Russian writing" would be fully accepted in the East Slavic lands being united under Moscow, the "new

Constantinople," in the fifteenth century. Grounded in the belief that Moscow was now the center of the true Orthodox faith, it could easily become an essential part of a new ideological vision seeking to stress the autonomous entry of Rus' into the Christian family of peoples.[18]

One should recall that a similar ideological attitude implicitly is offered by Hilarion's *Sermon on the Law and Grace*. Indeed, it is noteworthy that the main themes conveyed in the *Tale on Russian Writing*—above all, the superiority of the Christian age of Grace over that of Jewish Law, the conversion of Rus' as the confirmation of God's promise, and the exaltation of Grand Prince Vladimir as the lord's chosen instrument—are strikingly similar to the motives that pervade Metropolitan Hilarion's composition. One should not forget that in Hilarion's work, whose textual documentation not only dates from no earlier than the fifteenth century[19] but also betrays clear traces of redactional intervention,[20] a "Sermon on Law and Grace" is followed by the "Eulogy of Vladimir," which aims to underscore the idea that Rus' was converted directly by God through the inspired deeds of Saint Vladimir.[21]

II

One of the most celebrated works frequently linked by scholars with the ideological vitality of the Cyrillo-Methodian heritage in Muscovite Russia is Epiphanius the Most Wise's *Life of Saint Stephen of Perm*, written shortly after Stephen's death in 1396, although the textual documentation dates from the end of the fifteenth century.[22] The purpose of the present study is to elucidate the precise manner in which Epiphanius relied on the Cyrillo-Methodian heritage in his *Life of Saint Stephen* and to examine the implications of Epiphanius's response to this ideological legacy for his inquiry into the nature of, and the relations between, the "Russian" and "Permian" literary traditions.

It is well known and often stated that in the *Life of Saint Stephen*, which subordinates all thematic and compositional features to the central event in Stephen's life—namely, his missionary activity among the inhabitants of the Permian lands, known as the Komi or Zyrians—Epiphanius uses traditional arguments not only to compare the saint with Constantine-Cyril but even to insist that the feats of the former were more outstanding than the accomplishments of the latter. As Epiphanius declares, Saint Cyril had been helped by his brother Methodius, whereas Saint Stephen invented the "Permian alphabet" and translated the sacred books into the "Permian language" with no assistance save from God.[23]

In discussing the importance given to a comparison of Saints Stephen and Cyril, scholars long have pointed out that Epiphanius used as a source a treatise entitled *On the Letters*, attributed by the textual tradition of the work to a certain "Monk Hrabr."[24] It is generally accepted that the relationship between Epiphanius and Monk Hrabr ought to be viewed in terms of the influence exerted on a late fourteenth-century hagiographic composition by an early tenth-century work, that is, a work completed shortly after the translation of the Cyrillo-Methodian community to the Bulgaria of Boris and Symeon.[25] Yet insofar as the place of the Cyrillo-Methodian tradition in the *Life of Saint Stephen* is concerned, it appears that insufficient attention has been paid to (1) the textual tradition of Monk Hrabr's treatise, (2) the particular correspondences between Epiphanius and Monk Hrabr and the implications of these textual coincidences, and (3) Epiphanius's reliance on Cyrillo-Methodian sources other than Monk Hrabr.

As regards the question of "influences" on the *Life of Saint Stephen* beyond the textual tradition of Monk Hrabr, as early as 1964 Ihor Ševčenko perceptively noted that Epiphanius "not only copied—and improved upon—some parts of the tenth-century treatise *O pismenex* by Monk Hrabr ... but also (a fact which seems to have passed unnoticed) freely adapted the first chapter of the Slavic *Vita Constantini* and applied some of its quotations and phraseology to Stephen."[26] Ševčenko refers here not only to certain striking "parallels" found in the section of Epiphanius's work allegedly dependent on Monk Hrabr,[27] but also to the specific combination of 1 Timothy 2:4 and Ezekial 33:11 found at the very beginning of *Vita Constantini*[28] and in another part of the *Life of Saint Stephen*.[29] In 1964, in a similar vein, Dmitri Obolensky pointed out that the *Life of Saint Stephen*[30] parallels not only Chapter 15 of *Vita Constantini*[31] but also the East Slavic *Primary Chronicle*[32]—namely, in reference to the spread of Slavic letters in the reign of Grand Prince Vladimir (*sub anno* 6496 [988 A.D.])—when Epiphanius combines quotations from Isaiah 35:6 and 29:18[33] to express the "bounty of the vernacular tradition."[34]

It is difficult to overestimate the importance of these biblical citations for works such as the *Life of Saint Stephen* and *Vita Constantini*. Indeed, according to Riccardo Picchio, it is precisely the particular conflations of biblical references found at the very beginning of *Vita Constantini*[35] and in the opening lines of Chapter 15 of *Vita Constantini*[36] which offer the reader "spiritual leitmotifs" that reveal the higher meaning of Constantine-Cyril's missionary activity in general and his apostolic mission among the Slavs in particular. It should be noted, however, that a multitude of additional textual correspondences could be made between the *Life of Saint Stephen* and not only other "classical" texts of the Cyrillo-Methodian patrimony, such as *Vita Methodii*, the *Encomium for Saint Cyril*, and the *Encomium for Saints Cyril and Methodius*,[37] as well as a number of East Slavic writings, including Hilarion's *Sermon on Law and Grace*, Nestor's *Life of Saint Theodosius*,[38] Cyril of Turov's *Discourse on the Removal of the Body of Christ from the Cross*,[39] and the *Discourse on the Life and Death of the Grand Prince Dmitrii Ivanovich*,[40] but also medieval Serbian texts such as Domentijan's *Life of Saint Symeon* and *Life of Saint Sava*, as well as the two *Lives* of Stephen Nemanja written by his sons Rastko (Saint Sava) and Stephen the First-Crowned (Stefan Prvovenčani).[41] It appears that at issue here may not be direct textual relationships[42] but rather a stockroom of scriptural formulae and thematic-stylistic commonplaces that could be used in the presentation of certain motifs.[43] In the particular case of the *Life of Saint Stephen*, therefore, a particular repertoire of biblical formulae—especially in the section of the *Life* entitled "On the Summoning and on the Conversion of Many Nations"[44] (that is, the section in which the parallel between Saints Stephen and Cyril is established)[45]—serves to underscore a single fundamental idea indissolubly linked with Cyrillo-Methodian ideology: Stephen, like the apostles, like teachers such as Saint Cyril, and like many other spiritual predecessors raised up by God, is an instrument of Grace sent to spread the Word of God among a newly chosen people, namely, the Permians.[46] Because all pagans must be liberated from both spiritual and material "speechlessness,"[47] Stephen has created a Permian alphabet and translated the sacred books into the Permian language. He thereby offers further proof that the redeeming intervention of divine Grace is not limited to any one historical period, for even "in the final days of the last age,"[48] God seeks to lead all to knowledge and salvation.

There is no question, therefore, but that the spiritual dignity of Permian letters, whose creation is held to be grounded in a practice sanctioned by a long tradition,[49] was inextricably bound with the theological justification for Saint Stephen's mission to the Permian lands. In response to those who might have questioned the appropriateness of using divine Scriptures written in a Permian alphabet, it could be asserted that it was the apostolic duty of the Church to employ "new tongues" so that all people could understand Christ's teachings. More specifically, in presenting Stephen's work among the Permians and the language questions involved, Epiphanius appears to have had recourse to a well-established ideological scheme that reflected various stages of the Cyrillo-Methodian legacy. Yet, as I have already indicated, when discussing the precise manner in which Saint Stephen's apostolate to the Permian lands was modeled on Constantine-Cyril's mission to the Slavs, it seems appropriate to talk in terms not of direct textual borrowings or direct textual transmission, but rather of the continuity of a tradition and the existence of a highly formalized literary system in which sets of lexicalized formulae and images are linked with connotative functions.

Nowhere is this more clearly in evidence than in the "motive of language acquisition" presented as a prerequisite for embarking on an apostolic mission. In both hagiographic works—*Vita Constantini* and the *Life of Saint Stephen*—it should be noted that the mastery of a language triad does not merely point to the general significance of the number 3 for the works[50] but rather conveys a particular symbolic message. Thus, in Chapter 8 of *Vita Constantini*, Constantine's acquistion of a new trinity of languages—namely, Hebrew, Samaritan, and "Russian"—demonstrates a level of spiritual preparation sufficient for his mission to the Khazars. In similar fashion—and even more significant to the *Vita*—Constantine's ability to decipher the enigmatic verses on "Solomon's Chalice" in Chapter 13 reveals the teacher's "gift of tongues," which is coupled with his "gift of prophecy," and his readiness to undertake an apostolic mission to the newly elected Slavic people.[51] In this regard, one should remember that several versions of the story on "Solomon's Chalice" in the East Slavic apocryphal tradition indicate that the three lines on the chalice were written in three languages.[52]

The fullest elaboration of this crucial motive is found in the *Life of Saint Stephen*. Indeed, it is Epiphanius's description of Stephen's linguistic studies that, through its use of citations from Mark 16:17 and Acts 2:4, offers what appears to be the "spiritual leitmotif" for the entire work. After briefly describing Stephen's origins, his childhood and youth, and his deeds as monk and deacon, Epiphanius abruptly switches to his ordination as priest and his spiritual and linguistic preparation for his inspired apostolic mission. Stephen studied the "Russian" language, and in preparation for his obligation to teach the Permians and turn them from unbelief to Christ, he learned the Permian tongue. However, before embarking on his apostolate to the Permian lands, which clearly is patterned after Constantine's mission to the Slavs, Saint Stephen required additional understanding and therefore undertook the study of Greek. As Epiphanius writes:

> But desiring greater knowledge, [Stephen] also learned Greek writing as the model of wisdom, and studied Greek books, and he read them thoroughly and always kept them with him. And he was able to speak in three languages; and he also was able to master three ways of writing, that is, Russian, Greek and Permian. And thus the word was fulfilled which says

that "they shall speak in new tongues" and, again, that "he gave [them] to speak in other tongues." And the thought strongly seized him to go to the Permian land and teach them.[53]

Here Jesus's promise from Mark 16:17 ("in my name they will cast out demons; *they will speak in new tongues*"), which is fulfilled on the day of Pentecost with the descent of tongues of fire upon the Apostles in Acts 2:4 ("and they . . . began *to speak in other tongues,* as the Spirit *gave them* utterance"), suggests that through his mastery of a language triad consisting of "Russian, Greek, and Permian," Saint Stephen, too, had been granted full apostolic dignity as a teacher and spiritual successor to the apostles and other men chosen as instruments of Grace to spread the Word of God. Like the invention of the Slavic alphabet, the inspired creation of Permian letters thus was to be viewed as a second Pentecost, that is, a vital instrument in repealing the original confusion of tongues which had emerged from the Tower of Babel.[54] One should note, moreover, that the language trinity mastered by the "apostle to the Permians"—more specifically, the peculiar network of relationships among Russian, Greek, and Permian presented in the *Life of Saint Stephen*—assumes critical importance for the structures of Epiphanius's thought.[55]

III

Let us now turn to the problem of determining the significance of Monk Hrabr's treatise *On the Letters* for Epiphanius's work. As indicated above, scholars long have pointed to the central role played by Monk Hrabr's apology in the section of the *Life of Saint Stephen* entitled "On the Summoning and on the Conversion of Many Nations." Above all, scholars have stressed two basic points:

1. By relying on the "five-century[*sic*]-old argument of the so-called Monk Hrabr,"[56] Epiphanius is able to praise alphabets, such as "Russian" or Permian, created by a single holy man (i.e., Saint Cyril or Saint Stephen) in contradistinction to an alphabet, such as Greek, which was the work of numerous heathens over many generations.
2. The use of Monk Hrabr's tract permits Epiphanius to place his hero within a historical context of apostleship and to link the Permian tongue to a sequence of languages.[57]

It appears, however, that a number of factors regarding this textual relationship have not been considered adequately:

1. It is important to remember that, in large part, Hrabr's apology does not harken back to the language controversies in ninth-century Great Moravia, but rather echoes the new situation in which the "Cyrillo-Methodian language" found itself in tenth-century Bulgaria. In other words, within the context of debates on religious and cultural acceptability, the particular relation of the "national" Slavic tongue to the "supra-national" Greek language emerges as the central issue in the treatise.[58]
2. Although one cannot easily deduce to what extent the oldest codices of Hrabr's apology (fourteenth–fifteenth century) betray a faithful transmission of an earlier (allegedly tenth-century) work,[59] it is clear that in the treatise—as it has come down to us—the Slavic tongue is presented not only in opposition to, but in imitation of, the prestigious Greek language. This means that, because the Slavic language formed part of a providential trinity of languages governed by the principle of imitation, Hrabr often felt compelled to stress similarity even in a discussion of what appeared to be distinctions between Slavic and Greek.[60]
3. There appear to be significant differences between a large part of the textual documentation of Hrabr's treatise and the textual portions of Epiphanius's which allegedly rely on Hrabr. These differences relate to a number of important areas, which include: (a) the first human language—in Hrabr's opinion it is Syriac,[61] while in Epiphanius's view it is Hebrew;[62] (b) the designation for the alphabet invented by Saint Cyril—according to Hrabr it is called "Slavic," whereas Epiphanius uses the term "Russian"; and (c) the degree of importance attached to a providential trinity of languages—its significance is stressed by Hrabr, while Epiphanius is concerned more with a general succession of languages.

As to these areas of alleged discrepancy, Alda Kossova has shown that many of the portions of Epiphanius's work that seem to deviate from the contents of Hrabr's apology in fact betray textual material common to both the *Life of Saint Stephen* and the so-called Russian Revision of Hrabr's treatise *On the Letters*.[63] Even if one cannot determine the precise textual relationship of Epiphanius's composition to the "Russian Revision" of Monk Hrabr's apology,[64] it is evident that they both sought to advance a "Russocentric" conception of the Slavic language, which may have emerged on East Slavic soil, in deliberate opposition to earlier "Bulgarocentric" or "Serbocentric" conceptions. By presenting Saint Cyril as the inventor of "Russian writing," or as the translator of sacred books (together with Methodius) from the Greek language into "Russian," the *Life of Saint Stephen* seems in agreement with other fifteenth-century documents that aimed not only to stress the antiquity of "Russian letters" but also to identify the purest form of the Slavic tongue with the language of the Russian lands.[65]

Having discussed the general problem of possible textual borrowings in Epiphanius's *Life of Saint Stephen* and outlined some of the textual coincidences between Epiphanius's *Life* and the "Russian Revision" of Monk Hrabr's treatise, we are now in a position to focus on the nature of the correspondences between Epiphanius and Hrabr. In other words, we can now seek to determine whether—and if so, to what extent and why—Epiphanius might have seen fit to rely on the textual material and intent conveyed in the apology *On the Letters*. However, in any discussion of Monk Hrabr's impact on the *Life of Saint Stephen* it is critically important to distinguish between *actual textual parallels*[66] and dependence on (or repudiation of) a *particular ideological scheme*.[67] It seems to me that it is the latter type of "influence" that has received scant attention from scholars but is of special significance for Epiphanius's thought. Let us now attempt to elucidate the impact of Hrabr's ideological scheme and then offer some concluding remarks on the implications of Epiphanius's acceptance or rejection of its component parts.

The major elements of Hrabr's ideological scheme that coincide with what is found in the *Life of Saint Stephen* are the following:

1. The interrelated motifs of God's constant and redeeming intervention and the continuity of apostleship. Since God wants all men to come to a knowledge of the truth and be saved, he has raised up first Saint Cyril and then Saint Stephen as teachers and inventors of new alphabets.
2. The notion that a writing system created even "at the eleventh hour" is justifiable if it liberates men from heathen "speechlessness." Hence, both Russian and Permian writings are more honored than Greek writings, for only they were invented by inspired men in the age of Grace.
3. The polemical attitude of those who implicitly repudiate Cyrillo-Methodian ideology and—because they employ an authoritative language consecrated by tradition—reject the legitimacy of a

"new language" to spread the Gospel. In Hrabr's treatise the Greeks reject the Slavic alphabet, for it did not exist "from the beginning"—as Hebrew, Latin and Greek letters did—and was not to be found in the inscription placed on Christ's cross.[68] In Epiphanius's work Moscow offers itself as a new and imperious Byzantium that practices cultural imperialism and asserts the superiority of its own language,[69] questioning the appropriateness of a Permian alphabet invented at the end of the last age and wondering why the prestigious Russian letters should not be employed instead.[70]

No less important, however, are the motifs in Epiphanius's *Life of Saint Stephen* which violate the ideological scheme in Hrabr's treatise. They include:

1. In both Monk Hrabr and Epiphanius the "new language" is presented as part of a providential continuity. Nevertheless, the significance in the attached by the author of the *Life of Saint Stephen* to the notion of a particular spiritual lineage—and, above all, the necessity of including the new tongue within a special trinity of languages which reveals two separate phases of divine revelation[71]—is at odds with what is contained in the majority of codices of Monk Hrabr's tract. In Hrabr's *On the Letters*, Saint Cyril appears compelled to have the Slavic letters rely on Greek in the way that the Greek letters had imitated Hebrew:

From the first letter [Saint Cyril] began as in Greek. For they [the Greeks] have "alpha," while [Saint Cyril began] from "az'." Thus both begin from "A." And as they [the Greeks], imitating the Hebrew letters, created [their own letters], so [Saint Cyril imitated] Greek [letters]. For the Hebrews have "aleph" as the first letter, which means "learning."; and when they introduce a child [to learning], they say "learn!," that is, "aleph." And the Greeks, imitating [this] said "alpha." . . . For Saint Cyril, imitating them, created the first letter "az'."[72]

It is not by chance that what is found in the *Life of Saint Stephen* is decidedly different, for Epiphanius seeks to present an inventor of the Permian alphabet for whom it is not nearly so critical to imitate "Russian" (i.e., Slavic) and thereby pattern himself after the inventor of Russian writing who in his time had relied on Greek letters.[73] It appears that the apostle to the Permians aims to break down the significance of a peculiar language geneology governed by the principle of successive imitation. In particular, the practical result of Saint Stephen's activity—as presented in Epiphanius's *Life*—is to deemphasize the authority and prestige of Russian.

2. The violation of Hrabr's ideological scheme is most clearly evident in Saint Stephen's choice of letters for the new Permian alphabet. In Hrabr's view, Saint Cyril had invented thirty-eight letters for the Slavs, "twenty-four on the model of Greek letters and fourteen others according to the Slavic speech."[74] Yet here, when discussing what would appear to be an important distinction between Greek and Slavic—the former seems to have twenty-four letters, whereas the latter has thirty-eight letters—Monk Hrabr felt obliged to stress similarity between the two languages:

Others say, "Why did [Saint Cyril] create thirty-eight letters? For one can write with fewer [letters], as the Greeks do with twenty-four." Yet those [who say such things] do not know how many letters the Greeks write with. For they [the Greeks] have twenty-four letters, but these [letters] are not sufficient for their writing. Therefore, they have added eleven dipthongs with the three numerical signs for six, ninety and nine hundred. And together there are thirty-eight [letters].[75]

According to Epiphanius, Saint Stephen, too, invented twenty-four letters, "some according to the model of the Greek letters[76] and the others according to the speech of the Permians."[77] Epiphanius's statement is especially noteworthy, for although one finds here an apparent textual coincidence with Monk Hrabr's apology, there is also a violation of its ideological scheme. Like Saint Cyril, Saint Stephen draws upon the prestigious Greek linguistic tradition;[78] indeed, the number of letters in Permian and Greek is to be the same. Nevertheless, in terms of Hrabr's ideological framework, one should have expected a reliance not on Greek but on the "Russian" tradition established by Saint Cyril. The "apostle of the Permian people" fashioned by Epiphanius apparently sees no need to stress similarity between Permian and Russian; indeed, even when likeness is emphasized in the *Life of Saint Stephen*, it frequently is by virtue of their common inadequacy or appearance "at the eleventh hour."[79]

Thus, in Epiphanius's *Life of Saint Stephen* one is confronted with a selective reliance on Monk Hrabr coupled with a Russocentric vision of the Orthodox Slavic tradition. The "Russian" tongue, invented by Saint Cyril, not only represents a venerable linguistic medium consecrated by a long tradition but is also more honored than Greek because it originated in the age of Grace.[80] Saint Stephen's gift of apostleship, however, could not take place until he had mastered Greek; moreover, notwithstanding the imperious attitudes emanating from Moscow, not Russian but Greek came to be considered the model of imitation for Stephen's invention of a Permian alphabet;[81] and finally, many of the books necessary for the mission had to be translated not from Russian but from Greek.[82]

IV

It can be said, therefore, that Epiphanius's partial reliance on the message and scheme conveyed in Hrabr's treatise *On the Letters* could serve several useful purposes. First, it could confirm the prestige of the Permian mission—in particular, the invention of the Permian alphabet—by establishing a parallel between Stephen and Cyril based on the continuity of God's redeeming intervention and the continuity of apostleship. Second, and equally important, it could help refute the imperious claims made by the ideologues from Moscow, the new and intolerant Byzantium, regarding the legitimacy of the Cyrillo-Methodian legacy in general and Stephen's apostolic activity in particular. At the same time, it should be noted that differences with Hrabr's scheme also assisted in legitimizing the appropriateness of the Permian mission: by affirming the special role of a Greek model, Stephen implicitly deflated the alleged authority and prestige of a Russian cultural tradition identified with the policies and aspirations of Moscow.

One should remember that a constant in Epiphanius's work is strong opposition to any attempts to extol Muscovite power.[83] Neither the dignity conferred upon the Russian lands as a center for propagating the Christian faith nor a Russocentric conception of the Cyrillo-Methodian heritage could bring the author of the *Life of Saint Stephen* to apotheosize the Muscovite prince or state. Indeed, it is possible to say that Epiphanius's exaltation of Saint Stephen, not only "apostle to the Permian lands" but also a fellow Rostovian, served as yet another pretext for criticizing Moscow for its aggressive designs even in the religious sphere. Ever the patriot from Rostov and always ready to condemn Muscovite religious imperialism, Epiphanius offered a polemical response to the increasing pan-Russian threat from Moscow to spiritual and cultural autonomy in the local centers. In his celebrated enumeration of Christian lands and their respective patron saints—which, though it betrays textual material common to both the *Sermon on Law and Grace* and the *Discourse on the Life and Death of the Grand Prince Dmitrii Ivanovich*, conveys a message substantially different from that found in these two works[84]—Epiphanius referred not only to the "land of Rus'" (Saint Vladimir), but also "Moscow" (Saint Peter) and the "land of Rostov" (Saint Leontius).[85] Epiphanius was unwilling to accept the notion of a unified Russian land subject to Moscow and sought, instead, to assert the prestige of the local spiritual and cultural traditions such as those of Rostov. In the structures of Epiphanius's "orthodox" patriotism, Moscow alone was not to be identified with the rising prestige of Russian spirituality; for him the idea of the Muscovite realm as the sole spiritual heir of Rus' was totally unacceptable.

It is important, moreover, to see Stephen's exaltation of the Greek tradition—often at the expense of the Russian patrimony—against the backdrop of the Byzantino-Slavic spiritual unity proclaimed and promoted by the Hesychasts.[86] In this regard, it is not by chance that, when referring to the time of Stephen's death (1396), Epiphanius listed the names of the Byzantine emperor Manuel II Palaeologus and Patriarch Anthony IV before all others.[87] The Muscovite grand prince Basil[88] (together with Cyprian, metropolitan of all Rus'),[89] mentioned only after the patriarchs of Jerusalem, Alexandria, and Antioch, was presented with many princes and other grand princes such as Vitovt of Lithuania, Michael of Tver', Oleg of Riazan, and Andrew of Rostov. Finally, Epiphanius's reference to Stephen's passing "in the seventh year of [Basil's] rule" in no way diminished the political supremacy of the Tatar khans, for—as is also noted—the teacher of the Permian people died "in the sixteenth year of the reign of tsar Tokhtamysh, who ruled the horde of Mamai," while the empire beyond the Volga was ruled by a second tsar Temir Qutlug."[90] Clearly, one is confronted both here and elsewhere in the *Life of Saint Stephen*[91] with not only an attempt to neutralize the claims of the Moscow grand prince to uniqueness and to deflate Muscovite spiritual and political authority, but also a kind of profession of faith proclaiming the indisputable supremacy of the "Roman" *basileus* and Byzantine patriarch over all Orthodox peoples. It appears, therefore, that Epiphanius—whose work reveals not only the impact of, but also a profound insight into, some of the major tenets of Hesychast thought, including its Platonizing tendencies[92]—asserted, perhaps in conscious opposition to alternative positions, the vision of a united Christian *ecumene* that sought to reaffirm the rightful place of the emperor and patriarch in the "Byzantine Commonwealth."[93]

At the same time, however, by justifying Stephen's mission to the Permians sent from the Russian lands, Epiphanius implicitly raised the spiritual authority of the Russian Church, which in the late fourteenth and the early fifteenth century had not yet obtained either autonomous status or the spritual leadership of Orthodox Slavdom.[94] In other words, Stephen's missionary activity could be viewed as a deliberate effort by Russian Orthodox Christianity to bring the light of God's Word to a heathen people.[95] Yet equally important, and paradoxically, Epiphanius's dependence on Hrabr's ideology—more specifically, his identification of the adversaries of Stephen's mission as authorities from Moscow (that is, the "new Byzantines")—also unwittingly elevated the prestige of the Muscovite prince and state. Epiphanius's *Life of Saint Stephen* thus served to elucidate the situation that developed in the Russian lands in the second half of the fifteenth century— especially after the fall of Constantinople (1453)—when Moscow, inexorably expanding its rule over older and illustrious principalities, not only asserted a spiritual and political unity in the Russian lands under its leadership but also proclaimed an official ideology that affirmed its role as the very heart and center of Orthodox Christendom. The above-mentioned authorities from Moscow, the "new Constantinople," soon would condemn the use of the Permian language and destroy the liturgical books written in it.[96] The imperious ideology of the multinational Muscovite state and its church might later praise Stephen's missionary activity in the Permian lands but would repudiate its practical achievements, which had deliberately been modeled on the accomplishments of Cyril and his brother Methodius.

It is thus noteworthy that Epiphanius could highlight both the "Cyrillo-Methodian claim of a full franchise for every national language"[97] and Moscow's denunciation of this claim by relying on the textual tradition of Monk Hrabr's treatise. On the one hand, the author of the *Life of Saint Stephen* could praise the Russian lands that in the spirit of the Cyrillo-Methodian tradition and in accordance with God's plan for salvation, had sent an apostle to the heathens; on the other hand, he could condemn Stephen's adversaries in Moscow who, in the cultural imperialism they practiced, appeared to repudiate the Cyrillo-Methodian legacy. Epiphanius might assert a Russocentric conception of the "language of Saint Cyril" and stress Constantine-Cyril the Philosopher's prominent role in affirming a Russian culture but could not accept any attempts either to minimize the universal significance of Cyrillo-Methodian ideology or to claim Cyril's achievements exclusively for the Russian lands.

Notes

1. See I. Ševčenko, "Three Paradoxes of the Cyrillo-Methodian Mission," *SR* 23, no. 2 (1964): 220–236, esp. p. 225. Cf. B. O. Unbegaun, "L'héritage cyrillo-méthodien en Russie," *Cyrillo-Methodiana,* ed. M. Hellman et al. (Cologne and Graz, 1964), pp. 135–149; D. Obolensky, "The Heritage of Cyril and Methodius in Russia," *DOP* 19 (1965): 47–65.

2. This is the designation found in the title to some of the textual witnesses of *Vita Constantini:* "Житіе и жизнь, и подвизи . . . отца нашего Константіна философа, пръваго наставника и оучителѧ словѣньскоу языкоу." [In quoted matter, Cyrillic superscript letters have been set in italics and titlos have been replaced with the appropriate letters in angle brackets.—*Editor*] (P. A. Lavrov, *Materialy po istorii vozniknoveniia drevneishei slavianskoi pis'mennosti,* [=*Slavistic Printings and Reprintings,* no. 67] [The Hague and Paris, 1966], p. 1). Here and in subsequent references I shall quote *Vita Constantini* after Lavrov's edition of the fifteenth-century ms. 19 of the Manuscript Section of the Lenin State Library, *fond* 173 (formerly ms. 19 of the Moscow Theological Academy), pp. 1–36. On the crucial terms "pastor" and "teacher," in relation to the designation "apostle," see R. Picchio, "The Function of Biblical Thematic Clues in the Literary Code of 'Slavia Orthodoxa,'" *Slavica Hierosolymitana* 1 (1977): 11–13.

3. Many Cyrillo-Methodian writings, including Chapter 14 of *Vita Constantini* and Chapter 5 of *Vita Methodii,* assign to Constantine-Cyril the Philosopher a singular role in the divinely-inspired action of inventing letters so that the Slavs might come to a knowledge of the Word of God. It is noteworthy that Constantine Kostenechki, who compiled his *Skazanie iz'iavlenno o pismenekh"* in the 1420s in the Serbian lands, offers a detailed commentary on the invention of Slavic letters and the first Slavic edition of the divine Writings in which "Cyril the Philosopher" plays a preeminent role but where no mention is made of Methodius. This omission is all the more curious in that Kostenechki's account stresses the fact Cyril did not act alone but chose "wondrous men" who aided in the preparation of the Slavic Scriptures: see H. Goldblatt, *Orthography and Orthodoxy: Constantine Kostenečki's Treatise on the Letters,* [=Studia Historica et Philologica, no. 16] (Florence, 1987), 118–120, 231–241. However, in approximately the same period—but in the East Slavic area—Epiphanius the Most Wise asserts that Cyril is slightly "less equal" than Stephen of Perm precisely because in creating the alphabet and translating the sacred books he frequently was helped by his brother Methodius, whereas Stephen had no assistance but from God in inventing Permian letters: see Ševčenko, "Three Paradoxes," p. 225; Obolensky, "The Heritage of Cyril and Methodius," pp. 63–64.

4. In this regard, scholars have placed considerable emphasis on the prominent role occupied by the Thessalonican brothers and their mission in the East Slavic *Primary Chronicle* (*s.a.* 6406 [898 A.D.]) and the fact that the vast majority of manuscripts containing *Vita Constantini* and a number of other Cyrillo-Methodian writings, as well as all extant copies of *Vita Methodii,* come from the East Slavic area. See B. St. Angelov and Kh. Kodov, eds., Kliment Okhridski, *Săbrani săchineniia,* vol. 3: *Prostranni zhitiia na Kiril i Metodii* (Sofia, 1973), pp. 30–59, 160–168; Obolensky, "The Heritage of Cyril and Methodius," p. 64.

5. See M. S. Iovine, "The History and the Historiography of the Second South Slavic Influence" (Ph.D. diss., Yale University, 1977), esp. pp. 1–65.

6. See D. S. Likhachev, "Nekotorye zadachi izucheniia vtorogo iuzhnoslavianskogo vliianiia v Rossii," in *Issledovaniia po slavianskomu literaturovedeniiu i fol'kloristike: Doklady sovestskikh uchenykh na IV Mezhdunarodnom s"ezde slavistov* (Moscow, 1960), pp. 95–151; idem, "Neskol'ko zamechanii po povodu stat'i Rikkardo Pikkio," *TODRL* 17 (1961): 675–678; Iovine, "The History and the Historiography of the Second South Slavic Influence," pp. 45–49.

7. See R. Picchio, "'Prerinascimento esteuropeo' e 'Rinascita slava ortodossa,'" *Ricerche Slavistiche* 6 (1958): 185–199; H. Goldblatt, "La rinascita slava ortodossa (sec. 14–15), in *Storia della civiltà letteraria russa*, ed. M. Colucci and R. Picchio (in press).

8. See B. St. Angelov, "Kirillometodievoto delo i ideiata za slaviansko edinstvo v staroslavianskite literaturi," in *Slavistichen sbornik* (Sofia, 1958), 2: 45–48. In this period one can observe attempts to establish this connection not only in the East Slavic area but in the Balkan Slavic lands as well. Thus, for example, in Chapter 4 of his *Skazanie iz'iavlenno o pismenekh"*, Constantine Kostenechki links the activity of "Cyril the Philosopher" with a conception of the Slavic language which, "in the beginning," had as its basis the "most refined and beautiful Russian tongue" (тън'- чаишіи и краснѣишіи роуш'кыи езыкь). As Kostenechki points out, the patrimony of Cyril belongs to all the Slavs, "but more to Rus'" (нь ѡбаче Роусь вещ'ше): see V. Jagić, *Codex Slavenicus rerum grammaticarum*, Slavische Poropläen, no. 25 (Berlin, 1968), pp. 108–110. On Kostenechki's "Russocentric" conception of the Slavic language, see Goldblatt, *Orthography and Orthodoxy*, pp. 233–237.

9. "Обрѣте же тоу еуаггеліе и ψалтирь роуськыми писмены писано." (Lavrov, *Materialy*, p. 12). As I indicated in an earlier study, one should reflect on the possibility that the extant testimonies of *Vita Constantini* may be the result of the activities of reshaping and compiling in the Russian lands in accordance with the new ideological demands of the fifteenth century. Indeed, given that there is no direct evidence of textual transmission before the fifteenth century, it seems advisable to consider the phrase "rous'kymi pismeny" not so much a relatively very early "miscopying," or "enigmatic anomaly" due to corruption in the tradition, as a reading that conveys a precise message and that performs an important contextual function in all surviving codices of *Vita Canstantini:* see H. Goldblatt, "On the 'rous'kymi pismeny' in the *Vita Constantini* and Rus'ian Religious Patriotism," in *Studia Slavica Mediaevalia et Humanistica Riccardo Picchio dicata*, ed. M. Colucci, G. Dell'Agata, and H. Goldblatt (Rome, 1986), pp. 311–328, esp. 317–321. Cf. R. Jakobson, "Minor Native Sources for the Early History of the Slavic Church," in Roman Jakobson, *Selected Writings*, vol. 6: *Early Slavic Paths and Crossroads*, ed. S. Rudy (Berlin, New York, and Amsterdam, 1985), pp. 186–187; R. Picchio, "Chapter 13 of *Vita Constantini*: Its Text and Contextual Function," *Slavica Hierosolymitana* 7 (1985): 133–152.

10. Obolensky, "The Heritage of Cyril and Methodius," p. 62.

11. See, for instance, ms. 8 of the Barsov Collection: "Сихъ же стиховъ никтоже може протолковати. но протолкова древле. иже приходи в Русь философъ оучитъ Володимира. ему же бѣ има Коурилъ." (Lavrov, *Materialy*, p. xlvi).

12. See, for example, Epiphanius the Most Wise's comparison of "Russian writ-

ing" and the "Hellenic tongue": "Тѣм'же мню, яко русскаа грамота ч<е>стнѣиши есть ел'линьскіа, с<ва>тъ бѡ моужь сотворилъ ю есть, Кѵрила рекоу ѳилѡсоѳа, а греческоую алѳавитоу ел'лини некрещени, погани соуще, составливали соуть." (V. G. Druzhinin, ed., *Zhitie sv. Stefana, episkopa permskogo, napisannoe Epifaniem Premudrym* [St. Petersburg, 1897]. Rpt.: Apophoreta Slavica, no. 2 ['s-Gravenhage, 1959], p. 72. Cf. Angelov, "Kirillometodievoto delo," pp. 47–48.

13. Obolensky, "The Heritage of Cyril and Methodius," p. 62.

14. Two codices of the *Skazanie o gramote rous'tei* date from the fifteenth century; one textual witness goes back to the sixteenth century; and three testimonies date from the seventeenth century. At least two copies bear the title *O prestavlenii svętago Kirila ouchitelę sloven'skomou ęzyku*, but the work is best known to scholars under the title, *Skazanie o slavianskoi pis'mennosti*, or Jagić's designation, *Skazanie o slavianskikh knigakh, perenesennoe na pochvu russkuiu: sopostavlenie sv. Vladimira s sv. Kirillom* (Jagić, *Codex Slovenicus*, 20–22). For the text of the *Skazanie o gramote rous'tei* and commentary, see, most recently, F. Maresh, "Skazanie o slavianskoi pis'mennosti," *TODRL* 19 (1963): 169–176.

15. For a good summary of the discussions on the historical authenticity of the *Skazanie o gramote rous'tei*, see O. Kralik, "Povest' vremennykh let i legenda Kristiana o sviatykh Viacheslave i Liudmile," *TODRL* 19 (1963): 185–191. Cf. Goldblatt, "O 'rus'kymi pismeny,'" pp. 322–323.

16. On these differences, see Goldblatt, "On 'rus'kymi pismeny,'" pp. 324–325.

17. The idea of linking the *Skazanie o gramote rous'tei* to the "Russian episode" in *Vita Constantini*—or even the possibility that it represents an amplification of the account in *Vita Constantini* (Chapter 8)—is given added credence by the fact that the oldest copy of the work is found in the above-cited ms. 19 of the Manuscript Section of the Lenin State Library, *fond* 173, immediately after what is generally considered the earliest East Slavic testimony of the *Vita Constantini* (Lavrov, *Materialy*, pp. 36–37).

18. The motif of autonomous entry contrasts sharply with the account given in the *Primary Chronicle* (*s.a.* 6406 [898 A.D.]), where the claim that the beginnings of Christianity and literacy in Rus' are grounded in the Cyrillo-Methodian tradition is accompanied by an insistence on the apostolic origins of evangelization among the Slavs (*Povest' vremennykh let,* ed. V. P. Adrianova-Peretts and D. S. Likhachev [Moscow and Leningrad, 1950], 1: 52–54. See Goldblatt, "O 'rus'kymi pismeny,'" pp. 325–326.

19. I have excluded from consideration here one witness of the so-called Fragments of the Second Redaction (BAN 4.9.37, fol. 2r-v), which dates from the second half of the thirteenth century: see A. M. Moldovan, ed., *Slovo o zakone i blagodati* (Kiev, 1984), pp. 20–24, 71, 73.

20. One should note that the "first redaction" (or "extensive redaction"—that is, the version that contains all four sections of the work indicated by its title—is preserved only in a single fifteenth-century codex, now in the State Historical Museum in Moscow (GIM, Collection of the Synodal Library, No. 591). For "archaeographic information" on the extant testimonies of Metropolitan Hilarion's *Slovo o zakone i blagodati* and an analysis of the manuscript tradition, see Moldovan, *Slovo o zakone i blagodati*, pp. 4–65. Cf. N. N. Rozov, "Rukopisnaia traditsiia 'Slova o zakone i bla-

godati,'" *TODRL* 17 (1961): 71–85; L. Müller, ed., *Des Metropoliten Ilarion Lobrede auf Vladimir den Heiligen und Glaubnisbekenntnis* (Wiesbaden, 1962), pp. 33–51.

21. See R. Picchio, "The Function of Biblical Thematic Clues," pp. 20–23.

22. The *Slovo o zhitii i uchenii sviatogo Stefana byvshago v Permi episkopa* has come down to us through an "extensive version" in about twenty textual witnesses, the oldest of which can be dated to 1480. The work also has survived in an "abbreviated version" (including the version found in the *Prolog*), contained in approximately thirty codices that reveal numerous redactional variants. The best edition of the work (in its "extensive version") remains that of V. G. Druzinin, *Zhitie sv. Stefana, episkopa permskogo, napisannoe Epifaniem Premudrym* (St. Petersburg, 1897), rpt. Apophoreta Slavica, no. 2 ('S-Gravenhage, 1959). (All citations from the *Zhitie sv. Stefana* will rely on Druzhinin's publication; page numbers will be given in parentheses.) Even this edition, however, is based on a *codex optimus* and offers a scanty list of textual variants: for a description of the four codices used by Druzhinin, see pp. iii–vii of the 1897 publication. It therefore is important to stress that opinions on the *Zhitie sv. Stefana*, both past and present, have been advanced in the absence of either a *recensio codicum* or a systematic *collatio*, which would seek to establish a *constitutio textus*. For a bibliography on Epiphanius the Most Wise and his work, see N. F. Droblenkova, "Epifanii Premudryi," *TODRL* 40 (1985): 89–91.

23. Druzhinin, *Zhitie sv. Stefana*, pp. 71–72.

24. As early as the 1870s, V. Kliuchevsky, in his *Drevnerusskie zhitiia sviatykh kak istoricheskii istochnik* (Moscow, 1871), p. 5, alluded to a connection between the two works. Cf. K. Kuev, *Chernorizets Khrabăr* (Sofia, 1967), pp. 172–179. For the texts and examination of *O pismenekh'* see, *inter alia*, Jagić, *Codex Slovenicus*, pp. 9–31; Kuev, *Chernorizets Khrabăr;* R. Picchio, "Questione della lingua e Slavia Cirillometodiana," in *Studi sulla questione della lingua presso gli Slavi*, ed. R. Picchio (Rome, 1972), pp. 86–108; A. Giambelluca Kossova, *Chernorizets Khrabăr. O pismenekh'* (Sofia, 1980); B. N. Floria, *Skazaniia o nachale slavianskoi pis'mennosti* (Moscow, 1981). All quotations from Monk Hrabr's treatise will refer to Kossova's critical edition.

25. On the early Bulgarian (rather than Moravian!) origins of Monk Hrabr's treatise, either in Saint Clement's school (at Ohrid) or in the literary circle of Tsar Symeon (at Preslav), see V. Tkadlčik, "Le moine Chrabr et l'origine de l'écriture slave," *BzySl* 25 (1964): 75–92; Kuev, *Chernorizets Khrabăr*, pp. 20–44; F. Dvornik, *Byzantine Missions among the Slavs. SS. Constantine-Cyril and Methodius* (New Brunswick, 1970), pp. 250–251; Floria, *Skazaniia o nachale slavianskoi pis'mennosti*, pp. 174–175.

26. Ševčenko, "Three Paradoxes," p. 225, n. 19.

27. "Но Б<о>гъ, м<и>л<о>стивыи чл<овѣ>колюбець, иже вса оустраѧа на пѡлʼзу людемʼ си, и не ѡставлѧа рѡда чл<овѣ>ча без разоума, но всачески приводѧ на разоумъ и на сп<а>сеніе, иже пощадѣ и помилова люди (69). Cf. *Vita Constantini* (Chapter 1): перʼмьскга языка, въздвиже и оустрои имъ, якѡж древле Веселеила въ І<зра>или" "Богъ милостивыи . . . жадаа на покааніе чловѣче, да быша спасени въси были и въ разоумъ истинныи пришли . . . но не оставлѧетъ чловѣча рода ѡтпасти ослабленіемъ . . . якоже испръва, таже и нынѣ . . . въздвигыи намъ оучителѧ сицего." (Lavrov, *Materialy*, p. 1). On the

scriptural correspondences between the two works, see Picchio, "The Function of Biblical Thematic Clues," pp. 6–13.

28. "Богъ милостивыи и щедръ, жадаа на покааніе чловѣче, да быша спасени въси были и въ разоумъ истинныи пришли [1 Tim. 2:4], не хощеть бо съмръти грѣшникомъ, но покааніа и животоу [Ez. 33:11]." (Lavrov, *Materialy*, p.1).

29. "Г<оспод>ь ... хотАи всѣмъ чл<овѣ>комъ сп<а>сенымъ быти и въ разоумъ истинныи пріити [1 Tim. 2:4]: не хотАи смер'ти грѣшнико*м*, но ѡбращеніа и покааніа ѡжидаа в' животѣ ихъ [Ez. 33:11]" (32). It is noteworthy that the final biblical citation in the *Zhitie sv. Stefana* is based on 1 Tim. 2:4: "слава хотАщемоу всА чл<овѣ>ки сп<а>сти і в разоумъ истин'ныи привести ... " (112).

30. "... и ясенъ будет Азыкъ гоугниваго [Is. 35:6]; тогда въ д<е>нь [ѡнъ] оуслышать глусіи словеса книжнаа [Is. 29:18]" (66).

31. "И ѡтверзошасА по пророчьскомоу словеси, оуши глоухыхъ оуслышати книжная словеса [Is. 29:18], и языкъ яснъ бысть гоугнивымъ [Is. 35:6]" (Lavrov, *Materialy*, 28).

32. "Сим же раздаяномъ на ученье книгамъ, събысться пророчество на русьстѣи земли, глаголющее: В оны днии услышать глусии словеса книжная [Is. 29:18], и яснъ будеть языкъ гугнивых [Is. 35:6]" (*Povest' vremennykh let*, 1: 81).

33. "... and the tongue of the stammerers shall speak plainly" (... καὶ τρανὴ ἔσται γλῶσσα μογιλάλων—Is. 35:6); "and in that day the deaf shall hear the words of the book" (καὶ ἀκούσονται ἐν τῇ ἡμέρᾳ ἐκείνῃ κωφοὶ λόγους βιβλίου—Is. 29:18).

34. Obolensky, "The Heritage of Cyril and Methodius," pp. 57–58, 65.

35. The combination of 1 Timothy 2:4 and Ezekiel 33:11, together with other scriptural references, forms what Picchio calls a "general thematic clue" for the *Vita Constantini*: see R. Picchio, "*VC* and *VM*'s Pauline Connotations of Cyril and Methodius' Apostleship," *Palaeobulgarica* 6, no. 3 (1982): 112–118; idem, "The Function of Biblical Thematic Clues," pp. 6–13. On the importance of these biblical references for the "Slavic thesis on the continuity of the apostleship," see Picchio, "Questione della lingua," pp. 34–48.

36. Picchio, "Chapter 13 of *Vita Constantini*," pp. 145–150. According to Picchio, the scriptural allusions to Isaiah in Chapter 15 of *Vita Constantini*, which are intended as an "allusion to the incumbent days of the spiritual salvation of the Slavs" (p. 150), fulfill the expectations raised by the citation of Is. 35:2 in *Vita Constantini*, Chapter 13: "... and my people shall see the glory of the Lord" (... καὶ ὁ λαός μου ὄψεται τὴν δόξαν κυρίου). Thus, although "this new reference to Isaiah [in *Vita Constantini*, Chapter 15] helps the reader grasp the higher meaning of the hagiographic account," it is the initial citation in Chapter 13 of *Vita Constantini* "which functions as a *thematic clue* governing the *Vita*'s section devoted to the apostolic mission among the Slavs" (ibid.).

37. See A. Giambelluca Kossova, "Zakonăt i blagodatta v 'Pokhvalno slovo za Kiril i Metodii,'" *Polota K"nigopis'naia* 14–15 (1985): 109–121.

38. See A. Giambelluca Kossova, "Per una letteratura analitica del 'Žitie prepodobnago Feodosija Pečerskogo' di Nestore," *Ricerche Slavistiche* 27–28 (1980–1981): 65–100, esp. pp. 75–82; idem, "Il messaggio evangelico di Feodosij di Kiev," *Cristianesimo nella storia* 11, no. 2 (1981): 371–399, esp. pp. 376–379.

39. See M. F. Antonova, " 'Slovo o zhitii i o prestavlenii velikago kniazia Dmitriia Ivanovicha, tsaria Rus'kago' (Voprosy atributsii i zhanra)," *TODRL* 28 (1974): 140–154, esp. pp. 144–145.

40. See V. P. Adrianova-Peretts, "Slovo o zhitii i o prestavlenii velikogo kniazia Dmitriia Ivanovicha, tsaria Rus'skago," *TODRL* 5 (1947): 73–96; A. V. Solov'ev, "Epifanii Premudryi kak avtor 'Slova o zhitii i prestavlenii velikago kniazia Dmitriia Ivanovicha, tsaria russkago,'" *TODRL* 17 (1961): 85–107; M. C. Ziolkowski, "The Style and Authorship of the Discourse on Dmitrij Ivanovič Donskoj" (Ph.D. diss., Yale University, 1977), esp. pp. 142–152, 181–199.

41. Picchio, "The Function of Biblical Thematic Clues," pp. 16–20; J. Børtnes, "The Function of Word-Weaving in the Structure of Epiphanius' *Life of Saint Stephen, Bishop of Perm'*," in *Medieval Russian Culture* [= California Slavic Studies, no. 12], ed. H. Birnbaum and M. Flier (Berkeley, Los Angeles, and London, 1984), pp. 318–319.

42. Cf. the opinion expressed by D. Obolensky: "Ševčenko ['Three Paradoxes,' p. 225] has pointed out further parallels between the *Vita Constantini* and the *Life of St. Stephen*, which strongly suggest that Epiphanius made use of the former document" (Obolensky, "The Heritage of Cyril and Methodius," p. 65, n. 76).

43. See Picchio, "The Function of Biblical Thematic Clues," p. 20.

44. "ѡ призваніи, і ѡ вѣрованіи мнѡгыхъ языкъ" (64–77). On Epiphanius's use of biblical citations, see F. Vigzell, "Tsitaty iz knig sviashchennogo pisaniia v sochineniiax Epifaniia Premudrogo," *TODRL* 26 (1971): 232–243; F. Kitch, *The Literary Style of Epifanij Premudryj: Pletenie Sloves* [= Slavistische Beiträge, no. 96] (Munich, 1976), 131ff.

45. For the comparison of Saint Stephen and Saint Cyril, see Druzhinin, *Zhitie sv. Stefana*, pp. 71–73.

46. It is important to note that Epiphanius places particular emphasis on the fact that—in contradistinction to the situation in Rus' and many other lands—no apostle had ever visited the Permian land, not even Saint Paul: see Druzhinin, *Zhitie sv. Stefana*, pp. 9–12. Cf. Børtnes, "The Function of Word-Weaving," pp. 332–333.

47. On the motif of "speechlessness" (Gr. ἀλογία; Slav. "bessloviesie") in the context of the Cyrillo-Methodian language question, see Picchio, "Questione della lingua," pp. 34–48; cf. Goldblatt, pp. 179–180, 316–317.

48. According to Epiphanius, the Permians were baptized "at the end of time" and "at the end of the seventh millennium": "Но егда бл<а>говоли Сп<а>съ нашь ... в' послѣднаа дни, въ скон'чаніе лѣт, во ѡстаточнаа времена, на исхо∂ числа сед'мыа тысаща лѣтъ, м<и>л<о>с<е>рдова> о нихъ Г<оспод>ь наш." (13). In order to legitimize the Permians' late entry into history—that is, "at the eleventh hour"—Epiphanius relies on the parable of the hired workers in the vineyard (Matt. 20:1-16): see Druzhinin, Zhitie sv. Stefana, p. 12. Cf. Børtnes, "The Function of Word-Weaving," pp. 322, 332–333. On the motif of the "seventh age" and the importance of the parable of the workers in the vineyard for Cyrillo-Methodian writings, see Picchio, "Questione della lingua," pp. 38–48; Kossova, "Zakonăt i blagodatta," pp. 111–112.

49. One can hardly agree with C. A. Ferguson's assertion that, in confronting the language problems involved in his mission, "[Saint Stephen] acted without benefit of

a sociolinguistic theory or frame of reference, and without any recorded body of previous sociolinguistic experience he could consult" (C. Ferguson, "St. Stephen of Perm and Applied Linguistics," in J. Fishman, C. Ferguson, and J. Das Gupta, eds., *Language Problems of Developing Nations* [New York, 1968], pp. 261-262).

50. Cf. R. Auty, "The Gospel and Psalter of Cherson: Syriac or Russian," in *To Honor Roman Jakobson. Essays on the Occasion of his Seventieth Birthday* (The Hague and Paris, 1967), vol. 1, p. 117.

51. See Picchio, "Chapter 13," pp. 148-151.

52. See ms. 8 of the Barsov Collection: "Суть же и стихи трие написани первыи на первои гранѣ. самарѣиски. вторыи на второи гранѣ еврѣискии. Третии на третьеи грани грѣчьскии." (Lavrov, *Materialy,* p. xlvi).

53. "Желаажс бωлшаго разоума, яко ωбразомъ любомоудрїа изоучисѧ и греческои грамотѣ, и книги греческїа избыче, и добрѣ почиташе ѧ, и пр<и>сно имаше ѧ оу себе. И баше оумѣѧ гла<гола>ти треми языки; тако же и грамоты три оумѣаше, яж<е> есть роусскыи и греческыи, пер'мьскыи, яко збытисѧ ω сем словеси ωномоу, гл<агол>ющоу, иже речеса: яко языки възгл<агол>ють нωвы; и пакы: инѣми языки гла<гола>ти оустрои. И добрѣ ωбдержаше и помыслъ, еже ити въ Пер'мьскоую землю и учити ѧ." (8).

54. See Obolensky, "The Heritage of Cyril and Methodius," pp. 54-56.

55. On Orthodox Slavic language triads, see Picchio, "Questione della lingua," pp. 37-38, 67-72; Goldblatt, *Orthography and Orthodoxy,* pp. 231-233, 350-352; D. Frick, "Meletius Smotricky and the Ruthenian Question in the Age of Counter-Reformation" (Ph.D. diss., Yale University, 1977), pp. 153-204, esp. pp. 181-185.

56. R. Jakobson, "The Kernel of Comparative Slavic Literature," in Roman Jakobson, *Selected Writings,* vol. 6: *Early Slavic Paths and Crossroads,* ed. S. Rudy (Berlin, New York, and Amsterdam, 1985), p. 48.

57. See Børtnes, "The Function of Word-Weaving," pp. 335-336.

58. For a discussion of this point, see R. Picchio, "Il posto della letteratura bulgara antica nella cultura europea del medio evo," *Ricerche Slavistiche* 27-28 (1980-1981): 37-41; H. Goldblatt, "The Language Question and the Emergence of Slavic National Languages," *The Emergence of National Languages,* ed. A. Scaglione (Ravenna, 1984), pp. 129-131.

59. See, in this regard, J. Vlášek, "Quelques notes sur l'apologie slave par Chrabr," *ByzSl* 28 (1967): 82-97; R. Picchio, "On the Textual Criticism of Xrabr's Treatise," in *Studies in Slavic Linguistics and Poetics in Honor of Boris O. Unbegaun,* ed. J. Allen et al. (New York and London, 1968), pp. 139-147; idem, "Questione della lingua," pp. 86-108; Floria, *Skazaniia o nachale slavianskoi pis'mennosti,* pp. 60-63.

60. On the place of this attitude in Orthodox Slavic language speculation of the fourteenth and fifteenth centuries, see Goldblatt, *Orthography and Orthodoxy,* pp. 20-24, 242-243, 350-354.

61. It is noteworthy that Constantine Kostenechki, too, stresses the prestige of the Syriac tongue. In his opinion, the "wondrous men" who invented the Slavic expressions "in the beginning" knew that the Slavic edition of the divine Scriptures had to be brought forth in a language that possessed a level of "literary subtlety" (*t''nkota knizhnaa*) equal to that of "Greek, Hebrew and Syriac." The author of the *Skazanie iz'iavlenno o pismenekh"* thus proposes a new "Orthodox" triad of languages in which he has elimi-

nated Latin and placed Syriac in its stead (Jagić, *Codex Slovenicus*, p. 108). On the prestige of Syriac in the Orthodox Slavic tradition, see Goldblatt, *Orthography and Orthodoxy*, pp. 231–233; Picchio, "Questione della lingua," pp. 29–30. Cf. Jakobson, "Minor Sources," pp. 186–187.

62. On the long exegetical tradition that focused on the question of whether Hebrew or Syriac was the first language, see Kuev, *Chernorizets Khrabăr*, pp. 68–70; Goldblatt, *Orthography and Orthodoxy*, pp. 231–233, 274.

63. See A. Giambelluca Kossova, "Ruskata prerabotka na 'Za bukvite' ot Chernorizets Khrabăr," *Literaturna misăl* 22, no. 4 (1978): 107–122; idem, "La rielaborazione russa del 'Trattato sulle lettere' di Černorizec Chrabăr," in *Konstantin-Kiril Filosof. Materiali ot nauchnite konferentsii po sluchai 1150 godishnata ot rozhdenieto mu* (Sofia, 1981), pp. 204–222; idem, *Chernorizets Khrabăr*, pp. 78–108. One should note that in the latter study Kossova examines not only East Slavic but also Balkan Slavic "revisions" of Hrabr's tract. Cf. Kuev, *Chernorizets Khrabăr*, pp. 167–182.

64. See Kossova, "La rielaborazione russa," pp. 204–206.

65. See Goldblatt, "On 'rus'kymi pismeny,'" pp. 317–328; idem, *Orthography and Orthodoxy*, pp. 233–236.

66. Thus, for example, in both Epiphanius and Hrabr one finds common textual material focusing on the notion of a Greek writing system that develops only gradually and with great difficulty. One could also refer here to the thematic parallel in Epiphanius's work and the "Russian Revision" of Hrabr's tract regarding the first language (Hebrew) and its invention by Seth, the son of Adam.

67. Here one might point to the motif of the twenty-four Greek letters which, though common to both Epiphanius and Hrabr, conveys a very distinct ideological message in each of the two works.

68. Kossova, *Chernorizets Khrabăr*, pp. 126–128.

69. I.e., a Russian language and tradition no less dignified and authoritative than Hebrew, Greek, and Latin: "аще ли и се требѣ есть, достоаше паче роус'скаа готова соущи грамота, юже предати имъ и наоучити а, соутʼ бѡ писмена книжнаа ихже издавна, и по пошлинѣ имоуще языци оу себе, якѡже се жидовьскы, ел'линьскы, римьскы." (70). See note 80 below.

70. See Druzhinin, *Zhitie sv. Stefana*, p. 70.

71. I.e., first from Hebrew into Greek, and then from Greek into Slavic (or "Russian"). On this fundamental motif, see Goldblatt, *Orthography and Orthodoxy*, pp. 20–24, 211–214, 350–353.

72. "ѡтъ пръваго же наченъ по гръчьскоу. ѡни оубо алфа, а съ азъ, ѡтъ аза начать ѡбое. И якоже ѡни подоблъше сѧ жидовьскымъ писменемъ сътворишѫ, тако и съ гръчьскымъ. Жидове бѡ пръвое писма имать алефъ, еже сѧ сказаеть ученіе съвращажще въводимоую дѣтищоу и глаголаще: учи сѧ, еже есть алефъ. И гръци подобаще сѧ томоу алфа рѣщѫ . . . Тѣмъ бо подоба сѧ сватыи Кирилъ створи пръвое писма азъ." (Kossova, *Chernorizets Khrabăr*, pp. 116–119).

73. In other words, what is primary in the corresponding passage from Epiphanius is not a particular triad of languages but rather a multitude of tongues among which the author includes Russian and Permian: "Оу жидовьскіа аз'букы, первомоу словоу имѧ алѳъ, а [у] греческіа аз'букы пер'вомоу словоу имѧ алѳавита; а сиріаньскыѧ, алеѳъбе; а [у] оугорьскіе аѳакавасака; а [у] русски азъ; оу пер'мь-

скіе абуръ; да не по единои, гл<агол>юще, оумнѡжитсѧ слово: мнѡзи бѡ соу*т* грамоты, и мнѡзи аз'боукы." (69–70).

74. "И сътвори имъ л̃. писмена и осмь, ѡва убѡ по чиноу гръчьскыхъ писменъ, ѡва же по словѣньстѣи рѣчи." (Kossova, *Chernorizets Khrabar*, p. 116.) Constantine Kostenechki also places the number of letters in the Slavic alphabet at thirty-eight and divides the letters into two groups, namely, into twenty-four "Greek" letters and fourteen "Slavic" (or "invented") letters (Jagić, *Codex Slovenicus*, pp. 111–112). See Goldblatt, *Orthography and Orthodoxy*, 242–243.

75. "Дроузии же глаголать: Почто есть л̃и. писменъ створиль, а можеть сѧ и меньшимь того писати, якоже и гръци к̃д. пишѫть? А не вѣдать колицѣмь пишѫть гръци. Есть бо убѡ к̃д. писменъ нж не наплънѣжть сѧ тѣми книгы, нж приложили сѫть двогласныхъ а̃i, и въ писменехъ же г̃.: ѕ̃. -е и ѳ̃. десатное и ѳ̃. сътное и събиражѫть сѧ ихъ л̃и." (Kossova, *Chernorizets Khrabăr*, pp. 122–124). On the importance of the principle of imitation for Orthodox Slavic language speculation of the fourteenth and the fifteenth century, see Goldblatt, *Orthography and Orthodoxy*, pp. 350–353.

76. In fact, on the basis of the edition and variants offered by Druzhinin, it is unclear *what* is being imitated: the number of Greek letters or the actual letters themselves. See note 77 below.

77. "Тако же и сесь [Stefan] сложилъ число*м* четыре межоу двѣма десатима сло*в*', подоб*ѧ*сѧ греческіа [азбоукы числу сло*в*, ѡва убо слова по чину греческих] письмень, ова*ж* убо по рѣчи пер'мьскаго азыка, пер'вое же слово: азъ, оустиха, якоже и оу греческіа азбоукы." (69). Note the conclusions offered by G. Lytkin, whose comparison of the orthographic signs in the Old Permian alphabet with both Greek and Slavo-Russian letters of the thirteenth and fourteenth centuries led him to assert that a significant number of Old Permian letters were created on the model of Greek letters, while the remaining letters were patterned after the Slavo-Russian alphabet (G. Lytkin, *Drevnepermskii iazyk* [Moscow, 1952], p. 26). Cf. Ferguson, "St. Stefan of Perm," p. 259.

78. See note 77 above.

79. See Druzhinin, *Zhitie sv. Stefana*, pp. 8, 58, 73. Note in this regard the parallel established by Epiphanius between the invention of Permian letters, which occurred "only *120 years* before the end of the last age" (70), and the creation of "Russian" letters, which took place *120 years* before the baptism of the land of Rus'" (73). See note 80 below.

80. "Тѣм'же мню, яко русскаа грамота ч<е>стнѣиши есть ел'линьскіа, с<вя>тъ бѡ моужъ сотворилъ ю есть, Кѷрила рекоу ѳилѡсоѳа, а греческоую алѳавитоу ел'лини некрещени, погани соуще, составливали соуть" (72). Nevertheless, the "Russian" letters were invented at a time when the land of Rus' was still pagan and not yet ready for baptism: "Кѷрилъ тои намъ грамотоу сотворилъ . . . въ княженіе кн<ѧ>зѧ великого всеѧ Роуси Рюрика погана соуща и некр<е>щена, за р̃к. лѣ*т* до кр<е>щеніа Роусскіа землѧ." (73).

81. Cf. note 77 above.

82. "Книгы писаше, с роус'скых перевода на пер'мьскіа, но и съ греческыхъ мнѡгажды на пер'мьскіа." (58). Cf. note 53 above.

83. See R. Picchio, *La letteratura russa antica* (Milan, 1968), pp. 127–133; Iovine,

"The History and Historiography of the Second South Slavic Influence," pp. 301–303.

84. See Ziolkowski, "The Style and Authorship of the Discourse on Dmitrij Ivanovič Donskoj," pp. 148–152.

85. "Хвалитъ бѡ ... Роускаа землѧ, великого кн<а>зѧ Володимера, кр<е>стившаго ю, Москва же бл<а>житъ и чтитъ Петра митрополита, яко новаг чюдотворца, Ростов'скаѧ же землѧ, Леѡн'тіа, еп<и>с<ко>па своего." (89–90).

86. On the connection made between Epiphanius and the Hesychast movement, which is often based on the writer's use of the "new style" usually referred to as "word-weaving" (*pletenie sloves*), see, *inter alia,* Likhachev, "Nekotorye zadachi,"; idem, *Kul'tura Rusi vremeni Andreia Rubleva i Epifaniia Premudrogo* (Moscow, 1962); Picchio, " 'Prerinascimento esteuropeo' "; idem, "L'intreccio delle parole' e gli stili letterari presso gli Slavi ortodossi nel tardo Medio Evo," in *Studi slavistici in ricordo di Carlo Verdiani,* ed. A. Raffo (Pisa, 1979), pp. 245–262; Iovine, "The History and Historiography of the Second South Slavic Influence," esp. pp. 197–204, 234–248, 251–255; 321–334; J. Meyendorff, *Byzantium and the Rise of Russia. A Study of Byzantino-Russian Relations in the Fourteenth Century* (Cambridge, 1981), esp. pp. 119–144; Børtnes, "The Function of Word-Weaving," esp. pp. 312–313, 330–331; G. Brogi Bercoff, "Sulla poetica nel Medio Evo slavo ortodosso: Il *Poslanie* di Epifanij a Kiril di Tver'," *Europa Orientalis* 4 (1985): 7–28.

87. Druzhinin, *Zhitie sv. Stefana,* p. 85. (For an English translation of the relevant passage, see Meyendorff, *Byzantium and the Rise of Russia,* p. 137.) Cf. Epiphanius's references to the time when Saint Cyril invented the "Russian" letters (73) and Saint Stephen invented the Permian alphabet (74), respectively. In both cases, the names of the Byzantine emperor and patriarch are mentioned first. One should recall, in this regard, the celebrated letter of Patriarch Anthony to the Muscovite grand prince Basil I, written some time between 1394 and 1397, in which the Muscovite ruler is reproached for not affirming the supreme authority of the Byzantine emperor and patriarch: see *Acta Patriarchatus Constantinopolitani,* ed. F. Miklosich and I. Müller (Vienna, 1862), pp. 188–192. On the claim of the Byzantine emperor and the patriarchate of Constantinople to universality and its connection with the "victory" of the Hesychasts: see D. Obolensky, "Byzantium and Russia in the Late Middle Ages," in *Europe in the Late Middle Ages,* ed. J. Hale et al. (London, 1965), pp. 248–275; idem, *The Byzantine Commonwealth: Eastern Europe, 500–1453* (London, 1971), pp. 264–265; Meyendorff, *Byzantium and the Rise of Russia,* pp. 96–118, 137–138, 254–256; Goldblatt, *Orthography and Orthodoxy,* pp. 12–16.

88. It is noteworthy that only in one of the textual witnesses utilized by Druzhinin is the Muscovite grand prince referred to with the designation "of all Rus' " (*vseia Rousi*). Druzhinin, *Zhitie sv. Stefana,* p. 85.

89. Interestingly, Epiphanius notes that Metropolitan Cyprian "was in Kiev in those days [of Saint Stephen's demise]," (85) thereby undermining, in some measure, the bond between Moscow and the "metropolitan of all Rus'." Cf. Epiphanius's reference to the metropolitan in the period when Saint Stephen invented the Permian letters: "... в лѣто [1375] ... на Роуси же, при велицѣмь кн<а>зи Дмитреи Ивановичи, архіеп<и>с<ко>поу же митрополитоу не соущоу на Руси в' ты д<ь>ни никомоу же ..." (74).

90. Meyendorff, *Byzantium and the Rise of Russia,* pp. 116–118, 137.

91. See note 79 above.
92. See Brogi Bercoff, "Sulla poetica nel Medio Evo slavo ortodosso."
93. Obolensky, *The Byzantine Commonwealth*, pp. 264–265.
94. See Picchio, *La letteratura russa antica*, pp. 116–120; Goldblatt, "La rinascita slava ortodossa."
95. See Picchio, *La letteratura russa antica*, pp. 120–133; Iovine, "The History and Historiography of the Second South Slavic Influence," pp. 296–303.
96. See Obolensky, "The Heritage of Cyril and Methodius," pp. 64–65.
97. Jakobson, "The Kernel of Comparative Slavic Literature," p. 48.

The Corpus of Slavonic Translations Available in Muscovy

The Cause of Old Russia's Intellectual Silence and a Contributory Factor to Muscovite Cultural Autarky

FRANCIS J. THOMSON

> A rhetor and a philosopher cannot be a Christian.
> —Avvakum Petrov[1]

The absence of intellectual learning in Old Russia[2] has frequently been the subject of comment. In 1901, Evgenii Golubinsky, Russia's most eminent church historian, pronounced the following judgment:

> Literacy and not enlightenment—all our history over the immense period spanning the time from Vladimir to Peter the Great is epitomized in these words.[3]

In 1937, Georges Florovsky began what remains the most penetrating history of Russian theology with the words:

> The history of Russian thought contains a good deal that is problematical and incomprehensible. The most important question is this: what is the meaning of Russia's ancient, enduring and centuries long intellectual silence?[4]

In 1946, George Fedotov in one of the most profound studies of early Russian religious culture wrote:

> The poverty of intellectual culture in ancient Russia is amazing. For seven centuries—that is, until the seventeenth—we know of no scientific work in Russian literature, not even a dogmatic thesis ... Russia, in fact, did not receive together with Greek Christianity the classical culture of Greece. ... The available Slavonic literature had an overwhelmingly practical and didactic character. Theoretical interests had not been awakened. And the Russian intellect was dwarfed in its development for a long time, not because of the predominance of mystical tendencies, as has often been claimed, but because of the absence of external occasions for exercise.[5]

In a written debate between Georges Florovsky and the historians Nikolay Andreyev and James Billington in 1962, Florovsky held the diametrically opposed view: Russia received not too little, but:

> too much at once—an enormous richness of cultural material, which simply could not be absorbed at once . . . Old Russia seems to have been charmed by the perfection, completeness and harmony of Byzantine civilization, and paralysed by this charm . . . the Byzantine achievement had been accepted but the Byzantine inquisitiveness had not.[6]

The solutions proposed by Andreyev and Billington were more prosaic: the former ascribed the intellectual silence to the fact that as a province of the Mongol Empire, Old Russia had been isolated from Western Europe,[7] whereas the latter attributed it to the fact that the two periods of the most intensive assimilation of Byzantine culture had coincided with the anti-intellectual movements of iconodulia and hesychasm respectively.[8] Florovsky rightly rejected the validity of Andreyev's and Billington's theses: the Mongol invasion, which destroyed neither Novgorod nor Pskov, did not isolate the East Slavs from the West, while the first and second periods of South Slav influence[9] also coincided with the Macedonian and Palaeologan renaissances, whose intellectual—as opposed to artistic[10]—achievements passed unnoticed in Kiev and Moscow.[11] In this connection it must at once be pointed out that intellectual silence by no means implies cultural silence, as Florovsky put it: "Old Russia indeed left a precious legacy, at least in the realm of art."[12] However, the debate remained inconclusive as no answers were forthcoming to Florovsky's questions: "Where was rooted the bias toward an aesthetic rather than a philosophical culture? In the Byzantine heritage itself, or in the attitude of the Russians?"[13]

In fact throughout the entire debate the basic question had been begged: did Old Russia receive and assimilate Byzantine culture? The general pattern of cultural reception takes the form of a progression from assimilation, via imitation to original creation.[14] If only part of the donor culture is assimilated, the recipient's subsequent imitation and creation will ignore the unassimilated aspects: the recipient has no knowledge of, and hence no attitude towards, the donor culture *per se*, but only towards what is assimilated. This reasoning is overlooked by Zdenko Zlatar who argues that "Kievan Russia chose the kind of inheritance it wanted and needed from Byzantium and . . . excluded the rest."[15] Zlatar's thesis is based upon the false premise that the East Slavs were fully acquainted with Byzantine culture. The key to a correct understanding of the evolution of Old Russian culture lies in establishing precisely which aspects of Byzantine culture were assimilated and hence served as the source of original East Slav creativity.

Zlatar's recent attempt to solve this problem, at least for Kievan Russia, is based mainly upon the corpus of surviving manuscripts of the Kievan period, since "what might have perished is in most cases a moot question."[16] This is, in fact, a simplistic approach since many works, whose language reveals that they were translated before the mid-thirteenth century, survive only in later codices.[17] It also ignores the evidence of quotations in the works of Kievan authors and the possibility that Byzantine works may have been read in the original Greek.

It is hardly surprising that several of Zlatar's conclusions about the corpus of available translations are inaccurate, for example, that only post-Nicene works were translated,[18] but no works by contemporary Byzantine authors.[19] Nevertheless his conclusion, the same as Fedotov's, that the vast bulk of the works available were biblical, liturgical, didactic, and edificative in nature is correct, although his explanation of this fact is not. According to Zlatar, both the Cyrillo-Methodian mission to Moravia (863) and the conversion of Boris of Bulgaria (ca. 865) preceded the compilation after 876 of Photius's *Bibliotheke*, which, in his opinion, led to the "reconciliation of Hellenism with Christianity."[20] The choice of works to be translated was thus marked by the "systematic exclusion of every work of classical scholarship," a policy that subsequently remained unchanged.[21] In view of the fact that, in his words, "the dating of the *Bibliotheca* is crucial for our purpose,"[22] it is strange that Zlatar accepts without question Cyril Mango's dating,[23] which is in fact a restatement of François Halkin's: in ca. 252 of the *Bibliotheke* Photius resumes a short Greek life of Gregory the Great[24] which contains episodes taken from John Hymmonides's Latin life of Gregory finished in 876.[25] In fact, however, both the short Greek life and the Latin one go back independently to an earlier source,[26] and the *Bibliotheke* must be dated to before 858,[27] prior to both the Moravian mission and Boris's conversion. If it had had the exaggerated importance which Zlatar ascribes to it, it would have led to the inclusion, not exclusion, of classical works.

The fact that the corpus of old Bulgarian translations available in Kievan Russia[28] resembles the library of a large provincial Byzantine monastery such as Saint John's on Patmos is explained by the fact that the choice of the works translated in Bulgaria had been dictated by the mission to convert the Bulgarians and had largely been governed by liturgical requirements as laid down by the typicon.[29] The conversion of Russia coincided with the disappearance of the first Bulgarian Empire, marked by the fall of Preslav to

Emperor John Tzimisces in 971 and the incorporation of the remaining Bulgarian lands into the Byzantine Empire after the surrender of Maria, widow of Tsar John-Vladislav, to Basil II in 1018. Despite relegation of Slavonic culture to second-rate status, Slavonic remained in use as a liturgical and literary language, although translation activity continued at a much reduced level.[30] There is no evidence that newly converted Kievan Russia took over Bulgaria's role as the mediator of Byzantine culture by making new translations.[31] The theoretical possibility that a knowledge of Christian *koine* and classical *attic* enabled Kievan authors to study Byzantine philosophy and classical antiquity in the original is ruled out by the fact that, with the possible exception of Metropolitan Hilarion of Kiev (1051–1054), not a single Kievan author reveals any direct acquaintance with a Greek work unavailable in translation.[32] The result was that Kievan Russia had access to the written aspects of Byzantine culture only through the medium of Bulgarian translations and hence did not assimilate the Byzantine intellectual tradition and consequently could not pass it on to Muscovy.

A knowledge of Greek must have been more widely available in Muscovy in view of the presence there of Greeks. Already in the fourteenth century, Greek monks are found in provincial cities, for example Nilus in Tver' in 1316–1317 and Malachi in Nizhny Novgorod in 1381. After the fall of Constantinople in 1453, a Greek colony came into existence in Moscow which included representatives of some of the leading Byzantine families with names such as Angelus, Lascaris, Rhalles, and Tarchaniotes. It is, however, striking that there is no evidence for the emigration of Byzantine intellectuals to Muscovy, although one Greek refugee—if his legendary life of the seventeenth century is to be believed—became a monk: Cassian of Uglich. Once again, however, it was a knowledge of *demotic* and perhaps in a few cases also *koine* that was available, not *attic*. The writings of churchmen such as Nilus of the Sora (ca. 1433–1508), Joseph Sanin of Volokolamsk (1439/1440–1515), Zenobius of Oten (ca. 1500–1568), and Avvakum Petrov (1621–1682) reveal no acquaintance with Greek works in the original. It is significant that Maximus Triboles "the Greek" went to Moscow in 1518 in response to a request from Basil III precisely because no translators were available. It is not until the mid-seventeenth century that a knowledge of *koine* and *attic* becomes more common in Muscovy; indeed it may be assumed a priori that the absence until then of schools providing a systematic education meant that it was virtually impossible to obtain such knowledge. Because Muscovy neither inherited the Byzantine intellectual tradition from Kiev nor was acquainted with the latter in the original, the sole means for it to be assimilated remained the medium of translation. The aim of this paper is to provide a survey of works available in translation in order to establish whether it was possible for the Muscovites on this basis to have become acquainted with that tradition.[33] Such a survey must not include all translations ever made from Greek into Slavonic since it is not axiomatic that all translations made in the South Slav world—where translation activity gradually revived after the establishment of the second Bulgarian Empire —symbolized by the coronation of Kalojan at Tărnovo on 8 November 1204, automatically went northwards. Two examples of major fourteenth-century translations that apparently never went to Muscovy since they have been traced solely in South Slav codices are Gregory of Nyssa's mystical treatise *On the Creation of Man*[34] and Euthymius Zigabenus's *Dogmatic Panoply*.[35]

* * *

During the fourteenth century the choice of works to be translated was still largely governed by liturgical requirements. The gradual replacement of the Constantinopolitan typicon[36] by that of Jerusalem,[37] which took place in Russia over the period from the late thirteenth to the early fifteenth century,[38] involved considerable changes in the prescribed readings.[39] The majority of the homilies translated at this time are connected with these changes: Anastasius Sinaita's *Homily on the Transfiguration*,[40] Andrew of Crete's *Homily on the Nativity of the Deipara*,[41] John of Damascus's *Homily on the Nativity of Saint Mary the Virgin*,[42] John Mauropus's *Eulogy of the Three Hierarchs*,[43] Pantoleon of Jerusalem's *Sermon on the Exaltation of the Holy Cross*,[44] and Severian of Gabala's *Sermon on the Epiphany*.[45] Most translations of saints' lives were also made for the same reason: Symeon Metaphrastes's *Life of Saint Stephen of Constantinople*,[46] the anonymous *Life of Saint Anthimus of Nicodemia*,[47] and other hagiographical works such as the *Miracle of Saints Gurias, Damonas and Abibus*.[48] The changes in liturgical practice also required the translation of guides to the new services, such as Patriarch Philotheus Coccinus's *Order of the Liturgy*[49] and Nicon of the Black Mount's *Tacticon*.[50]

John Chrysostom remained the most popular father, a major translation being that of a collection of his homilies known as the *Margarita*, whose basic contents consist of thirty entries: Homilies 1–5 and 11 on the Incomprehensible Nature of God, Sermons 1, 4–8 against Jews, Homilies 1–6 on: 'I saw the Lord' (Isaiah 6:1), Sermons 1–4 and 7 on Lazarus, 1–3 on

David and 1–4 on Job.[51] Considerable importance was attached to the translation of anti-Latin polemics, such as Nilus Cabasilas's *On the Procession of the Holy Ghost against the Latins*,[52] Michael Cerularius's *First Epistle to Patriarch Peter of Antioch*,[53] Dominicus of Grado's *Epistle to Patriarch Peter of Antioch*,[54] together with the latter's reply,[55] Nicetas of Nicaea's *Treatise on Azymes*[56] and the anonymous *How and Why the Latins Separated from Us and Were Erased from the Diptychs*,[57] although other polemical works also received attention, such as John of Jerusalem's *Homily on Sacred Images against Constantine Cabalinus and All Heretics*.[58]

An important contribution to systemic theology was the translation of John of Damascus's philosophical introduction to dogmatics, his *Dialectics*.[59] Questions of cosmogony clearly aroused interest, as found in Severian of Gabala's six *Homilies on the Creation*[60] and George Pisides's *Hexaëmeron*,[61] as did exegesis, as in Andrew the Presbyter's *Catena on the Acts of the Apostles*.[62] The catechetic needs of the faithful were not neglected as the dual translation—one Bulgarian,[63] the other Serbian[64]—of the *Succinct Exposition of the Orthodox Faith* ascribed to Patriarch Anastasius I of Antioch shows.

Considerable attention was paid to canon law. The principal work translated was Matthew Blastares's *Alphabetical Handbook of Canon Law*, to which were appended, among other things, John the Faster's third *Collection of Penitential Canons*, John of Citrus's *Replies to Archbishop Constantine Cabasilas*, and Leo VI's list of metropolitan and archiepiscopal sees known as the *Diatyposis*.[65] History is represented by Constantine Manasses's *Metrical History*[66] and an abridgment of John Zonaras's *Annals*.[67] A mirror for princes translated at this time, pseudo-Basil I's *Exhortations to His Son Leo*,[68] influenced the development of Muscovite political thought: about half of Metropolitan Macarius's address to Ivan IV at his coronation in 1547 is taken from it,[69] and it was published no fewer than five times in the seventeenth century.[70]

However, the greatest stimulus to translation among the South Slavs in the fourteenth century was the Hesychast movement. Collections of works by the leading Hesychasts—Gregory of Sinai,[71] Nilus Cabasilas[72] and Gregory Palamas[73]—were translated, although, strangely enough, this last collection seems not to have gone to Muscovy, where only some of Palamas's works were known, such as his *Refutation of the Epigraphs of Patriarch John Beccus*[74] and his *Dispute with the Impious Moslems*.[75] Other Hesychast works translated include David Disypatus's *History of the Origin of the Heresy of Barlaam and Acindynus*,[76] Patriarch Callistus I's *Life of Saint Gregory of Sinai*,[77] and many of the liturgical hymns and prayers composed by Patriarch

Philotheus Coccinus.[78] The Hesychasts' influence was not limited to the translation of their own works: those of the fathers who had most influenced them were also translated. These included whole collections of works by Dorotheus of Gaza,[79] Symeon the New Theologian[80] and Dionysius Areopagita (the latter together with Maximus the Confessor's commentary),[81] as well as Isaac of Ninevah's homilies,[82] Peter Damascenus's *Hypomnesis*,[83] Philip Solitarius's *Dioptra*,[84] Philotheus of Sinai's *Treatise on Asceticism*,[85] Diadochus of Photice's *Treatise on Spiritual Perfection*,[86] Abbot Zosimas's *Conversations*[87] and Nicetas Stethatus's three *Practical, Physical and Gnostic Centuries*, prefaced by his *Questions and Replies*.[88]

The fourteenth century also saw a considerable number of retranslations. Because translators rarely specify their motive for retranslating a work, in most cases the reason remains uncertain. In some cases it will simply have been because the earlier translation had not survived: for example, only a fragment of the tenth-century translation of Basil of Caesarea's ascetic works survives,[89] and a new translation was made.[90] In other cases the new translation may have been made either because the extant translation was only partial, as in the case of John of Damascus's *Exposition of the Catholic Faith*[91] and Nicon of the Black Mount's *Pandectes*,[92] or because it was of a variant redaction of the original, as in the case of Gregory the Monk's *Life of Saint Basil of Constantinople*,[93] the *Gospel of Nicodemus*,[94] and the *Tale of Alexander the Great*.[95] In a few cases the second translation was made merely because the original was found in a different context. For example, to his *Alphabetical Handbook of Canon Law* Matthew Blastares appended his revision of Nicetas of Heracleia's *Replies to Bishop Constantine*, the latter translated in this context,[96] even though they were already available as Chapter 58 of the Serbian nomocanon.[97] In addition, Amphilochius of Iconium's *Life of Saint Basil of Caesarea* was translated as a preface to Basil's ascetic works,[98] even though a translation already existed as an independent work.[99] In some cases the more literalist, hellenizing approach to translation typical of the fourteenth century, in accordance with which both the sense and the form of the original had to be preserved,[100] meant that earlier, freer translations were considered inadequate and needed to be replaced. This may well have been the reason for the new translations of John Climacus's *Ladder*[101] and Gregory the Great's *Dialogues on the Lives and Miracles of the Italian Fathers*.[102] In many cases, of course, a second translation was made simply because the translator was unaware of the existence of the earlier translation.

In the first half of the fifteenth century a similar South Slav translation activity continued, although on a reduced scale because of the fall of the Bulgarian Empire to Sultan Bayezid I in 1393. Translations included Thalassius the Libyan's four *Centuries*,[103] Maximus the Confessor's *Ascetic Treatise in Questions and Answers*,[104] and John Chrysostom's sixty-seven *Homilies on Genesis*.[105] In 1412, Gabriel of Hilandar retranslated a catena on Job because, as he put it, the earlier translation was both abridged and obscure.[106] However, the fall of Constantinople in 1453—recorded in translated literature by John Eugenicus's *Lamentation on the Fall of Constantinople*,[107] which influenced the development of the theory of Moscow as the Third Rome[108]—and the incorporation of the surviving rump of the Serbian state into the Ottoman empire in 1459 led to a rapid decline in South Slav translation activity and to the transfer of such work to Lithuania[109] and Muscovy.

That refugees from the South, both Greek and Slav, played a role in this transfer is beyond doubt. Thus Athanasius of Alexandria's *Disputation with Arius at the Council of Nicaea* was translated by the joint efforts of both Demetrius Tarchaniotes, who had arrived in the suite of Zoe Palaeologa in 1472 as the envoy of her brothers Andrew and Manuel, and Protopresbyter Theodore of the Church of the Annunciation.[110] The fact, however, that this translation was made not from Greek but from Latin illustrates another aspect of the transfer of translation activity to the North. The transfer did not involve a mere geographical displacement of the activity, but marked the beginning of a change in the object of that activity: no longer was it focused virtually exclusively on the world of Byzantine Christianity. Translations began to make their appearance in fields where other languages were the media for the transmission of knowledge.

A striking illustration of this shift in interest is provided by a series of translations made in Lithuania in the second half of the fifteenth century from Hebrew into Ruthenian.[111] Quickly finding their way to Muscovy, they included the *Secret of Secrets*, a mirror for princes falsely ascribed to Aristotle, with interpolations in Book 7 (which provides advice on how to keep healthy) from three of Moses Maimonides's medical treatises: *On Poisons*, *On Intercourse*, and *On Asthma*, as well as a physiognomy taken from Rhazes's *Book for Almansor*;[112] two books on astrology—Emmanuel ben Jacob Bonfils's *Hexapterygon*[113] and John of Holywood's (de Sacrobosco) *On the Sphere of the World*,[114] and excerpts from al-Gazzali's *Ethics and Logic*,[115] soon afterwards interpolated into a translation of Maimonides's *Logic*.[116] At least two of these translations, Maimonides's *Logic* and Bonfils's *Hexapterygon*, were associated by Archbishop Gennadius of Novgorod (1485–1504) with the Judaizers.[117] The *Secret of Secrets* influenced the development of Ivan Peresvetov's political ideas in the mid-sixteenth century.[118]

It was in the Archbishop Gennadius's entourage at Novgorod that the first East Slav translations from Latin into Slavonic were made by Demetrius Gerasimov, Gerasimus Popovka, Timothy Veniaminov, the Germans Bartholomäus Ghotan and Nicolaus Bülow, and the Western monk Benjamin. Their principal achievement is the first complete translation of the Bible into Slavonic,[119] for which they translated 1 and 2 Chronicles, Ezra, Nehemiah, Esther (the deuterocanonical 10:4 through Chapter 16), Jeremiah (1–35, 46–51), 1 and 2 Esdras, Tobit, Judith, the Wisdom of Solomon, and 1 and 2 Maccabees from the Vulgate and added Jerome's prefaces and Nicholas of Lyra's postscripts to the various Biblical books.[120] For comparative purposes, they referred to the Low German translation of the Bible published by Heinrich Quentell at Cologne (ca. 1478),[121] despite which the notion of producing a vernacular Russian version seems not to have occurred to them. The use of the Vulgate reveals their ignorance not merely of the Greek language, but also of the Orthodox canon of Scripture as they included 2 Esdras, not found in the Septuagint, and omitted 3 and 4 Maccabees found in the Septuagint but not included in the Vulgate.

Their translation of Book 8 on the computus and calendar of William Durandus the Elder's *Guide to the Divine Offices*[122] from one of the two editions that appeared at Strassburg in 1486[123] must be seen in connection with the request addressed by Metropolitan Zosimas of Moscow to Archbishop Gennadius to draw up new pascal tables now that the expected end of the world on 31 August 1492 had not taken place.[124] This the archbishop did with the aid of Nicolaus Bülow, and in the preface they explained the method for computing the tables on the basis of the 532-year cycle.[125] In his epistle to Michael Misjur Munexin (ca. 1521), Bülow translated the prediction of the Second Flood for 20 February 1524 as found in Johannes Stoeffler and Jacob Pflaumen's *New Almanach*, first published at Ulm in 1499,[126] and it is virtually certain that he was also responsible for the translation of the entire almanac.[127] Philotheus of Pskov's celebrated epistle to Munexin of 1524 in which he expatiates on the theory of Moscow as the Third Rome, that "meretricious substitute of the Byzantine oecumenical idea,"[128] was written as a direct response to the translation of the prediction of the Second Flood. Bülow's other translations include Samuel of Morocco's *Book on the Coming of the Messiah*, made from Quentell's 1493 Cologne edition,[129] and it is possible that he was also responsible for the 1534 translation of the first medical handbook available in Muscovy, Johann von Cuba's *Garden of Health*, made from one of the two Low German Lübeck editions in 1492 and 1520.[130]

Demetrius Gerasimov's translations from Latin included Donatus's *Minor Grammar of Latin*,[131] Nicholas of Lyra's *Treatise on the Messiah*,[132] Bruno of Würzburg's *Commentary on the Psalms*,[133] and perhaps Maximilian Transylvanus's account of Magellan's circumnavigation of the globe, *On the Moluccan Islands*, first published at Cologne in 1523.[134] His translation activity overlaps with that of Maximus Triboles "the Greek," since when the latter arrived in Muscovy in 1518, he knew insufficient Slavonic to translate into it and thus at first translated from Greek into Latin, which Gerasimov then rendered into Slavonic. The full range of Maximus's translations cannot be listed here,[135] but they include the Biblical books Esther[136] and 4 Maccabees,[137] a catena on the Psalms[138] and another on Acts,[139] homilies, saints' lives, apocrypha, including the *Gospel of Nicodemus*[140] and the *Sibylline Oracles*,[141] and various other works such as Enea Silvio de' Piccolomini's (Pius II's) *Treatise on the Fall of Constantinople*.[142] His translation of some of Theodore Balsamon's commentaries on individual canons[143] for Bassian Patrikeev's second version of the latter's revision of the nomocanon,[144] in which Patrikeev had deliberately altered or omitted canons to suit his non-possessor views, was to prove one of Maximus's fatal errors. The corpus of Maximus's translations confirms the judgment that Maximus was no Renaissance humanist: moreover, he did not contribute to the dissemination of such views in Muscovy.

Indirectly Maximus inspired one of the major translation projects of the sixteenth century, that undertaken by Prince Andrew Kurbsky after his flight to Lithuania in 1564.[145] Maximus had recounted to Kurbsky the old legend that at the fall of Constantinople the patriarchal library had been rescued and taken to the West where the books had been translated into Latin, printed, and sold cheaply.[146] Soon after his flight to the West, Kurbsky was requested by another exile in Lithuania, Artemius, formerly abbot of the Trinity Laura of Saint Sergius, then living at Słuck, to have Basil of Caesarea's works translated from a printed edition, either from Greek or from Latin. Kurbsky had to decline because of the lack of a qualified translator,[147] but the request gave Kurbsky the idea of a translation project to make the works of the fathers available to the Orthodox population of Lithuania, then under pressure from both Catholics and Protestants. To this end he undertook a study of Latin and purchased printed editions of the works of Basil of Caesarea, Cyril of Alexandria, Gregory of Nazianzus, John Chrysostom, and John of Damascus.[148] He also won a fellow-exile in Lithuania, Prince Michael Nogotkov-Obolensky, for his project. The latter matriculated at Cracow in the winter semester of 1571,[149] and after three years at the university left for Italy to continue his studies there, returning to Lithuania after some two years in 1576.[150]

The first major achievement of the project, a translation of a collection of John Chrysostom's works known as the *New Margarita*, was in fact completed before Obolensky's return from Italy. The purpose of the translation, made from the Latin translation in the 1558 Basel edition,[151] was, as the preface explains, to provide a translation of those of Chrysostom's works that were not already available in Slavonic. The conscientious way in which the translators approached their task is shown by the fact that entries 55–61 are homilies 45 on Matthew and 22–23, 44–47 on John, missing either wholly or in part in Maximus Triboles's translation of the homilies on Matthew and John.[152]

The second major achievement was a translation, begun in 1576–1577,[153] of the collected works of John of Damascus, probably from the Latin of the 1575 Basel edition.[154] Besides their own new translations—including the *Dialectics* and *Compendium on Heresies*, the previous translations of which were presumably either unknown or unavailable to them—they included in the collection their revisions of John the Exarch's translation of the *Exposition of the Catholic Faith*, the omissions of which they made good by translating the missing passages, and of the earlier translations of the homily *On Those Who Have Fallen Asleep in the Faith* and John of Jerusalem's *Homily on Sacred Images*.[155] The *Dialectics* has been supplemented by appending to it an abridged translation of Book 3 of Johann Spangenberg's *Questions of the Trivium*, in which syllogisms are explained and illustrated.

Among the translations of individual works with which Kurbsky has been credited are the second and fourth of Cicero's *Paradoxes of the Stoics*, the first East Slav translation of any work by a classical Latin author.[156] A curious paradox of Kurbsky's project is that the translations were never published and thus the aim of supplying the Orthodox in Lithuania with the works of the fathers remained unfulfilled.

The second half of the sixteenth century saw in Muscovy an increasing interest in translations of works of a more secular nature and the beginnings of translation from Polish. Some information about geography became available from the translation of Book 1 of Pomponius Mela's *Chorography*,[157] although more accurate information is found in Martin Bielski's *Kronika wssytkyego swyata*, translated from the 1564 Cracow edition,[158] which became one of Muscovy's main sources for Western European history, especially about the Reformation. Another translation from Polish was that of the

1549 Cracow edition of the Polish version of Petrus de Crescentiis's work on farming.[159]

Whereas in the sixteenth century the efforts to provide the Orthodox population of Lithuania with the works of the fathers had involved in the main translations from Latin, by the early seventeenth century the level of learning there had considerably improved and a whole series of translations from Greek was made. For the first time printed editions of the translations began to appear. At some time before 1607, Gabriel Dorofeevich of Lemberg translated John Chrysostom's fifty-five homilies on Acts, which were published after revision by Pambo Berynda at Kiev in 1624.[160] He was perhaps also the translator of John Chrysostom's treatise *On the Priesthood*, published at Lemberg in 1614.[161] Hieromonk Cyprian of Ostrog in 1610 translated Macarius of Egypt's fifty homilies, which were published in Vilnius in 1627,[162] and John Chrysostom's homilies on the Pauline epistles, which were published at Kiev in 1623, after having been checked against Henry Savile's 1612–1613 Eton edition of the Greek by Lawrence Zizanii, Zacharius Kopystensky, and Pambo Berynda.[163] In 1625 at Kiev appeared Zizanii's translation of Andrew of Caesarea's commentary on the Revelation of Saint John, which had been revised by Tarasius Zemka, who appended his translations of Ephraem Syrus's *Sermon on the Transfiguration*, John Chrysostom's first *Sermon on Pentecost*, and an excerpt from Oecumenius of Tricca's commentary on the Revelation of Saint John.[164] At Kiev in 1628 appeared the fourteenth-century translation of Dorotheus of Gaza's works, which had been revised and augmented by Berynda using Fronton du Duc's 1624 Paris edition.[165] A new departure was the publication by Andrew Skulsky of a free-verse rendering of the tragedy *The Suffering Christ*, ascribed to Gregory of Nazianzus, at Lemberg in 1630.[166] Not all translations, however, saw the light of day: those of Nicholas Cabasilas's *Commentary on the Liturgy*[167] and Germanus of Constantinople's *Ecclesiastical History and Mystical Contemplation*[168] remained unpublished. The absence of translations from Polish is, of course, due to the fact that in Lithuania the educated knew that language.

Relatively few translations appear to have been made in Muscovy in the early seventeenth century, no doubt due to the Time of Troubles and its aftermath. Moreover, what was translated remained unpublished. Theodore Gozvinsky in 1607–1608 translated Maximus Planudes's *Life of Aesop* and the Aesopian fables from Greek[169] and in 1609 Innocent III's *On Contempt for the World, or On the Misery of the Human Condition* from an unpublished Polish translation.[170] An abridged, somewhat free translation of

Philipp Melanchthon's *Elements of Rhetoric* was made by 1620.[171] An important source of geographical knowledge was the translation of one of the editions published by Jodocus and Henricus Hondius at Amsterdam between 1606 and 1630 of Gerard Mercator's atlas,[172] a work which, incidentally, did most to propagate in the West the myth that the works of the Western fathers Ambrose, Augustine, and Jerome were available in Slavonic translation and studied in Russia.[173] Whether Nicephorus Callistus Xanthopoulos's *Treatise on Sobriety and Purity of Heart* was translated as early as this is uncertain.[174] Gennadius Scholarius's prophecy about a *blond (rhousios)* people who would drive the Turk from Constantinople, his *Commentary on the Inscription in the Tomb of Constantine the Great*, naturally aroused great interest and was translated no less than four times in the seventeenth century, first in Lithuania in 1641,[175] then in 1650 by Arsenius Sukhanov,[176] and virtually simultaneously by Metropolitan Gabriel of Nazareth (a Serb) during his stay at Moscow in 1650–1651,[177] and finally at the turn of the century by Pernethius Neboza between 1695 and 1704.[178]

The second half of the seventeenth century saw a veritable explosion of translating activity in Muscovy from Greek, Latin, and Polish, much of it being undertaken by Greek, Polish, Moldavian, Ukrainian, and Belorussian immigrants. For the first time some of the translations were published at Moscow. In connection with Patriarch Nicon's proposed liturgical reforms, Arsenius "the Greek," who in 1649 had arrived in Muscovy, published in 1656 the *Skrizhal'*, an anthology of texts on the liturgy and sacraments, including John Nathanael's *Commentary on the Sacred Liturgy* from the 1574 Venice edition and Gabriel Severus's *Treatise on the Seven Sacraments* from the 1600 Venice edition. In 1660, he published the *Anfologion,* a collection of various religious translations, some of which he himself had made, such as John Geometra's *Paradise* and Damascenus Studites's *Passion of Saint Theodore the General.* Since the *Skrizhal'* contains Damascenus's *Oration on the Adoration of the Cross,* it is possible that Arsenius made the unpublished translation of a collection of Damascenus's works known as the *Treasure,* which includes these versions of the two works.[179] Another of Damascenus Studites's works translated at this time was his *Bestiary* from the 1643 Venice edition.[180] In 1655, Arsenius began the translation of Dorotheus of Monembasia's *History,* which was finished in 1665 by Dionysius "the Greek" (in fact a Macedonian Vlach), his successor as corrector at the Ecclesiastical Printing Press.[181]

In the same year that Arsenius arrived at Moscow (1649), so did the leading Ukrainian scholar Epiphanius Slavinetsky, some of whose many translations chiefly in the fields of theology and canon law were published. The 1656 *Skrizhal'* contains his translations of Athanasius of Alexandria's *Questions and Replies to Antiochus, Questions on Sacred Scripture,* and *Other Questions,* whereas the 1660 *Anfologion* has Justin Martyr's *Greek Questions to Christians.* In 1665 appeared a large volume of his translations including Athanasius of Alexandria's four *Homilies against the Arians* from the 1627 Paris edition, Basil of Caesarea's nine homilies on the *Hexaëmeron* from the 1532 Basel edition, and fifty of Gregory of Nazianzus's homilies from the 1630 Paris edition. His translation of Matthew Blastares's *Alphabetical Handbook of Canon Law,* for which he used the fourteenth-century translation as a guide,[182] was consulted at the synod of Moscow in 1666–1667, at which Patriarch Nicon was removed from office. He also translated Johann Löwenklau's (Leunclavius) work on canon and civil law published at Frankfurt in 1596.[183] According to the catalogue of works available in Slavonic translation drawn up for the Ecclesiastical Printing Press in 1665–1666, he also translated Pliny the Younger's *Panegyric,* Andrew Vesalius's work on anatomy, and part of Book 1 of Thucydides's *Histories,*[184] but no copies have ever been traced.

On Slavinetsky's death in 1675, his successor as chief corrector at the Printing Press, Euthymius, a monk of the Monastery of the Miracle of the Archangel Michael, continued his work. His theological translations include Cyril of Jerusalem's *Catechisms,*[185] Gregory Palamas's two *Treatises on the Procession of the Holy Ghost* from the 1624 London edition,[186] and Peter Mogila's *Confession of the Orthodox Faith*[187] from the 1665 Amsterdam edition. This latter translation was published at Moscow in 1696. His translations also include works on canon law, such as the *Nomocanon in Fourteen Titles* together with Theodore Balsamon's and John Zonaras's commentaries, for which he used Löwenklau's 1596 Frankfurt edition as well as William Beveridge's *Synodicon,* published at Oxford in 1672;[188] on liturgy, such as Patriarch Athanasius III Patellarus of Constantinople's *Commentary on the Order of the Patriarchal Liturgy;*[189] on history, including Matthew Cigalas's *New Synopsis* from the 1637 Venice edition;[190] and on sacred geography, for example, Arsenius Calloudes's description of the Holy Land for pilgrims from the 1679 Venice edition.[191]

Other translators from Greek include Metropolitan Dositheus Bărilă of Suceava, who had fled Moldavia in 1686 and who translated Ignatius of Antioch's *Epistles*[192] and a collection of thirty-five Chrysostomian homilies that had been published in modern Greek at Venice in 1675,[193] and another Moldavian, Nicholas Spătar (also known as Milescu from his estate at

Mileşti), who translated the first part of Paisius Ligarides's compendium of prophecies known as the *Chresmologion*.[194] One feature of many of these seventeenth-century Muscovite translations from Greek is their literal, hellenizing style that rendered the sense often obscure and was probably the reason why many remained unpublished. To give but one example: Patriarch Dositheus II of Jerusalem in 1685 sent a copy of the 1683 Jassy edition of Symeon of Thessalonica's works to Moscow and Euthymius was instructed to translate it. The result was so obscure[195] that Metropolitan Dositheus Bărilă was requested to revise it. He removed many Graecisms but even this was found unsatisfactory,[196] and Spătar in turn was entrusted with a further revision. The result is, if anything, even more obscure than Euthymius's original translation,[197] and none of the versions ever saw the light of day.

Besides this school of translators working from Greek, to whose production must be added the occasional translation made from the same language in the South that found its way to Muscovy, such as Agapius Landos's *Salvation of Sinners*,[198] there was another school of translators who worked from Latin, the leading spirit being Symeon Petrovsky-Sitnianovich of Polotsk, who emigrated to Moscow in 1664 and whose translations include Gregory the Great's *Pastoral Rule*,[199] an abridgment of Petrus Alfonsi's anti-Jewish *Dialogues*[200] and the information about Mahomet and Islam in the fourth part of Vincent of Beauvais's *Great Mirror*.[201] Other translators include Andrew Białobocki, a member of the Polish gentry who arrived in Moscow in 1681 and whose translations include Thomas à Kempis's *Imitation of Christ*[202] and Raymund Lull's *Brief Art* with Agrippa of Nettesheim's commentary,[203] and Palladius Rogovsky, who translated Nicephorus Callistus Xanthopoulos's *Ecclesiastical History* from one of the many printed editions of the Latin translation.[204] Anonymous translations from Latin include two pseudo-Augustinian works, the *Manual*[205] and the *Meditations*,[206] pseudo-Albertus Magnus's work *On the Secrets of Women*, translated in 1670 from the 1648 Amsterdam edition,[207] and pseudo-Vigilius of Thapsus's *Dialogue against the Arians*, translated in 1687 from the 1555 Cologne edition.[208]

Increasingly in the second half of the century the translations are of secular, not religious works, for example Erasmus's *On the Civility of Children's Manners*[209] and Thomas Edwards's *New, Brief and True Description of the Most Celebrated Italian Cities* from the 1595 Frankfurt edition.[210] Of vital importance for the development of geographical knowledge was the translation between 1655 and 1657 of the first four volumes of Willem and Joan Blaeu's atlas, which first acquainted the Muscovites with the Copernican system.[211] In several ways unique is the translation of Johann Jacobi of Wallhausen's *Kriegs-Kunst zu Fuss*. Not merely is it the first translation of a modern military work, it is the first secular work ever published in Muscovy and contains the first copper engravings to be included in a book published in Moscow.[212]

A number of Polish works were translated, including one that was to have an enormous impact on Ukrainian historiography in the seventeenth century and Russian in the eighteenth: Matthew Stryjkowski's *Kronika Polska, Litewska, Żmódzka i wszystkiej Rusi*, of which there are two complete translations, one ca. 1673–1679[213] and the other of 1688.[214] Also important for historiography was the translation in 1678 of the 1607 Cracow edition of Peter Skarga's abridgment of Cesare Baronius's *Ecclesiastical Annals*.[215] The growing interest in philosophy is illustrated by the translation in 1676 of Sebastian Petrycy's Polish version of the pseudo-Aristotelian *Economics* by Theodore Bogdanov[216] and the two translations of Andrew Glaber's Polish adaptation of the pseudo-Aristotelian *Problems*, one undated,[217] the other of 1677,[218] both from the 1567 Cracow edition. The first translation of classical poetry made in Muscovy was a prose version of Waleryian Otfinowski's Polish verse rendering of Ovid's *Metamorphoses*, published at Cracow in 1638.[219]

* * *

This survey of the translations available in Muscovy down to the beginning of Peter the Great's reign (1682 [1689]–1725) is by no means exhaustive, but a complete list would only illustrate Alphonse Karr's maxim: *Plus ça change, plus c'est la même chose*. The conclusions that can be drawn are the following: down to the mid-fifteenth century the translations are virtually exclusively ecclesiastical in content and made from Greek, mostly by South Slavs. The first translations that are neither ecclesiastical in content nor made from Greek appear only in the second half of the fifteenth century and then not in Muscovy but in Lithuania.[220] Translations from Latin begin to be made in Muscovy, at first in Novgorod, at the end of the fifteenth century, but are still largely ecclesiastical. In the second half of the sixteenth century, there is an increase in the number of secular works translated from Latin and Polish, but again most are translated in Lithuania, not Muscovy. It is not until the reign of Tsar Alexius (1645–1676) that there is a veritable explosion of translation activity in Muscovy, in which Greek, Polish, Moldavian, Ukrainian, and Belorussian immigrants play a significant part. Whereas the translations from Greek even then remain largely religious in content, those from Latin and Polish clearly reveal a burgeoning interest in secular knowledge. However, these secular translations have but a limited impact since they are not published; indeed, throughout the entire seventeenth century only three books not specifically religious were published in Moscow: Meletius Smotritsky's Slavonic grammar in 1648, Tsar Alexius's new code of law in 1649, and Jacobi's *Kriegs-Kunst zu Fuss*, also in 1649.[221] Although few, the translations show that during the transitional period of Alexius's reign secular ideas were spreading rapidly and that Peter the Great's policy of Westernization merely accelerated a process that was already well under way.

The corpus of translations from Greek includes not a single work of classical philosophy, without some grasp of which the great achievements of Greek patristic theology must perforce remain largely incomprehensible. It is hardly surprising that many of the major works of dogmatic theology, such as Athanasius of Alexandria's *On the Incarnation,* Basil of Caesarea's *Against Eunomius,* Gregory of Nyssa's *Refutation of Apollinarius,* and Epiphanius of Salamis's *Ancoratus,* remained untranslated. No attempt was ever made to translate the philosophical works of any of the leading Byzantine thinkers such as Michael Psellus, John Italus, Nicephorus Blemmydes, Theodore Metochites, or George Gemistus Plethon. There is not even a trace of the works of serious Byzantine historians from Procopius to George Phrantzes inclusive. Latin authors, secular or ecclesiastical, remained a closed book, and the very idea of classical antiquity as an essential part of culture was absent. The corpus of available translations did not provide an adequate foundation or stimulus for the development of serious original intellectual thought in the sphere of theology, let alone philosophy. Florovsky's claim that "there was enough stimulating challenge in that theological inheritance which was received from Byzantium and appropriated in Russian culture,"[222] is from the point of view of the Christian intellectual tradition factually true. The situation would have been different had a knowledge of Greek and Latin been widespread in Muscovy, but until the reign of Tsar Alexius, this was not the case. Slavonic acted as a barrier, not a bridge, to learning. As Peter Skarga bluntly put it in 1577: "Z Słowieńskiego języka nigdy żaden uczonym być nie może."[223] Where neither a profound knowledge of Greek nor the availability of translations was required for the assimilation of Byzantine culture, its reception was comprehensive, as Old Russia's rich artistic heritage reveals. Even here, however, the failure to assimilate the intellectual tradition meant that Old Russia never developed an original theory of art.[224]

Recently scholars have appealed to Iurii Lotman's semiotic theories in attempts to explain away Old Russia's intellectual silence. Zlatar dismisses the problem as *une question mal posée* on the grounds that it ignores Lotman's distinction between *functional* and *textual* cultures:[225] the former are *open* cultures in which history is viewed as a progression towards the fulness of Truth; hence, the value of a text is *functional* insofar as it contributes towards that progression; the latter are *closed* cultures in which history is viewed as the progressive loss of the fulness of Truth, the original Text; hence the value of a text is *textual* insofar as it reflects the original Text.[226] To talk of intellectual silence is to view Old Russian culture as though it were functional instead of textual. William Veder, however, appeals to Lotman's distinction between the varying roles of *canonical art:* in some cultures the purpose of a graphic text is to convey the fruit of the author's own intellectual activity; in others it is to stimulate the receptor's activity; hence, the recorded text does not have to contain the entire work.[227] For Veder, Orthodox Slav culture is of the second type, and this explains why even the most careful examination of the contents of many florilegia fails to establish any systematic organization of the contents. The contents merely reflect "the generation, by simple randomization, of an unlimited number of new textual structures on the basis of a limited number of available texts."[228]

Such appeals to Lotman's theories beg the most important questions: *why* was Old Russian culture *textual? Why* did the principle of *randomization* come into being?[229] This is hardly surprising since Lotman himself all too often merely restates the questions in different terms without providing the answers. Thus in dealing with the problem of the Byzantine influence on Russian culture,[230] he rejects the concept of the "influence" of one culture upon another and replaces it with the idea of a "dialogue" between a *transmitter* and a *receiver,* in which the latter, having assimilated the foreign text, transforms it on the basis of his own "primordial semiotic substratum" and then gives an answer which is *always* superior to the received text but not always given to the original transmitter.[231] This begs the questions: what did Old Russia assimilate? What was the substratum which transformed it? Florovsky rightly concluded the 1962 debate by remarking:

> What we actually most urgently need is not a general discussion of certain basic topics, but rather a patient study of sources, critically evaluated and impartially assessed.[232]

A study of the works available in translation clearly reveals that Old Russia never assimilated either classical antiquity or the intellectual tradition of Byzantium; hence, down to the mid-seventeenth century it lived in a state of cultural autarky characterized by intellectual silence, not as the result of any innate inability but because of the lack of a stimulus. This is not in any way to derogate from its achievements in other fields. When at last the stimulus to intellectual thought came, it came from the West, so that the emergence of Russian intellectual thought represents a break with its Byzantine-oriented past. For those who identified Old Russia's understanding of Orthodoxy (that is, without its intellectual tradition) with true Christianity, such a break was unacceptable. It is in this sense that Avvakum Petrov's words are to be understood: "A rhetor and a philosopher cannot be a Christian."

Notes

Manuscript Collections and Depositories Referred to in the Notes

AFM	Archives of the Ministry of Foreign Affairs, CSA
ANL	Austrian National Library, Vienna
Anzer	Trinity Hermitage on Anzer Island, SPL
Archangel	Archangel Seminary, SAS
ASRC	Archives of the Synod of the Russian Church, CSHA
Barsov	E. Barsov, SHM
BAS	Bulgarian Academy of Sciences, Sofia
Beloozero	Dormition Monastery of St. Cyril of Beloozero, SPL
BNL	Bulgarian National Library, Sofia
CSA	Central State Archives of Early Acts, Moscow
CSHA	Central State History Archives, Leningrad
Deipara	Monastery of the Deipara, Cetinje
Egorov	E. Egorov, LSL
Gil'ferding	A. Hilferding, SPL
Grigorovich	V. Grigorovich, Odessa Municipal Library
Hilandar	Hilandar Monastery, Athos
Iatsimirskii	A. Iatsimirskii, SAS
IH	Institute of History of the USSR, Soviet Academy, Leningrad
IRL	Institute of Russian Literature, Soviet Academy, Leningrad
JAS	Jugoslav Academy of Sciences, Agram
JRM	Jaroslavl-Rostov Museum of History, Art and Architecture, Jaroslavl
Khludov	A. Khludov, SHM
LAS	Lithuanian Academy of Sciences, Vilnius
Likhachev	N. Likhachev, IH
LSL	Lenin State Library, Moscow
Michael	St. Michael's Monastery with the Golden Dome, UAS
Miracle	Monastery of the Miracle of the Archangel Michael, Moscow, SHM
MSOC	Museum of the Serbian Orthodox Church, Belgrade
MTA	Moscow Theological Academy, LSL
Museum	Rumiantsev Museum, LSL
NLP	National Library, Plovdiv

Obolenskii	Prince M. Obolenskii, CSA
Peretts	V. Peretts, IRL
Piskarev	D. Piskarev, LSL
Pogodin	M. Pogodin, SPL
Popov	A. Popov, LSL
RAS	Rumanian Academy of Sciences, Bucharest
Resurrection	New Jerusalem Monastery of the Resurrection, SHM
Rila	St. John's Monastery, Rila
Rumiantsev	Count N. Rumiantsev, LSL
SA	Serbian Academy of Sciences, Belgrade
SAS	Soviet Academy of Sciences, Leningrad
Sevast'ianov	P. Sevast'ianov, LSL
SHM	State History Museum, Moscow
Siia	Trinity Monastery of St. Anthony on the Siia, SAS
SNL	Serbian National Library, Belgrade
Solovki	Transfiguration Monastery, Solovki, SPL
Sophia	Cathedral of St. Sophia, Novgorod, SPL
SP	Serbian Patriarchate, Belgrade
SPL	State Public Library, Leningrad
SRHA	Society of Russian History and Antiquities, LSL
STA	St. Petersburg Theological Academy, SPL
Synod	Synod of the Russian Church, SHM
Tolstoi	Count F. Tolstoi, SPL
Transfiguration	Monastery of the Transfiguration, Jaroslavl, JRM
Trinity	Trinity Laura of St. Sergius, LSL
Typography	Typography of the Synod of the Russian Church, CSA
UAS	Ukrainian Academy of Sciences, Kiev
Undol'skii	V. Undol'skii. LSL
Uvarov	Count A. Uvarov, SHM
Volokolamsk	Dormition Monastery of St. Joseph, Volokolamsk, LSL
VPL	Vilnius Public Library, LAS
Zographou	Zographou Monastery, Athos

1. "Chto est' taina khristianskaia i kak zhiti v věrě khristově," T. Chertoritskaia, ed., *Krasnorechie drevnei Rusi XI-XVII vv.* (Moscow, 1987), pp. 345-349. Cf. "ritor i filosof ne mozhet byt' khristiianin" (p. 347).

2. "Old Russia" is here used to mean the history of the East Slavs from their origins to the reign of Peter the Great with the exception of the territories of the future Ukraine and Belorussia from the fourteenth to seventeenth centuries when, as part of the Grand Duchy of Lithuania, they experienced a different cultural development. (The cessation of the provinces of Kiev, Braslav, Volhynia, and Podlasia to the Polish Crown by the Union of Lublin in 1596 had little impact on the cultural—as opposed to the political—situation). The term "Lithuania" is here used to denote these territories during this period. "Ruthenia" seems to me to be a more appropriate term, but it has not received wide acceptance.

3. E. Golubinskii, *Istoriia russkoi tserkvi* (Moscow, 1901–1916), vol. 1, pt. 1, p. 720. See also 1:xxi-xxii, 701–702, 869–870.

4. G. Florovskii, *Puti russkogo bogosloviia* (Paris, 1937), trans. as *Ways of Russian Theology*, 2 vols. (Belmont, 1979–1987), pt. 1, p. 1 (= *The Collected Works of Georges Florovsky*, vols. 5–6).

5. G. Fedotov, *The Russian Religious Mind*, 2 vols. (Cambridge, 1946–1966), 1:38, 39–40. Fedotov is using "scientific" in the sense of *naunchyi*.

6. G. Florovsky, "The Problem of Old Russian Culture," *SR* 21 (1962): 14.

7. N. Andreyev, "Pagan and Christian Elements in Old Russia," *SR* 21 (1962): 21.

8. J. Billington, "Images of Muscovy," *SR* 21 (1962): 29–30, 34.

9. The term "South Slav influence" is retained here merely because it is in current use. It is, however, a misnomer, since the South Slavs, as mediators of Byzantine Christianity, did not influence pagan East Slav culture; they replaced it.

10. W. Treadgold would not include art in the discussion of the concept of "renaissance," but this is an artificial limitation of the term. See "Introduction: Renaissances and Dark Ages" in *Renaissances before the Renaissance: Cultural Revivals of Late Antiquity and the Middle Ages*, ed. W. Treadgold (Palo Alto, 1984), p. 3.

11. G. Florovsky, "Reply," *SR* 21 (1962): 40–41.

12. "The Problem of Old Russian Culture," p. 15.

13. "Reply," p. 41.

14. See Francis Thomson, *Sensus or Proprietus Verborum*. "Medieval Theories of Translation as Exemplified by Translations from Greek into Latin and Slavonic," *Symposium Methodianum: Beiträge der Internationalen Tagung in Regensburg (17. bis 24. April 1985) zum Gedenken an den 1100. Todestag des hl. Method*, ed. K. Trost et al. (Neuried, 1988), p. 675 [= *Selecta Slavica*, vol. 13].

15. Z. Zlatar, "The Transmission of Texts and Byzantine Legacy [sic] to Kievan Rus'," *Australian Slavonic and East European Studies* 22, no. 2 (1988): 22.

16. Ibid., p. 4.

17. His results are further vitiated by the fact that his corpus of manuscripts is merely that recorded in O. Schmidt, ed., *Svodnyi katalog slaviano-russkikh rukopisnykh knig, khraniashchikhsia v SSSR, XI-XIII vv.* (Moscow, 1984), and he ignores all East Slav codices preserved outside the Soviet Union, not to mention codices now lost, but whose existence has been recorded—for example, those in the collection of Theodor Bause (1752–1812) which perished in the Moscow conflagration of 1812. The description of the codices in Schmidt must be supplemented by that in R. Marti, *Handschrift—Text—Textgruppe—Literatur. Untersuchungen zur inneren Gliederung der frühen Literatur aus dem ostslavischen Sprachbereich in den Handscriften des 11. bis 14. Jahrhunderts* (Wiesbaden, 1989), pp. 153–213 [= *Veröffentlichunger der Abteilung für slavische Sprachen und Literaturen des Osteuropa-Instituts (Slavisches Seminar) an der Freien Universität Berlin*, vol. 68].

18. Zlatar, "Transmission of Texts," p. 10.

19. Ibid., pp. 17-18. Also inaccurate is the claim that nothing was translated from Latin before 1240 (p. 10).

20. Ibid., p. 13.

21. Ibid., p. 14.

22. Ibid., p. 13.

23. C. Mango, "The Availability of Books in the Byzantine Empire, A.D. 750–850," in *Byzantine Books and Bookmen* (Dumbarton Oaks, 1975), p. 40.

24. R. Henry, ed., *Photius. Bibliothèque* (Paris, 1959–1977), 7:207–209.

25. F. Halkin, "La Date de la composition de la 'Bibliothèque' de Photius remise en question," *Analecta Bollandiana* 81 (1963): 414–415.

26. This has been pointed out by B. Hemmerdinger, "Le 'Codex' 252 de la bibliothèque de Photius," *Byzantinische Zeitschrift* 58 (1965): 1–2, and in more detail by J. Schamp, *Photius, historien des lettres. La "Bibliothèque" et ses notices biographiques* (Paris, 1987), pp. 71–73 [= *Bibliothèque de la Faculté de philosophie et lettres de l'Université de Liège*, vol. 248]. This explanation was already proposed in 1904 by H. Delehaye, "S. Grégoire le Grand dans l'hagiographie grecque," *Analecta Bollandiana* 23 (1904): 452. Zlatar seems to be unacquainted with the relevant literature.

27. Henry, ed., *Photius*, 1:1, 8:214. The preface and postface make it clear that it was compiled prior to Photius's departure on an embassy to the Assyrians. Since Photius undertook no such embassy after his appointment as patriarch of Constantinople (858–867, 877–886), it must antedate 858. The various embassies suggested— 838, 845, 850/851, 855/856—cannot be examined here. Suffice it to say that 838, favored by H. Ahrweiler and P. Lemerle, is unlikely since Photius's parents, as iconodules, suffered from iconoclastic persecution. Photius would scarcely have been sent on an imperial embassy before the restoration of icondulia in 840. See Photius's epistle to his brother Tarasius in J. Migne, ed., *Patrologiae cursus completus... Series Graeca* (Paris, 1860), 102:969–981; cf. 102:972. See also H. Ahrweiler, "Sur la carrière de Photios avant son patriarcat," *Byzantinische Zeitschrift* 58 (1965): 360–361; P. Lemerle, *Le Premier humanisme byzantin. Notes et remarques sur enseignement et culture à Byzance des origines au Xe siècle* (Paris, 1971), pp. 40, 179–180 [= *Bibliothèque byzantine, Série Etudes*, vol. 6].

28. For a description of the corpus, see F. Thomson, "The Nature of the Reception of Christian Byzantine Culture in Russia in the Tenth to Thirteenth Centuries and Its Implications for Russian Culture," *SG* 5 (1978): 107–139.

29. Ibid., pp. 117–118; Marti, p. 397.

30. See F. Thomson, "Continuity in the Development of Bulgarian Culture during the Period of Byzantine Hegemony and the Slavonic Translations of Works by the Three Cappadocian Fathers," in *Mezhdunaroden simpozium 1100 godini ot blazhenata konchina na sv. Metodii*, ed. N. Kochev (Sofia, 1989), 2:140–153.

31. Over seventy works have been claimed to have been translated in Kievan Russia; only one is justified, and that was not translated by an East Slav. See F. Thomson, "'Made in Russia': A Survey of the Translations Allegedly Made in Kievan Russia," *Millennium Russiae Christianiae, Münster 5. bis 9. Juli 1988* (in press), pp. 1–60.

32. See F. Thomson, "Quotations of Patristic and Byzantine Works by Early Russian Authors as an Indication of the Cultural Level of Kievan Russia," *SG* 10 (1983): 65–102; idem, "The Implications of the Absence of Quotations of Untranslated Greek Works in Original Early Russian Literature, Together with a Critique of a

Distorted Picture of Early Bulgarian Culture," *SG* 15 (1988): 63–91. In the entourage of the Greek metropolitans of Kiev, there were some East Slavs who knew *demotic*, but there is no evidence for a knowledge of *attic* or even *koine*. There may have been some Bulgarians in Kievan Russia who knew *koine*, but speculation is pointless as the sources are silent. See Thomson, "The Bulgarian Contribution to the Reception of Byzantine Culture in Kievan Rus': The Myths and the Enigma," *HUS* 12–13 (1988–1989): 216–218.

33. The principal investigation in this field remains A. Sobolevskii, *Perevodnaia literatura Moskovskoi Rusi XIV-XVII vekov. Bibliograficheskie materialy* (St. Petersburg, 1903), pp. 52–436 [= *Sbornik Otdeleniia russkogo iazyka i slovesnosti Imperatorskoi Akademii nauk*, vol. 74, i].

34. The earliest codex, Hilandar 405, is of the fourteenth-fifteenth century. For reasons of space, references have been limited in each case to the earliest codex of the translation known to me.

35. In view of its size, it is found in two parts. The earliest codices of the first (titles 1–11) are only of the sixteenth century—e.g., Hilandar 186; the second (titles 12–28), however, is found in the fourteenth-century RAS 296, part of which is preserved as Grigorovich 10/36. It should be noted, however, that an anti-Latin polemic falsely ascribed to Photius but in fact composed of five passages taken from the *Panoply*—one from title 13 on the *filioque* and four from 22 on azymes—is found in East Slav codices, the earliest of the fifteenth century—e.g., SRHA 189. It is also found interpolated into a late redaction of the anonymous *How and Why the Latins Separated from Us*, ed. *PSRL*, vol. 12 (St. Petersburg, 1901), pp. 54–61; cf. pp. 59–60. On this latter work, see n. 57 below.

36. The term *Studite typicon*, properly speaking, applies to the monastic, not the liturgical rule, and is thus incorrectly used in this context.

37. To be strictly accurate, by a combination of the Jerusalem and Constantinopolitan rules that originated in the eleventh century.

38. Even then it was not complete: one of the major differences between the typica is that in accordance with that of Jerusalem the *Gloria in excelsis* is sung at matins, whereas according to that of Constantinople, it is spoken. From the acts of the Synod of Moscow in 1551, it is clear that the *Gloria* was still being said. See ed. D. Kozhanchikov, *Stoglav* (St. Petersburg, 1863), c. vi, Q 43, pp. 19–283; cf. 55. Many, if not most, East Slav codices of the typicon contain contaminations of the two rules, and even their classification is disputed. Mansvetov distinguishes six redactions, whereas Dmitrievsky favors a basic distinction between the literal translations of one or the other typicon and all those with various accretions. The two basic translations of the Jerusalem typicon are by Archbishop Nicodemus of Serbia in 1319 and by the monk Athanasius in 1401 in the Constantinopolita monastery of the Deipara *tês Paribleptou*. See I. Mansvetov, *Tserkovnyi ustav (tipik)—ego obrazovanie i sud'ba v grecheskoi i russkoi tserkvi* (Moscow, 1885), pp. 269–281; A. Dmitrievskii, "Review of Mansvetov, *Ustav*," *Khristianskoe chtenie* 2 (1888): 549–550; L. Mirković, "Tipik archiepiskopa Nikodima," *Bogoslovje* 16 (1957): 12–19, 69–88; L. Kavelin, "O slavianskikh perevodakh tserkovnogo bogosluzhebnogo ustava," *ChOIDR* 61 (1867): 8–10.

39. For those laid down by the Constantinopolitan rule, see V. Vinogradov, *Ustav-*

nye chteniia (Sergiev Posad, 1914-1915), 1:21-79. Cf. those in the Jerusalem rule, 1:137-203 and the remarks by Vinogradov, 3:1-32.

40. South Slav codices of the fourteenth century—e.g., Deipara 73; East Slav codices of the fifteenth century—e.g., Anzer 83.

41. South Slav codices of the fourteenth century—e.g., BNL 1045; East Slav codices of the fifteenth century—e.g., Uvarov 509.

42. South Slav codices of the fourteenth century—e.g., JAS III.c.24 + 22; East Slav codices of the fifteenth century—e.g., Uvarov 63.

43. South Slav codices of the fifteenth century—e.g., Rila 4/5; East Slav codices of the sixteenth century—e.g., the Macarian menologium (30 January). The language definitely dates from the fourteenth century.

44. South Slav codices of the fourteenth century—e.g., JAS III.c.24 + 22; East Slav codices of the fifteenth century—e.g., Uvarov 63.

45. South Slav codices of the fourteenth century—e.g., BNL 1045; East Slav codices of the fifteenth century—e.g., Uvarov 63.

46. South Slav codices of the fourteenth century—e.g., Zographou 103; East Slav codices of the sixteenth century—e.g., Volokolamsk 214/629.

47. South Slav codices of the fourteenth century—e.g., JAS III.c.24 + 22; East Slav codices of the fifteenth century—e.g., Trinity 666.

48. South Slav codices of the fourteenth century—e.g., Sevast'ianov II.41/1467; East Slav codices of the sixteenth century—e.g., Macarian menologium (15 November).

49. The translation associated with Patriarch Euthymius of Tărnovo is in South Slav codices of the fourteenth century—e.g., Zographou 1; East Slav codices of the fifteenth century—e.g., Synod 268. A slightly earlier translation is found only in South Slav codices—e.g., Popov 101 of the fourteenth century, whereas that associated with Metropolitan Cyprian of Kiev is found only in East Slav codices—e.g., Synod 601 of the fourteenth century.

50. Both South Slav (e.g., Hilferding 40) and East Slav (e.g., Tolstoi I.312 [F.p.I.41]) codices of the fourteenth century. A different, abridged translation is in the fourteenth-century Serb codex ANL 42.

51. South Slav codices of the fourteenth century—e.g., Hilandar 404; East Slav codices of the fifteenth century—e.g., Undol'skii 181. Whether the translator, Dionysius, is to be identified with Patriarch Theodosius of Tărnovo's disciple Dionysius the Wondrous cannot be examined here.

52. South Slav codices of the fourteenth century—e.g., Synod 383; East Slav codices of the sixteenth century—e.g., Synod 45.

53. South Slav codices of the fourteenth century—e.g., SP 70; East Slav codices of the fifteenth century—e.g., SRHA 189. A second translation of a variant redaction is found in codices of the fifteenth century—e.g., Trinity 177.

54. Same codices as the first translation of Cerularius's epistle. See n. 53.

55. Same codices. See n. 53.

56. Earliest codices are East Slav of the fifteenth century—e.g., Trinity 760, but the language shows that it was translated in Bulgaria in the fourteenth. This Nicetas should not be confused with Nicetas Stethatus whose *Treatise against the Latins* was translated in the thirteenth century as part of the Serbian nomocanon.

57. South Slav codices of the fourteenth century—e.g., SP 70; East Slav codices of

the fourteenth-fifteenth centuries—e.g., Tolstoi III.65 (O.p.I.7); a second translation of a variant redaction is found in both South Slav (e.g., Iatsimirskii 49) and East Slav (e.g., SRHA 189), codices of the fifteenth century. The redaction in the Nicon Chronicle (see n. 35) is a conflation of both translations with several interpolations.

58. South Slav codices of the fourteenth century—e.g., Resurrection 105; East Slav codices of the sixteenth century—e.g., Macarian menologium (4 December). See below, n. 155.

59. It was translated together with his *Exposition of the Catholic Faith;* South Slav codices of the fourteenth century—e.g., MSOC 176; the latter translation seems not to have traveled to the north, as East Slav codices of the fifteenth century (e.g., Trinity 176) combine the fourteenth-century translation of the *Dialectics* with John the Exarch's tenth-century abridged rendering of the *Exposition.*

60. Both South Slav (e.g., Rumiantsev 921) and East Slav (e.g., Synod 367) codices are of the fifteenth century, but the language is of the fourteenth.

61. East Slav codices of the fifteenth century (e.g., Tolstoi I.144 [F.I.199]), but the translator's colophon shows that it was translated in 1385 by Demetrius Zographus. The language is Bulgarian, but so far, no South Slav codices have been traced.

62. The earliest codex of the fifteenth century is East Slav (Synod 18), but its orthography reveals that it was copied from an earlier Serb exemplar.

63. South Slav codices of the fourteenth century—e.g., Synod 38; East Slav codices of the sixteenth—e.g., Trinity 760.

64. South Slav codices of the fourteenth century—e.g., SP 70; East Slav codices of the sixteenth—e.g, Macarian menologium (31 August).

65. South Slav codices of the fourteenth century—e.g., SP 70; East Slav codices of the sixteenth—e.g., ASRC 253. See below, n. 182.

66. South Slav codices of the fourteenth century—e.g., Synod 38;East Slav codices only of the seventeenth century—e.g., Sophia 1497, but it was used by the compiler(s) of the 1512 Russian Chronograph. See O. Tvorogov, *Drevnerusskie khronografy* (Leningrad, 1975), pp. 33-41.

67. South Slav codices of the fifteenth century—e.g., MSOC 42. The original translation seems not to have traveled northwards, but a revised version known as the *Paralipomenon* is found in the early sixteenth-century East Slav codex Volokolamsk 230/566. The dating of the translation to ca. 1160—suggested by P. Potapov ("Sud'ba khroniki Zonary v slaviano-russkoi literature," *Izvestiia Otdeleniia russkogo iazyka i slovesnosti Rossiiskoi Akademii nauk* 22, no. 2 [1917]: 184-186) is still being repeated (e.g., by Tvorogov, p. 181), but it was made in either 1332 or 1344. See M. Weingart, *Byzantské kroniky v literatuře cirkevněslovanské. Přehled a rozbor filologický* (Pressburg, 1922), 1:117-120 [= *Spisy filosofické fakulty University Komenského,* vol. 2].

68. South Slav codices of the fourteenth-fifteenth centuries—e.g., Trinity 758 (a convolute: folios 282-580 are fifteenth-century East Slav); East Slav codices of the late fifteenth century—e.g., Synod 367.

69. E. Barsov, "Drevne-russkie pamiatniki sviashchennogo venchaniia tsarei na tsarstvo v sviazi s grecheskimi ikh originalami. S istoricheskim ocherkom chinov tsarskogo venchaniia v sviazi s razvitiem idei tsaria na Rusi," *Chteniia v Imperatorskom Obshchestve istorii i drevnostei rossiiskikh* 124 (1883): 56-60.

70. Ostrog, 1607; n.p., 1638; Moscow, n.d. (1661?–1663); Moscow, 1680; Kiev, 1680. There are also two eighteenth-century editions: St. Petersburg, 1718 and 1724. The 1776 edition is a new eighteenth-century translation.

71. South Slav codices of the fourteenth century—e.g., BAS 80; East Slav codices of the fourteenth-fifteenth centuries—e.g., Trinity 183.

72. South Slav codices of the late fourteenth century—e.g., Synod 383; East Slav codices of the sixteenth century—e.g., Synod 45.

73. South Slav codices only of the sixteenth century—e.g., BAS 82, but the language is of the fourteenth century.

74. South Slav codices of the late fourteenth century—e.g., Synod 383; East Slav codices of the sixteenth century—e.g., Synod 45.

75. East Slav codices of the fifteenth century—e.g., Volokolamsk 116/438. No South Slav codices have been traced, but the language and orthography of the earliest codices indicate a South Slav origin.

76. South Slav (e.g., JAS III.a.47) and East Slav (e.g., Pogodin 1941) codices of the fifteenth century.

77. South Slav (e.g, Rila 4/8) and East Slav (e.g., Synod 172) codices of the fifteenth century.

78. For the complicated textological tradition going back to the fourteenth century in both South Slav (e.g., Hilandar 342) and East Slav (e.g., Trinity 253) codices, see G. Prokhorov, "K istorii liturgicheskoi poezii: gimny i molitvy patriarkha Filofeia Kokkina," *TODRL* 27 (1972): 120–149. In some cases there are several translations of the same prayer. For an example, see idem, "Filofei Kokkin o plenenii i osvobozhdenii geraklitov," *TODRL* 33 (1979): 253–260. For Philotheus's *Order of the Liturgy*, see above, n. 49.

79. Both South Slav (e.g., NLP 103) and East Slav (e.g., Trinity 163) codices of the fourteenth century. See below, n. 165.

80. South Slav codices of the fourteenth century—e.g., BNL 672; East Slav codices of the fourteenth-fifteenth centuries—e.g., MTA 49.

81. South Slav codices of the fourteenth century—e.g., Gil'ferding 46; East Slav codices of the fifteenth century—e.g., Solovki 165/115.

82. South Slav codices of the fourteenth century—e.g., Trinity 172; East Slav codices of the fourteenth-fifteenth centuries—e.g., MTA 151.

83. Both South Slav (e.g., Trinity 179) and East Slav (e.g., Tolstoi III.46 [O.I.59]) codices of the fourteenth century.

84. Both South Slav (e.g., BNL 1025) and East Slav (e.g., Miracle 14) codices of the fourteenth century.

85. South Slav codices of the fourteenth century—e.g., BNL 672; East Slav codices of the fifteenth—e.g., Trinity 156. The relation between the version in the South Slav and that in the East Slav codices remains to be studied.

86. South Slav codices of the fourteenth-fifteenth centuries—e.g., Hilandar 468; East Slav codices of the fifteenth—e.g., Trinity 756.

87. Both South Slav (e.g., Hilandar 394) and East Slav (e.g., Trinity 753) codices of the fifteenth century, although the language is of the fourteenth century.

88. South Slav codices of the fourteenth century—e.g., BNL 672; East Slav codices of the fifteenth century—e.g., Trinity 756.

89. Two folios of the tenth century contain the end of rule 34 and the beginning of rule 35 of the longer version of his *Rules* in the common recension. They are in the Zographou Collection, the present number being perhaps eight. See H. Miklas "Ein Beitrag zu den slavischen Handschriften auf dem Athos," *Palaeobulgarica* 1, no. 1 (1977): 68, 73.

90. This time in the Studite recension. Both South Slav (e.g, Trinity 129) and East Slav (e.g., Uvarov 506) codices of the fourteenth century.

91. See above, n. 59.

92. In both South Slav (e.g., Likhachev I.502 [only cc. 1–29]), Egorov 1 [only cc. 31–63]) and East Slav (e.g., Synod 193) codices of the fourteenth century. The earlier abridged translation is found in both South Slav (e.g., Hilandar 175) and East Slav (e.g., Synod 836) codices of the thirteenth century.

93. South Slav codices of the fourteenth century—e.g., Pogodin 61; East Slav codices of the fourteenth-fifteenth centuries—e.g., Obolenskii 6. The earlier translation has not been traced to any codex earlier than the sixteenth century (e.g., Macarian menologium [26 March]), but was used by the compiler of the Russian Primary Chronicle in the description of Igor's expedition against Constantinople in 941, on which there is a considerable literature. See Thomson, "The Implications of the Absence of Quotations," p. 65.

94. South Slav codices of the fourteenth century—e.g., Deipara 55; East Slav codices of the sixteenth century—e.g., Trinity 774. The earlier translation (of a Latin version) has not been traced in codices prior to the fourteenth century—e.g., ANL 24; and there is no agreement as to either place or time of the translation, but in view of the Croat Glagolitic textual tradition, Croatia in the eleventh or twelfth century would seem most likely.

95. Both South Slav (e.g., SNL 117) and East Slav (e.g., Beloozero 11/1088) codices of the fifteenth century. The earlier translation has not been traced to any codex prior to the fifteenth century (e.g., AFM 279/658), but it had been interpolated into John Malalas's *Chronograph*, which was used by the compiler of the Russian Primary Chronicle and other early Russian chronicles. See Thomson, "The Implications of the Absence of Quotations," pp. 64–65.

96. For the codices, see above, n. 65.

97. Both South Slav (e.g., JAS III.c.9) and East Slav (e.g., Tolstoi I.311 [F.p.II.1]) codices of the thirteen century.

98. For the codices, see above, n. 90.

99. No codex prior to the fourteenth century has been traced (e.g., Trinity 8), but the language is of the tenth century. A third translation is found in the fourteen-century Serb codex Khludov 195.

100. This approach to translation is often mistakenly associated specifically with Hesychasm. See Thomson, *Sensus*, p. 676.

101. South Slav codices of the fourteenth century—e.g., Rila 3/10; East Slav codices of the early fifteenth century—e.g., Miracle 219. Rumiantsev 198, the earliest codex of the first version, is of the twelfth century. There are at least four different Slavonic versions of the *Ladder*. The extent to which the later versions may be considered independent translations, as opposed to revisions, of the earlier ones remains to be studied. Rila 3/10 and Miracle 219 are both codices of the fourth version, Heppell's

group 1. See M. Heppel[l], "Some Slavonic Manuscripts of the 'Scala Paradisi' ('Lestvica')," *ByzSl* 18 (1957): 248.

102. South Slav codices of the fourteenth century—e.g., ANL 22; East Slav codices of the fifteenth-sixteenth centuries—e.g., Solovki 244/68. They have, of course, been translated from the Greek version, not the original Latin.

103. Both South Slav (e.g., ANL 28) and East Slav (e.g., Trinity 753) codices of the fifteenth century.

104. Both South Slav (e.g., Hilandar 278) and East Slav (e.g., Trinity 175) codices of the fifteenth century.

105. South Slav codices of the fifteenth century—e.g., Hilandar 402 + 403; East Slav codices only of the seventeenth century—e.g., Uvarov 789.

106. Gabriel's autograph of 1412, Synod 202, was taken to Muscovy from Athos in 1655, and only then did the translation become known there. The first complete edition of Gabriel's preface is by D. Trifunović, "Zapisi inoka Gavrila, prevodioca Tumačenja Knjige o Jovu," *Literaturoznanie i folkloristika v chest na 70-godishninata na akademik Petăr Dinekov*, ed. A. Stoikov (Sofia, 1983), pp. 110–111. Miracle 6, the earliest codex of the previous translation, is of the fourteenth century, but the language is of the tenth century. In most scholarly literature, the catena is identified with Olympiodorus of Alexandria's *Commentary on Job*, but that is merely the most quoted source.

107. East Slav codices of the fifteenth century—e.g., Uvarov 18. In view of the absence of South Slav codices, it may well be one of the first translations made in Muscovy after 1453.

108. See N. Meshcherskii, "Problemy izucheniia slaviano-russkoi perevodnoi literatury XI–XV vekov," *TODRL* 20 (1964): 229–231.

109. On the meaning of "Lithuania," see above, n. 2.

110. Earliest codices of the sixteenth century—e.g., Trinity 178. The circumstances of the translation are related in a gloss on f. 427v in the seventeenth-century codex Uvarov 51, where Tarchaniotes is wrongly called Manuel, son of Demetrius, instead of the reverse. His father was the syncleticus Manuel Tarchaniotes Bullotes, who represented Emperor John VIII at the Council of Florence.

111. "Ruthenian" is used here merely to denote the official language of Lithuania from the fifteenth to the seventeenth centuries. Uncodified, it reveals considerable variations, and it became increasingly Polonized.

112. Codices of the sixteenth century—e.g., VPL 222.

113. Codices of the sixteenth century—e.g., LAS 272.

114. The present whereabouts of the sole codex traced, the sixteenth-century Kholm Orthodox Fraternity Museum 96, is uncertain. The questions whether in fact this was translated from the Latin original and whether it was one of the Hebrew translations are disputed and cannot be examined here.

115. Codices of the late fifteenth century—e.g, Michael 1655.

116. Codices of the seventeenth century—e.g., Synod 263.

117. See his epistle of 1489 to Joasaph, Prince Obolensky, former archbishop of Rostov (1481–1488, +1514), in N. Kazakova and I. Lur'e, eds., *Antifeodal'nye ereticheskie dvizheniia na Rusi XIV-nachala XVI veka* (Leningrad, 1955), pp. 316–320. Cf. p. 318.

118. See A. Zimin, *I. S. Peresvetov i ego sovremenniki. Ocherki po istorii russkoi obshchestvenno-politicheskoi mysli serediny XVI veka* (Moscow, 1958), pp. 352, 355, 397–399. Evidence that it influenced Prince Andrew Kurbsky or was even known to Maximus Triboles "the Greek" is inconclusive.

119. The Methodian translation has not survived and anyway did not include Maccabees.

120. All of these Biblical books were first translated together in one codex, a sixteenth-century copy of which exists (Pogodin 84); only subsequently were they inserted into the complete Bible, the earliest codex being Synod 915 of 1499.

121. No. 26 in vol. 1 of C. Borchling and B. Claussen, *Niederdeutsche Bibliographie. Gesamtverzeichnis der niederdeutschen Drucke bis zum Jahre 1800* (Neumünster, 1931–1936). It must not be confused with the Low Rhenish translation of the Bible published by Quentell at Cologne in 1478; see ibid., no. 27.

122. Sole traced codex is Pogodin 1121 of the seventeenth century.

123. Probably that by Johann Prüss, since its explicit coincides with the colophon of the translation, whereas the explicit of Georg Husner's edition adds: *Finitus quinta feria post diem sancti Kiliani,* which is not in the translation.

124. The view that the end of the seventh millennium (7000 = 1 September 1491 to 31 August 1492) would see the end of the world had led to pascal tables being computed only to the year 7000, e.g., those in the fifteenth-century codex Synod 951, ff. 261r–264r. The view was based on a combination of the six days of creation plus one of rest and the fact that "with the Lord one day is as a thousand years" (2 Peter 3:8). Cf. "a thousand years in thy sight are but as yesterday" (Psalm 90:4).

125. The preface, but not the tables. See A. Pavlov, *Pamiatniki drevne-russkogo kanonicheskogo prava,* vol. 1, ed. V. Beneshevich, 2d ed. (St. Petersburg, 1908), pp. 801–817 [= *Russkaia istoricheskaia biblioteka,* vol. 6].

126. This epistle has not survived, but the translation of the prediction is preserved as the preface to Philotheus of Pskov's epistle to Munexin. See A. Gol'dberg, "Tri 'Poslaniia Filofeia': (Opyt tekstologicheskogo analiza)," *TODRL* 29 (1974): 68–97, esp. p. 70. (In the event, February 1524 was a very dry month in Germany!)

127. Sole codex traced is Pogodin 1674.

128. D. Obolensky, "The Byzantine Impact on Eastern Europe," *Praktika tês Akademia Athênôn,* 55 (1980): 167. The best edition of the epistle remains that by V. Malinin, *Starets Eleazarova monastyria Filofei i ego poslaniia. Istoriko-literaturnoe issledovanie* (Kiev, 1901), pp. 37–47.

129. The earliest codex is SA 26 of the sixteenth century.

130. Earliest codices of the seventeenth century—e.g., Tolstoi II.42 (Q.XVII.12). The translation has also been ascribed to Theophilus Marquart and Gottlieb Lansmann. The question cannot be studied here.

131. Codices of the sixteenth century—e.g., Siia 189. By translating the paradigms, he has transformed it into a Slavonic grammar of sorts.

132. Codices of the sixteenth century—e.g., SA 26. It was translated in 1501.

133. Codices of the sixteenth century—e.g., Sophia 1255. It was translated in 1536.

134. Sole traced codex is SPL Q.IV.412 of the sixteenth century.

135. A. Ivanov, *Literaturnoe nasledie Maksima Greka. Kharakteristika, atributsii, bibliografiia* (Leningrad, 1969), pp. 39–88. Ivanov lists 113, but of these Maximus did

not translate the homilies and epistles of Gregory of Nazianzus (nos. 36–40) or the anti-Latin polemics (nos. 106–112), although he both turned his attention to the extant Slavonic translation of Gregory's works and probably compiled a collection of anti-Latin polemics from extant translations. See D. Bulanin, *Perevody i poslaniia Maksima Greka. Neizdannye teksty* (Leningrad, 1984), pp. 30–52, 82–94.

136. Ivanov, *Literaturnoe nasledie,* no. 70. This translation was included in the Ostrog Bible of 1581.

137. Ibid., no. 73.

138. Ibid., no. 1.

139. Ibid., no. 4.

140. Ibid., no. 113.

141. Ibid., no. 89.

142. Not in Ivanov; see B. Kloss, "Maksim Grek—perevodchik povesti Eneia Sil'viia 'Vziatie Konstantinopolia turkami'," *Pamiatniki kul'tury. Novye otkrytiia. Ezhegodnik 1974* (Moscow, 1975), pp. 55–61.

143. Ivanov, *Literaturnoe nasledie,* no. 8.

144. The second version is found in two sixteenth-century codices: Tolstoi I.169 (F.II.76) and AFM 181/1597. The original revision is in the sixteenth-century codex Piskarev 228/39. Matters were not improved by the fact that in the second version, Patrikeev included Maximus's account of the monastic life on Athos, in which he stressed his own non-possessor views. See Ivanov, *Literaturnoe nasledie,* no. 324.

145. In view of the fact that, first, on 19 September 1571 he made a formal legal declaration that he could not write Russian, see I. Auerbach, *Andrej Michajlovič Kurbskij. Legen in osteuropäischen Adelsgesellschaften des 16. Jahrhunderts* (Munich, 1985), p. 375, n. 2; second, he more than once admitted that he did know Slavonic well—for example, in his letter to Mark Sarygozin (G. Kuntsevich, *Sochineniia kniazia Kurbskogo* [St. Petersburg, 1914], 1:415–420, esp. p. 418); third, his signature, always in Latin script, reveals an unpracticed hand (see the reproduction in Auerbach, *Kurbskij,* p. 377). E. Keenan has concluded that Kurbsky "was not only illiterate, but analphabetic in all languages of Orthodox Slavic letters, it is simply inconceivable in the cultural context in which he lived that he could have dictated, suggested, overseen, initiated, or understood the production of the texts of the type attributed to him ("A Landmark of Kurbskii Studies," *HUS* 10 [1986]: 245). This is not merely an exaggeration, it is a non sequitur: the ability to suggest does not require the skill to perform. He several times repeats that he has learned some Latin—e.g., in his epistles to Sarygozin (Kuntsevich, p. 416), and unless all of his correspondence as well as the prefaces and postscripts to all of the translations attributed to him are dismissed as forgeries (*cui bono?*), their association with him cannot be denied. This does not mean, of course, that he himself translated them, but merely that they originated in the circle around him. He himself talks only of making the translations with the aid of assistants skilled in Latin. See the preface to I. Auerbach, *Andrej Michajlovič Kurbskij. Novyj Margarit. Historisch-kritische Ausgabe auf der Grundlage der Wolfenbütteler Handschrift* (Gießen, 1976), vol. 1, fasc. 1, ff. 1r–7v; cf. f. 5r [= *Bausteine zur Geschichte der Literatur bei den Slaven,* 9:i–iii].

146. See the preface to ibid., ff. 4v–5v. In the postscript to his translation of the works of John of Damascus, Kurbsky adds that Maximus had said that, having

translated the works, the Latins burned the Greek originals. See W. Eismann, *O silogizma vytolkovano. Eine Übersetzung des Fürsten Andrej M. Kurbskij aus den Erotemata Trivii Johann Spangenbergs* (Wiesbaden, 1962), pp. 76–80, esp. p. 78 [= *Monumenta linguae slavicae dialecti verteris. Fontes et dissertationes*, vol. 9]. In the preface to the *New Margarite*, Kurbsky refers to Maximus as "my dearly beloved teacher" (Auerbach, f. 5v). In *Andrej Michajlovič Kurbskij . . . Adelsgesellschaften*, Auerbach claims that Maximus taught Kurbsky theology and philosophy (p. 30). That is an unsubstantiated claim: there is no evidence whatsoever that Kurbsky is using the words "I heard from my dearly beloved teacher" other than in a metaphorical sense.

147. See his letter to Sarygozin in Kuntsevich, 1:415–417.

148. Ibid., pp. 416–417. See also the preface in Auerbach, *Novyj Margarit*, vol. 1, fasc. 1, f. 5v.

149. See A. Chmiel, *Album studiosorum Universitatis Cracoviensis* (Cracow, 1904), 3:80.

150. See the letter to Sarygozin in Kuntsevich, 1:417.

151. Compare the translation of the fifth entry in Auerbach, *Novyj Margarit*, vol. 1, fasc. 1, ff. 20r–26r with the Latin version edited with variants from the Venice 1504, 1548, 1574, Basel 1504, 1517, 1522, 1524, 1530, 1539, 1547, 1548, 1558, and Paris 1534, 1536, 1570, 1574 editions in ibid., vol. 3, fasc. 15, pp. 1–12. Only the readings of the 1558 Basel edition agree in every case. The earliest codex of the *New Margarite* is of the late sixteenth century: Bibliotheca Augusta, Wolfenbüttel, Codex Guelf. 64–43, Extravagantium.

152. In the case of the homilies on John, the Greek codex from which Maximus was translating was defective, and because of the missing folios the ending of Homily 22 and the beginning of Homily 23 were lacking. In the *New Margarite*, the missing ending and beginning have been translated from Latin so that entries 56 (Homily 22) and 57 (Homily 23) are half translated from Greek, half from Latin. See Auerbach, *Novyj Margarit*, vol. 2, fasc. 8, ff. 223v–227v, 227v–232r. For Maximus's translations, see Ivanov, *Literaturnoe nasledie*, nos. 6 (on John) and 7 (on Matthew).

153. This dating can be established from the fact that in the preface to the collection, Kurbsky states that in the revision of the *Exposition of the Catholic Faith* he has been assisted by Obolensky. See M. Obolenskii, "O perevode kniazia Kurbskogo sochinenii Ionna [sic] Damaskina," *Bibliograficheskie zapiski* 1, no. 12 (1858): 358–366, esp. p. 359. Obolensky only returned from Italy in 1576 (see above, n. 150) and died before August 1577. See Auerbach, *Kurbskij*, p. 137, n. 157.

154. That this was the edition used is shown by the fact that some of the glosses in the collection have been translated from the commentary by Jodocus Clichtoveus (= Josse Clichtove) found in that edition; moreover, only it (and neither the 1548 nor the 1549 Basel edition) contains the homily "On the Day of Judgment," which is included in the collection. The earliest codices of the collection are of the late sixteenth century, e.g., Miracle 34, although the codex Khludov 60 (sixteenth–seventeenth centuries) has the most complete text.

155. For the earlier translation of John of Jerusalem's homily, see above, n. 58. The false ascription of this homily to John of Damascus is found in Greek and from there taken over into Slavonic.

156. It is appended to the first part of his third epistle to Ivan IV of 1579, the earliest codices of which are of the seventeenth century, e.g., Uvarov 301. The question of the genuine nature of Kurbsky's correspondence cannot be discussed here. Suffice it to say that the argument advanced by Keenan (*The Kurbskii-Groznyi Apocrypha: The Seventeenth-Century Genesis of the "Correspondence" Attributed to Prince A. M. Kurbskii and Tsar Ivan IV* [Cambridge, 1971], p. 56, n. 23 [= *Russian Research Center Studies*, vol. 66]) against the ascription of this translation to Kurbsky's circle on the grounds that the first Polish translation of Cicero was by Stanisław Koszucki published at Vilnius in 1576 [in fact, it was at Łosk in either 1575 or 1576] and that it is unlikely that Cicero would have been translated earlier into Slavonic, is not merely hypothetical, it is incorrect. Koszucki's translation may not have been the first published one, but it was preceded by unpublished translations, including one by Martin Cromer, ca. 1532–1536. See K. Budzyk, ed., *Bibliografia literatury polskiej "Nowy Korbut"* (Warsaw, 1964), 2:412. The other translations of individual works ascribed to Kurbsky cannot be listed here.

157. The earliest codex is AFM 51/995 of the seventeenth century.

158. (The 1564 edition is entitled *Kronika, tho iesth Historya swiátá.*) Earliest codices of the seventeenth century—e.g., Tolstoy I.205 (F.IV.162). Whether it was first translated in Lithuania by command of King Sigismund II August of Poland and only revised and not translated in Moscow in 1584 cannot be examined here. The seventeenth-century codex SPL F.IV.688 does not contain another version of Bielski's chronicle, as sometimes claimed, but a copy of the Ukrainian chronicle of Leonid Bobolinsky, who made ample use of Bielski, but in the second edition of 1554. See below, n. 214.

159. The sole traced codex is Barsov 371 (sixteenth century).

160. See the prefaces reprinted by Kh. Titov, *Materiïaly dlia istorii knyzhnoï spravy na Ukraïni v XVI-XVIII vv. Vsezbirka peredmov do ukraïns'kykh starodrukiv* (Kiev, 1924), pp. 91–104 [= *Zbirnyk Istorychno-filologichnoho viddilu Ukraïns'koi Akademiï Nauk*, vol. 17].

161. It may, however, have been Hieromonk Paphnutius of Saint Onuphrius's Monastery, Lemberg. A second edition, revised by Epiphanius Slavinetsky, appeared at Moscow in 1664.

162. A second edition was printed at Kiev in 1634.

163. See the prefaces reprinted by Titov, pp. 52–85. A second edition, slightly revised by Stephan Iavorsky, was published at Moscow in 1709 and again (in two volumes) in 1765–1766.

164. For the prefaces, see Titov, pp. 135–146. It was reprinted at Moscow in 1712 and 1768. For his translation, Zizanii used F. Sylberg's 1596 Heidelberg edition.

165. See above, n. 79. There were at least twenty-one editions by 1800.

166. Whether Skul'sky was also the author is uncertain.

167. The sole traced codex is AFM 735/1257 (seventeenth century).

168. Also traced only to AFM 735/1257.

169. Earliest codices are of the seventeenth century—e.g., STA 157.

170. The earliest codex is Synod 451 of 1634.

171. The earliest codex is Synod 933 of 1620. It was clearly intended for teaching purposes, and there are several later redactions.

172. Earliest codices of the seventeenth century—e.g., Resurrection 159. Evgenii Bolkhovitinov claims that the translation was made in 1637 by Bogdan Lykov, but no evidence to support this theory has been found. See E. Bolkhovitinov, *Slovar' russkikh svetskikh pisatelei, sootechestvennikov i chuzhestrantsev, pisavshikh v Rossii* (Moscow, 1845), 2:37.

173. See the description of Muscovy in any of the numerous editions in Latin, French, German, Dutch, or English, e.g., the English one of 1636: *Atlas or a Geographicke Description of the Regions, Countries and Kingdomes of the World, Through Europe, Asia, Africa, Represented by New and Exact Maps* (Amsterdam, 1636), 1:106. Mercator had, of course, taken this story from Paolo Giovio's *Treatise on the Embassy of Grand Prince Basil of Muscovy to Pope Clement VII*, first published at Rome in 1525. Giovio had been told this by Basil III's envoy, Demetrius Gerasimov.

174. It has been traced only in Resurrection 94, a codex of 1788.

175. Codices of the seventeenth century—e.g., Typography 394.

176. His autograph exists: CSA f. 52, d. 8.

177. Codices of the seventeenth century—e.g., Pogodin 1561.

178. After his return from the Near East and before his death. It is in the eighteenth-century codex Pogodin 1745. The eighteenth-century codex Rumiancev 365 contains a fifth translation made in 1702. The prophecy is also found in Dorotheus of Monembasia's *History* (see below, n. 181) and Matthew Cigalas's *New Synopsis* (see below, n. 190).

179. The sole traced codex is Khludov 69 of the seventeenth century. It is unrelated to any of the other five translations of the *Treasure*.

180. Codices of the seventeenth century—e.g., Synod 388.

181. Codices of the seventeenth century—e.g., Synod 343. It is possible that Dionysius in fact only revised a completed translation. See below, n. 190.

182. See above, n. 65. Codices of the seventeenth century—e.g., Synod 155.

183. Codices of the seventeenth century—e.g., Synod 223-226 (one codex in four parts).

184. See the catalogue in V. Undol'skii, "Sil'vestr Medvedev, otets slaviano-russkoi bibliografii," *Chteniia v Imperatorskom Obshchestve istorii i drevnostei rossiiskikh* 7 (1846): 1–90; cf. 21–22.

185. His autograph exists: Synod 133.

186. Undol'skii 475 is partly his autograph.

187. Synod 571 is his rough copy; Synod 475, his fair copy.

188. Codices of the late seventeenth century—e.g., Synod 475.

189. This forms the basis of the second (1677) and subsequent Moscow editions of the *archieraticon*. In places, Euthymius adapted the order to current Muscovite practices, and there is a noticeable influence of Mogila's 1639 edition of the *hieraticon*.

190. The sole traced codes is AFM 579/1081 of the seventeenth century, although the seventeenth-century codex Synod 483 has a conflation of this translation with that of Dorotheus's *History*. See above, n. 181.

191. Synod 529 is his rough copy; Synod 543, his fair one.

192. Synod 436 is his autograph.

193. Synod 446 is his autograph.

194. Codices of the late seventeenth century—e.g., Synod 192.
195. Synod 283 is partly his autograph.
196. Codices of the late seventeenth century—e.g., Synod 727.
197. Codices of the late seventeenth century—e.g., AFM 277/256.
198. Translated on Athos by Samuel Bakačić in 1684 from the 1641 Venice edition, it is found in East Slav codices already in the late seventeenth century—e.g., Pogodin 1105. Although Bakačić was a Ruthenian, the language of his translation is Serbo-Slavonic.
199. Synod 663 is his autograph.
200. Synod 660 is his autograph.
201. Synod 663 is his autograph. See the *Speculum maius*, iv, 28, 39.
202. In Synod 825, a codex of the seventeenth-eighteenth centuries. It must be distinguished from the translation by Udrişte Năsturel published at Dealu Monastery in 1647.
203. Codices of the late seventeenth century—e.g., Uvarov 422.
204. The sole traced codex is Transfiguration 170 of the late seventeenth century.
205. Codices of the seventeenth century—e.g., Synod 459. Some codices (e.g., Archangel 98/475 of the late seventeenth century) have a note that Karion Istomin had translated it from a version in Belorussian, so that this may be a revised version of an earlier Ruthenian translation.
206. Codices of the late seventeenth century—e.g., Miracle 290. The association of these pseudo-Augustinian translations with Kurbsky is utterly devoid of substance.
207. Earliest codices are of the eighteenth century—e.g., Museum 2955.
208. Codices of the late seventeenth century—e.g., Synod 476.
209. Codices of the eighteenth century—e.g, Uvarov 1865. It may have been translated by Slavinetsky.
210. The sole known codex is Peretts 158 of the seventeenth–eighteenth centuries.
211. Epiphanius Slavinetsky translated vol. 1 from one of the first three Amsterdam Latin editions (1635, 1640, 1644), his autograph being Synod 779. Arsenius Koretsky-Satanovsky did vol. 2 from one of the same three editions, his autograph being Synod 781. Vols. 3–4 were translated from the Amsterdam editions of 1640 and 1645 respectively by the monk Isaiah of the Miracle Monastery. For his autographs, see Synod 780 and 41.
212. Printing was finished in 1647, but the engravings had to be ordered from Holland. As a result, the book did not appear until 1649. The author is frequently called von Wallhausen. Although it is true that he came from Wallhausen, his name was Jacobi.
213. Codices of the late seventeenth century—e.g., Tolstoi I.186 (F.IV.103).
214. Codices of the late seventeenth century—e.g., Uvarov 1382. There are also translations of excerpts: Books 11–25 are found in the codex Tolstoi I.244 (F.IV.171) of the seventeenth–eighteenth centuries, whereas Andrew Lyzlov in preparing his *Skifskaia istoriia* translated Books 1, chap. 2 and 4, chaps. 1–3, which are found in late seventeenth-century codices—e.g., Pogodin 1494. An eighteenth-century Ukrainian translation is found in UAS I.57387.48. The claim that the seventeenth-century

codex SPL F.IV.688 contains another translation is inaccurate: it contains Bobolinsky's chronicle, one principal source of which was Stryjkowski. See above, n. 158.

215. Codices of the late seventeenth century—e.g., Pogodin 1712. Some codices (e.g., Tolstoi I.230 [F.I.273] of the seventeenth-eighteenth centuries) have the same translation except for the first three centuries, which are in a different translation, although also made from the 1607 edition.

216. The sole traced codex is Piskarev 627 (eighteenth century).

217. Codices of the late seventeenth century—e.g., SRHA 162.

218. Codices of the late seventeenth century—e.g., Undol'skii 680.

219. The earliest codex is Synod 809 of the seventeenth-eighteenth centuries. The idea that it must have been made before 1691 because Silvester Medvedev (1641–1691) had a copy is erroneous; he had Otfinowski's edition. The second half of the seventeenth century also saw the translation from Polish of popular tales such as those about Melusine, Otto and Olunda, Peter of Provence, and the Beautiful Maguellone, as well as moralistic tales contained in the *Magnum speculum exemplorum* and the *Gesta Romanorum*, but these lie outside the scope of an inquiry into Russian's intellectual silence.

220. Previous translations from Latin can be divided into two categories: (1) Croat Glagolitic ones made for *Slavia romana*, which lie outside the scope of this survey except for the few—and these exclusively religious in content—that went to the East Slavs, e.g., the *Gospel of Nicodemus* (see above, n. 94); (2) a very few Orthodox South Slav ones, also exclusively religious in content. These include the allegedly "Moravian" or "Bohemian" translations, some of which were not in fact translated from Latin. See Thomson, "'Made in Russia': A Survey of the Translations," pp. 331–348.

221. On the date of publication of the latter work, see above, n. 212. Pseudo-Basil I's *Exhortations to His Son Leo*, published at Moscow, ca. 1661–1663 and 1680 (see above, notes 68 and 70), are devoted to the duties of a Christian monarch and have sections on faith, patience, humility, etc. so that it cannot be considered secular, whereas the contents of the various primers published at Moscow—namely, those of 1634 and 1637 by Basil Burtsov, of 1679 by Symeon Petrovsky-Sitnianovich, of 1694 and 1696 by Karion Istomin, and the anonymous ones of 1657, 1664, 1667, and 1669—clearly show that they were intended to teach both reading and religion. The customs tariff and regulations for admission to the tsar's service for the settlement of disputes where there are no witnesses published in 1654, the multiplication tables of 1682, and the military leaflet of 1699 can scarcely be classified as books.

222. Florovsky, "Reply," p. 42.

223. "O iedności kościola Bożego pod iednym pasterzem. Y o greckim od tey iedności odstąpieniu." Vilnius 1577, 360. It is significant that in his reply to Skarga's strictures about Slavonic, Ivan of Vishnia makes no attempt to refute them, but claims that learning is of the devil. See his *Zachapka mudrago latynnika z glupym rusinom* in I. Eremin, ed., *Ivan Vyshenskii. Sochineniia* (Leningrad, 1955), pp. 170–205. Cf. p. 194.

224. See the pertinent remarks by D. Murphy, *The Theory of the Visual Arts in Old Russia* (Princeton, 1985), pp. 182–185.

225. Zlatar, pp. 18–22.

226. See Iu. Lotman and A. Piatigorskii, "Text and Function," in D. Lucid, ed., *Soviet Semiotics: An Anthology* (Baltimore, n.d.), pp. 125–135.

227. See Iu. Lotman, "Kanonicheskoe iskusstvo kak informatsionnyi paradoks," *Problema kanona v drevnem i srednevekovom iskusstve Azii i Afriki. Sbornik statei* (Moscow, 1973), pp. 16–22.

228. W. Veder, "Old Russia's 'Intellectual Silence' Reconsidered," in M. Flier and D. Rowland, eds., *Medieval Russian Culture*, vol. 2 (Berkeley, Los Angeles, and London, in press).

229. In fact this theory of "randomization" applies only to the earlier period, and it is noteworthy that Veder refers only to the florilegia of the eleventh to the thirteenth centuries. It is scarcely a main characteristic of Muscovite literature of the sixteenth and seventeenth centuries.

230. See Iu. Lotman, "Problema vizantiiskogo vliianiia na russkuiu kul'turu v tipologicheskom osveshchenii," in *Vizantiia i Rus'. Pamiati Very Dmitrievny Likhachevoi, 1937–1981*, ed. G. Wagner (Moscow, 1989), pp. 227–236.

231. This is not the definition of a dialogue, but of two successive monologues.

232. Florovsky, "Reply," p. 42.

Церковнославянизмы в украинском языке

PAVEL SIGALOV

1. Оценка роли церковнославянских элементов в восточнославянских литературных языках никогда не была чисто лингвистической проблемой. Б. А. Успенский в книге, посвященной роли Тредиаковского в истории русского литературного языка, пишет, что в XVIII веке отношение к церковнославянизмам или к заимствованиям выражало мировоззрение человека так же, как в последующие века оно выражалось в отношении к монарху или к революционерам.[1] Для истории украинского литературного языка воздействие внешних факторов — общественно-политических событий — всегда играло важную, если не сказать — решающую, роль. Г. Шевелев говорит о парадоксальной «заслуге» Александра II в создании двухдиалектного характера украинского литературного языка (это можно сравнить с «заслугой» Николая II в создании революционной ситуации в России):

> Der entscheidende Faktor für eine Festigung der galizischen Elemente in der ukrainischen Schriftsprache war die scharfe Verschiedenheit des politischen Zustands in Rußland und in Österreich: Die Verbote der ukrainischen Sprache in den Jahren 1863 und 1876 im autokraten Rußland, und auf der anderen Seite die Freiheit, die ukrainische Sprache im konstitutionellen Österreich zu gebrauchen. Es mag sich paradox anhören, wenn man sagt, daß für die galizischen Einflüße auf die ukrainische Schriftsprache und folglich für ihren zweidialektischen Charakter letzlich Aleksander II. verantwortlich zu machen ist![2]

С другой стороны, в истории украинской литературы и литературного языка, как и в истории украинской культуры вообще, и в дореволюционное и в советское время нередко чисто языковое (литературное, культурное) событие оценивалось властями как политическое, вызывая соответствующие обвинения. Как писал Павло Филипович — поэт из группы «неоклассиков», переводчик западноевропейской литературы, пропавший в сталинских концлагерях, о себе и себе подобных: «Кінець! Мечем Дамокловим нависла Сувора резолюція ЦК. Дарма, що він, у піджаку старому, Пив скромний чай, приходячи додому, I жив працьовником з юнацьких літ, — Он муза аж здригнулась, як почула, Що ті переклади з Гомера і Катулла Відродять капіталістичний світ».³

Вполне понятно, что социально-политические факторы определяли и положение отдельных элементов украинской культуры; это касается и роли церковнославянизмов в формирующемся литературном языке. Эти факторы — а именно оценка языковой ситуации на современной Украине и прежде всего, взаимоотношения украинского и русского языков на Украине — и сейчас в значительной степени определяют использование церковнославянизмов в украинском языке. Роль церковнославянизмов в украинском и белорусском литературных языках резко отличается от роли этих элементов в русском литературном языке, что объясняется различной историей этих народов.

2. Весь мир отметил в 1988 году тысячелетие крещения Руси — отправного пункта в истории цивилизации и культуры трех народов-наследников Киевского государства: русского, украинского и белорусского.

Историю восточнославянских народов можно разделить на три периода:

а/ X–XIII века: Киевское государство, крещение Руси, формирование трех восточнославянских народов и их языков;

б/ XIV–XVII/XVIII века: создание Русского государства на северо-востоке, вхождение Украины и Белоруссии в состав — последовательно — Литовского, Польско-Литовского и Польского государств;

в/ XVII/XVIII века — настоящее время: вхождение Украины и Белоруссии в состав Русского (затем Советского) государства.

Эта периодизация *mutatis mutandis* (особенно это касается последнего периода) может быть принята и для характеристики восточнославянских литературных языков.⁴ В начальный период церковнославянский язык выступает как первый литературный (письменный) язык восточных славян. Второй период характеризуется действием и взаимодействием трех компонентов: церковнославянского языка, делового и разговорного языков каждого из трех восточнославянских народов. Третий период — эпоха создания современных русского, украинского и белорусского литературных языков. Именно в этот период резко разошлись пути формирования русского литературного языка, с одной стороны, и украинского и белорусского литературных языков, с другой. Решающей причиной такого расхождения явилась различная социально-политическая ситуация этих народов. Становление русского литературного языка, при всех сложностях, определялось только внутренними причинами различного (идеологического [Б. А. Успенский], культурного, литературного, собственно языкового) порядка, потребностями русского общества — в ситуации, когда русский язык был языком государственным, имперским. Это, бесспорно, сыграло важную роль в том, что между вторым и третьим периодами в русском литературном языке не было разрыва, и церковнославянские элементы (как бы ни оценивать их роль) явились важным компонентом формирующегося русского литературного языка. Как видим, церковнославянизмы являются существенным элементом преемственности, скрепляющим историю всех трех периодов, — этот вывод можно сделать из истории русского литературного языка. Что касается украинского литературного языка, то здесь можно говорить как бы о раздельном существовании первого и второго периодов, с одной стороны, и третьего периода, с другой стороны, — настолько велик разрыв между ними. Борис Унбегаун пишет: «Впоследствии однако сербский и украинский языки пошли по иному пути, отказавшись от церковно-славянского наследия».[5] Не касаясь истории сербского языка, об украинском можно было бы сказать, что он был вынужден — в прямом значении этого слова — отказаться от церковнославянского наследия. Этот разрыв, отсутствие преемственности обусловливались внешними и внеязыковыми факторами: ликвидацией самостоятельности Украины после ее добровольного вхождения в состав России, запрещением богослужения на церковнославянском языке украинского извода (1721), запрещением печатания на украинском языке (1876), постоянными преследованиями украинского языка, украинской литературы и культуры — вплоть до революции 1905 года. Известный украинский историк и государственный деятель М. Грушевский пишет:

> Почалось від контролю патріярха над православними, догматичними поглядами київських богословів, а скінчилось — в редакції геніяльного московського насильника Петра Вел. — забороною яких-небудь язикових відмін в українських виданнях, що майже на ціле століття загальмувала всякий друкарський рух, книжну справу і літературну працю на Україні. А коли, нарешті, світська книга якось визволилася з-під букви сеї заборони, українська думка, українське слово — і включно до українського акценту в вимові, мусіли пробиватися через сітку всяких заборон, обмежень і запідозрюваань, які неймовірно гальмували розвій українського культурного життя і відстрашували обивательську масу від будь-якої причетности до нього. Заборона 1876 року, що потривала без двох місяців цілих тридцять літ та вивела з лав українського активу цілий ряд поколінь, — була тільки найбільш яскравим і голосним явищем, — але подібних перепон, часом менш абсолютних і менш тривких, українське культурне життя за часи свого

зв'язку з Москвою знало безліч! І вони в загальній сумі утворили таку «натуральну» для багатьох ситуацію, де українська культура, що давніш ішла *попереду* Московщини в зв'язках з культурним світом, в культурних домаганнях і досягненнях, зійшла на провінціяльний додаток до «світової» російської культури.[6]

Эти внешние факторы явились причиной отсутствия преемственности между вторым и третьим периодами существования украинского литературного языка и — как следствие этого — значительно меньшего количества — по сравнению с русским — церковнославянизмов в нем. Идеологическая задача (если прибегнуть опять к выражению Б. А. Успенского), стоявшая перед украинским народом, была иной, чем у русского народа. Национальной идеологической задачей, задачей жизни и смерти украинского народа как самостоятельной этнической единицы, была необходимость создания литературного языка на народной основе. Во второй половине XVIII и начале XIX века, когда украинское дворянство обрусевало, украинскому народу грозила денационализация. На украинском языке говорило, в основном, крестьянство и мещанство. Ввиду близости украинского и русского языков, украинскому языку грозила опасность превращения в диалект русского языка. Многие современники (в том числе и украинцы) именно так расценивали перспективы существования украинского языка. Украинский поэт-романтик Амвросий Метлинский писал в начале 19 века в стихотворении «Смерть бандуриста»: «Вже не гримітиме, вже не горітиме, як в хмарі, Пісня в народі, бо вже наша мова конає!».[7] Характерны в этом смысле высказывания В. Г. Белинского:

> Предстоит важный вопрос: есть ли на свете малороссийский язык, или это только областное наречие? Из решения этого вопроса вытекает другой: может ли существовать малороссийская литература и должны ли наши литераторы из малороссиян писать по-малороссийски? Что до первого вопроса, на него можно отвечать и *да,* и *нет.* Малороссийский язык действительно существовал во времена самобытности Малороссии и существует теперь — в памятниках народной поэзии тех славных времен ... Но с Петра Великого началось разделение сословий. Дворянство, по ходу исторической необходимости, приняло русский язык и русско-европейские обычаи в образе жизни. Язык самого народа начал портиться, — и теперь чистый малороссийский язык находится преимущественно в одних книгах. Следовательно, мы имеем полное право сказать, что теперь уже нет малороссийского языка, а есть областное малороссийское наречие, как есть белорусское, сибирское и другие подобные им областные наречия.[8]

Это отношение к украинскому языку и украинской литературе Белинский демонстрирует в оценке поэмы Т. Г. Шевченко *Гайдамаки*:

> ...новый опыт *спиваний* г. Шевченка, привилегированного, кажется, малороссийского поэта, убеждает нас еще более, что подобного рода произведения издаются только для услаждения и назидания самих авторов: другой публики у них, кажется, нет. Если же эти господа *кобзари* думают своими *поэмами* принести пользу низшему классу своих соотчичей, то в этом очень ошибаются: их поэмы, несмотря на обилие самых вульгарных и площадных слов и выражений, лишены простоты вымысла и рассказа, наполнены вычурами и замашками, свойственными всем плохим пиитам, часто нисколько не народны, хотя и подкрепляются ссылками на историю, песни и предания, — и, следовательно, по всем этим причинам они непонятны простому народу и не имеют в себе ничего с ним симпатизирующего.[9]

Составители примечаний к *Полному собранию сочинений* Белинского отмечают, что «отзыв Белинского о Т. Г. Шевченко несправедлив и в значительной степени объясняется тем, что Белинский был мало знаком с его произведениями».[10] Добавим к этому, что Белинский, очевидно, был «мало знаком» и с украинским языком: из посвящения Квитки-Основьяненко «Любій моїй жінці» (дат. падеж) он восстанавливает им. падеж в виде «жинка, или жинца».[11] Я столь подробно цитирую Белинского потому, что его оценки и рекомендации очень характерны для оценки ситуации на русской Украине вплоть до начала века. Белинский не рекомендует писать произведения на украинском языке и восклицает: «Какая глубокая мысль в этом факте, что Гоголь, страстно любя Малороссию, все-таки стал писать по-русски, а не по-малороссийски!».[12] И не только Гоголь, но и другие писатели-украинцы в общественно-культурной ситуации того времени предпочитали писать по-русски (В. В. Капнист, В. Т. Нарежный), некоторые же писали по-украински и по-русски (Г. П. Данилевский, Г. Ф. Квитка-Основьяненко, Е. П. Гребенка, П. А. Кулиш, Т. Г. Шевченко, Марко Вовчок).

Национальная задача создания украинского литературного языка на народной основе была начата творчеством Тараса Шевченко, продолжена Марко Вовчок, Иваном Франко, Михайлом Коцюбинским, Лесей Украинкой и не завершена до настоящего времени. Эта национальная задача была не только внутренней. Формирование украинского литературного языка происходило, если можно так выразиться, в тени русского языка. Под этим я имею в виду, что писатели, живущие на русской Украине, знали русский язык и в своем творчестве так или иначе определяли свое отношение к нему: ориентируясь на него или отталкиваясь от него. К середине XIX века русский литературный язык уже сформировался и обслуживал все стороны жизни русского народа и Российского государства. В это время церковнославянизмы были уже органической частью русского литературного языка. Поэтому в контексте украинского языка церковнославянизмы могли восприниматься (и нередко воспринимаются и сейчас) как русизмы и оцениваться негативно. А между тем — потенциально — церковнославянизмы могли стать важной составной частью словаря будущего украинского литературного языка — и это хорошо понимал Т. Г. Шевченко, ибо речь шла о средствах, обслуживающих все сферы жизни украинского народа, все жанры украинской литературы. Если использовать традиционное деление литературных жанров и литературного языка на три стиля, то можно сказать, что в разработке нуждались высокий и средний стили. Низкий стиль традиционно считался полем приложения дефектологии и диалектологии, и, как кажется, *Енеіда* И. П. Котляревского была принята благосклонно именно потому, что украинский язык был использован в ней для сатирического и пародийного описания. С другой стороны, взрыв негодования у В. Г. Белинского поэма Т. Г. Шевченко *Гайдамаки* вызвала потому, что в темах, традиционно включавшихся в высокий стиль — трагические события, героические деяния, высокие чувства, — Шевченко осмелился писать «малороссийским наречием», нарушив этим правила игры. С какой иронией Белинский пишет о любви героя поэмы Яремы к Оксане: «А вот нечто в роде чувствительно нежном. Страстный любовник Яремо [так! — П. С.] пришел на свидание к своей возлюбленной; но ее еще нет. Яремо, по сему случаю, *воет элегию* [подчеркнуто мной — П.С.] на целой странице и уже собирается умирать, как вдруг шелест ... Опять картина, и какая живая! Вот уж подлинно, говоря поэтическим языком самого господина сочинителя: ушкварил!».[13]

3. В истории украинского литературного языка XIX века, т. е. в тот период, когда он формировался, известны три попытки включить церковнославянизмы в состав его лексики. Одной из таких попыток было так называемое галицкое язычие, существовавшее в австрийской Украине. М. М. Коцюбинский так характеризует его:

> Ще з кінця 60 роки в серед галицької інтелігенції почались суперечки, чи ми самостійний народ, чи тільки частина російського. Чи наша мова окремий «языкъ», чи «нарѣчіе» великоруського. Ці суперечки ділили людей на два ворожі табори і розкололи вкінці галицьку інтелігенцію на москвофілів і народовців. Були навіть такі, що визнавали галичан

за окрему «рутенську націю», окрему од українців і великоросів. Москвофіли хотіли писать мовою Пушкіна, якої, звісно, не знали, а виходило у них так зване «язичіє», мішанина україньського, російського і церковнослов'янського... Що б ви не взяли до рук з тодішньої літератури — скрізь реакційний дух, мертвота, засмічена московщиною та церковщиною мова.[14]

И далее он приводит образцы этой, действительно, макаронической речи. Отметим положительные интенции создателей галицкого язычия: они стремились сохранить церковнославянизмы как часть восточнославянского культурного наследия, как элементы языка богослужений православной церкви. Такая попытка могла возникнуть только на территории австрийской Украины: это был как бы отголосок ситуации, существовавшей в восточнославянских землях в XVI–XVII веках, — наступления католицизма, появления униатства, конкуренции латыни и церковнославянского языка, что имело одним из своих следствий усиление внимания к грамматике и словарю церковнославянского языка. Во второй половине XIX века противостояние немецкому и польскому языкам, австрийской и польской культурам, влиянию католической церкви и было толчком к созданию этого нежизнеспособного агломерата. Галицкое язычие не получило большой поддержки на австрийской Украине (ср. отрицательное отношение к нему Ивана Франко, ориентировавшегося на народный язык всей Украины: «Діалект, а ми його надишем Міццю духу і огнем любови І нестертий слід його запишем Самостійно між культурні мови»[15]). Вполне понятно, что в ситуации русской Украины русские и церковнославянские элементы галицкого язычия встретили отрицательную оценку (ср. выше высказывание М. М. Коцюбинского). Так и осталось галицкое язычие любопытным эпизодом в истории украинского литературного языка, хотя принципы его организации могли всплывать и позже: ср. литературную форму лемковского диалекта, которой написана книга И. Ф. Лемкина «История Лемковины».[16]

Второй попыткой включения церковнославянизмов в состав украинского литературного языка была деятельность и творчество Пантелеймона Кулиша — современника Т. Г. Шевченко. П. А. Кулиш занимался историей Украины, писал художественные произведения (наиболее известное из них — исторический роман *Чорна рада*), переводил на украинский язык Библию, переводил Шекспира, Байрона, Гете, Мицкевича, Пушкина.[17] Митрополит Илларион (Иван Огиенко) пишет о стремлении Кулиша использовать архаические и церковнославянские слова в своих произведениях и переводах, связать второй и третий периоды развития украинского литературного языка: «П. Куліш, збагачуючи нашу літературну мову, спробував був брати потрібний матеріял і з нашої старої мови; надто часто це робив він у своїх перекладах з Шекспіра, а особливо з Біблії. Громадянство не підтримало цю Кулішеву ідею про староруську мову, вбачаючи в таких архаїзмах просто церковнослов'янізми або москалізми».[18]

Третьей попыткой — и, как представляется, наиболее удачной — включения церковнославянизмов в украинский литературный язык было творчество Тараса Шевченко, чей язык стал основой украинского литературного языка. Если в раннем своем творчестве Шевченко редко прибегает к церковнославянизмам, то позже — при возрастании гражданских мотивов в его произведениях — он все чаще, для выражения благословляющего и обличающего пафоса, прибегает к хорошо знакомому ему средству — церковнославянской речи. Он хорошо знал язык Священного Писания и богослужений и многое просто цитировал. Об отдельных видах церковнославянизмов в его произведениях речь будет идти дальше, здесь же отметим, что использование церковнославянизмов у него носит преимущественно цитатный характер. Если в процессе освоения заимствования выделить три этапа: 1) цитата — в виде фразы или отдельного слова, ощущаемая как инородное, иноязычное явление, требующая перевода; 2) полуцитата — требует для своего употребления особого контекста или комментария; 3) слово данного языка — только его история, возможные фонетические особенности, семантика, стилистические ограничения свидетельствуют о его заимствованном характере, — то в творчестве Шевченко церковнославянизмы остаются, преимущественно, на начальном, первом этапе. Он цитирует не только церковнославянские выражения: в его произведениях мы находим цитаты на польском, латыни, еврейском языках (*Гайдамаки*), русские фразы («Катерина», «Сон»). Но все цитаты такого рода выступают не в авторской речи и используются для отрицательной характеристики их носителей. Для Шевченко церковнославянизмы (слова или выражения) — часть его собственного языка, позволяющая выразить то, что с помощью обычных слов сделать трудно, это как бы верхний регистр его собственного языка. И его не останавливало то, что такие слова могли совпадать с русскими словами, его не останавливало даже явно не украинское звучание отдельных грамматических элементов (например, суффиксов или окончаний). Иногда эти цитаты (в применении к Шевченко их, может быть, лучше назвать автоцитатами) вырастают до размеров целых фрагментов. Ср. в поэме *Марія:* тексту предшествует эпиграф — прямая цитата из церковнославянского языка, далее идет авторский текст, представляющий собой в языковом отношении прямое продолжение эпиграфа: «Все упованіє моє На тебе, мій пресвітлий раю, На милосердіє твоє Все упованіє моє На тебе, мати, возлагаю. Святая сило всіх святих, Пренепорочная, благая!». Отметим, что здесь произношение отдельных форм сходно в церковнославянском и украинском языках, отличаясь от русского: *моє, на тебе.* Ср. также формы *раю, мати.* Шевченко использует церковнославянизмы и для противоположной цели — для обличения: «Пребезумний в серці скаже, Що бога немаї, В беззаконії мерзіє, Не творить благая» («Псалми Давидові»); Умре муж велій в власяниці. Не плачте, сироти, вдовиці, А ти, Аскоченський, восплач Воутріє на тяжкий глас. І Хомяков, Русі ревнитель, Москви, отечества любитель, О юбкоборцеві восплач. І вся о Русская беседа, Во глас єдиний ісповєдуй Свої гріхи. І плач! І плач!» («Умре муж велій...»). В последнем случае (сатирическое стихотворение приведено полностью) мы встречаем полный набор семантических и формальных церковнославянизмов, включая ироническое новообразование — *юбкоборець,* созданное по образцам неологизмов Ивана Вишенского. Я привел крайние образцы использования церковнославянских элементов в творчестве Т. Г. Шевченко. В них и в других случаях введения церковнославянизмов в украинский текст отчетливо видна позиция поэта: он видит в церковнославянизмах важное выразительное средство, он считает возможным использование церковнославянизмов в контексте украинского языка. В дальнейшем это отношение Шевченко к церковнославянизмам не получило продолжения. В этом повинна, прежде всего, социально-политическая ситуация, в которой происходило формирование украинского литературного языка.

4. При изучении церковнославянизмов не всегда просто определить, представлено ли то или иное слово в литературном языке или же оно выступает только в данном писательском употреблении. В данной статье были использованы следующие источники: 1) Б. Д. Грінченко, *Словарь української мови,* I–IV (Київ, 1907–1909) (репринт [Київ, 1958]); 2) *Словник української мови,* I–XI (Київ, 1970–1980); 3) *Інверсійний словник української мови* (обратный словарь к предыдущему) (Київ, 1985); 4) Произведения классиков украинской литературы (Т. Г. Шевченко, И. Я. Франко, Леся Украинка, М. М. Коцюбинский, Панас Мирный); 5) Католический перевод Библии на украинский язык: *Святе письмо Старого і Нового Завіту,* переклад тексту Івана Хоменко (Рим, 1963).[19]

5. Лексические церковнославянизмы украинского языка относятся преимущественно к религиозно-моральной сфере. Они, как правило, выполняют номинативную функцию, среди них много грецизмов. Ср. *аналой, ангел, апостол, вівтарь, євангеліє, риза, псалом, спас, спасати, закон, ірод, милосердний*.

Заимствования из церковнославянского языка, в которых присутствуют формальные (т. е. фонетические и словообразовательные) приметы их происхождения, рассмотрим отдельно по каждой из этих примет. Заимствований такого рода в украинском языке значительно меньше, чем в русском. Ситуация формальных заимствований более сложная, чем ситуация лексических церковнославянизмов: они иногда семантически соотносятся с собственно украинскими словами. В плане формальном их положение иногда оказывается даже более сложным, чем в русском: они функционируют не только параллельно с украинскими формами, но и с заимствованными в украинский язык полонизмами и чехизмами, что иной раз создает совершенно уникальную картину.

Неполногласие. Как и в случае лексических церковнославянизмов, формы с неполногласием относятся, в основном, к религиозной лексике, ср. *храм*, которое, помимо значения «церковь», имеет значение «храмовой праздник»; *враг* — в церковнославянском значении этого слова — «черт», ср. *Скачи, враже, як пан каже; Не взяв його враг!* (Б. Д. Грінченко, *Словарь української мови*, I, 258, далее — *Грінченко*); в авторском словоупотреблении оно нередко выступает параллельно с *ворог:* ср. у Шевченко: *хитрий ворог, руки вражі* — «Псалми Давидові»; то же у Франко; *празник* — параллельно к *свято*. В двух случаях в состав гнезда входят не только церковнославянские, но и чешские формы (иногда через польское посредство): 1) гнездо с исходным словом *благо*, в котором, наряду с *благий, блажений* (ср. у Франко: *Блажений муж, що йде на суд неправих і там за правду голос свій підносить*) и многочисленными композитами (*благословити, благородний, благоговіти, облагодіяти* и т. д.), выступает и чехизм *благати*, ср. пол. *błagać* при *błogi;* 2) гнездо, в котором, наряду с собственно украинскими *володіти, володар, Володимир*, есть и богемизмы по происхождению *влада, власний, властивий* (ср. пол. *władza, własny, właściwy*) и церковнославянизмы *власть, владика* (о епископе), а также заимствование из русского языка *область*. В одном случае отмечен триплет: наряду с обычным *золото* иногда, особенно в сложениях и в авторском словоупотреблении, выступает *злото* и *злато* — по виду полонизм и церковнославянизм. Ср. у М. Рыльского: «Готичний присмерк, еллінську блакить, Легенд біблійних мідь, вісон і злато — Все можемо на полотні віддати Чи на папір слухняний перелить» (*Словник української мови*, III, 587, далее — *СУМ*) или у П. Тычины: «Сестру я вашу так любив, безцінно, злотоцінно» («О ніжна Інно»). Даже в случае если выбор формы определяется размером, остаются две возможности — *злато* и *злото*, причем, как представляется, *злато* является более книжной формой. Ср. также варьирующуюся первую часть сложения при второй, церковнославянской, части: *златоглавий, злотоглавий, золотоглавий*. Параллельно к этому триплету выступает дублет *серебро* — *срібло*, где второе слово является полонизмом либо церковнославянизмом по происхождению (с последующей диссимиляцией). Слова этих двух групп нередко выступают вместе, можно предположить, что их форма иногда определяется их взаимодействием. Ср. «О Грузіє! В твоїх-бо горах ще стільки злота й срібла!» (П. Тичина, *СУМ*, IX, 619). Любопытна диалектная форма *верем'я* 'хорошая погода', встречающаяся в художественной литературе, при отсутствующем в литературном языке *время*. Вполне возможно, что это сохранившаяся восточнославянская форма, но не исключено, что перед нами диалектное изменение церковнославянского слова в восточнославянское. Ср. то же с польской формой: диалектное *королі* вместо литературного *кролі*.

В подавляющем же большинстве своем неполногласные формы представляют собой либо устаревшие слова, выступающие нередко как часть выражения, то есть как часть цитаты, либо заимствования из русского языка в специальном значении, то есть, опять же, в цитатном употреблении. Ср. примеры церковнославянизмов:

1. *Страж* — в значениях «1. Особа перев. озброїна, яка стереже, охороняї кого-, що-небудь від нападу, ворожих дій і т.ін. 2. Книжн. Той, хто захищає, оберігає що-небудь, пильно стежить за недоторканістю чогось» (*СУМ*, IX, 747), ср. также *страж порядку;* слово *страж* семантически и стилистически противостоит слову *сторож*.

2. *Древо*. В номинативном значении не выступает, но ср. у Шевченко: «Над водою посаджене древо зеленії», хотя это, скорее всего, требование размера, ср. в народной песне: «Червоная калинонька, А білеє древце. Чом не ходиш, не говориш, Моє миле серце?» Но характерна сама возможность такого употребления. Слово может использоваться в образном значении или в цитате, ср. «Де він [Каменяр] розбитими паралічем руками Прекрасне древо правди посадив» (Л. Забашта, *СУМ*, II, 410); «Є навіть райки, яблука гіркущі. На древі зла прищеплене добро» (Л. Костенко, *Маруся Чурай*).

3. *Прах.* В первоначальном значении, параллельно к *порох*, является устаревшим. В переносном значении выступает в высоком либо сниженном стиле, ср. «Я п'ю, не дорікай мені. Мій прах создатель замісив На чистому вині» (А. Кримський, *СУМ*, VII, 519).

4. *Глас.* В номинативном значении — лишь в фраземе-цитате *глас вопіющого в пустині:* ср. другой пример цитатного употребления: *возвишати глас* (Л. Костенко, *Маруся Чурай*). Другое заимствованное из церковнославянского значение — только мн. число — «Назва ладу в церковній музиці, а також назва мотивів, що складають систему церковного співу» (*СУМ*, II, 80), ср. у И. Франко: *гавкають на всі гласи* («Абу-Касимові капці»). Ср. другие заимствования с этим корнем: *гласити/огласити, оглашений, гласний, гласність.*

5. *Глава.* Слово обычно имеет значение 'часть книги', но в авторском тексте возможны и другие употребления с целью создания высокого стиля: «Верба сріблиться, наче борода Чи шевелюра на главі пророчій» (М. Рильський); «Минає ніч, простує до садочку Глава арабів, старшина йменитий» (А. Кримський, оба примера — *СУМ*, II, 78).

6. *Град.* Слово в церковнославянской форме выступает лишь в названиях городов, ср. *Новоград-Волинський, Павлоград,* или в функции, близкой к этой, ср. *В Путивлі-граді* (Шевченко). *В Київ-граді* (Воронько, *СУМ*, II, 153). Ср. пример цитатного употребления: «В душі знов образи взискуїмого града» (Рильський, «Колишеться човен»).

Приведенными словами фактически и ограничивается количество форм с неполногласием в украинском языке. Отметим, что там, где неполногласные формы употребляются параллельно с полногласными, первые, как правило, принадлежат к более высокому или образному пласту лексики. Употребление таких форм нередко носит характер цитирования. Кроме этих примеров, можно привести еще некоторое количество случаев индивидуального употребления, ср. *ворожда* (Коцюбинский), *срамотні* (Шевченко), *брашно* (Костенко) и т. д., а также некоторые заимствования из русского: *здравниця, гражданка,* ср. также полукальку — *градобудівництво.*

Особо следует остановиться на формантах с неполногласными сочетаниями: префиксах *пре-* и *пред-.* Адъективный суффикс *пре-* выступает в некоторых явных заимствованиях из церковнославянского, ср. *пречистий* (обычно в форме женского рода как один из эпитетов Богоматери, а также как название праздника Богоматери — *Перша Пречиста, Друга Пречиста* — Грінченко, III, 405), ср. также *Пренепорочная* (Шевченко), *премудрий, преподібний, пресловутий.* Но очень широкое употребление этого префикса и в литературном и в диалектном языке, причем нередко от просторечных и сниженных прилагательных, заставляет усомниться в его чисто церковнославянском происхождении. Ср. *пребагатий, превеликий, презлющий, препаршивий, препоганий, препоганющий, превражий* (*превражий сину!* — ругательство), *прегарний, предовгий, предовжелезний, пездоровенний, прецікавий* и т. д.

В русском языке префикс субъективной оценки *пре-* малопродуктивен.[20] Продуктивность этого типа в украинском объясняется, очевидно, тем, что здесь встретились две волны: церковнославянская и польская: в польском языке этот тип был продуктивен, ср. современные формы *przedziwny, przepiękny, przemiły, przecudny*. Единичные глаголы с приставкой *пре-* в украинском являются церковнославянизмами: *преклонити, прелюбодіяти,* существительные — церковнославянизмами (*престол*) либо полонизмами (*пречуття* — наряду с *передчуття* — из польского *przeczucie*). Несколько слов с суффиксом *пред-* являются заимствованиями из церковнославянского (*предвічний, представити, предстати, предтеча, пред'явити*) либо из русского (*предводитель*).

Начальные ра-, ла-. В украинском единственный пример — *раб-* параллельно к *невільник*. Сначала, очевидно, в религиозном значении, ср. «*Г(с̃)и помози рабу своєму Юрью Болковичю создавшєму ц̃рквь и олтарь ст̃аго архиєрђя х(с̃)ва Николы*» (б. м. н., бл. 1350)»,[21] ср. обычное *рабъ Божіи*. Любопытно сохранение в украинском языке, правда, редкого *роб* в значении 'раб, работник': «*Не роби твої, щоб помикав нами!*» (Загребельний, *СУМ*, VIII, 252), а также диалектное существительное общего рода *роба* 'роботяща, працьовита людина' при обычном *нероба* — лентяй.

Начальные є, ю, а. Единичные примеры для каждого случая. Для первого — гнездо с *єдин*, эти слова восходят к церковнославянским и польским заимствованиям.[22] Начальное *ю* — *юний, юність, союз* — в начале корня, ср. также префикс *со-*. Начальное *а*: *аз* — как название буквы, в переносном значении — *ні аза не знати, починати з азів; азбука;* книжное *агнець*.

Сочетание *жд* (из *dj). Оно выступает лишь в единичных заимствованиях: *вождь, нужда,* ср. производное *нужденний*.

Слова со *щ* (из *tj или *kt/gt) более многообразны. Отметим уникальный в славянских языках случай, когда в одном языке представлены и исходная (в данном случае — восстановленная) форма и рефлексы всех трех групп славянских языков, ср. *могти/помогти — поміч —* полонизмы *міць, міцний* и церковнославянизм *мощі* (ср. у Шевченко —

немощен — «*Буває в неволі іноді згадаю*»). Ср. также *священний* (с параллельным причастием *свячений* — о ноже, *свячена вода*), *священник, священнодійство*. Часты формы с *-щ-* у Шевченко: *обіщався* («Причинна»), *помощники* («Неофіти»), *просвіщенні* («Кавказ») и даже *дщере* («Псалми Давидові»). Особый интерес представляет адъективный класс с суффиксом *-ущ-/-ащ-*. Как известно, система причастий русского языка, кроме страдательных прошедшего времени, заимствована из церковнославянского. В украинском этих классов нет, есть лишь отдельные заимствования: *трудящі, бувший*. Ср. цитатное использование таких форм в авторском употреблении: *хліб насущний* (Шевченко, «Кавказ»), *глас вопіющого в пустині* (Костенко, *Маруся Чурай*), *псу смердящому* (Тичина, «З мого щоденника») и мн. др. Прилагательные с суффиксом *-ущ-/-ащ-* могут быть разделены на две группы: 1) образованные от глаголов и 2) образованные от прилагательных. Обе эти группы продуктивны как в диалектном, так и в литературном языке. Слова первой группы обозначают усиленный глагольный признак (*невмирущий* — тот, который *никогда* не умрет, *видющі очі* — глаза, которые *хорошо* видят). Слова второй группы имеют значение суперлатива (*багатющий, злющий*). Между обеими группами есть определенная семантическая перекличка, но является ли она результатом их общего происхождения — на этот вопрос ответить трудно. Иногда это принимается как очевидное: «Русский и украинский языки, имеющие словообразовательный тип увеличенных имен прилагательных с суффиксом *-ущ-* (*-ющ-, -уч-, -юч-*), противостоят остальным славянским языкам, в которых такой тип отсутствует. Ср. р. *толстущий, большущий, злющий*; укр. *завзятущий, триклятущий, худющий, злющий, хитрющий, багатющий, товстущий, товстючий, злючий, худючий*. Различие вызвано ареальным развитием в русском и украинском языках увеличительных прилагательных с суффиксом *-ущ-* (*-уч-*) под влиянием отглагольных относительных прилагательных типа *могущий, кипучий*».[23] Вопрос нуждается в специальном изучении, но, как представляется уже сейчас, дело обстоит сложнее, чем считают авторы «Исторической типологии славянских языков». В. В. Виноградов пишет: «Быть может, прав был проф. С. К. Булич, предполагая, что формам на *-ющий, -ящий* значение превосходной степени могло быть придано влиянием такого увеличительного суффикса, как например, *-ища, -ище*: *ручища, домище* и т. д.».[24] Если предположить, что в исходе обеих адъективных групп лежат церковнославянские действительные причастия настоящего времени, то неясно, почему отадъективные прилагательные образуются только с помощью суффикса *-ущ-* (так в обоих языках, ср. рус. *большущий, злющий, толстущий*; укр. *багатющий, злющий, поганющий*)? Почему этот тип в украинском более продуктивен, чем в русском? Конечно, можно предположить, что эти языки использовали восточнославянские и церковнославянские действительные причастия настоящего времени противоположно: в русском формы на -*щий* являются причастиями, а формы на -*чий* — прилагательными (*лежащий* — *лежачий*), а в украинском — наоборот — тип причастий на -*чий* и прилагательных на -*щий*. Прилагательные на -*щий* в русском и на -*чий* в украинском в таком случае следовало бы признать вторичными, результатом адъективизации причастных типов. Но причина столь различного распределения причастных и адъективных типов между русским и украинским языками остается непонятной, и трудно предположить, чтобы не усвоенный в украинском тип причастий на -*щий* сразу стал адъективным. Если вернуться к параллелизму между увеличительными существительными и прилагательными, о чем говорили Булич и Виноградов, встает вопрос о происхождении увеличительного суффикса существительных. В этом смысле интересны факты украинского и польского языков. Дело в том, что увеличительный суффикс *-išče* является общеславянским. В западнославянском же ареале (включая украинский) параллельно может выступать и суффикс -*isko*. Так, в украинском можно отметить такие параллельные формы: *бабисько* — *бабище, чубисько* — *чубище, кабанисько* — *кабанище, дідисько* — *дідище, хлопчисько* — *хлопчище*. В польском сейчас выступают только формы на -*isko*, но в старопольском до XIV века были обычны в этом значении только формы с суффиксом *-išče*. По мнению С. Роспонда, суффикс *-išče* первоначально имел пространственное значение, значение аугментативности для него вторично.[25] В. Ташицкий, специально изучавший типы с суффиксами *-išče/-isko* в западнославянских языках, приходит к выводу, что суффикс увеличительности *-išče* образовался из адъективного суффикса *-ist-*.[26] Как бы ни оценивать происхождение увеличительного суффикса существительных — из *-sk-* или из *-st-*, — очевидно, что он ничего общего с причастным суффиксом не имеет. Можно предположить, что в русских и украинских прилагательных с суффиксом -*ущий/-ащий* исходной была отадъективная группа, т. е. что суффикс этой группы не восходит к причастному. Подобно суффиксу аугментативов, он, очевидно, связан с адъективным суффиксом -*st*-. Позже он был перенесен на отглагольные образования, что вызвало его взаимодействие с причастным типом.

6. Как известно, церковнославянские по происхождению типы состав-

ляют важную часть русской словообразовательной системы. В украинском языке это влияние значительно слабее; церковнославянские словообразовательные типы представлены, чаще всего, как бы в начальной стадии воздействия — наличием некоторого количества образований по данному типу. Ср. *приязнь, неприязнь, боязнь* (суффикс -*знь*); *гординя, благостиня, милостиня* (суффикс -*иня*). Что же касается типов с суффиксами абстрактности -*ство* и -*ость*, которые иногда считают заимствованными из церковнославянского языка,[27] то это общеславянские типы, продуктивные в современном украинском языке, а их бóльшая представленность в книжном языке объясняется абстрактным значением. Общеславянский по происхождению тип с суффиксом -*тель* продуктивен в русском языке и непродуктивен в украинском. «На происхождение суффикса -*тель* в русском языке в науке существует две точки зрения. По мнению одних ученых, суффикс -*тель* известен русскому языку искони. Другие считают, что суффикс -*тель* как активная словообразовательная единица утвердился в русском языке под влиянием церковнославянского языка как языка образца, по которому формировался русский литературный язык. Окончательно усвоенным системой русского словообразования суффикс -*тель* может считаться с того момента, когда он начинает сочетаться с основами чисто русских глаголов — с XVII в.».[28] Украинский язык, как представляется, подтверждает вторую точку зрения, которая, кстати, не отрицает общеславянского характера суффикса. В украинском этот тип не утвердился до сих пор. Отсутствие чередования *е/і* в открытом-закрытом слогах (*вчителя — вчитель*), как будто бы, предполагает заимствованность этого типа, ср. в польском слова с суффиксом -*ciel*: *właściciel, nauczyciel, wielbiciel* и чехизм *obywatel*. Но это отсутствие чередования в украинских формах может быть объяснено и аналогией — выравниванием формы именительного падежа по образцу форм косвенных падежей, ср. отсутствие чередования в одиночном слове с омоморфом: *нетель — нетеля*. Образования с суффиксом -*тель* в современном украинском языке (*Інверсійний словник української мови* приводит 110 слов с суффиксом -*тель*[29]), как правило, являются заимствованиями из церковнославянского, русского и польского языков (для последнего ср. чехизм по происхождению *обиватель* и, возможно, *урвитель*). Такие слова относятся обычно к религиозной (ср. *хранитель, сквернитель, даритель, спаситель, просвітитель, святитель, сотворитель*) либо книжно-официальной лексике (ср. *засідатель, обожатель, стяжатель, почитатель, родитель* и т. д.);

ср. также такие пары, как рус. *житель — небожитель, спасатель — спаситель* и укр. *мешканець — небожитель, рятівник — спаситель*.

Заимствованных префиксальных типов (о типе с приставкой *пре-* речь шла выше) нет, есть лишь отдельные вкрапления со следующими префиксами: а) *со-: совість, сотворити, собрат*, ср. у Л. Костенко — *собраття, согрішити, союз, соратник*, ср. цитатное употребление предлога у Т. Г. Шевченко: *Або три царіє со дари* — «А. О. Козачковському»; б) *воз-: воскреснути, воскресіння;* очевидно, полукальки церковнославянского *возз'єднати, возз'єднання; воздух* — в церковном значении. Часто эти формы использует Т. Г. Шевченко: *восхвалимо тебе, боже* («Псалми Давидові»); *воспоїм благая* — там же; *апостол...возгласив* («Неофіти») и др. Любопытно, что в украинском переводе Библии нам встретилось лишь несколько примеров употребления этого, характерного для религиозных текстов, типа: *возношення, возносити, воскрешати;* в) *из-*, фонетически изменяющийся в *з/с*, ср. *сповідати, сповідь, скінчити* (из *исконьчити*), *зоставити* (из *из/о/оставити*). Часты эти формы у Т. Г. Шевченко, ср. *та язви мира ізціли* — «Єретик»; *ізбави нас* — «Псалми»; *А радость матері Марії неізреченная* («Марія»). В этом и предыдущем случае виден цитатный характер употребления этих форм Т. Г. Шевченко. Иногда фонетические варианты украинского префикса *з/с* принимаются за церковнославянский элемент; так, например, оценивается глагол в фразе из *Енеїди* Котляревского *Ізбий Енея з пантелику* авторами изданной в Польше истории украинского языка.[30]

Иногда высказывается мнение, что церковнославянским по происхождению является в украинском языке префикс *без-*.[31] Этот префикс выступает в двух словообразовательных типах, ср. *безголовий — безбілетний*. Оба этих типа восходят, в своих началах, к предложным сочетаниям: *без голови — без білету*. С. П. Обнорский в статье «Префикс *без-* в русском языке»[32] предполагает, что тип *без-ный* является в русском языке вторичным по сравнению с типом *без-ый* и утвердился под влиянием церковнославянского языка. Ср. рус. (включая диалектные формы) *бескостый — бескостный, бескрылый — бескрыльный, безлистый — безлистный*; укр. *безсилий — безсильний, безголосий — безголосний*, но только *безгласний*. То же, как представляется, можно утверждать и об украинском языке: не сам по себе суффикс *без-* (общеславянский) был заимствован из церковнославянского, а словообразовательный тип *без-ний* (также общеславянский) утвердился в украинском языке благодаря церковнославянскому. Это же можно сказать о некоторых церковнославянских адъективных сложениях (с начальным *благо-, бого-, веле-, все-*), которые способствовали оформлению типа сложных прилагательных в украинском языке.

7. Таким образом, можно говорить об относительно слабой (по сравнению с русским языком) представленности в украинском языке лексических и фонетических церковнославянизмов, относящихся, как правило, к религиозной и книжной сферам лексики и выполняющих, большей частью, понятийную функцию. Нередко церковнославянизмы — самостоятельно или в более широком контексте — употребляются как цитаты, что зависит от уровня знакомства говорящего (пишущего) с религиозно-книжной культурой, с темой высказывания и подготовленностью аудитории. В плане словообразовательном можно, как кажется, отметить роль четырех адъективных типов церковнославянского языка (на *пре-, -ущ-, без-ный* и композита) в становлении соответствующих типов украинского языка (с учетом замечаний, сделанных выше). Другие же словообразовательные типы остаются на начальном уровне заимствования — некоторое количество однотипных дериватов. Как кажется, украинский язык по отношению к церковнославянскому языку в значительной степени находится в ситуации, в которой оказался древнерусский язык в начальный период своих контактов со старославянским языком.

8. В книге, посвященной украинскому литературному языку нового времени,[33] профессор Шевелев противопоставил украинский литературный язык как двухдиалектный (zweidialektische) русскому языку как двухъязычному (zweisprachliche); в создании украинского литературного языка принимали участие два диалекта: юго-восточный и галицийский, тогда как в создании русского участвовали два языка: русский и церковнославянский. Основное различие между этими ситуациями, помимо генетического, он видит в том, что разнодиалектные элементы литературного языка не имеют жанрового противопоставления, тогда как разноязычные элементы литературного языка обслуживают разные жанры. Дав интересную картину галицийского влияния на украинский литературный язык, он говорит, что устранение галицийских заимствований и введение русизмов и церковнославянизмов (в составе русизмов) в литературный язык Советской Украины в 30-е и последующие годы привели к изменению структуры украинского литературного языка: из языка двухдиалектного он превратился в язык двухъязычный. Эта оригинальная и эффектная классификация, как представляется, все же недостаточно верно описывает ситуацию. Во-первых, само понятие двух-

или полидиалектного литературного языка представляется спорным — по крайней мере, применительно к украинскому языку. Сам Г. Шевелев показал, что речь идет о галицийском *влиянии* на формирующийся литературный язык, а не о равном *участии* нескольких диалектов в образовании украинского литературного языка. Во-вторых, то же можно сказать о понятии двухъязычности языка: один язык должен быть основным, испытавшим влияние второго языка. Противопоставление двухдиалектного украинского языка двухъязычному русскому литературному языку у Г. Шевелева как бы *a priori* определяет негативное отношение к заимствованию церковнославянизмов в украинский литературный язык, так как это разрушает его структуру и уподобляет русскому литературному языку. В украинском языке есть некоторое количество церковнославянизмов, обозначающих, большей частью, новые понятия и ставших частью украинского словаря, ср. *вчитель, храм, совість, собор*. Они никак не изменили структуру украинского литературного языка. Не их, конечно, имеет в виду Г. Шевелев: он говорит об использовании заимствований, которые обозначают понятия, уже имеющие названия в украинском языке, т. е. о возможности стилистического дифференцирования. Некоторое количество таких пар уже есть в языке: *спасати — рятувати, страж — сторож, раб — невільник, прах — порох*. Можно ли говорить, что их появление меняет структуру украинского литературного языка? Церковнославянский язык — язык украинской православной церкви, один из языков украинской средневековой культуры; отсюда, как представляется, открытость украинского словаря церковнославянскому воздействию и понятность такого рода употребления на цитатном и лексическом уровне. Определенное количество со вкусом отбираемых церковнославянизмов, используемых для обслуживания верхнего регистра украинского литературного языка, вряд ли может изменить его структуру. Бесспорно, попытки внедрения русских и церковнославянских слов (как русских) в 30-е и последующие годы, вызванные политическими причинами, и малограмотные упражнения отдельных писателей отрицательно сказывались на украинском литературном языке. Но я не думаю, что все это было способно изменить структуру украинского литературного языка. Украинскому литературному языку угрожает не опасность из двухдиалектного превратиться в двухъязычный. Ему угрожает более серьезная опасность — вообще утратить права литературного языка и превратиться в социальный диалект русского языка. Об этом речь будет идти дальше.

9. Борис Унбегаун предлагает для характеристики восточнославянских литературных языков другую терминологию: он называет русский язык двухмерным (two-dimensional), противопоставляя его одномерным (one-dimensional)[34] украинскому и белорусскому литературным языкам. Определение «меры в языке» не дается, и используется этот термин нестрого: очевидно, как наличие торжественного, высокого стиля, обслуживаемого в русском языке, в значительной степени, средствами церковнославянского языка. Но этот стиль, этот регистр есть и в украинском и белорусском литературных языках, просто для его выражения используются иные средства. Кроме того, вопреки интенциям Унбегауна, имеется возможность оценочного использования предложенных им терминов. На страницах советской (даже специальной) печати можно встретить утверждения о какой-то особой лингвистической предрасположенности русского языка для выполнения функции языка межнационального общения в СССР (В. Костомаров, И. Протченко).

10. Как говорилось в начале статьи, место церковнославянизмов в современном украинском литературном языке определяется языковой ситуацией на Украине, то-есть, прежде всего, взаимоотношениями украинского и русского языков.

Положение украинского языка на Украине сейчас очень сложно. Об этом говорят не только диссиденты, но — в последнее время — и официальная советская пресса. На Украине (особенно в ее восточной и центральной частях) украинский язык сейчас не престижен. Престижным является русский язык. Близость этих языков приводит к тому, что украинский язык фактически функционирует как социальный диалект русского языка: немаркированно он употребляется только в селах и небольших городах. В городах немаркированным является употребление русского языка, украинский же выступает в специальных ситуациях: в официальном употреблении, недавними выходцами из села, национально определившейся интеллигенцией. Это большая и больная проблема. Приведу несколько фактов из советской печати. Писатель Юрий Щербак в интервью, посвященном двухлетию Чернобыля, приводит записки, которые он получает от слушателей, среди них и такая: Что делают писатели, чтобы сохранить украинскую природу и украинский язык?[35] — читатели говорят о языковом Чернобыле. Другой писатель, Борис Олейник, выступая на XIX Всесоюзной конференции КПСС, сказал:

Одно из тяжких наследий культа — извращение ленинской национальной политики. Не стоит искать виноватых по регионам. Ведь беда универсальная. В этом плане одинаково печальны и следствие, и причина. Следствие, в частности, на Украине таково: национальный язык очутился почти на околице духовной и материально-производственной деятельности народа. Он постепенно как-то уходит из делопроизводства, из государственного и партийного обихода. Более того, во многих городах уже не существует школ на родном языке. Почти во всех высших учебных заведениях студенты лишены возможности учиться на языке своих матерей, не говоря уже о детских садах.[36]

В современных условиях единственным выходом из положения является признание украинского языка государственным языком Украины.

В силу всего этого частный вопрос о церковнославянизмах обычно рассматривается в контексте всей языковой ситуации на Украине; вот почему отношение к ним нередко негативное: они рассматриваются как русизмы. Но церковнославянизмы — это общее наследие всех восточнославянских народов, церковнославянский язык — это язык православной церкви, и использование церковнославянизма в украинском языке должно оцениваться не по тому, есть ли он в русском языке, а по тому, нужен ли он украинскому языку. Нет никакого сомнения, что церквнославянизмы — потенциальный источник обогащения украинского языка. Использование церковнославянизмов зависит от контекста и вкуса автора. В качестве примера именно такого использования церковнославянизмов можно назвать одно из самых значительных произведений украинской литературы последних лет — роман в стихах Лины Костенко *Маруся Чурай.*

Примечания

This article was accepted for publication in 1989.

1. Б. А. Успенский, *Из истории русского литературного языка XVIII–начала XIX века* (М., 1985), стр. 5.
2. George Y. Shevelov, *Die Ukrainische Schriftsprache 1798–1965* (Wiesbaden: Otto Harrassowitz, 1966), стр. 163.
3. Павло Филипович, «Епітафія неоклясикові». В: Юрій Лавріненко, *Розстріляне відродження, Антологія 1917–1933,* (Instytut Literacki, printed in Germany, 1959), стр. 218–219.
4. См., например, периодизацию истории украинского языка в соответствующих статьях Г. Шевелева и Р. Смаль-Стоцкого в *Ukraine. A Concise Encyclopedia,* ed. by Volodymyr Kubijovyč, vol. 1 (University of Toronto Press, 1963). стр. 481–511.
5. B. O. Unbegaun, «Язык русского права». In: B. O. Unbegaun, *Selected Papers on Russian and Slavonic Philology* (Oxford, 1969), стр. 314.

6. Михайло Грушевський, «Ганебній пам'яті». В: Юрій Лавріненко, *Розстріляне відродження*, стр. 924.

7. Цит. по книге George Y. Shevelov, *Die Ukrainische Schriftsprache 1798–1965*, стр. 1.

8. В. Г. Белинский, «Ластовка. Сватанье». В: В. Г. Белинский, *Полное собрание сочинений*, т. V, *Статьи и рецензии 1841–1844* (Изд. АН СССР, М., 1954), стр. 176–177.

9. В. Г. Белинский, «Гайдамаки. Поэма Т. Шевченка». В: В. Г. Белинский, *Полное собрание сочинений*, т. VI, *Статьи и рецензии 1842–1843* (М., 1955), стр. 172.

10. Ibid., стр. 731.

11. В. Г. Белинский, «Ластовка. Сватанье...», стр. 179.

12. В. Г. Белинский, ibid., стр. 178.

13. В. Г. Белинский, «Гайдамаки...», стр. 174.

14. М. М. Коцюбинський, «Іван Франко». В: М. М. Коцюбиньский, *Вибране* (Львів, 1983), стр. 324–325.

15. Іван Франко, «Антошкові П. (Азъ Покой)». В: Іван Франко, *Гримить* (Київ, 1986), стр. 203.

16. И. Ф. Лемкин, *История Лемковины* (Нью-Йорк, 1969).

17. О П. А. Кулише см. George Luckyj, *Panteleimon Kulish. A sketch of his life and times* [= *East European Monographs,* No. CXXVII] (Boulder, 1983).

18. Митрополіт Іларіон, *Історія української літературної мови* (Вінніпег, 1949), стр. 285.

19. Последний источник особенно интересен, так как по нему можно судить о роли церковнославянизмов в украинском католическом богослужении, что заслуживает самостоятельного анализа. Видно, что автор перевода Иван Хоменко избегает церковнославянизмов. В тексте можно отметить следующие формы: с неполногласием: слова с *благо* — *благоугодний, благоговіти, благословити, благословенний; владика, храм, празник; предкладати;* слово с начальным *ра-: раб;* слова с -*щ*- (из **tj*): *священик, причастия жерущий, ссущий;* слова с префиксом *со-: союз, сотворити, согрішити;* с префиксом *воз-: возносити, возношати, воскрешати;* сложные слова: *всепалення, лжепророк, всемогутній, жертвоприношення.* В большинстве своем это слова, вошедшие не только в литературный, но и в диалектный язык.

20. В. В. Виноградов, *Русский язык (грамматическое учение о слове)*, изд. 2-е (М., 1972), стр. 207.

21. *Словник староукраїнської мови XIV–XV ст.*, т. II (Київ, 1978), стр. 286.

22. *Етимологічний словник української мови*, т. II (Київ, 1985), стр. 179.

23. *Историческая типология славянских языков*, под ред. А. С. Мельничука (Киев: Наукова думка, 1986), стр.95.

24. В. В. Виноградов, op. cit., стр. 198.

25. Stanisław Rospond, *Gramatyka historyczna języka polskiego* (Warszawa, 1971), стр. 200–201.

26. Witold Taszycki, "Przyrostek -isko, -išče w językach zachodniosłowiańskich" (*Slavia*, 4[1925/26]:213–227); Jan Łoś, *Gramatyka polska, Część druga, Słowotwórstwo* (Lwów etc., 1925), стр. 87.

27. Ср., например, М. А. Жовтобрюх, Б. М. Кулик, *Курс сучасної української літературної мови*, т. 1 (Київ, 1965), стр. 44.

28. *Очерки по исторической грамматике русского литературного языка XIX века. Изменения в словообразовании и формах существительного и прилагательного в русском литературном языке XIX века* (Москва, 1964), стр. 23.

29. Стр. 743.

30. T. Lehr-Spławiński, P. Zwoliński, S. Hrabec, *Dzieje języka ukraińskiego w zarysie* (Warszawa, 1956), стр. 50.

31. *Історія української мови. Лексика і фразеологія*, ред. В. М. Русанівський (Київ, 1983), стр. 696.

32. С. П. Обнорский, «Префикс *без-* в русском языке». В: С. П. Обнорский, *Избранные работы по русскому языку* (М., 1960).

33. George Y. Shevelov, *op. cit.*, стр. 162–168.

34. B. O. Unbegaun, «The Russian Literary Language: A Comparative View». In: *The Modern Language Review*, vol. 68, no. 4 (1973), стр. xix–xxv.

35. Газета *Московские новости*, № 17, 24 апреля 1988, стр. 14.

36. Газета *Известия*, № 184, 2 июля 1988, стр. 7.

Pavel Sigalov/Summary: Church Slavonicisms in Ukrainian

The role of Church Slavonicisms in the East Slavic literary languages was determined not only by linguistic but also by socio-political and cultural factors. In modern times, when literary Russian, Ukrainian, and Belorussian were formed, the divergent development, evident from the fourteenth century on, resulted in sharp differentiation with respect to the role of Church Slavonicisms between Russian on the one hand, and Ukrainian and Belorussian literary languages on the other. Whereas in modern literary Russian, Church Slavonicisms retained their major stylistic function, in literary Ukrainian they were often perceived as "Russianisms." As a result, there are relatively few phonetic and lexical Church Slavonicisms in Ukrainian. They are usually connected with religious and bookish lexical areas and often have a denominative function. The strikingly different role of Church Slavonicisms in literary Ukrainian and literary Russian was chiefly determined by extra-linguistic factors.

PART III
Christianity and Medieval Cultural Paradigms

Солярно-лунарная символика в облике русского храма

BORIS USPENSKII

1. Маковки русских церквей украшает крест с полумесяцем — или, говоря точнее, крест, в основании которого помещен полумесяц.

Каково происхождение этой традиции?

Символика креста естественно вписывается в христианские представления, она соответствует самой функции христианского храма и, кажется, не нуждается в разъяснении. Но что означает полумесяц? Почему столь устойчиво само это сочетание? Вопрос этот волновал еще Максима Грека, который посвятил ему специальное рассуждение «Сказание о том, что под крестом на церкви окружен аки месяц млад». И, наконец, встает еще один вопрос: является ли эта композиция чисто русским явлением?

Обычно считают, что эта символика, это сочетание знаменует победу православия над мусульманством, освобождение от татарского владычества. Это мнение не выдерживает критики. Несомненно, интересующее нас явление возникло еще в домонгольский период. Об этом красноречиво свидетельствует крест с полумесяцем на куполе владимирского Дмитровского собора (1194–1197 гг.); этот крест, несомненно, сохраняет свою первоначальную форму. Такую же форму имел и крест на церкви Спаса Нередицы в Новгороде (1199 г.). Наконец, такое же изображение встречается в древнейший период на миниатюрах и на клеймах икон (где представлено изображение храма), а также на каменных резных крестах. Так, мы встречаем его на миниатюрах Добрилова евангелия 1164 г., Симоновой псалтыри XIII в., сочинений Григория Двоеслова XIII в., Федоровского евангелия 1325–1327 гг., Сильвестровского сборника XIV в., так называемого Служебника Антония Римлянина XIV в., Хроники Георгия Амартола XIV в., Часослова 1423 г., Коневской псалтыри XV в.; на клеймах московской иконы Николы Зарайского XIV в. и новгородской иконы Николы с житием XIV–XV в.; на каменных крестах — Перынском кресте XIV в., кресте церкви Рождества Богородицы на Молоткове XIV в. и др. Равным образом мы встречаем это изображение на граффити и на актовых печатях.

Итак, безусловно неправомерно трактовать интересующее нас изображение как символ торжества православия (христианства) над мусульманством. Столь же неправомерна, по-видимому, и попытка увидеть здесь символическое изображение торжества христианства над язычеством — некоторые исследователи усматривают здесь изображение змея, попираемого крестом.

Но как же трактовать это изображение? Крест имеет для нас прежде всего христианские ассоциации; между тем, полумесяц, очевидно, изображает луну, т. е. представляет собой символ несомненно языческого происхождения. Достаточно напомнить хотя бы о лунницах, т. е. подвесках в форме полумесяца, которые носили славяне язычники (то, что на них изображена именно луна, хорошо осознавалось, как это видно из поучений против язычества). Как же в таком случае объяснить это сочетание христианской и языческой символики? Говорит ли оно о двоеверии, т. е. о функциональном объединении христианского и языческого начала? Но почему же тогда это сочетание узаконено в храмовом декоре? Почему оно настолько распространено?

2. Для ответа на этот вопрос следует принять во внимание, что не только полумесяц, но и крест соотносится с астральной — или, точнее, с солярно-лунарной — символикой.

Общеизвестно, что символика креста предшествует христианству: крест — это солярный символ, символ солнца. Эта символика едва ли не универсальна и во всяком случае имеет исключительно широкое распространение. Не случайно четырехконечный (равноконечный) крест встречается, например, на японских буддийских храмах. Изображение креста обнаружено и на древних американских монументах, предшествующих появлению в Америке европейцев (в частности, в Мексике, на полуострове Юкатан), и старинные историки для того, чтобы объяснить это явление, вынуждены были предположить, что в Америке задолго до Колумба проповедовал апостол Фома и его ученики.

Соответственно объясняется и обычай носить крест на груди или на шее, который также наблюдается и вне христианского культа. Так, главный жрец Мемфиса носил крест как нагрудное украшение; в Риме носили крест на шее весталки; наконец, крест могли носить и славяне язычники (об этом свидетельствуют археологические данные). Все это легко объяснимо, если иметь в виду, что крест выступает во всех этих случаях как солярный символ.

Солярная символика особенно ясно и выразительно представлена в свастике. В самом деле, свастика — это типичный солярный знак, где передается при этом круговое движение солнца. Вместе с тем, свастика — это, конечно, разновидность креста: этот знак, собственно, и именуется крестом — такого рода крест, поскольку он известен в христианском искусстве, носит название *crux gammata* или «крюковидный крест». В качестве солярного символа свастика была распространена в Индии, и это хорошо известно благодаря тому, что именно отсюда заимствовали этот знак нацисты; в несколько меньшей степени известно то обстоятельство, что свастика как солярный знак была распространена у славян — изображение свастики до сих пор можно увидеть на славянских избах (например, в Татрах у польских гуралей).

3. Итак, сочетание креста и полумесяца целиком вписывается в космологическую, языческую по своему происхождению символику: крест и полумесяц символизируют солнце и луну.

Но вместе с тем оба символа имеют и другой, христианский смысл: крест очевидным образом выступает как символ Христа, тогда как луна в христианской традиции символизирует Богородицу.

Такое толкование прямо соответствует каноническим текстам и поддерживается ими: текстам, где Христос называется «солнцем правды» или «солнцем праведным» (*sol justitiae*) (Малахия 4:2), а Богородица предстает как «жена, облеченная в солнце; под ногами ее луна, и на голове ее венец из двенадцати звезд» (Откр. 12:1). Иллюстрацией к этому последнему образу может служить хотя бы икона Остробрамской Божьей Матери, где Богоматерь изображена с месяцем и ее изображение окружают 12 звезд; отсюда же объясняется и иконография так называемой Богоматери смирения (*Madonna humilitatis*) в западной традиции.

Итак, лунарная символика непосредственно связана с Богородицей, так же как солярная символика связана с Христом. Эту связь очень хорошо ощущал, например, Стефан Яворский, когда говорил в «Слове о победе под Полтавой» (1709 г.): «Сам Христос Спаситель, иже есть солнце, и луна — пресвятая дева Мария, стали и пособствовали победить гордаго сего». Но, конечно, всего нагляднее и убедительнее эта символика выражена в песнопении, которое поется на Страстной неделе — на утренней службе в Великую Субботу: «Заходиши под землю, солнце правды; тем же рождшая тя луна печальми оскудевает, вида твоего лишаема». Этому тексту предшествует следующий текст, который поется накануне — на повечерии в Великий Пяток (т. е., в Страстную Пятницу): «Солнце не заходяй, Боже предвечный и творче всех тварей, Господи, како терпиши страсть на кресте, чистая плачущи глаголаше». Итак, в этом последнем песнопении Богородица называет Христа «солнцем не заходящим». Эти слова перекликаются с песнопением, которое приведено выше и определяет его восприятие; однако в нем Христос предстает как солнце, заходящее под землю, а Богородица — как луна, его родившая, которая оскудевает от скорби, лишаясь его вида. Мы видим, что наименование Христа «солнцем» естественно соотносится с наименованием Богородицы «луной».

Итак, Христос ассоциируется с солнцем и, соответственно, крест как солярный знак оказывается символом Христа. Именно таким образом нужно понимать изображение креста на куполе христианского храма (между тем, полумесяц как лунарный знак обозначает здесь Богородицу). Совершенно так же может трактоваться, между прочим, и изображение петуха на куполе храма в западной христианской традиции (католической и протестантской): в самом деле, петух — это тоже типичный солярный символ. Таким образом, как крест, так и петух на куполе христианского храма изображает солнце и через него Христа, т. е. Солнце Правды: это разные реализации одной идеи.

В древнерусской учительной литературе можно встретить мнение, что когда Христос воскрес, солнце, не заходя, стояло всю неделю (см., например, «Устав людем о велицем посте» в Соловецкой кормчей 1493 г. и другие сочинения). С этим полемизирует Максим Грек в «Сказании к глаголющим, яко всю Светлую неделю солнце не заходя стояло, и того ради глаголют един день всю Светлую неделю». Тем не менее, это мнение в какой-то мере соответствует литургической практике, поскольку на пасхальной неделе каждый день служится как воскресенье. Достаточно характерно и народное представление о том, что солнце играет на Пасху. Итак, воскресение Христа соотносится с солнцем — и это вполне понятно, поскольку с солнцем ассоциируется сам Христос.

4. Ассоциация Христа — и креста как христианского символа — с солнцем очень отчетливо проявляется в богослужебном действе. Так, старообрядцы-беспоповцы расходятся в своей практике каждения; они кадят с помощью кации, которую держат за ручку, а не обычной кадильницы, которая висит на цепочках. Одни старообрядцы кадят крестом (т. е. крестообразно, изображая крест), другие же — «обносом», т. е. обводят кацеей посолонь (по солнцу, изображая движение солнца).[1] Существует специальная полемика по этому поводу, однако для нас важно то обстоятельство, что оба действия предстают как функционально равнозначные — солнце и крест выступают как эквивалентные символы.

Но и в обычной — не старообрядческой — православной службе мы можем наблюдать ту же самую эквивалентность. Так, в определенные моменты литургического действа священник из алтаря, стоя в царских дверях — там, куда входит Царь Славы, т. е. Христос, — благославляет молящихся знаком креста (осеняет их крестом); затем его сменяет дьякон, который, держа в руке орарь, обводит им посолонь (по солнцу). И в этом случае, опять-таки, крест и солнце предстают как синонимичные явления.

Еще более заметна ассоциация Христа (а соответственно, и креста) и солнца в народных верованиях. Достаточно характерен обычай молиться на восток, повсеместно распространенный у русских; в ряде мест принято молиться как на восходящее, так и на заходящее солнце — по сообщению этнографа, «при виде восходящего, а также заходящего солнышка ... некоторые из крестьян благоговейно снимают шапки и истово крестятся 'на солнышко'». Церковь могла осуждать этот обычай, помня о его языческом происхождении, — т. е. связывая его не с христианскими каноническими текстами (где Христос именуется «солнцем»), а с дохристианскими верованиями. Так, в древнерусском «Поучении отца духовного к детям духовным» осуждаются те, кто «кланяется солнцу или луне или звездам или иному чему, то есть поганой [языческий] закон».

Во второй половине XVII в. дьякон Федор Иванов — известный старообрядческий деятель, сподвижник протопопа Аввакума — свидетельствует о том, что многие поселяне, а также попы и дьяконы, «живучи по селам своим, покланяются солнцу, где с ними не лучится образа, иконы Христовы и креста его»; итак, солнце явно соотносится как с иконой Христа, так и с крестом, т. е. символическим изображением Христа. До нас дошло дело о старообрядце Василии Желтовском (1680-е гг.), который не ходил в никонианскую (новообрядческую) церковь, говоря: «Бог наш на небеси, а на земле Бога нет», и «крестился, смотря на солнце». Естественно, что у старообрядцев, лишенных возможности ходить в церковь, соответствующие представления — идущие из глубокой древности — актуализируются.

Вообще солнце может называться в народе «богом» так же, как и икона. Так, по этнографическим свидетельствам, «в восточной Сибири поселяне говорят о солнце: Бог глядит с неба». Согласно другому свидетельству (из Вологодской губернии), «клясться именем Бога — большая клятва, но *право* [т. е. клятва со словом *право*] считается 'выше солнца'»; здесь явно отразилось не только восприятие солнца как Бога, но и наименование его «богом» (вместе с тем, в этом свидетельстве прослеживаются, видимо, реликты древней языческой клятвы солнцем). Ассоциация Бога и солнца проявляется и в русском свадебном обряде, а именно в мотивировке ритуального закрывания волос у замужней женщины: полагают, что «на женский волос не должно солнце светить», т. е. женщина не может показывать волосы солнцу; вместе с тем, даже и дома женщина не может с открытой головой «пред образа стать», т. е. молиться перед иконами — итак, солнце и икона (а иконы именовались в России «богами») и в этом случае предстают как соотнесенные явления.

Ассоциация Христа и солнца может поддерживаться каноническими текстами. Так, например, юродивый Иоанн Большой Колпак, живший при царе Федоре Иоанновиче, любил подолгу смотреть на солнце, размышляя о «праведном солнце», т. е. о Христе как Солнце Правды. Подобным же образом ассоциация Христа и солнца может поддерживать восприятие креста как солярного символа, как это отчасти видно и из приведенных выше примеров: древняя традиция восприятия такого рода приобретает в этих условиях новый смысл.

Не приходится думать, однако, что народные верования, о которых только что шла речь, непосредственно обусловлены каноническими текстами. Нет, здесь просто естественно контаминируются христианские и языческие представления — христианство, так сказать, наслаивается на язычество, т. е. христианские идеи и образы усваиваются на фоне языческого культурного субстрата. Не случайно церковь, как мы видели, может осуждать обычай молиться, обращаясь к солнцу, справедливо усматривая здесь языческий по своему происхождению обряд.

Народные представления могут оказываться при этом даже сильнее церковных установлений. Так, когда в 1479 г. при освящении московского Успенского собора митрополит Геронтий стал ходить с крестом вокруг храма «не по солнечному всходу» (т. е. не посолонь, а против солнца), то великий князь Иван Васильевич немедленно воспротивился этому, заявив, что за то «гнев Божий приходит». Митрополит Геронтий был не русским, а греком, и исходил, естественно, из практики греческой церкви. Когда митрополит и его сторонники пытались обосновать свою позицию ссылкой на эту практику, им было отвечено, что поскольку Христос есть «солнце праведное», ходить против солнца означало бы идти против Христа. Хождение вокруг храма против солнца тогда не было принято, но в середине XVII в. патриарх Никон все-таки привел русский обряд в соответствие с греческой практикой. И совершенно так же мотивировали свой отказ ходить в новоосвященные церкви старообрядцы: они отказывались ходить в эти церкви именно потому, что они освящены против солнца. Подобным же образом старообрядцы не признают новообрядческого крещения и венчания, в частности, и потому, что новообрядцы обходят вокруг купели (при крещении) или вокруг аналоя с крестом и Евангелием (при венчании) против солнца, а не посолонь. Хождение против солнца воспринимается как выступление против Христа.

5. Итак, сочетание креста и полумесяца читается, так сказать, в двух кодах, может интерпретироваться в двух концептуальных системах — языческой и христианской. В одном случае это сочетание предстает как солярно-лунарная символика, в другом же случае оно символизирует соединение Христа и Богородицы. Поскольку, в свою очередь, Христос ассоциируется с солнцем, а Богородица с луной, это сочетание оказывается очень устойчивым.

Уместно отметить в этой связи, что такое сочетание зафиксировано на русских лунницах, т. е. подвесках языческого происхождения: наряду с лунницами в форме полумесяца, есть и такие подвески, в которых между рогами полумесяца помещен крест. Мы можем предположить, что в том случае, когда лунница не имела изображения креста, она могла носиться вместе с крестом, образуя таким образом интересующую нас композицию.

До сих пор речь шла о русских примерах. Однако наряду с этим, сочетание креста и полумесяца можно встретить — правда, совсем не так часто — и в византийском искусстве. Оно встречается здесь как на изображении храмов (см., например, миниатюры Менология Василия II Болгаробойцы X–XI вв. или Гомилии Иакова XII в.), так и в качестве отдельного изображения. Мы находим его, в частности, в Равенне на рельефе каменного саркофага епископа Феодора (460–470 гг.) или на серебряной монете императоров-соправителей Василия II и Константина VIII (975–1025 гг.). До нас дошли относительно поздние (XVI в.) афонские резные кресты, близкие по форме к интересующему нас изображению. Характерно, наконец, что Максим Грек, рассматривая кресты такого рода в уже упоминавшемся «Сказании о том, что под крестом на церкви окружен аки месяц млад», отнюдь не трактует их как местное русское явление, но не сомневается в их греческом происхождении.[2]

Мы можем предположить, следовательно, что купольные кресты с полумесяцем пришли на Русь из Византии. Вместе с тем, поскольку солярно-лунарная символика имеет вообще универсальное распространение, постольку как в Византии, так и на Руси — независимым образом — могло реализоваться двойное прочтение соответствующей композиции: и как собственно христианских, и как солярно-лунарных символов.

6. Но почему же церковь — сначала в Византии, а затем и на Руси — использует столь двусмысленную символику — символику, в принципе допускающую двойное истолкование? Можно ли усматривать здесь своеобразное проявление двоеверия? Думается, что нет.

Необходимо напомнить, что целый ряд обрядов и символов христианской Церкви обнаруживает несомненное языческое происхождение. Это обусловлено вполне сознательной практикой Церкви, которая имеет, вообще говоря, очень древнюю традицию и которую можно было бы условно определить как своего рода «воцерковление язычества» — речь идет о традиции усвоения более ранних, дохристианских форм, переосмысления их, наполнения языческих форм новым — христианским — содержанием. В сущности, это миссионерская традиция. Действительно, с распространением христианства — в самые разные исторические периоды — Церковь определенно и, видимо, вполне сознательно приспосабливалась к язычеству, в частности, к языческим празднествам и в какой-то степени даже к языческим обрядам. Иначе говоря, она сознательно приспосабливалась к уже существующим формам, стремясь придать им новый смысл, переосмыслить их в новом семантическом ключе.

По словам современного историка церкви (о. Александра Шмемана), «христианство восприняло и сделало своими многие 'формы' языческой религии ... потому .., что весь замысел христианства в том и состоит, чтобы все 'формы' в этом мире не заменить новыми, а наполнить новым и истинным содержанием. Крещение водою, религиозная трапеза, помазание маслом — все эти основоположные религиозные акты Церковь не выдумала, не создала, все они уже имелись в религиозном обиходе человечества».[3] И еще: « ... в борьбе с язычеством, в ... завоевании мира, Церковь не усумнилась обратить на служение христианству многие 'естественные' формы религии, бывшие обычными для язычества. Язычники праздновали 25 декабря рождение Непобедимого Солнца, христиане к этому дню приурочили празднование Рождества Христова, научившего людей 'поклоняться Солнцу Правды, его познавать с высоты востока', у язычников 6 января был праздник 'богоявление': эта же дата стала датой и христианского Богоявления. Церковный культ 'бессребренников' имеет много общего с языческим культом Диоскуров, форма христианского 'жития' — с образцами языческих 'восхвалений героев', и, наконец, объяснение христианских таинств оглашенным — с 'мистериальной' терминологией языческих посвящений».[4] Говоря о приспособлении христианских праздников к языческим, можно указать, далее, что праздник Усекновения главы Иоанна Предтечи (29 августа) был установлен александрийской церковью в противовес празднествам александрийского нового года; праздники Рождества Богородицы (8 сентября) и Зачатия Богородицы (12 января) были установлены в Азии в противовес олимпийским играм; праздник Преображения Господня (6 августа) — армяно-каппадокийского происхождения и установлен в Армении в противовес языческому празднику роз; день архангела Михаила (8 ноября) — александрийского происхождения и заменил собой древнейший праздник Крещения Господня, установленный египетской церковью в противовес крокиям и торжествам в честь Усири. Таким образом, Церковь как бы давала христианское освящение народным празднествам; естественно, что при этом должны были сохраняться те или иные языческие обряды, которые получали, однако, новое содержание, переосмысляясь в плане христианских представлений.

Точно так же и христианские храмы ставились, как правило, на месте языческих капищ, а языческие жрецы по мере распространения христианства становились христианскими священнослужителями. Сходным образом, наконец, христианские святые оказываются заместителями языческих богов, впитывая в себя, соответственно, те или иные черты языческого происхождения.

Практика «воцерковления язычества», восходящая, как мы видели, к первым векам христианства, сохранялась в византийской, а затем — последовательно — и в русской церкви. Эта практика идет из глубокой древности; вместе с тем, она может периодически возобновляться — циклически повторяться — по мере распространения христианского вероучения.

Соответственно, целый ряд обрядов, как общих, так и местных — и вообще целый ряд моментов культового поведения — обнаруживает несомненное языческое происхождение. Сюда относится, например, обычай носить нательный крест, заменивший языческие наузы, культовая роль яиц, а также восковых свечей, некоторые моменты отношения к иконам (в частности, наименование их «богами», принятое у русских). Таким же образом объясняется, думается, и интересующая нас символическая композиция — сочетание креста и полумесяца, которое приобретает в христианском культе принципиально новое содержание.

Примечания

1. Движение по солнцу соответствует по направлению движению часовой стрелки.
2. Подобное изображение встречается и в других христианских традициях, в частности в армянском церковном искусстве: мы находим его как на куполах древних армянских церквей, так — с теми или иными элементами орнаментализации — и на армянских каменных резных крестах (так называемых хачкарах). В болгарском иллюминированном списке летописи Манассии (XIV в.) есть соответствующее изображение болгарского храма. Нам известно также изображение храма в Валенсии (1547 г.), где интересующая нас композиция представлена в необычном — так сказать, перевернутом — виде: купольный крест на этом храме состоит из креста и полумесяца, однако крест в данном случае находится не над полумесяцем, а под ним (т. е. полумесяц находится не в основании креста, а на его вершине).
3. А. Шмеман, *Исторический путь Православия* (Нью-Йорк, 1954), стр. 137.
4. Ibid., стр. 232.

Boris Uspenskii/Summary: Solar and Lunar Symbolism in the Exterior of the Russian Church

Cupolas of Russian churches are crowned with a cross and a crescent. This combination of symbols can be given both a pagan and a Christian interpretation. In the first instance, this linkage represents solar-lunar symbolism; in the second it stands for Christ and the Mother of God. Since Christ is associated with the sun and the Mother of God with the moon, this linkage becomes an exceptionally stable one. Such reinterpretation of pagan symbols should not be viewed as Russian double faith (*dvoeverie*); rather it is an example of a conscious use by the Church of the old pre-Christian symbols by informing them with new Christian meanings.

The Notion of "Uncorrupted Relics" in Early Russian Culture

GAIL LENHOFF

"If a person's body has not been preserved in the flesh, then for the Muscovites he is no saint!"[1]

—Pakhomii Logofet

The meek hieromonk, Father Iosif, who was the librarian and had been the dead man's favorite, tried to counter the slanderers, arguing that "it isn't like this everywhere" and that the preservation of righteous men's remains is not part of Orthodox dogma... But the words of the humble father failed to convince, and actually provoked a mocking retort. "This is all pedantry and innovation. Why bother listening?" The monks agreed. "We keep to the ancient ways..."[2]

—F. M. Dostoevsky

Kiev's conversion profoundly altered the social codes prevailing at the time. The newly baptized community began to emulate Christian behavioral models and to repudiate ancient customs that now fell into the categories of "sinful" or "profane" conduct. Among the norms that underwent recoding, none are more revealing than those dictating the interaction between the living and the dead. For the Byzantine and Kievan Christian every tomb was a text that, when read correctly, permitted the perceiver to distinguish the remains of saints from the remains of ordinary mortals or demon-possessed imposters. The fate and status of a corpse were ascertained with reference to a set of binary indicators dictated by canon law and by common Orthodox tradition. At the same time, the Eastern Slavs, like other peoples who joined the Byzantine spiritual commonwealth, adapted the model to local conditions, developing a distinctive paradigm that valorized the miraculous preservation of a corpse as a sign of a person's sanctity.

Two major stages in the East Slavic cult of relics will be analyzed in this paper. The initial Kievan model retained its dominance from the conversion to the first quarter of the fourteenth century, when it was superseded by a Muscovite model that held sway through the remainder of the pre-Petrine period. I hope to demonstrate that Kievan attitudes to relics are a combined response to the Byzantine and the pagan Slavic traditions, whereas the Muscovite model defines itself in opposition to Kievan syncretic practices (*dvoeverie*). Our discussion must begin with an outline of the Byzantine cult whose norms were transposed by the Kievans and restored by the Muscovites.

The Byzantine Paradigm

Powers of Relics. In the Middle Byzantine period relics, like icons, served as a tangible reminder of the saint's example and as an aid to salvation. Relics were believed to have the power to protect and heal those who touched or possessed them. The typical miracles (analogous to those worked by Christ in the Gospels) which would be anticipated are outlined in Saint Ireneus's *Adversus Haereses:*

> For they [the relics] are able to give sight to the blind, hearing to the deaf, to put all demons to flight . . . The infirm, or the lame, or those paralysed, or those disturbed in other parts of the body, are cured: it often happens that those who have contracted some bodily illness or have had some kind of accident, are restored in this way to good health.[3]

Byzantine Christians also believed in the power of relics to repel the enemy, to bring good harvests, to defend a righteous victim in legal disputes, to overthrow unjust rulers, and even to strengthen the pillars of the churches in which they were housed.[4]

Functions. The ritual for the consecration of a new church in Byzantium required the formal deposition of relics. The canons of the Seventh Ecumenical Council (787) provide for the distribution of *antimensia,* pieces of cloth containing fragments of relics pounded into a powder with fragrant gum and annointed with holy oil by a bishop. *Antimensia* were sent in place of an altar to domestic chapels or any place not consecrated by a bishop where Christians might wish to perform the liturgy.[5] Relics were also installed in the altar, beneath the sanctuary floor, in special tombs or side chapels, and by the entrance of Byzantine churches so that they could be venerated by the faithful. Parts of a saint were placed in small caskets that could be displayed for veneration on designated feast days or carried in religious processions. Fragmentary relics were worn in phylacteries (*enkolpia*) by the clergy and the laity.[6] Relics were an especially coveted gift offered by dignitaries of the Church and the Empire to mark special occasions (official visits, holidays, diplomatic agreements). Owned by individuals as well as by ecclesiastical institutions, they could also serve as a source of ready capital.[7]

The popular faith in the power of relics led to chaotic scenes at the funerals of Byzantine ascetics who had lived exemplary lives or were associated with miracles. A number of hagiographers describe how laymen and clergymen attempted to seize their own personal mementos of the saint. For example, the monk Kallinikos reports that when Hypatios (d. 446), hegumen of the Rufinianai Monastery at Chalcedon, was being placed in his sarcophagus,

> ... the crowd tore at his funeral bed in order to obtain some fragment of his robes for a blessing. One person cut the shroud with a knife; a second went for [Hypatios's] mantle; a third plucked out hairs from his beard. With great difficulty we managed to put an end to this—not without a number of people strongly resisting our efforts.[8]

Presence in Absence. Three interconnected principles underlie the veneration of relics by the Byzantine Church. Each principle ultimately derives from the example and mysteries of Christ's life—the model that lies at the basis of the cult of saints and provides the standard for assessing Christian miracles. The first principle may be expressed as the principle of "presence in absence." The saint has passed away, and his tomb is generally associated with a single shrine (*locus sanctorum*), yet the sharing of relics permits the saint to be omnipresent and to patronize congregations and petitioners without regard to temporal or geographical limitations.[9] The obvious analogy here is the Host. The faithful literally approach the absent saint, visualize his or her presence with their spiritual eyes, and physically experience the saint's power to intercede. As Gregorios of Nyssa writes in his encomium for Saint Theodoros:

> Those who behold [the relics] embrace them as though the actual living body, applying all their senses, eyes, mouth and ears; then they pour forth tears [for the saint's] piety and suffering, and bring forth their supplications to the martyr as though he were present and complete.[10]

The Part as the Whole. The second principle is that the part constitutes the whole: the slightest fragment of a relic has the power of the saint himself.[11] Evidently untroubled by the ancient taboos on desecrating a corpse, the Eastern Church began as early as 356 to translate and distribute the remains of the apostles and martyrs.[12] "Early Greek relic veneration" writes E. E. Golubinsky, "is marked by efforts of individuals and churches to obtain as many different parts [of saints and their appurtenances] as possible . . ."[13]

This attitude persisted into the Early and Middle Byzantine periods. Otto Meinardus's annotated inventory of the extant relics of 475 Greek Orthodox saints shows only twenty-seven instances where the entire body or most of the body is located in a single place. Over half of these saints (fifteen) were canonized in the sixteenth century or later. Approximately a fourth of the saints preserved *in toto* (seven) died in the fourth and fifth centuries. The remains of only three saints canonized in the period from the seventh through the fifteenth century have been preserved more or less intact.[14]

Bones versus *Flesh*. A third principle in the Byzantine cult of relics is a stress on the preservation of the bones rather than the preservation of the saint's body as though it were still alive. This attitude was common to the early Christians and is shared by the Western Church. To some degree it represents a reaction against the Egyptian custom of enbalming a corpse and displaying it to mourners.[15] The majority of Byzantine relics, like the majority of Early Christian and Latin relics, consisted of bare bones.[16] A fragrant odor or a sweet-smelling unguent exuded by the bones was a sign of sanctity. A foul odor spoke against the sanctity of the deceased.[17]

Only in special cases did the Byzantine clergy strive to preserve a saint's body intact, and even here the exceptions testify to the rule. Ten months after Saint Theodora of Thessalonica (d. 892) was buried in a common grave, the tombstone shattered. This was taken as a divine indication that Theodora should be buried separately. Her body, found to be uncorrupted, was carefully wrapped in a sheet so that no part would be lost before it could be translated to the new grave. At present, however, only bones remain; some parts are in her monastery at Thessalonica, whereas others are claimed by four different cloisters.[18]

The principle was carried to an extreme on Mount Athos where the fragrant odor of the bones was especially prized. The Russian pilgrim Barsky reported that it was the custom to exhume the dead after three or four years so that the bones could be ritually washed: "... when God wished to glorify a righteous man, [the bones] would exude a fragrance, which happened in many cases."[19]

The Kievan Model

Foreign versus *Native Relics*. From the time of Kiev's conversion to Orthodoxy, and until well into the seventeenth century, the Greeks provided Rus' with fragmentary relics.[20] The Laurentian chronicler reports that the newly baptized prince Vladimir returned from Cherson with relics of Pope Clement I and his disciple Phoebus (d. ca. 100).[21] Novgorod, Vladimir, Suzdal', Rostov, and Tver' princes similarly acquired relics from Byzantium and Palestine for their central cathedrals, some as gifts, others through purchase.

In 1211, the Novgorodian pilgrim Dobrynia Iadreikovich (later Archbishop Antonii) returned from Constantinople with a model of the Holy Sepulcher which he presented to Novgorod's Cathedral of Saint Sophia.[22] Grand Prince Vsevolod Iur'evich of Vladimir acquired a plank from the tomb of Saint Demetrios of Thessalonica that "exuded fragrant myrrh that healed the sick" and was placed in the local Church of Saint Demetrios together with the martyr's shirt.[23] In 1218, the arms or hands of Saint Longinus the Centurion and parts of Saint Mary Magdalene were brought by Nikolaos, the Greek bishop of Polotsk from Constantinople to Prince Konstantin Vsevolodovich in Vladimir for the same church,[24] Bishop Kirill of Rostov, consecrated in 1231, is praised for adorning the Cathedral of the Theotokos with "many relics of the saints in splendid caskets."[25] In 1362, Archbishop Dionisii of Suzdal' purchased in Constantinople a list of fifteen items associated with Christ's passion (including the sponge, blood, hairs from his beard, and the crown of thorns).[26] In 1347, Emperor Johannes VI Kantakuzenos sent Muscovite Grand Prince Simeon Ivanovich a cross, alleged to have been made from the True Cross, and the relics of a number of martyrs (including Saints Theodoros Stratilates, Prokopios, and Kerykos). In 1397 and 1399, Emperor Manuel II Palaiologos and the patriarch sent icons and relics to a number of Russian princes, including Mikhail Aleksandrovich of Tver', in gratitude for alms.[27] Kievan and Muscovite Christians of all classes wore phylacteries and collected fragments of relics to which they attributed powers of healing, salvation, and protection.[28]

From the very inception of Kievan Christianity, however, the Eastern Slavs consistently distinguished between relics acquired from other lands and the remains of their native saints. When it came to glorifying local saints, the Kievans seemed unable to take on faith the evidence of life in mere bones or to accept entirely the principle of presence in absence, the primary evidence for which is a decided preference for the whole rather than the part. This attitude had profound consequences for the history of canonization in Rus' and for the cults of individual saints.

From 988 to 1318, fifteen native saints were venerated.[29] Of this number the remains of eleven are identified as uncorrupted. They include (in order of their veneration) the Kievan princes Boris and Gleb Vladimirovichi (d. 1015), Princess Olga (d. 969), Bishop Nikita of Novgorod (d. 1108), Prince Mstislav Vladimirovich of Kiev (d. 1132/1133), Bishop Leontii of Rostov (d. 1077), Prince Vsevolod Mstislavovich of Novgorod (d. 1138), Prince Mikhail Vsevolodovich of Chernigov and his boyar Fedor (d. 1246), Prince Aleksandr Iaroslavich "Nevsky" (d. 1263), and Prince Mikhail Iaroslavich of Tver' (d.

1318). Of the four cases that diverge from the norm, the remains of Feodosii Pecherskii (d. 1074) were found to be partially preserved, and the account of Prince Igor Olegovich of Chernigov (d. 1147) does not provide sufficient information to judge the state of the remains (the Hypatian chronicler uses the word *moshchi.*[30] Only Antonii (d. 1073), founder of the Kiev Cave Monastery, and Grand Prince Vladimir Sviatoslavovich of Kiev (d. 1015) constitute clearcut exceptions to the rule and were glorified with some hesitation, as we shall discuss below.

The Miraculous Preservation of the Corpse. The process of selecting candidates for sainthood in Kievan Rus' generally began with an exhumation of the remains. A number of Kievans eventually recognized as saints were not glorified until centuries after their deaths. Prior to the fifteenth century such deferrals were the rule when the burial site was unknown, when the state of the remains could not be verified, and when the remains gave no "sign" of sanctity. The earliest recorded case of a Kievan martyrdom involved a Varangian immigrant to Rus' who was lynched by a mob when he refused to surrender his son to be sacrificed to pagan gods. The martyrdom of father and son was not formally recognized for several centuries evidently because, as the Laurentian Chronicle entry for 983 explains "no one [knew] where [the bodies] had been placed, for the people were ignorant pagans."[31]

A similar principle is reflected in the choice of the first two East Slavic saints to be officially glorified as martyrs: the junior princes Boris and Gleb, who were murdered by their half brother Sviatopolk in the struggle for the throne of Kiev that followed Vladimir's death in 1015. A third son of Vladimir, Prince Sviatoslav, killed under the same circumstances as Boris and Gleb, was never venerated as a martyr: his body had been lost in the mountains, thereby precluding the discovery of miraculous signs. The bodies of Boris and Gleb, in contrast, were discovered to be preserved uncorrupted. This sign, together with subsequently witnessed healing miracles, led to their glorification as saints.[32]

By the same token, both Olga and her grandson Vladimir were eventually glorified, by analogy to Constantine and Helena, as "Equal to the Apostles," but Olga was the first to be venerated. This initial preference for Olga cannot be explained by her contribution to the spread of Russian Christianity, for Vladimir's role was unquestionably the greater of the two. Healing miracles, which did not play a role in Olga's glorification, are mentioned only in sixteenth-century copies of her *vita.* The clue is to be found in the most ancient North Russian manuscript (fifteenth century), which reports that "when Vladimir unearthed the body of Olga, his grandmother [and discovered that it was] uncorrupted, [he then] placed it in a wooden coffin in the Church of the Tithe."[33] Later copies describe a small window cut in the tomb to allow Olga's remains to be viewed by the faithful.[34]

The fact that Olga displayed special signs of sanctity, while Vladimir did not, was a source of perplexity to the Kievans. The earliest surviving eulogy for Vladimir expresses regrets that Vladimir's remains had not been associated with any posthumous miracles. The author, identified as the monk Iakov, goes so far as to place the blame on the Kievan people, arguing that "had we been more zealous in our prayers to God [for Vladimir] on the day of his death, God would have [rewarded] our efforts by glorifying [Vladimir with a miraculous sign] . . . "[35]

While the majority of Kievan Christians placed special emphasis on uncorrupted relics, the monks in the Kievan Cave Monastery appear to have been divided on this question. Their attitudes can be deduced by considering the cases of two saints who were venerated within the monastery before their formal glorification: Antonii, the hermit who founded the monastery, and Feodosii, his disciple and the first hegumen.

Feodosii's case confirms the Kievan preference for uncorrupted remains over other kinds of miraculous signs. A *vita*, preserved in the *Uspenskii sbornik*, documents a wide variety of miracles worked by the hegumen in his exemplary life. But this biography was written before the official investigation of Feodosii that led to his formal glorification. The account of how the saint's remains were unearthed is contained in the Laurentian Chronicle entry for 1091, several decades after the saint's death in 1074. The hegumen ordered the exhumation because he wanted to rebury Feodosii in the main cathedral. The monks who opened the grave stated their findings in the most positive terms that the evidence permitted, reporting that "the bones had not disintegrated and the hair on the hegumen [Feodosii's] head had dried up." For some, but not for all, this partial state of preservation confirmed Feodosii's sanctity: the date of the translation (14 August) was initially celebrated in the Cave Monastery as the anniversary of the saint. But it was not until 1108 that Hegumen Feoktist of the Cave Monastery formally requested Grand Prince Sviatopolk Iziaslavich to enter Feodosii's name into the calendar on 3 May, the anniversary of the saint's death.[36]

Antonii's cult reflects a very different theological model than the cult of Feodosii. He is referred to as a saint in the *Kiev Cave Patericon,* yet no miracles were recorded and his remains were never found. The place and exact day of his death were not known, and sources conflict on the year.[37] Antonii's stature among the monastic community suggests that the hermit was not simply forgotten, but actually chose to die in seclusion and to be buried in an unmarked grave. The precedent was set by his patron, Antony the Great of Egypt (d. 356), who likewise led a secluded ascetic life and arranged for two trusted monks to conceal the place of his death, saying:

> ... do not permit anyone to take my body to Egypt, lest they set it in the houses [i.e., embalm the corpse and display it to the mourners]. It was for this reason that I went to the mountain and came here. You know how I always corrected the ones who practiced this and ordered them to stop that custom. Therefore perform the rites for me yourselves and bury my body in the earth. And let my word be kept secret by you, so that no one knows the place but you alone. For in the resurrection of the dead I shall receive my body incorruptible once again from the Savior.[38]

In this context Antonii's anonymous death and perhaps even the lack of testimony regarding miracles incarnate the spirit of anchoritic monasticism. The emphasis on material preservation of the corpse in this world is rejected by the ascetic and shifted to the true resurrection in the world to come.

If my reading of the sources is correct, we may distinguish three positions on sainthood within the Kiev Cave Monastery community: those who venerated a saint without demanding exhumation and repudiated the display of preserved remains on the precedent of the early Christian martyrs and ascetics; those who, like the Greeks, accepted preserved bones as a sufficient miraculous sign; and those who hesitated to recommend formal glorification unless the relics were uncorrupted in the strictest sense of the word. That the last position was the norm among the Kievan clergy and lay population is evident both from the statistical preponderance of uncorrupted relics and from the circumstances of individual cases.

Uncorrupted Relics and the Kievan Throne. The insistence on uncorrupted, "whole" relics militated against the fragmentation and distribution of local saints' bodies. Instead, the faithful who wished to be cured or to petition the saint for other kinds of aid visited the saint's shrine. In the eleventh and twelfth centuries, before the Tatar invasions, the shrines of saints were less a source of prestige and revenue for leading monasteries than an index of political power. The almost magical bond between the artifacts and the fortunes of the prince in whose principality they were located may be seen when we follow the handling of Boris's and Gleb's relics.

Their half brother and self-styled avenger, Iaroslav the Wise, erected the first church in their honor at Vyshgorod. Iaroslav's sons and grandsons followed this precedent. In 1072, after losing and reclaiming the throne of Kiev, Iziaslav Iaroslavich built a new church and had the saints' relics moved there. Boris's relics, which had been buried in a wooden coffin, were transferred to a stone sarcophagus befitting his princely status. A year later, Iziaslav was driven out of Kiev by his brothers, Sviatoslav and Vsevolod. One of the first acts initiated by Sviatoslav during his brief reign was the erection of a new church dedicated to Boris and Gleb. His successor, Vsevolod, attempted to complete the church; but it caved in when the finishing touches were put on it, and he died before he could repair the damage. His successor, Sviatopolk Iziaslavich, wanted to build his own church for Boris and Gleb but did not dare to move the saints' relics, allegedly because of his dubious character. Sviatopolk flatly refused to let Oleg, son of Sviatoslav, restore his father's church because it had been built by another prince.[39]

Even Vladimir Monomakh did not dare to defy openly Sviatopolk's proscriptions regarding the saints' relics. During the period when he ruled Pereiaslavl', he is said to have traveled secretly to the grave of Boris and Gleb by night to adorn it with gold and silver. When he ascended the Kievan throne, Monomakh immediately ordered that the relics be translated from Iziaslav's old church to the church restored by David and Oleg Sviatoslavichi of Chernigov. According to the Hypatian Chronicle, the princes bickered about the exact place where the coffins would be located. Oleg and David wanted to have them in a side chapel built especially for that purpose by their father, whereas Vladimir wanted the coffins in the center of the church. Lots were cast, and the coffins were placed in the side chapel. Vladimir had the last word, however, for he proceeded to have "silver slabs [forged for the coffins], making a likeness of the saints on them, gilding them," then adding "a fence with gold and silver . . . decorated . . . with large crystal openwork, with much gold on top, and gilded candlesticks, in which he placed burning candles."[40] The chronicler attributes Vladimir's motives, typically, to his desire to praise the Lord, but cannot resist adding that travelers from Byzantium and other lands came to marvel at such unheard-of splendor in Monomakh's domain, implying that the shrine was a source of great prestige for the ruler.[41]

The Miraculous Junction of the Part to the Whole. During the battles against the Tatars, a number of princes suffered what was interpreted by the Church as a martyr's death and were, accordingly, counted among the ranks of the saints. Certain of these martyrs, among them Prince Iurii (Georgii) Vsevolodovich of Vladimir (d. 1238), lost their heads in battle and therefore presented less than whole remains. According to the legend, Rostov bishop Kirill found Iurii's decapitated body in a pile of corpses, recognizing the prince by his royal clothing, and brought it back to Rostov, placing it in the

Cathedral of the Theotokos. Iurii's head miraculously joined to his body in the tomb so that not the slightest evidence of any injury remained. His uncorrupted remains were then returned to Vladimir in 1239 at the order of his brother, Iaroslav Vsevolodovich, and interred in the Cathedral of the Dormition for veneration by the faithful.[42]

The legend of Saint Merkurii of Smolensk depicts a similar miracle whereby a damaged corpse is reconstituted in connection with an apocryphal battle against Batu. Appearing to the youth Merkurii in a vision, the Virgin Mary told him that he would defeat the Tatars, but that after his victory, he was to hand his sword to a soldier, who would cut off his head. The prediction was fulfilled. Following his decapitation, Merkurii picked up his severed head and returned to Smolensk. Still holding his head, he lay down in front of the city gates and died. The now whole corpse was interred in state, with the dead hero's spear and shield upon his coffin, in the Smolensk Cathedral of the Theotokos, where the saint's relics took on the function of a palladium.[43]

The Sanctification of Unsaintly Behavior. The awe before uncorrupted relics inevitably led to instances where a person whose life was unknown, or one whose life had been anything but saintly, inspired a cult and was formally canonized. Such cases occurred with the greatest frequency in northeast Rus'. Each principality evidences distinctive patterns of canonization, but all stress the preservation of the saint's corpse. In Rostov, the remains of one bishop after another, beginning with Leontii and Isaiia, were discovered to be uncorrupted.[44]

In Iaroslavl', where the local pantheon is much more limited, the most revered saints were princes, usually two or three members of a single family whose remains were miraculously and wholly preserved. The princes Vasilii and Konstantin were locally glorified shortly after their preserved bodies were discovered by workers rebuilding a burned cathedral in 1501. Since they had died at an early age in a battle against the Tatars, very little was known about them. Their *vita* consists of a list of buildings (falsely ascribed to Konstantin) and a few platitudes on their virtues as ideal Christian princes.[45]

One of the most extraordinary dossiers in the history of East Slavic canonization belongs to twice-married prince Fedor Rostislavich "Chernyi" of Iaroslavl' and Smolensk whose days were spent in civil wars, often fighting for, or with, Tatar armies, but whose miraculously preserved remains inspired a local cult. Fedor's remains were never buried in the earth, as is the Orthodox practice, but were kept in a vault above the ground of Iaroslavl's

Savior Monastery and evidently observed for signs of decay. The bodies of his two sons, David and Konstantin, who were buried beside him, also remained uncorrupted. When after 164 years no thaumaturgic powers had been evidenced, Archimandrite Khristofor decided that the princes should be properly interred. During the ceremonies, the son of a local priest and other parishioners were miraculously healed by touching the coffin. Thus, Fedor, together with his sons, was formally glorified and became one of the most widely venerated saints of Muscovite Rus'.[46]

Archaic Cultural Codes and the Kievan Model

Self-Definition of New versus *Old Behavior.* The sources of the Kievan preoccupation with the preservation of the dead "as though still living" are difficult to isolate. The Orthodox liturgy stresses the concept of resurrection, and the Hymn of the Resurrection is sung weekly. Easter has a central place in the Slavic calendar. The striking frescos of the dead rising for the Last Judgment, which adorned the western wall of churches, together with icons depicting eschatological themes, must have created an acute consciousness of life after death. All of these liturgical and iconographic images of the dead rising were common to Byzantium, however, and so they alone cannot explain the Kievan model.

A more plausible motivation is the Kievans' desire to define their own behavior in opposition to pagan behavior. Paradigms of pagan beliefs and practices with regard to the dead are provided in the Primary Chronicle, in homilies, and in accounts of Kievan saints' lives. Archeological evidence, as well as the reports of less partisan witnesses (travelers, for example), suggests that such descriptions should not be regarded as definitive or objective without careful corroboration. As Lotman and Uspensky have shown, self-descriptive paradigms give rise to models that both reject the codes of the previous period and inadvertently regenerate them.[47]

The Pagan Paradigm. By way of example, let us consider two paradigms for pagan burial from the Primary Chronicle. The first describes the "bestial" customs of certain tribes:

> When someone died, they made a funeral feast (*trizna*), then lit a bonfire and placed the corpse on it. When the [body] had been cremated, they gathered up the bones and placed them in a small urn by the roadside. The Viatichi still do this today, as do the Krivichi and other pagans who do not know God's laws, but make their own laws.[48]

The second describes the funeral of the well-known prince Oleg in 912:

Oleg died, and all the people mourned him with much lamenting, and they took him and buried him on a hill called Shchekovitsa. His grave is there to the present day and is revered as "Oleg's grave."[49]

From these passages, as well as from disparaging remarks made by chroniclers and preachers in connection with other "unclean" burial practices, we can reconstruct a series of oppositions that determined the Kievans' view of themselves as enlightened Christians rejecting the dark practices of the past. The handling, placement, and concealment of the corpse acquired particular importance, although archeological findings suggest that pagan customs varied and, not infrequently, overlapped with Church protocol.[50]

1. Whole versus Part. The pagan tribes are stigmatized here for destroying the corpse in contrast to the Christians, who valorize the body's integrity. In the new Kiev, a whole corpse laid out in a coffin for viewing replaces the bones and ashes collected in an urn.

2. Churchyard versus crossroads. The pagan urn containing the bones is placed in an area traditionally regarded as the domain of the devil and associated with movement and, therefore, with decaying and mortal things.[51] The believing Christian is buried in a sacred area that has precise boundaries identifying it with static, eternal values and providing the preconditions for a miraculous state of preservation.

3. Grave versus Mound. The high burial mounds of the pagan kings (cf. the burial of Askol'd, Dir, Igor) are contrasted to the grave of the Christian princess Olga. Olga is buried by a priest in a grave *na meste* i.e., without a burial mound or the small wooden structure erected on it for the soul to rest during its journey to the other world.[52]

Such oppositions encouraged Kievan Christians to valorize whole remains and to interpret literally references to resurrection in ritual texts and art forms inherited from the Byzantine Church. The analogy between the physical incorruptibility of a corpse and the spiritual incorruptibility of the righteous was projected onto the concept of the saint. Data on the canonization of Kievan saints testify that, although certain monks appear to have recognized that saintliness was something quite distinct from preservation, the princes and the laity perceived incorruptibility as the primary sign of a saint.

Ancestor Worship and Relic Veneration. At the same time we can distinguish relics of pre-Christian worship in areas that the Church did not single out in its description of pagan behavior. The primary archaic code involves the Kievan worship of dead ancestors, in particular among the princes. Before the conversion to Christianity, as Komarovich has shown, the princes believed that their dead ancestors would protect and guide them in times of need. Such aid was contingent upon the descendants' fulfilling certain obligations to the dead: blood revenge and a proper burial in the ancestral grounds (including the pre-burial funeral feast and post-burial lamentation).[53] The influence of ancestor worship is evident in the statistical predominance of princes among the Kievan saints. Some two-thirds of the saints venerated before the fourteenth century, as we have seen, are identified as princes who died in battle. The etiquette for burying one's dead ancestors encouraged the attention to a corpse that was a precondition to discovering its incorruptibility. Ancestral veneration also established a precedent for treating the burial site as a shrine to which the supplicant would come for miraculous aid.[54] Olga's *vita,* as noted above, testifies that her remains were exhumed by Vladimir and reburied in the Church of the Tithe in order to assure that the ancestral obligation had been met according to the now-operative burial code. In 1044, Iaroslav Vladimirovich exhumed the remains of the princes Iaropolk and Oleg Sviatoslavichi, baptized their bones, and reburied them in the Church of the Tithe which, under the new dispensation, also served as the ancestral mausoleum of the Kievan princes.[55] In this way, the intersection of Christian and pagan codes generated syncretic behavior that violated Orthodox tradition (the baptism of the dead) while trying to observe it.

A further product of ancestral worship is the strong identification between the corpse of the prince and the state of the realm. Not only must the corpse be preserved in ancestral ground, it must also be preserved whole. The hand of Gleb, for instance, was believed to have special healing powers: in the account of the 1072 *translatio* to a church built by Iziaslav Iaroslavich, then grand prince of Kiev, Gleb's hand is used by the metropolitan to bless the Kievan princes in order of rank; Sviatoslav Iaroslavich then takes the hand, presses it to his injured neck and forehead, and lays it back in the coffin.[56] Yet there was no question of its separation from the saint's corpse (a concept that would have been perfectly acceptable to the Greeks) or of distributing parts to each of Iaroslav's sons (as practiced in Scandinavia).[57] The bodies of Boris and Gleb, as we have seen, were placed in a series of churches identified with the current grand prince of Kiev until they disappeared during the chaos of the Tatar invasions.

The Muscovite Model

Recoding the Signs of Sanctity. Muscovy continued to valorize uncorrupted relics and retained the Kievan preference for whole relics of native saints. But the Muscovites reinterpreted the concept of incorruptibility, adopting the original Greek position that it was not synonymous with preservation in the flesh. They also qualified the notion of integrity, permitting objects contiguous to the saint's remains to be distributed. These modifications can be accounted for by the gradual politicization of the canonization process that shifted the distribution of categories of saints.

Miraculous Preservation of the Bones. Comparison of Kievan saints with saints venerated locally in Muscovy reveals fairly radical typological differences. Almost two-thirds of Kievan saints were princes, and about the same percentage were preserved in the flesh. In the Muscovite period, however, there is a sharp increase in two categories of saint—the *prepodobnyi* (monk) and the *sviatitel'* (hierarch)—accompanied by a decrease in the number of saints with uncorrupted remains.[58] The lower percentage of saints with uncorrupted relics is attributable not to a loss of faith in the significance of *netlennost'*, but to Moscow's intertwined secular and ecclesiastical political agenda. Beginning in the fourteenth century, the higher clergy, as well as the Muscovite princes, attempted to glorify a number of people whose work had promoted the welfare of the land. Many of the relics were not preserved in the flesh. A few, like Stephen of Perm, could not even be associated with documented miracles. In accounts of these saints' canonization, in their *vitae*, and in *encomia* composed for their services, the belief that a saint's relics must be preserved "as though in life" is presented as an ignorant superstition.

The cult of Metropolitan Petr is a case in point. The metropolitan died in 1326 and was glorified without the usual official exhumation in 1339 at the direction of Metropolitan Feognost and with the approval of the Constantinople patriarch.[59] In 1472, Metropolitan Filipp ordered that the dilapidated Dormition Cathedral be leveled and a new church be constructed in its place. During the construction, the coffins of the metropolitans who had been buried in the old church (Petr, Iona, Fotii and Kiprian) were opened. The Sophia II Chronicle describes the findings in some detail. Iona was preserved in his entirety; Fotii's legs were preserved, whereas Kiprian's and Petr's coffins contained only bones. Iona's relics were displayed and, after manifesting miraculous healing powers, a day was set for the metropolitan's glorification. Petr's coffin was exhumed during the night. His relics were not displayed to the people, but transferred to a casket (*larets*) placed beside Iona's grave. Pakhomii Logofet, the Serbian monk and hagiographer, was commissioned to compose two kanons in honor of the *inventio* and to compose a sermon "on the church's position and on the *inventio* of the wonderworker [Petr] and on Iona's *inventio*." In his sermon he reproaches the people for their insistence that saints must manifest uncorrupted relics: "They do not understand that bare bones can also work [miracles] of healing."[60]

The Separation of the Part from the Whole. The consolidation of the Muscovite state did not, as one might expect, result in mass translations of the relics of important regional saints from their shrines to Moscow. Instead, the princes, like the clergy and laymen, made pilgrimages to local shrines to ask for the help of saints in personal and political affairs. When there were no counterindicating miraculous signs, pilgrims were permitted to take or purchase pieces from objects that had some connection with the saint. The *vita* of the fool-in-Christ Isidor of Rostov (who died in the second half of the fifteenth century) notes that "Many who have faith take home small pieces of [the saint's] coffin or shroud which are efficacious against toothache, eye problems, fever and sepsis."[61]

The opposition between the uncorrupted body, which could not be broken up, and articles associated with the saint, which could be fragmented for distribution, is unusually clear in the case of Prince Andrei of Smolensk. According to his *vita*, he appeared one day in Pereiaslavl' without any visible means of support or identification and was taken on as the sexton of Saint Nicholas's Church where he worked for thirty years. When he died, he left behind a golden chain and ring with a note indicating his origins. His remains were wrapped in a birchbark shroud and buried in a common grave. Some time before 1505, miracles were witnessed at the grave: the relics were discovered to be uncorrupted; local veneration was authorized, and hymns for an office were also composed. Ivan III Vasil'evich was permitted to take the saint's ring and chain on condition that he provide a yearly allowance for the care of the grave. In 1539, the Pereiaslavl' hegumen Daniil (himself later glorified) requested permission to exhume Andrei's body. The investigator confirmed that the prince had been preserved without decay. His corpse exuded fragrant myrrh, the thick reddish hair had been preserved, and his garments shone radiantly. Andrei's body was kept intact, and pieces of the shroud, which proved to have miraculous powers of healing, were distributed to the faithful.[62]

Such liberties were not always condoned. When the relics of Saint Nikita of Pereiaslavl' were disinterred, for example, a boyar requested a piece of the birchbark shroud in which the saint's body had been wrapped "as a blessing for myself and my household." According to the *vita,* at that very moment a terrible storm arose, and the people who had been digging for the saint's grave were swept away by heavy winds. Some of them lost their minds. Others became ill, but were cured when the bishop and the priests prayed to the saint to forgive their desecration of his relics. The grave was completely filled in, covering the coffin of the saint. From that time on, Saint Nikita's relics remained in the earth in a small chapel, together with the hairshirt and manacles that he wore during his life as a hermit. Only holy water from a well dug by the saint was permitted to be given to the faithful. Among those who requested this miraculous water was Ivan IV Vasil'evich, who made rich gifts to the monastery, including the funding of a new dormitory, to show his gratitude for the recovery of his son.[63]

Muscovite Self-Definition. While the Kievan model addressed itself to pre-Christian codes, the Muscovite model defined itself in opposition to Kievan behavior, complicating the paradigm. The binary model of true versus false beliefs was reshaped to conform with the official perception of a split between the ignorant (the advocates of pagan, perverted, or anti-Muscovite traditions) and the educated (the advocates of Muscovite Orthodox and autocratic interests). A broad segment of the East Slavic population—especially in outlying regions—held to the traditional Kievan paradigm: they valorized uncorrupted remains and viewed local saints as protectors of regional interests. But their beliefs were now identified with pagan beliefs.

The Pagan Paradigm. The Muscovite paradigm draws its examples of pagan behavior, in part, from data gathered by the clergy on relics of pagan behavior in the countryside and, in part, from its own political agenda. The norms of good behavior, set in opposition, are drawn from traditions of the Byzantine Church rejected or overlooked by Kiev and restored by Muscovy.

1. Burial in Consecrated or Unconsecrated Earth. Ignorant or superstitious Christians are accused of giving their dead to sorcerers to be buried in pagan mounds, woods, fields, and other places outside the boundaries of the Christian cemetery—a clear parallel to the placing of remains in "unclean" locations such as crossroads.[64]

2. Bones *versus* Flesh. The ignorant (Kievan and provincial) Christian's insistence on the whole preservation of a corpse is represented as primitive literalism. The educated recognize that preservation of bones with a fragrant odor is a miraculous sign

of sanctity and perhaps even a more reliable sign than preservation in the flesh in correspondence to the teachings of the Greek Church.

3. Whole and Part. The ignorant (Kievan and provincial) Christians are implicitly accused of over-valorizing the bond between the saint and his native region by artificially restricting saintly patronage. This archaic behavior is combatted by encouraging the distribution of objects contiguous with the saint. Through the distribution of such contiguous parts, the painting of new composite icons and the composition of new hymns for the saint's proper, local saints are portrayed as patrons of Muscovite Rus', regardless of where their shrines are located.[65]

Uncorrupted Remains in the Collective Cultural Memory

From the medieval period to the present day, the concept of uncorrupted remains retains its force in the popular imagination, superseding other codes for interpreting the status of the dead. The superseded codes range from archaic (syncretic) behavior to behavior defined as "scientific" (i.e., progressive, anti-religious). An example of the first situation may be seen in the history of Artemii Verkol'sky, a thirteen-year-old peasant boy who was killed by a bolt of lightning in 1545. In accordance with the popular belief that persons who died unnatural deaths were unclean and in the service of the devil, his body was left unburied in a forest. The discovery of the uncorrupted relics created a conflict between those who had relegated Artemii to the ranks of the devil's servants and those who believed that his incorruptible relics were a sign of sainthood. The awe before the relics was sufficient for the latter viewpoint to prevail. Miracles were documented, and in 1640 local veneration of Artemii (f.d. 23 June) was formally approved. Five years later, a church in his name was erected on the "unclean" place where the body had been abandoned.[66]

The second situation—the recoding of uncorrupted relics to fit binary models aimed at reforming or abandoning archaic beliefs—may be seen in the years following the October Revolution. Wishing to define their new social order as progressive (i.e., opposed to the superstitions of the pre-Revolutionary period), the new government ordered the graves of Russian saints to be opened in order to determine whether their relics were really preserved in the flesh. Allegedly uncorrupted remains that showed signs of decay were exhibited as "proof" in museums of atheism; uncorrupted remains were disposed of (some destroyed, many of them simply hidden away and eventually returned to the Church by uneasy local custodians). The very same authorities who initiated the wholesale debunking of sacred relics created secular relics, displaying the mummified bodies of dead leaders in a mausoleum for public viewing.

The last example illustrates the total inversion of the initial model: the preserved relics testify to the triumph of positivistic values that reject the notion of resurrection after death. Any effort to reinforce new behavior by appealing to "archaic" values, however, constitutes *de facto* evidence that the values in question are still in force.[67] Such is, indeed, the case with the notion of uncorrupted relics. Originally expressed in the veneration of persons whose remains had been preserved, it took deep root in the collective cultural memory as a powerful metaphor for transcendence which could be recoded to fit the varied needs and value systems of successive epochs.

Notes

1. From a sermon commissioned in 1472 for the *inventio* of two Muscovite metropolitans. Cited in *PSRL* 6:196.

2. F. M. Dostoevskii, *Brat'ia Karamazovy*, cited from the *Polnoe sobranie sochinenii* (Moscow, 1972–1989), 14:300.

3. *PG* 7, col. 824. Cited in the translation of Benedicta Ward, *Miracles and the Medieval Mind* (Philadelphia, 1987), p. 35.

4. E. E. Golubinskii, *Istoriia kanonizatsii sviatykh v Russkoi Tserkvi* (Moscow, 1903), pp. 37–39; George P. Majeska, "St. Sophia in the Fourteenth and Fifteenth Centuries: the Russian Travellers on the Relics," *DOP* 27 (1973): 87.

5. *The Seven Ecumenical Councils*, ed. and tr. Henry R. Percival, A Select Library of the Nicene and Post-Nicene Fathers of the Christian Church, Second Series, vol. 14 (Edinburgh; rpt. Grand Rapids, Michigan, 1988), pp. 560–561 (Canon 7). By the mid-thirteenth century *antimensia* were used for the celebration of the liturgy in consecrated Orthodox churches as well. See E. E. Golubinskii, *Istoriia russkoi tserkvi*, 2d ed. (Moscow, 1904) vol. 1, pt. 2, pp. 181–185; Konrad Onasch, *Kunst und Liturgie der Ostkirche in Stichworten* (Vienna, Cologne, Graz, 1981), pp. 25–26.

6. On the portable reliquaries, see "Enkolpion" in ibid., pp. 101–102; G. F. Korzukhina, "O pamiatnikakh 'korsunskogo dela' na Rusi (po materialam mednogo lit'ia)," *Vizantiiskii vremennik* 14 (1958): 129–137.

7. On Greek gifts and sales of relics to the Russians, see N. F. Kapterev, *Kharakter otnoshenii Rossii k pravoslavnomu vostoku v XVI i XVII stoletiiakh*, 2d ed. (Sergiev Posad, 1914), pp. 60–102.

8. Cited from Callinicos, *Vie d'Hypatios*, tr. and ed. G. J. M. Bartelink, [= *Sources chrétiennes* 177] (Paris, 1971), 51:10, pp. 290–291. Parallel descriptions may be found in the following Byzantine saints' lives: Theodosios the Cenobiarch (d. 529) in A.-J. Festugière, tr., *Les moines d'orient* 3, no. 3 (1963): 157; Patriarch Eutychios of Constantinople (d. 582) in: *PG* 86, 2, 97–98 (cols. 2383–2386); Eustratios of Augaros

(d. ca. 867) in: A. I. Papadopoulos-Kerameus, ed., *Analekta hierosolymitikes stachyologias* (St. Petersburg, 1897), 4:39 (pp. 393–394); Patriarch Ignatios of Constantinople (d. 877) in: *PG* 105, cols. 559–560; Basileos the Younger (d. 954) in *Acta Sanctorum Martyrium III*, 38 (pp. *33–*34); Nikon "Metonoeite" (d. 998), in Sp. Lampros, ed. *Neos Hellenomnemon* 3 (1906): 182–183. See Dorothy Abrahamse, "Rituals of Death in the Middle Byzantine Period," *Greek Orthodox Theological Review* 29, no. 2 (1984): 130, notes 19 and 20.

9. These issues are raised in fourth-century polemics. Saint Jerome uses the phrase *quasi praesentem viventemque* in his treatise *Contra Vigilantium* in: *PL* 23, 5 (col. 358). The theme recurs in the accounts of late Roman and Byzantine pilgrims to the Holy Land as well as in hagiography, homilies, and epistles mentioning relics. See E. D. Hunt, "The Traffic in Relics: Some Late Roman Evidence," in *The Byzantine Saint*, ed. Sergei Hackel (London, 1981), pp. 175–179.

10. *PG* 46, col. 740. Cited in the translation of ibid., p. 179.

11. This principle is discussed by Gaudentius, Bishop of Brescia [*Sermo* 17, *PL* 20, col. 965]; Paulinus of Nola [*Carmen* 27 in *Corpus scriptorum ecclesiasticorum latinorum* 30, ed. G. de Hartelm (Vienna, 1894), 440–455 (pp. 281–282)]; and by Victricius, Bishop of Rouen in *De laude sanctorum* [*PL* 20, cols. 443–458]. See Hippolyte Delehaye, *Les origines du culte des martyrs*, 2d ed. (Brussels, 1933), pp. 61–66; Hunt, "The Traffic in Relics," p. 175, note 28.

12. In 356, the relics of Timothy were translated to Constantinople, followed in 357 by the relics of the apostles Andrew and Luke. See A. Heisenberg, *Grabeskirche und Apostelkirche* (Leipzig, 1908), 2:112 and Delehaye, *Les origines*, pp. 55–59.

13. Golubinskii, *Istoriia kanonizatsii*, p. 37.

14. Otto Meinardus, "A Study of the Relics of Saints of the Greek Orthodox Church," *Oriens Christianus* 54 (1970): 132. This count is tentative since in a number of cases one monastery may claim to possess the whole body of the saint, but other monasteries claim to possess parts. One must also allow for the loss of relics due to looting (particularly in 1204 and 1453), theft, sale, and fires.

15. Athanasius writes: "Antony frequently asked a bishop to instruct the people on this matter, and he similarly corrected laymen and chastised women, saying, 'It is neither lawful nor at all reverent to [display the bodies of deceased holy men]. The bodies of the patriarchs and the prophets are preserved even to this day in tombs, and the Lord's own body was put in a tomb, and a stone placed there hid it until he rose on the third day.' And in saying these things he showed that the person violates the law who does not, after death, bury the bodies of the deceased, even though they are holy." [*PG* 26, col. 969]. Cited from Athanasius, *The Life of Antony and the Letter to Marcellinus*, tr. R. Gregg (New York, 1980), ch. 90, p. 96. On the Synodal canons for this protocol, see Bernhard Kötting, *Der frühchristliche Reliquienkult und die Bestattung im Kirchengebäude* (Cologne-Opladen, 1965), pp. 32–36.

16. The earliest saints mentioned as being preserved in the flesh are the prophet Zacharias and the martyr Julitta (d. 304). A list describing the remains of Greek and Athonite saints, most consisting of bones, is given by Golubinskii in *Istoriia kanonizatsii* p. 36. Benedicta Ward mentions a few Western saints, such as Cuthbert of Lindisfarne (d. 687) and William of Norwich (d. 1144), whose uncorrupted relics

were taken as a sign of extraordinary importance, but Ward regards this as the exception to the rule [*Miracles and the Medieval Mind*, pp. 56–66, 72].

17. Paul the Younger's hagiographer reports that the saint's tomb was opened in private in case the remains had a foul odor "lest a sign of mortality prove a source of scandal or harm his reputation." Cited from Hippolyte Delehaye, ed. *AB* 11 (1882): 167; see also Abrahamse, "Rituals of Death," p. 133.

18. *La Translation de S. Théodore Studite et de S. Joseph de Thessalonique*, ed. C. Van Vorst, *AB* 32 (1913): 50–61; see also Abrahamse, "Rituals of Death," and Meinardus, "A Study of the Relics," p. 253.

19. *Stranstvovaniia Vasiliia Grigor'evicha Barskogo po sviatym mestam Vostoka s 1723–1747 gg.*, ed. N. Barsukov (St. Petersburg, 1885–1887), pt. 3, p. 41; see also Golubinskii, *Istoriia kanonizatsii*, p. 29.

20. As late as 1632, long after the Russian Church became autocephalous, the Kievan metropolitan Isaiia Kopinskii wrote to Patriarch Filaret complaining that there were no fragmentary relics suitable for use in the *antimensia* (see above, n. 5) and for the consecration of oil "because few Greeks visit us and they have traditionally supplied us with holy relics." Cited from Kapterov, *Kharakter otnoshenii Rossii*, pp. 74–75.

21. *PSRL*, vol. 1: *Lavrent'evskaia letopis'*, 2d ed. (Moscow, 1962), col. 116, and *PSRL*, vol. 2: *Ipat'evskaia letopis'*, 2d ed. (Moscow, 1962), col. 101. Saint Clement and his relics (probably not genuine) were of special significance to the Slavs. Saint Constantine believed that he discovered them in Cherson in 861 and returned them to Rome. See F. Dvornik, *Byzantine Missions among the Slavs* (New Brunswick, N.J., 1970), pp. 66–67, and note 36. The relic taken by Vladimir is identified in a later chronicle record as Saint Clement's skull [*PSRL* 2:340–341].

22. *NPL*, p. 250.

23. *PSRL* 1:414, 437.

24. Ibid., 441.

25. Ibid., 458.

26. Ibid., 8:74–75.

27. See Makarii, *Istoriia Russkoi Tserkvi*, 3d ed. (St. Petersburg, 1886), 3:254–255 for sources.

28. On phylacteries in the early medieval period, see B. I. Lesiuchevskii, "Vyshgorodskii kul't Borisa i Gleba v pamiatnikakh iskusstva," *Sovetskaia arkheologiia* 8 (1946): 225–245; Korzukhina, "O pamiatnikakh," pp. 129–137, and M. A. Aleshkovskii, "Russkie gleboborisovskie enkolpiony 1072–1150 godov" in *Drevnerusskoe iskusstvo. Khudozhestvennaia kul'tura domongol'skoi Rusi* (Moscow, 1972), pp. 104–125. The later period is discussed by I. Zabelin in *Domashnii byt russkikh tsarits v XVI i XVII st.* (Moscow, 1872), pp. 615–616.

29. The following list is based on Golubinskii's *Istoriia kanonizatsii*, pp. 40–60, while taking into account more recent scholarship. See Richard D. Bosley, "The Saints of Novgorod: à propos of A. S. Chorošev's Book on the Church in Medieval Novgorod," *Jahrbücher für Geschichte Osteuropas* 32 (1984): 1–15.

30. *PSRL* 2:408.

31. Ibid., 1:83.

32. *Zhitiia sviatykh muchenikov Borisa i Gleba i sluzhby im,* ed. D. Abramovich (Petrograd, 1916), pp. 20–21, 55–56. See G. Lenhoff, *The Martyred Princes Boris and Gleb: A Socio-Cultural Study of the Cult and the Texts* (Columbus, Ohio, 1989), pp. 48–50.

33. Cited from I. Serebrianskii, *Drevne-russkie kniazheskie zhitiia. Obzor redaktsii i teksty* (Moscow, 1915), p. 7.

34. Ibid., pp. 11–12.

35. "Pamiat' i pokhvala kniaziu Vladimiru" cited from Golubinskii, *Istoriia russkoi tserkvi,* 1, 1: 263. Golubinskii dates the beginnings of the cult around 1240. John Fennell, who called my attention to this citation, believes that the evidence points to 1284. See his "The Canonization of Saint Vladimir" in *Tausend Jahre Christentum in Rußland: zum Millennium der Taufe der Kiever Rus',* ed. K. Ch. Felmy (Göttingen, 1988), pp. 299–304. An updated account of the issues connected with this cult can be found in O. V. Tvorogov's entry in *Slovar' knizhnikov i knizhnosti Rusi,* no. 1 (XI–pervaia polovina XIV v.), ed. D. S. Likhachev (Leningrad, 1987), pp. 288–290.

36. *PSRL* 1:211, 212, 283.

37. See Richard Bosley, "A. A. Šachmatov's These einer verschollenen Vita des Heiligen Antonii" in *Sprache und Literatur Altrußlands,* ed. G. Birkfellner (Münster, 1987), pp. 1–5.

38. *PG* 26, cols. 971–973. Cited from Athanasius, *The Life of Antony,* ch. 91, p. 97.

39. Abramovich, ed., *Zhitiia . . . Borisa i Gleba,* pp. 18–19, 21–22, 54–56, 64.

40. Ibid., pp. 64–66 (cited in the English from Marvin Kantor, ed. and tr., *Medieval Slavic Lives of Saints and Princes* [= *Michigan Slavic Translations* 5] [Ann Arbor, 1983], p. 231); see also *PSRL* 2:280–281.

41. Ibid., 282.

42. Iurii/Georgii Vsevolodovich was officially glorified in 1645 when his remains were verified as uncorrupted: his relics were translated to a silver sarcophagus and a *vita* was composed. His service and legend may be found in *Mineia: Fevral'* (Moscow, 1981), pp. 143–155; see also Golubinskii, *Istoriia kanonizatsii,* p. 141 and Serebrianskii, *Drevne-russkie kniazheskie zhitiia,* pp. 149–150, "Teksty," p. 182.

43. L. T. Beletskii, "Literaturnaia istoriia povesti o Merkurii Smolenskom. Issledovaniia i teksty," *Sbornik Otdeleniia russkogo iazyka i slovesnosti Rossiiskoi Akademii nauk,* 99, no. 8 (1922): 50–57.

44. On Leontii see G. Iu. Semenchenko, "Drevneishie redaktsii zhitiia Leontiia Rostovskogo," *TODRL* 42 (1989): 241–254, and G. Lenhoff, "Canonization and Princely Power in Northeast Rus': The Cult of Leontij Rostovskij" in *Welt der Slaven* 37 (1992): 359–380. On Isaiia, see "Zhitie sviatogo Isaii, episkopa Rostovskogo" in *Pravoslavnyi sobesednik* (1858), pt. 1, pp. 434–450.

45. An unscholarly edition of the *vita* has been published in *Iaroslavskie eparkhial'nye vedomosti* (1874), pt. neoffitsial'naia: no. 40, pp. 314–317; no. 41, pp. 321–333; no. 42, pp. 332–334; no. 43, pp. 337–341; no. 44, pp. 348–350.

46. Texts of Fedor's *vita* have been published in the appendix to Serebrianskii, *Drevne-russkie kniazheskie zhitiia,* pp. 90–99, in Metropolitan Makarii's *Velikiia Minei Chetii. Sentiabr', dni 14–24,* (St. Petersburg, 1869), pp. 1255–1282, and in *PSRL* 21:307–314. New editions of previously unpublished manuscripts are currently

being prepared by B. M. Kloss. For the most updated account of the textological issues, see Gail Lenhoff, "Die nordostrussische Hagiographie im literarischen Prozeß: die Vita des Fürsten Fedor Černyj" in *Gattungen und Genealogie der slavisch-orthodoxen Literaturen des Mittelalters (Dritte Berliner Fachtagung 1988)*, ed. K.-D. Seemann (Berlin-Wiesbaden, 1992), pp. 63–104.

47. Iu. M. Lotman and B. A. Uspenskii, "Rol' dual'nykh modelei v dinamike russkoi kul'tury" in *Trudy po russkoi i slavianskoi filologii* 28 [= *Acta et commentationes universitatis Tartuensis* 414] (Tartu, 1977): 3–36.

48. *PSRL* 1:14.

49. Ibid., 39.

50. A. Kotliarevskii, O pogrebal'nykh obychaiakh iazycheskikh slavian (Moscow, 1868), pp. 335–243 (and passim); M. Karger, *Drevnii Kiev. Ocherki po istorii material'noi kultury drevnerusskogo goroda* (Moscow and Leningrad, 1958), vol. 1, ch. 4 ("Kievskii nekropol' IX-X vv."), pp. 157–230; V. L. Ianin, *Nekropol' Novgorodskogo Sofiiskogo sobora* (Moscow, 1988), pp. 182–191.

51. On the crossroads, see D. K. Zelenin, *Ocherki russkoi mifologii. Vypusk pervyi: umershie neestestvennoiu smert'iu i rusalki* (Petrograd, 1916), p. 55; B. A. Uspenskii, "K probleme khristiansko-iazycheskogo sinkretizma v istorii russkoi kul'tury" in *Vtorichnye modeliruiushchie sistemy* (Tartu, 1979), 62.

52. *PSRL* 1:68. On the small house constructed above pagan graves, see Kotliarevskii, *O pogrebal'nykh obychaiakh*, pp. 119–120.

53. V. L. Komarovich, "Kul't roda i zemli v kniazheskoi srede XI-XIII vv.," *TODRL* 16 (1960): 84–104.

54. On the connection between ancestor worship and the veneration of princes as saints, see Lenhoff, *The Martyred Princes*, pp. 32–41, 82–87.

55. *PSRL* 1:155.

56. Abramovich, ed. *Zhitiia . . . Borisa i Gleba*, pp. 21–22, 56.

57. The body of pagan Norwegian king Hálfdan "Whiteleg" (d. 860) was "assigned to four places: the head was laid in a mound at Stein in Hringariki, but each other [men who wanted a part of the body] carried away their share and interred them in burial mounds in their homelands." Cited from Snorri Sturluson, *Heimskringla*, trans. L. M. Hollander (Austin, Texas, 1964), p. 45.

58. An eighteenth-century manuscript, published by N. Barsukov in *Istochniki russkoi agiografii* (Saint Petersburg, 1882; appendix, 3–4), lists thirty-one saints venerated locally in Moscow. They include seven princes, one princess, two martyrs, four fools-in-Christ, and twelve hierarchs. With the exception of Fedor, the servant of Prince Mikhail Vsevolodovich of Chernigov, all of the remaining saints are canonized monks or nuns. See also Günther Stökl, "Staat und Kirche im Moskauer Rußland," *Jahrbücher für Geschichte Osteuropas* 29 (1981): 482–483.

59. "Prestavlen'e Petra, mitropolita vseia Rusi" in Makarii, *Istoriia russkoi tserkvi*, vol. 4, supp. 3, pp. 312–316 (first redaction by Prokhor of Rostov); Metropolitan Makarii, *Velikie Minei Chetii. Dekabr', dni 18–23*, (Moscow, 1907), cols. 1620–1646 (a redaction of Metropolitan Kiprian's life).

60. *PSRL* 6:195–196. The Nikon Chronicle version glosses over the public scepticism about Petr's sanctity. His relics, described as "shining like a light and exuding a powerful fragrance," are compared with the coffin that had allegedly been burnt

during Tokhtamysh's invasion of Moscow. See *PSRL* 11–12:146. A later source claims that Anastasiia, the wife of Ivan IV, had a vision in which Metropolitan Petr appeared to her and ordered her personally to seal his coffin so that no one could disturb his remains (Golubinskii, *Istoriia kanonizatsii,* pp. 67–69).

61. Cited from ms. TsGADA, RO MGAMID 181, 692 (dated 1560), f. 374 v.

62. Andrei's history, which was sometimes copied out and circulated separately, was also integrated with the *vita* of Saint Daniil of Pereiaslavl'. It is published in S. I. Smirnov, ed. *Zhitie prepodnobnogo Daniila, pereiaslavskogo chudotvortsa* (Moscow, 1908), pp. 62–65. Iona, archimandrite of the Chudov Monastery, expressed doubts about the miracle. Daniil's hagiographer notes in passing that Andrei may have been obliged to flee Smolensk because of some internecine feud in which he attacked or betrayed a close relative (*brat*). Compare Golubinskii, *Istoriia kanonizatsii,* pp. 86–87.

63. Cited from the ms. in BAN 31.6.22, ff. 11v–12r (dated by B. M. Kloss as 1657–1659). On the miracle of the child's recovery, which was added to *Stepennaia kniga* see G. Kuntsevich, "Zhitie sv. Nikity Pereiaslavskogo. Chudo o vode," *Zhurnal Ministerstva narodnogo prosveshcheniia,* 341 (1902), sec. 2, 1–7, and G. Lenhoff, "The Cult of Nikita Pereiaslavskii," in *Daemons: A Symposium* (forthcoming).

64. On 25 March 1534, Makarii, then archbishop of Novgorod, send a charter urging the eradication of such continuing pagan customs as burial in mounds and fields by direction of sorcerers. See *Dopolneniia k aktam istoricheskim, sobrannye i izdannye Arkheograficheskoiu Kommissieiu* (St. Petersburg, 1846) vol. 1, no. 28, p. 28; Kotliarevskii, *O pogrebal'nykh obychaiakh,* pp. 93–95.

65. The term "pantheon" is used by A. S. Khoroshev, *Politicheskaia istoriia russkoi kanonizatsii (XI-XVI vv.),* p. 125, and by others who stress the analogy between pagan and Christian supernatural patronage. The appropriation of regional saints by Muscovy is discussed in general histories such as Makarii, *Istoriia russkoi tserkvi;* V. O. Kliuchevskii, *Drevnerusskie zhitiia sviatykh kak istoricheskii istochnik* (Moscow, 1871) (Chapters 6 and 7); Golubinskii, *Istoriia kanonizatsii,* pp. 92–109. Among the many individual studies, see U. Bamborschke et al., *Die Erzählung über Petr Ordynskij. Ein Beitrag zur soziologischen Erforschung altrussischer Texte,* [= *Veröffentlichungen der Abteilung für slavische Sprachen und Literaturen des Osteuropa-Instituts an der Freien Universität Berlin* 48] (Berlin and Wiesbaden, 1979), pp. 155–181; Stökl, "Staat und Kirche"; Fedor Poliakov, "Die Auffassung der byzantinischen Mission in der lokalen hagiographischen Überlieferung über den Heiligen Leontij von Rostov" in *Tausend Jahre Christentum,* pp. 481–493; as well as my work on Leontii, Fedor, and Nikita (see above, notes 44, 46, and 63).

66. S. V. Bulgakov, *Nastol'naia kniga dlia sviashchenno-tserkovno-sluzhitelei,* 2d ed. (Khar'kov, 1900), p. 215. The folk distinction between *roditeli* (one's ancestors who must be venerated according to custom) and *zalozhnye* (corpses that are unclean because the person died unnaturally) is a syncretic distortion of the Christian tradition prohibiting the burial of certain persons (suicides, non-Christians, unrepentant sinners) in a Christian cemetery. The bodies of *zalozhnye* were not buried because it was believed that the earth would not accept them (Zelenin, *Ocherki russkoi mifologii,* pp. 1–40).

67. The recent parliamentary debate on whether Lenin's corpse should be given

a proper burial, eerily reminiscent of the debate about the corpses of the Iaroslavl' princes in 1463 (see above, n. 46), and the process of returning sacred relics (among them the relics of Fedor and his sons) to the Church for public veneration confirms the validity of Lotman's and Uspenskii's model (see above, n. 47).

Justice in Avvakum's Fifth Petition to Tsar Aleksei Mikhailovich

PRISCILLA HUNT

Avvakum's Fifth Petition to Tsar Aleksei Mikhailovich is a crucial document in his polemic with the State. That he not only sent it to the tsar but also circulated it in a sbornik meant for his followers indicates that he intended it for a broader audience.[1] Written in 1669, a year after Avvakum's exile to Pustozersk, it represents his last words to Aleksei Mikhailovich and his final response to the Church Council of 1666–1667, which the tsar organized to condemn the Old Belief and its adherents.

This study will show that the purpose of the petition is to discredit the judgment against the Old Believers and prove the illegitimacy of the tsar; the petition represents Avvakum's enemies as the heretics and schismatics, and the Old Believers persecuted by them as the true inheritors of the Church and its ideals of justice. Ultimately, I believe, the petition claims that Avvakum is the rightful heir to the messianic function of the tsar and has taken his place as the dispenser of justice.

The petition evaluates both Avvakum's and the tsar's exercise of justice against the religious sanctions for judgment in the Russian Christian tradition. In its first part, Avvakum establishes the "mystical body of Christ" as the archetype for ideal justice and indicates how his and the tsar's actual relationship to the Church define their respective relationships to this "body." In the second part, he recounts three visions that reveal the state of his and the tsar's own bodies at the Second Coming, in order to verify the tsar's illegitimacy and his own messianic role.[2]

Avvakum's tradition lacked theological or philosophical treatises on justice. The criteria for justice were implicit in Christian myth. For example, in the metaphorical language of Revelation, Christ's creation of absolute community is synonymous with the exercise of absolute justice during his Second Coming in glory. The central metaphors for community in Revelation (e.g., 19:7–8, 21:1–2) are the Transfiguration of Being, the Sacred Marriage of the Lamb and his Bride, and the New Jerusalem. The establishment of this ideal community depends on the exercise of just judgment as enacted, for example, in the Supper of the Great God and the final battle between good and evil at Armageddon (Rev. 16:16; 19:17-21).

Revelation further describes the penitential cleansing process through which man overcomes his egoism and contributes to community and justice. The blood of the Lamb symbolizes the expiatory sacrifice of Christ the Son (Rev. 12:10-11). Revelation presents this sacrifice as necessary to Christ's emergence as Pantocrator and Father whose exercise of justice serves not the self but the whole. In Revelation 17, His sacrifice overcomes the Harlot and the Beast who have polluted the imperial city of Babylon and who epitomize the egoism and lust that destroy community.

Finally, the imagery of Revelation and its interpretation by Saint Paul indicate that the Last Judgment involves moral accountability. It brings the person face to face with the actions he performed in his life, and makes him transparent to himself as well as to others. At the Second Coming, as Paul prophesied, God will lay bare the inner councils of the heart, and man will know even as he is known (I Cor. 13:12; cf. Rev. 21:21, 22, 22:4, 12).

Avvakum's visions, placing himself and the tsar in an eschatological dimension, support the prophecies that Avvakum makes in the first part of the petition. Avvakum opens the petition by reminding the tsar and his broader audience of the traditional sanctions for judgment. He provides the criterion in terms of which his visions will later judge Aleksei Mikhailovich.

Generally speaking, Russian tradition exercised a taboo against judgment.[3] It assumed that only a saint could sufficiently approximate the ideal of Christ to be a just judge. In particular, it associated the prerogative of judgment with a certain kind of sainthood deriving from the radical imitation of Christ's humiliation and sacrifice (*kenosis*). This humiliation identifies the saint with the community and makes him a source of human brotherhood. His sacred status gives him the role of teacher and judge of local political authority and entitles him to speak the "truth" to the prince or the king. Through his advice, he assures that the ruler's power serves the community and is sanctioned by it.[4]

The holy fool expresses Christ's *kenosis* in a radical form; in him humility extends to self-humiliation, including the violation of religious taboos and self-pollution. As a reward for his expiatory identification with the outer extent of human sin, he embodies the outer limits of human community and is entitled to act as the king's conscience.[5] Avvakum identifies himself with a similar kind of kenotic sainthood in the first part of his petition, thereby justifying his teachings to and judgment on Tsar Aleksei Mikhailovich.

Russian tradition made another exception to the taboo against judgment specifically for the tsar. It sanctioned his exercise of both judgment and mercy in relation to his subjects by identifying him with the archetype of Christ. The tsar was expected to reenact through personal piety the sacrifice of Christ for mankind. He was to dedicate himself to penitential actions that would demonstrate his human brotherhood with his subjects and his fear of God. His piety legitimized his institutionally defined authority. His self-sacrifice guaranteed that his acts of judgment served the higher interests of the human community. Tradition interpreted the tsar's judgments as analogous to the judgment of Christ the Pantocrator, cleansing and renewing the world. The earthly power of a pious Russian tsar mirrored the heavenly king's power that would be fully revealed at time's end.[6]

Avvakum's petition demonstrates that he in his role as kenotic saint as self-appointed confessor to the tsar has taken the tsar's place as the mythic focus of community. Avvakum believed that the priesthood and especially the tsar's confessor were the guarantees of the tsar's mythic charisma. In his petition, he associates the tsar's loss of charisma and of the capacity to serve justice with his repudiation of his penitential relationship with Avvakum. For Avvakum, the break of their penitential tie testified to the tsar's repudiation of the religious ideal of community in Christ. Avvakum believed that the tsar's "worldly" attitudes deprived him of the power to create social integrity. Detaching his office and the state itself from rituals and symbols of human brotherhood, the tsar transformed institutional "structure" into something "external" to his people.

Avvakum, in his petition, looks to himself and his spiritual family to fill the vacuum created by the tsar's apostasy from the traditional ideal of community. He presents his spiritual family as the sacred alternative to a state that he believes has become profane and secular because it rejects the transcendent *communitas* values conveyed by Christian myth. He envisions his "family" as the inheritor of the traditional function of the Muscovite state to lead its people to millennial truth and justice on earth.[7] United not by "external" political or social structures, but by the inner ties of penitential ritual, it came close to realizing in everyday life the ideals of Christian myth.

In the first part of the petition, Avvakum exposes the tsar for failing to live up to the likeness of Christ. He thus discredits Aleksei Mikhailovich's right to judge the Russian Church and its defenders. By portraying his own kenotic humiliation, however, he sanctions his right to judge the tsar.

Beginning with the opening lines, the petition addresses the tsar's relation to the community, which Avvakum sees as the historical expression of the mystical body of Christ. Avvakum reminds the tsar of his spiritual links with the pre-Nikonian Church in which he himself was born, and with all those who, like himself, were baptized according to its sacraments. They include the tsar's forebears as well as the "true believers" he condemned as heretics at the Council of 1666–1667. By referring to the tsar's repudiation of the old ritual as a "separation from the body of the Church," Avvakum reminds the tsar that the pre-Nikonian Church embodies Christ's mystical body.

> Мнагажды писахом тебе прежде и молихом тя, да примиришися богу и умилишися в разделении твоем от церковного тела ... вниди паки в первое свое благочестие, в нем же ты порожден еси с преже бывшими тебе благочестивыми цари, родители твоими и прародители; и с нами, богомольцы своими, во единой святой купели ты освящен еси ...[8]

Avvakum's reference to the "body" and his insistence that the tsar "shares one baptismal font" with those he persecutes allude to Saint Paul's evocation of this mystical body (I Cor. 12:12–13):

> Якоже бо тело едино есть и уды имать многи, вси же уди единаго тела, мнози суще, едино суть тело тако и Христос. Ибо единем духом мы вси во едино тело крестихомся ... и вси единем духом напоихомся ...[9]

Although Avvakum does not directly refer to the greater context of this passage, it is nonetheless essential to his argument. Especially significant is Paul's idea that the seemingly lowliest and most unclean parts deserve the most honor and are most necessary to creating the body's wholeness: "... мнящиеся уди тела неможнейши быти, нужнейши суть, и ихже мним безчестнейших быти тела, сим честь множайшую прилагаем" (I Cor. 12:23–24). This subtext implies that when the tsar persecutes Avvakum and other true believers, treating them as lowly outcasts and outsiders, he is separating himself from those who have the most power to enhance the mystical body of Christ and create community. They, the most dishonored members of the body of the Church, should be his "intercessors," endowing his power with legitimacy.

Avvakum next confronts Aleksei Mikhailovich with his violation of the sanctions for judgment by appealing to the traditional doctrine of the tsar's dual nature.

> Господин убо есть над всеми царь; раб же со всеми есть Божий. Тогда ж наипаче наречется господин, егда сам себе владеет и безместным страстем не работает, но споборника имея благочестива помысла,

непобедимаго самодержца бессловесных страстей, иже всех матеря похоти всеоружием целомудрия низлагает. Честь царева суд любить, по пророку.[10]

The tsar should act as both "master" and "slave" in order to imitate Christ, who, despite his divine mystical body that reigns over creation, took on a lowly human form so that mankind could fully commune with him: "... себе умалил, зрак раба приим, в подобии человечестем быв ... смирил себе ... до смерти ..." (Phil. 2:7). Avvakum stresses that the tsar's mastery over his own passions—his willingness to put away the needs arising from his private body for the sake of his subjects—entitles him to be "master" over his subjects. His self-mastery or "chastity" (целомудрие), marks him as a "slave" of God and alone identifies him with his people, entitling him to be a "master."

Avvakum concludes his traditional formulation of the criterion for the tsar's legitimacy with a phrase from Psalm 99:4, which emphasizes his concern with the tsar's exercise of judgment. The part of the passage he leaves out (shown in italics) is the key to his message: "И честь царева суд любить: ты уготовал еси правоты, *суд и правду бо якоже ты сотворил еси*." [my italics, P.H.]

This admonition provides the tsar and Avvakum's larger audience with the reasons why Aleksei Mikhailovich has "separated" himself from the body of the Church (and, implicitly, of Christ). Avvakum suggests that the tsar's judgment against his forefathers' spiritual traditions and the present-day "true believers" serves his personal self-interest, rather than the well-being of his kingdom. With this, Avvakum indirectly accuses the tsar of moral "promiscuity" and calls into question the legitimacy of his judgment and even of his very reign.

Finally Avvakum urges the tsar to bear in mind that the Last Judgment and Second Coming represent the standard against which he should measure his own exercise of judgment. If the tsar does not strive to maximize ideal community in Christ now, he will inevitably face the consequences when the community he has violated triumphs at the end of time:

Ты, самодержче, суд подымеши о сих всех, иже таково дерзновение подавый на ны ... Вонми, государь, с коею правдою хочеши стати на страшном суде Христове пред тмы ангельскими и пред всеми племены ...[11]

Avvakum reproaches the tsar with his hardness of heart and his unwillingness to repent. He emphasizes that the tsar carried out his reform of the

Church to conform to Greek rite in the face of irrefutable evidence that the Russian rite is the only one that is consonant with orthodoxy: "Ведаешь ли, писано се во Истории о белом клабуце и, ведая, почто истинну в неправде содержиши?"[12] Thus the tsar's reforms are based on conscious falsehood and require him to act against his conscience.

Avvakum takes on the responsibility of confronting the tsar with the consequences of his falsehood, since the tsar himself has made a point of not doing so. The tsar's violation of the truth and lack of repentance, Avvakum suggests, mean that he will not participate in the resurrected body of Christ at the Last Judgment: "И ты не хвалися. Пал ся еси велико, а не востал искривлением Никона . . . а не исправлением . . . умер еси по души ево учением, а не воскрес . . ." The tsar and his followers, Avvakum insists, will be subject to the logic of apocalyptic justice revealed in Revelation. Christ in judgment will "double unto them double":

> Там будет и тебе тошно, да тогда не пособишь себе ни мало . . . им же судом судиша нас, тако ж и сами от Христа и святых его осудятся, а в ню меру мериша нам, возмерится им от сына Божия . . .[13]

Thus, in the first part of the petition, Avvakum establishes the mystical body of Christ as the sacred criterion for the tsar's right both to represent and judge his community. He evaluates the sovereign against this criterion and finds him wanting. Avvakum then counterposes his critique of the tsar with an image of himself and his co-sufferers which fulfills to the maximum degree the sacred prerequisites for participation in Christ's mystical body. This image entitles them to judge the tsar in the name of the Church. Moreover, it depicts them as creators of community with power to define the subjective forces that heretofore had bound together the abstraction of the State.

Avvakum asserts that "justice" has nothing to do with "worldly" (self-interested) power, but can flourish only in the context of sacrifice. The proof of one's authority to judge the Church is one's willingness to suffer for its sake as Christ did:

> Вся церковная права суть разумевающим истинну и здрава обретающим разум по Христе Исусе, а не по стихиям сего мира, за ню же мы страждем и умираем и крови своя проливаем.[14]

Avvakum then demonstrates how he and his co-sufferers embody in extreme form what the tsar fails to embody at all, the attributes associated with Christ's *kenosis* or "slavery": an expiatory humility extending to humiliation. He presents himself and them as the weakest and most unclean parts of Christ's mystical body and therefore the most necessary.

Avvakum prophesies their ritual pollution after death, when their bodies, denied the rite of burial, will be desecrated by birds and beasts: "А по смерти нашей грешная телеса наша — добро так, царю, ты придумал со властьми своими, что псом пометати или птицам на растерзание отдати."[15] Avvakum gives a positive interpretation to this pollution when he suggests that it likens them to the early martyrs whose dead bodies were thrown into "dishonorable places," in "ditches" with "excrement." He emphasizes the expiatory nature of this humiliation, explaining that by refusing to allow their bodies to be buried in the earth, the early martyrs demonstrated their great "humility":

> Вемы бо, да и ты слышишь по вся дни во церкви, яко святым мучеником ни единому честнаго погребения не бысть . . . но метаху их в бесчестныя места . . . Земли же есть и добровольне себе святии отцы погребати себе не повелеша, великаго ради смирения . . . [16]

Avvakum also emphasizes his radical humility by underscoring his refusal to judge his oppressor as a man and his desire to turn the other cheek in order to save him. He indicates that the more the tsar afflicts him, the more he strives to win the tsar's repentance by suffering for his sake:

> И елико ты нас оскорбляеши больши и мучишь и томишь, толико мы тебя любим, царя . . . Ну, государь, да хотя меня к собакам приказал выкинуть, да еще благословляю тя благословением последним, а потом прости, уж тово чаю только.[17]

His willingness to defer his own judgment to the Last Judgment of Christ again underscores his humility.

Avvakum's refusal to judge Aleksei Mikhailovich demonstrates that he has put aside anger and the desire for vengeance in the hope of eliciting the tsar's repentance. He thus establishes the moral conditions that allow him to portray himself as Aleksei Mikhailovich's just and disinterested judge when he has established that the tsar is beyond both repentance and deliverance from divine wrath.

According to Avvakum, his own and his comrades' expiatory suffering identifies them with the human Christ: "с ним бо стражем и умираем." The Church's official anathema on them, depriving them of the sacraments and casting them out, paradoxically enables them to experience Christ's *kenosis* and share in its power to create community:

> А еже нас не велишь, умерших, у церкви погребати, и исповеди и святых таин лишать в животе сущих еще коих, да Христос нас не лишит благодати своея: той есть присно с нами и будет . . . и никто ж . . . отлучити нас от него возможет.[18]

Avvakum sees the fate of the early martyrs as the key to his own. He, like them, will participate in the resurrection despite (indeed because of) their willingness to allow their bodies to be polluted:

> ... да Христос их нигде на забыл. Тако ж и нас негли не забудет надежда наша и купно с первыми соберет кости наша в последний день и оживотворит мертвенная телеса наша духом святым.[19]

Avvakum asserts that the suffering that he and his brethren have endured has made them a source not only of community in Christ, but also of His Truth and Justice. Only by listening to them can the tsar fulfill his role as the vehicle of God's justice on earth. If he does not listen now, he will be forced to confront his own violation of justice at the Last Judgment:

> Аще правдою спросиши, и мы скажем ти о том ясно с очей на очи и усты ко устом возвестим ти велегласно. Аще ли же ни, то пустим до Христова суда ...[20]

Avvakum makes it clear in the first part of his petition that he and his brethren embody what the tsar lacks and should therefore be his teachers. They are vehicles of the piety that the tsar has repudiated and that alone guarantees justice. The next step is to show that they have abrogated to themselves the tsar's authority to judge in the name of God and that of the community of the Church and the Russian people.

Avvakum prepares for this final step by presenting himself with his co-sufferers against the tsar as dangerously polarized opposites instead of brothers. Avvakum insists that even if the tsar denies his spiritual relationship with the Old Believers now, treats them as adversaries, and exiles them to the distant corners of his kingdom, their community with each other will be realized at the Last Judgment when they will stand together before God's truth: "Ты царствуй многа лета, а я мучуся многа лета, и поидем вместе в домы своя вечныя, еда Бог изволит ..."[21] If the tsar refuses to repent now when Avvakum is reaching out to him in brotherly love, he will suffer the consequences for violating this love and their interrelationship later when Avvakum participates in divine judgment. Avvakum foresees himself and his fellow sufferers at the Last Judgment personally holding the tsar responsible for the latter's acts of false judgment against them: "Здесь ты нам праведнаго суда со отступниками не дал, и ты тамо отвещати будеши сам всем нам ..."[22]

Avvakum warns the tsar that this moment of final accounting is at hand after which it will be too late to repent. He alerts Aleksei Mikhailovich that according to Christ's prophesy in Matthew 24:3–7, the Second Coming will be preceded by an intense crisis in community: its polarization into opposites that cease to communicate with one another, the majority of sinners against the righteous few.

Avvakum's words imply that the tsar's seduction of his people away from the true Church is bringing about this prophesied division. By polluting the only Christian kingdom that remains faithful to Orthodoxy, he deprives the whole Christian world of its last hope and gives it over to corruption. He thus is dividing the fallen Christian Church from the righteous remnant who dare to stand apart from it and alone bear responsibility for the world's redemption.

Avvakum now brings forth three visions that verify the eternal nature of the opposition between the tsar and himself, which he describes in the first part of the petition.[23] The first concerns the tsar. It reveals that the condition of the mystical body at the Last Judgment is an "answer" to his relationship to the Church and the Old Believers now. It indicates that the time in which the tsar could respond to the influence of his self-appointed father confessor, Avvakum, repent and change, has already passed. In the other two visions, Avvakum sees his own deified body. They verify his earlier prophecy that he will participate in the Last Judgment and especially the divine retribution against the tsar. Taken together, these visions measure the tsar and Avvakum in terms of each other, and realize the consequences of the tsar's violation of their relationship during historical time.

On the most obvious level of interpretation, Avvakum's vision of the tsar addresses the sovereign's relationship to the Church. The tsar's angelic body is corrupted because God has doubled unto him double for his corruption of the Church's mystical body:

> ... и видех тя пред собою или ангела твоего умиленна стояща ... И увидех на брюхе твоем язву зело велику, исполнена гноя многа, ... и начах язву на брюхе твоем, слезами моими покропляя, руками сводити, и бысть брюхо твое цело и здраво ... И паки поворотих тя вверх спиною твоею, видех спину твою сгнившу паче брюха, и язва больши первыя явихся. Мне ж так же плакавшуся, руками сводящу язву твою спинную, и мало мало посошлася и не вся исцеле.[24]

The concrete symbolism and logic of this vision derive from Revelation's metaphors for the Last Judgment. The sores on his stomach and back are signs of God's wrath. "... И иде первый ангел и излия фиал свой [ярости Божия] ... и бысть гной зол и лют на человецех имущих начертание зверино ..." (Rev. 16:1–2).

The fact that the tsar bears the mark of the Beast has broad implications.

In Revelation, the Beast and his symbolic wife, the Harlot, are responsible for the corruption of the universal empire and its transformation into the moral equivalent of Babylon. The Beast is the incarnation of the appetites, gluttony, and aggression, whereas the Harlot embodies promiscuous sexuality. They are symbols for the "passions," "lusts," and pride of self-aggrandizement that destroy community.

The sores also symbolize punishment for altering the revealed Word: "Со-свидетелствую бо всякому слушащему словеса пророчества книги сея: аще кто приложит к сим, наложит Бог на него язв написанных в книзе сей . . ." (Rev. 22:18–19). The tsar's sores signify that his likeness to the Beast is what caused him to allow the Nikonians to add "from themselves" to the Church books, corrupt the truth, and bring judgment on himself. The symbolism of the sores also concerns the tsar's relationship to his people. They are on his stomach because they are "doubling unto him double" for his appetites and passions: he "worships his belly"; he "drinks the blood" of his people and judges them falsely in order to consume them and aggrandize himself.[25] The sores testify to the tsar's lack of chastity, or his moral promiscuity.

The sores that Avvakum sees on the tsar's back double unto Aleksei Mikhailovich double for his actions against Avvakum. In his First Petition to the tsar (1664), Avvakum refers to the "sores of injustice" inflicted on his back by the tsar's representative in Dahuria, Afanasii Pashkov.[26] The sores that the tsar bears are divine justice for the afflictions he directly and indirectly visited on Avvakum in retaliation for the latter's defense of "justice" against corrupt authority.

The conclusion Avvakum draws from his vision of the tsar is that this sovereign and his kingdom are beyond healing; no matter what the extent of his suffering and tears for the tsar's sake, they will be of no avail. The tsar will not renew himself by identifying with his community and his self-assumed spiritual father, Avvakum:

> И очютихся от видения того, не исцелих тя всего здрава до конца. Нет, государь, больмо покинуть мне плакать о тебе, вижу, не исцелеть. Ну, прости ж, Господа ради, дондеж увидимся с тобою.[27]

The irredeemable nature of the tsar's corruption has cosmic implications. His final pollution of the only Christian kingdom fulfills the scriptural prophecy about the polarization of the world at the onset of the end of time. It makes imminent the ultimate battle between the Antichrist (the Harlot and the Beast) and Christ and the saints. Avvakum's vision of the tsar, associating Aleksei Mikhailovich with the Beast, implies the latter's fate during this ultimate battle on Judgment Day. The next two visions that Avvakum reports reveal his own participation in the winning side of the cosmic conflict when justice will prevail.

Avvakum first recounts an ecstatic experience of his mystical body during the Lenten fast of 1669 when he was incarcerated at Pustozersk. He then describes a second experience of bodily ecstasy that occurred earlier, in 1666, when he was in prison at the Nikolo-Ugreshkii monastery after he had been subjected to anathema. The vision of 1669 delivers the main force of his message:

> Нынешня 177 году, в великий пост на первой неделе по обычаю моему хлеба не ядох . . . прииде на мя озноба зело люта, и на печи зубы мои розбило с дрожи . . . и толико изнемог, яко отчаявшу ми ся и жизни сея, уже всех дней не ядшу ми дней с десять и больши. И лежащу ми на одре моем и зазирающу себе, яко в таковыя великия дни правила не имею . . . Божиим благоволением в нощи вторыя недели, против пятка, распространился язык мой и бысть велик зело, потом и зубы быша велики, а се и руки быша и ноги велики, потом и весь широк и пространен под небесем по всей земли распространился, а потом Бог вместил в меня небо, и землю, и всю тварь.

Avvakum interprets this vision for the tsar immediately afterwards in a series of statements that place the two men in opposition to one another:

> Видишь ли, самодержавне? Ты владеешь на свободе одною русскою землею, а мне сын Божий покорил за темничное сидение и небо и землю; ты, от здешняго своего царства в вечный свой дом пошедше, только возьмешь гроб и саван, аз же, присуждением вашим, не сподоблюся савана и гроба, но наги кости мои псами и птицами небесный растерзаны будут и по земле влачимы так добро и любезно мне на земле лежати и светом одеянну и небом прикрыту быти; небо мое, земля моя, свет мой и вся тварь—Бог мне дал, якож выше того рекох.[28]

Avvakum presents this vision as evidence that he has taken the tsar's place and is an inversion of Aleksei Mikhailovich. It verifies that the tsar represents a profane and false king, whereas Avvakum is a true and sacred one. Avvakum argues that his vision shows that he rules both heaven and earth, whereas the tsar merely rules the Russian land. Avvakum controls the greater community of life, of which the tsar's kingdom is a mere particle. Although the tsar is free to persecute him and rule by force, Avvakum in chains has a much greater authority that does not rely on external means, but is derived from his inner identification, through suffering, with the Russian land.

Like his vision of the tsar, Avvakum's vision of himself expresses the logic of divine judgment. Avvakum, however, is subject not to the logic of doubling associated with punishment, but to the logic of reversal and inversion, which is associated with the justice of reward. In order to understand the symbolic language of this vision, it is useful to examine briefly the archetypal expression of this logic in the metaphors of Revelation.[29]

Revelation models a process of transformation associated with expiation and the cleansing of sin and with marriage of the self to the community. It metaphorically traces the path from Adam to the glorified Christ and lays bare the underlying dynamism of sacred history.[30] It presents expiatory suffering as the key to this transformational process and understands it as the median stage in a dialectic of moral opposites leading to their inversion.

Revelation embodies the initial stage of sinfulness in the images of the Beast and the Harlot. They symbolize unrestrained appetite, both sexual and aggressive. The process of transforming their drives to serve the community gives rise to a median stage associated with expiation. A reversal of the initial stage, it is embodied in the images of the sacrificial Lamb, the Brethren, and the Mother of the Manchild (Rev. 12:10–11), which symbolize that the instinctual drives are sacrificed for the community: concretely, this sacrifice includes sexual abstinence and fasting, as well as allowing oneself to be eaten (Rev. 17:6). The end of this process and the reward for penitential suffering is the transformation of the instincts into spiritual force. This occurs through a reversal of the median stage of self-mortification, which is also an inversion of the initial state of destructive egoism. Revelation manifests this stage in images of resurrection, transfiguration, and justice.

The archetypal Supper of the Great God represents a reversal of the Fasting of the Brethren and an inversion of the rapacity of the Beast, for in it the angel with the sword proceeding out of his mouth and the fowl of the air devour the kings and captains and mighty men of Babylon. Their "devouring," however, is cleansed or spiritualized; it creates rather than destroys community. It is associated in Revelation with the divine act of judgment that doubles unto the sinner double and devours the devourers (Rev. 19:17–21).

The archetypal Marriage of the Lamb and his Bride and the pregnancy of the Mother of the Manchild represent a reversal of the abstinence of the Mother of the Manchild and an inversion of the destructive sexual lust of the Harlot. They symbolize sexuality transfigured and dedicated to community. Revelation associates Sacred Marriage with the unity of heaven and earth and the coming of the New Jerusalem (Rev. 12:1–2; 19:7–8; 21:1–2).

Avvakum's visions of 1669 and 1666 embody the dynamism of the apocalyptic transformational process. They testify that he has inverted the initial state of man, overcome his nature in Adam, and communed with the transfigured Christ.[31] In relation to the rest of the petition, his visions also represent him as an inversion of the unrepentant tsar who bears the marks of the apocalyptic Beast. Their metaphorical language reveals his participation in the Sacred Feast and Sacred Marriage, thereby suggesting that because of his personal piety, he, not the tsar, embodies the community and is the source of justice.

When Avvakum interprets his visions to the tsar in the petition, he demonstrates that they are the reward for his expiatory suffering, according to the apocalyptic logic of justice. Referring to his vision of 1669, he stresses the process of reversal that has taken place, characteristic of the final stage of the penitential process: his being cast out of the official Church leads to the merging of the self with the community; and his being deprived of official status and authority leads to his empowerment. He alludes to the humiliation of his body as described earlier in the petition, in order to suggest that it is a prerequisite for the reconstitution of his mystical body and its merging with the cosmos revealed in the vision. When Avvakum insists that "God gave" him heaven and earth, he is referring to the fact that his own communion with the Lamb of God has identified him with the cosmos.

Avvakum notes that this vision occurred during his severe penitential exercises during the second week of Lent. At this time the Christian dedicated himself to overcoming his sin in Adam by communing with the suffering human Christ. The vision signifies his arrival at the end of this process. The image of his body exploding with life incarnates the dynamism that liturgical texts associate with Easter Day, the Resurrection of Christ, and the world's ultimate resurrection.

Avvakum's second vision confirms his participation in the resurrected Christ. The sacred time in which this vision occurred, the day of the Lord's Ascension, is crucial to its meaning; in it Christ repeats his words to the apostles immediately after his resurrection from the grave: "Не бойся, аз есмь с тобою." The words of the scriptural subtext which Avvakum fails to report, as is usual with him, contain the crux of his message. In Matthew's account (28:20) Christ asserts: "и се аз с вами есмь бо вся *дни до скончания века*" (my italics). Christ's unspoken words to Avvakum are the promise that Avvakum will be present with Him at His Second Coming.

When interpreting his vision of 1669, Avvakum suggests that it reveals the power of sacrifice by alluding to scripture. His explanation that the expansion of his cosmic body means that the "son of God subjugated" (*no-*

корил), heaven and earth to him recalls Saint Paul's epistle to the Philippians in which Paul describes Christ's power to deify the body of man and reward him for accepting the way of the cross: "по деиству еже возмогати ему и покорити себе всяческая" (3:21). Avvakum's vision of his own body "subjugating" heaven and earth affirms that he has perfected this way of the cross and has achieved "разум по Христе Исусе."

Avvakum's expiatory suffering distinguishes him from the false Christian who, as Paul writes, is an enemy of his cross, fails to expiate his sin, and is therefore doomed: "имже Бог чрево, и слава в студе их иже земная мудрствуют" (Phil. 3:19). Avvakum's allusion to Philippians 3:21 in the context of setting up a series of contrasts between the tsar and himself suggests that the tsar himself is the sort of false Christian that Paul had in mind. Avvakum's earlier vision of Aleksei Mikhailovich's corrupted body confirms this suggestion. Avvakum thus emphasizes that his vision of himself results from the process of expiation that sets him apart from the tsar.

Avvakum's vision of 1669 not only manifests his movement from the median to the final stage of the transformational process symbolized by Revelation, but also signifies his inverted relation to the tsar who remains untransformed in the initial stage of this process. Avvakum's first vision symbolizes the consequences of the tsar's refusal to expiate his sin: his embodiment of the absolute, polarized evil manifested by the Beast's (and implicitly the Harlot's) lustful, devouring nature. Avvakum's vision of his cosmic body contains the message that his nature is polarized at the other end of the dialectic of transformations: his sexual lust and aggressive drive have been transfigured into spiritual force.

In an epistle to his spiritual children, Avvakum interprets his vision of 1669 as proof of his cleansed sexuality or spiritual "pregnancy."[32] He stresses that the image of his body's union with heaven and earth symbolizes his power to create a spiritual community that overcomes the vast physical separation between himself and them. He imagines himself with a mystical womb that contains this community, and he suggests that this womb is implicit in his vision of his mystical body which he reports to the tsar.

> Да хоть мы в далнем разстоянии, да слово Божие живо и действенно, проходит до членов же и мозгов и до самыя души ... кровию своею помазую душа ваша и слезами помываю. Никто же от еретик восхитит вас ... от руки моея ... хощу неповинных представити вас в день просвещенный праведному Судии. Да и бывало таково время: Христос, бдящу ми, и вселел вас всех во утробу мою. И царю Алексею говорено о том.[33]

Avvakum derives his notion of his mystical "womb" from the Pseudo-Chrysostom, who describes the contents of the confessor's "heart":

> ... аще бо бы лзе с҃рдце раздравше, ти покаяния показати вам, то видели ся бысте все вънутрь седяше в мне и с женами и с детьми, тако бо сила есть любовная н҃бсъ ширшю творить. Душю и утробу вместитеся в ны, рече апостол ... не стужити си в нас бо весь град коринфскыи имяше в с҃рдци своем, ти рече че стужите си, раширитесь и вы но азъ того не могу рещи.[34]

Avvakum's description of his mystical body in the vision of the Fifth Petition echoes the Pseudo-Chrysostom's words. The evocation of his own "broadness" (when he describes himself as *широк* and *пространен*) and of God "placing" in him heaven and earth (*вместил в меня*) recall the Pseudo-Chrysostom's description of love's power to create a "broadness" (*ширшю*) and "place" (*вместитеся*) in man's soul and mystical womb.

The actual vision alludes directly to the source that inspired the Pseudo-Chrysostom's words, Paul's Second Epistle to the Corinthians (6:11–13). Avvakum's expanding mouth mirrors Paul's "open lips" and fulfills Paul's promise to his addressees that they will "broaden" like himself: "Уста наша отверзошася к вам, коринфиане, сердце наше распространися ... Тоже же возмездие, якоже чадом глаголю, распространитися и вы." Moreover, implicit in the image of Avvakum's expanding mouth is his "enlarged heart," which he, in the spirit of the Pseudo-Chrysostom, envisions as a mystical "womb" pregnant with his spiritual children.

Avvakum's vision of 1666 complements the later vision's allusion to his mystical pregnancy. In it, the resurrected Christ is accompanied by the Queen Mother of God and the heavenly powers. This collective image of Christ's power is related to the apocalyptic archetype of the Marriage of the Lamb and his Bride, which symbolizes the resurrection and the coming together of heaven and earth in the New Jerusalem. Their presence fulfills the implications of Avvakum's own mystical resurrection.

Avvakum does not include these archetypes in the original version of this vision contained in a 1666 letter to his family.[35] By adding them to the later version of 1669, Avvakum deepens its apocalyptic significance and places it on a level with his other visions in the petition. The presence of these archetypes also provides a concrete measure of his differences from the tsar.

The Queen Mother of God and the heavenly powers commune with him in his vision because he has purified his sexuality and transformed it into spiritual power. Their presence underscores the success of his expiatory suffering, the redemptive force of his piety. The archetypes of this vision indicate his successful "inversion" of his primal nature in Adam. They mark his opposition to the tsar who, because of his destructive aggression and lust, bears the marks of the Beast in Avvakum's first vision.[36] Avvakum means this portrayal of himself and the tsar as inverted versions of each other to justify his claim to Aleksei Mikhailovich's traditional role as the charismatic focus of the Russian people.

Avvakum's vision of 1669 also serves to justify his notion that he, rather than the tsar, is the earthly vehicle of divine justice, entitled to judge the tsar himself. The image of Avvakum's expanding tongue and teeth symbolizes the act of just judgment as it is archetypically expressed in Revelation by the image of the sacred Feast, the Supper of the Great God.

The fact that this image stands for cosmic eating or devouring can be inferred from the logic of Avvakum's self-presentation. He describes how, immediately before he has the vision, he shakes so violently from the stress and hunger brought on by his Lenten Fast that his teeth shatter against the stove. His mystical vision reverses this situation: his teeth are made whole and, implicitly, instead of refraining from eating, he mystically devours the world.

Whom Avvakum mystically devours can also be inferred from the logic of reversal. This vision of his resurrected body after death represents a reversal of the state of his body in death. Avvakum imagines that it will be desecrated by birds and beasts according to the will of the tsar: "аз же присуждением вашим, не сподоблюся савана и гроба, но наги кости мои псами и птицами небесными растерзаны будут . . ."[37] Implicitly, Avvakum's mystically reconstituted body in its turn desecrates the tsar through Avvakum's own act of judgment. His mystical mouth, along with the birds and beasts of heaven, devours the tsar's dead body.

The implicit association of the image of his cosmic tongue and teeth with birds and beasts feasting on carrion, as well as with judgment, links it archetypally to the apocalyptic Supper of the Great God. In another writing, when Avvakum imagines his own role in this great Feast of vengeance upon his enemies, he brings to the surface the image implicit in his vision: "телеса их птицы небесныя и звери земныя есть станут . . . потерпим, братия, не поскучим, господа ради."[38] Avvakum's implicit participation in spiritual "devouring" again reveals him to be an inversion of the tsar, whom Avvakum exposes in his first vision as a devourer in a carnal sense.

As an inverted version of the profane tsar, Avvakum represents himself as a sacred king in Christ.[39] His revelations of his own spiritualized body indicate that he and his followers have assimilated to themselves the tsar's traditional charisma and his mythical association with Christ in Judgment. They give him the right to repudiate the reigning tsar. Although his visions symbolize apocalyptic reality, Avvakum believes that they reveal eternal truth, and therefore condone his present relation to the tsar and his followers (the addressees of his petition).[40] The image of his cosmic tongue and teeth, on the one hand, symbolizes his "open mouth" and reciprocity with his disciples, and thus justifies Avvakum's teaching to his spiritual children. On the other, it symbolizes judgment on the tsar at the Supper of the Great God and condones Avvakum's verbal acts of judgment against the tsar and the Nikonians, beginning with the petition itself.

In this petition, Avvakum emerges as a kind of "pretender" to sacred kingship, taking over the mythic potential of Aleksei Mikhailovich to renew his people and define their social and political space as a "community" through the exercise of justice.[41] His visions implicitly make the claim that his own penitential community has taken over the eschatological sanction of the official Muscovite state and is the only vehicle of the truth and justice that will reign at the end of time.[42]

Avvakum's Fifth Petition presents his solution to the breakdown of the theocratic State.[43] It expresses Avvakum's perception that the tsar has refused to let his spiritual life be guided by his confessor and his conscience by the ideal of the Last Judgment. The Fifth Petition reveals that the Nikonian reforms are symptomatic of a deeper crisis in the relationship of the tsar to his people, their traditions, and their Christian symbols of community. It offers Avvakum and his penitential family as the solution to this crisis and thus plays a central role in Avvakum's polemic with the Nikonian state.

Notes

1. For Avvakum's Fifth Petition to Tsar Aleksei Mikhailovich, see *ZhPA*, pp. 195–202. The original text which Avvakum sent to the tsar has been found. Avvakum included the Fifth Petition in the Druzhinin *Pustozerskii sbornik,* and also in the Prianishnikov *sbornik.* Avvakum's followers also appreciated the importance of the Fifth Petition and its relation to Avvakum's *Life.* This is evident from a special manuscript cycle including both texts that Demkova believes originated in the Old Believer center in Mezen during Avvakum's lifetime. See N. S. Demkova, *Zhitie Protopopa Avvakuma (tvorcheskaia istoriia proizvedeniia)* (Leningrad, 1974), especially pp. 22–24, 107. My article, "The Life of the Archpriest Avvakum and the Kenotic Tradition" [*Canadian-American Slavic Studies* 25, nos. 1–4 (1991): 205–229], addresses the interrelationship of the *Life* and Avvakum's Fifth Petition.

2. This study does not accept Ponyrko's thesis in "D'iakon Fedor—so-avtor Protopopa Avvakuma," *TODRL* 31 (1976): 362–365 that Avvakum's co-exile at

Pustozersk, Fedor, wrote the first half of the Fifth Petition. I hope to demonstrate that the two parts are organically connected.

3. "The evangelical precept of non-judging, through all the age of Russian Christianity, remained, if not the prevalent, the most characteristic feature of the national mind." G. Fedotov, *The Russian Religious Mind* (Belmont, Mass., 1975), 2:59; cf. 2:58, 84.

4. Fedotov, 2: 59 notes the tension in Russian tradition between the taboo against judgment and the obligation to teach. An example of a teacher and judge of secular power is the kenotic saint Theodosius of the Caves Monastery whose humility invested him with the authority to intercede for those being wronged by the courts and to accuse the local prince of murder in the name of God's justice. See Fedotov, *The Russian Religious Mind*, 1:94–132, especially 124–126.

5. See Fedotov, 2:316–344.

6. See M. Cherniavsky, *Tsar and People* (New Haven, 1961); I. Ševčenko, "A Neglected Byzantine Source of Muscovite Political Ideology," in *The Structure of Russian History*, ed. M. Cherniavsky (New York, 1970), pp. 80–108. See also A. M. Panchenko and B. A. Uspenskii, "Ivan Groznyi i Petr Velikii: kontseptsii pervogo monarkha," *TODRL* 37 (1983): 54–78, where the authors discuss the ideology of the tsar's "justice" during the reign of Ivan IV and point out Ivan's association with apocalyptic archetypes such as the Archangel Michael and the Pantocrator.

7. I am indebted to Victor Turner, *The Ritual Process* (Chicago, 1969) for my understanding of Avvakum's response to the secularization of the ideology of the state and king. My terms "structure" and *communitas* refer to Turner's definition of the dialectically interacting elements that create social and political cohesion.

8. *ZhPA*, p. 195.

9. All biblical citations are from *Biblia sirech Knigi sviashchennago pisaniia vietkhago i novago zavieta* (St. Petersburg, 1891).

10. Avvakum's formulation echoes closely that of the sixteenth-century eulogy to Ivan III on the occasion of the birth of Ivan IV: "Such must be moreover the soul of the tsar which has so many cares which, like a mirror, is ever cleansed and continually shines with divine rays so that it learns the judgment of things . . . Verily are you called a tsar for you reign over the passions . . . you are crowned with the diadem of chastity and arrayed in the purple robe of justice." Cited in M. Cherniavsky, *Tsar and People*, p. 46.

11. *ZhPA*, p. 196.

12. See S. A. Zen'kovskii, *Russkoe staroobriadchestvo* (Munich, 1970), pp. 25–40, for a discussion of the Tale of the White Cowl and its ideological importance for the Zealots of Piety and the Old Believers.

13. *ZhPA*, p. 196.

14. See Rev. 18:6 where John describes the retribution against the Harlot: "i usugubite ei sugubo po delom eia: chashei, eiuzhe cherpa (vam) cherplite ei sugubo."

15. Ibid., p. 198.

16. Ibid.

17. Ibid., pp. 198–199.

18. Ibid., p. 198.

19. Ibid.
20. Ibid., p. 197.
21. Ibid., p. 199.
22. Ibid., p. 197.
23. Avvakum believes that these visions are from God rather than himself. He prefaces his vision of the tsar and then again his two visions of himself by attestations that he was already "dead" to the world and the self when he received them: "Prosti, Mikhailovich-svet, libo potom umru, da zhe by tebe vedomo bylo, da nikak ne lgu, nizh pritvoriaiasia govoriu: v temnitse mne, iako v grobu, sidiashchu, chto nadobna? Razve smert'? Ei, tako." (*ZhPA*, p. 198).
24. *ZhPA*, p. 199.
25. See A. N. Robinson, *Bor'ba idei v russkoi literature XVII veka* (Moscow, 1974), pp. 279-287 (Ch. 5, "Literaturnaia polemika ob ideal'nom 'obraze' cheloveka i izobrazitel'noe iskusstvo") and A. S. Eleonskaia, *Russkaia publitsistika vtoroi poloviny XVII veka* (Moscow, 1978), pp. 90-96 for discussions of Avvakum's and the Old Believers' characterizations of the tsar and Nikonians in metaphorical terms focusing on their appetites and especially their "stomachs." For Avvakum's relation to the tsar, see also A. N. Robinson, *Zhizneopisaniia Avvakuma i Epifaniia* (Moscow, 1963), pp. 27-38; and, *Bor'ba idei*, pp. 246-278 where Robinson shows that Avvakum's interpretation of the parable of Lazarus and the rich man has direct implications for the tsar.
26. *ZhPA*, p. 187.
27. Ibid., p. 199
28. Ibid., p. 200.
29. The length of this study does not allow me to elucidate this logic at great length. My interpretation of it derives from an examination of the way the metaphorical language of Revelation expresses the universal language of myth and the sacred. I understand the metaphors of this Book to be "ritual symbols" in the sense defined by V. Turner, *The Ritual Process*, p. 52: "Such symbols then unite the organic with the socio-moral order, proclaiming their ultimate religious unity over and above conflicts between and within these orders . . . powerful drives and emotions associated . . . especially with the physiology of reproduction . . . are divested in the ritual process of their antisocial quality . . . " This occurs through a dialectical process. On the dialectic of opposites which leads to inversion, see E. and P. Maranda, *Structural Models in Folklore and Transformational Essays* (The Hague, 1971).
30. See A. M. Farrer, *A Rebirth of Images* (Middlesex, 1949) for an analysis of the way the metaphors of Revelation recapitulate those of Genesis and the Prophets.
31. Avvakum's image of Adam and of basic human nature is functionally equivalent to the archetypes of the Beast and the Harlot in Revelation, which are subject to transformation through the dialectic described above. In his exegesis of Genesis, Avvakum explains that Adam fell because of his "lack of restraint" over his appetites. Avvakum portrays Adam as a "drunkard," covered with his own diarrhea and vomit after "overeating" the forbidden fruit. See *Russkaia istoricheskaia biblioteka*, vol. 39 (Leningrad, 1927), col. 667 (hereafter referred to as *RIB*). In an exegesis of Psalm 113, Avvakum characterizes himself and all mankind as sons of Adam and all-

devourers: "... ne khoshchem bo obshche stiazhaniia imet', no vsia khoshchu mne sobrat', iako nesytyi vseiadets. Ashche by mi vozmozhno, vsia by veshchi morskiia i zemskiia vo utrobu svoiu vmestil." See "Poslanie Simeonu, Ksenii Ivanovne i Aleksandre Grigor'evne," in ZhPA, p. 273. Avvakum's interpretation of the cause of the fall and Adam's resulting indigestion draws on an apocryphal account of the fall, "O ispovedanii Evgine i o v"spros vnuchat eia, i o bolezni Adama" in N. Tikhonravov, *Pamiatniki otrechenennoi russkoi literatury* (Moscow, 1863), vol. 1, reprinted in Slavistic Printings and Reprintings (The Hague, 1970), pp. 298–304.

32. Besides the interpretation of his vision which Avvakum gives to his spiritual children, he informs the addressees of the Fifth Petition that his miraculous bodily "all-encompassingness" has a precedent in the apocryphal "otkrovenie Avraama" found in the Palei, when "the angel Altez ... lifted Abraham up" and "showed him all of creation since the beginning of time." See *ZhPA*, p. 201. Avvakum's evocation of his similarity to Abraham is meant to suggest that his mystical charisma is a sign that he is finishing God's work of redemption, just as Abraham's vision was a sign that he was beginning the same. This is discussed in my unpublished paper "The Ideology in Avvakum's Life."

33. See N. Subbotin, *Materialy dlia istorii raskola za pervoe vremia ego sushchestvovaniia* (Moscow, 1874–1890), vol. 8, p. 97. Avvakum's characterization of himself as a confessor is traditional. S. Smirnov in his study, *Drevne-russkii dukhovnik* (Moscow, 1914; rpt. 1970), notes that the father confessor takes his spiritual children's sins on his neck (like a sacrificial lamb) in order to expiate them before the Last Judgment: "... na moei vyi sogresheniia tvoiia, chado, i da ne istiazhet tebe o sich Khristos Bog, egda priidet vo slave svoei na sud strashnii" (p. 42). The confessor was expected to direct his spiritual child to the Jerusalem on high: "... sluzhit' vozhdem ei [sem'e] v vyshnii Ierusalim', otkryt' Bozhie tsarstvo, privesti ee k prestolu Bozhiiu i skazat': se az i deti, iazhe mi esi dal" (p. 42). Smirnov discusses the mystical notion of the father confessor and Avvakum's appeal to it (p. 49).

34. See S. Smirnov, pp. 202–205. Avvakum's apocryphal source is "Slovo Ioana Zlatousta. Pouchenie ko vsem krestiianom" in a fourteenth–century redaction of *Zlataia Tsep'*. I have modernized the script.

35. See *ZhPA*, p. 218.

36. The Beast's sexual lust is implicit in his association with the Harlot who "rides" him. See Rev. 17:7.

37. *ZhPA*, p. 200.

38. See *RIB*, pp. 783–784. In another writing, Avvakum alludes to his personal participation in the judgment against the tsar and the Nikonians. This passage expresses his idea that he personally will exact judgment on the tsar even more concretely than his remarks in the first part of his Fifth Petition: "Daite tolko srok, sobaki, ne uidete u menia: nadeiusia na Khrista, iako budete u menia v rukakh! vydavliu ia iz vas sok-ot!? (*RIB*, pp. 488–489).

39. On the sacredness of the king (tsar) in Russian culture, see M. Cherniavsky, *Tsar and People*, pp. 44–71; and V. M. Zhivov, B. A. Uspenksii, "Tsar' i Bog: Semioticheskie aspekty sakralizatsii monarkha v Rossii," in *Iazyki kul'tury i problemy perevodimosti* (Moscow, 1987), pp. 47–149. See also J. Hubbs, *Mother Russia* (Bloomington, 1988).

40. In another writing Avvakum indicates that he considers his future moral reality applicable to the present as well. He speaks of his and his followers' "resurrection" as an eternal fact which has already taken place: "... v nashemu polku i mertvykh net. Voskresokhom be so Khristom, k tomu uzhe ne umrem...." See N. S. Demkova, "Neizvestnye i neizdannye teksty iz sochinenii protopopa Avvakuma," *TODRL* 21 (1965): 238.

41. See B. Uspenksii, "Tsar' i samozvanets: samozvanchestvo v Rossii kak kul'-turno-istoricheskii fenomen," in *Khudozhestvennyi iazyk srednevekov'ia* (Moscow, 1982), pp. 201–235; and A. M. Panchenko, "Buntashnyi vek," in *Russkaia kul'tura v kanun Petrovskikh reform* (Leningrad, 1984), pp. 3–36. For a discussion of the phenomenon of the pretender in Western tradition see Norman Cohen, *Pursuit of the Millennium* (London, 1957).

42. M. Cherniavsky, *Tsar and People,* p. 71 speaks of the eschatological *raison d'être* of the Muscovite state.

43. S. Zenkovsky, *Russkoe staroobriadchestvo* (Munich, 1970) describes the Old Believers' "theocratic, utopian hopes in Russia's messianic mission."

Традиционность и уникальность сочинений протопопа Аввакума в свете традиции Третьего Рима

MARIA PLIUKHANOVA

50-е–70-е годы XVII в. — наиболее яркий и роковой период в истории традиций древнерусской религиозной словесности и, вероятно, традиций древнерусского Православия вообще. Никогда еще традиции не ощущались с такой силой, никогда прежде они не были сформулированы с такой определенностью и никогда их судьба не внушала столь острого беспокойства.

Идеологи этой эпохи оказались во власти опасений, что нарушена или вот-вот нарушится правильная связь религиозных обычаев и письменных текстов с истинными образцами. За этим стояло предчувствие наступления нового времени, но не только это. Тревога за благоверие подобала теократическому государству — Третьему Риму, она была заложена в сценарии судьбы Третьего Рима еще Филофеем. По Филофею, миссия последнего оплота благоверия — Московского государства — это борьба за чистоту веры, возглавляемая царем; в этой борьбе Третий Рим погибнет и на этом кончится история.[1] Благочестивая тревога обусловила в свое время созыв Стоглавого собора, где (по словам «Стоглава») царская душа совокупилась с церковным устроением. Религиозно-государственный подъем середины XVI века быстро спал, что естественно, поскольку идея богоизбранности русского государства, которой он питался, была не исторического, а эсхатологического свойства. Это была богоизбранность скорее для высокоторжественной гибели, чем для исторического бытия. Новый подъем, ознаменовавший первую половину царствования Алексея Михайловича, достиг большой высоты, но и он ослабел бы вскоре, если бы не упорство Аввакума и его последователей.

Обе стороны, вошедшие в конфликт к середине XVII в., оберегали величие русского православия — благочестие Третьего Рима; Никон и Алексей Михайлович восстанавливали подобающее новому Царьграду соответствие греческим образцам.[2] Противники реформ охраняли решения Стоглавого собора, в которых, по их мнению, выразились святость и боголепие Московского царства — Третьего Рима. Неистовая забота о традиции имела революционные последствия.

Никоновские реформы, вынужденные искать опору в украинской учености (за отсутствием своей, московской), расширили путь для секуляризации и европейских влияний. Для русской литературы они имели следствием такое новшество, как, например, заимствованная школьная поэзия Симеона Полоцкого. Эффект деятельности другой стороны — совершившаяся в великом творчестве Аввакума «самоубийственная смерть» традиций древнерусской словесности, рассмотрению которой и посвящена предлагаемая работа.

* * *

Аввакум был древнерусским книжником в полной мере. Его произведения насыщены цитатами, отсылками, пересказами источников, иногда даже и более, чем это было в обычае у его предшественников. Задача взращивания новых идей не стояла перед Аввакумом: «А я, грешный, кроме писаново не хочу собою затевать: как написано, так верую; идеже что святыя написали, мне так и добро ... » (стлб. 815).[3] Так называемые еретические мнения Аввакума по сложнейшим догматическим вопросам — о троичности, о сошествии в ад, о боговоплощении — отразившиеся в полемических трактатах против дьякона Федора, есть результат невольного выхода из-под контроля книжной традиции в стихию устного спора. Устное обсуждение этих догматов людьми, не совсем изощренными в богословии, вероятно, неизбежно должно было привести к отклонениям. Когда же при изложении догматов Аввакум возвращался к книжным источникам — как, например, во введении к *Житию*, где он постарался коснуться всех основных спорных вопросов, — высказывания его становились догматически безукоризненными. Другой причиной догматических заблуждений Аввакума были ошибки в дониконовых книжных изданиях, чрезмерно почитавшихся среди сторонников старой веры.[4]

Аввакум не предполагал новизны и неожиданности даже в откровении. Чудесные видения горних сил он (вполне справедливо) считал связанными с книжной традицией и порицал недисциплинированного, некнижного визионера за произвол в его видениях: « ... И ты так же учи книжным разумом, и Писанием свидетельствуй о истине, а не мраковидным видением ... Егда видение с Писанием сходно, то разумеем, яко от Бога есть; егда же несогласно, то прелесть есть. ... Держатися подобает писанных» (стлб. 876–877).

Как истинный книжник древней Руси, Аввакум не создавал и не хотел создавать своего богословия. Древнерусские книжники, «делатели девятого часа», унаследовали сложившееся вероучение и разработанную систему авторитетных текстов; им не пришлось быть свидетелями сложностей исторического становления христианской словесности. Как показывает Г. П. Федотов,[5] особенности древнерусского православия определяются не новизной идей, а особенностями выбора, акцентирования и сочетания традиций, обусловленными особенностями субстрата. Чрезвычайная новизна аввакумова творчества, самого образа его мыслей — при установке на сугубую традиционность — должна рассматриваться, прежде всего, как обусловленная сдвигами внутри системы традиций.

Важное свойство иерархии традиций в древнерусской христианской словесности заключалось в том, что вершинные традиции имели священный характер и не подлежали активной разработке. Как отмечал Д. С. Лихачев: «Часть жанров были строго ограничены существующими произведениями, и создание новых произведений в них было невозможно».[6] В древнерусской словесности этот вершинный слой был особенно велик. Именно в него вторгался своей деятельностью Аввакум.

* * *

Простой экскурс в историю русских книжных обычаев с помощью справочника Филарета (Гумилевского) *Обзор русской духовной литературы*[7] позволяет видеть, что никто из русских книжников в пределах Руси не позволял себе создавать толкования на сколько-нибудь обширные фрагменты Священного Писания. Максим Грек, высокоученый пришелец с Афона, наделенный за всю историю древнерусской словесности, вероятно, наивысшими учительными правами, писал толкования лишь на отдельные труднопонятные словосочетания из Писания,[8] но не на целые тексты и даже группы текстов, как это делал Аввакум. Толкования на священные книги считались на Руси уже осуществленным делом великих отцов Церкви.

В недавней работе А. А. Алексеева о судьбе Песни Песней и толкований ее на русской почве содержится ряд наблюдений над особенностями освоения и распространения толковой литературы на Руси. Как видно из статьи, инициатива русских книжников проявлялась в переводах, компилировании, сокращении, редко — редактировании и весьма редко — в отрывочных самостоятельных толкованиях.[9]

В свою *Книгу толкований* Аввакум включил толкования на некоторые псалмы, на некоторые главы из Книги притчей Соломоновых, Книги Премудрости Соломоновой, Книги пророка Исаии. Сюда же вошло нравоучение с толкованием на фрагмент Евангелия от Матфея. В той мере, в какой Аввакум подчиняется дисциплине книжной традиции или хочет указать на преемственную связь с нею, толкования его по направлению и объему имитируют толкования отцов Церкви. Например, в первой части толкования на псалом 44 Аввакум аккуратно и последовательно разъясняет каждый стих, иногда, но отнюдь не всегда, воспроизводя традиционные толкования Исихия (на стих 4), Евсевия (на стих 11), Афанасия Великого (на стихи 12–14).[10] Бороздин полагает, что Аввакум просто помнил эти тексты по Толковой Псалтыри, хорошо ему известной. Соединяя свои экзегезы со святоотеческими, Аввакум не стесняется причислять себя таким образом к рангу великих учителей. Однако обстоятельства, толкнувшие его на это, были, судя по текстам его толкований, чрезвычайно серьезными.

Аввакум отдает лишь часть своих сил разъяснению буквального и нравоучительного смысла священных текстов. Внимание его сосредоточено на анагогическом смысле — на пророчествах Ветхого Завета о Новом Завете. В соответствии с традицией, события, образы, явления ветхозаветные мыслятся им как предшествующие новозаветным, параллельные им и пророчествующие о них. Но двумя параллельными рядами не исчерпывается священная история. Аввакум склонен добавлять третью параллель, по отношению к которой и вторая оказывается пророчеством. Материал для параллелей третьего ряда толкователь черпает из событий ему современных (Псалом 20, стих 6):

> Псалом: Врази мои реша мне злая: когда умрет и погибнет имя его. Толк: Было и самому сему глаголющему пророку от Саула, тестя его, не сладко; гоняше его и глаголаше: когда сын Iессеов умрет и погибнет имя его! Писано о сем в Царствах Первых книг. И жидовя о Христе такоже глаголаху: доколе вземлеши душа наша? И Анна Ртищева мне говорила: а и Аввакум протопоп! коли тебя извод возмет! (стлб. 443).

События новозаветных и текущих времен, будучи поставлены в параллель друг другу, взаимоуподобляются в деталях, даже обмениваются деталями, наименованиями и стилем описания (стих 9):

Псалом: Слово законопреступно возложиша на Мя; еда спяй не приложит воскреснути. Толк: Жиды лгаху Пилату на Христа, вадяще, да распнет Его, и ругающеся глаголаху: аще снидет со креста, упова на Бога, да видим и веру имем Ему! А нынешние жиды, в огонь сажая правоверных християн, тоже ругаяся говорят: аще-де праведен и свят, и он-де не згорит. Акой и не згорит, и оне, иссекши бердышами, и паки дров насеченных накладут, да в пепел правоверных жгут, яко и там на кресте Христа мертва мужик стрелец рогатиною пырнул. Выслужился блядин сын, пять рублев ему государева жалованья, да сукно, да погреб! Понеже радеет нам, великому государю. Ох, ох, бедныя! (стлб. 444).

Если ветхозаветный текст поддается истолкованию в качестве эсхатологического пророчества, то толкователь минует новозаветный этап священной истории и применяет пророчество прямо к своему времени. Таковы толкования на стихи из Книги Премудрости (Гл. 5:23–24; 6:1–3). Разъясняя стих «Сопротив станет им дух силы ... », Аввакум описывает, как Христос исцеляет в текущее время казнимых и как Он венчает мученическим венцом новых мучеников; затем, рисуя дела мучителей, автор постепенно, через посредство глаголов совершенного вида, переходит к картинам будущего: «изорвут .., изсекут .., наваляют .., пировать станут ... Да и сядет діявол-от посреде их на пиру-том ...» (стлб. 499). Прорицания Аввакума о будущем продолжаются прорицаниями Апокалипсиса. Так Аввакум, не довольствуясь сотрудничеством с отцами Церкви, вступает в сотрудничество с апостолом. Он убежден, что наступившее время не уступает по своей значимости новозаветным временам. Это убеждение выражается в построении дальнейших толкований на Книгу Премудрости. Последовательно вводимые тексты — Премудрости, Аввакума, Апокалипсиса, опять Аввакума — соприравниваются благодаря одинаковым зачинам и сходной структуре. «Сущее: Слышите убо, царие, и разумейте ... Толк: Слышите, царие, и князи, и судии земстии ... Слышите, что Богослову сказано во осмой на десять главе: и слышах глас ин с небесе ... [Аввакум:] Слышите, царие, и разумейте ... » (стлб. 500–503) — Аввакум говорит как пророк и вместе с пророком.

Итак, Аввакум нарушил принятый среди русских книжников обычай удаленного, благоговейного молчания перед священными книгами. Он преодолел и ту дистанцию, которая была установлена, по отношению к Писанию, отцами Церкви. Новый толкователь вплотную приблизился к Священному Писанию и соединил свой голос с голосами пророков и апостолов. То, что с одной стороны видится как нарушение духовной дисциплины и отречение от предания, с другой — должно оцениваться как прямая и адекватная реакция на общепринятое среди современников Аввакума представление о наступившем времени как последнем. Последнее время столь же священно, как ветхозаветное и новозаветное, поэтому анагогические толкования Св. Писания должны быть распространены так, чтобы обнять и его события.

* * *

Аввакумова *Книга бесед* составлена из произведений, свободных по композиции и стилю и разнообразных тематически. Беседы — вид церковного красноречия, традиционно не связанный жесткими формальными требованиями. Исходя из позднейших принципов жанровых классификаций, беседы можно поместить между толкованиями и «словами». Как толкование, беседа обычно исходит из текстов Священного Писания, но, в отличие от толкований, она не следует за Писанием, а, удаляясь от него, развивает темы, важные для слушателей. В отличие от «слов», беседы не привязаны к событиям церковного года.[11] При таком широком понимании к жанру бесед можно было бы причислить и некоторые русские памятники, в том числе «Слово о законе и благодати» Илариона (понимаемое как беседа на послание Павла к Галатам); однако древнерусская традиция во всех случаях предпочитала название «Слово».

Работая над созданием *Книги бесед,* Аввакум несомненно имел в виду *Книгу бесед* Иоанна Златоуста на 14 посланий ап. Павла (Киев, 1623). Аввакум особенно любил эту книгу, в его черновых записях сохранилось множество выписок из нее.[12]

Беседы на послания Павла считались высшим духовным подвигом Златоуста. Согласно житию Златоуста, сам апостол Павел являлся к нему по ночам и, беседуя с ним, помогал ему в создании книги.[13] Киевское издание *Книги бесед* начиналось с изображения ночной беседы Иоанна с Павлом. Аввакум не использует тексты Златоуста ради приближения к истине через их посредство, что соответствовало бы обычаям, а сам вступает в беседу с Павлом, имитируя Златоуста и заявляя тем самым претензию на его духовный авторитет.

Среди своих бесед Аввакум помещает толкование на фрагмент послания Павла к Римлянам. Автор не следует здесь урокам Златоуста; связь его с апостольскими посланиями оказывается более непосредственной, чем отношения к ним древнего Павлова собеседника и почтительного толкователя. Язык апостолов становится языком самого Аввакума. Послание к Римлянам он толкует, по большей части, текстами второго послания Павла к Коринфянам, которые воспроизводит от своего имени. Например: на слова «хвалимся в скорбех ... » (Рим. 5:3):

> Двадесять два лета плаваю и так и сяк, иногда наг, иногда гладен, иногда убит, иногда на дожде, иногда на мразе, иногда на чепи, иногда в железах, иногда в темнице, кроме повседневных нападений и разлучений жены и детей. Кто изнемогает, и не изнемогаю? Кто соблажняется, и аз не разжизаюся? (стлб. 365) [первая часть — приблизительно цит. 2 Кор. 11:27; вторая часть — точно — 2 Кор. 11:29].

Беседы Аввакума, в отступление от традиций Златоуста, часто не привязаны к Писанию. Например, Беседа 3 (рассуждение о бесчинствах монашества и о наступлении сил зла) не заимствует темы из Писания и цитирует его не много, но она начата вступительными словами Евангелия от Луки. Это введение долженствует, очевидно, указать на высокое значение того, что описывается далее. То есть беседы Аввакума претендуют не на подчиненность Писанию, а, скорее, на рядоположенность ему.

Вся родословная Аввакума и его творений, развернутая во введении к *Книге бесед,* насыщена цитатами и реминисценциями.

Первое утверждение «гад есмь или свинья»: под воздействием следующей за ним реминисценции из притчи о блудном сыне, преобразует свой конкретный низменный смысл в более высокий, символический. Далее самоуничижение и потерянность Аввакума — блудного сына — соприравниваются греховности апостола Павла через внедрение в текст большой цитаты из послания к Римлянам с помощью слов: «С Павлом реку». Затем греховность Аввакума, поправшая в нем человека, противопоставлена человеческой сущности Иова, Моисея и т. д., вплоть до пророка Аввакума, которого, как напоминает автор, ангел принес в ров к Даниилу; каждый из них «бысть человек». «Но не я, окаянный Аввакум: я и сам сижу в рове, душею и телом обнажився». Эта фигура (не я, я и сам) — отрицательный параллелизм, только утверждающий сходство протопопа с соименным ему пророком и с Даниилом, сидящими во рву (стлб. 241–244). Далее, характеризуя безобразность грешников словами Златоуста, он призывает к плачу и начинает плач — свой, Иова и Иеремии одновременно. То есть, предстоящие беседы, как определены они в родословии введения, — это собеседования с Павлом, наподобие Златоустовых и, вместе с тем, библейский пророческий плач над миром, от которого отвернулся Бог.

Во введении к *Книге бесед* проявляются свойства, вообще характерные для творчества Аввакума. Все имена библейских персонажей, сюда включенные, встречаются разрозненно в других произведениях, где через аналогии, сравнения, противопоставления служат самоопределению автора. Введение построено на универсальном для Аввакума приеме: текст, определяющий гадость и мерзость текущего существования, в словесном отношении часто просторечный и грубый, вдвигается в контекст Священного Писания и святоотеческих творений. Читатели нового времени, воспитанные на стилистической концепции классицизма, воспринимают такие соединения как сильный стилистический контраст. Но природа этого приема не литературно-художественная. Аввакум видит в безобразиях, бесчинствах и мучениях своего времени соответствие священным бедствиям, страданиям и подвигам времен апостольских и пророческих, поскольку его, аввакумово, время столь же священно, так же близко связано со Вторым пришествием, как были связаны с Первым пришествием предварявшее его время пророков и примыкавшее к нему время апостолов.

Беседы Аввакума посвящены, преимущественно, обличениям никонианской церкви, и этим они отличаются от трудов Златоуста, где разоблачениям конкретных бесчинств уделяется ничтожное место, а основные силы сосредоточены на размышлениях о христианской жизни и на разъяснении священных текстов.

Беседы и толкования под пером Аввакума стали по существу жанрами историческими, поскольку они характеризуют свое время и определяют смысл и место его в общем плане истории.

* * *

Причинами, казалось бы, простыми и практическими объясняется безразличие Аввакума к ведущей форме древнерусского церковного красноречия — «словам» на события церковного года. Аввакум, расстриженный священник, насильственно удален от церковной упорядоченной жизни (он, впрочем, служил и в Пустозерске). Эта удаленность от церковного календаря имеет не только личный страдательный смысл. Аввакум вообще, в отличие от высокопочитаемых им древнерусских хранителей благоверия, мало обращается к образам и представлениям годового праздничного цикла. В нарушение обычая, он не указывает, на какой церковный праздник выпало описываемое событие. Исключительное значение имеют для него только посты, особенно — Великий пост.

В Великий пост 1671 г., описанный Аввакумом в специальной записке, пустозерские узники почти совершенно отказались от пищи (стлб. 719–722). Во время Великого поста 1669 г. изнемогшему от голода Аввакуму привиделось, как Господь вместил в него небо и землю — что описано в пятой челобитной царю Алексею Михайловичу (стлб. 763–764). Во время Петрова поста — согласно *Житию* — Аввакум был расстрижен и солнце померкло (*П.сб.*, стр. 14).[14] Посты перестают быть только частью нормального годового цикла, их значение историзируется; настроения, состояния и поступки, подобающие посту, наиболее соответствуют особенностям наступившего исторического периода.

В пятой челобитной царю Алексею Михайловичу представшее Аввакуму видение горних сил связывается с Вознесением. Но это не столько приурочение к праздничному дню, сколько отсылка к новозаветным текстам. Христос говорит Аввакуму слова, сказанные перед Вознесением апостолам: «Не бойся, Аз есмь с тобою» (стлб. 766). Ср. Матф. 28:20: «И се Аз с вами есмь во вся дни до скончания века».

Роль Аввакума по отношению к Вознесению больше, чем роль священника, празднующего и вспоминающего, произносящего «Слово», — это соучастие в событии.

Таким образом, обычное церковное время, столь важное для древнерусской церковной словесности и для обыденной жизни, выпадает из сферы внимания Аввакума, а вместе с ним выпадает и важнейшая традиция древнерусского церковного красноречия.

* * *

Чтобы определить традиции многочисленных и разнообразных посланий Аввакума, нужно было бы анализировать каждое в отдельности. Мы рассмотрим здесь только одно, но весьма представительное — «Послание Стаду верных или Кораблю Христову». Оно принадлежит к группе посланий, обращенных ко всем исповедникам старой веры, подобно апостольским посланиям, адресованным «принявшим с нами равно драгоценную веру». Послания этой группы, как особо важные, обычно известны в нескольких авторских редакциях и во многих списках («Послание Стаду верных» — в двух редакциях).

«Послание Стаду верных или Кораблю Христову» ориентировано на вполне конкретное Слово Златоуста. Подражание Златоусту здесь носит и биографический характер (в посланиях Аввакум вообще часто сопоставляет свою судьбу с судьбой Златоуста, см. стлб. 567 и др.).

По житию Златоуста, в час наиболее тяжелых испытаний, перед изгнанием, Иоанн обращается к пастве с проповедью, посвященной прославлению Церкви как сообщества верующих, неколебимого в вере и в единстве. Проповедь начинается знаменитыми словами:

> Многы волны и люто потопление, но не боимся егда погрязновения, на камени бо стоим; да ся пенит море и бесит, камени не может раздрушити, да востанут волны, но Исусова корабля не могут потопити.[15]

К этим словам Златоуста отсылает Аввакум свою паству — в обращении из пустозерской тюрьмы. Тема любви к пастве и обращение «Возлюбленные мои!» — дополнительные свидетельства контакта со Златоустовым «Словом». Корабль в обоих случаях сохраняет символический смысл — это община верующих. Но у Златоуста это наиболее устойчивая сила мира — Церковь, соединенная верой и любовью. «Корабля не могут потопить» — корабля-церкви, крепость которой держится на камне веры. Цитата Златоуста вводится Аввакумом с указанием на неустойчивость корабля-церкви: «Не сего дни так учинилось кораблю Христову влаятися» (мыкаться); далее свойство вечной крепости и невредимости под ударами волн приписывается лишь камню-Христу; судьба корабля не обозначена. Истинно верующие останутся с Христом («на камени бо стоим»). Изменение, внесенное в символику Златоустова фрагмента, позволяет Аввакуму представить земную церковь частью гибнущего мира; исповедники истинной веры, мученики обретут жизнь, соединясь с Христом. Отсюда различия во всех остальных темах Слова Златоуста и послания Аввакума. Златоуст говорит о несокрушимости Церкви, преодолении страха смерти любовью к пастве и о готовности своей умереть за нее; в нравоучительной части он разоблачает корыстолюбие, намекнув на гонения, претерпеваемые от царицы, призывает женщин к скромности и послушанию. Аввакум пишет о близости Судного дня: «Судия бо близ, при дверех есть, сотворити кончину веку сему суетному» (стлб. 812). «Никонианский дух — самого антихриста дух». Страх смерти, по Аввакуму, преодолевается смертью, в наступившее время живые «равны с погребенными» (стлб. 814); нравоучения Аввакума касаются того, как достойнее пострадать. Рисуя живописные картины претерпеваемых им самим мучений, Аввакум вновь приближается к своему образцу и перифразирует его повторно, но в новом регистре: вся сила правоверия оказывается сосредоточенной в одном Аввакуме, на него налетает буря — дьявол. «Многие волны и люто потопление; но не боюся погрязновения, на камени бо стою». Камень и здесь — Христос. «А я за Него держюся, никово не боюся» (стлб. 816). В отличие от Златоуста, он совсем не склонен придавать значение каким-либо земным сообществам, даже общине хранителей староверия. Этот специфический эсхатологический индивидуализм отличает Аввакума не только от предшественников, но и от последователей — от создателей староверческих общин.

Уже при самом начале раскола символ корабля-церкви в бурном море вошел в число символов, важнейших для защитников старой веры. Братья Плещеевы, ученики Ивана Неронова, писали своему учителю в 50-е годы: «Ей государь, ей в правду ныне люта зима и горько потопление, еже церковь объят: якоже бо море зримо, от самыя бездны глубины возмутившееся, тако и дух антихристов широким путем и пространным, ведущим к погибели, нача крепко возмущати истинный корабль Христов». Братья описывали плач и отчаяние пловцов и говорили о наступлении последних дней.[16]

В сборнике произведений Спиридона Потемкина есть послание, иногда приписываемое Аввакуму, но, по-видимому, принадлежащее самому Спиридону. Оно не является ответом на вышеприведенное письмо, но направлено одному из братьев Плещеевых и оспаривает близкое Плещеевым представление о гибели Церкви: отпадают и гибнут отступники, Церковь же — в своем истинном благоверии непреклонна и недвижима.[17]

В дальнейшем, как этого хотел Потемкин, корабль-церковь отождествлялся с общиной хранителей истинного благоверия. Гибель постоянно угрожает ему («От самыя преисподния геены, волны сия на корабль благоверия гремеша и гремят...»[18]), но корабль не погибнет. Идея церковности, поколебавшись, восстановилась, вернув себе первозданную форму, почти такую, какую имела во время Златоуста.

Текст о корабле из Слова Златоуста стал основой старообрядческого духовного стиха: «Многие на мя волны восстают и лютое потопление, и да не убоимся мы погрязновения, на камени бо стоим. Море ся пенит и да не устоит: не может бо погрузити Исусова корабля».[19]

Разрушая образ Церкви, созданный в Слове Златоуста, Аввакум демонстрирует исключительность своих эсхатологических умонастроений. Златоустов символ корабля в бурном море тоже имел эсхатологический смысл, но это была эсхатология христианина, поглощенного исторической жизнью Церкви.

* * *

Утверждать, что Аввакум нарушает обычаи древнерусской словесности потому, что он писатель эсхатологический, недостаточно. Эсхатологична вся христианская словесность, русская же — начиная от Нестора — в особенности привержена эсхатологическим идеям, образам и символам. Определяющим фактором приходится считать не просто наличие или отсутствие эсхатологизма, а степень напряженности его и какие-либо специфические его особенности.

Несомненно, в XVII веке русская словесность как никогда энергично и обильно выражала эсхатологические умонастроения. Небывалое распространение получили списки эсхатологических «откровений», как известных со времен Нестора, так и влившихся в русскую традицию в XVI в. Неизменность интереса русской аудитории к эсхатологии сказалась на деятельности Московского печатного двора, который многократно тиражировал слова Ефрема Сирина и другие сочинения о гибели мира.[20] Литература Смутного времени широко и ярко применила для описаний Смуты эсхатологические образы. Она не была более эсхатологичной, чем, например, хроника Нестора или «слова» Серапиона Владимирского о татарском нашествии. Но самое поле применения эсхатологического материала оказалось как никогда широким, поскольку ни одна предшествующая эпоха русской истории не имела своей литературы такого масштаба и не достигала такой высоты самосознания.

В России с особым вниманием отнеслись к эсхатологическим идеям, которые были высказаны некоторыми украинскими богословами в пылу полемики против унии, лютеранства и папства. Не имевшие для Украины принципиального значения, в Москве они получили особый вес и развитие. В 1644 г. здесь была напечатана так называемая «Кириллова книга», содержащая, кроме изложения основ православной веры, проясняемых в процессе полемик с иноверными, обширное 15 огласительное слово Кирилла Иерусалимского с толкованиями Стефана Зизания. Это — энциклопедия признаков кончины мира, среди них — помрачение веры, начавшееся, по Зизанию, в Риме с утверждением папства: Римское царство — антихристово царство.[21] Уния среди православных на Украине понималась как расширение власти римского костела, т. е. антихристова царства.

В 1648 г. в Москве была напечатана *Книга о вере* с украинскими по происхождению трактатами о сущности православия (главным образом — Захарии Копыстенского) и с украинским эсхатологическим уклоном. Как показали исследователи,[22] на последнем этапе поготовки, уже на московской почве в книгу вошла особая русская эсхатологическая концепция (в 30 гл.). В главе 30 заметна тенденция, характерная для идей Филофеева типа, не различать религиозные и политические представления. Движение антихристова царства — римского костела на восток видится ориентированным по национально-государственным границам. Вера в Малой Руси объявляется погибшей, невзирая на то, что православие среди украинцев остается распространенным. Хранителем веры оказывается лишь Русское Московское государство. X. Роте проницательно характеризует концепцию 30 главы как историко-политическую и националистическую,[23] однако он не прав, отрицая ее эсхатологический смысл. Он очевиден, заявлен и вытекает из контекста. Хотя, действительно, кажется невероятным, что на Московском печатном дворе, чья деятельность отвечала интересам высших церковных и светских властей и служила утверждению и прославлению русского благоверия, возникла потребность предполагать опасность для этого благоверия в самом ближайшем времени. «А по исполнении лет числа, тысячи шести сот шестидесяти шести, не непотребно и нам от сих вин опасение имети, да на некое бы что зло пострадати, по преждереченных исполнения писания свидетельств ... ».[24] Это, разумеется, национализм, но теократического и эсхатологического свойства, где судьба государства отождествлена с судьбой веры, а национальная мания величия выливается в предчувствие близкой гибели.

Итак, эсхатологические настроения достигли в России к середине века особого напряжения не потому, что жизнь как-нибудь особенно ухудшилась (напротив, она была менее катастрофична, чем обыкновенно), но именно в силу развития религиозно-исторического самосознания, отраженного и укрепленного развитием словесности. Национальное религиозно-историческое самосознание, получившее форму и стимулы к росту в эпоху Филофея и Макария, в период деятельности кружка ревнителей церковного благочестия, соединившего Алексея Михайловича, Никона и Аввакума, начало достигать своего совершенства, то есть высшего эсхатологического накала.

Предсказание *Книги о вере* об угрозе для веры в России было признано сбывшимся уже в 50-е годы в писаниях Спиридона Потемкина против никоновых реформ.[25] Трехступенчатая схема эсхатологического движения стала общим местом старообрядческой словесности. Аввакум использует ее со ссылками на источник. В его сочинениях особенно ощутимой становится двойная, украинско-московская природа концепции.

Постепенное движение сил зла с Запада в Россию Аввакум изображает как перемещение апокалиптической блудницы, сидящей на звере. Она пьет кровь мучеников и поит из чаши вином ереси, «упоила римское царство, и польское, и многия окрестные веси, да и в Русь нашу приехала в 160 [т. е. 7160 — М.П.] году» (стлб. 433). Торжество ереси заставляет Аввакума ждать турецкого нашествия на Русь, по аналогии с судьбой Царьграда, взятого турками, согласно идеям Филофея, после греческого отступления от веры — заключения Флорентийской унии. «Чаю, подвигнет Бог тогоже Турка на отмщение кровей мученических. Пускай любодеицу-ту потрясет, хмель-ет выгонит из блядки!» (стлб. 569). Пустозерская братия с волнением следила за перемещениями турецкой армии в районе Каменец-Подольска.[26] «Тому лет двести семьдесят с лишком, варвар, Бахмет турский, взял Царьград ... Не коснел Христос, скоро указ учини. Блюдусь и трепещу. Та же собака заглядывает и в нашу бедную Россию».[27] Аввакум и его товарищи в Пустозерске ошибочно полагали, что турки казнили восточного патриарха, участвовавшего в суде над сторонниками старой веры в 1666–67 гг., считая, что они уже начали служить орудием гнева Божия.[28] Истоки этой ошибки тоже следует искать в московских идеях XVI — начала XVII вв., восходящих к формуле Филофея.

Специфика русского мессианского эсхатологизма сказывается и на выборе эсхатологических книжных традиций в сочинениях Аввакума. Обычный эсхатологический репертуар русской книжности — «слова» отцов Церкви, «откровения», — относительно мало внедряются в тексты Аввакума, хотя несомненно ему известны. Чаще всего, он опирается на свод эсхатологических учений, сделанный в гл. 30 *Книги о вере,* и на Апокалипсис. Отсюда он извлекает, преимущественно, указания о знаках последних времен и дисциплинированно их придерживается. Как и прочие пустозерские учителя, Аввакум не считает царство антихристово окончательно наступившим, ибо твердо помнит учение Ипполита и других о том, что Антихрист должен родиться от колена Данова в Галилее. В соответствии с учением Златоуста и «Кирилловой книги», он говорит о множественности и постепенности появления на путях истории антихристовых предтечей, почти отождествимых с настоящим Антихристом: «Все одны черти, блядины дети, и тогда, и ныне, и до кончины» (стлб. 463).

Из всех ролей эсхатологической мистерии, предусмотренных традиционными учениями, Аввакуму (и его соратникам) более всего подходят роли последних пророков (Апокалипсис, гл. 11). Согласно толкованиям на Апокалипсис Андрея Кесарийского, *Книге о вере* и прочим источникам, пророки Илья и Енох (иногда к ним добавляется Иоанн Богослов) будут посланы утверждать в вере верных и за свою проповедь примут смерть от Антихриста, затем воскреснут и вознесутся уже перед самым Вторым пришествием Христа. Аввакум совмещает в себе ветхозаветного и апокалиптического Илью. В толковании на Псалом 44 — одном из самых мрачных эсхатологических произведений Аввакума — он представляет себя Ильей, связанным, лишенным сил: «Воли мне нет, да силы — перерезал бы, что Илья пророк, студных и мерских жрецов всех, что собак» (стлб. 458). Несколько ниже, в том же сочинении, Аввакум описывает, в полном соответствии с традиционными источниками, явление Ильи, Еноха и Иоанна Богослова, их смерть и вознесение, и продолжающиеся при том казни на земле. Ко всему этому добавлено: « ... Как то и ныне на Москве жгут, и по городам жгут ... Толко последне-ет чорт не бывал еще» (стлб. 462 с примечаниями). Единственное маленькое отступление от традиционных учений, допущенное, по-видимому, ради усугубления сходства между апокалиптическими пророками и нынешними, — утверждение, будто Илья и Енох придут и будут проповедовать до пришествия антихристова.

Обычно произведения древнерусской словесности, испытывавшие влияние эсхатологических слов и пророчеств, заимствовали из них картины бедствий и мучений; это делает и Аввакум, но в незначительной степени. Ему не близок дух покаяния, скорби и отчаяния, свойственный таким, описывающим последние дни, «словам». При всей силе Аввакумова эсхатологизма, его произведения лишь во фрагментах могут быть отнесены к роду эсхатологических «откровений» и «слов»; главное его занятие — это проповедь в защиту истинной веры и деяния в борьбе за веру.

Защита и проповедь веры во имя Царства Небесного перед лицом гибнущего мира — эти сугубо позитивные, вскормленные московским мессианизмом, основы Аввакумовой эсхатологии — сближают ее с эсхатологией апостолов. Осознавая величие русского благоверия как последнего и священное значение последней битвы за него, он испытывает необходимость опираться на священные образцы проповеди христианской веры в ее величайшей чистоте — на послания и Деяния апостолов.

* * *

Множество серьезных исследований, посвященных *Житию* Аввакума, ставят своей задачей изыскание традиции, к которой восходит форма автобиографического жития. Исследовательская потребность рассматривать творчество Аввакума в его традиционности отчасти обусловлена возросшим в последние десятилетия уважением к старообрядцам как традиционалистам — хранителям древних культурных ценностей. Первым в ряду таких работ стоит исследование С. А. Зеньковского, показавшего, что в автобиографическом повествовании нет для древнерусской литературы ничего необыкновенного; напротив, автобиографическое начало сильно развито в писаниях Грозного, присутствует в житиях, завещаниях, «хожениях» и пр.[29] Автобиографизм, как это следует из наблюдений Зеньковского, не является специальным достоянием какой-либо определенной традиции.

Сам Аввакум чувствовал необходимость оправдаться в своем деле — писании *Жития* — которое, видимо, ему самому казалось не совсем обыкновенным. В одном из вступлений к *Житию* в последней редакции он сослался на авву Дорофея, рассказывавшего о себе в поучениях своим ученикам, что дает некоторое основание рассматривать *Житие* как исповедь духовному отцу. А. Н. Робинсон, имея в виду эти отсылки, проанализировал некоторые повествовательные аспекты *Жития*, определив его как исповедь-проповедь.[30] Определение традиций *Жития* не было для него первостепенной задачей, и он не сделал этого. Ссылка Аввакума на Дорофея почти фиктивна.[31] И проповедь Дорофея, и проповедническая литература вообще допускают лишь незначительные иллюстративные автобиографические вкрапления. Так что проповедь не могла подготовить почвы для Аввакумова *Жития*. Мысль Робинсона об исповедальном характере *Жития* развила Н. С. Понырко.[32] Она указала, что исповедь с благословения духовного отца может составлять часть духовного завещания. Определив *Житие* как духовное завещание, она вместила его, таким образом, в устойчивую традицию древнерусской словесности. Однако завещания в Древней Руси обязательно включали в себя также благословения, завещательные формулы, указания, что они составляются в преддверии смерти. Не имея ни одного из этих признаков, *Житие* Аввакума может считаться завещанием только метафорически.

Из всех авторских самооправдательных ссылок на традицию в *Житии* наиболее значимы ссылки на пример апостолов, тоже рассказывавших о своих деяниях (*П.сб.*, с. 80). Право на высказывание всего того, что сказано в *Житии*, Аввакум получает непосредственно от апостолов:

Иное было, кажется, и не надобно говорить, да прочтох Деяния апостольская и Послания Павлова — апостоли о себе возвещали жо, егда Бог соделает в них. Не нам, Богу нашему слава! (*П.сб.*, с. 59).

Эти объяснения находятся в соответствии с многочисленными параллелями к событиям текущей жизни, которые заимствованы Аввакумом из посланий и Деяний апостолов. Обычные переживания и обыденные обстоятельства поднимаются и освещаются в *Житии* своим соответствием со Священным Писанием.[33] Страх Аввакума и его товарищей — это апостольский страх, невежество Аввакума — Павлово невежество, крещение сына в дороге — крещение эфиопа апостолом Филиппом, и т. д. (*П.сб.*, стр. 20, 41, 60). Понимание своего служения как апостольского, оправданное эсхатологическим мироощущением Аввакума, уже разбиралось выше. Но соотнесенностью с Деяниями и посланиями апостолов не исчерпывается природа *Жития*.

Жития святых принадлежат к тем немногим жанрам древнерусской словесности, которые имеют свою четкую жанровую модель. Этой модели следует Аввакум, начиная повествование подобающими сообщениями о родителях и кончая необходимым для полноценного жития перечнем «посмертных» чудес.[34] *Житие* Аввакума является, таким образом, памятником автоагиографии.

С. А. Зеньковский, из двух пустозерских житий имевший в виду преимущественно *Житие* Епифания, выявил несколько древнерусских автобиографов, предшествовавших Епифанию и даже, возможно, на него повлиявших. Н. С. Демкова расширила эти наблюдения и определила группу севернорусских житий святых, составивших традицию для пустозерских автобиографий.[35] В ряду этих памятников значатся автобиографические записки Герасима Болдинского, Лазаря Муромского, Мартирия Зеленецкого, Елеазара Анзерского. Перечисленные повествования в основном представляют собой рассказы от первого лица о чудесных явлениях горних сил, прежде всего Богоматери, и о том покровительстве, которое оказывалось высшими силами келье или монастырю, основанному рассказчиком. Такие рассказы встречаются в патериках (особенно палестинской традиции) и прологах. К этой линии принадлежит и *Житие* Епифания. Недаром две из трех ссылок на книжные источники, сделанные Епифанием в *Житии* (третья — на Златоуста, все остальные цитаты и заимствования — слова молитв и псалмов), — это ссылки на патериковые рассказы.

Автобиографические записки — свидетельства о событиях, испытаниях, чудесах — могли быть включены в патерики или прологи без изменений, но для жития святого они были недостаточны. Из перечисленных, записки Мартирия и Лазаря функционировали как духовные завещания.[36] Записки Мартирия и Герасима позже были использованы агиографами в работе над житиями этих святых.[37] Составитель жития Елеазара Анзерского не пользовался запиской его, ему не удалось ее найти.[38] Пустозерское *Житие* Епифания тоже составило основу большого его жития, написанного в 30-е годы XVIII века в Выговской общине. Новое произведение в основном воспроизводило сведения «автобиографии», называвшейся здесь «книжицей», но сделало принципиально важное добавление: сообщило о чудесной смерти Епифания.[39] Житие святого вообще могло включать весьма большую долю автобиографического повествования — как, например, столь любимое на Руси житие Андрея Юродивого, с рассказами святого о своих чудесных видениях. Но оно не могло быть чисто автобиографическим, поскольку святость святого должна была быть засвидетельствована другими лицами, что выражалось описанием посмертных чудес, или хотя бы, она должна была быть признана миром, что выражалось актом составления жития другим лицом. Таким образом, автобиографические записки сами по себе не являлись житиями святых. Это был вспомогательный материал, способный служить для разных целей, в том числе, при условии переделки, для агиографии.

Повествование Аввакума, построенное в соответствии с агиографической моделью, включает и эпизоды патерикового типа, и его собственные свидетельства о совершенных им исцелениях, и даже свидетельство, полученное от других лиц о его чудесном и спасительном явлении: «Как моим образом человек ему явился во сне, и путь указал, в которую сторону итти» (*П.сб.*, с. 40). То есть, *Житие* Аввакума представляет собой беспрецедентный в истории древнерусской словесности случай автоагиографии. И это тем более поразительно, что оно существовало в близком соседстве и взаимодействовало с *Житием* Епифания — достаточно традиционным повествованием от первого лица.

Епифаний сообщает о чудесных исцелениях, им полученных, и о видениях, ему открывшихся; получивший небесные дары традиционно свидетельствует о них. Аввакум, как агиограф, опираясь на цитаты из Писания, свидетельствует о подобии земных событий и лиц — священным.

Если взглянуть на *Житие* Аввакума, отрешившись от его автобиографизма, то в качестве памятника древнерусской агиографии оно обнаружит свойство — стремление к чересчур высоким образцам — которое вообще характерно для Аввакумова творчества. В контексте правильного жития новозаветные параллели преобретают характер указания на образцы святости, которым следует прославляемый в житии святой. Образцы Аввакума стоят на вершине иерархии. Святость его — весьма редкая для древнерусской традиции — равноапостольная, и даже более того: страсти его — это страсти Христовы.

Как указал еще В. В. Виноградов и вслед за ним, в новейших исследованиях, П. Хант и Й. Бёртнес, центральная часть *Жития* — сцена расстрижения Аввакума — наполнена евангельскими реминисценциями. Страдания Аввакума уподобляются в ней страстям Христовым, и соборное осуждение, сопровождаемое помрачением солнца, становится символической смертью героя *Жития*.[40] П. Хант, опираясь на работы Г. П. Федотова по русскому религиозному сознанию, отметила небывалую для русской традиции степень приближения героя *Жития* к Христу — русская традиция вообще обычно не допускала идеи подражания Христу и, соответственно, описания подражаний-имитаций, но только последование Ему.[41]

П. Хант проанализировала и видение из пятой челобитной Аввакума к царю Алексею Михайловичу как еще один пример самоуподобления Богу[42] и совершенно справедливо связала его с эсхатологическим миросозерцанием Аввакума. Степень подобия Христу — Судье Страшного суда — в видении пятой челобитной, когда Аввакум почувствовал, как Господь вместил в него весь мир, — кощунственна. Так воспринял это видение уже Дмитрий Ростовский, указавший, что Аввакум уподобился в нем сатане.[43] Параллели же, проведенные в *Житии* между страданиями Аввакума и страстями Христа, допустимы в рамках христианской словесности, хотя и чужды русскому православию. В этом случае исключительный эсхатологизм Аввакума проявляется в кощунственном акте писания собственного жития как жития святого — т. е. в автоканонизации.

Таким образом, в произведениях Аввакума обнаруживаются отклонения от норм христианства. И если видение своей всеобъемлемости в пятой челобитной еще и можно считать эксцессом, преувеличением, из которого необязательно делать широкие выводы, то создание автобиографического жития — многолетняя, многоэтапная работа, и ее необходимо рассматривать как выражение основ мироощущения Аввакума, как строительство формы этого мироощущения.

* * *

В эсхатологии Аввакума, в основном канонической, есть представления и идеи совершенно неканонические, возникшие вследствие необходимости самостоятельно ответить на вопросы, которые не обсуждались отцами Церкви. Само возникновение таких вопросов у Аввакума и у его сторонников обусловливалось чувством национально-религиозной исключительности перед лицом всеобщей гибели.

Аввакума весьма занимала проблема судьбы блюстителей истинного благоверия в последние времена, мало освещенная отцами Церкви и апостолами. Для носителей благоверия в традиционных источниках была предусмотрена чисто страдательная роль: они терпят гонения, принимают мучения. Содержание последних дней для них — испытание в твердости веры. Со ссылками на Кирилла Иерусалимского, Ипполита, Иоанна Дамаскина и др., *Книга о вере* указывает: «Блажен обрящется той, иже тогда не соблазнится и претерпит таковую лютость гонения, и аще бы Господь Бог не прекратил оных дней, не бы убо спаслася всякая тварь...».[44]

Тема гонений не могла быть основной для Аввакума, воспитанного идеями Третьего Рима; главные силы он отдавал прославлению русского благоверия, последнего на земле.

Стойкость русского благоверия в лице его самого и его товарищей ощущалась Аввакумом как триумф, сравнимый с триумфом Нового и Ветхого Заветов. Смерть ревнителей — мученическая смерть в уподобление Христу — становилась завершением земных путей благоверия, торжественным приобщением к небесным чинам. «На что лутче сего? С мученики в чин, со Апостолы в полк, со святители в лик, победный венец, сообщник Христу, Святей Троице престолу предстоя со ангелы и архангелы и со всеми безплотными, с предивными роды вчинен!» (стлб. 571).

Никонианам, даже Антихристу в этих заключительных актах эсхатологической мистерии отводилась служебная роль: они были орудием последнего славного мучения, предваряющего и приготовляющего переход в Царствие Небесное. Антихрист в глазах Аввакума не мог сохранить значение всеобъемлющей силы зла. Аввакум считал, что власть его не распространится на истинных носителей благоверия. В качестве комментария к посланию ап. Павла к Галатам в связи с мыслью Павла о христианской свободной воле Аввакум помещает рассказ о привидевшейся ему встрече с Антихристом. Антихрист смутился перед Аввакумом и сказал: «Что ты, протопоп, на меня кричишь? Я нехотящих не могу обладать...», — и поклонился ему (стлб. 360).

Свобода от власти зла для «нехотящих», по Аввакуму, заключена в возможности выбора самоубийственной смерти.[45] Нехристианская по сути проповедь самоубийства, настойчиво осуществляемая Аввакумом в беседах, толкованиях и посланиях, и есть то звено в системе представлений его, где произошел разрыв с традицией. Смерть добровольная и смерть вынужденная уравниваются Аввакумом в общем значении победы в борьбе за истинную веру. Смерть полностью исключает опасность отступничества и обеспечивает сохранение величайшего сокровища — последнего благоверия.

В среде учеников Аввакума возник вопрос о возможности почитать сжегшихся и сожженных за веру как святых. В прямом ответе, где потребовалось коснуться обрядовых деталей, Аввакум высказался осторожно, но не избежал противоречия. Он указал, что не следует поклоняться образам сожженных, пока их не прославит Бог, однако кости их можно вместе с крестом класть в воду при освящении ее, можно кадить мощам с молитвой и целовать перекрестясь. Однако в экстатических описаниях торжества огненной смерти он забывал об осторожности и прославлял святость сгорающих. Так, участь прошедших через огонь он определяет ссылаясь на Златоуста: «Тогда бо плоть святых легка будет, яко воспренна»,[46] — и продолжает: «Полетим, братия, тогда Надежю своего встречать с веселием, и с Ним воцаримся во веки веком», — это уже картина Второго пришествия и соучастия в нем русских мучеников (стлб. 574). Ср. Апокалипсис 22:4–5: «И узрят лице Его ... и воцарятся во веки веков». Характерно здесь «мы», вмещающее Аввакума в число горящих: он полагает себя уже прошедшим величайшие муки, тождественные мукам в горниле огня.

Таким образом, Аввакум оказывается создателем учения, согласно которому мученическая смерть делает человека святым и, соответственно, самовольная мученическая смерть становится чем-то вроде автоканонизации.

По Аввакуму, немногие избранные и на земле могут стать окончательным и безусловным воплощением благоверия. Те испытания, через которые прошла их вера — соборное расстрижение для самого Аввакума, казнь отрезанием языка и руки для Епифания, Боровская тюрьма для боярыни Морозовой — функционально соответствуют огненной смерти — средству сохранения веры, предусмотренному для слабых.[47]

Этими особенностями эсхатологии Аввакума было вызвано создание автоагиографического произведения с изображением многих жизненных мук и вершины их — соборного суда — как страстей Христовых, и соединение его с *Житием* Епифания в единый комплекс, призванный прославить последние торжества благоверия на земле.

* * *

Историческую перспективу и историческое значение житиям придавало «Снискание и собрание о Божестве и о твари» — сочинение Аввакума, присоединенное им к двум житиям в авторских пустозерских сборниках (в автографах так называемые Пустозерский сборник Дружинина и Пустозерский сборник Заволоко),[48] а также большая цитата из «Слова о вочеловечении» Иоанна Златоуста, помещенная непосредственно перед началом биографического повествования в *Житии* Аввакума, и цитата оттуда же — в конце *Жития* Епифания.

Начальная цитата из Златоуста — это диалог между Богом Отцом и Богом Сыном о создании человека по образу и подобию Бога и о будущей судьбе мира как помрачении богоподобия и новом соединении божественного и человеческого начал во Христе. Заключительная цитата у Епифания возвращает вновь к теме божественного образа в человеке, составляющей суть «Слова о вочеловечении».[49] «Снискание и собрание о Божестве и о твари» включает тот же диалог между Отцом и Сыном с добавлением фрагментов из того же Златоустова «Слова» — о негодовании твари на преступление Адама, о подчинении Богом твари Адаму и о провидении Богом в Адаме грядущих Петра и Павла. «Снискание» помещает фрагмент «Слова о вочеловечении» в подобающий ему контекст, расширяет тему божественного диалога, лишь указанную в начале и конце житийного комплекса, до подобающих ей размеров. Божественный диалог предварен рассуждением о первых днях творения, наводящих на мысль о подобии Аввакумова «Снискания» Шестодневу. Но, в отличие от составителя Шестоднева, Аввакум не интересуется мироустройством, явлениями природы, организмом человека, разнообразием животных и пр. «Тварь» занимает его лишь в отношении к человеку. «Снискание» концентрируется на первом периоде истории, расценивая начальные обстоятельства применительно к последующим, более поздним событиям, вплоть до Страшного Суда. В «Снискании» использованы фрагменты книги Бытия, рассуждения отцов Церкви и апостолов, апокрифические сказания из Палеи и сведения из Хронографа. Два последних источника Аввакум не цитирует, а пересказывает, очевидно, по памяти, вводя в текст отсылки, часто произвольные. Ссылки на Хронограф особенно многочисленны, хотя в действительности хронографического материала в «Снискании» не столь много.

Аввакум, работая над «Снисканием», по-видимому, держит в памяти Хронограф как целое, как обширное повествование о судьбах человечества с первых дней творения до последних времен. Именно таким было построение Русского хронографа (ред. 1512 г.), который (как полагает Н. С. Демкова, исходя из анализа хронографического материала в произведениях Аввакума) и служил источником для Аввакума.[50]

В Русском хронографе по некоторым спискам тексту предпослан «Летописчик вкратце» — исчисление лет по периодам от Адама «до конца седмыя тысяща»,[51] т. е. до последних времен. Аввакум кончает «Снискание» кратким исчислением лет от Авраама до «сих мест» (*П.сб.*, стр. 112). Эта параллель — вовсе не доказательство влияния «Летописчика» на «Снискание», она только показывает общность масштабов временной перспективы в Русском хронографе и у Аввакума.

Пустозерские писатели — дьякон Федор и Аввакум — вообще часто обращались к Хронографу; они черпали оттуда эпизоды византийской истории, рассказывающие о борьбе с ересями, о столкновениях царей-еретиков с благоверными архиепископами, о преследованиях истинной веры, которые чинили властители-еретики, и об ужасных небесных карах, от которых они погибали или приходили в раскаяние.[52] История в глазах пустозерских учителей представлялась борьбой за чистоту благоверия, и такое представление о ней соответствовало направлению Хронографа, им воспитывалось.

Русский хронограф вошел в обиход отцов старообрядчества по причинам весьма конкретным. Дьякон Федор ссылается на «Гранограф» в «Ответе православных», перечисляя «свидетельства от Святаго Писания о крестном знамении».[53] В некоторых списках именно Русского хронографа редакции 1512 г. присутствует вводная часть — «Изложение о вере», где, со ссылкой на блаженного Феодорита, приведено рассуждение об истинности и о сути двуперстного крестного знамения.[54]

Появление в Хронографе этого рассуждения и, соответственно, обращение к нему защитников старой веры ни в коем случае не может считаться случайным. Связь с Хронографом через «Слово» Феодорита есть выражение глубинных отношений, связывающих Русский хронограф с идеологией пустозерских отцов.

В Русском хронографе впервые в крупных масштабах русские события были соединены с событиями мировой истории. Влившись в общий поток, они оказались подчиненными общей концепции хронографических сводов — идее сменяемости мировых царств согласно толкованиям на книгу пророка Даниила. Христианский период включал, по

Хронографу, события новозаветные, падение Иерусалима, падение Рима и затем длинное повествование о Византии и странах православного славянского мира. К концу Хронографа все православные страны оказывались пришедшими к своей гибели, последним и единственным в перспективе Хронографа оставалось Русское Московское царство, сосредоточившее в себе силу и величие мирового исторического движения и принявшее ответственность за судьбу мира в его последние дни. После известий о падении Царьграда Русский хронограф в ред. 1512 г. продолжался сообщениями только о русских событиях. В идеологическом отношении Хронограф, как и послания Филофея, служил подготовительным этапом для Стоглавого собора. Он был вовлечен в сферу идей «Стоглава». Свидетельство тому — появление в некоторых списках Хронографа «Изложения о вере» с защитой двуперстия по Феодориту, соответствующего решениям «Стоглава», которые тоже опирались на авторитет Феодорита.[55]

Таким образом, Русский хронограф повлиял на масштабы мировосприятия Аввакума и прямо, и косвенно; он вообще определял начальный этап того развития идеологии Третьего Рима, завершителем которого был Аввакум.[56]

Эта общность масштабов мировосприятия сказалась на сходстве введения к Хронографу и введения к *Житию* Аввакума, играющему одновременно роль введения ко всему Пустозерскому сборнику. И то и другое — исповедания веры с изложением троичного догмата и некоторых других положений, служивших в соответствующее время предметами полемических споров; оба введения включают стихи из книги Бытия о замысле Божием сотворить человека по образу и подобию Своему с толкованиями сходных традиций (у Аввакума — по «Слову о вочеловечении» Златоуста, в Хронографе — по Слову о четвертом дне творения Севериана Габальского,[57] близкому традиции «Слова о вочеловечении»). События основного повествования, освещаемые этими введениями, получают смысл борьбы за чистоту божественного образа в человечестве как борьбы за чистоту благоверия против отступничества и отступников. И если в Хронографе последней силой благоверия является Русское государство, то в Пустозерском сборнике последние столпы благоверия — это Аввакум и Епифаний; из-за отступничества царя и церковных властей судьба благоверия перестает совпадать с судьбой русского царства и сосредоточивается в двух *Житиях*.

Таким образом, Пустозерский сборник в его целостности создан Аввакумом, наподобие Хронографа, как описание начала и конца в историческом пути человечества — от сотворения человека по образу и подобию Божьему до последнего утверждения богоподобия в Аввакуме и Епифании. Эсхатологический национализм Третьего Рима развивается на конечном этапе в эсхатологический индивидуализм протопопа Аввакума.

* * *

Итак, протопоп Аввакум со всей свойственной ему энергией стремился придерживаться «писаного», блюсти установления христианской словесности, не удаляться от уже сказанного авторитетного слова. В этих стремлениях он проявлял небывалую для древнерусского книжника решительность.

Аввакум не последовал традициям древнерусской словесности и древнерусской святости в их благоговейно-отдаленном отношении к высшим священным образцам. Декларативно столь почитая древнерусское благоверие, Аввакум не подражал его носителям и почти никогда не ссылался на них в своих сочинениях. Образцы собственно русского ряда оказывались неудобными для него, поскольку были порождены серединной частью истории, в то время как деятельность Аввакума в его понимании принадлежала краю истории, поднимающемуся к сакральным вершинам.

Сбросив связывающие и сдерживающие оковы местной традиции, Аввакум вступил в столь непосредственное соприкосновение с высшими священными образцами, что оказался на грани христианских норм вообще. Как вероучитель, он претендовал на авторитет, недосягаемый в обычных исторических условиях, как деятель, он претендовал на статус святого, недосягаемый при жизни. Все эти претензии были порождены отнюдь не личной самонадеянностью, они естественно вытекали из понимания происходящего как последней битвы за благоверие, центр которой находится в Пустозерске, — понимания, подготовленного и вскормленного целым периодом культурно-исторического развития России. В эсхатологическом творчестве Аввакума констатируется конец этого периода, понимаемый как конец мира.

Стоя на краю истории, Аввакум добавлял к Священному Писанию последние события. Этот род книжной деятельности прервал все традиции уже хотя бы потому, что эсхатологический накал, достигнутый Аввакумом, не мог воспроизводиться и продлеваться. Характерно, что книжность Выго-Лексинской старообрядческой общины не стала наследницей Аввакума, но и не продолжила непосредственно древнерусских традиций. Для поддержания сколько-нибудь длительного существования выго-лексинской литературе потребовалась прививка новой киевской учености.

Творчество Аввакума стало литературным фактом и получило возможность воздействовать на литературный процесс лишь во второй половине XIX века, в эпоху позитивизма, когда в Аввакуме смогли увидеть бунтаря-демократа, а сверхнапряженные образы его писаний стали восприниматься в метафорическом плане. И до сих пор оно, в известной мере, оценивается как продукт художественной деятельности, а не как последний закономерный процесс в религиозной жизни Древней Руси.

Примечания

1. Эсхатологическая направленность идей Филофея анализировалась уже Малининым: В. Малинин, *Старец Елеазарова монастыря Филофей и его послания* (Киев, 1901). Об этом же и о восприятии в эпоху раскола формулы «Москва — Третий Рим» как эсхатологической см.: Г. Флоровский, *Пути русского богословия* (Paris, 1937), стр. 11. О влиянии комплекса представлений о Москве как Третьем Риме на старообрядчество: С. А. Зеньковский. *Русское старообрядчество: Духовные движения XVII в.* (München, 1970), Гл. 1.

2. В 20–50-е годы XVII в. в политике Московского правительства заметно влияние национально-мессианских представлений. С. А. Зеньковский (op. cit.) рассматривает в этом ключе «грекофильскую» деятельность Никона и царя Алексея Михайловича. Наиболее существенные меры, предпринимавшиеся правительствами первых Романовых для воплощения в жизнь формулы «Москва — Третий Рим» (или, что то же самое, — Новый Царьград) — это сосредоточивание в Москве святынь православного мира. См. Н. Каптерев, *Характер отношений России к православному Востоку в XVI и XVII столетиях* (М., 1885).

В ретроспективе первых вождей старообрядчества, пустозерских отцов, Московское царство 20–40-хх годов виделось воплощением последнего царства благоверия, описанного в «Откровении» Мефодия Патарского и в других источниках. В царе Михаиле Романове видели образ эсхатологического царя Михаила, которому суждено вручить свое царство Богу. Символом святости Московского царства считалась риза Господня, полученная московским правительством от шаха Аббаса в 1625 г. См. челобитные попа Лазаря царю и патриарху из Пустозерска 1669 г.: *Материалы для истории раскола за первое время его существования*, изд. Н. Субботин. т. 4 (М., 1876).

3. Сочинения Аввакума цитируются по изданию: *Памятники истории старообрядчества XVII века*, кн. 1, вып. 1 (Л., изд. АН СССР, 1927); номера столбцов (стлб.) указываются в тексте статьи после цитат.

4. См. П. С. Смирнов, *Внутренние вопросы в расколе в XVII веке* (СПб., 1898), гл. 4, раздел «Догматические споры», стр. 219–233.

5. G. P. Fedotov, *The Russian Religious Mind* (New York, 1960); Г. П. Федотов, *Святые древней Руси (X–XVII ст.)* (Paris, 1931).
6. Д. С. Лихачев, «Зарождение и развитие жанров древнерусской литературы». В кн.: Лихачев, *Исследования по древнерусской литературе* (Л., 1986), стр. 8.
7. Изд. 2, кн. 1–2 (СПб., 1884).
8. *Сочинения преподобного Максима Грека*, ч. 1–3 (Троице-Сергиева лавра, 1910–1911). Толкования см.: т. 3, послания 1–9.
9. А. А. Алексеев, «К истории русской переводческой школы XII в.», *ТОДРЛ*, т. 41 (1988): 171, 176, 187 и др.
10. А. К. Бороздин, *Протопоп Аввакум* (СПб., 1898), стр. 237.
11. В. Ф. Певницкий, *Церковное красноречие и его основные законы* (СПб., 1908), стр. 111–112, 119.
12. См.: И. М. Кудрявцев, «Сборник с подписями протопопа Аввакума и других пустозерских узников», *Записки отдела рукописей ГБЛ*, вып. 33 (М., 1972), стр. 148–212.
13. «Житие Иоанна Златоуста», *Великие Минеи Четии*, ноябрь 13–15 (СПб., 1899), стлб. 963–965.
14. *Житие* Аввакума в последней авторской редакции и другие произведения, входящие в Пустозерский сборник (так наз. сборник Заволоко) цитируются по изданию: *Пустозерский сборник. Автографы сочинений Аввакума и Епифания* (Л., 1975). Номера страниц указываются в тексте в скобках с отметкой — *П.сб.*
15. «Житие Иоанна Златоуста», стлб. 1032.
16. А. К. Бороздин, *Протопоп Аввакум* (СПб., 1898), приложение, стр. 3.
17. Ibid., стр. 5.
18. Иван Филиппов. *История Выговской старообрядческой пустыни* (СПб., 1862), стр. 88. Филиппов заимствует употребление символа из «Винограда Российского» Семена Денисова. В писаниях выговских отцов символ корабля в бурном море преобретает характер термина, означающего Выговскую общину.
19. Т. С. Рождественский, *Памятники старообрядческой поэзии* [= *Записки Московского Археологического института*, т. 6] (М., 1910), № 101.
20. Характеристику книжных изданий Печатного двора на эсхатологические темы см. С. А. Зеньковский, op. cit., стр. 97–100.
21. «Книга иже во святых отца нашего Кирилла архиепископа Иерусалимского, на осмый век», *Кириллова книга* (М., 1644), л. 48 об.
22. Литература вопроса указана: H. Rothe, "Zur Kiever Literatur in Moskau, 2," *Slavistische Studien zum IX. Internationalen Slavistenkongress in Kiev, 1983* (Köln, Wien, 1983), стр. 428.
23. Ibid., 428–429.
24. *Книга о вере* (М., 1648), л. 27.
25. П. С. Смирнов, *Внутренние вопросы...*, стр. 12–13; Н. Ю. Бубнов, «Спиридон Потемкин и его 'Книга'», *ТОДРЛ*, 40 (1985): 345.
26. Об отзвуках русско-турецких конфликтов начала 1670-х гг. в сочинениях Аввакума: P. Pascal, *Avvakum et les débuts du raskol*, ed. 3 (Paris, 1969), стр. 502.

27. «Письмо Аввакума к царевне Ирине Михайловне», *Житие протопопа Аввакума им самим написанное и другие его сочинения* (М., 1960), стр. 202.

28. См. Обращение к Симеону из *Книги Толкований* (стлб. 568– 569).

29. S. A. Zenkovsky, "Der Mönch Epifanij und die Entstehung der altrussischen Autobiographie," *Die Welt der Slaven* (Wiesbaden, 1956), Jrg. 1, H. 3.

30. А. Н. Робинсон. «Исповедь-проповедь (о художественности Жития Аввакума)». В кн.: *Историко-филологические исследования. Сб. статей к 75-летию акад. Н. И. Конрада* (М., 1967), стр. 358–370. Он же о пустозерском автобиографизме — в кн.: *Жизнеописание Аввакума и Епифания* (М., 1963), стр. 58–86.

31. См. комментарий к ссылке Аввакума на Дорофея: *Пустозерский сборник*, стр. 430.

32. Н. В. Понырко. «Житие протопопа Аввакума как духовное завещание», *ТОДРЛ*, 39 (1985): 379–387.

33. Роль библейских текстов в *Житии* замечательно охарактеризована В. В. Виноградовым в статье «О задачах стилистики: наблюдения над стилем *Жития* протопопа Аввакума», в кн.: В. В. Виноградов, *О языке художественной прозы* (М., 1980).

34. О посмертных чудесах и других чертах агиографии в *Житии*: см. А. Н. Робинсон, *Жизнеописание Аввакума и Епифания*, стр. 43–47, 64–82; Н. С. Демкова, *Житие протопопа Аввакума* (Л., 1974), стр. 156. Демкова отмечает усиление агиографической стилизации по ходу редактирования *Жития* Аввакумом (стр. 93 и др.).

35. Н. С. Демкова, *Житие протопопа Аввакума*, стр. 161–163.

36. См. Н. В. Понырко, op. cit.

37. В. Ключевский, *Древнерусские жития святых как исторический источник* (М., 1871), стр. 305, 346. «Автобиография» Герасима Болдинского по сообщениям Ключевского и Арс. Кадлубовского тоже представляла собой духовное завещание (А. Кадлубовский, *Очерки по истории древне-русской литературы. Жития святых* [Варшава, 1902], стр. 293).

38. «Житие преп. Елеазара Анзерского», *Православный собеседник*, ч. 1 (Казань, 1860). Ср.: «Келейная записка преподобного отца нашего Елеазара о зачатии жития его на Анзерском острове и о устроении скита, о разных видениях его и о прочем» — Рукописный отдел ГБЛ, Опт. (214) 273.

39. «Житие и подвиги чюдного отца инока Епифания, который скончался во благочестии в пустозерском городе с чюдными страдальцы протопопом Аввакумом и со священником Лазарем и с диаконом Феодором». — Отдел рукописей ГПБ, Q, I. 1062. — О нем см.: Н. В. Понырко, «Кирилло-Епифаниевский житийный цикл...», *ТОДРЛ*, 29 (1974).

40. В. В. Виноградов, «О задачах стилистики...», стр. 9–10. P. Hunt. "The Autobiography of the Archpriest Avvakum: Structure and Function," *Ricerche slavistiche*, 23 (1975–76):155–176; П. Хант, «Самооправдание протопопа Аввакума», *ТОДРЛ*, 32 (1977):70–84. Jostein Børtnes, "The Life of Avvakum," in *Visions of Glory* (Oslo, 1988), стр. 266–267; о том же в связи с тенденциями народной религиозности XVII– XVIII вв.: М. Плюханова, «О некоторых чертах личностного сознания в России XVII в.», *Художественный язык средневековья* (М., 1982), стр. 184–200.

41. P. Hunt, *A Penitential Journey: The Life of the Archpriest Avvakum* (in press).

Между прочим, этой особенностью русской традиции можно объяснить негативную реакцию некоторых русских ученых на понимание центральной части *Жития* как *passio* и вообще на анализ случаев самоуподобления Аввакума Христу. Н. С. Демкова, *Житие протопопа Аввакума,* стр. 148 (против Б. Илека); А. М. Панченко, *Русская культура в канун петровских реформ* (Л., 1984), стр. 33–35 (против П. Хант и М. Плюхановой); возражения Хант см. в ее статье "Eschatological Myth and the Writings of the Archpriest Avvakum" в настоящем сборнике; возражения Плюхановой — в рецензии на книгу А. М. Панченко, *Литературное обозрение* (1986), No. 8.

42. P. Hunt, "Eschatological Myth...".

43. [Дм. Ростовский.] *Розыск о раскольнической брынской вере...* (М., 1847), стр. 79–80.

44. *Книга о вере* (М., 1648), л. 270 об.

45. П. С. Смирнов, наиболее полно описавший учение Аввакума о самоубийственной смерти, считал, что оно находится в противоречии с его же идеей о бессилии Антихриста перед теми, кто хочет сохранить веру. См. П. С. Смирнов, *Внутренние вопросы в расколе в XVII веке,* гл. 1, стр. 62–66 и др. П. С. Смирнов не учитывал, что Аввакуму и его последователям, ощущавшим себя «на краю» времени, граница между жизнью посюсторонней и потусторонней казалась почти стершейся. См. об этом подробно: М. Плюханова, «О некоторых чертах народной эсхатологии в России XVII–XVIII веков», *Acta et commentationes universitatis Tartuensis,* 645 (Tartu, 1985), стр. 54–70.

Свобода от власти Антихриста мыслилась Аввакумом как свобода вообще, а не как возможность избежать его власти обязательно в этой, земной, жизни.

46. В оригинале — в беседе Златоуста, там, где говорится о легкости духовного тела, о святости не упомянуто. См. Кудрявцев, op. cit., стр. 193.

47. Аввакум в своих произведениях создает прижизненный культ боярыни Морозовой и ее соузниц, настойчиво отождествляя их пребывание в Боровской тюрьме с пребыванием трех отроков в печи вавилонской.

48. «Снискание» — сочинение почти неизученное. Небольшое описание и комментарий к «Снисканию» см.: *Пустозерский сборник,* стр. 179–185, 243–248. Здесь рассматриваем «Снискание» в контексте сборника Заволоко, то есть в Пустозерском сборнике последней авторской редакции, используя указанные замечания исследователей (Н. С. Демковой и др.), а также источниковедческие наблюдения А. К. Бороздина (Бороздин, *Протопоп Аввакум* [СПб., 1898], стр. 226–270).

49. «Слово о вочеловечении Господа нашего Исуса Христа и указание, яко над всякою страною предстательствуют ангелы». *Маргарит* (М., 1641), л. 469–490.

50. Н. С. Сарафанова (Демкова), «Произведения древнерусской письменности в сочинениях Аввакума», *ТОДРЛ,* 18 (1962): 333, 339.

51. «Русский хронограф», ч. 1. «Хронограф редакции 1512 года». *Полное собрание русских летописей,* т. 22 (СПб., 1911), стр. 19–20.

52. У дьякона Федора в послании сыну Максиму — о Константине Копрониме и Юлиане Отступнике и др.: *Материалы для истории раскола...,* т. 6 (М., 1881), стр. 217–219, ср. Хронограф, стр. 321–376. У Аввакума хронографический

материал в наибольшем количестве представлен в приложениях к толкованию на Псалом 44.

53. *Материалы...*, т. 6, стр. 274; то же в «письме», поданном собору 1666 г.: стр. 5.

54. «Хронограф», стр. 18–19.

55. *Стоглав* (Казань, 1862), глава 31, стр. 131–136.

56. Новейшее исследование показало, что соединение Русского хронографа с украинскими полемиками против унии произошло в русской рукописной традиции уже в 20–е годы XVII века, в составе *Просветителя Литовского* — сборника, ставшего потом основой «Кирилловой книги». В *Просветитель Литовский* входило и «Изложение о вере» — введение к Хронографу, и отдельные главы из Хронографа о ересях и борьбе с ними. — См.: Т. А. Опарина, «*Просветитель Литовский* — неизвестный памятник идеологической борьбы XVII века», *Литература и классовая борьба эпохи позднего феодализма в России* (Новосибирск, 1987), стр. 43–57.

57. «Хронограф», стр. 14–15; «Слово Севериана Габальского» — в кн.: *Творения Иоанна Златоуста*, т. 5 (Пг., б.г.), стр. 393, 408–409. Эта традиция толкований передавалась, по-видимому, через Палею. См.: А. Н. Попов, «Книга Эразма о св. Троице», *ЧОИДР*, кн. 4 (1880):2.

Maria Pliukhanova/Summary: Tradition and Originality: Archpriest Avvakum's Works in Light of the "Third Rome" Tradition

The writings of the Protopop Avvakum are examined as the ultimate stage in the religious life of Old Russia. Following tradition is evident in Avvakum's texts in his adherence to hagiographic canons and in his faithfulness to the concept of the Word's carrying unquestionable authority. Avvakum shared the eschatological expectations of his predecessors (*Russian Chronograph*), who interpreted current events as the final battle for the true faith ("Moscow, the Third Rome"). The exceptional intensity of his eschatological expectations resulted in Avvakum's equating his times with the Apostolic times and his identifying with the Apostles and even with Christ. In this Avvakum breaks with the Old Russian tradition of a respectfully distanced attitude toward sacred models and writes his own *Life* in the genre of autohagiography. His blasphemous attempt at self-canonization is accompanied by the no less blasphemous insistence on the sanctity of voluntary death. In Avvakum the eschatological nationalism of the Third Rome evolved into eschatological individualism.

The Evolution of Church Music in Belorussia

GUY PICARDA

The Greek-Rite Churches

The systematic study of church music in Belorussia is a relatively recent phenomenon. Texts from the seventeenth century in the *Litovskaia Metrika,* however, ecclesiastical reports and letters, such as those of Archimandrite Kimbar of Suprasl' (sixteenth century), and accounts of travelers such as Paul of Aleppo (1654) were already recording distinctions between a Ukrainian and a Belorussian tradition of church music. Manuscript collections of chants such as the Zhyrovitsy *Irmologion* (1649) provide alternative Belorussian (*belorusskoe*) and Ukrainian (*ukrainskoe*) variants of the hymn "Da ispolniatsia usta nasha" (Let Our Mouths).[1] Recent research into the field of comparative liturgy has highlighted differences of ritual and text existing between Vil'nia (Vilnius) and Kiev.[2] As for Muscovy or Great Russia, its musical traditions had by the seventeenth century evolved in a manner so different from those of its Western neighbors that the introduction of "heretical" chants from Belorussia and the Ukraine was one of the prime causes of the Old Believer schism (*raskol*) among Russian traditionalists.[3]

The existence of a variety of musical traditions among the Eastern Slavs of Rus' was noted by the earlier musical historians in this field—Dm. Razumovsky, Smolensky, Metallov, Preobrazhensky, Findeizen, and especially I. Voznesensky—more often as a peripheral departure from the "mainstream" of Great Russian church music, tainted with *nekanonichnyi* (uncanonical) and possibly Latin-rite usages. Moreover, their use after 1596 among the Uniates rendered them doubly heinous in the eyes of Synodal purists.[4]

Late nineteenth-century Belorussian ethnographers such as P. Shein, Ramanaŭ, and Nikifaroŭski contributed valuable research into the paraliturgical aspects of folk music and the hymns passed on by oral tradition or noted in handwritten *Bahahlasniki* (hymnbooks) widely popular among Belorussians and Ukrainians alike, but generally alien to the Great Russian tradition.

Perhaps the most significant contribution to the study of church music in Belorussia was the work of nineteenth- and twentieth-century bibliographers, in particular F. Dobriansky, A. Petrushevich, and latterly by Iu. Iasinoŭs'kyi, in identifying the few surviving *Irmologia* chantbooks and *Bahahlasniki* recorded in *belorusskaia skoropis'* (Belorussian cursive) and scattered in various libraries and collections throughout the Russian Empire.[5]

Despite the scope of all this research, an objective study of Belorussian church music was inhibited by the tsarist policy, particularly after the national uprisings of 1831 and 1863, of suppressing any manifestation of a distinctive Belorussian cultural or religious life and later by the constraints of dogmatic officialdom after the events of 1917. Only in the present century, and more particularly since the late 1960s, has any serious possibility existed of giving even a general outline of the development of liturgical music in Belorussia since its beginnings in the tenth century.

The Early Znamenny Chants

Christianity came to the East Slavic lands after 988 from Constantinople together with liturgical music, probably brought by Slavonic-speaking missionaries from Bulgaria and Serbia. The present study is not intended to deal at any great length with the early development of church music in Belorussia; little is known about it, and there is little to add to what has already appeared in earlier publications.[6]

Although for many centuries after its introduction, the Byzantine liturgy was sung at least partly in Greek, particularly during pontifical offices, the original Greek or South Slavic chants that accompanied it were soon adapted to local usages as they spread through the Ukraine across vast distances, northwest to Belorussia, and northeast to Novgorod, and thence "to all the cities and monasteries of the Great Russian eparchy."[7]

In Belorussia, churches were built and choir schools established in Polatsk (Polotsk) and Vitsebsk (Vitebsk) (992), Turaŭ (Turov) (1005), and Smalensk (Smolensk) (1101). In the latter city Bishop Manuil the Castrate, known as an eminent singer, had "come from Greece with two others."[8] Little is known of these early chants, and no manuscript chantbooks seem to have survived in Belorussia prior to the sixteenth century. Given the nature of later known chants, it may be assumed that, much like Gregorian plainchant in the West, there was an original, relatively uniform chant noted in Byzantine neumes of *kriuki*, of which variants developed according to conditions prevailing in different areas. Folk music and local particularisms doubtless had a part to play. A less rounded, more angular neumatic notation developed in the later medieval period; known as the *znamenny*, it gave its name to the chant. From this and other local sources, according to Voznesensky, a "South-Western" *znamenny* chant evolved, which became indigenous to the Ukrainians and Belorussians as the *kievski* chant. A few Belorussian collections of *znamenny* chants have survived in Galitsian and Polish libraries, probably dating from the late fifteenth and early sixteenth centuries. A summary transcription of one extract made by the late Professor J. Gardner reveals something of the similarities and distinctive features, in relation to other East Slavic versions.[9]

The divergence of the various East Slavic traditions was assisted by the division of the ecclesiastical jurisdiction between Kiev and Moscow in the late fifteenth century. Belorussia remained in the original Kievan Metropolitan See that inclined towards Union with Rome.

At about this time, local chants began to flourish and may have provided the corpus of *demestvenny* (court) chants to be found in some sixteenth-century *Irmologia*, possibly derived from the court chapels of the Magnates. The most prolific source of indigenous chants, however, was the growing number of monasteries such as those founded in the fifteenth and early sixteenth centuries in Vil'nia, Suprasl', Zhyrovitsy, Vitsebsk, and Mahiloŭ (Mogilev). Eastern monasteries to this day take pride in their particular customs and usages, and enterprising singers elaborated variants or original chants to promote the fame of their foundation as a seat of devotion and learning.[10]

There was, in addition, a considerable coming and going of prelates, choristers, icon painters, and pilgrims between the East Slavic lands and the Balkans, and visiting singers contributed many Greek (*hretski*), Serbian (*serbski*), and Bulgarian (*balharski*) chants to the earlier *znamenny* chantbooks.[11]

The Golden Age of the *Irmologion*

In times of national oppression, the Belorussians tended to look back with nostalgia to the days when their language was that of the governor and legislator, their culture flourished, and taxes were light.[12] Officialdom's attempts to belittle or dismiss the past achievements of the Belorussian people are at variance with the facts: the number, variety, and contents of the Belorussian *Irmologia* of the sixteenth and seventeenth centuries which have survived plunder and fire appear to justify folk memories of a Golden Age, at least in the field of church music.

The Renaissance and the religious upheavals of the sixteenth century brought to Belorussia Western linear notation, hymns, metrical psalms, polyphony, organs, and fresh aspects of Latin and Greek civilization. At some time between 1550, when at Suprasl' all the chantbooks were still in the *znamenny* notation, and 1598, the year of the first linear *Irmologion* in Suprasl', Western notation was introduced into Belorussian liturgical usage. This was possibly a result both of conversions to and from Calvinism and of the familiarity with the hymnody of the Niesviezh *Katechizm* (1563), printed in Belorussia, but in Polish, which was then in the ascendancy.

Compiled by a monk from Pinsk, Bahdan Anisimovich, and lavishly decorated with polychrome miniatures and delicately drawn headpieces, the manuscript of the monumental Suprasl' *Irmologion* (1598–1601) comprised both transcriptions of the earlier *znamenny* chants into linear notation and numerous chants indigenous to the monastery of Suprasl'—"siia est napeŭ M.S." (this is an M.S. chant)—or simply the letters "M.S.," *mirski* chants from the fortified town of Mir, and examples of *hretski napeŭ* and *balharski*, the former sometimes with a Greek text. There is no polyphony, and many items described as *suprasl'ski* or *suprazhski napeŭ* are, by their narrow melodic range, their length, and otherworldly monotone, more suited to the accompaniment of a Balkan-style drone than to four-part harmony.[13]

Although an *Irmologion,* as its name suggests, is essentially a collection of *irmosy* or the nine hymns sung during Matins, the earlier Belorussian *Irmologia* contain in addition all manner of chants for the Holy Liturgy, Vespers and Matins, Festival and Holy Week services, and are often, as a result of additions in other hands, relatively complete service books. Prior to 1697, all Belorussian service books with music were in manuscript.

Among the surviving volumes known to be of Belorussian origin and appearing as such in the catalogues of Kiev, Vilnius, Moscow, Leningrad, and Warsaw, still awaiting analysis are some twenty-five *Irmologia* from all parts of Belorussia. The relative paucity of Belorussian chantbooks, compared to the lavish numbers of Russian collections, is due partly to wartime destruction over the centuries, but mainly to the systematic burning of thousands of "Uniate" books in the nineteenth century by the fanatical Archbishop Joseph Semashko.

In addition to the ordinary chants of the Kiev Metropolia, usually called *kievski* (albeit differing from the later Synodal "kievski rospev"), and the usual *hretski, serbski,* and *balharski,* the Belorussian *Irmologia* comprise a number of palace, town, and regional chants: Royal (*kralevski*), Vil'nia (*vilenski*), Slutsk (*slutski*), Mahiloŭ (*mahiloŭski*), Belorussian (*belorusski*), Kuteino (*kutseeŭski*), as well as monastic chants—*suprasl'ski, zhyrovitski, kutsenski,* and even Jesuit (*iezavitski*) and others. In some of these chants at least—for example, the *slutski* "Izhe kheruvim"—folk melodies and rhythms are discernible.[14]

A great number of eighteenth-century *Irmologia* also were in manuscript form, church music printing having been first introduced in the East Slavic world through Suprasl' (1697), though the first printed *Irmologion* was published in L'viv (Lvov) in 1700. Supposedly the latter work was referred to by the Holy Synod to prepare its own standard Russian Orthodox *Irmologion* in 1772, though what precise use was made of the "Uniate" publication remains to be clarified.[15]

Present research has not yet cast any light on the existence in Belorussian *Irmologia* of any examples of Russian chants, though numerous examples of Ukrainian chants—*ukrainski, padhorski, kremenetski*—occur. However, an inventory of the Suprasl' monastic library during the Russian and Cossack invasions from 1645 to 1654, records the accession of "seven Muscovite *Irmologia*" to replace seven Suprasl' books taken to Moscow, as Konotop wrily observes "vidimo, v poriadke knigoobmena" (apparently by way of book exchange). By this late date, of course, the *znamenny* notation, particularly Muscovite *znamenny*, would not have been readily intelligible to Belorussian "Uniate" monks, and there is no record of any borrowings from these *Irmologia* in later Suprasl' compilations.[16]

The manner in which the chants of the Belorussian *Irmologia* were sung depended upon the character of the anthem and the frequency of its use. The three-fold hymn-like "Izhe kheruvimy" (We, the Cherubim) or "Sviatyi Bozhe" (Holy God), particularly if of local rather than of Balkan or ancient monastic origin, was often sung in four-part harmony in a style derived from Western motets, with a partitura noted in the *Irmologion* itself. The spread of *partesnoe penie* (part singing) was, according to Preobrazhensky, largely due to the influence of the ecclesiastical Union of Brest in 1589, and Razumovsky records that by the first third of the seventeenth century, choirs in Polatsk and Mahiloŭ were singing "na chatyry khory" (in four voices).[17] A fine example of a polyphonic "Cherubikon" is noted in the Suprasl' *Irmologion* of 1638.[18] Other chants, such as the *irmosy* themselves, where the melodics were complex and non-repetitive, were probably sung in unison, or, as in Galitsian Ukraine, by the church cantor or *dziak*. If a melody was well known or easy to follow, lead singers from the congregation would group about the *dziak* and join in, accompanying the melody in parallel thirds, or occasionally in fifths and octaves, after the manner known as "samuilka" or "ierusalimka." In this way chants of the *irmologia* came under the direct influence of folk music.[19]

Recent studies by Konotop and Iasinovs'kyi have identified a number of church musicians who, like Anisimovich of Suprasl', compiled the principal surviving Belorussian *Irmologia:* Feodar Semiianovich (Suprasl', 1638), Tsimafei Kulikovich (Bely Koviel, 1652), Inok Feafil (Suprasl', 1662), Parkhomii Patsenka (Slutsak, 1669), Haŭryla Arianasovich (Sava Staroŭsk, 1673), Antoni Kishych (Suprasl', 1674), Kyril Iliinski (Davyd Maradok, 1713), Ieramanach Tarasii (Minsk, ca. 1750), S. Tserakhovich ('Litva,' ca. 1750), Antonii Taranevich (Pinsk, 1759), Ieramanakh Aŭraamii (Vil'nia Sviatadukhaŭski, 1764). Little has yet come to light concerning their lives and activity, save that Haŭryla Arianasovich, like the singer Ian Kukiel, was a native of Polatsk, and after ordination 1667 in Charnihaŭ (Chernigov) province went to Moscow in 1669 and there compiled his *Irmologion* "s kievskaho napievu tak zhe i z belaruskaho" (with Kievan as well as Belorussian chants).[20]

A few other names of noted liturgical composers or singers from the seventeenth century have come down to us. At the conclusion of the Russian Wars of the mid-century, they found themselves in Moscow: Ian Kukiel of Polatsk (fl. 1657), the *dziak* Tyzenhaus of Vil'nia (fl. 1637), the organist Kazimer Vasileŭski of Smalensk (fl. 1670), Ian Kalenda, and Ian Kakhanoŭski (ca. 1600).[21] Belorussian artisans of every description, including musicians, were much sought after in Muscovy during the early seventeenth century, and many chose voluntarily to seek employment there. Later, during the wars of Tsar Aleksei Mikhailovich in 1654, as Paul of Aleppo relates, "countless thousands" of Belorussians, peasants as well as noblemen, were deported to Muscovy. Those who submitted to the tsar and embraced Orthodoxy were resettled in "houses which had become empty in the city, and the farms which were depopulated by the plague." Some 300,000 refugees, however, who had sought to escape were herded off "to Moscow and eternal life" in a muddy death-march whose survivors were sold off as slaves—"little children in lots of five or six, seven or eight at a dollar." Among these deportees there were evidently choristers, as Paul of Aleppo records: "for the most part, the Patriarch and the Emperor delighted in the chanting of the Cossack children, many of which the Emperor brought with him from Poland."[22] The plunder and depopulation brought about by these and later Russian forays at the turn of the century led to a general impoverishment of the economy and culture of Belorussia, not without effect on the artistic quality and the variety of content in the *Irmologia* of the eighteenth century.

The Role of the *Bahahlasnik*

Of great importance in Belorussian liturgical practice, and supplemental to the *Irmologion* and service-books proper, were the chants of the *Bahahlasnik* (Hymnbook). Strictly defined, the *Bahahlasnik* is a collection of paraliturgical hymns or *kanty* divided into festival hymns to the Savior, festival hymns to the *Theotokos,* hymns in honor of the major saints, and miscellaneous hymns, canticles, and responses for divine intercession, supplications, processions, and funerals. More loosely, the *Bahahlasnik* comprises almost any aspect of popular liturgical or paraliturgical singing, whether jotted down in rough exercise books—usually without notes—or communicated orally, but falling short of the ritual folk song with some religious element or refrain, say, "Khrystos uvaskros Syn-Bozhyi" (Christ the son of God is risen). Popular harmonizations of the Lord's Prayer or the Creed—particularly with recurring repetitions of the words "Otche nash" or "Veruiu," "Izhe kheruvim(y)," "Mnohaia lata," "Khrystos voskrese," often representing simplifications or variants of formal liturgical music or text—properly pertain to the *Bahahlasnik*. Similarly, hymns or *kanty* representing paraphrases of liturgical texts such as "O vspetaia Mati," "Neba i ziamlia," "So sviatymi upokoi," and "Vonmi Neba" are further examples of *Bahahlasnik* material.[23] Other instances include adaptations, often very beautiful, of Latin-rite Catholic hymns: "Dies irae," "Stabat Mater" ("Skorbnaia Matsi pad kryzhom staiala"), the old carol "Anhiel Pastyram skazaŭ," and in modern times even Baptist hymns.[24]

Both the language and the melodies of the *Bahahlasnik kanty* reflect the many influences at work in Belorussia over the centuries. The words of some of the *kanty* are pure Belorussian ("Vialik sviaty nam dzen'"); others, a mixture of Belorussian and Ukrainian, Belorussian and Old Slavonic, "ochen' plokho po-russki" and even worse Polish ("Ty nie hardzisza nikoha"). The finicky may seek to tidy them up, but many prefer the old words, however faulty. Poles and Ukrainians are often swift to claim authorship of the *kanty* (seldom the Russians, for whom they are "nekanonichnye"), only to discover that a Belorussian version presents substantial melodic and textual variants. The well-known carol "Nieba i ziamlia radasna spiavaiuts'," being a paraphrase of the Eastern-rite Christmas Eve Great Vespers *stikhira* "Nebo i zemlia dnes' prorocheski da vozveseliatsia," is almost certainly of East Slavic origin, whereas the Minsk version recorded by Ravienski is a distinctive melodic variant.[25]

The melodies of the *Bahahlasnik* chants are a unique bridge between fully liturgical anthems and pure folk music. The hurdy-gurdy singers' carol "U dome Davydavym" recorded in Ravienski's manuscript collection incorporates part of the tune of the third-toned *obikhod* Christmas *Kontakion* "Deva dnes'." The melody for "Ohn' hariashchi v serdtse moem" appears to owe much to the folk song "Zakhatsela babka dy razbahatsets'." Elsewhere, "Izhe kheruvim(y)" has been sung at Christmas to the tune of "Adeste Fideles," "Edinorodnyi Syne" to a variant of the carol "Neba i ziamla," and the *kant* to "Lasnianskaia Bozhae Matsi" according to a Don Cossack popular song of recent date, "Na Donu hulae kazak maladoi."

There is nothing new in this process; Preobrazhensky describes how already in the seventeenth century popular *kantychki* were being put to use as *Kherubika* in Belorussia and the Ukraine, whence (*kanonichnost'* notwithstanding) they passed into the liturgical use of the Russian Orthodox Church.[26]

Bahahlasniki began to be compiled in the late sixteenth century, and increased in popularity and numbers in the seventeenth and eighteenth centuries. The earliest copies were in manuscript, with or without notes, but in the eighteenth century a number of printed versions appeared in Suprasl' and reportedly in Polatsk. Few seem to have escaped the zeal of Semashko and his underlings. Among the early collections Kulikovich-Shchahloŭ mentions the *Bahaiaŭlenski Bahahlasnik* from Polatsk (1662) and the *Zhyrovitsy Bahahlasnik* (seventeenth century). More recently Kastsiukavets' in Minsk has recorded a further *Suprasl' Bahahlasnik* (eighteenth century), and mentions other later printed editions, none of which appears to have survived.[27]

The eighteenth century was, after the first two decades, with the downgrading of Belorussian as an official language in 1697 and the devastations of the Russian-Swedish wars, a period of decline. Few *Irmologia* of any great musical or artistic interest, comparable to the seventeenth-century Suprasl' and Zhyrovitsy collections, have come to light. The polonization of the nobility and the higher clergy, together with the introduction of a "low" or recited Mass in the numerically predominant Greek-Catholic Church, had an adverse effect on Belorussian liturgical singing. The *kanty* sung during the Liturgy were not infrequently in Polish, though traditional Belorussian hymns continued to be sung, particularly in remoter areas. The famous "O moi Bozha veru Tabe" was composed in Belorussian as late as 1824.[28] The *rococo* works of the Basilian monk Tsimafei Shchuroŭski (1740–1810) are occasionally pretty things, even in Polish (e.g., "Weselcie się nieba"), though intended for the Uniate faithful. Widely popular long after his death, his style seems to have influenced later compositions in Russo-Slavonic throughout the nineteenth century as, for example, the hymns to Saint Onufrius: "Pomoshchnika kto ishcheshi."[29] A number of Shchuroŭski's works were published in Krakow as a supplement to Mioduszewski's *Kościelny Śpiewnik* (1842), and his hymn to Saint Josephat provides an interesting example of eighteenth-century organ accompaniment to *kantychki* in the Greek-Catholic Church, as recorded in collections called *Hralniki,* of which little is known.[30]

Also born of these Basilian traditions is the beautiful and stirring "Izhe Kheruvimy" sung to the tune of the Vespers litany "Kyrie eleison," to this day deservedly popular among Belorussians and Ukrainians in a number of variants. Equally moving, and probably dating from the late eighteenth century, is the *Troparion* "Miloserdiia dveri" traditionally sung during the censing of the Church before the Liturgy in the Padlassian village of Klashchele, which suffered from a particularly brutal "dragonnade" in 1875. These and other late Greek-Catholic chants of the *Bahahlasnik* ("Sviaty Bozhe," "Otche nash," "Veruiu") are published in the series *Bielaruski Tsarkoŭny Speŭnik* (London, 1979).

Suppression and the Ethnographical Renaissance

The years 1772–1795 marked the progressive annexation of all Belorussia and its incorporation into the Russian Empire under Catherine II, the effect of which was to suppress most independent, political, religious, and cultural life for the impoverished inhabitants. An attempt by the Orthodox archbishop of Mahiloŭ, Varlaam Shyshatsky, to reestablish an independent Belorussian metropolis during Napoleon Bonaparte's campaign in 1812 failed after the retreat from Moscow, and Shyshatsky died a prisoner in exile.[31]

After the failure of the national uprising of 1831, the Belorussian Greek-Catholic Church was forcibly united with the Russian Synodal Church, and great numbers of "uncanonical" *Irmologia, Bahahlasniki,* and service books were destroyed or confiscated by the notorious Archbishop Joseph Semashko. The scope of this senseless act of vandalism can best be judged from the account given by the prelate himself to his spiritual superiors:

> No. 34: Register and Report to the Holy Synod of twentieth September 1855, under No. 2424, on the final withdrawal from use of Uniate liturgical books: . . . Further to three reports of 25th October 1853, 30th March and 8th November 1854, under Nos. 3461, 950 and 294 sent by me to the Holy Synod, on the presentation to me and effective consignment to the flames of: 217 Pontificals, 39 Trebniki, 287 Octoich, 154 Irmologia, 364 Triodia, 349 Minieia, 123 Triphologia, 37 Velichanie, 14 service books for [Saint] Josephat and 13 service books for the feast of the Holy Sacrament . . . Now there have further been presented to me and consigned to the flames: 4 Pontificals, 12 Trebniki, 44 Octoich, 32 Irmologia, 70 Triodia, 20 Menaia, 15 Triphologia and 4 Velichanie.[32]

Manuscript collections as well as printed books, some perhaps with decorations, miniatures, and woodcuts, were destroyed, and it is not known how many other musical and bibliographical treasures, in addition to the 1800 volumes destroyed by Semashko himself, perished all over Belorussia. Those remnants of a nation's musical heritage which escaped the flames were confiscated and stowed away in the Archives of the Holy Synod, Vil'nia Public Library, and Kievo-Pecherskaia Lavra, where they remain in exile to this day, despite growing demands from Belorussian intellectuals and workers alike for their return.[33]

In their place the Holy Synod provided the despoiled Belorussian churches with standard Russian chantbooks. Synodally trained choirmasters promoted the unified Russian Synodal chants of L'vov and Bakhmet'ev, though local chants from former times lingered on in the marshes of Palesse (Polessie). In churches too poor to support a choir, self-taught *dziaki,* assisted by a few female singers, made short work of distorting the official chants with long drawn-out notes and idiosyncratic harmonizations, to produce a whole cycle of intriguing vernacular variants of the Russian *obikhod* (Ordinary).[34]

During the 1863 Uprising, the Belorussian patriotic leader Kastus' Kalinoŭski urged his supporters to rally to the strains of the traditional *Trisagion* from the *Bahahlasnik* Office of *Supplikatsyia.* Barricaded in their churches singing Uniate *kantychki,* the villagers of Palesse defied the tsar's Cossacks, who had come to convert them in 1875 to the Muscovite faith.[35]

The Synodal authorities lost little time then in publishing their own *Bogoglasniki* in Russian, expurgating "unacceptable" Uniate Saints, and commissioning hymns in honor of Saint Apanas of Brest and other more acceptable saints to replace them.[36]

In the aftermath of these stormy political events, serious ethnographers began to make a systematic study of the East Slavic inhabitants of the area formerly claimed by Poland, but now redesignated as the *Severo-zapadnyi krai* (Northwest Territory) of the Russian Empire. These studies and collections of ethnographical material by Shein, Bessonov, Ramanaŭ, Dabravol'ski, and others extended to traditional paraliturgical *kanty* and prayers as they existed before the era of polonization, in a great variety of Belorussian dialects. Their scholarly research helped the confused Belorussian populace to re-appraise their true identity as distinct from Russians and Poles, and provided a solid base on which a national culture could flourish in the future. Invaluable also for the rebirth of a national school of church music was, as has been said, the work of bibliographers such as Dobrianskyi and

Petrushevich in rediscovering and identifying the old Belorussian *Irmologia* and *Bahahlasniki* during the 1880s.

In the wake of the Belorussian ethnographers of the late nineteenth and early twentieth centuries came a younger generation of musicologists with a more clear-cut perception of their field of research as part of the national musical heritage. In retrospect, they may be regarded as forming part of the *Nasha Niva* revival (1906-1918) and they continued to play an important role, despite strictures, after the formation of the Belorussian Soviet State. The most active of these, according to Aladaŭ, were N. Churkin, M. Ravienski, and A. Iahoraŭ. From their endeavors and those of other ethnographers the development of a national school of church music was derived.[37]

The Early Composers (1880–1918)

Prior to 1918 there were no music publishing houses in Belorussia, and the old Uniate press of Suprasl' had long ceased to function. Neither was there any national conservatory or school of music. Talented composers from Belorussia were constrained to study and publish their works in Moscow or Saint Petersburg. More seriously, the absence of any national Church, and the deliberate suppression of any Belorussian element in liturgical usage, of which Archbishop Semashko's campaign of book-burning and russification was the most striking example, militated against the establishment of any national "school" of church music before 1918. Thereafter, conditions if anything became worse. Church music may of course have been composed in Belorussia throughout the nineteenth century and may have passed into common usage as *Bogoglasnik* or *mestnye napevy* (local chants), but only a thorough study of parish church manuscript collections will reveal whether anything of value has been preserved.

Closely connected to the nineteenth-century ethnographic revival is the figure of Mikhal Antsaŭ (1869–1945). Born in Smalensk, he completed his musical studies at the St. Petersburg Conservatory under N. Rimsky-Korsakov in 1896, then returned to Belorussia where he became editor of *Vitebskie Gubernskie Vedomosti* and its supplement "Narodnyi Listok," publishing contributions on ethnographical subjects by Shein, Ramanaŭ, Nikifaroŭski, and others. He became known principally as a choral director and composer of church music, a number of collections of which were published in Moscow by Iurgenson. His *Liturgy* of Saint John Chrysostom appeared in 1902, and his output continued until 1918 when, in an era of secularization, he became caught up in the organization of the Vitsebsk National Conservatory and the Belorussian State Choir. Thereafter his compositions consist of lyrical songs to words by Belorussian poets—Kolas, Charot, Kupala—and a few commissioned political chorales.[38]

Antsaŭ's earlier choral style, as manifested in his *Liturgy,* is sonorous, cool, and inclined to didacticism: it reflects the proficiency, rather than the lyricism of the Russian "Saint Petersburg School," under whose aegis he received his training. Much of Antsaŭ's work today sounds gorgeously somber and dated, but occasionally, as in the latter part of his *Cherubikon No. 1,* he departs from the canons into a swirling pink and pale-blue world of high *rococo,* which although perhaps not concordant with the general taste of today, may well prove attractive to another generation. His harmonization is often original, and at times—as in his *Cherubikon No. 2* and his "Veruiu" —he evokes forms popular in Belorussian folk music, where women's and men's voices both sing in interweaving parallel thirds, a device later much favored by Turankoŭ and Kulikovich-Shchahloŭ. Regrettably for some seventy years, officialdom has prohibited the public performance of Antsaŭ's liturgical works and has remained disphonic on his achievements in this field.

In contrast, the liturgical works of Aliaksei Turankoŭ (1885–1958), one of the leaders of the young school of Belorussian choral music, have enjoyed a measure of international popularity, although they span only the seven years from 1912 to 1918. Born into a poor family that had settled in St. Petersburg, Turankoŭ displayed from an early age a particular affinity to Belorussian folk music. He received his formal training at the St. Petersburg Conservatory, and swiftly became involved in church music. His compositions proved popular, and a number of his anthems were published by Iurgenson. In addition to hymns for the Holy Liturgy and the All-Night Vigil service, he wrote music for Christmas, Holy Week, and Easter, of which his four-part "Razboinika blahorazumnaho" (The good thief) is one of his best known works. Like the works of his contemporary Mikola Ravienski, much of his music is for male-voice choir, though his more elaborate paraliturgical anthems such as "Sudi mi Hospodi" (Judge me, O Lord) are for mixed voices.

Although schooled in the traditional *pridvorny* style of the Russian Synodal Church, Turankoŭ exhibits a freshness and originality in his choral work similar to that in his Belorussian operas. This quality is derived in part from his interest in folk music. Even in an early composition, an "Izhe Kheruvimy" for male-voice choir (1914), he appears to allude to the Belorussian folk song "Kupalinka," and in the following year he turns, as Antsaŭ had done, to "samuilka"-style folk harmonization in parallel thirds, for his setting of "Khvali dushe moia Hospoda" (1915).[39] Whether by chance or design, a number of Turankoŭ's *Prychastnye stikhy* (Communion hymns) seem to reach back to the chant of the *Bahahlasnik*, in particular "Chashu spaseniia priimu" which evokes the refrain of "Matsi miloserdiia, more shchedrotam" (Mother of Mercy).

Intended for the smaller church choir, Turankoŭ's liturgical compositions are relatively easy to sing; they develop tunefully, are well structured and inventive in their harmonization. His style greatly impressed Kulikovich-Shchahloŭ, who wrote admiringly of Turankoŭ's command and handling of the Belorussian folk idiom. These promising beginnings were unfortunately cut short in 1918, and Turankoŭ's creative activity was thereafter restricted to secular operatic works, and the odd political commission like the trite sketch "Mister Dollar!"[40]

Any prospect of establishing a national liturgical tradition through a restored Belorussian Autocephalic Church ended with the arrest of Metropolitan Melkhisedek of Minsk in 1922. In Belorussia, as in the Ukraine and Russia, church music was out of favor, and involvement with it was dangerous; as an art, its development remained virtually paralyzed for the next half century.

Other composers active in Belorussia during the first half of the twentieth century are known to have written church music, in particular A. Iahoraŭ (1887–1959) and M. Matsison (1881–1940). Both are described in official publications as "Belorussian Soviet" composers, but such denominations can be broad enough to include an Armenian politician working in Belorussia (e.g., A. Miasnikov) whereas ethnic Belorussians working in Lithuania (e.g., K. Halkoŭski, "litoŭski Sovetski kampazitar") would be excluded. This renders it difficult to characterize a "national" composer within the framework of a spurious official nomenclature.

Alaksandar Iahoraŭ (Iegorov) (1887–1959) was born and brought up in St. Petersburg, completing his studies at the Conservatory in 1912. The name Iahoraŭ is common in the Smalensk region. From 1914 until 1920 he taught choral music at the Mahiloŭ High School, assisted Turankoŭ in the organization of the Homiel National Conservatory, and was, according to Aladoŭ, one of the most active in the collecting of Belorussian folk songs. From 1920 to 1951 he was a teacher at the Leningrad Conservatory, and he is generally referred to as being Russian.[41]

A number of his works were published in anthologies of church music by Iurgenson prior to 1918 in the *pridvornyi* Synodal style—"Dostoino est'," "Svete tikhii," "Nyne otpushchaeshi," "Vzbrannoi voevode," "Tebe poem,"

"Otche nash," none of which seems to display any Belorussian characteristics or influences.

From the Novgorod region, of Baltic descent, Mikhail Matsison (1881–1940) is a former student of the Moscow Synodal choir school. He taught musical theory at the Minsk Conservatory from 1924 until 1940. Iurgenson published a few of his works prior to 1918—"Blagoslovi dushe moia Gospoda" for Vespers and settings of *Troparia* and *Dogmatiki* in the Russian *znamennyi* chant, but nothing identifiably Belorussian.[42]

Ŭl. Teraŭski (1871–1938) is reputed to have written some church music, but Soviet sources have yet to elaborate on the full repertoire of his choral music. It may be that other works by composers of this period will come to light to give a fuller picture of the new awakening. But it may be premature to talk of a new dawn of Belorussian church music, when neither the nation nor the church was yet fully aware of its identity.

Western Belorussia: World War II and Its Aftermath

As a result of Polish, Soviet, Lithuanian, and Belorussian conflicts during the period 1919–1921, a substantial part of Belorussia, together with Galitsian Ukraine, formerly under relatively liberal Austrian rule, was incorporated into the new Polish Republic by the Treaty of Riga (1921). Belorussian and Ukrainian Orthodox believers, the latter principally from Volhynia, were pressed into a hybrid "Polish Orthodox" Church, served by russified Bishops and priests, mostly devoid of any serious interest in the languages or cultures of their flock.

Vil'nia, then in Poland, had traditionally been a center of Belorussian culture, and the Polish authorities prior to 1931 allowed a measure of freedom to their national minorities in religious and cultural affairs. Faced with a growing success of Baptist and Methodist missionaries, intelligently availing themselves of that freedom to distribute Gospels and sing hymns in the Belorussian language,[43] the "Polish Orthodox" hierarchy bestirred itself to produce an *Obikhod notnogo Tserkovnogo peniia* (Pinsk, 1929), which among a plethora of standard Russian Synodal chants gave a nod in the direction of *mestnye napevy* from Palesse. The three-volume collection included a number of modest but attractive local chants for "Nyne otpushchaeshi," "Sviatyi Bozhe," "Slava v vyshnykh Bohu," "Nyne sily nebesnyia," a Zhyrovitsy "Mnohaia leta," "Izbavi ot bed," "Ne otvrati litsa," and a few other items better known in Belorussia than in Moscow.

A *Bohohlasnik* (Warsaw, 1935) of indeterminate parentage followed, compiled from local sources by Fr. N. Lencheŭski, a priest from Volhynia, which included *kanty* with elements of Belorussian as well as the prevailing Russo-Slavonic: "O khto, khto Mikolaia liubits'," "O vspetaia Mati," "Spevaite liudzi," and others. More obviously Uniate survivals such as "Skorbnaia Matsi" (Stabat Mater) were not included, though the ever-popular *supplikatsii* were too well entrenched to be omitted.

At the level of professional musicians in western Belorussia, there was in the absence of an established Belorussian school of art music to look to the traditions of Galitsian Ukraine. These, it was doubtless reasoned, were probably not far removed from the liturgical usages in Belorussia prior to 1839. Hryhor Shyrma (1892–1978), later a leading Belorussian folklorist and Director of the Belorussian State Choir, was a distinguished church musician and choral director in Vil'nia during the 1930s.[44] Anton Valynchyk, a former student of the Warsaw Conservatory, conducted Church choirs in Kletsk, Slonim, Navahradak, and later in Zhyrovitsy, before becoming director of the "Nioman" ensemble and professor of music in the Hrodna (Grodno) Pedagogical Institute (1961–1976). He is known to have attempted church compositions using Belorussian elements, but none of his liturgical works have been published. A study of his endeavors in this field, and those of the lesser-known Iakub Semashko (fl. 1926–1940) of Dalatychy, one of the few Greek-Catholic parishes restored after 1921 in western Belorussia, is long overdue.[45]

The reunification of western and eastern Belorussia in 1939, albeit the result of a disreputable political double-deal between two totalitarian powers, had an incalculable effect on the Belorussian people's national consciousness. With the outbreak of the Second World War and the German occupation of Belorussia (1941–1944), particularly in the east, many restrictions imposed on the freedom of worship were erased, and in 1942 Metropolitan Panteleimon of Minsk, presiding over a Synod of Belorussian Bishops, once again reestablished the Belorussian Autocephalic Orthodox Church as a jurisdiction independent of Moscow.

Three of the leading members of the Union of Composers of the B.S.S.R. —A. Turankoŭ, M. Ravienski, and M. Kulikovich-Shchahloŭ, all of them distinguished folklorists and former church musicians, as well as operatic composers—elected to spend the War years in Minsk. Turankoŭ remained there after the Germans withdrew; Ravienski and Kulikovich-Shchahloŭ were evacuated to the West. Neither of the latter composers in his memoirs mentions his activity in the field of church music during the occupation, although it was a time of exceptional activity in other fields. As a result, their names have been consigned to official oblivion for almost fifty years, albeit they figured prominently in gubernatorial publications before 1941.

Mikola Ravenski (1886–1953) began his musical life as a chorister in Minsk Cathedral at the age of six. From 1901 until 1905, he directed a monastic choir in that city, and from 1905 until 1914 a church choir in Navahradak, where he also collected over 500 folk songs. In 1922, as Director of the Minsk Workers Club Choir, he published his first collection of folk songs, *Zbornik pesen z notami,* just one year after Teraŭski's pioneer publication.[46] Having completed his studies at the Moscow Conservatory with Ippolitov-Ivanov, himself an adept of Belorussian folk music, Ravenski returned to Minsk where, according to Dreizin, he wrote compositions for piano and strings, as well as a cantata. His involvement in operatic work, with the poet Ŭl. Duboŭka as librettist, almost ended in his being deported together with the latter to Siberia. Much of his work perished during the bombardments of Minsk in 1941 and 1944.

Evacuated to Berlin in 1944, and then to a refugee camp at Osterhofen, he became more consistently involved in the composition of liturgical music for the Belorussian Autocephalic Orthodox Church in exile. A number of his manuscripts, scored for a mixed-voice choir—"Vo tsarstvii Tvoem," *Cherubikon No. 1,* and "Veruiu" for Bass solo and choir—date from this period.

In 1950, Ravienski was appointed Director of the Belorussian Students Choir at the University of Louvain in Belgium. There he was able to reconstitute some of his lost collections of Belorussian folk songs, and to complete his *Liturgy* of Saint John Chrysostom (1952) for male-voice choir.

Familiar from childhood with the provincial Cathedral style (Bortniansky, Vedel', Verbitsky) and through later training with the innovative trends in Russian church music, as well as the traditions of folk music, Ravienski was acutely aware of the need for the Liturgy to be accessible to the common people. He retained in many of his simple and limpid settings of "Edinorodnyi Syne," "Otche nash," and "Da ispolniatsia usta nasha," the easy pattern of harmonization in parallel thirds followed in the *mestnyia napevy* of the Polessian *Obikhod*, and the earlier eighteenth-century tradition of "samuilka" singing. In his more elaborate anthems—"Vo tsarstvie Tvoem," *Cherubikon No. 1,* "Milost' mira," "Veruiu" and particularly in his Belorussian hymn "O Bozha Ŭseŭladny" (O God, all-powerful), Ravienski adopts a more liberated and innovative style, reminiscent of Turankoŭ and Ippolitov-Ivanov, to considerable effect.[47]

Steeped though he was in liturgical tradition, Ravienski was at some pains to incorporate elements of secular folk music into his compositions. This he did notably in his *Cherubikon No. 3,* taking as his theme the folk song "Tsi svet, tsi svitaie," which he ably disguises in a bland traditional form, waiting until the final three-fold "Alliluia" before he brings the folk theme clearly to the fore.

Apart from his *Liturgy,* Ravienski's output of church music was slight. He composed a "Slava vo vyshnich Bohu" for Vespers and Matins, "Mnohaia leta," and a few simple harmonizations of *obikhod* melodies for the ordination of a priest. His paraliturgical hymn to words by the poetess Natalia Arsen'eva—"Mahutny Bozha"—gained great popularity, and is widely sung in Belorussian churches abroad as a recessional. As in the field of folk music, he was a pioneer who has left memorable anthems illustrative of the tastes of his time and of his own lyrical spirituality.[48]

The Search for Authenticity

Contemporaneously with Ravienski in the immediate post-War period, another leading member of the Union of Composers of the B.S.S.R., Mikola Kulikovich-Shchahloŭ (1897–1969), devoted a great deal of thought to the problem of restoring authentically Belorussian traditions in the field of church music. Born of Don Cossack and Belorussian parents, and orphaned at an early age, he was brought up by his maternal aunt, the *igumenia* (Prioress) of a Convent of Orthodox nuns in Tula, where he sang in the choir. His exceptionally beautiful alto voice won the boy a choral scholarship at the prestigious Moscow Synodal Choir School, then under the direction of A. Kastal'sky, and he was chosen to accompany the choir on a tour of Western Europe as a *kanonarkh.*

After completing his studies in Moscow, he taught music for some years in the Ukraine before undertaking extensive research into the folk music of the Smalensk region, where his mother's family—Kulikovich—had originated. From 1937 in Minsk, where he became conductor of the Radio Symphony Orchestra, he composed a number of choral and operatic works in Belorussian, based on folk motifs, of which he had collected four volumes. His highly acclaimed opera *Katsaryna* was published in Moscow in 1940. He also became the leading Belorussian correspondent for *Sovetskaia Muzyka,* to which he contributed a number of articles on Belorussian operatic works and performances.[49]

During the German occupation of Minsk, Kulikovich-Shchahloŭ enlarged his extensive collection of folk songs, composed two operas on Belorussian historical themes, and wrote numerous patriotic songs, which achieved instant and wide popularity. In 1944, he was evacuated to Germany, continuing his choral and theatrical activities on a much reduced scale in a number of Belorussian refugee camps, before emigrating to the United States. There he organized concerts and conducted a number of church choirs in parishes of the Belorussian Autocephalic Orthodox Church. His last years he spent in Chicago, where he directed the choir of the Belorussian Greek-Catholic Holy Redeemer Church prior to his death in 1969.

In seeking to create an authentically Belorussian church music, Kulikovich-Shchahloŭ, like Ravienski and perhaps to a lesser extent the earlier composers such as Antsaŭ, turned in the first instance to folk music, and more particularly to folk harmonization, choosing to follow its fresher, bolder nuances, than to look back to the more predictable form of the "samuilka" style of the *Bahahlasnik* chants. In this he was following the example that Kompaneisky and Kastal'sky had set in the field of Russian church music.

By 1948, Kulikovich-Shchahloŭ had composed a full *Liturgy* of Saint John Chrysostom, a service of Vespers and Matins, an Easter *Canon*, and a system of eight-tone chants or *Oktoechos*, based entirely, and without any attempt at "rounding off" or liturgical refinement, on folk melodies and folk harmonizations.[50]

The latter experiment was a mixed success. The hymns of the *Oktoechos* tended to be monotonous and overly repetitive, with an unacceptable identity between chants proposed for the *Troparia*, the *Hospodi vozzvakh* and the *Irmosy*, which, if adopted as a system, would be alien to the traditions of the Eastern Church in Belorussia. But by applying the same *papeŭki* or folk motifs to non-recurring chants such as "Blahoslovi dushe moia," the *Cherubikon*, "Dostoino est'," the *Eucharist Canon*, and "Khvalite imia Hospodne," Kulikovich-Shchahloŭ achieved results with which he could be better pleased and which in due course he offered for publication. Indeed, he made use of folk themes from his own popular setting of M. Bahdanovich's poem, "Ad rodnykh niŭ, ad rodnai khaty" to particularly fine effect in the "Nyne otpushchaeshi" of his Vespers service. In the same way, his folk *Irmos* of the fifth tone was recast as an attractive "Milost' mira" (*belaruski napeŭ*). On the other hand, his folk *Irmos* of the fourth tone was more successful in capturing the cadences and flow of an ecclesiastical chant. It illustrates that folk motifs may have a creative part to play in the elaboration of an alternative *Oktoechos*.

In his "cathedral-style," whether applied to harmonizations of ancient chants or of free compositions, Kulikovich-Shchahloŭ was able to give full vent to his choral experience and creative talents. His *Troparion* for Christmas, "Rozhdestvo Tvoe Khriste Bozhe nash" (fourth-tone *obikhod* version of the Greek chant), the Easter *Svetilen* "Plotiiu usnuv" for alto *kanonarkh* and mixed choir, and his Pontifical "Dostoino est'" (folk version of the fourth-tone Greek chant) are broad and majestic works that match the best of Kastal'sky or Chesnokov, while maintaining a distinctively Belorussian identity. Other free compositions—*Cherubikon No. 1*, "Khrystos voskrese," "S nami Boh," his "Veruiu" for alto *kanonarch* and mixed choir (which may be ranked with Grechaninov's), and perhaps most of all his "Milost' mira," a strikingly modernistic work with a soprano solo,[51] show that in the field of church music, Kulikovich-Shchahloŭ is unquestionably the most impressive figure to have emerged to date in Belorussia.

The years 1958–1960 seem to have marked a watershed in the history of the development of Belorussian church music, by a seemingly concerted effort to return to the roots. Within the hierarchies of the Belorussian Autocephalic Orthodox and the Greek-Catholic Churches overseas—no national Church existed then in Belorussia—the question of a return to authenticity both in liturgy and language was attracting ever increasing attention.

In London a center for the study of Eastern liturgical music (CSELM) had been set up in 1957 under the auspices of the Belorussian Marian Fathers, formerly of Druia, with a view to creating a collection of all available church music, pertaining in particular to the Eastern Slavs.[52] Useful contacts were established with a group of Russian church musicians centered in Paris (Kedrov, Gardner, A. Shishkin, P. Spassky,[53] M. Kovalevsky among others), editing the *Notnyi Sbornik Russkogo Tserkovnogo Peniia* ("Collected Russian Church Chants") (1962), and the idea grew that a similar collection of Belorussian church music should be produced.

Sponsored by the future Apostolic Visitor of Belorussians, Tseslaŭ Sipovich, and supported by Kulikovich-Shchahloŭ, the project was beset by two major problems relating to choices of material and language: Old Slavonic or modern Belorussian. The difficulty over the selection of an eight-tone system to set up in place of the Synodal *obikhod* chants was resolved by Kulikovich-Shchahloŭ, who, having become familiar, through the bibliographical research of A. Kalubovich in America, with the existence in Soviet libraries of a number of old Belorussian *Irmologia*, firmly declared that only on these could a national system of eight-tone chants properly be based.[54] Early in 1960, in a series of articles in the leading Belorussian newspaper overseas, *Bats'kaŭshchyna*, he drew attention to the need for reform in the repertoire of the Belorussian Orthodox Church and called for the replacement of the works of Arkhangel'sky, Turchaninov, and Sarti by those of the Belorussian school of composers. In one article, "Pytanne belaruskae bahasluzhby"

("The problem of a Belorussian Liturgy"), he developed his ideas as a kind of manifesto, encouraging composers and choirmasters to turn also to the old *Bahahlasniki*, and to paraliturgical folk music such as carols and festival songs as sources for new melodies.[55]

Over the years 1959–1964 the London center sponsored five unofficial expeditions—three to the Soviet Union and two to the Bielastok region of Poland—to trace, if possible, the sixteenth and seventeenth-century *Irmologia* and to record what might remain of a vanishing oral tradition in the countryside. After a preliminary exploration, a research assistant from Paris brought back in 1960 an invaluable checklist of Belorussian liturgical chantbooks in the Library of the Ukrainian Academy of Sciences, including the former "Lithuanian" holding of the Vil'nia Public Library analyzed by Dobriansky in 1882. The following year, he recovered from Kiev a notebook including substantial transcripts from the *Suprasl' Irmologion* (1598) and an equally rare *Zhyrovitsy Irmologion* (1649) containing a number of identifiably Belorussian local chants, as well as extracts from other *Irmologia* in the Historical Museum in Moscow. Further notebooks were collected of unrecorded *Bahahlasnik* chants from Palesse. Because of their clandestine nature, these musicological forays were not without a measure of danger and involved identity checks, sustained police interrogations, thorough baggage and hotel room searches, and on one occasion expulsion under escort. Fortunately the *corpora delicti* escaped detection and "consignment to the flames." Copies were duly forwarded to Kulikovich-Shchahloŭ in Chicago, who then produced a series of outstanding harmonizations, including *zhyrovitski* "Nyne otpushchaeshi," *slutski* "Izhe kheruvimy," *iablachynski* "Izhe kheruvimy," *belaruski* "Da ispolniatsia usta nasha," all of which were published posthumously. Blending ancient chants with folk harmonization, they must be numbered among his finest ecclesiastical works.[56]

In the wake of Kulikovich-Shchahloŭ's "Pytanne belaruskae bahasluzhby," a number of articles on Belorussian church music, the *Suprasl' Irmologion*, and chants of the *Bahahlasnik* appeared in Belorussian overseas publications—*Bats'kaŭshchyna, Bozhym Shlakham,* and *The Journal of Byelorussian Studies*—between 1962 and 1970.

Meanwhile the whole subject of church music had remained dormant in the Soviet Union, with the exception of one or two publications by Uspensky and Brazhnikov. In Belorussia an even higher degree of stagnation has prevailed since the 1930s. However, by the late 1960s a parallel and apparently unrelated revival of interest in Belorussian and Ukrainian church music began to emerge,[57] thanks largely to the research of A. Konotop in Kiev,

Iu. Iasinoŭski in Lvov, N. Gerasimova-Persidskaia in Moscow, and L. Kastiukavets in Minsk.[58] This interest appears, however, to be purely academic; there has been little publication of original texts from the rediscovered *Irmologia* and *Bahahlasniki*. Nor is there any indication that Belorussian composers are making any practical use of this new material. The Metropolitan See of "Minsk and Belorussia" is but one of many "national" Churches under the Moscow patriarchate, in which the state of church music, to judge by the few available publications of works by Uspensky, Shishkin, and Pariisky, is hardly one of innovative development. The evolution of an indigenous school of Church singing calls for conditions that simply did not exist within the prevailing establishment.

Problems of a similar kind afflict the Białystok area of Poland, where there is a substantial and homogenous Belorussian minority and where there have recently been calls for the Liturgy and sermons to be in the Belorussian language. An interest in "multi-national" Orthodox church music has been stimulated since 1982 by an annual Hainoŭka Festival of liturgical music, but there are few signs of any active concern with the restoration of a Belorussian tradition in this field.[59]

With the death in 1969 of Mikola Kulikovich-Shchahloŭ, the creative role of the Belorussian emigration in the field of church music seemed to come to an end. One or two minor composers left a few inconsequential works in a style popular in the smaller provincial parish church. These were subsequently published.

By 1964, the London Center for the Study of Eastern Liturgical Music, after a brief period of collaboration with the Kedrov-Kovalevsky Paris group, merged into the editorial board of the projected Belorussian *Speŭnik*, under the chairmanship of Bishop Cheslaŭ Sipovich until his death in 1981. Progress on the project was held up for some time, owing to difficulties in producing and printing a bilingual Old Slavonic and Belorussian text. High costs rendered it necessary to adopt a laborious system of transfers and cut-out texts, but by 1979, the *Belaruski Tsarkoŭny Speŭnik* ("Belorussian Church Chantbook") began to appear as a continuing series of brochures comprising forty-six of these, with a total of 210 printed pages of music for the Holy Liturgy up to 1984. Such a pattern of publication, while presenting the appearance of a permanently incompleted work, enabled the editors to include new discoveries as they came to light. Two volumes for the *All-Night Vigil* and *Festival Offices* were begun, but inadequate material and technical problems impaired progress.

The preparation of the celebrations to mark the millennium of Christianity in the East Slavic lands lent momentum to the reemergence of a national tradition of church music in Belorussia. *Troparia* and *Kontakia* were written and set to music in honor of the country's Saints—Euphrosyne of Polotsk, Cyril of Turov, and Sophia of Slutsak—and the venerated Icons of Our Lady of Minsk and of Zhyrovitsy. Variants of the *obikhod* and *mestnye* chants were harmonized by local musicians such as L. Rakitski and V. Skarabahataŭ. Recognition was given to the existence of a school of Belorussian Church composers, and as a tribute, performances were given of the works of Turankoŭ and A. Valynchyk, as well as of more recent composers such as M. Mikalaevich, F. Makaroŭ, and N. Butoma. An impressive Belorussian Metropolitan Choir flourishes at the Cathedral of the Holy Ghost in Minsk, and the continued growth of provincial choirs seems assured in the prevailing liberal atmosphere. Roused from its torpor, the Russian Patriarchal Church sought to implement the reforms of Kastal'sky and the Moscow School, progressively abandoning the Italo-German "pridvornyi" style. "The liturgical chant of the Russian Orthodox Church," as the great Moscow conductor N. Matveev wrote recently, "has adopted a strictly national style which precludes anything baroque, artificial or sugary." Such a style is not necessarily concordant with the national traditions of the Church in Belorussia or the Ukraine. Conditions appear favorable for a parallel reform in these countries to adopt their own "strictly national style."

For one hundred and fifty years, since the "consignment to the flames" of a centuries-old national tradition, Belorussian Church singing has been pressed into the alien mold of the institutionalized "pridvornyi" style. Although some recent Belorussian composers have produced commendable works in this style, there seems little relevant left to say in this overworked idiom.[60]

A younger generation of musicians, in composing for liturgical purposes, may look back to seek inspiration from the old *Irmologia* and *Bahahlasniki*, or from folk music; they may look to the examples of Yugoslavia, Greece, and Bulgaria, as did the compilers of the seventeenth century, or they may look even further afield to modernist composers in the West. The choice ultimately must lie with them, but to make a choice they must first know the options.

The Latin-Rite Church

Culturally as well as geographically, Belorussia stands at the watershed of the Roman and Byzantine worlds—a characteristic shared with Finno-Carelia, Rumania, Yugoslavia, and the Graeco-Venetian lands. Though the main thrust of Christianity came by way of the Balkans and the Ukraine,

Latin Christianity penetrated into the East Slavic lands through the Baltic, Poland, and Moravia.

The Catholic Mass was, of course, from the outset sung in Latin, and liturgical music in Belorussia followed the standard Gregorian plainchant and later adopted polyphonic motets in the medieval and Renaissance styles. Some such chants passed by osmosis into the repertoire of the Greek-rite churches; Dobriansky noted the presence in seventeenth-century Eastern Church chantbooks versions of "Dies irae," "Stabat Mater," and "Te Deum laudamas" translated into Slavonic.[61]

No doubt there were Belorussian Catholic composers, but because the liturgical language was Latin, it is difficult to distinguish them from Lithuanians or Poles. Moreover, paraliturgical hymns in the vernacular were increasingly sung in Polish during the late sixteenth and early seventeenth centuries. Sebastian of Minsk (sixteenth century) and Mikola Mazovich were noted organists in their day, and the Jesuit composers Ionash Hrusheŭski (d. 1646) and Jakub Pashkievich (d. 1657) wrote *kantychki* for their school choirs.[62]

The earliest printed Catholic hymnal in the Belorussian language with notes, appears to have been published in Petrograd in 1917 by V. Gozhel'niarsky. Earlier collections of hymns had appeared without music—V. Lastoŭski's *Kantyczka abo sabrańnie* (Vil'nia, 1914), and *Boh z nami* (Vil'nia, 1915) as a section in a prayer book published through the munificence of Princess Mahdalena Radzivil. Most of the hymns are Belorussian variants of Lithuanian and Polish hymns (e.g., "Na tvar upaŭshy," "O Maryia Matsi Boha").[63]

A number of translations of west European hymns were published with notes by Msgr. P. Tatarynovich (1896–1978), who also set Belorussian words to Gregorian plainchant for the Mass in the vernacular during the 1950s. Later, Mikola Kulikovich-Shchahloŭ, with a characteristic Belorussian openness to East and West, harmonized six Catholic hymns, including a charming "Vitai Maryia" of his own composition.[64]

More recently the group "Belaruskiia Katoliki ŭ Anhlii" has prepared for publication a collection of six *Pes'ni da Naisviatoi Dzevy Maryi* in Belorussian, set to Gregorian plainchant (including "Salve Regina," "Alma Redemptoris Mater," "Regina caeli laetare") as well as a mass based on folk melodies.

Since the Second Vatican Council and the introduction of the vernacular for ordinary liturgical use, problems have arisen in Catholic Churches in Belorussia, where polonized priests seek to impose the Polish language on increasingly alienated congregations. The need for a corpus of genuinely Belorussian Catholic church music has become vital to the survival of a viable Latin-rite Church.[65]

The Evangelical Tradition

The Reformation brought to Belorussia forms of communal worship in which a use of the vernacular in preaching, in prayer, and in the singing of hymns and psalms played an essential part. Although early reformers such as Vasil Chapin'ski made good use of the Belorussian language, later pastors resorted to Polish, and the first Evangelical hymns in Belorussia appeared in the Niasvezh *Katekhizm* (1563) printed in that language.[66]

Little else seems to have been published in Belorussia prior to the twentieth century, when Baptist and Methodist missions in western Belorussia, then under Polish rule, began to publish Gospels and prayer books with vernacular texts. In 1925, American-backed Methodist missionaries, supported by a number of Belorussian notables grown weary of alien Russian Orthodoxy and Polish Catholicism—in particular, A. Ŭlasaŭ and the poet Halash Laŭchyk—assisted in the production of a hymnal with notes in the Belorussian language. A second hymnal appeared in 1927 without musical notes, and in 1930 a substantial collection of 152 hymns in Belorussian was published in Vil'nia with the title *Bozhaia Lira—Metadystychny Pesennik (Speŭnik) Belaruski z notami* ("The Divine Lyre"). Many of the tunes were taken from the Polish language *Polski Śpiewnik Metodistyczny* and were part of the ordinary world-wide evangelical repertoire, including a number of Catholic hymns (e.g., Cardinal Newman's *Ty Svetach moi*—"Lead Kindly Light"). Many traditional Christmas carols ("Tam ŭ Betleeme," "Holas naseststsa," "Try Manarkhi") and Easter hymns ("Viasioly dzen'") were included, together with some original Belorussian material ("Dai nam, Bozha, dobry chas").[67]

By far the most impressive collection of evangelical hymns is Pastor D. Ias'ko's *Himny Chrystsiian* ("Christian Hymns") published by the Belorussian Evangelical Baptist Fraternity in the United States and Canada in 1979, already well known in Belorussia. Catholic hymns and Orthodox liturgical chants have been included with a comprehensive selection of 604 hymns from many nations ranging from Brazil to New Zealand. Classical chorales by Melchior Teschner, J. S. Bach, Dm. Bortniansky, and F. Mendelssohn mingle with popular hymns such as *Chudoŭnaia Laska* ("Amazing Grace") and Belorussian Christmas and Easter carols, all competently translated into Belorussian. With its confident and ecumenical approach, Ias'ko's *Himny* is indicative of the coming of age of church music in Belorussia, whatever the rite, whatever the liturgical form.

Notes

1. [Paul of Aleppo], *Travels of Macarius, Patriarch of Antioch* (London, 1829), vol. 2, pp. 271–272; H. Pikhura, "Tsarkoŭnaia Muzyka na Belarusi," *Bozhym Slakham* no. 83 (1964): 12.
2. Bishop Česlaus Sipovič, *The Pontifical Liturgy of St. John Chrysostom* (London, 1978), 136 ff.
3. Dm. Razumovskii, *Tserkovnoe penie v Rossii* (Moscow, 1867–1869), 207 ff.; A. Preobrazhenskii, *Kul'tovaia muzyka v Rossii* (Leningrad, 1924), p. 57.
4. I. Voznesenskii, *Tserkovnoe penie pravoslavnoi iugozapadnoi Rusi* (Moscow, 1898), no. 1, pp. 17–20.
5. F. Dobrianskii, *Opisanie rukopisei Vilenskoi Publichnoi Biblioteki* (Vilnius, 1882), 287 ff.; Iu. Iasinoŭski, *Belaruskiia Irmoloi pomniki muzychnaha mastatstva 16–17 st.* (Minsk: Mastatstva Belarusi, 1984), no. 11, pp. 51–55.
6. H. Pikhura, "Tsarkoŭnaia muzyka," deals with the general background of the subject.
7. Razumovskii, p. 58.
8. N. Findeizen, *Ocherk po istorii muzyki v Rossii* (Moscow and Leningrad, 1928), p. 87.
9. Voznesenskii, 17–20; H. Pikhura, "Bohdan Anisimovich," *Bozhym Slakham*, no. 97 (1966): 8–12.
10. Iu. Iasinoŭski, p. 54.
11. Voznesenskii, 61 ff.
12. K. Kalinoŭski, *Muzhytskaia Praŭda*, no. 2 (August, 1862), in *Paŭstan'nie na Belarusi 1863 hodu*, ed. J. Zaprudnik and T. Bird (New York, 1980), p. 30.
13. H. Pikhura, "Bohdan Anisimovich," pp. 11–12; A. Konotop, "Suprasl'skii Irmologion," *Sovetskaia Muzyka* 1972, no. 2: 119 ff.
14. Iasinoŭski, p. 54.
15. Voznesenskii, pp. 6, 21.
16. A. Konotop, op. cit.
17. Dm. Razumovskii, p. 209.
18. A. Konotop, "Suprasl'skie Irmologii 1638–1639gg.," *Pamiatniki Kul'tury, Novye Otkrytiia 1980 g.* (Moscow, 1981), p. 235.
19. E. Spikula, "Byzantine–Slavonic Liturgical Music—The period of choral development," *The Ark* (Stanford), vol. 4, pp. 11–13.
20. Iasinoŭski, p. 54.
21. Findeizen, pp. 308–309.
22. "We saw them coming in, and bringing with them countless thousands of captives. We did not see one of them without a prisoner or two, or five or six, and more: and yet in consequence of the mud caused by the rains of late, and the death of their horses, they had abandoned the greatest part of their prisoners on the roads, and left them to die of cold and hunger . . . The grandees of the empire, and the

military and *Timariots*, in like manner filled up their farms with captives, and made them cultivate the land. For if anywhere the people ever lived despised and abject slaves, it was the hereditary cultivators of the soil for the Poles, who now became cultivators for the Muscovites. Our hearts were truly afflicted for these poor wretches; seeing the sales of their little children in lots of five or six, seven or eight, at a dollar." Cf. [Paul of Aleppo] *Travels*, vol. 2, pp. 209–210. For a different view of these "massive" movements of population "to Moscow and eternal life" during the "Struggle for reunion of Belorussia to Russia," see L. Abetsedarskii, "V svete neoproverzhimykh faktov," in *Dary Danaitsev* (Minsk, 1987), 60 ff.

23. *Bogoglasnik* (Warsaw, 1935), no. 1, p. 5; no. 18, p. 59; no. 59, p. 243.

24. Generally on the subject of *kantychki* see L. Kostiukevich, *Kantovaia kul'tura v Belorussii* (Minsk, 1975).

25. M. Ravienski, *Collected Folksongs* (MSS), no. 92. [Fr. Skaryna Library, London].

26. A. Preobrazhenskii, "Ot uniatskogo kanta do pravoslavnoi kheruvimskoi," *Muzykal'nyi Sovremennik*, vol. 4 (St. Petersburg, 1915–1916).

27. L. Kas'tsiukaviets', "Bahahlasnik," *ELMB*, vol. 1 (Minsk, 1984), pp. 255–256.

28. E. Karskii, *Belorussy*, vol. 3 (St. Petersburg, 1921), 150 ff.

29. *Bogoglasnik* (Warsaw, 1936), no. 60, p. 246; no. 86, p. 351.

30. M. Mioduszewski, *Śpiewnik Kościelny* "Dodatek ... z melodyjami" (Cracow, 1843): "Jeżeli nas Pan Bog pozwoli, to się wyda i Gralnik Koscielny, czyli melodyje Śpiewnika na organ," p. 25; Ks. Michal Dąbrowski, *O Swiętych męczenniku Josafacie Arcybiskupie Polockim, ul. przez X. Tym. Szczurowskiego ZSBW, Superiora Klasztoru Bialskiego* (Cracow, 1868) [two hymns with organ accompaniment].

31. H. Stammler, "Der Fall des Erzbischofs Varlaam Šišackij von Mogilev," *Ostmitteleuropa: Berichte u. Forschungen* (Stuttgart, 1981), pp. 78–92.

32. *Zapiski Iosifa Mitropolita Litovskago*, vol. 2 (St. Petersburg, 1883), pp. 616–617.

33. *List da Gorbacheva* (Minsk and London, 1987), p. 30; idem, *Belarus'* (New York, 1987), 1 ff.

34. Cf. "Vo tsarstvii Tvoem" (hrecki napeŭ), *Belaruski tsarkoŭny spieŭnik* (London, 1979–), no. 36.

35. K. Kalinoŭski, *Muzhytskaia Praŭda*, no. 6 (June, 1863), in *Paŭstanne na Belarusi 1863 hodu*, p. 37.

36. *Bogoglasnik*, compiled and scored by A. Rozdestvenskii (St. Petersburg, 1912).

37. N. Aladov, "Muzyka Belorusskoi respubliki," *Sovetskaia Muzyka*, nos. 9–10 (Moscow, 1939), pp. 61, 63.

38. N. Nisnevich, "Mikhail Antsaŭ," *ELMB*, vol. 1 (Minsk, 1984), p. 135. This device of singing in parallel thirds is common to many systems of folk music both in Western and Eastern Europe and is by no means confined to Belorussia. The Russian church composer Arkhangel'sky among others made frequent and effective use of it.

39. M. Kulikovich, "Aliaksei Turankoŭ," *Bats'kaŭshchyna*, no. 40 (426) (Munich, 1958), pp. 2–3; Dz. Zhuraŭleŭ, "Aliaksei Turankou," *ELMB*, vol. 5 (Minsk, 1987), p. 287.

40. Ju. Dreizin, "Muzykal'naia zhizn' Belorussii," *Sovetskaia Muzyka* (1934): 45.

41. [Anon.] "Aleksandar Iahoraŭ," *ELMB*, vol. 5 (Minsk, 1987), p. 677.

42. Dz. Zhuraŭleŭ, "Mikhail Matsison," *ELMB*, vol. 3 (Minsk, 1986), p. 489.

43. G. Picarda, "The Heavenly Fire: A Study of the Origins of the New Testament and Psalms" (1931), *Bozhym Slakham* (London, 1975), no. 1–2 (143–144), pp. 9–24.

44. Ul. Chemier, "Novyia harmonizatsyi belaruskikh pes'nia ŭ vykan'ni Choru R. Shyrmy, *Kalosse* (Vil'nia, 1939), no. 1, pp. 55–57.

45. [Anon.] "Anton Valynchyk," *ELMB*, vol. 1 (Minsk, 1984), p. 568.

46. Arkhiep. Afanasii Martos, *Belarus' v istoricheskoi, gosudarstvennoi i tserkovnoi zhizni* (Buenos Aires, 1966), pp. 268–284.

47. M. Ravenski, "Kampazitar M. Ravenski ab sabie," *Belaruski Rabotnik* (Berlin, 1944), no. 33, p. 6.

48. Ul. Nemirovich, "Na sluzhbe mastats'tva i idei," *Naperad*, no. 25 (Munich, 1953), pp. 20–24.

49. N. Shcheglov [Kulikovich] "U kompozitorov Belorussii," *Sovetskaia Muzyka*, 12 (1939): 68 ff.; "Muzykal'noe iskusstvo Zapadnoi Belorussii," *Sovetskaia Muzyka*, 11 (1939): 69 ff.

50. A. K., "Belaruskaia tsarkoŭnaia muzyka kampazitara M. Kulikovicha," *Bats'kaŭshchyna*, no. 12 (56) (1948): 4.

51. *Belaruski tsarkoŭny speŭnik*, no. 27 (London, 1979).

52. The records and library of the CSELM now form part of the holdings of the Francis Skaryna Byelorussian Library and Museum, London.

53. Piotr V. Spassky was one of the most distinguished and sensitive conductors of the famous Saint Alexander Nevsky Russian Orthodox Cathedral choir in the rue Daru, Paris. An admirer of Turankoŭ and of Belorussian *kantychki*, he would say of the latter that their melodies were steeped in the very essence of Orthodox Church music.

54. M. Kulikovich, "Tsi nia chas zakrunats' pytane?" *Bats'kaŭshchyna*, nos. 1–2 (485–486) (Munich, 1960): 3.

55. M. Kulikovich, "Pytanne belaruskai bahasluzhby," *Bats'kaŭshchyna*, nos. 12–13 (496–497) (Munich, 1960): 3.

56. Cf. *Belaruski tsarkoŭny speŭnik*, nos. 2, 18, 23, 34.

57. An important step was the facsimile publication of N. Diletski, *Hramatyka muzykal'na* (Kiev, 1978), a key work in the development of Ukrainian music.

58. L. Kostiukovets, *Kantovaia kul'tura v Belorussii* (Minsk, 1975).

59. X. Grzegorz Sosna, *Bibliografia: Dni Muzyki Cerkiewnej, Hajnowka 1982–1986*, Fr. Skaryna Library, London.

60. Cf. *Pokhvala Belorusskim Sviatym* (recording), izd. Moskovskoi Patriarchii, (Leningrad/Petrograd, 1987).

61. F. Dobrianskii, *Opisanie*, 210 ff.
62. Z. Ivinskis, "Kirchengesang in Litauen im 16–18ten Jahrhundert," *Commentationes Balticae*, vol. 1 (Bonn, 1953), 69 ff., at pp. 90–92, 102.
63. Cf. O.K. "Kastselnye pesni," *Homan*, no. 24 (220) (Vilno, 1918), p. 3.
64. Cf. *Znich*, no. 26 (Rome, 1953), p. 3; no. 57, p. 1.
65. Fr. F. Charniaŭski, *Letter from a Byelorussian Priest* (London, 1988).
66. H. Pikhura, *Tsarkoŭnaia Muzyka na Belarusi*, p. 12.
67. Cf. *Bozhaia Lira*, (Vil'nia, 1930), no. 125, p. 132.

Notes on the Contributors

Henrik Birnbaum is Professor of Slavic Languages and Literatures at the University of California, Los Angeles. Among his recent publications are *Praslavianskii iazyk. Dostizheniia i problemy v ego rekonstruktsii* (Moscow, 1987); *Novgorod and Dubrovnik: Two Slavic City Republics and Their Civilization* (Zagreb, 1989); and *Aspects of the Slavic Middle Ages and Slavic Renaissance Culture* (New York, 1991).

†*John Fennell* was Professor of Russian at Oxford University and Fellow of New College. He was co-editor of *Oxford Slavonic Papers* (1968–1986) and *Russia Mediaevalis*. Among his numerous books are *Ivan the Great of Moscow* (London, 1961), *The Emergence of Moscow, 1304–1359* (Berkeley, 1968), and *The Crisis of Mediaeval Russia, 1200–1304* (London and New York, 1983) [Russian translation: *Krizis srednevekovoi Rusi, 1200–1304* (Moscow, 1989)].

Boris Gasparov is Professor of Slavic Languages and Literatures at the University of California, Berkeley. His latest book-length studies are *Poetika "Slova o polku Igoreve"* [Poetics of "The Song of Igor's Campaign"] (Vienna, 1984) and *Poeticheskii iazyk Pushkina kak fakt istorii russkogo literaturnogo iazyka* [Pushkin's poetic language as a fact in the history of the Russian literary language] (Vienna, 1992).

Harvey Goldblatt is Professor of Slavic Languages and Literatures at Yale University. He is the author of *Orthography and Orthodoxy: Constantine Kostenečki's Treatise on the Letters* (Florence, 1987) and co-editor of *Aspects of the Slavic Language Question* (New Haven, 1984).

Priscilla Hunt is a Five College Associate in Amherst, Massachusetts. She is the author of a number of studies on the Archpriest Avvakum.

Gail Lenhoff is Associate Professor of Slavic Languages and Literatures at the University of California, Los Angeles. She is the author of *The Martyred Princes Boris and Gleb: A Socio-Cultural Study of the Cult and the Texts* (Columbus, 1989); and *Early Russian Literary Legends: the Lives of Prince Fedor the Black of Jaroslavl'* (Berlin, forthcoming).

Fairy von Lilienfeld is Professor of History and Theology at Friedrich-Alexander University, Erlangen-Nürnberg. Among her works are *Glaube und Tat: Nikolai Leskow, ein russischer Dichter christlicher Nächstenliebe* (Berlin, 1956); and *Nil Sorskij und seine Schriften: die Kriese der Tradition in Rußland Ivans III* (Berlin, 1963).

Paul Robert Magosci is Professor of History and Political Science at the University of Toronto, where he also holds the University Chair of Ukrainian Studies. Among his several books in Slavic studies are *The Shaping of a National Identity: Subcarpathian Rus', 1848-1948* (Cambridge, 1978); *Galicia: A Historical and Bibliographic Guide* (Toronto, 1983); *Ukraine: A Historical Atlas* (Toronto, 1985); and *Historical Atlas of East Central Europe* (Seattle, forthcoming).

†*John Meyendorff* was Professor of Church History and Patristics and Dean of St. Vladimir's Orthodox Theological Seminary in New York. His numerous publications include *A Study of Gregory Palamas* (London, 1962); *Christ in Eastern Christian Thought* (Washington, 1969); *St. Gregory Palamas and Orthodox Spirituality* (New York, 1974); *Byzantine Hesychasm: Historical, Theological and Social Problems* (London, 1974); *Byzantine Theology* (New York, 1974); *Byzantium and the Rise of Russia* (Cambridge, 1981); and *Imperial Unity and Christian Divisions* (New York, 1989).

Donald Ostrowski is Research Advisor in the Social Sciences at Harvard University and Research Associate of the Harvard Ukrainian Research Institute. His most recent articles include: "The Mongol Origins of Muscovite Political Institutions," *Slavic Review* 49 (1990); "Second-Redaction Additions in Carpini's *Ystoria Mongolorum*," *Harvard Ukrainian Studies* 14 (1990); and "A Metahistorical Analysis: Hayden White and Four Narratives of 'Russian' History," *CLIO* 19 (1990).

Aleksandr Panchenko is Senior Research Fellow at the Institute of Russian Literature of the Academy of Sciences (Pushkinskii Dom) in St. Petersburg. Among his numerous publications are *Russkaia stikhotvornaia kul'tura XVIII veka* [Russian poetic culture of the eighteenth century] (Leningrad, 1973); *Smekh v drevnei Rusi* [Laughter in old Russia; with D. S. Likhachev and N. V. Ponyrko] (Leningrad, 1984); and *Russkaia kul'tura v kanun petrovskikh reform* [Russian culture on the eve of the reforms of Peter the Great] (Leningrad, 1984).

NOTES ON THE CONTRIBUTORS

Jaroslaw Pelenski is Professor of Russian and East European History at the University of Iowa. He is the author of *Russia and Kazan: Conquest and Imperial Ideology (1438–1560s)* (The Hague and Paris, 1974) and editor of *The Political and Social Ideas of Vjačeslav Lypyns'kyj* (Cambridge, 1985).

Guy Picarda is a trustee of the Francis Skaryna Byelorussian Library and Museum in London. He is the editor of *Bielaruski Carkoŭny Śpieŭnik* [Belorussian church music collection] (1979) and *Bielaruski Duchoŭny Śpieŭnik* [Belorussian spiritual music collection] (1989).

Maria Pliukhanova is a Docent of Russian Literature at Tartu University, Estonia. She is the author of many articles on the Old Believers and on eighteenth-century Russian culture.

Pavel Sigalov is Professor of Modern and Classical Languages at the University of Wyoming. He works in the area of Russian and Slavic morphology and word formation. He is a co-author, with Boris Gasparov, of *Sravnitel'naia grammatika slavianskikh iazykov* [Comparative grammar of Slavic languages] (the author of volume II, Morphology) (Tartu, 1974) and many articles on Slavic linguistics.

Francis J. Thomson is Professor of English and Translation at the University of Antwerp. He is the author of many articles on translations into Slavonic. He is compiling a catalogue listing all translations from Slavonic made before the beginning of the eighteenth century.

Boris Uspenskii is Professor of Russian Linguistics at the Moscow University. His numerous publications include *Filologicheskie razyskaniia v oblasti slavianskikh drevnostei* [Philological studies in Slavic antiquities] (Moscow, 1982), and *Iz istorii russkogo literaturnogo iazyka XVIII-nachala XIX veka* [Aspects of the history of Russian literary language of the eighteenth and early nineteenth century] (Moscow, 1985).

Dean S. Worth is Professor of Slavic Languages and Literatures at the University of California, Los Angeles. His publications on Old and Middle Russian language and literature include *Sofonija's Tale of the Russian-Tartar Battle on the Kulikovo Field* (1957) (with Roman Jakobson); *The Origins of Russian Grammar: Notes on the State of Russian Philology before the Advent of Printed Grammars* (1983), and some thirty articles, including "The Birchbark Letters in Time and Space," *Wiener Slawistischer Almanach* 25/26 (1990).

INDEX*

Abramovich, D. I., 75
Adalbert of Trier, 53
Adam (Dubec), Bishop, 126
Afanasii, *see also* Athanasius
Afanasii the Recluse, Saint, 69
Agapius Landos, 193
Agrippa of Nettesheim, 193
Akindin, abbot, 63
Al-Gazzali, 186
Aladaŭ, N., 338, 340
Alaska 25
Aldeigja (Old Ladoga), 46
Aleksandr, *see also* Alexander
Aleksandr II, Emperor, 215
Aleksandr Nevskii, Prince, 18, 80, 81, 83, 85–86, 103, 109, 256
Alekseev, A. A., 299
Aleksei (Kabaliuk), Archimandrite, 132n
Aleksei (Alexis), Metropolitan, 18, 22, 107–108
Aleksei (Alexis) Mikhailovich, Tsar, 22, 194–195, 276–292, 297, 305, 309, 315, 322n, 333
Alexander, *see also* Aleksandr
Alexander, Emperor, 46
Alexandria, 12, 166
Alexis, *see* Aleksei
Ambrose, Saint, 191
Amphilochius of Iconium, 185
Amsterdam, 191, 212n
Anastasiia, Tsarina, 274n
Anastasius I of Antioch, Patriarch, 184
Anastasius Sinaita, 183
Andrei, *see also* Andrew
Andrei (Sheptyts'kyi), Metropolitan, 119, 133n
Andrei Bogoliubsky, Prince, 17, 44, 85, 106

Andrei Iurodivyi, 314
Andrei, Prince of Smolensk, 266, 274n
Andrew, *see also* Andrei
Andrew, the Apostle, 270n
Andrew of Caesarea (Andrei Kesariiskii), 190, 311
Andrew of Crete, Saint, 183
Andrew Glaber, 194
Andrew Palaeologus, 186
Andrew the Presbyter, 184
Andrew, Prince of Rostov, 166
Andreyev, Nikolai, 180
Anisimovich, Bahdan, 331, 333
Anna, Princess, 20, 35, 57
Ansgar, Saint, 43
Antál (Papp), Bishop, 133n
Anthony, *see also* Antonii, Antony
Anthony IV, Patriarch, 166
Antioch, 11, 12, 23, 166, 184, 192
Antonii Pecherskii, 64–72, 74, 257, 258–259
Antonii, Archbishop (Dobrynia Iadreikovich), 256
Antony the Great of Egypt, 259
Antsaŭ, Mikhal, 338, 339, 345
Apanas of Brest, Saint, 337
Arabia, 15
Arianasovich, Haŭryla, 333
Aristotle, 186
Arkhangel'sky, A. A., 346, 353n
Armenia, 3, 14, 73
Arndt, Johann, 25
Arsenius Calloudes, 192
Artemii Verkol'skii, Saint, 268
Artemius, abbot, 188
Askochens'kyi, V. I., 223
Asia Minor, 35
Askold, 42, 45–48, 53, 56, 263
Athanasius, *see also* Afanasii

* The index preserves the authors' usage (see pp. 7–8); in most instances, where the same name is spelled or transliterated in different ways, it is given according to its first appearance, with cross-references to alternate spellings, except when listed contiguously or where differences are insignificant. Slavic names appearing only in the Russian texts are given in the Library of Congress transliteration.

Athanasius of Alexandria, Bishop, 186, 192, 195
Athanasius III Patellarus, Patriarch, 192
Athanasius, monk, 201n
Athelstan (Guthrum), 46
Athos, 18, 25, 64, 65, 72, 206n, 208n, 212n, 255, 299
Augustine of Canterbury, Saint, 14
Augustine, Saint, 191
Austria, 91, 118, 119, 120–121, 122, 341
Austria-Hungary, 120–121, 122
Austrian Galicia, 134
Avvakum, Archpriest, 179, 182, 197, 276–292, 292–296n, 297–322, 325n

Babylon, 35
Bach, J. S., 351
Bahdanovich, M., 345
Bakačić, Samuel, 212n
Bakhmet'ev, N. I., 337
Bakhtin, M. M., 6
Balkans, 24, 54, 155, 169n, 330, 331, 332, 349
Balsamon, Theodore, 188, 192
Baltic region, 17, 55, 124, 350
Bardas Phocas, 35, 57
Baronius, Cesare, 194
Barsky, V. G., 255
Bartholomew, merchant, 91
Basil, *see also* Vasilii
Basil (Basileios) the Great, Archbishop of Caesarea, 71, 185, 188, 192, 195
Basil I, Emperor, 48
Basil II, Emperor, 15, 20, 35, 57, 182, 247
Basil III, Grand Prince, 20, 182
Batu, 261
Bause, Theodor, 199n
Bayezid I, Sultan, 186
Begunov, Iu. K., 80
Belgium, 343
Belgrade, 135n
Belinskii, V. G., 218–219, 220
Belorussia, 1, 2, 3, 19, 86, 198n, 216, 328–351
Benedict, Saint, 71
Benjamin, monk, 187
Berynda, Pambo, 190
Bessonov, P., 337

Biakont, Fedor, 107
Białobocki, Andrew, 193
Bielastok (Białystok), 347, 348
Bielski, Martin, 189, 210n
Billington, James, 180
Birka, 43
Bjǫrn (Berno Nortmannus), King, 46
Black Sea, 101n
Blaeu, Joan, 193
Blaeu, Willem, 193
Blastares, Matthew, 184, 185, 192
Blok, A., 27
Bobolinsky, Leonid, 210n
Bobrinskoi, Vladimir, 132n
Bogdanov, Theodore (Fedor), 194
Bogoliubovo, 44
Bohemia, 44
Boldinskii, Gerasim, 313–314, 324n
Bonfils, Emmanuel ben Jacob, 186
Boniface, Saint, 14
Boris (Godunov), Tsar, 21
Boris, Prince, Saint, 32, 38, 54, 55, 80, 256, 257, 259–260, 264
Boris, Tsar of Bulgaria, 157, 181
Borisov, N. S., 114
Borozdin, A. K., 300
Børtnes, Jostein, 315
Bortniansky, D. S., 343, 351
Brazhnikov, M. V., 347
Brest, 118
Briansk, 93
British Isles, 14
Bruno of Würzburg, 188
Bulgar, 34
Bulgaria, 13, 15, 17, 18, 32, 43, 54, 101n, 125, 157, 161, 181–182, 183, 185–186, 202n, 329, 330, 349
Bulich, S. K., 228–229
Bülow, Nicolaus, 187
Burtsov, Basil (Vasilii), 213n
Butoma, N., 349
Byron, George Gordon, 221
Byzantium, 13–20, 21, 22, 25, 26, 34, 35, 43–57 passim, 65, 66, 73, 76n, 77, 81, 88, 89, 94, 101n, 103, 105–107, 108, 141, 144, 145, 154, 163, 166–167, 177n, 180–182, 186, 195–197, 247–248, 252, 253–255, 260, 262, 263, 267, 270n, 329, 349

Cabasilas, Nicholas, 190
Cabasilas, Nilus, 184
Cahun, Léon, 98n
Callistus I, Patriarch, 184
Carpathian Mts., 17, 116–131, 133n (see also Transcarpathia)
Carpini, Johannes de Plano, 89–92, 98n
Cassian of Uglich, monk, 182
Catherine II, Empress, 336
Cerularius, Michael, 184
Chaadaev, P. Ia., 27
Chalcedon, 15, 254
Chapin'ski, Vasil, 351
Charot, M., 339
Chernigov, 83, 107, 256
Chernobyl, 234
Cherson, 57, 255
Chesnokov, P. G., 346
Chełm (Kholm), 118
Churkin, N., 338
Cicero, 189, 210n
Cigalas, Matthew, 192
Clement, see also Kliment
Clement I, Saint, 255, 271n
Clement of Ohrid, 171n
Clement Smoliatich, Metropolitan, 17
Columbus, Christopher, 242
Constance, 117
Constantine, see also Konstantin
Constantine I the Great, Emperor, 12, 53, 78, 79, 257
Constantine VII Porphyrogenitus, Emperor, 46, 48, 51–53
Constantine-Cyril, Apostle to the Slavs, 15, 21, 44, 117, 131n, 133n, 154–165, 167, 168n, 169n, 171n, 177n, 271n
  Cyrillo-Methodian tradition, 15, 16, 19, 21, 24, 28, 56, 181
Constantinople, 12–21 passim, 23, 43, 44, 45, 46, 47, 49, 51, 52, 56, 63, 65, 71, 75, 78, 79, 87, 89, 91, 107, 118, 167, 182, 183, 185, 186, 188, 190–192, 200, 201, 205, 256, 265, 270n, 297, 310, 329
Copernicus, Nicolaus, 193–194
Cosmas of Prague, 50
Cracow, 188–190, 194, 336
Crimea, 98n, 154
Croatia, 135n, 205n

Cromer, Martin, 210n
Cross, S. H., 50
Cuthbert of Lindisfarne, 270n
Cyprian of Ostrog, Hieromonk, 190
Cyprian, Metropolitan, 18, 19, 23, 28, 104–105, 107, 109–110, 111, 113, 166, 177n, 202n, 265
Cyril, see also Kirill
Cyril of Jerusalem, Archbishop, 192, 308, 316
Cyril of Alexandria, Bishop, 188
Cyril of Turov, Bishop, 158, 349
Cyril III, Metropolitan, 18, 83–90, 92, 97n, 103
Cyril, Saint, see Constantine–Cyril
Czechoslovakia, 32, 116, 121–125, 127–131, 133n, 155

Dabravol'ski, U. M., 337
Dahuria, 285
Dalatychy (Belorussia), 342
Damascenus Studites, 191
Damascenus, Peter, 185
Damian the Presbyter, 72
Daniel (Danylo Romanovych), Prince of Galicia, 18, 85, 86, 88, 103
Daniil of Pereiaslavl', Saint, 266, 274
Daniil Zatochnik, 31, 142
Danilevskii, G. P., 219
Danylo Romanovych, see Daniel
David (Fedorovich), Prince of Iaroslavl', Saint, 262
David (Sviatoslavich) of Chernigov, Prince, 260
David Disypatus, 184
Demetrios, see also Dmitrii
Demetrios of Thessalonika, Saint, 67, 68, 256
Demkova, N. S., 313, 319
Denisov, Semen, 323n
Denmark, 46
Derbent, 44
Diadochus of Photice, 185
Dionisii, Archbishop of Suzdal, 256
Dionysius Areopagita, 185
Dionysius the Greek, 191
Dionysius the Wondrous, 202n
Dir, 42, 44, 45–48, 56, 263
Dmitrievsky, A., 201n
Dmitrii, see also Demetrios
Dmitrii (Ivanovich), Grand Prince, 107

Dmitrii (Tuptalo), Metropolitan of Rostov, 315
Dnieper (Dnepr) r., 35, 45, 46, 48, 50, 56, 57, 83, 91, 93, 96, 100
Dobriansky, F., 329, 337, 347, 350
Dobrynia, 30, 31
Domentijan, monk, 158
Dominicus of Grado, 184
Donatus, 188
Dorotheus (avva Dorofei) of Gaza, Saint, 185, 190, 312
Dorotheus of Monembasia, 191, 211n
Dositheus (Bărilă), Metropolitan of Suceava, 192, 193
Dositheus II, Patriarch of Jerusalem, 193
Dostoevsky, F. M., 5, 252
Dreizin, Iu., 343
Druia, 346
Druzhinin, V. G., 318
Duboŭka, Ŭl., 343
Długosz, Jan, 47

Edwards, Thomas, 193
Efrem, *see also* Ephrem
Efrem, Eunuch, 71
Egypt, 65, 255, 259
Eleazar Anzerskii, Saint, 313–314
England, 14, 46
Ephrem, *see also* Efrem
Ephrem the Syrian (Ephraem Syrus), 190, 308
Epifanii, monk, 313–314, 317–318, 321
Epiphanius of Salamis, 195
Epiphanius (Epifanii) Slavinetsky, 108, 191, 210n, 212n
Epiphanius the Wise, 156–167, 168n–177n passim
Erasmus, 193
Eremiia, monk, 72
Ericsson, K., 44, 45, 55
Ethiopia, 14
Euphrosyne of Polotsk, Princess, Saint, 349
Euthymius (Evfimii), monk, 108, 192, 193, 211n
Euthymius, Patriarch of Trnovo, 202n
Euthymius Zigabenus, 183
Evgenii (Bolkhovitinov), Metropolitan, 211n

False Dimitri (Grigorii Otrep'ev), 21
Feafil (Feofil) of Iaroslavl', Saint, 333
Feofil, *see* Theophilus
Fedor, *see also* Theodore, Theodoros
Fedor (Ivanov), deacon, 245, 298, 319, 325n
Fedor (Rostislavich) "Chernyi", Prince of Smolensk, Saint, 261–262
Fedor (Ioannovich), Tsar, 246
Fedor, Chernigov boyar, Saint, 256
Fedorov, N. F., 4, 6
Fedotov, G. P., 179, 181, 199n, 293n, 299, 315
Feodorit, Archimandrite, 319–320
Feodosii Pecherskii, Saint, 38–39, 64, 68–72, 74–76, 257, 258, 293n
Feognost, Metropolitan, 99n, 265
Feoktist, abbot, 258
Feoktist, Archbishop, 93
Ferguson, C. A., 173–174
Filaret (Gumilevsky), Archbishop, 89, 299
Filin, F. P., 150n
Filipovich, Pavlo, 215
Filipp, *see also* Phillip
Filipp, Metropolitan, 265
Filippov, I., 324n
Filofei, *see* Philotheus
Findeizen, N. F., 328
Fine, J. V. A., 54
Finno-Carelia, 349
Florence, 19, 22, 117
Floria, B. N., 43–44
Florovsky, Georges, 23, 25, 27, 179, 180, 195, 196
Fotii, *see* Photius
France, 46
Frankfurt-am-Main, 52
Franko, Ivan, 219, 221, 223, 224
Frisia, 46
Fronton du Duc, 190
Fuhrmann, Joseph, 87, 91

Gabriel Dorofeevich of Lemberg, 190
Gabriel of Hilandar, 186, 206n
Gabriel of Nazareth, Metropolitan 191
Gabriel Severus, 191
Galicia, 17, 18, 85, 86, 88, 94, 104–106, 110, 117, 119, 123, 124, 133n, 134n, 221

Galicia-Volhynia, 17, 86, 99n, 103, 105, 106
Galitsian Ukraine, 330, 332, 341, 342
Gardner, J., 330, 346
Gennadius, Archbishop of Novgorod, 20, 186, 187
Genoa, 91, 101n
George Gemistus Plethon, 195
George Pisides, 184
Georgia, 14, 16, 73
Gerasimov, Demetrius (Dmitrii), 187, 188, 211n
Gerasimova-Persidskaia, N., 348
Germanus of Constantinople, Patriarch, Saint, 190
Germany, 14, 34, 50, 51, 52, 124, 207n, 342, 344–345
Gerontii, Metropolitan, 246
Giovio, Paolo, 211
Gładyszów, 127
Gleb, Prince, Saint, 32, 38, 54, 55, 80, 104, 256, 257, 259–260, 264
Glemp, Cardinal, 126
Glubokovsky, N. N., 25
Gnezdovo, 143
Goethe, J. W. von, 221
Gogol', N. V., 219
Goldblatt, H., 58
Golubinsky, E. E., 77, 85, 89, 92, 179, 254
Gorlice, 126, 127
Gozhel'niarsky, V., 350
Gozvinsky, Theodore, 190
Grabar, Olga, 132n
Graeco-Venetian lands, 349
Great Russia, 95n, 101n, 328, 329
Grebenka, E. P., 219
Grechaninov, A. T., 346
Greece, 11, 16, 17, 22, 33, 67, 75n, 182, 254, 255, 259, 264, 270n, 271n, 329, 349
Gregory, *see also* Hryhorii
Gregory the Great, 181, 185, 193
Gregory (Gregorios) of Nyssa, 183, 195, 254
Gregory Bolgarin, Metropolitan, 19
Gregory the Monk, 185
Gregory of Nazianzus, 188, 190, 192, 208n
Gregory Palamas, 184, 192

Gregory of Sinai, 184
Gregory Tsamblak, 17
Grinchenko, B. D., 223, 224
Grushevskii, M., 217

Hajdúdorog, 119, 125
Halfdan "Whiteleg," King, 273n
Halkin, François, 181
Halkoŭski, K., 340
Halych, 105
Hamartolos, George, 35
Harnack, Adolf, 25
Hasting-Askold, *see* Askold
Helena, Saint, 53, 78, 79, 257
Hellespont Straits, 101n
Henry Bonadies, 91
Hilarion, Metropolitan, 17, 34, 36, 37, 64, 77, 104, 144, 156, 158, 182, 302
Hlinka, Andrei, 135n
Hondius, Henricus, 191
Hondius, Jodocus, 191
Hrabr, monk, 157, 160–165, 167, 171n, 175n
Hrusheŭski, Ionash, 350
Hryhorii (Iakhymovych), Metropolitan, 119
Hungary, 13, 73, 117, 118–122, 125, 133n
Hunt, Priscilla, 315
Husák, Gustav, 136n
Husner, Georg, 207n
Hypatios, abbot, 254

Iahora, Alaksandr, 338, 340
Iakov, monk, 51, 78, 79, 247, 258
Ian Kukiel of Polatsk, 333
Iaropolk (Sviatoslavich), Prince, 34, 42, 54–55, 56, 145, 264
Iaroslav (Vladimirovich) the Wise, Prince, 15, 17, 38, 54–55, 78, 143, 144–145, 259, 264
Iaroslav (Vsevolodovich), Prince, 111, 261
Iaroslavl', 261–262
Ias'ko, D., 351
Iasinoŭski, Iu., 329, 333, 348
Ignatius of Antioch, Saint, 11, 192
Ignatius, Patriarch, 45, 46

Igor, Prince, 32, 36, 42, 47–50, 52, 56, 78, 145, 205n, 263
Igor (Olegovich), Prince of Chernigov, 257
Ilarion, Metropolitan, see Hilarion
Iliinski, Kyril, 333
Illarion (Ivan Ogienko), Metropolitan, 221–222
Illyricum, 43
India, 14, 243
Ingelheim, 44, 56, 61n
Innocent (Veniaminov), Metropolitan, 24–25
Innocent III, Pope, 190
Innocent IV, Pope, 103
Ioann, see also John, Ivan
Ioann Bolshoi Kolpak, 246
Ioann Damaskin, see John of Damascus
Ioann II, Metropolitan, 31
Ioann Zlatoust, see John Chrysostom
Iona, Metropolitan, see Jonas
Iov, Patriarch, 108
Ippolit, Saint, 310, 316
Ippolitov-Ivanov, M. M., 343
Irenaeus of Lyons, Saint, 253
Isaac of Nineveh (the Syrian), Saint, 185
Isachenko (Issatschenko), A. V., 149, 150n
Isaiah of the Miracle Monastery, 212n
Isaiia, Bishop, 261
Isaiia (Kopinskii), Metropolitan, 271n
Isidor of Rostov, Saint, 266
Isidore, Metropolitan, 19
Istomin, Karion, 212n, 213n
Istvan (Novak), Bishop, 133n
Italy, 20, 189, 209n
Iulitta, martyr, see Julitta
Iurgenson, P. (publishers), 338, 339, 340, 341
Iurii I (of Galicia-Volhynia), King, 103, 104–105
Iurii (Vsevolodovich), Prince, 260–261, 272n
Ivan, see also Ioann, John
Ivan (Martyniak), Bishop, 126
Ivan I Kalita, Grand Prince, 87, 104
Ivan III the Great, Grand Prince, 20, 246, 266, 293n
Ivan IV the Terrible, Tsar, 20, 184, 267, 293n, 312

Ivor, 50
Iziaslav (Iaroslavich), Prince, 38–39, 70–71, 259–260, 264

Jacobi, see John Jacobi
Jagiello, King, 18, 28
James the Monk, see Iakov
James Reverius of Acre, 91, 99n
Ján (Hirka), Bishop, 130–131, 137n, 138n
Japan, 25
Jeremiah II Tranos, Patriarch, 21
Jerome, Saint, 187, 191, 270
Jerusalem, 12, 34, 166, 183, 201n
Joasaph, Patriarch, 20
Jodocus Clichtoveus (Josse Clichtove), 209n
Johann Jacobi of Wallhausen, 194, 195, 212n
Johann von Cuba, 187
John, see also Ioann, Ivan
John, the Apostle (the Theologian), 311
John Chrysostom, 118, 183, 186, 188, 189, 190, 192, 290, 302–304, 305–307, 310, 313, 317, 318, 320, 338, 343, 345, 352
John Climacus, 185
John of Citrus, 184
John of Damascus, 183, 184, 185, 188, 189, 210n, 316
John I Tzimisces, Emperor, 56, 182
John VI Cantacuzenos, Emperor, 28, 256
John VIII, Emperor, 206n
John Eugenicus, 186
John the Exarch, 189
John Geometra, 191
John of Holywood (de Sacrobosco), 186
John Hymmonides, 181
John Italus, 195
John of Jerusalem, 184, 189
John Mauropus, 183
John Nathanael, 191
John the Faster, Patriarch, 184
John Paul II, Pope, 126, 136n
John Vladislav, Tsar of Bulgaria, 182
John Zonaras, 184, 192
Jonas, Metropolitan, 19, 107, 108, 265, 266
Joseph (Sanin) of Volokolamsk, abbot, 182

Josephat, Saint, 336
Josephus Flavius, 148
Julian the Apostate, 32
Julitta, martyr, 80, 270n
Justin Martyr, 192
Justinian, Emperor, 15

Kakhanoŭski, Ian, 333
Kalenda, Ian, 333
Kalinoŭski, Kastus, 337
Kallinikos, monk, 254
Kalojan, King of Bulgaria, 183
Kalubovich, A., 346
Kamenets-Podol'sk, 310
Kapnist, V. V., 219
Karakorum, 89
Karamzin, N. M., 27, 83, 109
Karr, Alphonse, 194
Kastal'sky, A., 344, 345, 346, 349
Kastsiukavets, L., 335, 348
Kazimierz (Kazimer), King of Poland, 105, 333
Kedrov, N. N., 346, 348
Keenan, E., 208n
Kerykos, Saint, see Kirikos
Khomenko, I., 223, 236n
Khomiakov, Alexis, 25, 223
Khorezm, 34
Khoroshev, A. S., 114n
Khristofor, Archimandrite, 262
Kiev, 4, 13, 15, 16–17, 18, 19, 24, 28, 32, 34, 35, 39, 42, 43, 45, 47, 48, 50–57, 63–74, 78, 79, 81, 83–95, 96n–101n passim, 102–112, 113n, 132n, 148, 177n, 180, 182, 190, 198n, 201n, 252, 253, 255–260, 262–265, 267, 268, 271n, 328, 330, 331, 347, 354
Kievan Rus', 1, 6, 30–39, 64, 102, 103, 106, 109–112, 117, 141–150, 180–182, 200, 255–257
Kimbar of Suprasl, Archimandrite, 328
Kiprian, see Cyprian
Kirikos (Cyricus), martyr, 80, 256
Kirill, see also Cyril
Kirill, Bishop of Rostov, 256, 260
Kirill Ierusalimskii, see Cyril of Jerusalem
Kishych, Antoni, 333
Klashchele, 336
Kletsk, 342
Kliazma r., 17

Kliment, Bishop, 87
Kliuchevsky, V. O., 84
Kolas, Iu., 339
Komarovich, V. L., 264
Komańcza, 126, 127
Kompaneisky, N. I., 345
Konotop, A., 332, 333, 347
Konstantin, see also Constantine
Konstantin VIII, Emperor, 247
Konstantin (Fedorovich), Prince of Iaroslavl', Saint, 261, 262
Konstantin (Vsevolodovich), Prince of Iaroslavl', 256, 261
Kopystenskii, Zakharii, 308
Koretsky-Satanovsky, Arsenius, 212n
Kossova, Alda, 161
Kostenechki, Constantine, 168n, 169n, 174n, 176n
Kostenko, Lina, 231, 235
Kostomarov, V., 234
Koszutski, Stanisłas, 210n
Kotliarevskii, I. P., 220, 231
Kotoshikhin, Grigorii, 142
Kotsiubinskii, M. M., 219, 220, 223
Kotsylovs'kyi, Josyfat, 133n
Kovalevsky, M., 346, 348
Krakow, see Cracow
Králík, O., 44
Krempna, 126
Krynica, 126, 127
Ksenofont, 149
Kukanlyk (Kaganlyk) r., 93
Kuksha, monk, 73
Kulaszne, 127
Kulikovich, Tsimafei, 333
Kulikovich-Shchahloŭ, Mikola, 335, 339, 340, 342, 344–348, 350
Kulish, P. A., 219, 221–222
Kupala, Ia., 339
Kurbsky, Andrew, Prince, 188–189, 207n–210n passim, 212n
Kvitka-Osnov'ianenko, G. F., 219
Kyi, 44, 45, 47, 55, 56, 58

Ladoga, 46
Lansmann, Gottlieb, 207n
Lastoŭski, V., 350
Laŭchyk, Halash, 351
Lazar' Muromskii, Saint, 313–314
Lemberg, see L'viv
Lemkin, I. F., 221

Lencheŭski, N., 341–342
Lenin, V. I., 274–275n
Leningrad (see also Petrograd, St. Petersburg), 331, 340
Leo (Leontius), Bishop of Kiev, 48
Leo VI, Emperor, 46, 48, 184
Leontii of Rostov, Bishop, 73, 166, 256, 261
Libutius, monk, 53
Ligarides, Paisius, 193
Likhachev, D. S., 49, 75, 78, 85, 87, 102, 299
Limonov, Iu. A., 85–86
Lithuania, 17, 83, 93, 94, 101n, 105, 106, 108, 109, 118, 166, 186, 188–191 passim, 194, 198n, 206n, 210n, 216, 340, 341, 347
Lithuania-Ruthenia, 105, 106, 110
Little Rus', 101n
Liubech, 64
London, 336, 346–347, 348
Longinus the Centurion, Saint, 256
Łosie, 127
Lotman, Iu. M., 195–196, 262, 275n
Louis the Pious, Emperor, 44, 56
Löwenklau (Lenclavius), Johann, 192
Ludmila, Saint, 44
Luke, the Apostle, 270n
Lull, Raymund, 193
Lunt, Horace G., 149
L'viv, 123, 132n, 190, 210n, 332, 337
L'viv-Halych, 119, 132n, 133n
L'vov, see L'viv
L'vov, F. P., 337
Lykov, Bogdan, 211n
Lytkin, G., 176n
Lyzlov, Andrew, 212n

Macarios of Antioch, Patriarch, 23
Macarius of Egypt, Saint, 190
Macarius, Metropolitan, 108, 184, 274n, 309
Macedonia, 180, 191
Machiavelli, 21
Magellan, 188
Magnus, pseudo-Albertus, 193
Mahiloŭ (Mogilev), 330–332, 336, 340
Maimonides, Moses, 186
Makarii, see Macarius
Maksim, see Maxim, Maximus
Maksimovich, M. A., 143

Malachi, monk, 182
Mamai, Khan, 166
Manasses, Constantine, 184
Mango, Cyril, 181
Mangu Temir, Khan, 81
Mansvetov, I., 201n
Manuel II Palaeologus, Emperor 166, 256
Manuel Palaeologus, 186
Manuel Tarchaniotes Bullotes, 206n
Manuel the Venetian, 91, 99n
Manuil the Castrate, Bishop of Smolensk, 329
Maria of Bulgaria, 182
Marmaroš Sighet, 132n
Marquart, Theophilus, 207n
Marwazī, geographer, 49
Mary Magdalene, Saint, 256
Masciuk, Vasylii, 133n
Matfei, monk, 72
Matsison, Mikhail, 340, 341
Matthew, Patriarch, 28
Matveev, N., 349
Maxim, Metropolitan, 81, 83–85, 87, 88, 90–94, 95n, 97n, 103
Maximus the Confessor, 185, 186
Maximus the Greek, 21, 153n, 182, 188–189, 207n, 208n, 209n, 241, 244, 247, 299
Mazovich, Mikola, 350
Medvets'kyi, Iakiv, 133n
Melanchthon, Philipp, 191
Melkhisedek, Metropolitan of Minsk, 340
Memphis, 242
Mendelssohn, F., 351
Mercator, Gerard, 191, 211n
Merkurii of Smolensk, Saint, 261
Metallov, V. M., 328
Methodius of Patara, 322n
Methodius of Thessalonika, Apostle to the Slavs, 15, 21, 44, 117, 131n, 133n, 156, 162, 168n
Metlinskii, A., 218
Meyendorff, John, 87–88, 106
Michael, see also Mikhail
Michael, Bishop of Kiev, 48
Michael the Genoese, 91
Michael (Aleksandrovich), Prince of Tver', 166, 256
Michalovce, 131

Mickiewicz, Adam, 221
Middle East, 15, 22, 24
Mikalaevich, M., 349
Mikhail, see also Michael
Mikhail (Vsevolodovich), Prince of Chernigov, 256
Mikhail (Iaroslavich), Prince of Tver', 256
Mikhail (Romanov), Tsar, 322n
Minsk, 333–335 passim, 340–344 passim, 348–350 passim
Mioduszewski, 336
Mirnyi, Panas, 223
Mogila, Peter, 192
Mogilev, see Mahiloŭ
Moisei the Hungarian, 74
Moldavia, 25, 192
Moravia, 13, 15, 28n, 43, 132n, 155, 161, 181, 350
Morozova, Fedos'ia, 317, 325n
Moscow, 18–22, 83, 89, 95n, 99n, 102–112, 113n, 155–156, 163, 165–167, 177n, 180, 182, 186, 187, 191–195 passim, 199n, 201n, 210n, 211n, 213n, 265, 266, 297, 308–309, 330, 331, 332, 333, 336, 338, 341, 342, 343, 344, 348, 349
Muscovite Russia, 4, 155–156, 163,165–67, 177n, 332, 337
Muscovy, 1, 3, 14, 16, 18–22, 86, 102–112, 114n, 118, 179–197, 206n, 214n, 252–253, 256, 262, 265–268, 269n, 278, 292, 328, 333
Mstislav (Vladimirovich), Prince, 256
Mtskheta, 16
Mukačevo, 119, 121, 123, 131n, 133n
Müller, Ludolf, 46, 61, 77
Munexin, Michael Misjur, 187, 207n
Myroslav (Marusyn), Archbishop, 126, 136n

Nadezhdin, N. I., 143
Napoleon Bonaparte, 336
Narezhnyi, V. T., 219
Năsturel, Udrişte, 212n
Navahradak (Nowogródek), 342, 343
Near East, 211n
Neboza, Pernethius, 191
Neronov, Ivan, Archpriest, 307
Nestor, chronicler, 63, 64, 70, 75, 76, 158, 308

Neva, r., 80–81
Newman, Cardinal, 351
Nicaea, 94
Nicephorus, see also Nikephoros
Nicephorus Blemmydes, 195
Nicephorus Callistus Xanthopoulos, 191, 193
Nicetas, see also Nikita
Nicetas of Heracleia, 185
Nicetas of Nicaea, 184, 202n
Nicetas Stethatus, 185, 202n
Nicholas, see also Nikola, Nikolai, Nikolaos
Nicholas (Kasatkin), Bishop of Japan, 25
Nicholas of Lyra, 187, 188
Nicodemus, Archbishop of Serbia, 201n
Nicon, see also Nikon
Nicon of the Black Mount, 183, 185
Nikephoros Gregoras, 92
Nikifaroŭski, M. Ia., 328, 338
Nikita of Novgorod, Bishop, 256
Nikita of Pereiaslavl', Saint, 266–7
Nikol'skii, N. K., 37, 43–44
Nikola (Nikolai), monk, see Sviatosha
Nikolai, Nikolaos, see also Nicholas
Nikolai II, Emperor, 215
Nikolaos, Bishop of Polotsk, 256
Nikon, see also Nicon
Nikon, Patriarch, 21, 22, 37, 71, 81, 87, 111, 191, 192, 247, 285, 292, 294n, 295n, 297, 306, 309, 322n
Nil Sorsky, Saint, 21, 182
Nizhny Novgorod, 97n, 182
Nogotkov-Obolensky, Michael, 188–189, 209n
Norway, 273n
Novgorod, 15, 17, 20, 30, 44, 53, 55, 56, 80, 81, 83, 85, 87, 88, 92, 93, 97n, 109, 110, 111, 142–143, 144, 180, 187, 194, 255, 256, 274n, 329
Nowica, 127
Nowy Sącz, 126
Nubia, 15

Obnorsky, S. P., 150, 231
Obolensky, D., 15, 28, 45, 51, 53, 157
Odessa, 100
Oecumenius of Tricca, 190
Ohrid, 16
Olchowiec, 127

Oleg, Prince, 45–48, 54–55, 56, 262–263
Oleg (Ioannovich), Prince of Riazan, 166
Oleg (Sviatoslavich), Prince, 260, 264
Oleinik, Boris, 234
Olga, Princess, 15, 33, 34, 38, 42, 50–53, 56, 57, 60, 61, 77–81, 256, 257–258, 263, 264
Olgierd, Grand Prince of Lithuania, 106
Olympiodorus of Alexandria, 206n
Onufrius, Saint, 335
Osterhofen, 343
Otfinowski, Waleryian, 194, 213n
Otto (Otton) I the Great, Emperor, 34, 42, 52, 53
Otto Meinardus, 254
Ovid, 194

Pachomios, *see also* Pakhomii
Pachomios, Saint, 71
Paisii Velichkovskii, Saint, 25, 29
Paisios, Patriarch of Alexandria, 23
Pakhomii Logofet (the Serbian), 108, 252, 266
Palesse (Polesie), 337, 341, 347
Palestine, 65, 255
Pannonia, 43
Panteleimon of Minsk, Metropolitan, 342
Pantoleon of Jerusalem, 183
Pap, Stepan, 137–138n
Paphnutius, Hieromonk, 210n
Pariisky, L. N., 348
Paris, 57, 60, 62, 209n, 346, 347, 348, 354n
Pashkievich, Jakub, 350
Pashkov, Afanasii, 285
Pasternak, Boris, 6
Patmos, 181
Patrikeev, Bassian (Vassian), 188, 208n
Patsenka, Parkhomii, 333
Paul of Aleppo, 328, 333
Paul the Younger, Saint, 271n
Paul, the Apostle, 12, 173n, 277, 279, 289, 290, 302–303, 316, 318
Pavel (Gojdič), Bishop, 125, 129
Pereiaslavl', 260, 266
Peresvetov, Ivan, 186
Perm, 156, 158–160, 167, 173n, 176n

Persia, 15
Peter, the Apostle, 12, 318
Peter I, Emperor, 1, 23–26, 27, 30, 31, 179, 194, 195
Peter (Petr), Metropolitan, 18, 86–87, 94, 101n, 103–105, 107, 108, 166, 265–266, 273–274n
Peter Paschami, 91
Peter of Antioch, Patriarch, 184
Pętna, 127
Petrograd (*see also* Leningrad, St. Petersburg), 350
Petrov, Avvakum, *see* Avvakum
Petrus Alfonsi, 193
Petrus de Crescentiis, 190
Petrushevich, A., 329, 338
Petrycy, Sebastian, 194
Pflaumen, Jacob, 187
Phillip, *see also* Filipp
Phillip, the Apostle, 313
Philotheus Coccinus, Patriarch, 23, 183, 184–185
Philotheus (Filofei) of Pskov, 20, 22, 187, 207n, 297, 309, 310, 320
Philotheus of Sinai, 185
Photius, Metropolitan, 19, 265
Photius, Patriarch, 45, 47, 48, 52, 181, 200n, 201n
Phrantzes, George, 195
Picchio, Riccardo, 157, 172n
Pinsk, 331
Pisani, Nicolas, 91, 99n
Pitirim, Bishop of Perm, 108
Pius II (Piccolomini), Pope, 188
Planudes, Maximus, 190
Pleshcheev, brothers, 307
Pliny the Younger, 192
Pochaina Creek, 50
Podlasia (Padlassia, Podlasie), 198n, 336
Pogodin, M. P., 213n
Poland, 13, 17, 18, 19, 21, 32, 70, 91, 105, 106, 108, 116–126, 128, 131, 135n, 136n, 137n, 198n, 210n, 330, 333, 334, 337, 341, 347, 348, 350, 351
Polikarp, monk, 63
Polish-Lithuanian Commonwealth, 105, 106, 118
Polotsk (Polatsk), 46, 256, 329, 332, 333, 335

Polyeuctus, Patriarch, 51, 52
Pomponius Mela, 189
Ponyrko, N. S., 292n, 312
Popovka, Gerasimus, 187
Poppe, A. V., 35
Potemkin, S., 307, 309
Prague, 125, 127, 136n
Preobrazhensky, A. V., 328, 332, 335
Preslav, 16, 181
Prešov, 121, 125, 127, 129–131, 135n, 136n
Priselkov, M. D., 37, 85, 87, 109
Pritsak, O., 46, 47, 52, 53, 60
Procopius, 195, 256
Prokhorov, G. M., 111
Prokopovich, Feofan, 23
Protchenko, I., 234
Przemyśl, 121, 122, 123, 124, 126, 131n, 132n, 133n, 135n
Psellus, Michael, 195
Pseudo-Basil I, 184, 213n
Pseudo-Chrysostom, 290
Pskov, 53, 81, 180
Pushkin, A. S., 26, 221
Pustozersk, 276, 286, 293n, 304, 310, 321
Putiata, 30

Quentell, Heinrich, 187

Radzivil, Mahdalena, Princess, 350
Ragnarr Loðbrók, 46
Rakitski, L., 349
Ramanaŭ, E. R., 328, 337, 338
Rastko of Serbia, see Sava
Ravienski, Mikola, 334, 335, 338, 339, 342–345, 353
Razumovsky, D. M., 328, 332
Regino of Prüm, abbot, 53
Rhazes, 186
Rhōs, 44–46, 56
Riasanovsky, A. V., 61
Riazan, 83, 108, 109, 166
Rimsky-Korsakov, N. A., 338
Riurik, 46, 47, 58
Robinson, A. N., 294n, 312
Rogovsky, Palladius, 193
Roman, Prince of Galicia-Volhynia, 17
Romania (Rumania), 135n, 349
Romanus II, Emperor, 53
Rome (and Roman Empire), 11, 12, 14, 15, 19–22, 81, 104, 118, 122, 125, 130, 132, 211n, 242, 270n, 330, 349, 355
Rospond, S., 229
Rostov, 91, 165–166, 255, 256, 260, 261, 266, 273, 274
Rothe, H., 309
Rublev, Andrei, 18
Runciman, Steven, 85
Rus', 1–6, 13, 16–17, 30–39, 42–57, 63, 66, 70, 73, 81, 83–95, 100n, 101n, 102–115, 117, 154–156, 166, 169n, 170n, 176n, 216, 247–248, 261, 299, 310, 312, 314, 322 (see also Kievan, Muscovite Rus')
Ruthenia, 108, 110, 198n
Rybakov, B. A., 46
Ryl'skii, M., 224
Rzepadź, 127
Rzeszów, 134n

St. Petersburg (see also Leningrad, Petrograd), 338, 339, 340
Sakharov, A. N., 49
Samuel of Morocco, 187
Sanok, 126
Sarti, Guiseppe, 346
Sarygozin, Mark, 208n
Sava, Saint, 158
Savile, Henry, 190
Scandinavia, 13, 45–46, 47, 50, 73, 264
Scherbak, Iurii, 234
Schmidt, O., 199n
Scholarius, Gennadius, 191
Sebastian of Minsk, 350
Semashko, Joseph, Archbishop, 331, 335, 336, 337, 338
Semashko, Iakub, 342
Semen, see also Simeon, Symeon
Semen, Bishop of Vladimir, 91, 93, 101
Semiianovich, Feodar, 333
Serapion, Bishop of Vladimir, 97n, 308
Seraphim of Sarov, Saint, 25
Serbia, 16, 17, 135, 168n, 185, 186, 329, 330
Serebriansky, N., 77
Sergius of Radonezh, Saint, 18
Severian of Gabala, 183, 184, 320

INDEX

Severus, Gabriel, 191
Shakespeare, William, 221–222
Shakhmatov, A. A., 43, 46, 55, 57, 109, 150
Shakhovskoi, Semen Ivanovich, 108
Shchuroŭski, Tsimafei, 335
Shein, P., 328, 337, 338
Sherbowitz-Wetzor, O. P., 50
Shevchenko, Ihor, 157
Shevchenko, T. G., 219–231 passim
Shevelev, G., 215, 232–233
Shishkin, A., 346, 348
Shmeman, Aleksandr, 248, 250
Shyrma, Hryhor, 342
Siberia, 24, 29, 343
Sigismund II Augustus, King of Poland, 210n
Silesia, 124
Silvester Medvedev, 213n
Silvestr, abbot, 43
Simeon, *see also* Semen, Symeon
Simeon (Ioannovich), Prince, 256
Simon, Bishop of Suzdal, 63
Sinai, 65
Skarabahata, V., 349
Skarga, Peter, 194, 195
Skoplje, 16
Skulsky, Andrew, 190, 210n
Slavinetsky, Epiphanius, 191, 192
Slonim, 342
Slovakia, 122, 124, 128–131, 135n, 137n
Slutsk, 331
Smirnov, P. S., 325n
Smolensk (Smalensk), 261, 274, 329, 333, 338, 340, 344
Smolensky, S. M., 328
Smotritsky, Meletius, 195
Socrates, 36
Solitarius, Philip, 185
Soloviev, S. M., 83–85, 88, 92
Soloviev, V. S., 6, 25
Sophia of Slutsak, Saint, 349
Soviet Union, 122–125, 127–128, 135n, 136n, 347
Spangenberg, Johann, 189
Spassky, P. V., 346, 354
Spătar, Nicholas (Milescu), 192
Spitsyn, A. A., 96n
Stalin, I. V., 122
Stanyslav, 123

Stefan Iavorskii (Stephan Iavorsky), 210n, 243
Stefan Zizanii, 308
Stephen, abbot, 68
Stephen of Perm, Bishop, 18, 24, 154, 156–167, 168n, 177n, 265
Stephen the First-Crowned, of Serbia, 158
Stoeffler, Johannes, 187
Strassburg, 187
Stryjkowski, Matthew, 194, 213n
Sukhanov, Arsenius, 191
Suprasl', 328, 330, 331, 332, 335, 338
Suzdal', 17, 81, 83, 86, 97n, 102, 103, 104, 109, 110, 111, 255, 256
Suzdal'-Vladimir, 102, 103, 109, 110, 111
Sveinald, 54
Sviatopolk (Iziaslavich), Grand Prince, 258, 260
Sviatopolk (Vladimirovich) the Accursed, 32, 55, 257
Sviatosha, Prince, 72–73
Sviatoslav (Iaroslavich), Prince, 260, 264
Sviatoslav (Igorevich), Prince, 33, 36, 42, 53–54, 56, 78, 145
Sviatoslav (Vladimirovich), Prince, 70, 257
Sweden, 21, 32, 43, 80
Świerczewski, Karol, 134n
Sylvan, 153n
Symeon, *see also* Semen, Simeon
Symeon Metaphrastes, 183
Symeon the New Theologian, 185
Symeon (Petrovsky-Sitnianovich) of Polotsk, 193, 213n, 298
Symeon of Thessalonica, 193
Symeon, Tsar of Bulgaria, 157, 158, 171n
Syria, 65, 73

Taranevich, Antonii, 333
Tarasii, Hieromonk, 333
Tarchaniotes, Demetrius, 186, 206n
Tarnow, 135n
Tashitskii, V., 229
Tatarynovich, P., 350
Tatishchev, V. N., 47
Tatra Mts., 243
Temir Qutlug, Khan, 166

INDEX

Teraŭski, Ŭl. T., 341, 343
Terek r., 100n
Terelia, Josyf, 136n
Teschner, Melchior, 351
Thapsus, Pseudo-Vigilius, 193
Theodora of Thessalonica, Saint, 255
Theodore, *see also* Fedor
Theodore, Bishop of Ravenna, 247
Theodore Metochites, 195
Theodore, Protopresbyter, 186
Theodore (Ioannovich), Tsar, 21
Theodoret of Cyrrhus, 25
Theodoros Stratilates, Saint, 254, 256
Theodosius Pecherskii, *see* Feodosii
Theognostos, *see* Feognost
Theoktistos, *see* Feoktist
Theophanes the Greek, 18
Theophilus, Emperor, 44, 56
Thessalonica (Saloniki), 16, 104, 148, 193, 255, 256
Thomas à Kempis, 193
Thomas, the Apostle, 242
Thucydides, 192
Tikhomirov, M. N., 46
Tikhon of Zadonsk, Saint, 25
Timothy, Bishop, Saint, 270n
Timour, Khan, 100
Tmutorakan, 71
Tokhta, 93, 94, 100n
Tokhtamysh, Khan, 166
Tolochko, P. P., 46, 47–48
Tolstoy, L. N., 4, 5, 26
Transcarpathia (Subcarpathian Rus'), 116, 123, 128, 131–132n, 133n, 135n
Transylvania, 132n
Transylvanus, Maximilian, 188
Treadgold, D. W., 199n
Trebizond, 16
Trediakovskii, V. K., 215
Triboles, Maximus (Michael), *see* Maximus the Greek
Trypho of Pechenga, Saint, 24
Tserakovich, S., 333
Tseslaŭ (Sipovich), bishop, 346
Tula, 344
Turankoŭ, Aliaksei, 339–340, 342, 343, 349
Turaŭ (Turov), 329
Turchaninov, P. I., 346
Turner, Victor, 293n, 294n

Trnovo, 16
Tver', 88, 103, 109, 110, 166, 182, 255, 256
Tychyna, P., 225
Tyzenhaus of Vil'nia, 333

Ukraine, 1, 2, 3, 19, 22, 24, 42, 86, 87, 107, 116, 119, 123, 134, 198n, 210n, 215–235, 308–309, 328, 329, 330, 332, 334, 335, 336, 340, 341, 342, 344, 347, 349
Ukrainka, Lesia, 219, 223
Ulasaŭ, A., 351
Ulm, 187
Unbegaun, Boris, 217, 233–234
United States of America, 133n, 345, 346, 351
Uście Gorlickie, 127
Uspenskii, B. A., 30–31, 144, 149, 215, 216, 218, 262, 275n
Uspensky, N. D., 347, 348
Uzï r., 100n
Uzbek, Khan, 32
Užhorod, 123

Vaclav, Prince, Saint, 44
Valencia, 250n
Valynchyk, Anton, 342, 349
Varda Foka, *see* Bardas Focas
Varlaam (Shyshatsky), Archbishop, 336
Varlaam, monk, 74
Vasiliev, V., 77
Vasilii *see also* Basil
Vasilii II, Grand Prince, 108
Vasilii I (Dmitrievich), Prince, 111, 166
Vasilii (Vsevolodovich), Prince of Iaroslavl', 261
Vasnetsov, V. M., 31
Vasyl' (Hopko), Bishop, 125, 129, 130
Vasyl'ko, Prince, 86
Vedel', A. L., 343
Veder, William, 196
Veniaminov, Timothy, 187
Venice, 22, 91, 98n, 99n, 101n, 191, 192, 209n
Verbitsky, M. M., 343
Vernadsky, G., 85, 89, 90, 93
Vesalius, Andrew, 192
Vilnius (Vil'nia), 190, 210n, 328, 331, 341, 352

Vincent of Beauvais, 193
Vinogradov, V. V., 228–229, 315
Vishensky, I., *see* Vyshenskii
Vitalii (Maksimenko), Archimandrite, 133n
Vitovt, Prince of Lithuania, 166
Vitsebsk (Vitebsk), 329, 330, 338
Vladimir (on the Kliaz'ma), 17, 83–95 passim, 102, 103, 105, 107, 109–111, 256, 261
Vladimir Monomakh, Grand Prince, 38, 39, 260
Vladimir (Sviatoslavovich), Prince of Kiev, 13–15, 20, 30–39, 42–43, 48–51, 54–56, 57, 77–82, 83–94, 95n, 97n, 98n, 99n, 101n, 104, 145, 154–156, 157, 166, 171n, 255, 257–258, 264, 271n
Voitiekh, Bishop, 155
Volga r., 17, 91, 166
Volhynia, *see also* Galicia-Volhynia, 86, 104–106, 110, 198n, 341, 342
Volkhov r., 56
Volodimir, *see* Vladimir Sviatoslavovich
Vovchok, Marko, 219
Voznesensky, I., 328, 330
Vsevolod (Iaroslavich), Prince, 260
Vsevolod (Iur'evich), Grand Prince, 256

Vsevolod (Mstislavovich), Prince of Novgorod, 256
Vyshenskii, Ivan, 213n, 223
Vyshgorod, 259

Warsaw, 125, 136n, 331, 341, 342, 353
William Beveridge, 192
William Durandus the Elder, 187
William of Norwich, 270n
William of Rubruck, 89
Wlasowsky, Ivan, 86–87, 88
Wrocław, 124

Yanin, V. L., 30, 31
Yugoslavia, 135n, 349

Zavoloko, I. N., 318
Zelenetskii, Martirii, 313–314
Zemka, Tarasius, 190
Zemskaia, E. A., 142
Zen'kovskii, S. A., 312, 313, 322n
Zenobius of Oten, 182
Zheltovskii, V., 245
Zhyrovitsy, 328, 330, 335, 341, 342, 349
Zizanii, Lawrence, 190
Zlatar, Zdenko, 180–181, 196
Zoe-Sophia Palaeologa, 20, 186
Zosimas, abbot, 185
Zosimas, Metropolitan, 187

Corrections to *Christianity and the Eastern Slavs,* Volume I (California Slavic Studies, Volume 16)

Francis J. Thomson, "The Corpus of Slavonic Translations Available in Muscovy"

page	line	reads	should read
181	25	ca.	c.
183	27	Nicodemia	Nicomedia
185	6	Ninevah	Nineveh
	25	the latter translated	the latter were translated
190	26	a free-verse rendering	a very free verse rendering
191	16	Pernethius	Parthenius
195	6	Although few, the translations show	The translations nevertheless clearly show
	28	factually true	factually untrue
208	24	*Legen*	*Leben*
210	11–12	may not have been the first	may have been the first
213	24	Thomson, "'Made in Russia': A Survey of the Translations"	Thomson, "A Survey of the Vitae Allegedly Translated into Slavonic in Bohemia in the Tenth and Eleventh Centuries," in Atti dell' 8° Congresso internazionale di studi sull' alto medioevo (Spoleto, 1987)
	34	service for the settlement	service and for the settlement